Disease
and
Demography
in the
Americas

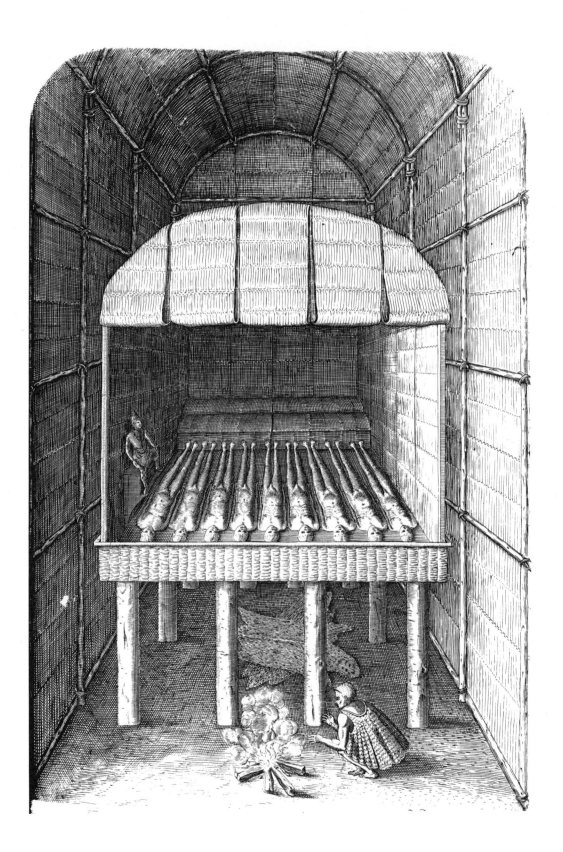

Disease
and
Demography
in the
Americas

Edited by John W. Verano
and Douglas H. Ubelaker

SMITHSONIAN INSTITUTION PRESS
WASHINGTON AND LONDON

© 1992 by the Smithsonian Institution

All rights reserved

Publisher's note: The Press is grateful to Diane Della-Loggia for discharging full and professional responsibilities for the editing and proofreading of this volume.

Library of Congress Cataloging-in-Publication Data

Disease and demography in the Americas / edited by John W.
   Verano and Douglas H. Ubelaker.
      p. cm.
      "One of a series of symposia produced as part of Seeds of
   Change, the National Museum of Natural History's
   commemoration of the Columbus Quincentenary"—
   Foreword.
      Includes bibliographical references and index.
      ISBN 1-56098-163-6 (cloth); 1-56098-401-5 (paper)
      1. Indians—Anthropometry—Congresses. 2. Indians—
   Diseases— Congresses. 3. Indians—Population—
   Congresses.
   4. Paleopathology—America—
   Congresses. 5. Epidemics—America—History—
   Congresses. 6. America—Antiquities—Congresses.
   I. Verano, John W. II. Ubelaker, Douglas H.
   III. National Museum of Natural History (U.S.)
   E59.A5D57 1992
614.4'27—dc20   91-32713

British Library Cataloging-in-Publication Data is available.

Manufactured in the United States of America.
96 95   5 4 3

♾ The paper used in this publication meets the minimum
requirements of the American National Standard for
Permanence of Paper for Printed Library Materials
Z39.48-1984.

Frontispiece: Burial practices among American Indians.
Cover illustration: Early contact between Indians and
Europeans in Florida.
Engraved and published by Theodore De Bry, Frankfurt,
1585 and 1591.

Contents

Foreword

HERMAN J. VIOLA
DIRECTOR, SEEDS OF CHANGE

Disease and Demography in the Americas is one of a series of symposia produced as part of Seeds of Change, the National Museum of Natural History's commemoration of the Columbus Quincentenary. Seeds of Change is the story of the processes of encounter and exchange set in motion by the Columbus voyages of discovery. Like pebbles thrown in a pond, "seeds of change"—plants, animals, diseases—were introduced, sometimes deliberately, sometimes accidentally, by Columbus and those who followed him. These "seeds" sent ripples around the globe, affecting the people as well as the flora and fauna of both the New World and the Old.

Although literally hundreds of examples could have been chosen to represent the Columbian exchange, the scholars working on Seeds of Change selected five: sugar, maize, the horse, the potato, and disease. Many will argue effectively that alternative plants and animals—tobacco, quinine, rubber, cattle, or a dozen others—were more important. Nonetheless, each of these seeds was chosen because of the human dimension in its story. Sugar led directly to the enslavement of Africans and the transformation of New World ecosystems; maize was one of the New World foods that fed the Africans that provided the manpower for American plantations; the potato, like maize, was developed by American Indians and has become a basic food of people around the globe; the horse was one gift from the Old World that America's Indians came to embrace and cherish. Even today members of many North American tribes regard the horse as a vital part of their culture.

Disease, the fifth "seed," is perhaps the most difficult of the components of the quincentenary story to grasp intellectually. Scholars have long known that Old World diseases such as smallpox, measles, even the common cold, wrought havoc with New World peoples and greatly favored the European settlers in displacing the Native Americans. Less well known is the fact that the New World was not a disease-free paradise. Indeed, as the papers presented in this conference indicate, the American Indians suffered from a variety of aches and ailments that afflicted individuals throughout the hemisphere. Unfortunately, the evidence needed to identify and describe those maladies is not easy to obtain. The conference and this volume mark a major attempt to bring together the resources and research of a variety of disciplines and scholars to resolve the riddle of New World disease and demographics. As conference directors John Verano and Douglas Ubelaker conclude, "while many . . . problems may never be resolved, much can be learned through interdisciplinary research and careful research design."

Disease and Demography in the Americas, like the exhibition at the Smithsonian Museum of Natural History that formed the basis for this stimulating conference, is an attempt to interpret the events of 1492 five hundred years after the Admiral of the Sea stepped ashore in the Bahamas and changed the course of world history.

1

Introduction

DOUGLAS H. UBELAKER
AND JOHN W. VERANO

This volume results from a symposium, "Disease and Demography in the Americas, Changing Patterns Before and After 1492," held November 2 and 3, 1989, at the Lecture Hall of the S. Dillon Ripley Center of the Smithsonian Institution. The symposium was sponsored by the Office of Quincentenary Programs of the National Museum of Natural History, as part of a series of academic symposia and public programs related to its upcoming exhibition Seeds of Change.

The idea for this symposium evolved over the years among several of us who have observed the growing research intensity in these and related fields. Those of us who have dual interests in skeletal biology or paleopathology as well as demography have long recognized that researchers in these respective areas do not communicate well with each other, in spite of the obvious overlap of interests. Much of the demographic literature depicts pre-European contact America as "a disease-free paradise," while the literature in physical anthropology and paleopathology regularly documents a variety of disease conditions in ancient America. Conversely, demographic reconstructions from ancient samples seem at odds with standard interpretations from ethnohistory and demography. What is fact and what is theory? The symposium was designed to stimulate discussion among disciplines that may lead to clarification of these issues. Clearly, America before European contact was not disease free, but what were the health problems? How did they vary in time and space? How did they compare in type and severity with those of post-European America, and how did they relate to new diseases introduced from Europe? These issues were largely explored on the first day of the symposium by scholars representing different geographical areas of the New World as well as different research orientations. This session was moderated by Dr. Arthur Aufderheide of the School of Medicine, University of Minnesota, Duluth, who himself has learned a great deal about ancient disease in the Americas, most recently in Chile.

The second day of the symposium shifted to the important question of population size and related demographic issues. Research in this area continues to produce important new information, as well as controversy, since many of the strongly held positions on population size contradict one another, or at least show great variability. Without doubt,

American Indian population size decreased substantially following European contact, but questions remain on the size of the aboriginal population, fluctuation in population size prior to European contact, the extent to which disease impact preceded actual population contact, the magnitude and severity of the epidemics, and regional or local variability in the timing and rate of population decline. The scholars assembled for this discussion represent all aspects of this debate, speak from different data bases, and undoubtedly create divergent impressions of precontact population size and the subsequent European impact. The goal of this discussion was not to emerge with a unified point of view but to clarify the issues and logic involved and point the way toward greater understanding. This session was appropriately moderated by Dr. Alfred Crosby of the University of Texas, Austin, whose research and publications are well known by all who work in this field.

The symposium was conceived through the efforts of many people. Our organizational efforts were greatly enhanced by the staff of the Office of Quincentenary Programs at the Museum of Natural History and the Smithsonian's Office of Conference Services. In particular, Carolyn Margolis, project coordinator for Seeds of Change, and Cheryl Laberge and Karen Bennett of the Office of Conference Services coordinated every detail from securing funding for the symposium to arranging for food service and lodging for our participants. They have been marvelous to work with, and we are all in debt to their effort. The participants who have joined together for this symposium are some of the very best international scholars available in the areas of research covered by this symposium. We are grateful for their involvement. There are, of course, many others whose points of view could not be included due to limitations of time and resources, and we regret that the program could not be even more inclusive.

The timely publication of this volume would not have been possible without the excellent editorial work of Diane Della-Loggia, who copyedited the manuscripts, communicated with the individual authors, and kept the production of the volume moving forward. Karen Ackoff prepared all the illustrations, and Lorraine Jacoby edited the bibliographical entries. We would also like to thank

Daniel Goodwin of the Smithsonian Institution Press for his interest and assistance in carrying this project through.

The organization of this volume loosely follows that of the symposium. The first part of the volume explores the evidence for mortality and morbidity in the New World before and after 1492. Patterns of disease and demography, revealed largely through analysis of well-documented and dated samples of human remains, are presented for geographic areas—Andean South America, and the Southeast, Southwest, Plains, Northeast, and California areas of North America—by specialists working in those areas. The paper by Georgieann Bogdan and David Weaver was not presented at the symposium but was included in the volume because of its relevance to the issue of treponemal disease in the precontact Americas.

The second part of the volume presents the evidence for temporal shifts in population size, again following a regional organization. Following a discussion of population estimates in historical context, scholars present the evidence from the Amazon Basin in South America, Andean South America, the Caribbean, and Northeast, Southeast, Southwest, Plains, and Northwest Coast areas of North America. These chapters present perspectives from different data bases, including ethnohistorical sources, archeological surveys, computer simulations, and epidemiological theory.

We hope that collectively the assembled essays convey the diversity and intensity of current research in this area. Readers should be aware that scholars were selected for inclusion not because they shared a particular point of view with the organizers, but because they are in the forefront of their fields and have unique perspectives on the problem of disease and demography in the Americas. While this approach may sacrifice some cohesion of the essays within the volume, we feel it adds a sense of excitement about the innovative and diverse research that is underway and provides perspective on the issues. We feel that real progress on these issues can be made only when scholars working in different academic areas share their data and perspectives. Such interdisciplinary research may pave the way toward new understanding of the demographic and disease impact of Christopher Columbus's venture into the New World 500 years ago.

— I —

Disease before
and
after Contact

2

Skeletal Paleopathology

Probabilities, Possibilities,
and Impossibilities

DONALD J. ORTNER

Much of the evidence for the presence of disease in the New World, both before and after 1492, is based on data obtained from research on archeological human skeletal samples. This source of data has considerable potential in clarifying the biological and cultural impact of disease in Native American groups. However, it is important to evaluate carefully what can be learned, what can be suggested, and what cannot be learned about disease on the basis of research in skeletal paleopathology.

The current literature on the subject is a rather uncomfortable mixture of interesting data and ideas along with statements that are not well supported by sound research methodology and careful interpretation of evidence. Sorting out the good research from inadequate research can be a challenge. However, clear evidence of sound methodology, careful observation, and thoughtful interpretation of results are often apparent particularly if one is familiar with some of the basic issues and methods in skeletal analysis.

There are a number of limitations in using skeletal remains to reconstruct the presence and impact of pathological conditions in the past. About 15 percent of all skeletons in a typical archeological sample from North America will show evidence of significant disease. Most of these cases will be divided about equally among three general disease categories—trauma, infection, and arthritis. All the remaining general orthopedic disease categories occur but are rare. Infectious diseases are of particular significance following European contact in 1492.

One of the limitations in studying infectious disease in archeological skeletal samples is that acute diseases are very rarely expressed in either the gross or microscopic morphology of the skeleton. Almost all the infectious pathological conditions that are evident are chronic diseases. This means that most of the great epidemics that have punctuated human history will leave, at best, nonspecific and indirect evidence in a skeletal sample. Infectious diseases caused by viruses very rarely affect the skeleton. Viral diseases such as smallpox and measles had a particularly devastating effect on Native American populations subsequent to A.D. 1500 but there is no clear evidence of either disease in archeological skeletal samples. But the extraction of human immunoglobulins from archeological human skeletons (Tuross 1991) raises the possibility of identifying antibodies to viral diseases in archeo-

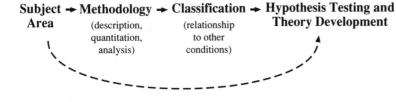

Subject → Methodology → Classification → Hypothesis Testing and
Area   (description,   (relationship   **Theory Development**
              quantitation,   to other
              analysis)   conditions)

Fig. 1. Stages (solid arrows) in the development of theory in paleopathology. Careful scholarship in paleopathology requires thorough attention to methodology and classification. It is tempting to move on to hypothesis testing and theory development (dashed line) before establishing a sound methodology and creating a classificatory system that defines significant relationships.

logical remains. Several laboratories claim to have recovered human DNA from archeological tissues, including bone (Pääbo 1987; Hagelberg, Sykes, and Hedges 1989). Viral DNA may also be identifiable, so archeological evidence of viral disease may be directly accessible in the near future.

The infectious diseases that do affect the skeleton are those caused primarily by bacteria. But even these infectious organisms rarely affect the skeleton unless there is long-term survival with the disease. Most evidence of infectious disease in archeological human skeletons is the result of chronic bacterial infections in which the host's immune response did not entirely eliminate the infectious agent but was not overwhelmed by the agent either. Long-term survival of the host and the agent provides the time necessary for the skeletal system to become involved.

The limited number of infectious diseases that affect the skeleton highlights the importance of asking two basic questions in skeletal paleopathology—where are the diseases that occur in a skeletal sample and what do they mean particularly to longevity and the biological function of the individual during life? In this context it is important to emphasize that the cause of skeletal disease in an archeological case is not necessarily the cause of death, although it may be a contributing factor.

METHODS IN SKELETAL PALEOPATHOLOGY

In skeletal paleopathology the basic method is observation. In this paleopathology resembles other sciences, such as systematic biology, geology, and paleontology, which have only limited access to experimental methods. Figure 1 illustrates the broad stages in the development theory. For the subject area, in this case skeletal paleopathology, scientists try to develop a methodology that permits useful statements about their observations. On the basis of descriptive features scientists classify the observations into categories that appear to be related. Where possible they use quantitative methods to attempt to analyze and integrate their data with those of others. Finally, they relate the findings to existing theory, perhaps with some modification or enrichment of appropriate elements of relevant theory.

Normally, of course, there is feedback between the various stages of research, and it is important to emphasize, in addition, that science is most often an iterative process and not a matter of reaching, once and for all, some immutable conclusion. Problems in skeletal paleopathology develop when short-cuts are used in the theory-building process, that is, when one attempts to overextend the data by conclusions that are not justified by the quantity or quality of the data. In skeletal paleopathology, as in other biomedical disciplines, one should be cautious about engaging in theory development without having done an adequate job in the previous stages of the research process.

The initial step in the research process is careful description of the pathological condition in an archeological skeleton. What is the nature of the abnormality? Possibilities include abnormal size, abnormal shape, abnormal bone destruction, and abnormal bone formation. The location within the skeleton and within a specific bone is important and, if the condition involves more than one area in the skeleton, the distribution pattern is critical. For example, some diseases predilect the appendicular skeleton (e.g., treponematosis); others more commonly affect the axial skeleton (e.g., tuberculosis). Some diseases tend to involve the metaphysis (e.g., bone tumors) while others more often affect the diaphysis (e.g., infection).

Classification of pathological conditions is a

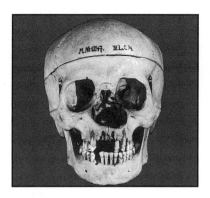 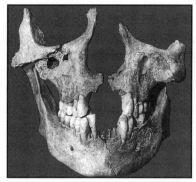

Fig. 2. Left, nasomaxillary involvement in syphilis with pathological enlargement of the piriform aperture and partial destruction of the nasal bones, nasal septum, and conchae. (Male, estimated age of 30 years, catalog no. 1247, Federal Pathologic Anatomy Museum, Vienna, Austria.) Right, nasomaxillary involvement in leprosy with remodeling of the piriform aperture and anterior maxilla. (Male, estimated age of 20 years, burial no. S-64 from the medieval cemetery of the hospital of St. James and St. Mary Magdalene in Chichester, England. Skeletal sample curated by the Department of Archeological Sciences, University of Bradford, England.)

major challenge in many cases. One of the problems is that different diseases can affect the skeleton in similar ways. This is well illustrated by destructive lesions of the nasal aperture. Such abnormalities can be caused by many pathological conditions, including treponematosis (fig. 2), leprosy (fig. 2), tuberculosis (fig. 3), leishmaniasis, cleft palate and lip, cancer, and trauma. These conditions present skeletal evidence so similar that even experienced physical anthropologists often have difficulty in sorting it out.

One of the problems in trying to classify a pathological condition is that only one stage is presented in what would have been an on-going process. It is somewhat analogous to reconstructing the plot of a feature-length movie on the basis of a few segments of film taken from anywhere in the picture. For example, there are two possible models for interpreting a porous enlargement of bone tissue in the skull, one expression of which is known as porotic hyperostosis. This condition is associated with a number of pathological conditions, most commonly with anemia, particularly in infants and small children.

During infancy and early childhood virtually all marrow spaces are required for blood formation. Increased blood-cell turnover creates the demand for added red marrow space for hematopoiesis. Enlargement of marrow spaces tends to take place in all marrow areas but is particularly apparent in the skull.

As with many other abnormal conditions, other pathological conditions can stimulate conditions that resemble those resulting from anemia. On the skull these include both scurvy and infection. In figure 4, two models are presented for different pathological processes that can result in a similar bony change.

The first model illustrates the addition of porous inflammatory bone on the outer surface of the outer table. As the bone increases in thickness, remodeling begins to take place, particularly in the healing phase; and although there is no increase in hematopoietic marrow at all, the thickness of some bones is enlarged and the outer surface is porous. Toward the end stage of the disease the inner table is remodeled away, leaving a porous outer surface with openings that are continuous with the diploë. In this model, the disease process begins on the outer, compact-bone surface but eventually may become continuous with the diploë.

The second model shows abnormal change that is initiated in the diploë. The porous outer table is the result of remodeling that converts the outer table to diploë in order to create additional space for hematopoietic tissue. In early stages the pores penetrate the outer table so there is no solid layer of bone as is the case in the upper model. In

Fig. 3. Nasomaxillary involvement in cranial tuberculosis (lupus vulgaris) with partial destruction of nasal bones, conchae, nasal septum, maxilla, and palate. (Male, 15 years of age with tuberculosis for 10 years, catalog no. 1 FT 2(1), Pathology Museum, The Royal College of Surgeons of Edinburgh, Scotland.)

fected (fig. 5). Abnormal inflammatory bone is added on top of existing tissue. There has been some remodeling of the original outer table, with blood vessel channels becoming continuous through the table, but the table is still largely intact. In the second case (fig. 6) the inner table is present although thinner than normal, but the outer table has virtually been obliterated and replaced by spongy bone with only a remnant of the original outer table and minimal evidence of any new outer table.

Reconstructing the pathogenesis in these two cases depends on the ability to determine whether the pathological process began in the diploë or on the external surface of the outer table. It is at least conceivable that in or near the end stage of both pathological processes the dry-bone morphology would be indistinguishable.

the end-stage, the gross surface and sectional morphology may be very similar to the appearance of model one, although the process was fundamentally different. Figures 5-6 show archeological probable examples of both models.

The first case (fig. 5) is a child's skull, from an archeological site in Florida, that shows porous lesions on the skull surface and a thickened skull (Ortner and Putschar 1981:138). Superficially it resembles the porous abnormal bone seen in infant and childhood anemia. The second case (fig. 6) is a child from the American Southwest that is a probable case of iron deficiency anemia (Ortner and Putschar 1981:262). In addition to the porous thickened skull, the long bones have an abnormally enlarged marrow space and thinned cortical bone.

Sections of these cases show a clear difference. In the first case, the hemopoietic marrow is not af-

FACTORS THAT AFFECT THE EXPRESSION OF DISEASE IN THE SKELETON

There are many factors that affect pathogenesis in a person with a pathological condition including: (1) the age of onset; (2) the individual's nutritional status; (3) the immune response of the person, which determines how effectively they will meet the challenge of pathological agents; (4) the biology of infectious agents, one component of which is virulence; (5) the portal of entry, such as the respiratory system, the digestive system, the urogenital system, or directly through the skin by way of a cut or open sore; (6) the effectiveness of any method of treatment; and (7) social conditions that can affect the transmission of disease (e.g., clothing that limits transmission of disease via skin contact) or the host

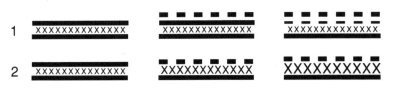

Fig. 4. Models for the development of porotic hyperostosis—thickened, porous lesions of the skull vault. Normal bone tissue is represented by the left diagram in both models. In both processes the skull is thickened and the outer surface is porous. A cross-section of end stages of both processes may be very similar.

LEGEND

compact bone tables of the skull
diploë or hematopoietic marrow
porous inflammatory bone

 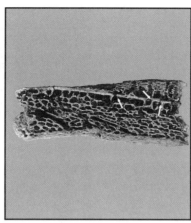

Fig. 5. Porous, inflammatory, reactive bone on the skull vault. Left, top view; right, cross-section. The outer table is largely intact although there are vascular channels through it (arrows) providing communication between the diplöe and the reactive bone tissue. (Three-year-old child from a post-Columbian site on the Canaveral Peninsula, Fla., catalog no. 377545, National Museum of Natural History, Smithsonian.)

response (e.g., social breakdown that diminishes the will to live).

Treponematosis is a disease system that illustrates many of these factors. There are four syndromes associated with treponematosis. All four are caused by organisms that are indistinguishable from each other by current clinical procedures (Grmek 1989:135). Three syndromes—venereal syphilis, yaws, and bejel (endemic syphilis)—can affect the skeleton and do so in about 15 percent of affected individuals. The fourth, pinta, does not affect the skeleton. Only venereal syphilis is associated with a congenital expression of the disease with transplacental transmission from the infected mother to the developing fetus. Yaws and bejel are usually acquired as childhood diseases with transmission typically occurring in play groups. Syphilis is acquired venereally with an onset that usually begins after childhood.

A fair amount of printers ink has been used to explore the history of syphilis. Of particular interest has been the transmission of the disease syndrome between Europe and the New World. This is, in fact, an important and interesting question. A far more interesting question is why what appears to be a single organism results in different pathogenic processes and different patterns of skeletal involvement. Three archeological cases of probable treponematosis illustrate aspects of this problem.

The first specimen is that of a male American

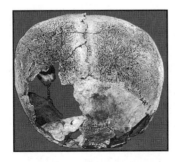 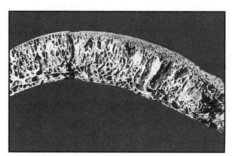

Fig. 6. Thickened parietal bones in a probable case of iron deficiency anemia. Left, cribriform outer surface; right, broken section. The inner table is very thin, while the outer table is not distinguishable due to the extensive remodeling. The temporal bone is much thicker than normal with greatly enlarged space for hematopoietic marrow. (Two-year-old child from the pre-Columbian site of Pueblo Bonito, N. Mex., catalog no. 327107, National Museum of Natural History, Smithsonian.)

Indian from the Fisher site, Virginia, that is dated between A.D. 1000 and 1400. The age of this particular individual is estimated in the 30–40 year range. Pathological features in this case include disseminated, remodeled, healed lesions occurring on the frontal bone of the skull and in the postcranial skeleton as well. The lesions are classic granulomatous foci that are indicative of chronic infectious processes. The type and distribution of lesions is typical of treponematosis that affects the skeleton.

The upper extremity exhibits multiple areas of destructive foci that are in the process of healing and thickening of the diaphyses. The joints are unaffected. The radiological evidence demonstrates reactive bone deposition (sclerosis) around most lytic foci that provides clear evidence of the chronic nature of the disease process. There is no involvement of the spine. There is slight involvement of some of the ribs. In the lower extremity, the tibias exhibit the addition of bone on the anterior surface that creates the impression of bowing. However, this appearance is entirely due to appositional bone being added on the anterior surface creating a thickened and rather lumpy surface (fig. 7). This condition is apparent but less severe on the femora. The bones of the feet are involved in this case as well.

The disease process is clearly systemic, implying hematogenous dissemination. The involvement of the frontal bone, the tibias, the absence of significant involvement in the axial skeleton—all fit the typical pattern of treponematosis. This is one of the most convincing candidates for treponematosis in pre-Columbian, New World archeological skeletal samples.

The skeleton of a child between three and four years of age was also recovered from the Fisher site, a few feet from the adult male skeleton described above. Particularly striking in this case is the evidence of defective enamel formation (fig. 8) that has resulted in substantial destruction of some dental crowns by caries superimposed in areas of defective enamel (hypoplasia). Deciduous incisor crowns are involved, suggesting that the abnormality was present at the time of birth. The long bones of this individual, particularly the tibias, exhibit perosteal reactive bone indicative of a longstanding, disseminated, inflammatory condition. The combination of dental hypoplasia and periosteal reactive bone formation in the long bones is strongly suggestive of congenital syphilis. This diagnostic option is in-

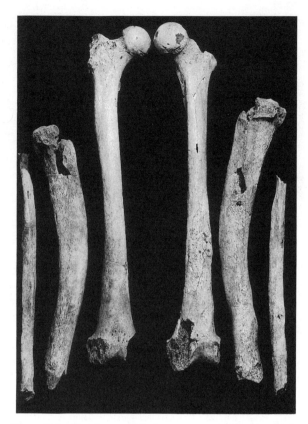

Fig. 7. Major long bones of the lower extremity showing the development of reactive periosteal bone in a probable case of syphilis. Reactive bone is particularly pronounced on the anterior aspect of the tibias (shown lateral view). (Catalog no. 385788, National Museum of Natural History, Smithsonian.)

creased by the evidence of treponematosis in the adult male skeleton from the same site and time period. Although the argument is somewhat circular, these two cases support the conclusion that the treponemal syndrome associated with this pre-Columbian site is syphilis since that syndrome is the only one reported to induce a congenital expression.

Yaws affects the skeleton in areas that generally overlap with the pattern of involvement seen in syphilis. There may be some subtle differences in the pattern, frequency, and severity of lesions in the skeleton (Steinbock 1976:114, 144), but the morphological overlap is considerable. For example, in the case of 30 individuals from archeological material excavated in Guam and Australia, yaws was diagnosed largely on the basis of geographical association. However, a strong case can be made for treponematosis in all 30 examples.

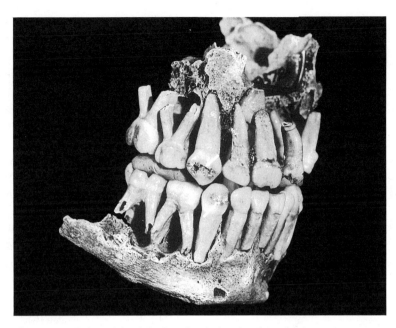

Fig. 8. Lateral view of the right dental arch showing the enamel defects (arrows) in the crown that are the possible result of congenital syphilis (catalog no. 385786, National Museum of Natural History, Smithsonian.)

The pattern of granulomatous lesions in the skull and appendicular skeleton is very similar to that seen in syphilis. About one-third of the cases studied had an additional feature of destructive lesions involving the joints and para-articular metaphyseal and enthesial bone tissue. This feature is unlike any joint involvement in syphilis (Charcot joint) and can affect large areas of bone.

An example of this aspect of skeletal involvement in yaws is seen in an archeological skeleton of an adult Australian Aboriginal female (fig. 9). The skull exhibits healed lytic foci that are typical of treponematosis. Lesions of the appendicular skeleton are also like those seen in clinical cases of treponematosis. However, many of the joints and para-articular areas exhibit major destruction of bone tissue accompanied by considerable reactive repair, a type of articular and para-articular surface destruction that is unknown in syphilis. This feature in some yaws cases may make it possible to differentiate between archeological cases of yaws and syphilis in some specimens.

The difference between the skeletal manifestations of yaws and syphilis raises a very important and interesting biological problem: why is this type of joint destruction seen in yaws and not in syphilis?

Since the treponemal bacteria that causes all the syndromes of treponematoses appears to be identical, other factors must explain the different skeletal involvement in the two treponemal syndromes.

CONCLUSIONS

It is helpful to distinguish between the theoretical potential of skeletal paleopathology and the current state of the research in that field. Clearly there are serious problems in the literature that reflect deficiencies in methodology and theory. Incorrect diagnosis of pathological cases is a common problem. This occurs in a variety of contexts including the failure to understand the diagnostic options for pathological conditions that are attributable to a specific disease and attempting a specific diagnosis for nonspecific pathological conditions. In addition there are definite limits on the types of diseases that can be identified in skeletal specimens. For infectious disease one rarely encounters conditions other than chronic, bacterial diseases. Fungal organisms can cause skeletal disease, but infection from these agents is rare even in areas where it is endemic. The potential of a major breakthrough in identifying

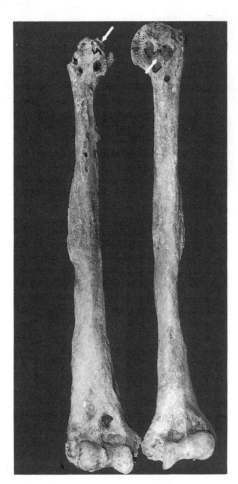

Fig. 9. Anterior view of the humeri in a probable case of yaws from a postcontact site in Coolah, Australia (retouched). The diaphysis of the right is especially enlarged. Of particular interest is the evidence of remodeled destructive foci of proximal articular and para-articular surfaces (arrows). This type of joint involvement is not typical of skeletal manifestations in syphilis. (Catalog no. 136, Shellshear Museum, University of Sydney, Australia.)

other types of infectious diseases using biochemical methods seems real and promising through both recovery and analysis of DNA and immunoglobulins.

The ethnohistorical record demonstrates that many infectious diseases were introduced into the New World by European contact from 1492 on. Almost certainly some infectious diseases were present in both Europe and the New World at that time.

Treponematosis was certainly present in the New World before 1492 (Baker and Armelagos 1988). Whether it was in Europe remains a question. There are at least two reports of probable pre-1500 cases (Anderson et al. 1986; Dawes and Magliton 1980). Unequivocal cases of syphilis reliably dated to before 1492 are uncommon in New World archeological skeletal samples. Many of the New World cases reviewed in Baker and Armelagos (1988:711–717) exhibit lesion types and patterns that are suggestive of treponematosis but could be the result of other pathological conditions.

Archeological evidence of tuberculosis in New World, pre-Columbian archeological human skeletals seems convincing (Ortner and Putschar 1981:166–176). Its antiquity in the Old World is well established, with skeletal evidence extending to at least the Neolithic period (Grmek 1989:133; Ortner and Theobald 1991). The association of tuberculosis with the early domestication of bovids in the Old World seems plausible (Manchester 1983:39). Its relationship with animal vectors in the New World is more problematic.

Research and discussion has focused on another interesting problem in paleopathology, the history of the inflammatory, erosive, joint diseases such as rheumatoid arthritis (Dieppe 1989). These joint diseases are thought to have a defective genetic substrate probably associated with an infectious triggering agent. Some syndromes, such as ankylosing spondylitis, are present in the New World well before 1492. The existence of pre-Columbian rheumatoid arthritis is being debated (Rogers and Dieppe 1989; Rothschild, Woods, and Turner 1989). The major theoretical problem for those who argue that it was present long before Columbus and before its appearance in Europe (e.g., Rothschild and Woods 1990) is why it remains a much more serious problem among contemporary Native American groups than in the White population. Cockburn (1963:34) proposed that infectious agents tend to be less virulent through time as the host population evolves a more effective immune response. If some variant of this hypothesis is relevant in the inflammatory, erosive, joint diseases, one would expect a host population with longer exposure to the agent to have a lower prevalence of the disease than a population that was first exposed more recently.

It is one of the unfortunate ironies of scientific research that scientists are acquiring the knowledge and methodological tools to do a much more effective job of interpreting evidence of disease in archeological specimens at a time when the pressure for reburial will make many archeological samples inaccessible for research.

It must be remembered that infectious organisms evolve as does the host population. Diseases that disappeared before the advent of good medical descriptions are unlikely to be identified. However, very few cases of skeletal disease look fundamentally different from the conditions encountered today. To tap more fully this important source of information on human biological history, research methodology and the classificatory system must receive careful attention.

REFERENCES

Anderson, T.
1986 Suspected Endemic Syphilis (treponarid in Sixteenth-century Norway. *Medical History* 30:341–350.

Baker, B. J., and G. J. Armelagos
1988 The Origin and Antiquity of Syphilis. *Current Anthropology* 29:703–720.

Cockburn, A.
1963 The Evolution and Eradication of Infectious Diseases. Baltimore: The Johns Hopkins Press.

Daws, J. D., and J. R. Magilton
1980 The Archeology of York. Vol. 12, fasicle I: The Cemetery of St. Helen-on-the-Walls, Aldwark, York, England: Archeological Trust.

Dieppe, P.
1989 The History of Rheumatoid Arthritis. Pp. 35–38 in The Antiquity of the Erosive Arthropathies. P. Dieppe and J. Rogers, eds. The Arthritis and Rheumatism Council for Research, Conference Proceedings No. 5.

Gremk, M. D.
1989 Diseases in the Ancient Greek World. Baltimore: The Johns Hopkins University Press.

Hagelberg, E., B. Sykes, and R. Hedges
1989 Ancient Bone DNA Amplified. *Nature* 342:485.

Manchester, K.
1983 The Archaeology of Disease. Bradford, England: The University of Bradford.

Ortner, D. J., and W. G. J. Putschar
1981 Identification of Pathological Conditions in Human Skeletal Remains. Washington: Smithsonian Institution Press.

Ortner, D. J., and G. Theobald
[1991] History of Human Diseases During Prehistory and Antiquity in the Old World. In the History and Geography of Human Disease, P. 5. Kenneth F. Kiple, ed. New York: Cambridge University Press.

Pääbo, S.
1987 Molecular Genetic Methods in Archaeology: A Prospect. *Anthropologischer Anzeiger* 45:9–17.

Rogers, J. M., and P. A. Dieppe
1989 Symmetrical Erosive Arthritis in Ohio Woodland Indians. *Journal of Rheumatology* 16:1012.

Rothschild, B. M., and R. J. Woods
1990 Symmetrical Erosive Disease in Archaic Indians: The Origin of Rheumatoid Arthritis in the New World? *Seminars in Arthritis and Rheumatism* 19:278–284.

Rothschild, B. M., R. J. Woods, and K. R. Turner
1989 Reply. *Journal of Rheumatology* 16:1012–1013.

Steinbock, R. T.
1976 Paleopathological Diagnosis and Interpretation. Springfield, Ill.: Charles C. Thomas.

Tuross, N.
1991 Recovery of Bone and Serum Protein from Human Skeletal Tissue: IgG, Osteonectin and Albumin. In Human Paleopathology: Current Syntheses and Future Options. D. J. Ortner and A. C. Aufderheide, eds. Washington: Smithsonian Institution Press.

—— 3 ——

Prehistoric Disease and Demography in the Andes

JOHN W. VERANO

Andean South America has a rich archeological record that documents the rise and collapse of some of the most complex societies to emerge in the pre-contact New World. Large sedentary populations, ceremonial architecture, and complex societies appeared earlier on the desert coast of Peru than in any other part of the New World. Changes in settlement pattern and subsistence strategy, and their effects on human health and demography, have become important research areas in archeology and physical anthropology (Cohen and Armelagos 1984; Cohen 1989; Ubelaker 1984). The impact of European and African disease imports on New World populations during the early contact period was strongly affected by variables such as settlement pattern, population density, and frequency of contact between indigenous groups. Community health and previous disease experience were also important factors in determining the response of native New World peoples to European contact.

THE ANDEAN AREA

The Andean area is generally defined as the portion of South America that formed the Inca empire at its period of greatest expansion. At the time of first European contact in 1532, the Inca empire stretched nearly 5,000 kilometers north to south, from the present-day Ecuador-Colombia border to the Maule River in central Chile. East to west it extended from the Pacific coast to the eastern slopes of the Andean Cordillera, roughly 300 to 600 kilometers. It was linked by a network of some 15,000 kilometers of roads, making communication and travel surprisingly rapid, despite the rugged terrain and great variation in altitude characteristic of the Andes. The Inca empire itself was quite short-lived, existing for less than 100 years before being conquered by Spaniards in 1532. However, much of its cultural and administrative foundations were rooted in a long sequence of complex societies, several of which had, like the Inca, periodically united large areas of the Andean highlands and coast.

Population at Contact

The Inca were excellent administrators and conducted frequent censuses of their population. Unfortunately, these census data, which were kept by Inca professionals on groups of knotted cords called quipus, were lost during the disruption and chaos of the early colonial period. The first population figures documented for Peru come from the census taken in 1571. By this time disease, conquest, civil wars, forced population movements, and disruption of native societies had resulted in major population decline throughout the Andean area.

Given the lack of reliable data from the precontact and early postcontact period, estimates of the population of the Inca empire have varied widely. Based on comparisons of the 1571 census figures with population estimates for selected Inca provinces at around 1525, Rowe (1947:184–186) proposed a mean depopulation ratio of 4:1 during the early contact period and estimated the population of the Andean area in 1525 at about six million. C. T. Smith (1970) is in general agreement with Rowe's figures. However, other scholars have proposed substantially higher numbers. Cook (1981) placed the population of the Andean area at about 13 million in 1520, with approximately nine million people living within the present-day borders of Peru. Other estimates of the precontact population of Peru have ranged from 2 million to 32 million (Dobyns 1966; Cook 1981:13). The most reasonable estimate of population size of the Andean area in 1520 probably lies somewhere between 6 and 13 million.

European disease appears to have preceded actual European contact in the Andean area. In the mid-1520s, nearly a decade before Francisco Pizarro met the Inca emperor Atahualpa in Cajamarca, the Andean area experienced a major epidemic, probably smallpox, which spread south from Ecuador. The epidemic was carried rapidly through the Inca empire, assisted undoubtedly by its excellent road and communication system. Beginning in the 1530s, repeated epidemics, combined with the ravages of conquest, civil war, famine, and social disruption, led to a major decline in the native Andean population, particularly in the densely populated coastal valleys of Peru (Dobyns 1963; Cook 1981). While there has been substantial population recovery over the past two centuries, the cultural and genetic complexion of much of the Andean area has been permanently transformed as a result of European contact.

Pre-Inca Population

Andean South America is littered with ruins, abandoned agricultural terraces, and irrigation canals that provide evidence of dense and long-term human occupation of the region. The vast majority of these sites predate the Inca empire, and some of the largest Andean cities were already abandoned or in decline at the time of the expansion of the Inca empire in the fifteenth century A.D. (Rowe 1963; Isbell 1988).

Coastal Peru provides the most detailed archeological evidence for the initial transition from migratory hunter-gatherers to sedentary populations, which began on the coast at around 6000 B.C. (Benfer 1984; Quilter 1989). The Peruvian coast also documents the emergence of the earliest complex societies in the New World, which appear between about 2500 and 1500 B.C. (Moseley 1975; Donnan 1985; Fung Pineda 1988). These sites are characterized by large-scale monumental architecture and a degree of planning that suggests centralized control over labor and subsistence activities (Moseley 1975, 1985; Pozorski 1982; Pozorski and Pozorski 1987). Although there continues to be debate about the level of social complexity reflected in these early sites, it is clear that large, sedentary populations appeared surprisingly early in Andean South America.

Following the period of early florescence of complex society in the Andes, there is abundant evidence of intensification of agricultural production, reflected in the construction of agricultural terraces and raised fields in the highlands (Kolata 1983; Erickson 1987) and irrigation canal networks in coastal valleys (Kosok 1965; Mosely and Deeds 1982). Archeological site surveys in both coastal and highland valleys indicate that there was substantial fluctuation in population size through time, with some areas showing periods of dense occupation followed by collapse and decline, long before the period of initial European contact (Willey 1953; Kolata 1983; Wilson 1988).

PREHISTORIC DISEASE

Most studies before 1950 focused on the identification of chronic infectious diseases, such as syphilis, tuberculosis, and leprosy, and degenerative diseases, such as arthritis and dental pathologies in prehistoric South American remains (Stewart 1950a, 1950b). Much of the early debate over syphilis and leprosy, while lively, was based more on artistic depictions than skeletal remains, and subsequent research has failed to produce unequivocal evidence for either leprosy or syphilis, although some form of treponemal disease appears to have been present in prehistoric populations of northern Chile (Allison et al. 1982; Standen, Allison, and Arriaza 1984).

In contrast, the presence of tuberculosis has been positively identified histologically in mummified remains from Peru (Allison, Mendoza, and Pezzis 1973), and skeletal changes characteristic of tuberculosis have been noted in several prehistoric Andean populations (Allison et al. 1981; Allison 1984; Buikstra and Williams 1991). There is also some evidence that leishmaniasis (*uta*), an insect-borne disease endemic in portions of Peru and Brazil in the twentieth century (Omran 1961), afflicted some prehistoric Andean populations as well (Weiss 1961; Urteaga-Ballon 1991). Studies of coprolites from coastal Peruvian archeological sites indicate that pre-Hispanic populations were afflicted with various intestinal parasites, including tapeworm (*Diphyllobothrium pacificum*), pinworm (*Enterobius vermicularis*), whipworm (*Trichuris trichuria*), and roundworm (*Ascaris lumbricoides*) (Callen and Cameron 1960; Patrucco, Tello, and Bonavia 1983). Hookworm (*Ancylostoma duodenale*) has also been recovered from the intestinal lumen of a precontact south coast Peruvian mummy (Allison et al. 1974). Coprolite samples (Patrucco, Tello, and Bonavia 1983) document the presence of tapeworm and roundworm in cultural strata dating to 2700–2800 B.C., and pinworm at approximately 2300 B.C., providing evidence of substantial antiquity for these parasites on the Peruvian coast.

Early observers such as René Verneau (Stewart 1950b) and Aleš Hrdlička (1911, 1914) were impressed by a lack of evidence of chronic infectious and degenerative disease in prehistoric South American skeletal remains. It is difficult to evaluate these findings, because the samples examined by Verneau, Hrdlička, and their contemporaries consisted of disassociated skeletal elements collected from looted cemeteries of uncertain cultural association and dating. Unfortunately, such problems affect the majority of collections of Andean skeletal remains in museums worldwide, making it difficult to make reliable statements about the frequency of specific diseases on a population basis.

Research on human skeletal and mummified remains by Robert Benfer and associates on the central coast of Peru, by Marvin Allison, Jane Buikstra, Arthur Aufderheide, and associates in southern Peru and northern Chile, by Douglas Ubelaker in Ecuador, and by John Verano on the north coast of Peru is providing some of the first quantitative data on patterns of health and disease through time in the Andean area. A growing sample of scientifically excavated skeletal collections, rare in the Andean area until the 1980s, has made such studies possible.

Ecuador

Ubelaker has published descriptions of skeletal samples from prehistoric Ecuador (Ubelaker 1980a, 1980b, 1981, 1983, 1988a, 1988b, 1988c), as well as summaries of his research on prehistoric demography and skeletal biology (Ubelaker 1984, 1988d). In a review of temporal trends in disease and demography in Ecuador (Ubelaker 1990) he concludes that while early populations of coastal Ecuador had low levels of infectious disease, anemia, dental caries, and various measures of nutritional stress, samples of human remains from later time periods show regular temporal increases in the frequencies of these problems. These frequency increases are notable in coastal populations and correlate with an increase in sedentism and a less varied diet. Moreover, Ubelaker has found a significantly higher frequency of porotic hyperostosis in coastal populations, and he suggests that parasitism, due to hookworm and possibly other parasites that require warm and damp conditions to propagate, may have been a significant contributing factor. This finding of higher frequencies of porotic hyperostosis in coastal populations is consistent with observations on prehistoric Peruvian skulls by Hrdlička (1914:57–59) and Weiss (1961:125–127). Porotic hyperostosis in prehistoric Ecuador reflects chronic anemia produced by viral, bacterial, and parasitic diseases stimulated by increased sedentism, population density, and sanitation problems (Ubelaker 1990). The similar pattern in the distribution of porotic hyperostosis in coastal and highland Peru may also reflect differences in settlement density, sanitary conditions, and parasite infestation. Other variables, such as the degree of social stratification, agricultural intensification, and differential access to dietary resources may also explain frequency differences observed between different coastal samples.

Central Peru

The early transition from migratory hunting and gathering to sedentary village life and incipient agriculture has been studied on the central coast of Peru at the site of La Paloma, which dates between 5000 and 2500 B.C. (Benfer 1981, 1984; Quilter 1989). Based on the age distribution of burials in different occupational levels and relative frequency of skeletal stress indicators, Benfer concluded that although the earliest inhabitants of La Paloma were severely stressed, there was evidence of decreased infant mortality, greater adult life expectancy, and some indications of improved nutritional status with the adaptation to sedentism and incipient food production.

Southern Peru and Northern Chile

Allison and associates have published a number of studies of prehistoric disease in populations of southern Peru and northern Chile (Allison 1984; Allison and Gerszten 1982; Allison, Mendoza, and Pezzia 1973; Allison et al. 1974, 1979, 1981; Dalton, Allison, and Pezzia 1976; Elzay, Allison, and Pezzia 1977). This work is important in that it involves the study of mummified tissues as well as skeletal remains. The extremely dry south coast of Peru and coastal Chile provide an exceptional preservational environment, and natural mummification of bodies is common. Through the study of mummified tissues, Allison and colleagues have been able to document the presence of chronic infectious diseases such as tuberculosis (Alison, Mendoza, and Pezzia 1973) and blastomycosis (Alison et al. 1979) as well as acute infectious diseases such as bronchopneumonia and lobar pneumonia (Allison 1984). Such findings are exceptional in the field of paleopathology, because the presence of acute infectious disease can rarely be identified from the skeleton alone. Based on autopsies of mummified remains from Peru and Chile, Allison (1984:521) concludes that:

> acute respiratory disease in the form of pneumonia was a major cause of death in individuals from both coastal and mountain cultures and indeed was the major cause of death among all people from all time periods independent of diet, involvement, or social organization. It would be no exaggeration to say that for the past 8000 years most Americans have died of the same causes, acute and chronic respiratory diseases.

Based on a study of 16 populations from coastal Peru and Chile ranging from approximately 2000 B.C. to the early colonial period, Allison (1984) examined patterns of demography and disease through time. He found childhood mortality to be high, with nearly 50 percent of children dying before 15 years of age in most samples. No evidence of a general improvement in health was observed with the adoption of sedentism and intensification of agricultural production. On the contrary, sedentary village life was generally detrimental to health, due to crowding and sanitation problems, and the increasing social stratification seen at some later sites resulted in health benefits only for the elite minority. "It would appear that the larger political organizations of pre-Columbian times, the last of which was the Inca, were able to store and distribute agricultural products to provide a less than optimal diet to a large potential labor force, but at the expense of its health" (Allison 1984:527).

Northern Peru

Despite intensive archeological investigations on the north coast of Peru since the 1960s, research on prehistoric demography and skeletal biology of north coast populations remains at a preliminary stage. Descriptions of some important early skeletal remains have been published (Chauchat and Dricot 1979; Chauchat and Lacombe 1984; Vidal Vidal and Schwidetzky 1987), but most other data on prehistoric populations of the north coast are derived from studies of surface-collected material from looted cemeteries of uncertain temporal and cultural association (Verano 1987, 1991b). The looting of archeological sites by artifact collectors, a tradition that began in the early colonial period, continues to be a major problem in Peru in 1990. The great majority of prehistoric cemeteries on the north coast have been heavily damaged by looting. While many museums contain skeletal material collected from these sites, very few of these collections were made systematically, and most are mixed samples from various sites and time periods.

Fieldwork conducted by John Verano on the north coast of Peru has involved both cemetery excavations and controlled surface collections of looted cemeteries. Although the principal focus of this research has been on prehistoric population relationships and mortuary practices (Verano 1987; Verano and Cordy-Collins 1986), data on skeletal pathology and paleodemography were collected as well (Verano 1990, 1991a, 1991b). Much of this work has centered on the site of Pacatnamu.

Pacatnamu is a Middle Horizon and Late Intermediate period ceremonial center situated on a blufftop overlooking the Pacific Ocean at the mouth of the Jequetepeque River on the north coast of Peru. The archeological site consists of a complex of more than 50 mud brick pyramid mounds and associated courtyards and walled enclosures, covering an area of approximately one square kilometer. Although much of the visible architecture appears to have been ceremonial in function, extensive refuse deposits at the site suggest that Pacatnamu had a substantial resident population (Donnan 1986). More than 40 cemeteries have been identified within the architectural complex and outside its outer wall (Verano and Cordy-Collins 1986; Verano 1987). During a five-year multidisciplinary study of the site (Donnan and Cock 1986), the physical characteristics, population affinities, and health status of the prehistoric population was analyzed.

Pacatnamu has suffered centuries of depredation by artifact hunters, and looting has been frequent since the early 1970s (Verano 1987:67). The surfaces of most cemeteries at the site are littered with human skeletal remains and fragments of ceramics and textiles. Examination of artifact material on the surface revealed that most cemeteries at the site are single component, used for relatively brief periods of time during one of the two major occupational phases, the Middle Horizon, A.D. 600–900, and the Late Intermediate period, 1100–1400. The single-component nature of these cemeteries made systematic surface collection of skeletal remains feasible, permitting between-cemetery comparisons of physical characteristics and skeletal pathology (Verano 1987).

Disturbance of graves with the resultant disassociation of skeletal material by looters limits paleopathological observations considerably. However, the frequency of certain skeletal stress indicators such as porotic hyperostosis and cribra orbitalia can be assessed in disassociated material. Porotic hyperostosis and cribra orbitalia, porous lesions found on the external table of the skull vault and orbital roofs, are generally considered to repre-

sent a physiological response to iron deficiency anemia, which can be caused and exacerbated by a variety of factors, including dietary deficiencies, intestinal parasites, infectious disease, and the synergistic effects of these factors (Huss-Ashmore, Goodman, and Armelagos 1982; Goodman et al. 1984; Stuart-Macadam 1985, 1987a, 1987b; Kent 1986; Walker 1986).

Preliminary examination of skeletal material on the surface of looted cemeteries at Pacatnamu suggested that there was substantial between-cemetery variation in the incidence of these skeletal stress indicators. This initial impression was confirmed by systematic surface collection. In table 1 the incidence of porotic hyperostosis and cribra orbitalia is presented for six cemetery samples from Pacatnamu. Five of these cemeteries had been disturbed and were surface collected; one (H45CM1) was intact and was fully excavated. The three Middle Horizon cemeteries show very low incidence of both porotic hyperostosis and cribra orbitalia. The Late Intermediate period cemeteries, in contrast, show substantial variability in frequencies, with very high incidence of both conditions in two cemeteries.

Although five of the six cemeteries sampled had been looted, fragments of ceramics and textiles left behind by looters, as well as the form and construction of tombs, provided information on the relative social status of individuals buried in the different cemeteries. The three Middle Horizon cemeteries showed similar tomb construction, and fragments of ceramics found on the surface of cemeteries S2 and S20 were comparable in form and workmanship to complete examples recovered from excavated graves in H45CM1. In comparison to materials recovered from the few elite Middle Horizon tombs that have been excavated by archeologists at Pacatnamu (Ubbelohde-Doering 1960, 1966) the quality of grave goods and energy expenditure in tomb construction in S2, S20, and H45CM1 indicated that these were not elite cemeteries.

Comparison of artifact material from looted tombs in the three Late Intermediate period cemeteries revealed significant differences in the quality of grave goods. While tombs in cemetery S9 contained fragments of elite fineware ceramics and elaborate polychrome cotton and wool textiles, tombs in cemeteries S1 and S8 contained only utilitarian ceramics and simple plainwave cotton textiles, many of which showed evidence of extensive

TABLE 1

*Cribra Orbitalia and Porotic Hyperostosis
in Pacatnamu Cemeteries*

	Cribra Orbitalia		Porotic Hyperostosis	
	Frequency	Percentage	Frequency	Percentage
Middle Horizon Occupation, A.D. *600–900*				
Cemetery S2				
Juveniles	1/4	25.0	0/6	0.0
Adults	0/25	0.0	3/25	12.0
Cemetery S20				
Juveniles	0/2	0.0	0/2	0.0
Adults	1/32	3.1	1/32	3.1
Cemetery H45CM1				
Juveniles	0/23	0.0	1/23	4.3
Adults	0/39	0.0	0/39	0.0
Late Intermediate Period Occupation, A.D. *1100–1400*				
Cemetery S1				
Juveniles	7/10	70.0	6/16	37.5
Adults	8/28	28.6	9/28	32.1
Cemetery S8				
Juveniles	6/14	42.9	5/9	55.6
Adults	9/41	22.0	3/41	7.3
Cemetery S9				
Juveniles	1/5	20.0	0/5	0.0
Adults	0/15	0.0	0/15	0.0

patching and repair. The differences in the quality of grave goods in cemeteries S1, S8, and S9 clearly reflect differential access to elite goods and imply that substantial status differences existed between individuals buried in S9 and those buried in S1 and S8. The high frequency of porotic hyperostosis and cribra orbitalia seen in individuals from cemeteries S1 and S8 suggest that many of these individuals suffered from significant health problems as well. Possible factors responsible for the elevated frequency of porotic hyperostosis and cribra orbitalia in S1 and S8 might include differences between elites and commoners in diet, residence pattern, sanitary conditions, parasite infestation, exposure to infectious disease, or a combination of factors. Interestingly, the earlier Middle Horizon burials at Pacatnamu do not appear to show similar evidence of nutritional stress in nonelite burials. One possible explanation is that there was increased social stratification during the Late Intermediate period

occupation of Pacatnamu, resulting in a deterioration in health conditions among the nonelite population. This would be consistent with data from other Late Intermediate period north coast sites such as Chan Chan, where residence patterns and mortuary behavior indicate increased social stratification compared to earlier time periods (Moseley 1982; Topic 1982).

CONCLUSION

Differences in the frequency of porotic hyperostosis in highland and coastal Andean skeletal samples suggest that parasite ecology, in addition to other factors, such as settlement density and sanitary conditions, may have been a significant determinant of community health in prehistoric Andean populations. On the other hand, variability in the frequency of porotic hyperostosis among different coastal population samples, and between contemporary cemeteries at a single site such as Pacatnamu, suggest that additional factors such as the degree of social stratification, local differences in residential pattern and settlement density, and differential access to dietary resources, also need to be considered in reconstructing the dynamics of community health at complex sites. The Pacatnamu data are consistent with Allison's (1984) assertion that social stratification seen in some late prehistoric Andean societies resulted in health benefits only for the elite minority.

While the study of La Paloma (Benfer 1984) suggests that there was some improvement in general health and life expectancy with the initial adaptation to sedentism and food production on the central coast of Peru, surveys of long-term temporal trends in skeletal pathology (Allison 1984; Ubelaker 1990) point to a general deterioration in health conditions with increasing sedentism, agricultural intensification, and population growth. Studies of mummified human remains from coastal Peruvian and Chilean sites indicate that both chronic infectious diseases, such as tuberculosis, and acute pulmonary infections were significant factors in morbidity and mortality in prehistoric Andean populations. Coprolite studies have documented the presence of various intestinal parasites in Andean populations as early as 3000 B.C., and some data suggest that parasite infestation may have been an important contributing factor in elevated frequencies of porotic hyperostosis in later prehistoric coastal Ecuadorian and Peruvian populations.

The paleopathological evidence indicates that prehistoric Andean populations faced significant health challenges in their adaptation to sedentism, agricultural production, and population growth. With increasing population size and density came inevitable problems of sanitation, parasitism, and increase in infectious disease. Agricultural intensification and social stratification led to a less varied diet for many, exacerbating the effects of infectious disease and parasitism. Dense late-prehistoric populations in Andean coastal valleys were particularly vulnerable to rapid disease spread and depopulation following initial contact with European pathogens in the sixteenth century.

Andean South America suffered severe demographic decline during the early colonial period, largely as a result of the introduction of European diseases, although, as in other areas of the New World, the impact of disease varied due to differences in local settlement pattern and population density, as well as with differences in the timing and intensity of European contact and colonization.

REFERENCES

Allison, M. J.
 1984   Paleopathology in Peruvian and Chilean Populations. Pp. 531–558 in Paleopathology at the Origins of Agriculture. M. N. Cohen and G. J. Armelagos, eds. Orlando, Fla.: Academic Press.

Allison, M. J., and E. Gerszten
 1982   Paleopathology in South American Mummies: Application of Modern Techniques. 3d ed. [Richmond, Va.]: Virginia Commonwealth University.

Allison, M. J., E. Gerszten, J. Munizaga, C. Santoro, and D. Mendoza
 1981   Tuberculosis in Pre-Columbian Andean Populations. Pp. 49–61 in Prehistoric Tuberculosis in the Americas. J. E. Buikstra, ed. Evanston, Ill.: Northwestern University Archaeological Program.

Allison, M. J., E. Gerszten, H. J. Shadomy, J. Munizaga, and M. Gonzales
 1979   Paracoccidiodomycosis in a Mummy. *Bulletin of the New York Academy of Medicine* 55:670–683.

Allison, M. J., D. Mendoza, and A. Pezzia
 1973   Documentation of a Case of Tuberculosis in Pre-Columbian America. *American Review of Respiratory Diseases* 107:985–991.

Allison, M. J., A. Pezzia, Ichiro Hasegawa, and Enrique Gerszten
 1974   A Case of Hookworm Infestation in a Pre-Columbian American. *American Journal of Physical Anthropology* 41(1):103–105.

Allison, Marvin J., G. Focacci, M. Fouant, and M. Cebelin
 1982   La Sífilis una enfermedad americana?. *Revista Chungará* 9:275–284. Universidad de Tarapacá, Arica, Chile.

Benfer, Robert A.
 1981   Adaptation to Sedentism and Food Production: The Paloma Project, II. *Paleopathology Newsletter* 37:6–8

 1984   The Challenges and Rewards of Sedentism: The Preceramic Village of Paloma, Peru. Pp. 531–558 in Paleopathology at the Origins of Agriculture. M. N. Cohen and G. J. Armelagos, eds. Orlando, Fla.: Academic Press.

Buikstra, Jane E., and Sloan Williams
 1991   Tuberculosis in the Americas: Current Perspectives. Human Paleopathology: Current Syntheses and Future Options. Donald J. Ortner and Arthur

C. Aufderheide, eds. Washington: Smithsonian Institution Press.

Callen, E. O., and T. W. M. Cameron
1960   A Prehistoric Diet Revealed in Coprolites. *The New Scientist* 8:35–37, 39–40.

Chauchat, Claude, and Jean M. Dricot
1979   Un Nouveau type humain fossile en Amérique du Sud: l'Homme de Paiján (Pérou). *Comptes-rendus de l'Académie des Sciences* 289:387–389.

Chauchat, Claude, and J. P. Lacombe
1984   El Hombre de Paijan: El más antiguo Peruano? *Gaceta Arqueológica Andina* 11:4–6, 12.

Cohen, Mark N.
1989   Health and the Rise of Civilization. New Haven: Yale University Press.

Cohen, Mark N., and George J. Armelagos
1984   Paleopathology at the Origins of Agriculture. Orlando, Fla.: Academic Press.

Cook, Noble D.
1981   Demographic Collapse: Indian Peru, 1520–1620. New York: Cambridge University Press.

Dalton, H. P., M. J. Allison, and A. Pezzia
1976   The Documentation of Communicable Diseases in Peruvian Mummies. *Medical College of Virginia Quarterly* 12:43–48.

Dobyns, Henry F.
1963   An Outline of Andean Epidemic History to 1720. *Bulletin of the History of Medicine* 37:493–515.

1966   Estimating Aboriginal American Populations: An Appraisal of Techniques with a New Hemispheric Estimate. *Current Anthropology* 7(3):395–416.

Donnan, Christopher B., ed.
1985   Early Ceremonial Architecture in the Andes. Washington: Dumbarton Oaks Research Library and Collection.

1986   Introduction in The Pacatnamu Papers. Vol. 1. C. B. Donnan, and G. A. Cock, eds. Los Angeles: Museum of Cultural History, University of California Los Angeles.

Donnan, C. B., and G. A. Cock, eds.
1986   The Pacatnamu Papers. Vol. 1. Los Angeles: University of California Museum of Cultural History.

Elzay, R. P., M. J. Allison, and A. Pezzia
1977   A Comparative Study on the Dental Health Status of Five Pre-Columbian Peruvian Cultures. *American Journal of Physical Anthropology* 46:135–139.

Erickson, Clark L.
1987   The Dating of Raised-field Agriculture in the Lake Titicaca Basin, Peru. Pp. 373–384 in Pre-Hispanic Agricultural Fields in the Andean Region. Pt. ii W. M. Denevan, K. Mathewson, and G.

Knapp, eds., *British Archaeological Reports, International Series* 359 (ii). Oxford.

Fung Pineda, Rosa
1988   The Late Preceramic and Initial Period. Pp. 67–96 in Peruvian Prehistory: An Overview of pre-Inca and Inca society. R. W. Keatinge, ed. New York: Cambridge University Press.

Goodman, A. H., D. L. Martin, G. J. Armelagos, and G. Clark
1984   Indications of Stress from Bone and Teeth. In Paleopathology at the Origins of Agriculture. Mark Nathan Cohen and George J. Armelagos, eds. New York: Academic Press.

Hrdlička, A.
1911   Some Results of Recent Anthropological Exploration in Peru. *Smithsonian Miscellaneous Collections*, 56 (16). Washington.

1914   Anthropological Work in Peru in 1913, with Notes on the Pathology of the Ancient Peruvians. *Smithsonian Miscellaneous Collections*, 61 (18). Washington.

Huss-Ashmore, R., A. H. Goodman, and G. J. Armelagos
1982   Nutritional Inference from Paleopathology. *Advances in Archaeological Method and Theory* 5:395–474.

Isbell, William H.
1988   City and State in Middle Horizon Huari. Pp. 164–189 in Peruvian Prehistory: An Overview of pre-Inca and Inca Society. Richard W. Keatinge, ed. New York: Cambridge University Press.

Kent, Susan
1986   The Influence of Sedentism and Aggregation on Porotic Hyperostosis and Anaemia: A Case Study. *Man* 21(4):605–636.

Kolata, Alan L.
1983   The South Andes. Pp. 241–281 in Ancient South Americans. Jesse D. Jennings, ed. San Francisco: W. H. Freeman.

Kosok, Paul
1965   Life, Land and Water in Ancient Peru. New York: Long Island University Press.

Moseley, Michael E.
1975   The Maritime Foundations of Andean Civilization. Menlo Park, Calif.: Cummings Publishing Company.

1982   Introduction: Human Exploitation and Organization on the North Andean Coast. Chan Chan: Andean Desert City. M. E. Moseley and K. C. Day, eds. Albuquerque: University of New Mexico Press.

1985   The Exploration and Explanation of Early Monumental Architecture in the Andes. Pp. 29–57 in Early Ceremonial Architecture in the Andes. C. B. Donnan, ed. Washington, Dumbarton Oaks Research Library and Collections.

Moseley, Michael E., and Eric E. Deeds

1982   The Land in Front of Chan Chan: Agrarian Expansion, Reform, and Collapse in the Moche Valley. Pp. 225–253 in Chan Chan: Andean Desert City. M. E. Moseley and K. C. Day, eds. Albuquerque: University of New Mexico Press.

Omran, Abdel-Rahim

1961   The Ecology of Leishmaniasis. In Studies in Disease Ecology. Jacques M. May, ed. New York: Hafner Publishing Company.

Patrucco, Raul, Raul Tello, and Duccio Bonavia

1983   Parasitological Studies of Coprolites of Pre-Hispanic Peruvian Populations. *Current Anthropology* 24(3):393–394.

Pozorski, Sheila, and Thomas Pozorski

1987   Early Settlement and Subsistence in the Casma Valley, Peru. Iowa City: University of Iowa Press.

Pozorski, Thomas

1982   Early Social Stratification and Subsistence Systems: The Caballo Muerto Complex. Pp. 225–253 in Chan Chan: Andean Desert City. M. E. Moseley and K. C. Day, eds., Albuquerque: University of New Mexico Press.

Quilter, Jeffrey

1989   Life and Death at Paloma: Society and Mortuary Practices in a Preceramic Peruvian Village. Iowa City: University of Iowa Press.

Rowe, John H.

1947   Inca Culture at the Time of the Spanish Conquest. Pp. 183–330 in Handbook of South American Indians. Vol. 1. J. H. Steward, ed. *Bureau of American Ethnology Bulletin* 143. Washington.

1963   Urban Settlements in Ancient Peru. *Ñawpa Pacha* 1:1–27.

Smith, C. T.

1970   Depopulation of the Central Andes in the 16th Century. *Current Anthropology* 11:453–464.

Standen, Vivien, Marvin J. Allison, and Bernardo Arriaza

1984   Patologías óseas de la población Morro-1, Asociada al Complejo Chinchorro: Norte de Chile. *Revista Chungará* 13:175–185. Universidad de Tarapacá, Arica, Chile.

Stewart, T. D.

1950a   Deformity, Trephining, and Mutilation in South American Indian Skeletal Remains. In Handbook of South American Indians. Vol. 6. J. H. Steward, ed. *Bureau of American Ethnology Bulletin* 143. Washington.

1950b   Pathological Changes in South American Indian Skeletal Remains. In Handbook of South American Indians. Vol. 6. J. H. Steward, ed. *Bureau of American Ethnology Bulletin* 143. Washington.

Stuart-Macadam, P.

1985   Porotic Hyperostosis: Representative of a Childhood Condition. *American Journal of Physical Anthropology* 66:391–398.

1987a   A Radiographic Study of Porotic Hyperostosis. *American Journal of Physical Anthropology* 74:511–520.

1987b   Porotic Hyperostosis: New Evidence to Support the Anemia theory. *American Journal of Physical Anthropology* 74:521–526.

Topic, John

1982   Lower-class Social and Economic Organization at Chan Chan. Pp. 145–175 in Chan Chan: Andean Desert City. M. E. Mosely and K. C. Day, eds. Albuquerque: University of New Mexico Press.

Ubbelohde-Doering, Heinrich

1960   Bericht über archäologische Feldarbeiten in Peru, III. *Ethnos* 25(3–4):153–82.

[1966] On the Royal Highways of the Inca. New York: Praeger.

Ubelaker, D. H.

1980a   Human Skeletal Remains from Site OGSE-80, a Preceramic Site on the Sta. Elena Peninsula, Coastal Ecuador. *Journal of the Washington Academy of Sciences* 70(1):3–24.

1980b   Prehistoric Human Remains from the Cotocollao Site, Pichincha Province, Ecuador. *Journal of the Washington Academy of Sciences* 70(2):59–74.

1981   The Ayalán Cemetery, a Late Integration Period Burial Site on the South Coast of Ecuador. *Smithsonian Contributions to Anthropology* 29. Washington.

1983   Human Skeletal Remains from OGSE-172 an Early Guangala Cemetery Site on the Coast of Ecuador. *Journal of the Washington Academy of Sciences* 73(1):16–27.

1984   Prehistoric Human Biology of Ecuador: Possible Temporal Trends and Cultural Correlations. In Paleopathology at the Origins of Agriculture. M. N. Cohen and G. J. Armelagos, eds. New York: Academic Press.

1988a   Human Remains from OGSE-46 La Libertad, Guayas Province, Ecuador. *Journal of the Washington Academy of Sciences* 78(1):3–16.

1988b   A Preliminary Report of Analysis of Human Remains from Agua Blanca, a Prehistoric Late Integration Site from Coastal Ecuador. *Journal of the Washington Academy of Sciences* (78(1):17–22.

1988c   Prehistoric Human Biology at La Tolita, Ecuador, a Preliminary Report. *Journal of the Washington Academy of Sciences* 78(1):23–37.

1988d   Skeletal Biology of Prehistoric Ecuador: An Ongoing Research Program. *Journal of the Washington Academy of Sciences* 7(1):1–2.

1990   Porotic Hyperostosis, Parasitism and Sedentism in Ancient Ecuador (Abstract). *American Journal of Physical Anthropology* 81(2):309–310.

Urteaga-Ballon, Oscar
1991   Medical Ceramic Representations of Nasal Leishmaniasis and Surgical Amputation in Ancient Peruvian Civilization. In Human Paleopathology: Current Syntheses and Future Options. Donald J. Ortner and Arthur C. Aufderheide, eds. Washington: Smithsonian Institution Press.

Verano, John W.
1987   Cranial Microvariation at Pacatnamu: A Study of Cemetery Population Variability. Ph.D. Dissertation in Anthropology, University of California, Los Angeles.

1990   The Moche: Profile of an Ancient Peruvian People. *National Museum of Natural History Anthropological Notes* 12(1):1–3, 14–15. Washington.

[1991a] Human Skeletal Remains from Chotuna. In C. B. Donnan, ed. Excavations at Chotuna and Chornancap, Lambayeque Valley, Peru. Los Angeles: University of California, Museum of Cultural History.

[1991b] Physical Characteristics and Skeletal Biology of the Moche. In The Pacatnamu Papers, Vol. 2. C. B. Donnan and G. C. Cock, eds. Los Angeles: University of California, Museum of Cultural History.

Verano, J. W., and A. Cordy-Collins
1986   H1M1: A Late Intermediate Period Mortuary Structure at Pacatnamu. In The Pacatnamu Papers. Vol. 1. C. B. Donnan and G. A. Cock, eds. Los Angeles: University of California, Museum of Cultural History.

Vidal Vidal, Hilda, and Ilse Schwidetzky
1987   The Andean Countries: Ecuador, Peru, Bolivia. Pp. 177–218 in Rassengeschichte der Menschheit, 12. Lieferung, Amerika II: Mittel- und Südamerika. Ilse Schwidetzky, ed. Munich, Germany: R. Oldenbourg Verlag.

Walker, Phillip L.
1986   Porotic Hyperostosis in a Marine-dependent California Indian Population. *American Journal of Physical Anthropology* 69:435–354.

Weiss, Pedro
1961   Osteologia Cultural: Practicas Cefálicas. Pt. 2. Lima: Universidad Nacional Mayor de San Marcos, Anales de la Facultad de Medicina.

Willey, Gordon
1953   Prehistoric Settlement Patterns in the Viru Valley, Peru. *Bureau of American Ethnology Bulletin* 155. Washington.

Wilson, David J.
1988   Prehispanic Settlement Patterns in the Lower Santa Valley, Peru. Washington: Smithsonian Institution Press.

4

Population Decline and Extinction in La Florida

CLARK SPENCER LARSEN,
CHRISTOPHER B. RUFF,
MARGARET J. SCHOENINGER,
AND DALE L. HUTCHINSON

The first well-documented encounters between Europeans and Indians occurred during Spanish explorations of the region in the early sixteenth century. The exploratory expeditions led by Juan Ponce de León, Pánfilo de Nárvaez, and Hernando de Soto in 1513, 1528, and 1539–1540, respectively (Sauer 1971; Oviedo 1945; Smith 1968), and the ill-fated colonization effort by Lucas Vásquez de Ayllon in 1526 (Jones 1978) provide little information on the long-term consequences of contact with Europeans for native populations. Quite likely, epidemic disease introduced from the Old World by early explorations had devastating effects (Milner 1980).

Because relatively few infectious diseases affect bone (Kelley 1989), human remains from the early sixteenth-century Indian cemeteries provide little information about epidemics. However, these remains do bear witness to the violent nature of early contacts between Indians and Europeans. Skeletal elements show evidence of sword cuts from the Florida Gulf coast, including partially severed arm (humerus) and shoulder (scapula) bones (Hutchinson 1990), and there are patterns of trauma in human remains from the King site in northwestern Georgia (Blakely 1989). The cemetery most likely dates to the time of the 1539–1540 de Soto entrada. Included in the human remains from the cemetery are individuals who exhibit cut marks from sword blows.

Written details about the effects of European interaction with Indians in La Florida come primarily from those areas that were subject to missionization later in the sixteenth century. Following the establishment of a large permanent Spanish colony at Saint Augustine in 1565, missions were established among four provinces: Guale (the Georgia coast), Timucua (Florida east of the Aucilla River), Apalachee (between the Aucilla and Ochlockonee Rivers), and, to a lesser extent, Apalachicola (on the Apalachicola River) (Thomas 1987, 1988; Vernon 1989). At the peak of the mission system in the mid-seventeenth century, 38 missions served approximately 25,000 Indians (fig. 1) (Thomas 1988).

The four provinces of La Florida have been intensively investigated by archeologists, especially during the 1980s (see Thomas 1987, 1988 for reviews). However, Guale is the only province where

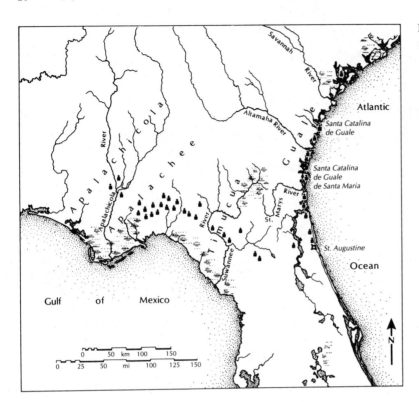

Fig. 1. Missions of La Florida, mid-16th to late 17th centuries.

large samples of human remains from precontact and contact-period mortuary localities have been investigated by biological anthropologists. Therefore, the discussion will focus primarily on Guale; but where appropriate, historical, archeological, and biological data from the other provinces will be drawn upon.

ARCHEOLOGICAL AND
ETHNOHISTORICAL CONTEXT

Archeological evidence indicates that the prehistoric Georgia coast was occupied by foraging populations with a particular focus on coastal marine resources (fishes, shellfish, and other invertebrates) (Reitz 1988). During the twelfth century, or slightly before, evidence suggests that in addition to foraging, maize agriculture rapidly took on an important role in subsistence economy. Although the evidence based on botanical remains is scarce, the appearance of large, nucleated settlements, increase in population size, and presence of communities that were likely sedentary is a pattern that is consistent with the emergence of complex societies

and agricultural production in other areas of eastern North America during the remaining centuries before the arrival of Europeans (Griffin 1966; Larsen 1982; Smith 1986, 1989; Steponaitis 1986).

When the Spaniards arrived along the Georgia coast in the sixteenth century, they encountered Indian populations with a broad-based subsistence economy that included hunting, gathering, fishing, and farming. Maize and other crops were grown in sufficient quantities for storage, and these agricultural products were collected and redistributed by chiefs (Jones 1978). During the contact period, the demand for food tribute by Spanish military and other personnel, as well as encouragement by mission priests to grow crops, probably contributed to an increase in production of maize and other agricultural foods.

Native labor was a central element in the Spanish economic interests in La Florida. A number of accounts note the use of Indian laborers and suggest that they were often subject to harsh, abusive treatment. In Apalachee, mission clergy were in conflict with administrative leaders about use of Indians for personal gain. For example, administrators relied on Indians to carry heavy loads, sometimes over long distances (Hann 1988). One friar complained that on one expedition only 10 of the 200 Indians that left Apalachee carrying cargo returned. Individuals who were not among those returning had died of starvation, exposure, and related deprivation (Hann 1988:20).

Indian populations of La Florida suffered tremendous losses due to European-introduced acute infectious diseases. However, this region, like others in the New World, was not a disease-free haven prior to European contact. In this regard, ample evidence exists for the presence of both nonspecific infectious diseases (Larsen 1982, 1984) as well as specific infectious diseases (Powell 1990). An increase in frequency of nonspecific bone inflammations in precontact agricultural populations on the Georgia coast suggests a decline in health (Larsen 1982, 1984). Crania from the Irene Mound site, about A.D. 1200–1450, a mortuary locality at the mouth of the Savannah River on the north Georgia coast, have been examined. Differential diagnosis of this skeletal series revealed the presence of two diseases of radically different mortal and morbid effects, namely tuberculosis and endemic treponematosis (Powell 1990).

The immunological experience with either nonspecific infectious disease or tuberculosis and endemic treponematosis did nothing to prepare the Indian populations occupying La Florida for the invasion of European diseases. The seventeenth century in Guale saw remarkable population losses during and following epidemics (Jones 1978). At least two epidemics hit La Florida between 1613 and 1617. By some accounts, at least half the mission Indians as well as some Spanish military personnel died during these years (Hann 1988). The epidemic of 1649–1650 resulted in tremendous loss of life.

In late 1655, the governor wrote that since the beginning of the year a series of "small-pox plagues" had contributed to substantial mortality (Hann 1986b). So high were the population losses that Rebolledo remarked in 1657 that very few Indians remained in either Timucua or Guale "because they have been wiped out with the sickness of the plague and small-pox which have overtaken them in the past years" (quoted in Hann 1986b:378). By 1659, it was reported that a measles epidemic resulted in the deaths of more than 10,000 Indians throughout Spanish Florida (Jones 1978). An unidentified epidemic (cf. Dobyns 1983) so reduced the native labor force in 1672 that in

1674 the labor necessary for construction of the fort at Saint Augustine was simply not available (Hann 1988). It is likely that these epidemics, spanning a period of somewhat less than 60 years, do not represent all the epidemics that contributed to depopulation in Guale in particular and La Florida in general (see also Dobyns 1983).

Throughout the seventeenth century, there was a reduction in number of missions and mission settlements. By 1675, six settlements remained in Guale, and within five years, this number had reduced to just four north of Cumberland Island (Jones 1978). Although this reduction in number of villages reflects deaths due to disease, in part it also likely reflects the consolidation or nucleation of populations that is common in other mission regions (see Hann 1988) and in other areas of the New World at the time. The increased concentration of Indian populations around mission centers could only have exacerbated an already precarious situation by providing conditions that were conducive to the maintenance and spread of crowd-related infectious diseases, a reduction in sanitation, and perhaps, water contamination. Moreover, the use of Indians as vehicles for transport of cargo from the provinces to Saint Augustine resulted in exposing them to infectious diseases (Hann 1988).

Other factors contributed to the decline of local populations. Periodic Indian rebellions erupted in response to demands by the Spaniards, including religious conversion and labor and food tribute (Jones 1978; Hann 1988). Within just a few years after the arrival of Franciscan missionaries, the first major uprising occurred in Guale in 1576. Attacks by Indian warriors on European intruders continued to at least 1582. Another rebellion in 1597 led to Spanish military retaliation in the form of burning of towns and valuable stored crops (Jones 1978). These retaliations must have led to food shortages and other problems for the Indians.

In 1670, with the establishment of a permanent English colony at Charleston, South Carolina, the region along the Atlantic seaboard extending south to Saint Augustine became contested by Spain and England. As a direct result, attacks by English military and English-ally Indians on the missions and settlements in the region increased. In 1680, following a decade of harassment, a force of several hundred British-ally Yamasee Indians descended on the principal Guale mission, Santa Catalina de Guale, on Saint Catherines Island, Georgia. The mission inhabitants fled to Sapelo Island, immediately to the south. Continued exhibitions of force, coupled with periodic predation by both English and French pirates on missions, led the Spanish governor to advise Indians and priests to move closer to the protection of Saint Augustine (Bushnell 1986).

Thus, in 1686, the remaining Guale population left Sapelo Island and reestablished Santa Catalina de Guale on Amelia Island, Florida. This mission, Santa Catalina de Guale de Santa Maria, was occupied during a period of relative quiet (Bushnell 1986). However, in 1702, it too was attacked by British-led forces, and the surviving population subsequently relocated in Saint Augustine, thus bringing an end to Guale as a tribal entity and region.

HUMAN REMAINS FROM GUALE

Large samples of human remains representing precontact preagricultural and agricultural populations have been recovered from the Georgia coastal region. Various aspects of health and disease, and bone morphology, especially in relation to an understanding of behavioral and biological adaptation to the shift from a lifeway based on food collection to that based at least in part on maize agriculture, have been examined (Larsen 1982, 1984). Findings suggest that prior to contact, there was a deterioration in quality of life that was accompanied by a general decrease in mechanical demand with this behavioral shift. These data form an essential backdrop to any understanding of the impact of the arrival of Europeans, and especially, the establishment of missions during the late sixteenth century.

The contact period is represented by two large series of human remains recovered from Spanish mission sites. One sample was recovered from Santa Catalina de Guale (n = 431) (Russell, Choi, and Larsen 1990). Although this mission was likely established as early as 1566, analysis of grave inclusions and other material culture from the mission cemetery located beneath the floor of the church suggests that the human remains date to the period 1607–1680. However, the presence of at least two superimposed church construction phases indicates that some of the burials may be earlier in the mission period (David Hurst Thomas, personal communication 1989).

The other contact skeletal sample includes individuals recovered from Santa Catalina de Guale de Santa Maria (n = 120) (Hardin 1986; Larsen and Saunders 1987). This mission sample dates between 1686 and 1702.

For the purposes of the following discussion, the human skeletal samples are divided into four temporal periods, including precontact preagricultural (pre-A.D. 1150), precontact agricultural (1150–1500), early contact (1607–1680), and late contact (1686–1702). Conditions in precontact and contact Guale are compared regarding physical activity and workload, nutritional quality and dietary stress, and growth disruption. Data relating in particular to demographic change as well as other aspects of adaptation and stress are presented elsewhere (see Larsen et al. 1990; Fresia, Ruff, and Larsen 1990; Simpson, Hutchinson, and Larsen 1990; Russell, Choi, and Larsen 1990).

Physical Activity and Work Demand

The historical documentation outlined above indicates that the arrival of Spanish colonizers and the establishment of missions in La Florida saw dramatic behavioral changes in Indian populations. Most accounts that discuss physical activity indicate that there was an increase in demand on Indians for labor. On the other hand, study of these records suggests that native populations were concentrated around mission centers, and as a result, may have been relatively more sedentary than their prehistoric predecessors. At least some individuals were used in projects involving long-distance travel, such as carrying supplies and agricultural produce from outlying missions to the administrative center at Saint Augustine.

Evidence of behavioral change in precontact and contact Guale populations can be studied by two indicators of behavioral pattern—long bone cross-sectional geometry and osteoarthritis.

CROSS-SECTIONAL GEOMETRIC PROPERTIES By the application of biomechanical beam theory developed by civil and mechanical engineers (Timoshenko and Gere 1972), several important properties in long bone cross-sections reflecting mechanical loading patterns and bone strength can be measured in a relatively straightforward fashion. Findings from this kind of analysis are important because they reflect behavioral differences that are difficult to distinguish in other kinds of skeletal analyses (Ruff and Larsen 1990).

Strength of long bones is determined by two primary cross-sectional geometric properties. These properties include (1) areas and (2) second moments of area (also called moments of inertia) of bone in a cross-section. Cross-sectional area is proportional to strength in axial compression and tension and second moments of area are proportional to strength in torsion (twisting) and bending of the long bone shaft (Ruff and Hayes 1983). Because bone is a living tissue and will adapt to imposed mechanical loads, decline in bone strength should reflect a decline in mechanical demand. Conversely, an increase in bone strength should reflect an increase in mechanical demand. This method of structural analysis assumes that geometric properties are more important than material properties (such as bone density) in interpreting mechanical function (Ruff and Larsen 1990).

Bone size (length) and cross-sectional geometric properties of humeri (arm) and femora (thigh) have been analyzed for all four time periods (Ruff, Larsen, and Hayes 1984; Ruff and Larsen 1990; Larsen and Ruff 1991; Larsen, Ruff, and Griffin 1990). Analysis of bone length and cross-sectional geometry standardized over bone length shows respective declines in body size and bone strength relative to body size prior to contact. The reduction in body size reflects a decrease in nutritional quality, and the geometric alterations reflect a decline in mechanical demand with the shift from foraging to agricultural lifeways (Ruff et al. 1984). In the early contact period, there is a clear reversal of this trend (except in the female humerus). That is, there is an increase in body size and bone strength relative to body size (Ruff and Larsen 1990). This trend continues in the late contact period.

One possible explanation for the increase in bone strength is that mechanical demand increased in the historic period Guale. However, in both early and late contact populations, there is an increase in circularity of the hip area of the femur that most likely reflects a decrease in general activity level. The increase in cross-sectional areas and second moments of area may reflect in part an increase in sedentism and carbohydrate consumption. This combination could have resulted in greater weight gain and body size (not reflected in bone length) in the more sedentary mission population in spite of the generally lower activity levels (Ruff and Larsen 1990). Indeed, other workers have reported that in

Native American populations undergoing similar transitions, there is clear evidence of weight gain. Hrdlička (1908), for example, noted that native populations undergoing less strenuous activities in a sedentary context, such as in reservations, show relative gain in body weight. Johnston and Schell (1979) reported that despite a heterogeneity in North American Indians, there is a tendency for high body weight and obesity in virtually all populations studied. They report that this tendency is even more pronounced in populations undergoing the shift from reservation to urban settings. Thus, the establishment of missions in Guale likely resulted in increased sedentism, weight gain, and hence, increase in cross-sectional geometric properties relative to bone length or stature.

This is not to say that the evidence contradicts reports that show increased labor demands on native populations. At least some of the males from the early contact period, for example, show evidence in the shape of the femur midshaft for a marked increase in activity that reflects long-distance travel (Ruff and Larsen 1990; see also Ruff 1987). These findings are consistent with the use of some of the males from various provinces of La Florida for labor-related projects involving travel over lengthy distances.

OSTEOARTHRITIS Study of joint-related pathology reflecting use of articular joints provides additional information about activity patterns in past human populations (Jurmain 1980; Merbs 1983; Larsen 1987). Analysis of osteoarthritis—exhibited as either breakdown of bone on articular joint surfaces or buildup of bone along articular margins or a combination of both—shows a decline in frequency in the agricultural period relative to the pre-agricultural period prior to contact (Larsen 1982, 1984). In sharp contrast to this trend, there is a marked increase in osteoarthritis prevalence in the late contact period (table 1) (Griffin and Larsen 1989; Larsen, Ruff, and Griffin 1990).

The decrease in frequency in the period before the arrival of Europeans has been interpreted as reflecting a decline in mechanical demand following the adoption of agriculture (Larsen 1982, 1984). If the late contact population is sedentary, then, should there be further reductions in frequency of osteoarthritis? However, osteoarthritis is a disease that reflects heavy, repetitive use of articular joints (Eichner 1989). Native laborers were used in types

TABLE 1

La Florida Osteoarthritis Prevalence

Articular joint	Before 1150		1150–1500		1686–1702	
	%	Number	%	Number	%	Number
MALES						
Cervical	40.0	(20)	11.3	(53)	44.4	(27)
Thoracic	12.5	(16)	11.8	(51)	65.4	(26)
Lumbar/sacral	34.6	(26)	16.3	(80)	52.9	(51)
Shoulder	10.5	(38)	1.7	(120)	11.1	(27)
Elbow	13.7	(51)	6.1	(114)	10.3	(29)
Wrist	2.6	(39)	0.9	(106)	10.0	(30)
Hand	0.0	(28)	2.0	(100)	3.2	(31)
Hip	0.0	(51)	9.1	(110)	6.4	(31)
Knee	18.6	(59)	12.6	(111)	7.4	(27)
Ankle	4.1	(49)	9.2	(109)	10.0	(30)
Foot	0.0	(26)	1.1	(93)	41.6	(24)
FEMALES						
Cervical	17.2	(29)	1.4	(73)	42.3	(26)
Thoracic	6.7	(30)	1.4	(72)	57.5	(33)
Lumbar/sacral	19.5	(51)	9.9	(111)	54.5	(55)
Shoulder	2.4	(83)	0.7	(144)	56.0	(25)
Elbow	9.6	(94)	0.0	(167)	2.9	(34)
Wrist	2.6	(77)	0.0	(140)	5.3	(38)
Hand	0.0	(50)	0.8	(129)	5.3	(38)
Hip	4.3	(93)	0.0	(148)	0.0	(36)
Knee	15.0	(94)	3.4	(147)	8.6	(35)
Ankle	4.5	(88)	0.0	(139)	15.6	(32)
Foot	0.0	(48)	0.0	(120)	11.1	(27)

Sources: Larsen 1982; Griffin and Larsen 1989.

of labor that would likely place severe mechanical demands on their articular joints, such as those associated with lifting and transport of heavy loads. Viewed in this context, the increase in articular joint pathology probably reflects an increase in frequent, heavy lifting or other stereotypic, repetitive motion.

Nutritional Quality

The native populations in La Florida quite likely experienced dramatic changes in diet, changes that were probably not for the better and may have contributed to the decline of these populations (Schoeninger et al. 1990). In order to describe with more precision the relative contributions of various components of diet in precontact and contact native populations in the region, stable isotope ratios of carbon and nitrogen and dental caries prevalence have been analyzed.

CARBON AND NITROGEN STABLE ISOTOPE RATIOS   In most studies of North American material, carbon stable isotope ratios in bone collagen ($^{13}C/^{12}C$) are used to determine the relative contribution of maize to diet (Vogel and van der Merwe 1977; Bender, Baerreis, and Steventon 1981; Buikstra et al. 1987; Smith 1989). For the Georgia-Florida coast, marine foods, which are also reflected in stable carbon isotope ratios, confound this kind of application (Schoeninger et al. 1990). The use of nitrogen stable isotope ratios ($^{15}N/^{14}N$) as an indicator of the contribution of marine foods (Tauber 1981; Schoeninger, DeNiro, and Tauber 1983) permits use of carbon isotope ratios in tracking the introduction and increased dependence on maize as a dietary item (Schoeninger et al. 1990).

Comparison of average $\delta^{13}C$ (a ratio of $^{13}C/^{12}C$) values for the precontact preagricultural, precontact agricultural, early contact, and late contact periods shows a trend for more positive values

TABLE 2

La Florida Carbon and Nitrogen Stable Isotope Summary Statistics

Period	δ¹³C			δ¹⁵N		
	Mean	Number	Range	Mean	Number	Range
Before 1150	−14.5	(20)	−18.6, −13.4	12.8	(20)	10.6, 14.4
1150–1500	−13.0	(9)	−16.4, −10.0	10.7	(9)	9.5, 13.3
1607–1680	−11.5	(22)	−14.3, −9.6	9.4	(22)	7.4, 10.8
1686–1702	−11.5	(21)	−12.6, −10.0	10.0	(22)	8.3, 11.6

Sources: Schoeninger et al. 1990; Larsen et al. 1990.

prior to contact and into the contact period. Comparison of average $\delta^{15}N$ (a ratio of $^{15}N/^{14}N$) values shows, on the other hand, a trend for less positive values prior to contact that continues into the contact period (table 2). These findings suggest that there is a dietary change involving a concomitant decreasing reliance on marine resources and increasing reliance on terrestrial plant resources, namely maize (Schoeninger et al. 1990). Moreover, although maize is an important source of food, marine resources continue to provide a significant proportion of protein in diet, even during the contact period. Therefore, consistent with the archeological and ethnohistoric data, there is a restructuring of diet involving an increased dependence on cultigens both prior to the arrival of Europeans and after the establishment of missions among native populations.

DENTAL CARIES Dental caries is a disease process characterized by the focal demineralization of dental hard tissues by acids produced as a byproduct of bacterial fermentation of dietary carbohydrates. Maize contains a simple sugar—sucrose—that is readily metabolized by oral bacteria. This sugar has been implicated by numerous researchers in a variety of cross-sectional and longitudinal studies as a major culprit in promoting dental caries (Newbrun 1982; Powell 1985; Larsen 1987). Therefore, the increased consumption of this food should result in an increase in prevalence of this disease after the increase in reliance on maize during the twelfth century, throughout the remainder of the prehistoric period, and during the period of missionization.

Comparison of caries prevalence among the four periods supports the hypothesis of increasing

consumption of maize. That is, there is a marked increase in frequency of carious teeth in the precontact agricultural period that almost certainly reflects an increase in maize consumption. The early contact period shows a slight decline in caries prevalence. The most striking change in comparison of the periods is the tremendous jump in frequency of carious teeth in the late contact period relative to the early contact period. Over one-third of late contact period teeth are carious, a frequency that is among the highest reported for any archeological sample in eastern North America (Larsen, Shavit, and Griffin 1991).

The increased prevalence of caries may reflect a dramatic increase in maize consumption in the late contact period. There probably was an increase in consumption of maize during this time, thus explaining at least partially the increase in this pathological condition. However, average stable carbon isotope ratios in comparison of the early and late contact periods are identical, indicating that diet changed relatively little if at all. Most certainly, these data suggest that if there was an increase in maize consumption it was not large enough to result in such a marked increase in prevalence of dental caries. Therefore, other factors must have contributed to change in caries prevalence from the early to late contact periods.

Food texture has been implicated as one factor that influences dietary cariogenecity (Powell 1985). Diets with rough textured foods or with foods containing abrasives (for example, sand in shellfish, or stone particles from stone-grinding implements used to grind maize) are less cariogenic because they tend to cleanse teeth during mastication, thereby preventing or at least reducing the aggregation of bacteria and the development of caries-promoting plaque. Foods that are less abrasive, due either to the nature of the food itself or the abrasives contained within, tend not to cleanse the teeth. Consumption of less abrasive foods promotes the buildup of plaque and, therefore, contributes to cariogenesis. Perhaps, then, late contact populations were either eating relatively less abrasive foods or were practicing a different food preparation technology resulting in reduced abrasion.

With the use of scanning electron microscopy microscopically visible occlusal surface pits and scratches have been compared in a series of permanent maxillary first molars from precontact preagricultural, early contact, and late contact individuals (Teaford 1991). Results of this analysis indicate the presence of a far greater number of pits relative to scratches in the precontact sample than in the contact samples. These findings strongly suggest that precontact foods were more abrasive than contact period foods. Moreover, comparison of scratch widths shows a consistent pattern of reduction in comparison of the three periods (average scratch widths in microns: precontact = 1.62, early contact = 1.47, late contact = 1.19) (Teaford 1991). Within the contact period, although the early and late contact teeth have virtually identical numbers of scratches and pits, the scratch widths reduce. It is possible that the reduction in scratch widths in these two agricultural populations may reflect a reduction in abrasiveness of diet perhaps as a result of change in food preparation technology.

Stress and Growth Disruption

The study of hard tissue responses to specific stressors (insults that have the potential of causing physiological disruption) in archeological materials has led to a much greater understanding of conditions that adversely affect the health and well being of the living populations that they represent (Larsen 1987; Goodman et al. 1988). These responses arise from a variety of circumstances, including undernutrition, infection, trauma, and degenerative changes (Goodman et al. 1988).

POROTIC HYPEROSTOSIS   Porotic hyperostosis is a descriptive term that characterizes specific pathological modifications of the flat bones of the outer surfaces of the cranial vault (especially parietals, occipital, frontal), the roof areas of the eye orbits (also known as cribra orbitalia), and, less frequently, postcranial skeletal elements. In general, the bone surfaces are porous and sievelike, but the degree of porosity varies according to the severity of stress as well as the degree of healing and remodeling following the stress episode. Most workers agree that the skeletal changes are related to hyperactive bone marrow and red blood cell production in response to any anemia, but especially during early childhood (Martin, Goodman, and Armelagos 1985; Stuart-Macadam 1989).

Porotic hyperostosis has been observed in a number of late prehistoric crania from Georgia coastal sites on Saint Simons Island (Zahler 1976) and at Irene Mound (Powell 1990). Crania from the Irene Mound site show a very low prevalence of porotic hyperostosis (8.3%). These findings suggest that iron deficiency anemia may not have been a significant problem during the period of time preceding contact with Europeans (Powell 1990; Larsen et al. 1990).

The frequency of porotic hyperostosis in the precontact preagricultural period is quite low, 6.5% (table 3). This is followed by a slight decline in frequency during the precontact agricultural period. In sharp contrast to a low prevalence of porotic hyperostosis in both precontact periods, the contact periods show a high prevalence. Like the precontact series, the contact series—especially from Saint Catherines Island—is underrepresented by juveniles. This underrepresentation likely obscures the true prevalence of this pathological condition for this and other periods. Nevertheless, these data are strongly suggestive of an increase in porotic hyperostosis after contact. Thus, iron deficiency anemia apparently became a problem only during the period of contact.

It is exceedingly difficult to pinpoint the exact cause for the increase in anemia in the contact period. With regard to other geographic areas, some workers have suggested that the adoption of maize-based diets may have resulted in iron deficiency anemia due to the role of maize in inhibition of iron absorption (El-Najjar 1977). However, the presence of very low prevalence of porotic hyperostosis in the Irene Mound series (Powell 1990) and the precontact agricultural period in general suggests that additional or other factors are likely operating.

An increasing body of evidence has demonstrated that porotic hyperostosis is symptomatic of a variety of circumstances contributing to iron bio-

TABLE 3

La Florida Porotic Hyperostosis Prevalence

Age	Before 1150		1150–1500		1607–1680		1686–1702	
	%	Number	%	Number	%	Number	%	Number
0–4.9	66.7	(6)	60.0	(5)	50.0	(4)	66.7	(12)
5–9.9	25.0	(4)	0.0	(3)	50.0	(2)	85.7	(7)
10–14.9	50.0	(2)	20.0	(5)	0.0	(0)	67.7	(3)
15–19.9	0.0	(4)	4.2	(24)	0.0	(0)	50.0	(4)
20+	0.0	(76)	3.7	(108)	21.3	(28)	10.6	(66)
Total	6.5	(92)	6.2	(145)	26.5	(34)	27.2	(92)

Sources: Larsen et al. 1989; Larsen et al. 1990; Larsen, unpublished.

[1] Includes crania from the Groves Creek, Seven Mile Bend, and Little Pine Island sites in addition to the Georgia coastal sites listed in Larsen (1982).

availability reduction (see reviews in Larsen 1987; Stuart-Macadam 1989). For example, living conditions such as trash disposal practices, sanitation, and food preparation techniques are essential factors for understanding this stressor (Walker 1985). In some contexts, iron absorption seems to be considerably reduced by consumption of maize. However, the eating of maize with other foods such as fish appears to promote iron absorption (Layrisse, Martinez-Torres, and Roche 1968). Therefore, it is possible that marine resources in precontact Guale diet may have served to increase iron absorption, thus preventing iron deficiency anemia.

How, then, can the dramatic increase in prevalence of porotic hyperostosis in the early and late contact periods—despite the continued use of marine resources—be explained? Diet may not necessarily be the most important factor in the explanation of iron deficiency anemia in past populations. In a large series of crania from the Channel Islands area of southern California, Walker (1986) reported a very high frequency of porotic hyperostosis in a fishing-based island population. Half of juvenile crania (<10 years) exhibited porotic hyperostosis. He suggests that aggregation of human populations around limited and heavily used water resources and subsequent contamination may have resulted in diarrheal infections, and hence iron deficiency anemia.

It is possible that the increase in frequency of porotic hyperostosis in the early and late contact series may be related to conditions similar to those observed in the southern California coastal region. At missions in La Florida, wells were constructed that served as sources of fresh water (Thomas 1988). If these wells functioned as primary water sources for mission populations, then their contamination could likely lead to diarrheal infections resulting in iron deficiency anemia. On Saint Catherines Island, there is some evidence to suggest that a freshwater stream near the mission was dammed and utilized as a primary water source for its occupants (David Hurst Thomas, personal communication 1989). Immediately surrounding this locality is an abundance of midden, including food remains, that suggests that trash was deposited in and around this water source during the occupation of the mission. Although purely suggestive, this trash may have contributed to a contamination of this water source, thus providing a possible avenue for infections leading specifically to iron deficiency anemia. It seems plausible, therefore, that the concentrations of populations around mission centers may have been conducive to generally deteriorating levels of sanitation, including those areas associated with water sources.

ENAMEL HYPOPLASIA Enamel, the outer covering of tooth crowns, offers an important record of metabolic insult and growth disruption during the period of development of the dentition. If disruptions occur in the process of enamel formation, then macroscopically visible defects in enamel thickness called hypoplasias may arise. Although these defects can occur as small pits, circumferential lines or furrows are more frequently present in archeological teeth. Hypoplasias are associated with three conditions, including hereditary anomaly, localized trauma, and systemic metabolic stress. If several teeth are affected that develop at the same time, then the defects are probably associated with systemic metabolic stress (Goodman and Rose 1991). Clinical associations have been found that link hypoplasias with a variety of nutritional disorders or diseases or both (Cutress and Suckling 1982; Larsen 1987; Goodman and Rose 1991 for reviews). Given the nonspecificity of hypoplasias, they should be considered as indicators of generalized or nonspecific physiological disruption (Kreshover 1960; Goodman and Rose 1991).

Hypoplasia data on six permanent teeth (maxillary and mandibular first and second incisors, canines) are available for precontact preagricultural, precontact agricultural, early contact, and late contact dentitions (see Hutchinson and Larsen 1988, 1990 for methods). Chronological history of defect events was determined by matching location of individual hypoplasias against a dental developmental sequence provided by Massler, Schour, and Poncher (1941), and modified for use by Swärdstedt (1966) and Goodman, Armelagos, and Rose (1980). Several researchers have suggested that because enamel deposition occurs in consecutive layers commencing at the occlusal surface and continuing to the cervical region of the tooth, period of duration of stress events can be approximated by measurement of hypoplasia width (Blakey and Armelagos 1985; Hutchinson and Larsen 1988). On the other hand, Suckling, Elliott, and Thurley (1986) have shown in laboratory animals that severity of stress is an important factor in determining the extent and width of hypoplastic lesions. Regardless of how stress is measured, either by duration or severity of the episode, it is reasonable to suggest that wider hypoplasias represent relatively greater stress than narrower hypoplasias.

The most obvious hypoplasia width difference among the four periods is the consistently smaller widths in the precontact preagricultural group compared to the other three periods (table 4). Thus, there is no clear change in widths in comparison of the three periods following the precontact preagricultural period. However, there is one tendency found in comparison of the early and late contact periods. In particular, four of the six teeth show a greater width of hypoplasias in the late period than in the early period, suggesting increased stress in the former. The tooth with the greatest hypoplastic width is the late contact period maxillary central incisor (I_1).

These data are generally consistent with the finding of increasing stress levels in late precontact and contact period Guale. The largest relative increase in width of hypoplasias is during the precontact agricultural period, suggesting that stress increased in these populations prior to the arrival of

TABLE 4

La Florida Hypoplasia Event Mean Widths

Tooth	Before 1150 (n = 141) Width in mm	Number[1]	1150–1500 (n = 140) Width in mm	Number[1]	1607–1680 (n = 229) Width in mm	Number[1]	1686–1702 (n = 41) Width in mm	Number[1,2]
Maxilla								
I1	.56	(53)	.70	(65)	.58	(77)	.86	(18)
I2	.47	(49)	.64	(66)	.70	(77)	.65	(17)
C	.56	(67)	.68	(81)	.73	(128)	.54	(17)
Mandible								
I1	.51	(40)	.57	(65)	.41	(84)	.68	(9)
I2	.44	(57)	.56	(77)	.46	(90)	.72	(10)
C	.50	(79)	.79	(97)	.73	(138)	.78	(26)

Sources: Hutchinson and Larsen 1988, 1990, unpublished.

[1] Number of individuals with at least one hypoplastic event.

[2] Partial sample.

Europeans. The common denominator for the periods following the precontact preagricultural period is maize agriculture. Therefore, the increase in stress may have been related to this single stressor. However, other stressors both before and after contact were present in these populations, including nonspecific and specific forms of infectious disease. Therefore, it is not possible to pinpoint a single cause for the increasing hypoplasia widths except to say that stress as a general phenomenon increased in these populations. The data comparisons for the contact period populations are suggestive of greater stress during late contact times.

CONCLUSIONS

The results of this research both confirm and at the same time broaden understanding of what administrators, priests, explorers, and others in La Florida put to paper regarding their observations of deteriorating conditions in Indian populations. The skeletal record of the Indian population provides a direct link representing a retrospective cumulative record of events occurring during growth and development and adulthood at both the individual and population level.

Historical and archeological records provide information on diet in native populations (Reitz 1988; Hann 1986a). A reading of these records indicates that a wide range of foods, both plant and animal, were consumed by precontact and contact populations in the region. Yet, the shortcoming of these records is that they do not give information on the relative importance of specific foods in the diet (such as marine versus terrestrial foods) and thus they cannot be used to address issues relating to nutritional quality. The study of bone chemistry has provided precise information on diachronic trends in food consumption patterns (Schoeninger et al. 1990) and has shown specifically that there was a reduction in breadth of foods consumed as well as a general reduction in dietary quality with an increased emphasis on plant carbohydrates, namely maize. Therefore, nutrition comes primarily within the purview of the study of human remains.

This discussion of population biology in La Florida has been mostly restricted to Guale. This record is probably representative of the general conditions of change in lifeway and workload as well as decline in health and quality of life for the

Indians of La Florida as a whole. However, some preliminary evidence provided by the study of a small series of Apalachee human remains from San Pedro de Patale (Storey 1986; Jones et al. 1990) has indicated that, in comparison with Mississippian populations in the region, health may have actually improved. Indeed, the fact that the late sixteenth-century population that inhabited this mission numbered between 1,000 and 2,000 Indians (Hann 1988) argues for a relatively successful lifeway.

If it becomes possible to study larger samples of human remains from premission and mission period sites in Apalachee, then the presence of a thriving, albeit reduced, population at the same time that Guale and Timucua were approaching collapse is interesting and points to the potential for variability of biological change in La Florida. A large cemetery at the principal Apalachee mission, San Luis de Talimali, has been discovered, but limited test excavation has produced only a couple of dozen teeth and fragmentary bones from disturbed contexts, thereby preventing meaningful biocultural interpretation (Larsen 1989).

A consensus has emerged that disease brought by Europeans to the New World was the prima facie cause for the extinction of some native populations. In references to the southeastern United States, "No other factor seems capable of having exterminated so many people over such a large part of North America" (Crosby 1986:213). Yet, equally important to understanding the proximate cause of this decline is the suite of other factors that provided the context for and ultimate causation of this devastation, including excessive workload and activity-level alterations, reduced nutritional quality, hostile European-Indian interactions, warfare, soil depletion, reduced sanitation, population nucleation, social disruption, physiological stress, and so forth. Therefore, it is essential that scholars move away from monocausal explanations of population change to reach a broad-based understanding of decline and extinction of Native American groups after 1492.

REFERENCES

Bender, M. M., D. A. Baerreis, and R. L. Steventon
    1981   Further Light on Carbon Isotopes and Hopewell Agriculture. *American Antiquity* 46:346–353.

Blakely, Robert L., ed.
1989   The King Site: Continuity and Contact in Sixteenth-Century Georgia. Athens: University of
Georgia Press.

Blakey, Michael L., and George J. Armelagos
1985   Deciduous Enamel Defects on Prehistoric Americans from Dickson Mounds: Prenatal and Post-
natal Stress. American Journal of Physical Anthropology 66:371–380.

Buikstra, Jane E., Jill Bullington, Douglas K. Charles, Della C.
Cook, Susan R. Frankenberg, Lyle W. Konigsberg, Joseph B.
Lambert, and Liang Xue
1987   Diet, Demography, and the Development of Hor-
ticulture. Pp. 67–85 in Emergent Horticultural
Economies of the Eastern Woodlands. William F.
Keegan, ed. Southern Illinois University at Carbondale
Center for Archaeological Investigations, Occasional
Paper 7.

Bushnell, Amy Turner
1986   Santa Maria in the Written Record. Florida Museum
of Natural History, Department of Anthropology, Miscellaneous Project Report Series 21.

Crosby, Alfred W.
1986   Ecological Imperialism: The Biological Expansion
of Europe, 900–1900. New York: Cambridge University Press.

Cutress, T. W., and G. W. Suckling
1982   The Assessment of Non-carious Defects of Enamel. International Dental Journal 32:119–122.

Dobyns, Henry F.
1983   Their Number Become Thinned: Native American Population Dynamics in Eastern North America. Knoxville: University of Tennessee Press.

Eichner, Edward R.
1989   Does Running Cause Osteoarthritis? The Physician
and Sportsmedicine 17:147–154.

El-Najjar, Mahmoud Y.
1977   Maize, Malaria, and the Anemias in the Pre-Columbian New World. Yearbook of Physical Anthropology 20:329–337.

Fresia, Anne E., Christopher B. Ruff, and Clark Spencer Larsen
1990   Temporal Decline in Bilateral Asymmetry of the
Upper Limb on the Georgia Coast. In Archae-
ology of Mission Santa Catalina de Guale. Vol. 2:
Biocultural Interpretations of a Population in
Transition, Clark Spencer Larsen, ed. Anthro-
pological Papers of the American Museum of Natural
History, No. 68:121–132.

Goodman, Alan H., G. J. Armelagos, and J. C. Rose
1980   Enamel Hypoplasias as Indicators of Stress in
Three Prehistoric Populations from Illinois. Human Biology 52:512–528.

Goodman, Alan H., and Jerome C. Rose
1991   Dental Enamel Hypoplasias as Indicators of Nutritional Stress. Pp. 279–293 in Advances in Dental
Anthropology, Marc A. Kelley and Clark Spencer
Larsen, eds. Wiley-Liss, Inc., New York.

Goodman, Alan H., R. Brooke Thomas, Alan C. Swedlund, and
George J. Armelagos
1988   Biocultural Perspectives on Stress in Prehistoric,
Historical, and Contemporary Population Research. Yearbook of Physical Anthropology 31:169–
202.

Griffin, James B.
1966   Eastern North American Archaeology: A Summary. Science 156:175–191.

Griffin, Mark C., and Clark Spencer Larsen
1989   Patterns in Osteoarthritis: A Case Study from the
Prehistoric and Historic Southeastern U.S. Atlantic Coast. American Journal of Physical Anthropology
78:232.

Hann, John H.
1986a Demographic Patterns and Changes in Mid-Seventeenth Century Timucua and Apalachee. Florida Historical Quarterly 64:371–392.

1986b The Use and Processing of Plants by Indians of
Spanish Florida. Southeastern Archaeology 5:91–
102.

1988   Apalachee: The Land Between the Rivers. Gainesville: University Presses of Florida.

Hardin, Kenneth W.
1986   The Santa Maria Mission Project. Florida Anthropologist 39:75–83.

Hrdlička, Aleš
1908   Physiological and Medical Observations among
the Indians of the Southwestern United States and
Northern Mexico. Bureau of American Ethnology
Bulletin 34. Washington.

Hutchinson, Dale L.
1990   Postcontact Biocultural Change: Mortuary Site Evidence. Pp. 61–70 in Columbian Consequences.
Vol. 2: Archaeological and Historical Perspectives
on the Spanish Borderlands East, David Hurst
Thomas, ed. Washington: Smithsonian Institution
Press.

Hutchinson, Dale L., and Clark Spencer Larsen
1988   Determination of Stress Episode Duration from
Linear Enamel Hypoplasias. Human Biology
60:93–110.

1990   Stress and Lifeway Change: The Evidence from
Enamel Hypoplasias. In The Archaeology of Mis-
sion Santa Catalina de Guale. Vol. 2: Biocultural
Interpretations of a Population in Transition,
Clark Spencer Larsen, ed. Anthropological Papers of
the American Museum of Natural History 68:50–65.

Johnston, Francis E., and Lawrence M. Schell
  1979   Anthropometric Variation of Native American Children and Adults. Pp. 275–291 in The First Americans: Origins, Affinities, and Adaptations, William S. Laughlin and Albert B. Harper, eds. New York: Gustav Fischer.

Jones, B. Calvin, Mark Williams, Katherine Bierce-Gedris, John H. Hann, Rebecca D. Storey, and John Scarry
  1990   San Pedro de Patale: A Seventeenth-century Mission in Leon County, Florida. *Florida Archaeology* 5.

Jones, Grant D.
  1978   The Ethnohistory of the Guale Coast Through 1684. In The Anthropology of St. Catherines Island, 1: Natural and Cultural History, by David Hurst Thomas, Grant D. Jones, Roger S. Durham, and Clark Spencer Larsen. *Anthropological Papers of the American Museum of Natural History* 55:178–210. New York.

Jurmain, Robert D.
  1980   The Pattern of Involvement of Appendicular Degenerative Joint Disease. *American Journal of Physical Anthropology* 53:143–150.

Kelley, Marc A.
  1989   Infectious Disease. Pp. 191–199 in Reconstruction of Life from the Skeleton, Mehmet Yasar Iscan and Kenneth A. R. Kennedy, eds. New York: Alan R. Liss, Inc.

Kreshover, Seymour J.
  1960   Metabolic Disturbances in Tooth Formation. *Annals of the New York Academy of Sciences* 875:161–167.

Larsen, Clark Spencer
  1982   The Anthropology of St. Catherines Island, 3: Prehistoric Human Biological Adaptation. *Anthropological Papers of the American Museum of Natural History* 57:155–270. New York.

  1984   Health and Disease in Prehistoric Georgia: The Transition to Agriculture. Pp. 367–392 in Paleopathology at the Origins of Agriculture, Mark N. Cohen and George J. Armelagos, eds., Orlando, Fla.: Academic Press.

  1987   Bioarchaeological Interpretations of Subsistence Economy and Behavior from Human Skeletal Remains. Pp. 339–445 in Advances in Archaeological Method and Theory, Vol. 10, Michael B. Schiffer, ed. San Diego, Calif.: Academic Press.

  1989   Human Remains from Mission San Luis. Pp. 51–54 in Town Plan and Town Life at Seventeenth-Century San Luis, by Richard Vernon, *Bureau of Archaeological Research, Division of Historic Resources, Florida Archaeological Reports* 13.

Larsen, Clark Spencer, ed.
  1990   The Archaeology of Mission Santa Catalina de Guale. Vol. 2: Biocultural Interpretations of a Population in Transition. *Anthropological Papers of the American Museum of Natural History.* 68.

Larsen, Clark Spencer, Beverly Barber, Joseph Brandon, Wendy Brown, Jory Clebanoff, Paul Enwia, Kathryn Klokkenga, Joanna E. Lambert, Mara Lin, James McAndrews, Daniel R. Swendsen, and Chris Teteak
  1989   Human Remains from the Seven Mile Bend Site, Bryan County, Georgia. Contract report to Fred C. Cook, Brunswick, Georgia.

Larsen, Clark Spencer, and Christopher B. Ruff
  1991   Biomechanical Adaptation and Behavior on the Prehistoric Georgia Coast. Pp. 102–113 in What Mean These Bones? Studies in Southeastern Bioarchaeology, Mary Lucas Powell, Patricia S. Bridges, and Ann Marie Mires, eds. Tuscaloosa: University of Alabama Press.

Larsen, Clark Spencer, Christopher B. Ruff, and Marc C. Griffin
  1990   Behavioral Adaptation at Contact: Biomechanical and Pathological Evidence from the Southeastern Borderlands. (Paper presented at the meetings of the American Association of Physical Anthropologists, Miami, Florida.)

Larsen, Clark Spencer, and Rebecca Saunders
  1987   The Santa Catalina de Guale (Amelia Island) Cemeteries. (Paper presented at the meetings of the Southeastern Archaeological Conference, Charleston, South Carolina.)

Larsen, Clark Spencer, Margaret J. Schoeninger, Dale L. Hutchinson, Katherine F. Russell, and Christopher B. Ruff
  1990   Beyond Demographic Collapse: Biological Adaptation and Change in Native Populations of La Florida. Pp. 409–428 in Columbian Consequences. Vol. 2: Archaeological and Historical Perspectives on the Spanish Borderlands East, David Hurst Thomas, ed. Washington: Smithsonian Institution Press.

Larsen, Clark Spencer, Rebecca Shavit, and Mark C. Griffin
  [1991]   Dental Caries Evidence for Dietary Change: An Archaeological Context. Pp. 179–202 in Advances in Dental Anthropology, Marc A. Kelley and Clark Spencer Larsen, eds. New York: Wiley-Liss, Inc.

Layrisse, M., C. Martinez-Torres, and M. Roche
  1968   Effect of Interaction of Various Foods on Iron Absorption. *American Journal of Clinical Nutrition* 21:1175–1183.

Martin, Debra L., Alan H. Goodman, and George J. Armelagos
  1985   Skeletal Pathologies as Indicators of Quality and Quantity of Diet. Pp. 227–279 in The Analysis of Prehistoric Diets, Robert I. Gilbert and James H. Mielke, eds. Orlando, Fla.: Academic Press.

Massler, M., I. Schour, and S. G. Poncher
  1941   Developmental Pattern of the Child as Reflected in the Calcification Pattern of the Teeth. *American Journal of Diseases of Children* 62:33–67.

Merbs, Charles F.
  1983   Patterns of Activity-induced Pathology in a Cana-
          dian Inuit Population. *National Museum of Man,
          Mercury Series, Archaeological Survey of Canada Paper*
          119. Ottawa.

Milner, George R.
  1980   Epidemic Disease in the Postcontact Southeast: A
          Reappraisal. *Mid-Continental Journal of Archaeology*
          5:39–56. (Reprinted in: Native American Demog-
          raphy in the Spanish Borderlands, Clark Spencer
          Larsen, ed., 1991, Garland, New York.)

Newbrun, Earnest
  1982   Sugar and Dental Caries: A Review of Human
          Studies. *Science* 217:418–423.

Oviedo, Gonzalo Fernández de
  1945   Historia general y natural de las Indias: Islas y
          Tierra-Firme del Mar Oceano. Asunción, Para-
          guay: Editorial Guarania.

Powell, Mary Lucas
  1985   The Analysis of Dental Wear and Caries for Di-
          etary Reconstruction. Pp. 307–338 in The Analy-
          sis of Prehistoric Diets, Robert I. Gilbert and James
          H. Mielke, eds. Orlando, Fla.: Academic Press.

  1990   On the Eve of Conquest: Life and Death at Irene
          Mound, Georgia. The Archaeology of Mission
          Santa Catalina de Guale. Vol. 2: Biocultural In-
          terpretations of a Population in Transition, Clark
          Spencer Larsen, ed. *Anthropological Papers of the
          American Museum of Natural History* 68:26–35.

Reitz, Elizabeth J.
  1988   Evidence for Coastal Adaptation in Georgia and
          South Carolina. *Archaeology of Eastern North Amer-
          ica* 16:137–158.

Ruff, Christopher B.
  1987   Sexual Dimorphism in Human Lower Limb Bone
          Structure: Relationship to Subsistence Strategy
          and Sexual Division of Labor. *Journal of Human
          Evolution* 16:391–416.

Ruff, Christopher B., and Wilson C. Hayes
  1983   Cross-sectional Geometry of Pecos Pueblo Femora
          and Tibiae—A Biomechanical Investigation, I:
          Method and General Patterns of Variation. *Ameri-
          can Journal of Physical Anthropology* 60:359–381.

Ruff, Christopher B., and Clark Spencer Larsen
  1990   Postcranial Biomechanical Adaptations to Subsis-
          tence Strategy Changes on the Georgia Coast. The
          Archaeology of Mission Santa Catalina de Guale.
          Vol. 2: Biocultural Interpretations of a Population
          in Transition, Clark Spencer Larsen, ed. *An-
          thropological Papers of the American Museum of Natu-
          ral History* 68:94–120.

Ruff, Christopher B., Clark Spencer Larsen, and Wilson C.
Hayes
  1984   Structural Changes in the Femur with the Transi-

tion to Agriculture on the Georgia coast. *American
Journal of Physical Anthropology* 64:125–136.

Russell, Katherine F., Inui Choi, and Clark Spencer Larsen
  1990   The Paleodemography of Santa Catalina de
          Guale. The Archaeology of Mission Santa Catalina
          de Guale, 2: Biocultural Interpretations of a Popu-
          lation in Transition, Clark Spencer Larsen, ed. *An-
          thropological Papers of the American Museum of Natu-
          ral History* 68:36–49.

Sauer, Carl Ortwin
  1971   Sixteenth Century North America. Berkeley: Uni-
          versity of California Press.

Schoeninger, Margaret J., Michael J. DeNiro, and Henrik
Tauber
  1983   Stable Nitrogen Isotope Ratios of Bone Collagen
          Reflect Marine and Terrestrial Components of
          Prehistoric Human Diet. *Nature* 220:1381–1383.

Schoeninger, Margaret J., Nikolaas J. van der Merwe, Katherine
Moore, Julia Lee-Thorp, and Clark Spencer Larsen
  1990   Decrease in Diet Quality Between the Prehistoric
          and Contact Periods. The Archaeology of Mission
          Santa Catalina de Guale. Vol. 2: Biocultural In-
          terpretations of a Population in Transition, Clark
          Spencer Larsen, ed. *Anthropological Papers of the
          American Museum of Natural History* 68:78–93.

Simpson, Scott W., Dale L. Hutchinson, and Clark Spencer
Larsen
  1990   Coping with Stress: Tooth Size, Dental Defects,
          and Age-at Death. The Archaeology of Mission
          Santa Catalina de Guale. Vol. 2: Biocultural In-
          terpretations of a Population in Transition, Clark
          Spencer Larsen, ed. *Anthropological Papers of the
          American Museum of Natural History* 68:66–77.

Smith, Bruce D.
  1986   The Archaeology of the Southeastern United
          States: From Dalton to de Soto, 10,500–500 B.P.
          Pp. 1–92 in Advances in World Archaeology, Vol.
          5, Fred Wendorf and Angela E. Close, eds. Orlan-
          do, Fla.: Academic Press.

  1989   Origins of Agriculture in Eastern North America.
          Science 246:1566–1571.

Smith, Buckingham, ed.
  1968   Narratives of the Career of Hernando De Soto in
          the Conquest of Florida. Gainesville, Fla.: Kallman
          Publishing Company.

Steponaitis, Vincas P.
  1986   Prehistoric Archaeology in the Southeastern
          United States, 1970–1985. *Annual Review of An-
          thropology* 15:363–404.

Storey, Rebecca
  1986   Diet and Health Comparisons Between Pre- and
          Post-Columbian Native Americans in North Flor-
          ida. (Paper presented at the meetings of the Amer-

ican Association of Physical Anthropologists, Albuquerque, New Mexico.)

Stuart-Macadam, P. L.
1989 Nutritional Deficiency Diseases: A Survey of Scurvy, Rickets, and Iron-Deficiency Anemia. Pp. 201–222 in Reconstruction of Life from the Skeleton, Mehmet Yasar Iscan and Kenneth A. R. Kennedy, eds. New York: Alan R. Liss, Inc.

Suckling, Grace, D. C. Elliott, and D. C. Thurley
1986 The Macroscopic Appearance and Associated Histological Changes in the Enamel Organ of Hypoplastic Lesions of Sheep Incisor Teeth Resulting from Induced Parasitism. *Archives of Oral Biology* 31:427–439.

Swärdstedt, Torsten
1966 Odontological Aspects of a Medieval Population in the Province of Jämtland/Mid-Sweden. Stockholm: Tiden-Barnängen Tyrckerier.

Tauber, Henrik
1981 ^{13}C Evidence for Dietary Habits of Prehistoric Man in Denmark. *Nature* 292:332–333.

Teaford, Mark F.
1991 Dental Microwear: What Can It Tell Us About Diet and Dental Function? Pp. 341–356 in Advances in Dental Anthropology, Marc A. Kelley and Clark Spencer Larsen, eds. New York: Alan R. Liss, Inc.

Thomas, David Hurst
1987 The Archaeology of Mission Santa Catalina de Guale, 1: Search and Discovery. *Anthropological Papers of the American Museum of Natural History* 63:47–161.

1988 Saints and Soldiers at Santa Catalina: Hispanic Designs for Colonial America. Pp. 73–140 in The Recovery of Meaning: Historical Archaeology in the Eastern United States, Mark P. Leone and Parker B. Potter, eds. Washington: Smithsonian Institution Press.

Timoshenko, S. P., and J. M. Gere
1972 Mechanics of Materials. New York: Van Nostrand Reinhold.

Vernon, Richard
1989 Town Plan and Town Life at Seventeenth-century San Luis. *Bureau of Archaeological Research, Division of Historical Resources, Florida Archaeological Reports* 13.

Vogel, J. C., and Nikolaas J. van der Merwe
1977 Isotopic Evidence for Early Maize Cultivation in New York State. *American Antiquity* 42:238–242.

Walker, Phillip L.
1985 Anemia Among Prehistoric Indians of the American Southwest. Pp. 139–164 in Health and Disease in the Prehistoric Southwest, Charles F. Merbs and Robert J. Miller, eds. *Arizona State University Anthropological Paper* 34.

1986 Porotic Hyperostosis in a Marine-dependent California Indian Population. *American Journal of Physical Anthropology* 69:345–354.

Zahler, James W., Jr.
1976 A Morphological Analysis of a Protohistoric-Historic Skeletal Population from St. Simons Island, Georgia. (Unpublished M.A. thesis, in Anthropology, University of Florida, Gainesville.)

5

Health and Disease in the Late Prehistoric Southeast

MARY LUCAS POWELL

The old concept of the aboriginal New World as a "disease-free paradise" was based upon an extensive body of recorded observations, beginning in 1492, that Native Americans were devastated by introduced Old World diseases. The relatively small size of most pre-Columbian populations, with the exception of the largest urban concentrations in Mexico, did not provide the appropriate epidemiological setting for the appearance and maintenance of virulent acute infectious diseases, such as smallpox, to which Old World populations had become gradually adapted through centuries of repeated exposure. However, the aboriginal New World peoples were without doubt exposed to a wide variety of zoonoses (diseases primarily affecting animals, with humans as secondary "accidental" hosts), environmental pathogens, such as soil fungi and endogenous staphylococcal and streptococcal bacteria (St. Hoyme 1969).

In addition to these, paleopathological research has demonstrated the existence of two chronic infectious diseases—tuberculosis and treponematosis—that had established endemic focuses in many regions of the aboriginal Western hemisphere. Reported regional variations in their prevalence and severity reflect to some extent differences in sample integrity and methods of observation. Yet key social and ecological factors (such as general levels of health and the presence of certain soil fungi) also would have exerted strong effects upon their expression. Neither the origins nor the demise of these indigenous diseases is as yet fully understood, but their established presence held profound implications for life, debility, and death in precontact populations and for their exposure to related Old World pathogens after 1492.

THE DISEASES IN QUESTION

Tuberculosis

Tuberculosis is a chronic disease caused by the gram-negative microorganism *Mycobacterium tuberculosis* and, rarely, closely related mycobacterial species. In endemic contexts, most people in each generation are initially infected in early childhood, typically from inhalation of pathogen-laden droplets exhaled from individuals with active pulmonary lesions. If general levels of health are good, more than half of those infected will never develop any clinical symptoms of disease, but individuals with faulty immune response (due either to poor nutrition or other infections) may develop primary lesions in their lungs or hilar lymph nodes. If death does not ensue, the mycobacteria may be walled up within fibrous capsules in the body, halting further progression of the disease. However, the microorganisms can remain viable for decades, even with late twentieth-century medical therapy, and severe systemic stress in later life may reactivate the disease process. Localized focuses may rupture and spread mycobacteria via direct or hematogenous dissemination throughout the body, producing lesions in all types of tissue including bone and infecting new victims (Hoeprich 1977; Myers 1951; Robbins and Cotran 1979). In longstanding cases, overstimulation of immune responses in hypersensitized tissues may result in such proliferation of granulomatous tissue within the lungs that pulmonary capacity is compromised and death results.

Because of the extremely long viability of the encapsulated organisms, this disease may be passed from one generation to the next in very small populations even if reinfection from outside sources is rare (Myers 1951). Tuberculosis was a major cause of death in children, adolescents, and young adults before the development of effective surgical and antibiotic therapies, and the mortality from pulmonary tuberculosis ranged from 111 to 289 per 100,000 population in Europe and the United States in the first years of the twentieth century (Ortner and Putschar 1981).

Within the skeleton, the thoracic and lumbar vertebrae, ribs, and sternum are at high risk of hematogenous infection from active pulmonary lesions, because of the pathogen's affinity for cancellous bone containing hemopoetic (red) marrow. Cavitation of vertebral bodies leads to spinal collapse, resulting in the anterior kyphosis that characterizes Pott's disease. Very little perifocal reactive bone formation accompanies localized cavitations in long bone epiphyses or metaphyses, and periosteal reaction is also rare. The hip and knee joints are often affected in tuberculous infants, children, and adolescents, with adult onset rare (Ortner and Putschar 1981).

In general, the disease process leads predominantly to destruction of existing bone tissue, rather than to proliferation of new bone tissue, a pattern with important implications for paleopathological diagnoses in archeological series. The bones predominantly affected are fragile and prone to poor preservation and were often not systematically collected in archeological excavations. Skeletal lesions occur in only a small minority of cases, with estimated prevalence rates ranging from 3 to 7 percent by most authorities (Ortner and Putschar 1981; Steinbock 1976), though Kelley and Micozzi (1984) have suggested that rib lesions may occur twice as frequently in pulmonary tuberculosis, which comprises 90 percent of human cases.

Treponematosis

According to the "unitarian" view of treponematosis first set forth by Butler (1936), this multifaceted disease has been present in one form or another in human populations throughout the world since long before recorded history. The four modern syndromes "produce a pathological gradient extending from the cutaneous manifestations of pinta to the ulcers of yaws involving both skin and bone, to similar lesions of endemic syphilis affecting the skin, bone, and cardiovascular system, and finally to the lesions of venereal syphilis affecting all of the organs just mentioned in addition to the nervous system" (Steinbock 1976:92).

Hudson (1958, 1965) and Cockburn (1963) have argued that these clinical entities are all caused by the spirochete *Treponema pallidum*, one member of a vast family of bacteria that includes a wide range of saprophytic organisms, whose different strains produce the different syndromes depending upon the host population's epidemiological context. In this view, "every human population or subpopulation has the kind of treponematosis that is appropriate to its physical and socio-cultural status" (Steinbock 1976:93). Brothwell (1981) and Hackett (1963) argue that in fact different species of *T. pallidum* are implicated: *T. pallidum* for venereal syphilis, *T. pallidum* or *T. pallidum endemicum* for endemic nonvenereal syphilis, *T. carateum* for pinta, and *T. pertenue* for yaws. The similarity of the lesions in the four syndromes is remarkable, and organisms cultured from them have not been distinguished microscopically or immunologically from one another (Grin 1952; Hackett 1976; Turner and Hollander 1957).

The three nonvenereal treponemal syndromes are typically contracted in early childhood through direct contact with infectious skin lesions, not through venereal contact. Prevalence levels in endemic areas approaches 100 percent, and bone involvement of some sort (minor in most cases) occurs in 50–75 percent of late cases, resulting from hyperallergic response by sensitized hosts (Hackett 1951). Invasion of major organ systems is rare, in contrast to the well-known effects of venereal syphilis upon the cardiovascular system, the brain, and the motor nerves. The remainder of this discussion will focus upon the syndromes that affect bone, thus excluding pinta despite its exclusively New World distribution.

Venereal syphilis may severely dampen human fertility through miscarriages and stillbirths of infected fetuses. However, congenital cases of yaws and nonvenereal syphilis are very rare despite the apparent immunological identity of the treponemal pathogens, because of an important aspect of the epidemiology of endemic treponematosis. Where endemic treponematosis predominates, the great majority of conceptions occur in women whose disease was acquired at least a decade prior to menarche: as a result, the very low level of spirochetes in their bloodstreams greatly reduces the likelihood of passage through the placenta to infect the fetus. In contrast, because venereal syphilis is most typically transmitted to women through the same behavioral act that results in pregnancy, a woman may literally become pregnant and syphilitic at the same moment, thus exposing her fetus to very high levels of pathogens circulating through the maternal bloodstream across the placenta (Grin 1956; Ortner 1986). As Hackett (1976:8) notes, "transmission of [venereal] syphilis to the fetus is unusual if the mother had the disease for more than five years before the infant was conceived." The known association between elapsed time since maternal infection and the probability of fetal infection prompted physicians practicing before the introduction of antibiotic therapy to counsel syphilitic couples to postpone childbearing for a number of years after marriage (Morton 1913; Stokes 1928).

Bone lesions of treponematosis may be either nonspecific (periostitis, osteitis, and more rarely, osteomyelitis) or pathognomonic (gummateous osteoperiostitis, and caries sicca) (Hackett 1951, 1976; Hudson 1958; Grin 1953, 1956). They do not occur during the primary stage of disease but may appear along with skin and muco-cutaneous lesions late in the secondary stage. Tertiary stage lesions may recur intermittently throughout the life of the individual, eventually producing in some cases massive distortion of long bone shafts from repeated episodes of periostitis. The direct impact upon mortality is negligible, because the endemic syndromes do not invade vital organ systems, but the gummateous skin lesions invite superinfection by bacterial and mycotic agents and so may invite death by secondary effect.

Bones lying close underneath the skin (for example, the cranial vault, the superior aspects of the clavicle, and the anterior crest of the tibia) may develop lesions through spread of infection from adjacent skin lesions. The oral and nasal cavities are often affected in yaws and less often in endemic syphilis, and significant disfigurement may result (called gangosa in tertiary yaws). The lesions are self-limiting even without medical treatment, with eventual repair occurring to some extent. Plantation physicians in the South prevented yaws from tropical Africa from establishing an endemic presence in slave populations by the simple expedient of keeping infectious lesions clean and bandaged (Parramore 1970; Savich 1978).

Widespread but limited morbidity, rather than elevated mortality (Hackett 1951:13; E. H. Hudson 1961:3), is the hallmark of the two well-studied Old World endemic syndromes and probably characterized the prehistoric New World variety as well.

A Comparison of Morbidity, Mortal Effects, and Visibility

These two diseases, tuberculosis and treponematosis, have different implications for morbid and mortal impacts upon host populations, as well as different levels of visibility in archeological skeletal series. The general level of health in hosts is a crucial factor in the clinical expression of tuberculosis, but not of treponematosis, with individuals and populations severely stressed by malnutrition and other infections at highest risk of death from pulmonary failure. Endemic treponematosis typically produces clinical symptoms in far more individuals within each generation than does tuberculosis, but almost none of them die from it, even indirectly.

The clinical and archeological visibility of the two diseases on a gross level is inversely proportional to the risk of dying, because of their differences in pathophysiology. This is an important point to remember in paleopathological analysis: while the prevalence of diagnostic skeletal morbidity does reflect to some measure the prevalence of specific disease experience, the distribution of mortality within a population may have been significantly shaped by a quite different set of diseases, completely invisible from the skeletal record alone.

A second point of differential visibility concerns both diseases but more particularly treponematosis: the pathognomonic bone lesions reported in the clinical literature are almost exclusively those documented radiographically or discovered at autopsy in serologically positive cases. As such, they tend to be fairly extensive and destructive in nature, or else they would not have been discovered. Examination of dry bone specimens reveals a wealth of minor osteoblastic (proliferative) skeletal reaction that is not well visualized radiographically, often in regions rarely examined in autopsies: the pleural aspects of the ribs (a frequent site of tuberculosis lesions, according to Kelley and Miccozi 1984), and the shafts of the long bones (frequently affected by treponemal periostitis— Hackett 1976). Within a given population sample, then, paleopathologists may therefore actually see more skeletal evidence of infectious disease experience (albeit most of it relatively minor in nature) than clinicians conducting radiographic examinations or autopsies of known cases. The majority of this minor skeletal reaction is so nondiagnostic in nature that, without the presence of clearly pathognomonic lesions in at least a few cases, the same etiology for these minor cases would not be seriously considered.

NEW WORLD TUBERCULOSIS

Numerous cases of skeletal tuberculosis have been convincingly diagnosed in archeological series from North and South America (Buikstra 1981; Kelley and Eisenberg 1987; Lichtor and Lichtor 1957; Merbs and Miller 1985; Milner 1982, 1983; Milner and Smith 1990; Murray 1985; Powell 1988, 1990a; Ortner and Putschar 1981; Ritchie 1952; Steinbock 1976). Hrdlička (1909:1) expressed the opinion that "tuberculosis was rare, if it did exist," and Morse (1961) held serious doubts about the archeological contexts and accuracy of diagnosis of early reported cases (Ritchie 1952; Lichtor and Lichtor 1957). The earliest well-documented cases in the New World are reported by Allison et al. (1981) from Chile, one isolated spine dated about 160 B.C. and three cases from Casserones dated about A.D. 290. The desiccated lungs of a young Peruvian child who died of terminal miliary tuberculosis about A.D. 700 yielded identifiable acid-fast bacilli (Allison, Mendoza, and Pezzia 1973). The North American cases postdate A.D. 850, representing sites from Ontario and New York in the Northeast, to Ohio and Illinois in the Midwest, to Arizona and New Mexico in the Southwest. Only the states of Arkansas, Tennessee, Alabama, and Georgia in the Southeast have reported cases (table 1).

Murray (1985) reports two cases of spinal tuberculosis in adult females (Burial 2, 35–40 years and Burial 5, 17–25 years) among 15 burials examined from the Parkin site, a Late Mississippian community on the Saint Francis River in northeast Arkansas. Given the late occupation of this site (A.D. 1350–1650) and the possibility of direct or indirect contact with the Hernando de Soto expedition (Morse and Morse 1983), these cases could represent very early examples of introduced European disease. No definitely pre-Columbian cases of tuberculosis have been reported elsewhere in Arkansas.

TABLE 1

Tuberculosis in the Late Prehistoric Southeast

State	Site	Culture	Time	References
Alabama	Moundville	Mississippian	1050–1650 .	Powell 1988, 1990a
Arkansas	Parkin	Mississippian	1350–1650	Murray 1985
Georgia	Irene Mound	Mississippian	1200–1450	Powell 1990b
Tennessee	Averbuch	Mississippian	1275–1400	Kelley and Eisenberg 1987
	Arnold	Mississippian	about 1200	Widmer and Perzigian 1981

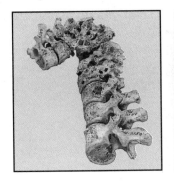 

Fig. 1. Tuberculosis. Left, spinal tuberculosis (Pott's disease), showing lytic destruction of upper thoracic vertebrae. Moundville, Alabama. Right, sacroiliac lesion showing joint involvement. Irene Mound, Georgia.

In Alabama, 10 individuals from the large Mississippian site of Moundville displayed rib lesions of the type claimed by Kelley and Micozzi (1984) to represent chronic pulmonary tuberculosis (Powell 1988). In one of these cases, extensive lytic destruction of upper thoracic vertebrae had resulted in marked anterior kyphosis (fig. 1). This young adult male had survived the onset of clinical disease for several years, as evidenced by the sclerotic nature of these lesions and the formation of numerous pscudo-arthroses between posterior spinal elements that would normally never come into contact. Of the 10 cases, two are subadults (0–6 months and 7–8 years), two died during the third decade, three during the fourth decade, two during the fifth decade, and one adult could not be precisely aged. Males and females are equally represented. These 10 identified cases may seriously underrepresent the true prevalence of skeletal tuberculosis at Moundville, because although the entire sample examined by Powell numbered 564 individuals, only 38 percent were represented by thoracic and 30 percent by lumbar vertebrae (Powell 1988:157).

Because the Moundville site does contain some evidence of protohistoric occupation (the Moundville III, A.D. 1500–1550, and IV, 1550–1650, phases), the chronological provenience of each of the 10 cases was carefully checked, using the most comprehensive listing of seriated grave lots (Vincas P. Steponaitis, personal communication 1989). Only one case (Md 1522) was directly in association with seriated grave vessels, assigned to the Moundville II-III phases, 1250–1550. Of the nine remaining cases, two (Md 1049 and Md 2615) were adjacent to burials assigned to Moundville I-II, 1050–1400, one (Md 2337) could be indirectly dated in similar fashion to Moundville II, three (Md 1571, Md 1583,

and Md 1603) to Moundville II-III, and two (Md 2150 and Md 2414) to the Moundville III phase. One case (Md 2208) could not be assigned to any particular phase.

Because no direct radiocarbon dates are available for these 10 cases, it cannot be ascertained how many actually postdate 1492 and therefore possibly reflect exposure to European tuberculosis. The preponderance of archeological evidence from the site suggests that they all predate that decisive date (Steponaitis 1989; Welch 1989; Peebles 1987).

The 10 cases of New World tuberculosis from Irene Mound, located near the mouth of the Savannah River on the north Georgia coast, have a definitely precontact context, with burials placed in this mortuary locality between A.D. 1200 and 1450 (Larsen 1982; Powell 1990a, 1990b). The 280 skeletal individuals examined exhibited more complete anatomical representation than did the Moundville skeletons, and therefore the number of identified cases probably reflects more accurately the actual prevalence of skeletal tuberculosis in this Georgia population.

Three of the 10 cases display lytic vertebral lesions (two of these also with rib lesions), one case exhibits extensive sacroiliac joint involvement (fig. 1), one shows both rib and scapula lesions, and five have rib lesions only. The most extensively affected case, a male in his early 20s, bears lesions on L2-L5, several ribs, and the pleural aspects of one scapula and his sternum. The 10 cases are sharply divided by age: two teenagers, four young adults (20 to 30 years), and four older adults (40 to 50 years). Five females and three males were affected, and no sex estimate was possible for the young adolescent.

Tuberculosis has been diagnosed in another clearly pre-Columbian context at the Averbuch site in central Tennessee representing the Middle Cumberland manifestation of the Mississippian culture radiocarbon dated to 1275–1400 (Eisenberg 1986; Kelley and Eisenberg 1987). This population apparently suffered from higher levels of severe systemic stress than did the Moundville or Irene Mound populations, judging from its much higher prevalence of skeletal lesions (cribra orbitalia and porotic hyperostosis) resulting from severe iron-deficiency anemia and other indicators of poor health. Several cases described by Kelley and Eisenberg (1987) display lesions suggestive of blastomycosis, a mycotic infection from the soil-borne fungus *Blastomyces dermatitidis* endemic in the Southeast. Differential diagnosis between tuberculosis and blastomycosis is often difficult (Buikstra 1977). Because both diseases are opportunistic in nature, that is, exposed individuals whose immune responses are already severely stressed by malnutrition or other factors are at particularly high risk from clinical expression of disease, Kelley and Eisenberg suggest that several of the Averbuch cases show simultaneous infection by both mycotic and mycobacterial pathogens, an epidemiologically sophisticated assessment.

An additional case of tuberculosis from another Middle Cumberland context in Tennessee, the Arnold site, dated about 1200, has been reported by Widmer and Perzigian (1981). This young adult female (represented only by the spinal column) displays extensive lytic destruction of T10-T12, resulting in kyphosis.

New World tuberculosis has been reported at four post-1200 but unquestionably pre-Columbian contexts in the Midwest, just outside the traditional boundaries of the Southeast: in Missouri, Kane Mounds (Milner 1982); in Illinois, the East Saint Louis Stone Quarry Site cemetery (Milner 1983) in the American Bottom, the Schild and Yokem sites in the Illinois River Valley (Buikstra and Cook 1981), and the Norris Farms #36 site (Milner and Smith 1990); and in Ohio, the Turpin site (Widmer and Perzigian 1981). Norris Farms #36 shows the highest prevalence (27 cases with clearly diagnostic lesions, plus 5 additional possible cases, in a population sample of 264 individuals) of any of the sites listed in this review as yielding tuberculous cases. The generally poor health of this Oneota agricultural population reflected the combined effects of sedentism and restricted access to food resources due to continual violent interactions with neighboring groups (Milner and Smith 1990), a situation conducive to opportunistic diseases.

In summary, the paleopathological evidence for tuberculosis in the late prehistoric Southeast (and Midwest) is both widespread and convincing.

NEW WORLD TREPONEMATOSIS

Baker and Armelagos's (1988) extensive review of the paleopathological literature on treponematosis from the pre-Columbian Americas includes cases reported from Alabama, Arkansas, Georgia, Florida, Illinois, North Carolina, Tennessee, Kentucky, Iowa, Virginia (table 2), New York, Ohio, Missouri, Oklahoma, California, Colorado, New Mexico, and Arizona, as well as from Canada (Saskatchewan), Mexico, and Central (Guatemala) and South (Peru, Argentina, and Colombia) America.

It is important to note that in the majority of these reports, only cases displaying the "classic" lesions are discussed: those with caries sicca, gummateous osteoperiostitis, grossly deformed long bone shafts (most frequently the tibiae), or significant nasal-palatal destruction. This emphasis is understandable, in the light of the differential visibility of bone lesions by radiography, by standard autopsy procedures, and by gross examination of dry bones. However, it may give an erroneous impression of the true extent of the disease within a population, an impression that can be corrected by reference to medically informed paleoepidemiological models, such as Cook's (1976) detailed discussion of treponemal disease in a Woodland Illinois population. In many populations in the world in the mid-twentieth century, the number of cases of endemic syphilis surpassed the number of cases of venereal syphilis (Hudson 1961:2).

Examples of prehistoric treponemal disease from Florida date as early as 3300 B.C. at the Archaic Tick Island (Bullen 1972), and abound from post-A.D. 1000 sites on both east and west coasts (Iscan and Miller-Shaivitz 1985). The Archaic population represented at Morton Shell Mound in coastal Louisiana (Robbins 1978) displayed similarly convincing lesions, as did several skeletal individuals from the Archaic Indian Knoll site in Kentucky (Brothwell and Burleigh 1975; Kelley 1980). The persistence of this infectious disease into the late prehistoric period is also well attested for the late

TABLE 2

Treponematosis in the Late Prehistoric Southeast

State	Site	Culture	Time	References
Alabama	Moundville	Mississippian	A.D. 1050–1650	Moore 1907; Haltom and Shands 1938; Powell 1988, 1990a
Arkansas	Nodena	Mississippian	A.D. 1400–1700	Powell 1989
	Northeast Ark.	Mississippian?	late prehistoric?	Ortner and Putschar 1981; Wakefield, Dellinger, and Camp 1937
Florida	Tick Island	Archaic	3300 B.C.	Bullen 1972
	Palmer Mound, Bayshore Homes, Hog Island	Weeden Island	A.D. 850–1350	Bullen 1972
	Lighthouse Mound, Browne Mound	St. Johns	A.D. 850–1350	Bullen 1972
	Highland Beach		A.D. 600–1200	Iscan and Miller-Shavitz 1985
Georgia	Irene Mound	Mississippian	A.D. 1200–1450	Powell 1990b
Kentucky	Indian Knoll	Archaic	4000–1000 B.C.	Kelley 1980; Brothwell and Burleigh 1975
	May's Lick	Mississippian	A.D. 1325	Brothwell and Burleigh 1975
	Hardin Village	Fort Ancient	A.D. 1200–1600	Cassidy 1972
Louisiana	Morton Shell Mound	Archaic	2500–500 B.C.	Robbins 1978; Neuman 1984: 198–202
Mississippi	Austin	Late Woodland/ Mississippian	A.D. 800–1200	Ross-Stallings 1989
	Lake George	Late Woodland/ Mississippian	A.D. 500–1500	Egnatz 1983
North Carolina	Hardin	Late Woodland/ Mississippian	A.D. 1350–1450	Reichs 1989
South Carolina	No paleopathological cases reported			Lawson 1709
Tennessee	Averbuch	Mississippian	A.D. 1275–1400	Eisenberg 1986
	various sites	Mississippian	late prehistoric	Jones 1876
Virginia	Fisher	Late Prehistoric	A.D. 1000–1400	Ortner 1986

prehistoric Fort Ancient peoples of Kentucky (Cassidy 1972) and adjacent Ohio (Mills 1906; Orton 1905).

Reichs (1989) has described in detail an extensively affected case from the late prehistoric Hardin site (A.D. 1350–1450) in North Carolina. Ross-Stallings (1989) diagnosed several cases from the Austin site (A.D. 800–1200) in Mississippi, and two individuals from the Lake George site (A.D. 500–1500) in that state displayed lesions that "resemble known cases of yaws" (Egnatz 1983:441).

In Arkansas, treponematosis has been identified at the Nodena site (Powell 1989), dated A.D. 1400–1700 (Morse and Morse 1983). One adult female displays a healed posterior cranial vault lesion of caries sicca (fig. 2), and another exhibits ex-

tensive nasal-palatal lesions suggestive of gangosa. Postcranial lesions of treponemal character are also abundant. Ortner and Putschar (1981) and Wakefield, Dellinger, and Camp (1937) report additional cases from other sites in northeast Arkansas. These cases have not been dated individually, so their precontact context is not certain.

In Alabama, the Moundville site yielded numerous cases with cranial and postcranial lesions indicative of treponematosis (Moore 1907; Haltom and Shands 1938; Powell 1988). One of the four cases illustrated by Powell (1990a) may have a postcontact date (Md 1381, late Moundville III), according to Steponaitis's (1989) seriation by grave vessels, but the other three are seriated before A.D. 1500 (Md 1322 and Md 1364, seriated indirectly through

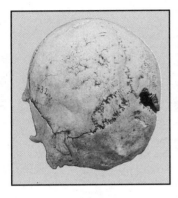 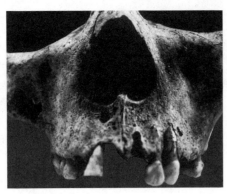

Fig. 2. Treponematosis. Left, caries sicca (healed cranial vault lesion). Nodena, Arkansas. Right, nasal lesions showing remodeling of the nasal margin. Irene Mound, Georgia.

association with other burials, and Md 1394, seriated directly, to Moundville II or early Moundville III).

The pre-Columbian context of treponematosis is unequivocal at Irene Mound in Georgia, dated A.D. 1200–1450 (Powell 1990a, 1990b). In addition to the distinctive cranial lesions, one adult female displays marked remodeling of the nasal margin and several small lytic lesions penetrating the palate (fig. 2). Only a few adults exhibit extreme distortion of their tibia shafts from repeated episodes of periostitis (fig. 3), but less extensive cases are abundant, as they were at Moundville.

The English explorer John Lawson remarked of the Santee Indians of South Carolina in the early eighteenth century, "the Natives of America have for many Ages (by their own Confession) been afflicted with a Distemper much like the *Lues Venerea,* which hath all the symptoms of the Pox, being dif-

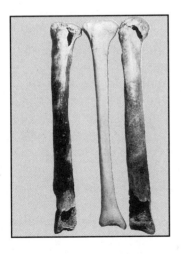

Fig. 3. Treponematosis. Bilateral tibia shaft expansion from periositis. Bone in center shows normal development. Irene Mound, Georgia.

ferent in this only: for I never could learn, that this Country-Distemper, or Yawes, is begun or continued with a Gonorrhea; yet it is attended with nocturnal Pains in the limbs, and commonly makes such a progress, as to vent Part of the matter by Botches, and several Ulcers in the Body, Oftentimes Death ensuing. I have known mercurial Unguents and remedies work a cure, following the same methods as in the Pox . . ." (Lawson 1709:18). Although no diagnosis of prehistoric treponematosis in South Carolina appears in the paleopathological literature, it seems only logical to assume that the disease was present there as in adjacent states.

The earliest diagnosis of treponemal disease from the prehistoric Southeast was published by the physician Joseph Jones (1876), prompted by his familiarity with the skeletal impact of venereal syphilis gained from his medical practice. His detailed descriptions of bone lesions from the stone box graves of various late prehistoric sites in the Middle Cumberland region of Tennessee comprise a model of logical deduction rarely equaled in modern paleopathology. Eisenberg (1986) recognized treponemal disease as one of the infectious disease stressors of the Middle Cumberland Averbuch population.

The preponderance of evidence suggests that the New World treponematosis was not essentially a venereally spread disease. Ortner (1986), however, presents a convincing case of congenital treponemal disease in a secure pre-Columbian context from the late prehistoric Fisher site in Virginia, dated 1000–1400. The skeleton of a child aged three to four years displays a combination of dental (extensive severe deciduous enamel hypoplasia) and skeletal (widespread periostitis) lesions that, taken together, closely match cases of modern congenital syphilis. An adult male skeleton in close proximity to this child displays chronic granulomatous lesions on the skull and postcranial elements. Citing Hackett (1963) on the immunologic identity of the spirochetes recovered from soft-tissue lesions of the modern treponemal syndromes, Ortner (1986:2) argues that "one possibility is that the childhood onset of the non-venereal syndromes allows time for a more adequate immune response of survivors by the time sexual maturity and childbearing occurs." Grin (1956) also favors this epidemiological (rather than immunological) explanation for the rarity of congenital transmission of endemic treponematosis.

The adult case alone presents a further bit of convincing evidence in the continuing debate about New World treponemal disease, because of the clearly diagnostic nature of its lesions in a securely pre-1492 context. However, the presence of the congenitally infected child is even more significant, because it illustrates the capacity of the New World treponeme to effect an atypical mode of infection (transplacental rather than epidermal), given the appropriate epidemiological circumstances. It was undoubtedly this flexibility that permitted the New World strain of *T. pallidum* to venereally colonize post-1492 Europe, although at least some of its very first Old World victims may have been infected through nonvenereal routes. Stewart and Spoehr (1952) argued that the treponemal epidemics that affected both Old and New World populations soon after 1492 resulted from a mutual exchange of isolated strains of the same spirochete, whose millennia-long separation resulted in negligible cross-immunity (unlike the Old World endemic and venereal strains today).

IMPLICATIONS FOR POSTCONTACT
DISEASE EXPERIENCE

Tuberculosis first appeared in ancient Egypt and gradually spread throughout Europe, as attested by paleopathological and historical evidence (Morse, Brothwell, and Ucko 1964; Morse 1967). The Europeans who invaded the Americas therefore represented host populations with sufficient time-depth of exposure to the disease for natural selection to have winnowed out the most susceptible genotypes. Stead (1974) reports significant differences in the immune response to primary tuberculosis infection between European and Asian populations with long exposure and Eskimo and American Indian populations with relatively little experience with the disease, at least with the Old World variety.

Tuberculosis was present among the Plains Indians of Saskatchewan from 1860 to 1880, but it "was not important as a cause of death" (Ferguson 1934:18) until after enforced settlement on reservations in 1879. In the next few years a tuberculosis epidemic swept through this region, and by 1896 the death rate was 9 percent of the total population. Cockburn (1963:93) attributes this disastrous impact to "many causes: inadequate diet following the disappearance of the buffalo, poor housing, overcrowding and general spiritual demoralization" in a population with little time-depth of experience with the disease.

Re-infection later in life of persons previously sensitized to tuberculosis may result in clinical disease, particularly in individuals under severe physical and psychological stress (Jaffe 1972:955). It has been estimated that up to 80 percent of new clinical cases represent flareups of earlier infections that had been suppressed by vigorous immune response (Hoeprich 1977:323; Robbins and Cotran 1979:397). Among Southeast Indians challenged by aggressive invasion and catastrophic cultural collapse, exposure to the Old World strain of tuberculosis may have provoked a particularly strong pathological response because of their previous exposure to the endemic New World variety.

Hackett (1951, 1963, 1976), Hudson (1958, 1965, 1968), and others in discussions of human treponematosis have noted the seemingly identical nature of the pathogens associated with the four modern syndromes. Within epidemiological regions, exposure in childhood to one of them appears to confer some positive degree of cross-immunity against later exposure to a different syndrome, but the strength of this protection is quite variable. Re-infection of latent cases or super-infection of active cases may create serious health problems, because re-activation of a hyperallergic response in sensitized tissues may result in destructive tertiary-stage gummateous and osteo-periostitic lesions (Grin 1956:969). This phenomenon could explain the vulnerability of Native Americans to venereal syphilis introduced by Old World invaders, even in regions with considerable experience of the indigenous treponematosis.

Given the mutable nature of treponemal strains under the selective pressures of different climatic and cultural variables (such as scanty versus extensive clothing for children), the development of the venereal syphilis that swept Europe in the early 1500s out of an endemic focus in the New World is epidemiologically plausible. As Hudson (1968:9) notes, "medical history offers instances of endemic syphilis initiated by the introduction of cases of venereal syphilis, as well as venereal infections arising from a background of endemic syphilis or yaws." The pre-Columbian presence in Europe of an endemic treponematosis has not been proven conclusively, but even if one did exist, it would not necessarily have conferred adequate cross-protection against a New World strain isolated for millennia from a common ancestor.

So while New World aboriginal pathogens and human populations may have become very well co-adapted to their own particular varieties of tuberculosis and treponematosis through the selective pressure of centuries of exposure, this epidemiological equilibrium was not adequate to protect Native Americans from devastation by the Old World versions of these diseases. In fact, previously sensitized aborigines probably stood at higher risk from re-activation of latent disease when newly exposed to different strains. The reciprocal impact upon Old World populations has been well documented through studies of the spread of venereal syphilis across the Old World after 1492 (Baker and Armelagos 1988; McNeal 1976; Crosby 1972). What happened to the New World strains of tuberculosis and treponematosis? They, like their human hosts, seem to have been submerged by the westward flood of plagues and peoples into the Western hemisphere.

REFERENCES

Allison, M. J., D. Mendoza, and A. Pezzia
1973   Documentation of a Case of Tuberculosis in Pre-Columbian America. *American Review of Respiratory Disease* 107:985–991.

Allison, M. J., E. Gerzten, J. Munizaga, C. Santoro, and D. Mendoza
1981   Tuberculosis in Pre-Columbian Andean Populations. Pp. 49–61 in Prehistoric Tuberculosis in the Americas, J. E. Buikstra, ed. Evanston, Ill.: Northwestern Archaeological Program.

Baker, B. J., and G. J. Armelagos
1988   The Origin and Antiquity of Syphilis. *Current Anthropology* 29(5):703–737.

Brothwell, D.
1981   Microevolutionary Change in the Human Pathogenic Treponemes: An Alternative Hypothesis. *International Journal of Systemic Bacteriology* 31:82–87.

Brothwell, D., and R. Burleigh
1975   Radiocarbon Dates and the History of Treponematoses in Man. *Journal of Archaeological Science* 2:393–396.

Buikstra, J. E.
1977   Differential Diagnosis: An Epidemiological Model. *Yearbook of Physical Anthropology* 20:316–328.

———, ed.
1981   Prehistoric Tuberculosis in the Americas. *Northwestern University, Archaeological Program, Scientific Papers* 5. Evanston, Ill.

Buikstra, J. E., and D. C. Cook
1981   Pre-Columbian Tuberculosis in West-central Illinois. Pp. 115–139 in Prehistoric Tuberculosis in the Americas. J. E. Buikstra, ed. *Northwestern University, Archaeological Program, Scientific Papers* 5. Evanston, Ill.

Bullen, A. K.
1972   Paleoepidemiology and Distribution of Prehistoric Treponemamiasis (syphilis) in Florida. *The Florida Anthropologist* 25:133–175.

Butler, C. S.
1936   Syphilis sive morbus Humanus—a Rationalization of Yaws So-called. Lancaster, Pa.: The Science Press Printing Company.

Cassidy, C. M.
1972   Comparison of Nutrition and Health in Pre-agricultural and Agricultural Amerindian Skeletal Populations. (Unpublished Ph.D. Dissertation in Anthropology, University of Wisconsin, Madison.)

Cockburn, A.
1963   Infectious Diseases, Their Evolution and Eradication. Springfield, Ill.: C. C. Thomas.

Cook, D. C.
1976   Pathologic States and Disease Processes in Illinois Woodland Populations: An Epidemiologic Approach. (Unpublished Ph.D. Dissertation in Anthropology, University of Chicago.)

Crosby, A. W.
1972   The Columbian Exchange: Biological and Cultural Consequences of 1492. Westport, Conn.: Greenwood Press.

Egnatz, D. G.
1983   Analysis of Human Skeletal Material from Mound C. Pp. 421–441 in Excavations at the Lake George

Site, Yazoo County, Mississippi, 1958–1960, by S. Williams and J. T. Brain. Appendix A, *Papers of the Peabody Museum of Archaeology and Ethnology, Harvard University* 74. Cambridge, Mass.

Eisenberg, L. E.
1986   Adaptation in a "Marginal" Mississippian Population from Middle Tennessee Biocultural Insights from Paleopathology. (Unpublished Ph.D. Dissertation in Anthropology, New York University, New York City.

Ferguson, R. G.
1934   Some Light Thrown on Infection, Resistance, and Segregation by a Study of Tuberculosis Among Indians. Pp. 18–26 in *Transactions of the American Clinical and Climatological Association.* Philadelphia.

Grin, E. I.
1952   Epidemiology and Control of Endemic Syphilis: Report on a Mass-treatment Campaign in Bosnia. *World Health Organization Monograph* 11. Geneva.

1956   Endemic Syphilis and Yaws. *Bulletin of the World Health Organization* 15:959–973.

Hackett, C. J.
1951   Bone Lesions of Yaws in Uganda. Oxford, England: Blackwell Scientific Publications.

1963   On the Origin of the Human Treponematosis. *Bulletin of the World Health Organization* 29:7–41.

1976   Diagnostic Criteria of Syphilis, Yaws, and Treponoid (treponematoses) and of Some Other Diseases in Dry Bones. Berlin: Springer-Verlag.

Haltom, W. L., and A. R. Shands
1938   Evidence of Syphilis in Mound Builders' Bones. *Archives of Pathology* 25:228–242.

Hoeprich, P. D., ed.
1977   Infectious Diseases, a Modern Treatise, 2d ed. Philadelphia: Harper and Row.

Hrdlička, A.
1909   Tuberculosis Among Certain Indian Tribes of the United States. *Bureau of American Ethnology Bulletin* 42. Washington.

Hudson, E. H.
1958   Non-venereal Syphilis, a Sociological and Medical Study of Bejel. Edinburgh, Scotland: E. and S. Livingston.

1961   Endemic Syphilis—Heir of the Syphiloids. *Archives of Internal Medicine* 108:1–4.

1965   Treponematosis and Man's Social Evolution. *American Anthropologist* 67:885–901.

1968   Christopher Columbus and the History of Syphilis. *Acta Tropica* 25(1):1–16.

Iscan, M. Y., and P. Miller-Shavitz
1985   Prehistoric Syphilis in Florida. *Journal of the Florida Medical Association* 72:109–113.

Jaffee, H. L.
1972   Metabolic, Degenerative, and Inflammatory Diseases of Bones and Joints. Philadelphia: Lea and Febiger.

Jones, J.
1876   Explorations of the Aboriginal Remains of Tennessee. *Smithsonian Contributions to Knowledge* 22(259). Washington.

Kelley, M. A.
1980   Disease and Environment: A Comparative Analysis of Three Early American Indian Skeletal Collections. (Unpublished Ph.D. Dissertation in Anthropology, Case Western University, Cleveland, Ohio.)

Kelley, M. A., and L. E. Eisenberg
1987   Blastomycosis and Tuberculosis in Early American Indians: A Biocultural View. *Midcontinental Journal of Archaeology* 12(1):89–116.

Kelley, M. A., and M. S. Micozzi
1984   Rib Lesions and Chronic Pulmonary Tuberculosis. *American Journal of Physical Anthropology* 65:381–386.

Larsen, C. S.
1982   The Anthropology of St. Catherine's Island. 3: Prehistoric Human Biological Adaptation. *Anthropological Papers of the American Museum of Natural History* 57:159–207. New York.

Lawson, J.
1709   A New Voyage to Carolina, Containing the Exact Description and Natural History of that Country. London: [no publisher.]

Lichtor, J., and A. Lichtor
1957   Paleopathological Evidence Suggesting Pre-Columbian Tuberculosis of the Spine. *Journal of Bone and Joint Surgery* 39-A(6):1398–1399.

McNeal, W. H.
1976   Plagues and Peoples. New York: Anchor Press.

Merbs, C. F., and R. J. Miller, eds.
1985   Health and Disease in the Prehistoric Southwest. *Arizona State University Anthropological Research Papers* 34.

Miller-Shavitz, P., and M. Y. Iscan
1991   The Prehistoric People of Fort Center: Physical and Health Characteristics. In What Mean These Bones? Studies in Southeastern Bioarchaeology, M. L. Powell, P. S. Bridges, and A. M. Mires, eds. Tuscaloosa: University of Alabama Press.

Mills, W. C.
1906   Baum Prehistoric Village. *Ohio Archaeological and Historical Publications* 15:45–136.

Milner, G. R.
1982   Measuring Prehistoric Levels of Health: A Study of Mississippian Period Skeletal Remains from the

American Bottom, Illinois. (Unpublished Ph.D. Dissertation in Anthropology, Northwestern University, Evanston, Ill.)

1983   The East St. Louis Stone Quarry Site Cemetery. Urbana: University of Illinois Press.

Milner, G. R., and V. G. Smith
1990   Oneota Human Skeletal Remains. In Archaeological Investigations at the Morton Village and Norris Farms 36 Cemetery. *Illinois State Museum, Reports of Investigations* 45:111–153. Springfield.

Moore, C. B.
1907   Moundville Revisited. *Journal of the Academy of Natural Sciences of Philadelphia* 13:337–405.

Morse, D.
1961   Prehistoric Tuberculosis in America. *American Review of Respiratory Diseases* 83:489–504.

1967   Tuberculosis. Pp. 149–171 in Diseases in Antiquity, D. R. Brothwell and A. T. Sandison, eds. Springfield, Ill.: C. C. Thomas.

Morse, D. F., and P. A. Morse
1983   Archeology of the Central Mississippi Valley. New York: Academic Press.

Morse, D., D. R. Brothwell, and P. J. Ucko
1964   Tuberculosis in Ancient Egypt. *American Review of Respiratory Diseases* 90:524.

Morton, H. H.
1913   Genitourinary Diseases and Syphilis. 3d ed. Philadelphia: F. A. Davis.

Murray, K.
1985   Bioarchaeology of the Parkin Site, Cross County, Arkansas. *The Arkansas Archeologist* 27/28:49–61.

Myers, J. A.
1951   Tuberculosis Among Children and Adults. 3d. ed. Springfield, Ill.: C. C. Thomas.

Neuman, Robert W.
1984   An Introduction to Louisiana Archaeology. Baton Rouge: Louisiana State University Press.

Ortner, D. J.
1986   Skeletal Evidence of Pre-Columbian Treponemal Disease in North America. (Paper read at the Annual Meeting of the Paleopathology Association, Madrid.)

Ortner, D. J., and W. G. J. Putschar
1981   Identification of Pathological Conditions in Human Skeletal Remains. *Smithsonian Contributions to Anthropology* 28. Washington.

Orton, S. T.
1905   A Study of the Pathological Changes in Some Mound Builder's Bones from the Ohio Valley, with Especial Reference to Syphilis. *University of Pennsylvania Medical Bulletin* 18:36–44.

Parramore, T. C.
1970   Non-venereal Treponematosis in Colonial North America. *Bulletin of the History of Medicine* 44:571–581.

Peebles, C. S.
1987   The Rise and Fall of the Mississippian in Western Alabama: The Moundville and Summerville Phases, A.D. 1000 to 1600. *Mississippi Archaeology* 22(1):1–31.

Powell, M. L.
1988   Status and Health in Prehistory: A Case Study of the Moundville Chiefdom. Washington: Smithsonian Institution Press.

1989   The Nodena People. Pp. 65–95, 127–150 in Nodena, an Account of 90 Years of Archaeological Investigation in Southeast Mississippi County, Arkansas. Dan F. Morse, ed. *Arkansas Archaeological Survey, Research Series* 30. Fayetteville.

1990a   Endemic Treponematosis and Tuberculosis in the Prehistoric Southeastern United States: The Biological Costs of Chronic Endemic Disease. In Human Paleopathology Current Syntheses and Future Options, D. J. Ortner and A. C. Aufderheide, eds. Washington: Smithsonian Institution Press.

1990b   On the Eve of the Conquest: Life and Death at Irene Mound, Georgia. In The Archaeology of Santa Catalina de Guale, C. S. Larsen, ed. *Anthropological Papers of the American Museum of Natural History*. New York.

Reichs, K. J.
1989   Treponematosis: A Possible Case from the Late Woodland of North Carolina. *American Journal of Physical Anthropology* 79(3):289–303.

Ritchie, W. A.
1952   Paleopathological Evidence Suggesting Pre-Columbian Tuberculosis in New York State. *American Journal of Physical Anthropology* n.s. 10(3):305–317.

Robbins, L.
1978   Yawslike Disease Process in a Louisiana Shell Mound Population. *Medical College of Virginia Quarterly* 14:24–31.

Robbins, S. L., and R. S. Cotran
1979   Pathologic Basis of Disease 2d ed. Philadelphia: W. B. Saunders.

Ross-Stallings, N. A.
1989   Treponemal Syndrome at the Austin Site (22TU54). (Paper read at the 46th Annual Meeting of the Southeastern Archaeological Conference, Tampa, Fla.)

Savich, T. L.
1978   Medicine and Slavery, the Diseases and Health

Care of Blacks in Antebellum Virginia. Urbana: University of Illinois Press.

Stead, W. W.
1974   Mycobacterial Diseases. In Harrison's Principles of Internal Medicine. 7th ed., M. M. Wintrobe et al., eds. New York: McGraw-Hill.

Steinbock, R. T.
1976   Paleopathological Diagnosis and Interpretation. Springfield, Ill.: C. C. Thomas.

Steponaitis, V. P.
1989   Contrasting Patterns of Mississippian Development. (Paper read in an advanced seminar on "Chiefdoms: Their Evolutionary Significance," School of American Research, Santa Fe, N.M.)

Stewart, T. D., and A. Spoehr
1952   Evidence on the Paleopathology of Yaws. *Bulletin of the History of Medicine* 26:538–553.

St. Hoyme, L.
1969   On the Origins of New World Paleopathology. *American Journal of Physical Anthropology* 31:295–302.

Stokes, J. H.
1928   Modern Clinical Syphilology. Philadelphia: W. B. Saunders.

Turner, T. B., and D. H. Hollander
1957   Biology of the Treponematoses. *World Health Organization Monograph* 35. Geneva.

Wakefield, E. G., S. C. Dellinger, and J. D. Camp
1937   A Study of the Osseous Remains of the "Mound Builders: of Eastern Arkansas. *American Journal of the Medical Sciences* 193:448–495.

Welch, P. D.
1989   Chronological Markers and Imported Items from the Roadway Excavations at Moundville. (Paper read at the 46th Annual Meeting of the Southeast Archaeological Conference, Tampa, Fla.)

Widmer, L., and A. J. Perzigian
1981   The Ecology and Etiology of Skeletal Lesions in Late Prehistoric Populations from Eastern North America. Pp. 99–113 in Prehistoric Tuberculosis in the Americas, J. E. Buikstra, ed. Evanston, Ill.: Northwestern University Archaeological Program.

6

Health and Disease in the Southwest before and after Spanish Contact

ANN L. W. STODDER

DEBRA L. MARTIN

Understanding the linkage of biological and cultural processes is essential in addressing the impact of European contact in the New World. Substandard health and disease states not only compromise the adaptive response of the individual to stressful social and political conditions but also modify activities and responses at the household, community, and polity levels. While archeological and ethnohistoric reconstruction can infer many aspects of demography and diet, disease and nutritional adequacy can only be directly assessed through the study of human biological remains.

In examining the patterns of prehistoric Pueblo health and adaptation, paleoepidemiological evidence for dental pathology, anemia, developmental arrest, rates of traumatic injury, and evidence for skeletal infection including tuberculosis and treponematosis are studied. Data from protohistoric and contact-period skeletal populations from Pecos, Gran Quivira, San Cristobal, and Hawikuh indicate that the rates of infectious disease and trauma increased during this period of massive economic, demographic, and social disruption.

The contact period in the northern Southwest is generally considered to begin with Marcos de Niza's expedition to Zuni in 1539. Francisco Vásquez de Coronado and his army followed in 1540, but the first Spanish colony in the Pueblo area was not founded until 1598. Colonists, soldiers, and missionaries were temporarily ejected by the Pueblo Revolt in 1680, but reconquest was complete by 1696. During the Revolt the Indians burned the official archives of the military, civilian, and ecclesiastical offices of the colony, leaving a huge gap in the ethnohistoric record for the 1500s and 1600s.

Studies of late prehistoric Puebloan subsistence economy and sociopolitical organization indicate that the protohistoric Pueblos and their non-agricultural neighbors were participants in a populous, complex, and far-reaching economic and political network (Riley 1982; Upham and Reed 1989; Cordell 1989; Snow 1981; Spielmann 1989; Wilcox 1981; Wilcox and Masse 1981; "Population and Spanish Contact in the Southwest," this vol.).

Underlying prehistoric population size and the rates and processes of Indian population decline is the issue of the timing of the arrival of Old World disease in the northern Southwest. Decimation of other New World populations by epidemics spreading beyond the frontiers of direct European-native contact has been addressed through archeological study by Ramenofsky (1987) and documented for northern Mexico through Reff's (1985, 1987, 1988) reading of the Jesuit archives.

Dobyns (1966, 1983) asserts that the Pueblos and other Indian populations in the Greater Southwest were decimated in a hemispheric pandemic shortly after Hernando Cortés's landing in Veracruz, about 20 years before any Europeans ventured as far north as New Mexico. If so, then even the large, apparently healthy and prosperous Pueblo towns described in Spanish chronicles represented only the remnants of precontact population. Upham (1986) has suggested the epidemic disease may have reached the Pueblos between 1541 and 1580, when there were no European entradas into New Mexico.

PRECONTACT ADAPTATION AND HEALTH

At least partial explanation for the trends in infectious disease, nutritional stress, and population decline during the sixteenth and seventeenth centuries, even given the introduction of new and devastating diseases, can be found in the adaptation and resulting health patterns of Southwestern agriculturalists that had been established for hundreds of years. These endemic health patterns must be understood before the biological impact of Spanish contact and colonization can be assessed.

Integral to the long-lived adaptive pattern of Southwestern agriculturalists is the utilization of environmental diversity through a mixed gathering-hunting and food-producing strategy. Flexibility and the production of surplus crops were important responses to both long- and short-term ecological instability. Prehistoric adaptation in the Southwest is also characterized by demographic instability. The archeological record is filled with evidence of local site abandonments, relocations, and large-scale regional migrations and shifts in settlement patterns.

Prehistoric Diet

Despite a few arguments to the contrary (Kent 1986), it seems safe to characterize prehistoric Pueblo (Anasazi and Mogollon) diet as based primarily on corn, with lesser amounts of squash and beans. Crops were supplemented by seasonally and locally available gathered and hunted resources and by pioneer or ruderal species, including the nutritionally valuable amaranth and chenopodium, which flourish as weedy annuals in disturbed areas like agricultural fields. Rabbits, deer, and other fauna were also attracted to the field, and larger species like elk, bison, and antelope were hunted.

Dietary reconstruction studies for the Kayenta Anasazi of Black Mesa (A.D. 200 to 1150), based on stable carbon isotope studies of human bone and on faunal and botanical food remains, indicate that 80–90 percent of the dietary protein was obtained from plants with the C-4 carbon uptake pathway: maize and amaranth (Martin et al. 1990). Decker (1986) estimated that 60–90 percent of the dietary protein at Grasshopper, a Mogollon Pueblo (A.D. 1275–1400), was composed of C-4 plants. Stable carbon isotope data from Basketmaker III through Pueblo III (A.D. 400–1300) skeletal remains indicate that corn comprised an average of 80 percent of Anasazi diet (Decker and Tieszen 1989).

Minnis's (1989) study of coprolite data from Four Corners area sites (Chaco Canyon, Canyon de Chelly, Mesa Verde, Black Mesa) indicates that there was a general stability in dietary mix over time at specific localities. Corn was always dominant, but local dietary differences were environmentally determined. Variation in diet also occurred due to cultural selection of different crops or specific varieties of corn determined by local climatic conditions (Matthews 1988) and by annual differences in productivity. In this region of frequent fluctuations in weather patterns (Dean et al. 1985; Euler et al. 1979), the potential impact of droughts and unfavorable climatic fluctuation on crop production and settlement patterns, on nutritional status, fertility, and morbidity can hardly be overstated.

Dental Health

Consistent dietary reliance on corn is reflected in the high rates of dental pathology. The rate of caries involvement ranges from 9 to 85 percent of individuals in the samples. Abscesses were observed in 11 to 66 percent of the individuals (table 1).

As Merbs (1989) notes, there is no comparative data for hunter-gatherer populations from the Southwest. Archaic and other nonsedentary peoples comprise a very small proportion of the human remains recovered in the Southwest (Stodder 1989a). The dental pathology data can be put in

TABLE 1

Prevalence of Caries and Abscesses in Permanent Dentition

Location	Date	Caries		Abscesses		Reference
		Number	Percent Affected	Number	Percent Affected	
Navajo Reservoir	400–1100	47	15	48	23	Berry 1985
Dolores	700–1100	24	71	25	32	Stodder 1987
Black Mesa	700–1100	64	26	64	21	Martin et al. 1990
Swarts Ruin	600–1000	62	26	62	11	Howells 1932
Turkey Creek	1000–1285	91	9	105	32	Berry 1983
Point of Pines	1000–1450	76	29	91	35	Berry 1983
Chaco Canyon	700–1300	27	85	46	63	Akins 1986
Salmon Ruin	900–1100	20	20	23	35	Berry 1983
Pindi Pueblo	900–1100, 1300–1600	52	13	52	19	London and Tobler 1979
Grasshopper	1275–1400	168	52	203	28	Berry 1983
Paako, Tijeras	1100–1600	149	23	149	13	Ferguson 1980
San Cristobal	1300–historic	136	57	136	46	Stodder 1989b
Hawikuh	1300–historic	98	53	95	58	Stodder 1989b
Gran Quivira	1315–1550	51	69			Swanson 1976
	1550–1672	41	85			
	1315–1672	97	81	111	66	
Pecos Pueblo	Precontact	126	48	126	41	Hooton 1930
	1550–1600	59	61	68	44	
	1600–1800	68	43	68	46	

perspective by comparing it to hunter-gatherer and horticultural populations from other areas. For example, Schmucker (1985) documented the greater prevalence of dental pathology in agriculturalists from Gran Quivira compared to California hunter-gatherers.

It is generally assumed that later, larger populations should exhibit greater dental pathology associated with high carbohydrate diet and agricultural intensification. This appears to be supported in the caries data. There is a general chronological trend to higher rates of caries and abscesses. Low rates of dental pathology are reported for the remains from the Navajo Reservoir sites, from the Mogollon site Turkey Creek and for Pindi Pueblo, which has both early and late components. The Dolores Anasazi exhibit a very high caries rate for an early pueblo population, partly because the sample is comprised predominantly of young adults (Stodder 1987). The striking difference in dental health between the Dolores and Black Mesa Anasazi may not be solely an artifact of sample age bias. Settlement patterns in these two localities are interpreted quite differently (Nichols and Powell 1987; Kane 1988). The Dolores Anasazi may have

been more sedentary and had a more carbohydrate-heavy diet than their contemporaries on Black Mesa.

The abundant dental pathology in burials from Chaco Canyon is notable in contrast to the quite moderate rates of caries and abscesses in the sample from Salmon Ruin, a Chacoan outlier. The Chaco people also exhibit a high rate of antemortem tooth loss; 63 percent of the adults had lost one or several teeth (Akins 1986).

High rates of dental pathology at the protohistoric and contact-period sites, especially in the postcontact (1550–1672) population of Gran Quivira, suggest a very high carbohydrate diet. Gran Quivira adults lost an average of 5.5 teeth per individual prior to death (Swanson 1976). Adults at Hawikuh and San Cristobal lost an average of 4.3 and 3.9 teeth during life (Stodder 1989b).

Anemia

Two types of cranial lesions often observed in Southwestern skeletal remains, cribra orbitalia and porotic hyperostosis, indicate iron deficiency anemia during childhood (Stuart-Macadam 1985,

1987a, 1987b). The prevalence of anemia in Southwestern populations has most often been attributed to the low iron content of the maize-based diet (El-Najjar, Lozoff, and Ryan 1975) and to parasitic infection. But given the variety of factors that mitigate iron absorption and utilization, particularly the synergism between infectious disease and malnutrition, it is unlikely that any single factor can account for the presence of anemia in a given population. Clearly, infants born to iron-deficient mothers, children at weaning age, females of reproductive age, and any individual with dysentery or another condition resulting in blood loss or fever is at increased risk for anemia.

The frequencies of cranial lesions indicative of anemia in the 0 to 10-year-old segments of Southwestern skeletal populations range from 15 to 88 percent, as listed in table 2. While some of the differences are due to observer variability, these data do indicate that there was an endemic problem throughout the prehistoric and protohistoric eras. Rather than a simple trend of increase over time, these data suggest that specific dietary mix, habitation structure type, infectious disease load, and community ecology and hygiene codetermined the frequency of anemia in prehistoric communities.

The low frequencies of anemia observed at Gran Quivira and Navajo Reservoir were explained by the greater ease of access to game for populations living in upland settings than for people in canyon-bottom environments like Canyon de

Chelly (El-Najjar, Lozoff, and Ryan 1975). However, this interpretation seems to be contradicted by coprolites from these sites that contain equivalent frequencies of corn while animal bones occurred nearly twice as often in samples from the canyon sites (Reinhard 1986). The dense population in cliff dwellings might be more relevant than diet in explaining the high frequencies of anemia in the Canyon de Chelly and Mesa Verde region populations, as the opportunity for disease transmission is greater than in a more dispersed settlement pattern.

Examining the age patterns of unremodeled (active) lesions is helpful in interpreting the occurrence and etiology of anemia in prehistoric communities. In table 3 the frequency of anemia in subadult age groups is given for samples from Black Mesa, the Mesa Verde Region, Grasshopper, Arroyo Hondo, San Cristobal, and Hawikuh. The most commonly observed peak age of anemia is in the one to three-year age range when iron deficiency is attributable to weaning diet and diarrheal syndromes and increased exposure to infection with loss of natural immunity acquired at birth.

In the Black Mesa and Arroyo Hondo children anemia peaks under one year of age. No unremodeled lesions were observed beyond age 2.9, and this was also observed in the children from Chaco Canyon (Akins 1986). The occurrence of unremodeled lesions is earliest and most restricted in the Arroyo Hondo children in whom, "the typical pattern of peak lesion onset has been preempted by

TABLE 2

Frequencies of Anemia in 0–10 Year Olds

Location	Dates	Number	Percent Affected	Reference
Canyon de Chelly	300 B.C.–A.D. 700	50	72	El-Najjar, Lozoff, and Ryan 1975
Black Mesa	A.D. 700–1100	55	85	Martin et al. 1990
Navajo Reservoir	A.D. 700–1100	44	16	El-Najjar, Lozoff, and Ryan 1975
Chaco Canyon	A.D. 700–1100	31	68	Akins 1986
Pueblo Bonito	900–1100	20	45	Palkovich 1984
Mesa Verde Region	700–1300	80	79	Stodder 1987
Canyon de Chelly	900–1300	15	88	El-Najjar, Lozoff, and Ryan 1975
Grasshopper	1275–1400	367	15	Hinkes 1983
Arroyo Hondo	1300–1600	54	22	Palkovich 1987
Gran Quivira	1300–historic	66	18	El-Najjar, Lozoff, and Ryan 1975
San Cristobal	1300–historic	64	87	Stodder 1989b
Hawikuh	1300–historic	31	74	Stodder 1989b

Note: Includes unremodeled and remodeled cribra orbitalia and porotic hyperostosis.

TABLE 3

Frequencies of Anemia (Unremodeled Cranial Lesions) in Subadults

Age in Years	Black Mesa Martin et al. 1990	Mesa Verde Stodder 1987	Grasshopper Hinkes 1983	Arroyo Hondo Palkovich 1980, 1987	San Cristobal Stodder 1988	Hawikuh Stodder 1988
	55	95	386	54	66	40
0–½		50%	5%	26%	33%	40%
0–1	100%[1]	69%	6%	28%	55%	42%
1–2.9	54%	83%	33%	7%	77%	89%
3–4.9	0%	68%	20%	0%	29%	50%
5–9.9	0%	81%	15%	0%	26%	50%
10–15.9	0%	53%	5%	0%	0%	22%

[1]N = 2.

maternal malnutrition resulting in low birth weight fetuses more likely to be at risk to immediately acquired infections and dietary inadequacies" (Palkovich 1987:535).

Children in these six populations also exhibit different degrees of association between anemia and skeletal indicators of infection, suggesting differences in the etiology of anemia. Nonspecific skeletal infection and anemia co-occur in 61 percent of the subadults from Black Mesa (Martin et al. 1990), in 33 percent of subadults from Hawikuh, and in 9 percent of subadults from San Cristobal (Stodder 1989a). In contrast no association between anemia and infection is apparent in subadults from Mesa Verde or Chaco Canyon. At Grasshopper both infection and anemia were relatively rare (Hinkes 1983). This suggests that anemia at Hawikuh and Black Mesa was more often a product of infection, perhaps combined with dietary deficiencies, than in other populations. Cribra orbitalia and porotic hyperostosis are ubiquitous in most prehistoric Southwestern populations, but the conditions underlying the anemia were not the same in every community.

Developmental Arrest: Dental Enamel Hypoplasia

Several studies of Southwest skeletal populations report the occurrence of dental enamel hypoplasias. Pits or grooves form in the enamel as the result of arrest and recovery of enamel matrix formation during a period of illness, malnutrition, or other metabolic insult.

Prenatal stress incidents are recorded in hypo-plastic defects in the deciduous dentition. Deciduous enamel hypoplasias are present in 23 percent of the children from Black Mesa (Martin et al. 1990), in 10 percent of Grasshopper children (Hinkes 1983), in 6 percent from San Cristobal, and 30 percent of the Hawikuh children (Stodder 1989b). These developmental arrest indicators suggest considerable in utero stress and significant health problems among reproductive age women.

The peak ages of dental enamel hypoplasia formation in the permanent incisors and canines of several populations have been studied (Stodder 1987, 1989b). The Black Mesa and Mesa Verde Anasazi exhibit the same bimodal peak. There is an earlier 2.5–3 year peak typically observed in the incisors and a later 4–4.5 year peak in canine hypoplasia formation (Goodman and Armelagos 1985). A shift to later hypoplasia formation, age 3–4.5, is evident in the Pueblo III Mesa Verde sample. A similar shift was observed in the later, Pueblo II, component of the Black Mesa skeletal assemblage (Martin et al. 1990). One explanation for these diachronic changes is a shift to older weaning ages and longer birth intervals among the later occupants of the Black Mesa and Mesa Verde areas.

The protohistoric Pueblos exhibit the same basic pattern in hypoplasia formation as the Anasazi, but the San Cristobal sample also has a weaker peak around age 1. In the Hawikuh sample there is an even broader age distribution of arrest-causing stress incidents: an early peak in the 6-month to 1-year period, a 3–3.5 year peak, and a sustained period of stress from age 4 to 5.5 years. These anomalous patterns in the protohistoric populations probably reflect increased levels of infectious disease in infants and children (Stodder 1989b).

The data on these general indicators of health and nutritional status demonstrate the interrelated nature of several aspects of prehistoric Southwestern adaptation: local environment and dietary mix, settlement system and habitation type, and community ecology. Within the framework of long-term, stable adaptation some basic patterns are evident: high dental pathology, fairly high anemia rates, developmental arrest at weaning and in the postweaning periods. There is a considerable range of variability in reported frequencies of all conditions (including skeletal infection), and there are subtle but significant differences in the patterns, etiologies, and demographic implications of stress and morbidity in different communities.

CONTACT AND COLONIZATION

There were several distinct phases of contact between Europeans and Pueblos. A period of indirect contact—the spread of Old World epidemic diseases among natives (Dobyns 1983)—is thought to have followed European arrival on the continent prior to the first entrada into the Pueblo region. Marcos de Niza's appearance near Zuni in 1539 initiated a period of direct but intermittent contact between Indians and the various expeditions sent north from Mexico. Direct, prolonged contact began in 1598 with Juan de Oñate's establishment of the first Spanish settlement in the Rio Grande valley near what is now San Juan Pueblo. Contact was intermittent during the 20 years spanned by the Pueblo Revolt and the several reconquest attempts. Reconquest and recolonization set the stage for the final subjugation of the revolt and reorganization of Indian settlements.

The multiple factors in Pueblo health and population decline after contact include frequent and severe drought and demographic instability in the form of large- and small-scale abandonments and migrations, battles and violent interaction between Spaniards and Indians and among Indian groups, starvation, and diseases both endemic and epidemic.

Postcontact Diet

The nature and intensity of Indian-European interaction varied, but conflict and disruption of native economy and subsistence were the common result. The Spaniards were impressed by the apparent surplus of food at the Pueblos, and even before colonization the Europeans constituted a drain on Indian food supply.

After the establishment of the colony and Franciscan missions in various Pueblos, the Spaniards demanded tribute in the form of labor, food, and goods including textiles and buffalo hides (Scholes 1935; Spielmann 1989). Indians worked in carpentry and textile workshops, and as blacksmiths and domestic servants. Spanish colonial laws pertaining to wages for Indian labor were not enforced in the far-removed colony (Barber 1932; Scholes 1935). Tracts of land were granted to influential colonists, encomenderos (Simmons 1979). Other lands were given to the missions, where converted Indians planted orchards and fields next to the churches and friaries also built by Indian labor.

The Spaniards brought new crops—wheat and fruit trees—as well as livestock to New Mexico, but it is doubtful that the content of the Indian diet was altered (Scholes 1935). Metal farming implements and livestock probably had far more impact on local ecology and economy (Schroeder 1972; Espinosa 1988), by hastening soil degradation and erosion, by providing horses that undoubtedly affected the balance of power between the Pueblos and the non-sedentary Apachean and Plains peoples, and by introducing new sources of disease carried by domestic animals.

Heavy reliance on corn is indicated in paleo-ethnobotanical data from Gran Quivira (Spielmann 1989), and by the bone strontium analysis of Pecos remains (Schoeninger 1989). Spielmann (1989) estimates that as much as 20 percent of the dietary protein at Pecos and Gran Quivira was provided by meat obtained through trade with Plains people. These eastern frontier Pueblos (and perhaps others like San Cristobal and Galisteo) may have altered their trading patterns to obtain hides, which were demanded as tribute, rather than meat. Faunal remains from Gran Quivira indicate a shift in the pattern of resource exploitation—an increase in small mammals, and a decline in bison remains, without a concomitant increase in other large game (Spielmann 1989). The combined factors of labor drain, trade for nonsubsistence items, drought, and reduced agricultural productivity suggest that "nutritional health decreased dramatically in the seventeenth century" (Spielmann 1989:110).

Data from the postcontact population of Gran Quivira exhibit an extremely high rate of dental pathology: 85 percent of the adults had caries, a substantial increase over the already high precontact rate of 69 percent (table 1). Periodontal disease and the rate of caries in deciduous dentition also increased (Swanson 1976). The prevalence of both caries and abscesses increases in the contact period among Pecos population as well (Hooten 1930). Infant mortality increased at Gran Quivira, and life expectancy declined (Spielman 1989; Turner 1981).

The San Cristobal and Hawikuh skeletal samples, which date from late prehistoric to the time of the Pueblo Revolt (1475–1680), also exhibit high rates of dental pathology, somewhat lower than at Gran Quivira. San Cristobal has an extremely high rate of anemia (tables 2–3), which is associated with skeletal infection in only 9 percent of the cases, suggesting that undernutrition may have been an important etiological factor. Hawikuh also has a high rate of anemia. Although more of the anemia may be related to infection, it is clear that while the Western Pueblos were considerably removed from the main area of European activity and resource and labor extraction, they were not protected from regional drought and famine.

During the seventeenth century many Pueblos were deliberately abandoned, perhaps as many as half in the Rio Grande area by 1640, and some groups became nomadic (Schroeder 1972). European and Indian food supplies and fields were frequently raided by Apaches (Simmons 1979). After the Revolt the various reconquest parties encountered starving groups of Indians in the hills around abandoned and burned pueblos (Espinosa 1988). Rather than benefiting from new agricultural technology, crops, and beasts of burden, it seems that food was in short supply and of poor quality in sixteenth- and seventeenth-century New Mexico.

Warfare and Violence

Little is known about warfare in the prehistoric Southwest (Cordell 1984). Woodbury (1959) asserts that archeologists have ignored or misinterpreted evidence of prehistoric conflict and aggression—burned rooms, unburied bodies, skeletons exhibiting evidence of violent death—and that warfare was probably a fairly normal part of ancient Southwest life. The frequencies of traumatic injury (which include accidental injuries) reported for skeletal populations range from a low of 5 percent in the Black Mesa population to a high of 41 percent in the Gallina skeletal remains (table 4). Gallina sites feature defensive architecture and evidence of massacres and cannibalism (Chase 1976; Flinn et al. 1976).

In addition to direct confrontations between Spaniards and Indians in the sixteenth and seventeenth centuries, inter-Pueblo feuding and factionalism was heightened. Pueblo-Plains interaction became increasingly hostile (Spielmann 1989).

The second highest trauma frequency is in the San Cristobal population. Prior to the site's abandonment around the time of the Pueblo Revolt, San Cristobal was the only Tano town still occupied in the Galisteo Basin, prey to Apache and Pecos hostil-

TABLE 4

Frequencies of Traumatic Injury

Location	Dates	Number	Percent Affected	Reference
Black Mesa	700–1100	167	5	Martin et al. 1990
Chaco Canyon	700–1300	135	17	Akins 1986
Gallina sites	700–1300	41	41	Stodder 1989a
Paako	1100–1600	57	19	Ferguson 1980
Arroyo Hondo	1300–1600	89	12	Palkovich 1980
Tijeras Pueblo	1300–1600	64	16	Ferguson 1980
Cochiti	1300–1600	101	9	Heglar 1974
San Cristobal	1300–historic	229	23	Stodder 1989b
Hawikuh	1300–historic	182	16	Stodder 1989b
Pecos Pueblo	1300–historic	581	9	Hooton 1930

ity (Lang 1977). Friendlier relations are thought to have been maintained among the Western Pueblos and Athapaskans, where there was less disruption by Spaniards (Ferguson 1981). This may explain the relatively low overall rate of trauma at Hawikuh.

The clearest reflection of this violent era is in the rates of cranial trauma. In the Pecos Glaze IV population (1500–1600) cranial trauma affected 8 percent of the adults. In the Glaze V and VI populations (post-1600), the frequency doubled to 16 percent (Hooten 1930). In contrast, the Pueblo III–IV Paako and Tijeras Pueblo skeletal samples have rates of 3.5 and 2 percent cranial trauma (Ferguson 1980). Cranial trauma is evident in 20 percent of the adult males from San Cristobal and 17.5 percent of adult males from Hawikuh (Stodder 1989b).

INFECTIOUS DISEASE AND HISTORICAL EPIDEMIOLOGY

Neither archeological nor skeletal evidence delineates when Old World epidemic diseases were first imported into the northern Southwest. As elsewhere in the New World, there was a dramatic decline in the size of Southwest Indian populations following contact. Multiple epidemics are documented in the seventeenth and eighteenth centuries, but the timing of initial demographic collapse is more easily modeled and inferred than documented. Skeletal remains have quite limited potential to reveal acute infectious disease (Ortner and Putschar 1981; Larsen 1987) such as those imported to the New World. But the changes in patterns of endemic disease can be traced and interpreted in the context of known events of the contact period.

Endemic Disease

The frequencies of infection reported in studies of 17 Southwestern skeletal samples are listed in table 5. These include conditions like periostitis, osteitis, mastoiditis, and otitis media, which cannot be attributed to specific infectious agents. Several types of viruses are thought to have been present in the precontact Southwest including staphylococcal and streptococcal viruses, some forms of herpes and hepatitis, poliomyelitis, pertussis, and rhinoviruses. Tick-borne fevers, rabies, sylvatic plague, tularemia, giardiasis, and amoebic dysentery were also probably present (Van Blerkom 1985). Coccidioidomycosis is thought to have been present prehistorically, but no cases have been observed in Southwest skeletal material (Merbs 1989). Domesticated turkeys and dogs may have transmitted parasitic infec-

TABLE 5

Frequencies of Skeletal Infection

Location	Dates	Number	Percent Affected	Reference
Navajo Reservoir	400–1100	82	2	Berry 1983
Dolores	400–1100	64	11	Stodder 1987
Black Mesa	700–1100	173	23	Martin et al. 1990
Chaco Canyon	700–1300	135	17	Akins 1986
Salmon Ruin	900–1100	97	6	Berry 1983
Turkey Creek	1000–1285	245	5	Berry 1983
Grasshopper	1275–1450	442	12	Berry 1983
Point of Pines	1000–1450	117	13	Berry 1983
Pindi Pueblo	900–1100, 1300–1600	86	14	London and Tobler 1979
Paako	1100–1600	57	4	Ferguson 1980
Tijeras Pueblo	1300–1600	64	3	Ferguson 1980
Arroyo Hondo	1300–1600	101	13	Palkovich 1980
San Cristobal	1300–historic	210	23	Stodder 1989b
Hawikuh	1300–historic	143	36	Stodder 1989b
Pecos	1300–1600	295	3	Hooton 1930
	1550–1600	115	2	
	1600–	93	6	

tions like salmonella and shigella (Kunitz and Euler 1972). Bison and other wild game may have transmitted diseases as well. Studies of coprolites from Anasazi settlements reveal at least eight species of helminthic parasites (Reinhard and Clary 1986; Reinhard 1988).

Comparing the prehistoric samples in table 5, the data from Turkey Creek, Grasshopper, and Point of Pines indicate that the rate of infection among the Mogollon increased over time. Infection is more than twice as common in Chaco Canyon inhabitants than in the outlier population from Salmon Ruin. The Black Mesa population has a high rate of skeletal infection that is described as chronic but relatively mild (Martin et al. 1990).

The very low infection rate reported for Pecos suggests methodological differences in categorizing skeletal pathologies, but the rates of nonspecific infection (periostitis and osteomyelitis) doubled after 1600 (Hooton 1930). The other late populations—San Cristobal and Hawikuh—have high rates of skeletal infection, which are expected in large, densely settled populations. The infection rates also reflect the increased susceptibility to disease among both Eastern and Western Pueblo populations during this period when the endemic problems of drought and famine were superimposed upon the economic disruption caused by the Spanish drain on food and labor.

Tuberculosis and Treponemal Infections

Two specific types of infectious disease were endemic in the precontact Southwest, tuberculosis and treponemal disease. The recorded cases of these are listed in tables 6 and 7.

The possibility of an epidemic wave of tuberculosis in the San Cristobal population is suggested by a cluster of five tubercular adults in a single burial area, one of seven middens at the site (Stodder 1989b). In a sense tuberculosis can be considered an index of economic status and population density. Massive social and economic disruptions such as warfare, migrations and population dislocations, overwork, famine or undernutrition and crowded living conditions all increase the numbers of susceptible individuals in a given population and can result in tuberculosis morbidity becoming widespread (Youmans 1979). Contact with disease reservoirs in cattle may also have increased the rate of infection. Hrdlička (1908) observed tremendously high rates of this disease in economically depressed early twentieth-century Indians, especially the Hopi.

Estimates of the proportion of individuals with tuberculosis who develop skeletal lesions range from fewer than 1 percent (Daniel 1981) to 5–7 percent (Steinbock 1976). The presence of tuberculosis in at least one infant from San Cristobal suggests

TABLE 6

Cases of Tuberculosis

Location	Dates	Number	Age	Areas Affected	Reference
Black Mesa	875–975	1	16	Lumbar vertebrae	Sumner 1985
Pueblo Bonito	900–1100	1	8–10	Thoracic, lumbar	El-Najjar 1979; Ortner and Putschar 1981
Chavez Pass	900–1100	4	adult	Thoracic, lumbar, ribs	Merbs 1989; El-Najjar 1979
Pinedale 4	900–1100	1	adult	Thoracic vertebrae	El-Najjar and Bussey 1980
Talus Unit (Chaco)	900–1300	1	4	Thoracic vertebrae	Akins 1986
Tocito Site	900–1300	1	4–5	Thoracic, lumbar	Fink 1985
Point of Pines	1285–1450	1	adult	Sacroiliac region	Micozzi and Kelly 1985
Gran Quivira	1315–1400	1	adult	Thoracic vertebrae	Coyne 1981
San Cristobal	1300–historic	5	adult	Vertebrae, ribs, hip, sacroiliac, foot	Stodder 1989b
			infant	widespread	
Hawikuh	1300–historic	1	adult	Vertebrae, ribs, sacroiliac	Stodder 1989b
Pecos Pueblo	1550–1700+	2	adult	Vertebrae	Hooten 1930

TABLE 7

Cases of Treponemal Infection

Location	Dates	Number	Cranial Involvement	Postcranial Involvement	References
Arizona Basketmaker	A.D. 200–700	1 adult	X	X	Williams 1932; Baker and Armelagos 1988
Vandal Cave	400–700 or 1100–1300	1 adult		X	Cole et al. 1955
Canyon de Chelly	900–1100	1 adult	X		El-Najjar 1979
Los Muertos	1100–1450	"several"		X	Baker and Armelagos 1988
Kinishaba	1100–1300	1 adult	X	X	Cole et al. 1955
Smokey Bear Ruin	1250–1350	1 adult		X	El-Najjar 1979
Tuzigoot Ruin	1000–1525	1 adult	X		Denninger 1938
Tijeras Pueblo	1300–1600	1 adult	X	X	Ferguson 1980
Pecos Pueblo	1100–historic	3 adults	X	X	Hooten 1930
San Cristobal	1300–historic	2 adults		X	Moodie 1923
Hawikuh	1300–historic	2 adults		X	Stodder 1989b

that life expectancy and mortality rate in children were affected in addition to loss of productivity and fertility associated with the mortality in young adults and chronically debilitating nature of the disease in all age groups.

Skeletal infections attributed to syphilis or to treponemal disease have been identified in Anasazi, Mogollon, and Hohokam skeletal remains from at least 11 localities. In some studies (Cole et al. 1955; Moodie 1923) cranial and postcranial lesions are attributed to venereal syphilis. In later studies (Ferguson 1980; Stodder 1989b) the general term treponemal disease is used. Postcranial involvement is more typical of nonvenereal treponematosis (Steinbock 1976; Baker and Armelagos 1988).

Baker and Armelagos (1988) conclude that there is abundant evidence of endemic, nonvenereal treponematosis in the New World (including the Southwest), but they do not accept the presence of venereal syphilis there prior to contact. In particular they note the absence of dental stigmata associated with congenital syphilis, noting the apparent exception of one child from Virginia (Ortner and Putschar 1981). One child from Hawikuh has notched permanent incisors, which appear to be Hutchinson's incisors (Stodder 1989b), but the postcranial remains of this child were not preserved and dental anomalies alone cannot be considered pathognomic (Steinbock 1976). No individuals in the Hawikuh and San Cristobal populations exhibit caries sicca, cranial lesions indicative of

venereal syphilis, but there is a possible case from prehistoric Pecos (Hooten 1930).

Powell (1988:725) asserts that endemic (not just venereal) treponemal disease could cause dental defects if the level of pathogenicity were sufficiently high in the mother to cause transplacental infection. While theoretically possible, especially given the similarities between venereal and nonvenereal treponemal strains, one would not expect such a high rate of pathogenicity of endemic disease in a woman of reproductive age, because these diseases are usually acquired quite early in life (Powell 1988). In a community like Hawikuh, which appears to have had a very high endemic disease load, there could have been severe enough treponemal infection in a young mother to have caused congenital dental defects.

Protohistoric populations exhibit increased infectious disease loads over most prehistoric Southwest populations. In addition it seems likely that either the pathogenicity or prevalence (or both) of tuberculosis and treponematosis were increased in these populations experiencing demographic disturbance, warfare, famine. Changes in host resistance through malnutrition and in the sizes and structure of a population disrupt the equilibrium between an endemic pathogen and the host population (McGrath 1988). Endemic diseases that had been present in Southwestern populations for centuries may well have become epidemic in the sixteenth and seventeenth centuries.

Old World Disease in the Northern Southwest

The earliest epidemic of Old World disease mentioned in the written records of New Mexico ethnohistory is in the 1630s, well after initial contact. Dobyns (1983) proposes that disease spread as far north as the Pueblos as early as the 1520s, initiating at least two major waves of epidemic disease prior to the de Niza and Coronado expeditions (table 8).

Prior to direct contact and during the period of intermittent contact between Indians and exploration parties, it is thought that disease spread northward from the Basin of Mexico through Indian networks (Upham and Reed 1989; "Native American Trade Centers as Contagious Disease Foci" and "Population and Spanish Contact in the Southwest," this vol.). During the sixteenth century Hawikuh and Pecos were the key west and east points in trade networks that connected the Pueblos to Mesoamerica and to the southern Plains (Riley 1975). Marcos de Niza was told by Indians (presumably Pimans) some 30 days' journey from Hawikuh that they "worked there tilling the soil and doing other tasks, and for their services the inhabitants gave

them hides of the cattle and turquoises" (Hammond and Rey 1940:68).

If economic interaction along the north-south route brought Old World disease to Hawikuh, then the east-west trade networks from Hawikuh to Pecos would have spread infection to non-Puebloan peoples in the region and to the southern Plains groups who traded with Gran Quivira, San Lazaro, San Marcos, San Cristobal, Picuris, and Taos (Spielmann 1983, 1989; Baugh and Nelson 1987).

After the founding of the Spanish settlements and missions there was substantially more contact between the Eastern Pueblos and Europeans. The Hopi were not subject to any sustained contact until after the Pueblo Revolt (Adams 1981). After the battle with Coronado the Zuni were left relatively alone until the first missions were built there in 1629 (Ferguson 1981). A regular three-year cycle of supply trips between the New Mexico missions and mining communities in northwest New Spain was established by the Franciscans (Scholes 1939). The inland road through Mexico doubtless eased the route to New Mexico. By 1630 some 90 churches had been built and there were 66 Franciscans in the province

TABLE 8

16th and 17th-century Epidemics in the Greater Southwest and Northern New Spain

	Greater Southwest Proposed—Dobyns 1983	Northern New Spain Documented—Reff 1985, 1987, 1988
1520–1524	Smallpox pandemic	Smallpox pandemic
1531–1533	Measles	
1559	Influenza ?	
1575–1580		Typhus
1590	Influenza	Measles, smallpox
1593–1597		Measles, smallpox
1601–1602		Smallpox
1604		Smallpox ?
1607–1608		Smallpox
1612–1613		Smallpox
1615	Plague	
1617	Plague	Smallpox
1623–1625		Smallpox, typhus
1635	Measles	
1636–1637	Scarlet fever	
1636–1641	Smallpox	Smallpox, others
1645–1647		Malaria
1652		Smallpox
1660s		Influenza

of New Mexico. The Euro-American population remained small, probably less than 100 (Scholes 1935), and dependent on Indian labor and food. Throughout the 1620s and 1630s reinforcements of colonists and soldiers arrived from Mexico.

Epidemic disease could have been repeatedly imported during the seventeenth century. The demographic disturbances documented during this period, ranging from the complete abandonment of many Pueblos to the migration of individuals and domestic groups from one settlement to another (Lycett 1989), must have been a significant factor in the spread of disease. As many as half of the Rio Grande Pueblos were abandoned between 1600 and 1643 (Schroeder 1972). Gran Quivira was abandoned in 1672 (Turner 1981). The population of Pecos was reduced by 40 percent between 1622 and 1641 (Kessell 1979).

As shown in table 9, the documentary evidence for epidemics in the pre-Revolt period is minimal. In 1638 the Franciscan Juan de Prada wrote that the Indian population had been greatly diminished due to "the very active prevalence during these last years of smallpox and the sickness the Mexicans call *cocolitzli*" (Forrestal 1954:5). *Cocolitzli*, a Nahuatl term, has been interpreted as referring to "the great introduced epidemics . . . and perhaps smallpox in general" (Cook 1946:332), and to "general sickness and plague" in central Mexico (Gibson 1964:448). Epidemics of smallpox may have been combined with (or confused with) influenza, chicken pox, measles, or scarlet fever (Crosby 1972). The census of the missions just prior to the Pueblo Revolt states that the Hopi Pueblos "had 14,000 gentiles, but a pestilence consumed them" (Bancroft 1889:173).

Jesuit missionary records for New Spain (Northern Mexico) indicate that smallpox, typhus, measles, and other diseases proceeded ahead of the mission frontier in the late sixteenth and early seventeenth centuries. Newly arriving at some settlements, the Jesuits observed mass graves and Indians worshiping dieties devoted to specific disease symptoms (Reff 1985).

No mass graves or other obvious deviations in mortuary behavior are described in reports on the rather few protohistoric Pueblos that have been excavated, but much of the information from these sites remains unstudied. A change in mortuary behavior seems to have taken place at Hawikuh

TABLE 9

New Mexico Epidemics Documented in Mission Records and Other Reports

Year	Location	Event
1636	Widespread	Smallpox or scarlet fever, *cocolitzli* (Forrestal 1954:5)
1640	Widespread	"Peste" killed 3,000 (Simmons 1966)
1695	Santa Fe	Unnamed epidemic among Spaniards.
1719	Nambe	Smallpox killed 21 children, 24 adults, January.
1728–1729	Galisteo	Many deaths during December epidemic.
	Jemez	Measles, 109 Indians died in December. Spread throughout New Mexico.
	Acoma	Measles, December–January.
	Jemez	Indians reported to flee from Jemez, Zia, Santa Ana, Cochiti.
1733	Santa Ana	Smallpox, April–August.
	Jemez	Smallpox, June–July.
	Santa Fe	Many deaths, May–June.
1734	Zuni	Smallpox, 200 deaths recorded.
1737	Santa Fe	67 deaths, October–November.
1738	Pecos	Smallpox, January–March.
1748	Pecos	Epidemic, August.
	Santa Fe	68 deaths, July–September.
1770	Santa Clara	Unnamed epidemic affecting children.
1772	Laguna	"La peste." 44 adults, 21 children died, January 4–March 31.
1781	Sandia	Smallpox, January–October. Also at Hopi, Bernalillo, Corrales, Alameda (Simmons 1966; Adams 1981:326)
	Santo Domingo	More than 230 Indians died, February 4–March 4.
	Santa Clara	Smallpox, December 1781–March 1782.
1785	Tome	10 deaths, "dolor de costado," May.
1799	Santa Cruz	Smallpox, November 1799–March 1800.
1800	Santa Clara	Smallpox, January.
1804	Santa Fe	24 deaths, February.
	Santa Cruz	Increased number of deaths in burial book, May–June.
1805	Santa Cruz	Increased number of deaths in burial book, April–May.
	Santa Clara	Measles.

(continued)

TABLE 9   *(Continued)*

Year	Location	Event
	Cochiti	Measles, April.
	Santa Fe	122 deaths, April–June.
1816	San Juan	Smallpox, spring.
	Santo Domingo	Smallpox.
	Picuris	Increased number of deaths in burial book.
	Santa Fe	78 deaths, September 4–19
1831	San Miguel del Vado	Smallpox, December 1831–March 1832.
1840	San Miguel del Vado	Smallpox, February–June.
	San Juan	Smallpox in children, fever in adults.
1853	Zuni	Smallpox (Hodge, Hammond, and Rey 1945:279) also at First Mesa (Adams 1981:326).
1896	Cochiti	Malaria (Dumarest 1919).
1898	Zuni	Smallpox (Hodge, Hammond, and Rey 1945:279).

Sources: Chavez 1957 except where noted.

around 1630 when cremation ceased (Smith, Woodbury, and Woodbury 1966). Chroniclers of the Coronado expedition of 1540 wrote that the Zuni cremated their dead (Hammond and Rey 1940; Schroeder 1979b). No cremations are associated with Hawikuh wares, which were produced beginning in around 1630 (Smith, Woodbury, and Woodbury 1966). Of the 205 cremations with temporally diagnostic associated ceramics, 89 percent were accompanied by Matsaki wares, which date between 1475 and 1650. The concentration of cremations in the Matsaki era might suggest a disease-oriented method of disposal, but a more detailed consideration of mortuary patterns at the site is needed to address this question. Both the cessation of cremation and the production of Hawikuh wares are probably related to the construction of the first missions at Halona and Hawikuh in 1629.

The period between the Revolt and the final reconquest was one of even greater demographic displacement and probably of very high mortality. At the time of the Revolt the Zuni left their six villages and lived on nearby Corn Mesa; when they returned in 1696 only one village was occupied (Ferguson 1981). There was much factionalism among Indian groups in addition to multiple skirmishes

during the several attempts to reconquer the upper Rio Grande (Espinosa 1988).

Following the reconquest the Spaniards embarked on a program of resettlement and reduction of the Indian populations into a smaller number of larger settlements. The change in settlement pattern probably increased disease levels on a local basis, but the increased distance between Pueblos and restrictions on inter-Pueblo travel imposed by the Spaniards (Wilcox 1981; Schroeder 1972) may have reduced the potential for the spread of epidemics. Smallpox periodicity rates in unvaccinated populations are inversely related to the amount of isolation experienced by a settlement or social group (Mielke et al. 1984).

Post-Revolt mission records, primarily the burial books, indicate many epidemics in the 1700s and 1800s, some of which are listed in table 9. Some outbreaks appear to have been localized, but the measles epidemic of 1728–1729 and the smallpox epidemic of 1780–1781 were obviously quite widespread. More complete data might indicate a more typical periodicity for small pox, which appears to have been endemic in the eighteenth century. It is doubtful that inoculation was employed at all in colonial New Mexico, but after the epidemic in the 1780s vaccination was started in the early 1800s (Simmons 1966; Bloom 1924), and the periodicity seems to have lengthened.

Epidemics and Population Reduction

Indian population decline in the Southwest was the combined result of epidemic disease and other factors. The rates and patterns of depopulation have been variously suggested by extrapolating from other areas with better documentation, and by assembling and interpreting the counts made by Spanish explorers and Franciscans. These data cannot be used without careful assessment of their meaning and reliability.

Even for the eighteenth century it is difficult to document the demographic effect of epidemic disease on Pueblo and other Indian populations. Censuses were taken for groups of settlements based on church locations, but the specific settlements included in the groups changed from year to year. Regional population estimates are useful, but site-specific figures are not. The impacts of documented epidemics on population size are not reflected in pre- and post-epidemic census figures for specific Pueblos (Palkovich 1985).

This problem is mirrored in the whole demographic picture of the prehistoric and historic Pueblos, which is one of seemingly continual demographic flux and ongoing processes of migration and settlement shifts. Population estimates at the settlement level are complicated by the difficulty in estimating momentary population at a given site. The number of Pueblo settlements declined after contact and there is a general trend to larger and fewer habitation sites. In settlements that continued to be occupied into the historic period, the area that was occupied within each site was smaller (Lycett 1989).

The simultaneous processes of migration, site abandonment, and growth of localized populations through aggregation occurred within the overall, large-scale trend of population decline, but site-specific data are not always interpreted within this framework. In his study of population figures for Pecos Pueblo, Kessel (1979) notes that the trend of population decline in the second quarter of the 1600s had been completely reversed by 1680. Zubrow (1974) compiled the population estimates for 19 other Pueblos and shows that the Pecos pattern was typical. Do these studies truly reflect a period of stabilization in population early in the contact period, as suggested by Wilson (1985)? The stabilization of population at these seventeenth-century towns (all still inhabited except Pecos) was at least in part the product of people abandoning smaller settlements and moving to these Pueblos. Local aggregation masks the regional trend of population decline.

Paleodemographic reconstructions based on skeletal series from this period are also complicated by the imposition of in- and out-migration on what appears to be a trend of biologically based population decline. Being neither closed nor stationary populations they violate the assumptions underlying the use of the paleodemographic life table (Moore, Swedlund, and Armelagos 1975). If the rates of growth or decline for specific sites are estimated, then paleodemographic data can be interpreted within that framework and combined with paleoepidemiological data on age and sex-specific patterns of morbidity (Johansson and Horowitz 1986; Goodman et al. 1984). It is important to look not only at the impact of specific events like epidemic outbreaks but also at longer-term pro-cesses that influence the age and mortality structures of populations and result in the decline of Indian populations over several generations (Lycett 1989).

REFERENCES

Adams, E. C.
1981   The View from the Hopi Mesas. Pp. 321–335 in The Protohistoric Period in the American Southwest. A.D. 1450–1700. D. R. Wilcox and W. B. Masse, eds. *Arizona State University Anthropological Research Papers* 24.

Akins, N. J.
1986   A Biocultural Approach to Human Burials from Chaco Canyon, New Mexico. *Reports of the Chaco Center* 9. National Park Service, Santa Fe.

Baker, B. J., and G. J. Armelagos
1988   The Origin and Antiquity of Syphilis, Paleopathological Diagnosis and Interpretation. *Current Anthropology* 29:703–720.

Bancroft, H. H.
1889   History of Arizona and New Mexico. San Francisco: The History Company.

Barber, R. K.
1932   Indian Labor in the Spanish Colonies. *New Mexico Historical Review* 7:105–142, 311–347.

Baugh, T. G., and F. W. Nelson, Jr.
1987   New Mexico Obsidian Sources and Exchange on the Southern Plains. *Journal of Field Archaeology* 14:313–329.

Berry, D. R.
1983   Disease and Climatological Relationship Among Pueblo III-Pueblo IV Anasazi of the Colorado Plateau. (Unpublished Ph.D. Dissertation in Anthropology, University of California, Los Angeles.)

1985   Dental Paleopathology of Grasshopper Pueblo, Arizona, Pp. 253–274 in Health and Disease in the Prehistoric Southwest. C. F. Merbs and R. J. Miller, eds. *Arizona State University Anthropological Research Papers* 34.

Bloom, L. B.
1924   Early Vaccination in New Mexico. Albuquerque: The Historical Society of New Mexico. Publication 7.

Chase, J. E.
1976   Deviance in Gallina: A Report on a Small Series of Gallina Human Skeletal Remains. Pp. 66–93 in Archaeological Excavations in the Llaves Area, Santa Fe National Forest, New Mexico, 1972 and 1974. U.S. National Forest Service, Southwest Region. Archaeological Report 13. Albuquerque.

Chavez, A.
1957   Archives of the Archdioceses of Santa Fe. *Publications of the Academy of American Franciscan History, Bibliographical Series* 8. Washington.

Cole, H., J. Harkin, B. Kraus, and A. Moritz
1955   Pre-Columbian Osseous Syphilis. *Archives of Dermatology and Syphilology* 71:213–238.

Cook, S. F.
1946   The Incidence and Significance of Disease Among the Aztecs and Related Tribes. *The Hispanic American Historical Review* 26:320–335.

Cordell, L. S.
1984   Prehistory of the Southwest. Orlando, Fla.: Academic Press.

1989   Durango to Durango: An Overview of the Southwest Heartland. Pp. 17–40 in Columbian Consequences, D. H. Thomas, ed. Washington: Smithsonian Institution Press.

Coyne, S. A.
1981   Variations and Pathologies in the Vertebral Columns of Gran Quiviran Indians. Pp. 151–155 in Contributions to Gran Quivira Archeology. A. C. Hayes, ed. *National Park Service Publications in Archaeology* 17. Washington.

Crosby, A. W.
1972   The Columbian Exchange, Biological and Cultural Consequences of 1492. Westport, Conn.: Greenwood.

Daniel, T. M.
1981   An Immunochemist's View of the Epidemiology of Tuberculosis. Pp. 35–49 in Prehistoric Tuberculosis in the Americas. J. E. Buikstra, ed. *Northwestern University Archeological Papers* 5. Evanston, Ill.

Dean, J. S., R. C. Euler, G. J. Gumerman, F. Plog, R. H. Hevly, and T. Karlstrom
1985   Human Behavior, Demography, and Paleoenvironment on the Colorado Plateaus. *American Antiquity* 50:537–554.

Decker, K. W.
1986   Isotopic and Chemical Reconstruction of Diet and Its Biological and Social Dimensions at Grasshopper Pueblo, Arizona. (Paper presented at the Annual Meeting of the Society for American Archaeology, New Orleans.)

Decker, K. W., and L. L. Tieszen
1989   Isotopic Reconstruction of Mesa Verde Diet from Basketmaker III to Pueblo III. *The Kiva* 55(1):33–46.

Denninger, H. S.
1938   Syphilis of Pueblo Skull Before 1350. *Archives of Pathology* 26:724–727.

Dobyns, H. F.
1966   Estimating Aboriginal American Population, an Appraisal of Techniques with a new Hemispheric Estimate. *Current Anthropology* 7(4):395–416.

1983   Their Numbers Become Thinned. Knoxville: University of Tennessee Press.

Dumarest, N.
1919   Notes on Cochiti, New Mexico. *American Anthropological Association Memoirs* 6(3).

El-Najjar, M. Y.
1979   Human Treponematosis and Tuberculosis: Evidence from the New World. *American Journal of Physical Anthropology* 51:599–618.

El-Najjar, M. Y., and S. Bussey
1980   Burials. In Conservatism on the Puerco River, Excavations at Four Small Farming Villages. S. Bussey, ed. *New Mexico State University Cultural Resources Management Report* 380. Las Cruces.

El-Najjar, M. Y., B. Lozoff, and D. Ryan
1975   The Paleoepidemiology of Porotic Hyperostosis in the American Southwest: Radiological and Ecological Considerations. *American Journal of Roentgenology, Radium, and Thermal Nuclear Medicine* 125:918–924.

Espinosa, J. M.
1988   The Pueblo Revolt of 1696. Norman: University of Oklahoma Press.

Euler, R. C., G. J. Gumerman, T. Karlstrom, J. Dean, and R. H. Hevly
1979   The Colorado Plateaus: Cultural Dynamics and Paleoenvironment, *Science* 205:1089–1101.

Ferguson, C.
1980   Analysis of Human Skeletal Remains. Pp. 121–148 in Tijeras Canyon. L. S. Cordell, ed. Albuquerque: University of New Mexico Press.

Ferguson, T. J.
1981   The Emergence of Modern Zuni Culture and Society: A Summary to Zuni Tribal History, A.D. 1450–1700. Pp. 336–353 in the Protohistoric Period in the North American Southwest, A.D. 1450–1700. D. R. Wilcox and W. B. Masse, eds. *Arizona State University Anthropological Research Papers* 24.

Fink, T. M.
1985   Tuberculosis and Anemia in a Pueblo II–III Anasazi Child from New Mexico. Pp. 359–379 in Health and Disease in the Prehistoric Southwest. C. F. Merbs and R. J. Miller, eds. *Arizona State University Anthropological Papers* 34.

Flinn, L., C. G. Turner, and A. Brew
1976   Additional Evidence for Cannibalism in the Southwest: The Case of LA 4528. *American Antiquity* 41:308–318.

Forrestal, P.
1954   Benavides' Memorial of 1630. Washington: Academy of American Franciscan History.

Gibson, C.
1964   The Aztecs Under Spanish Rule, a History of the Indians of the Valley of Mexico, 1519–1810. Palo Alto, Calif.: Stanford University Press.

Goodman, A. H., and G. J. Armelagos
1985   The Chronologic Distribution of Enamel Hypoplasia in Human Permanent Incisor and Canine Teeth. *Archives of Oral Biology* 30(6):503–507.

Goodman, A. H., D. L. Martin, G. J. Armelagos, and G. Clark
1984   Indications of Stress from Bone and Teeth. Pp. 13–50 in Paleopathology at the Origins of Agriculture. M. N. Cohen and G. J. Armelagos, eds. New York: Academic Press.

Hammond, G. and A. Rey
1940   Narratives of the Coronado Expedition, 1540–1542. (*Coronado Historical Series* 1). Albuquerque: University of New Mexico Press.

Heglar, R.
1974   The Prehistoric Population of Cochiti Pueblo and Selected Interpopulation Biological Comparisons. (Unpublished Ph.D. Dissertation in Anthropology, University of Michigan, Ann Arbor.)

Hinkes, M.
1983   Skeletal Evidence of Stress in Subadults: Trying to Come of Age at Grasshopper Pueblo. (Unpublished Ph.D. Dissertation in Anthropology, University of Arizona, Tucson.)

Hodge, F. W.
1937   History of Hawikuh. Los Angeles: The Southwest Museum.

Hodge, F. W., G. Hammond, and A. Rey
1945   Fray Alonso Benavides' Revised Memorial of 1634. Albuquerque: University of New Mexico Press.

Hooton, E.
1930   The Indians of Pecos Pueblo. New Haven, Conn.: Yale University Press.

Howells, W. W.
1932   The Skeletal Material of the Swarts Ruin. Pp. 115–170 in A Typical Mimbres Site in Southwestern New Mexico. *Papers of the Peabody Museum of Archeology and Ethnology,* Harvard University.

Hrdlička, A.
1908   Physiological and Medical Observations Among the Indians of the Southwestern United States. *Bureau of American Ethnology Bulletin* 34. Washington.

Johansson, S. R., and S. Horowitz
1986   Estimating Mortality in Skeletal Populations: Influence of the Growth Rate on the Interpretation of Levels and Trends During the Transition to Agriculture. *American Journal of Physical Anthropology* 71:233–250.

Kane, A. E.
1988   McPhee Community Cluster Introduction. Pp. 4–59 in Dolores Archeological Program: Anasazi Communities at Dolores, McPhee Village. A. E. Kane and C. R. Robinson, comps. Denver: U. S. Bureau of Reclamation. Engineering and Research Center.

Kent, S.
1986   The Influence of Sedentism and Aggregation on Porotic Hyperostosis and Anemia: A Case Study. *Man* 21:605–636.

Kessell, J. L.
1979   Kiva, Cross, and Crown. Washington: U.S. Department of the Interior. National Park Service.

Kunitz, S. J., and R. C. Euler
1972   Aspects of Southwestern Paleoepidemiology. Prescott College Anthropological Reports 2. Prescott, Arizona.

Lang, R.
1977   Archaeological Survey of the Upper San Cristobal Arroyo Drainage. Galisteo Basin, New Mexico. Santa Fe: School of American Research. Contract Archaeology Program.

Larsen, C. S.
1987   Bioarchaeological Interpretations of Subsistence Economy and Behavior from Human Skeletal Remains. Pp. 339–445 in Advances in Archaeological Method and Theory, Vol. 10. M. Schiffer, ed. New York: Academic Press.

London, M., and K. Tobler
1979   Pindi Site—Paleopathology. Abstract. (Manuscript on file, Maxwell Museum of Anthropology, University of New Mexico, Albuquerque.)

Lycett, M.
1989   Spanish Contact and Pueblo Organization: Long-Term Implications of European Colonial Expansion in the Rio Grande Valley, New Mexico. Pp. 115–126 in Columbian Consequences. D. H. Thomas, ed. Vol. 1. Washington: Smithsonian Institution Press.

McGrath, J. W.
1988   Multiple Stable States of Disease Occurrence. *American Anthropologist* 90:323–334.

Martin, D. L., A. H. Goodman, G. J. Armelagos, and A. L. Magennis
1990   Black Mesa Anasazi Health: Reconstructing Life from Patterns of Death and Disease. (Draft submitted to the Center for Archaeological Research, Southern Illinois University, Carbondale.)

Matthews, M. H.
1988   McPhee Community Cluster Macrobotanical Data Base: Testing the Concept of Agricultural Inten-

sification. Pp. 1099–1127 in Dolores Archaeological Program; Anasazi Communities at Dolores: Phree Village. A. E. Kane and C. R. Robinson, comps. Denver: U.S. Bureau of Reclamation, Engineering and Research Center.

Matthews, W., J. L. Wortman, and J. S. Billings
1893   Human Bones of the Hemenway Collection in the U.S. Army Medical Museum. *Memoirs of the National Academy of Sciences* 6:141–286. Washington.

Merbs, C. F.
1989   Patterns of Health and Sickness in the Precontact Southwest. Pp. 41–56 in Columbian Consequences, Vol. 1. D. H. Thomas, ed. Washington: Smithsonian Institution Press.

Micozzi, M. S., and M. A. Kelley
1985   Evidence for Pre-Columbian Tuberculosis at the Point of Pines Site, Arizona: Skeletal Pathology in the Sacroiliac Region. Pp. 347–358 in Health and Disease in the Prehistoric Southwest. C. F. Merbs and R. J. Miller, eds. *Arizona State University Anthropological Research Papers* 34.

Mielke, J. H., L. B. Jorde, P. G. Trapp, D. L. Anderton, K. Pitkanen, and A. W. Eriksson
1984   Historical Epidemiology of Smallpox in Aland, Finland: 1751–1890. *Demography* 21:271–295.

Minnis, P.
1989   Prehistoric Diet in the Northern Southwest: Macroplant Remains from Four Corners Feces. *American Antiquity* 54(3):543–563.

Moodie, R. L.
1923   Paleopathology: An Introduction to the Study of Ancient Evidences of Disease. Urbana: University of Illinois Press.

Moore, J. A., A. C. Swedlund, and G. J. Armelagos
1975   The Use of Life Tables in Paleodemography. *American Antiquity* 40:57–70.

Nelson, N. C.
1916   Chronology of the Tano Ruins, New Mexico. *American Anthropologist* 18(2):159–180.

Nichols, D., and S. Powell
1987   Demographic Reconstructions in the American Southwest: Alternative Behavioral Means to the Same End. *The Kiva* 52(3):193–207.

Ortner, D. J., and W. G. J. Putschar
1981   Identification of Pathological Conditions in Human Skeletal Remains. *Smithsonian Contributions to Anthropology* 28. Washington.

Palkovich, A. M.
1980   Pueblo Population and Society: The Arroyo Hondo Skeletal and Mortuary Remains. Santa Fe: School of American Research Press.

1984   Agriculture, Marginal Environments, and Nutritional Stress in the Prehistoric Southwest. Pp. 425–

438 in Paleopathology at the Origins of Agriculture. M. N. Cohen and G. J. Armelagos, eds. New York: Academic Press.

1985   Historic Population of the Eastern Pueblos: 1540–1910. *Journal of Anthropological Research* 41:401–426.

1987   Endemic Disease Patterns in Paleopathology: Porotic Hyperostosis. *American Journal of Physical Anthropology* 74:527–538.

Powell, M. P.
1988   Comment on the "The Origin and Antiquity of Syphilis." *Current Anthropology* 29:724–725.

Ramenofsky, A. F.
1987   Vectors of Death, The Archaeology of European Contact. Albuquerque: University of New Mexico Press.

Reff, D. T.
1985   The Demographic and Cultural Consequences of Old World Disease in the Greater Southwest, 1520–1660. (Unpublished Dissertation in Anthropology, University of Oklahoma, Norman.)

1987   The Introduction of Smallpox in the Greater Southwest. *American Anthropologist* 89(3):704–708.

1988   Old World Diseases and the Protohistoric Period in the Greater Southwest. (Paper presented at the Southwest Symposium, Arizona State University, Tempe.)

Reinhard, K. J.
1986   Diet and Iron Deficiency in the Southwest: The Coprolite Evidence. (Paper presented at the Second Conference on Health and Disease in the Prehistoric Southwest. Albuquerque, New Mexico.)

1988   Cultural Ecology of Prehistoric Parasitism on the Colorado Plateau as Evidence by Coprology. *American Journal of Physical Anthropology* 77:355–366.

Reinhard, K. J., and K. H. Clary
1986   Parasite Analysis of Prehistoric Coprolites from Chaco Canyon. Appendix E in A Biocultural Approach to Human Burials from Chaco Canyon, New Mexico, by N. J. Akins. *National Park Service, Division of Cultural Research. Reports of the Chaco Center* 9, Santa Fe.

Riley, C. L.
1975   The Road to Hawikuh: Trade and Trade Routes to Cibola-Zuni During Late Prehistoric and Early Historic Times. *The Kiva* 41:137–159.

1982   The Frontier People: The Greater Southwest in the Protohistoric Period. *Occasional Paper* 1. Carbondale: *Center for Archeological Investigations, Southern Illinois University.*

Schmucker, B. J.
1985   Dental Attrition: A Correlative Study of Dietary and Subsistence Patterns. Pp. 275–322 in Health

and Disease in the Prehistoric Southwest. C. F. Merbs and R. J. Miller, eds. *Arizona State University Anthropological Research Papers* 34. Tempe.

Schoeninger, M.
1989   Reconstructing Prehistoric Human Diet. Pp. 38–67 in The Chemistry of Prehistoric Human Bone. T. D. Price, ed. New York: Cambridge University Press.

Scholes, F. V.
1929   Documents for the History of the New Mexican Missions in the Seventeenth Century. *New Mexico Historical Review* 4:45–58.

1935   Civil Government and Society in New Mexico in the Seventeenth Century. *New Mexico Historical Review* 10:71–111.

1937   Church and State in New Mexico, 1610–1650. (*Historical Society of New Mexico Publications in History* II.) Albuquerque: University of New Mexico Press.

Schroeder, A.
1972   Rio Grande Ethnohistory. Pp. 42–70 in New Perspectives on the Pueblos. A. Ortiz, ed. Albuquerque: University of New Mexico Press.

1979a   History of Archeological Research. Pp. 5–13 in Handbook of North American Indians, Vol. 9: Southwest. A. Ortiz, ed. Washington: Smithsonian Institution.

1979b   Pueblos Abandoned in Historic Times. Pp. 236–254 in Handbook of North American Indians, Vol. 9: Southwest. A. Ortiz, ed. Washington: Smithsonian Institution.

Simmons, M.
1966   New Mexico's Smallpox Epidemic of 1780–1781. *New Mexico Historical Review* 41:319–324.

1979   History of Pueblo-Spanish Relations to 1821. Pp. 178–193 in Handbook of North American Indians, Vol. 9: Southwest. A. Ortiz, ed. Washington: Smithsonian Institution.

Smith, W., R. Woodbury, and N. Woodbury, eds.
1966   The Excavation of Hawikuh by Frederick Webb Hodge. Report of the Hendricks-Hodge Expedition. *Contributions of the Museum of the American Indian, Heye Foundation* 20, New York.

Snow, D. H.
1981   Protohistoric Rio Grande Pueblo Economics: A Review of Trends. The Protohistoric Period in the North American Southwest, A.D. 1450–1700. D. R. Wilcox and W. B. Masse, eds. *Arizona State University Anthropological Research Papers* 24.

Spielmann, K. A.
1983   Late Prehistoric Exchange Between the Southwest and the Southern Plains. *Plains Anthropologist* 28(102):257–272.

1989   Colonists, Hunters, and Farmers: Plains Pueblo Interaction in the Seventeenth Century. Pp. 101–114 in Columbian Consequences, Vol. 1. D. H. Thomas, ed. Washington: Smithsonian Institution Press.

Steinbock, R. T.
1976   Paleopathological Diagnosis and Interpretation. Springfield, Ill.: Charles C. Thomas.

Stodder, A. L. W.
1987   The Physical Anthropology and Mortuary Practice of the Dolores Anasazi: An Early Pueblo Population in Local and Regional Perspective. Pp. 309–504 in Dolores Archaeological Program Supporting Studies: Settlement and Environment. K. L. Petersen and J. D. Orcutt, comps. Denver: U.S. Bureau of Reclamation Engineering and Research Center.

1988   The Status of Bioarchaeological Research in the American Southwest. (Paper presented at the Annual Meeting of the Society for American Archaeology, Phoenix, Arizona.)

1989a   Bioarcheological Resources Survey of the Basin and Range Region. Pp. 141–190 in Human Adaptations and Cultural Change in the Greater Southwest, by A. H. Simmons et al. *Arkansas Archeological Survey Research Series* 32.

1989b   Pueblo Health and Disease in Protohistoric New Mexico. Submitted to Health and Disease in the Prehistoric Southwest. Vol. II. S. Rhine and R. T. Steinbock, eds. *University of New Mexico, Maxwell Museum of Anthropology Technical Bulletin Series*.

Stuart-Macadam, P.
1985   Porotic Hyperostosis: Representative of a Childhood Condition. *American Journal of Physical Anthropology* 66:391–398.

1987a   A Radiographic Study of Porotic Hyperostosis. *American Journal of Physical Anthropology* 74:511–520.

1987b   Porotic Hyperostosis: New Evidence to Support the Anemia Theory. *American Journal of Physical Anthropology* 74:521–538.

Sumner, D. R.
1985   A Probable Case of Prehistoric Tuberculosis from Northeastern Arizona. Pp. 340–346 in Health and Disease in the Prehistoric Southwest. C. F. Merbs and R. J. Miller, eds. *Arizona State University Anthropological Research Papers* 34.

Swanson, C. E.
1976   Dental Pathologies in the Gran Quivira Population. (Unpublished M.A. Thesis in Anthropology, Arizona State University, Tempe.)

Turner, C. G.
1981   The Arizona State University Study of Gran Quiviran Physical Anthropology. Pp. 119–121 in

Contributions to Gran Quivira Archeology. A. C. Hayes, ed. *National Park Service Publications in Archeology* 17. Washington.

Upham, S.
1986   Smallpox and Climate in the American Southwest. *American Anthropologist* 88:115–128.

Upham, S., and L. S. Reed
1989   Regional Systems in the Central and Northern Southwest: Demography, Economy, and Sociopolitics Preceding Contact. Pp. 57–76 in Columbian Consequences, Vol. 1. D. H. Thomas, ed. Washington: Smithsonian Institution Press.

Van Blerkom, L. M.
1985   The Evolution of Human Infectious Disease in the Eastern and Western Hemispheres. (Unpublished Ph.D. Dissertation in Anthropology, University of Colorado, Boulder.)

Wilcox, D.
1981   Changing Perspectives on the Protohistoric Pueblos, A.D. 1450–1700. Pp. 378–409 in The Protohistoric Period in the North American Southwest, A.D. 1450–1700. D. R. Wilcox and W. B. Masse, eds. *Arizona State University Anthropological Research Paper* 24. Tempe.

Wilcox, D., and W. B. Masse
1981   A History of Protohistoric Studies in the North American Southwest. Pp. 1–27 in The Pro-

tohistoric Period in the North American Southwest, A.D. 1450–1700. D. R. Wilcox and W. B. Masse, eds. *Arizona State University Anthropological Research Paper* 24. Tempe.

Williams, H. U.
1932   The Origin and Antiquity of Syphilis: the Evidence from Diseased Bones. *Archives of Pathology* 13:779–814, 931–983.

Wilson, J. P.
1985   Before and After the Pueblo Revolt: Population Trends, Apache Relations and Pueblo Abandonments in Seventeenth Century New Mexico. *Papers of the Archeological Society of New Mexico* 11:113–120. Albuquerque.

Woodbury, R. B.
1959   A Reconsideration of Pueblo Warfare in the Southwestern United States. Actas del Congreso XXXIII de Americanistas: 124–133.

Youmans, G. P.
1979   Tuberculosis. Philadelphia: W. B. Saunders.

Zubrow, E. B.
1974   Population, Contact and Climate in the New Mexican Pueblos. *Anthropological Papers of the University of Arizona* 24. Tucson.

7

Demography of Prehistoric and Early Historic Northern Plains Populations

DOUGLAS W. OWSLEY

Osteological and bioarcheological research on Plains populations can contribute much to an understanding of the biological consequences of Euro-American contact on Native American populations, especially in regard to the demographic impact of the introduction of infectious diseases. During the historic period, Northern Plains villagers located along the Missouri Trench were characterized by increased mobility and instability, as evidenced by rapid village abandonment and relocation (Ramenofsky 1987). Population loss was staggering and followed the introduction and diffusion of acute infectious diseases, including cholera, measles, smallpox, and whooping cough (Lehmer 1971, 1977a; Ramenofsky 1987; Trimble 1979, 1989). In South Dakota, European explorers and traders noted the large population of the Arikara nation, the predominant group along the Missouri River. According to the fur trader Jean Baptiste Trudeau, "in ancient times the Arikara nation was very large; it counted thirty-two populous villages . . ." (Nasatir 1952:299). In A.D. 1700, the Arikara are thought to have numbered 15,000 people, including 4,000 warriors (Beauregard 1912; Holder 1970).

Population estimates for the late eighteenth century were considerably lower. In 1785, the Arikara occupied seven villages and listed 900 men-at-arms. Trudeau's tabulation for 1795 mentioned 500 warriors (Beauregard 1912). The Arikara maintained only three villages in 1804 (Lehmer and Jones 1968). The population estimate in 1804 was 2,600, 500 in 1888, and by 1904, only 380 (Bradbury 1904; Fletcher 1907; Will and Hyde 1917).

Many have linked the beginning of this downward spiral to the last half of the eighteenth century and especially to the smallpox pandemic of 1780–1781. This epidemic was devastating; estimates suggest that from 50 to 75 percent of the Arikara population died (Lehmer and Jones 1968; Stearn and Stearn 1945). Lehmer (1971, 1977a), in particular, strongly supported this view. He gave considerable attention to defining the effects of infectious disease on Plains village tribes. While noting historical evidence for the diffusion of smallpox into the Missouri Valley before the 1780–1781 epidemic, Lehmer focused his attention on this catastrophic event and on the early nineteenth century. Lehmer (1971) believed that Indian contacts and experience in the Plains were unique. Unlike other parts of the Americas, European intrusion into and settlement of the Northern Plains lagged far behind the introduction of Euro-American material culture, horses, and economic influences. Nearly a century of indirect contact allowed Indian populations time to accommodate with European innovations (Lehmer 1971). The decades before 1780 were stable and, if anything, a time of cultural florescence. Epidemic diseases were thought to postdate the introduction of European trade goods about 1675 and the initial exploration of the region a half-century later (Ramenofsky 1982). According to Lehmer (1971:172), "The village tribes of the Middle Missouri subarea rode a wave of prosperity and cultural elaboration through the third quarter of the 18th century. Then another European introduction, epidemic diseases, came close to wiping out the population, and left the survivors with a badly disorganized remnant of their former culture."

Although dramatic events occurred during the last half of the eighteenth century, some evidence suggests that population decline began earlier. Dobyns (1983) argues that pathogens were introduced as early as A.D. 1520 and began at that time to spread widely through native populations. Although he was concerned primarily with population dynamics and trends in eastern North America, the implication is that lethal pathogens, especially "virgin soil epidemics," spread to and decimated Native Americans far beyond the geographic limits of face-to-face contact between Europeans and aboriginal groups (Dobyns 1983). Using archeological evidence of lodge size and settlement areas, Ramenofsky (1982, 1987) has argued that disease-induced depopulation in the Northern Plains began by at least the seventeenth century. The settlement record for the Middle Missouri subarea suggests population growth until the mid to late seventeenth century.

The earliest historically documented accounts of European contact with the Middle Missouri village tribes were those of Étienne Veniard, sieur de Bourgmont in 1723 and Pierre Gaultier de Varennes, sieur de La Vérendrye in 1738 (Lehmer 1971; Nasatir 1952; Wood and Thiessen 1985). Osteological research has provided evidence for the presence of Euro-American resident traders prior to this date (Jantz 1989). Before direct contact, long-established trading patterns involving Indians as middlemen brought European goods to the villages. The geographic location of the Middle Missouri villages provided a base that facilitated the

movement of horses from the Southwest and trade goods from the Northeast, as well as the exchange of horticultural surpluses for products of the hunt (Ewers 1955; Wood 1980). These exchange networks were potential routes for the early transmission of infectious disease. Sustained European presence resulted in the catastrophic effects of smallpox and other diseases during the late eighteenth and early nineteenth centuries (Trimble 1979).

Of the main historical questions about this catastrophic demographic change, timing is foremost. When approximately did this downward trend in population size begin? Further, was the postcontact period characterized solely by decline in population? Finally, can paleodemographic research identify temporally patterned changes in age-specific mortality rates? Osteological research provides the best approach to these questions because early census counts for the Middle Missouri villages postdate direct contact by more than a half-century.

Investigators (Campbell 1989; Taylor 1989) have examined the historical demography of nomadic Plains groups during the nineteenth century using census counts and reports by traders, Indian agents, and others. The effects of introduced infectious diseases varied considerably among bands. Trimble (1979, 1989), using the ethnohistorical record combined with epidemiological theory, examined the role of acute crowd infections, particularly smallpox, among the Arikara, Mandan, and Hidatsa during the early nineteenth century. Employing a disease-ecology model, he considered interactions between disease and the cultural and biological environment. Historical documentation has provided information on diseases that reached epidemic proportions in regions adjacent to the Plains (Dobyns 1983; Ramenofsky 1987; Trimble 1989; Vehik 1989), and Ramenofsky (1987) used archeologically determined settlement patterns to assess the possibility of diffusion into the Plains.

Specific questions concerning the timing and nature of demographic change before direct contact can be investigated through comparative analyses of demographic data from temporally sequential populations representing the prehistoric, protohistoric, and early historic periods. The demographic data are focused on populations of the Middle Missouri subarea, as represented by sedentary horticultural populations of the Plains Coalescent tradition and Woodland period hunter-gatherers. Information for Central and Southern Plains village populations is also helpful in the resolution of these questions.

REGIONS AND CULTURES STUDIED

Northern Plains Woodland

Demographic data from four sites, comprising nine burial mounds, located on the first high terrace overlooking the Missouri River near the North Dakota–South Dakota state line are available. The archeological classification is the Sonota complex, a Middle Woodland cultural tradition dating approximately A.D. 1–600. These people were organized into small groups that exploited the plains-riverine environment, with primary subsistence oriented toward communal hunting of bison (Neumann 1975). Demographic data reported by Bass and Phenice (1975) and Owsley (1985–1989) for Boundary Mounds 1, 2, and 3 (32SI1) are used in the analysis. In addition, mortality data for 26 Archaic and Woodland sites from eastern North and South Dakota and northwestern Minnesota allow limited comparison of Missouri Trench populations with prehistoric groups of the Northeastern Plains (Williams 1989).

Northern Plains Village

Plains village cultures after A.D. 1550 in the Middle Missouri subarea of South Dakota have been classified into three archeological variants of the Coalescent tradition: Extended, Postcontact, and Disorganized (Lehmer 1971). The three centuries that followed 1550 represent a time of dynamic change as ancestral Arikara Indian populations refined their adaptation to the Middle Missouri environment. Extended Coalescent (1550–1675) groups expanded their geographical distribution and gained control of the Middle Missouri Valley in South Dakota through the displacement of resident groups. This was a time of cultural florescence most dramatically evident slightly later in protohistoric period sites of the Postcontact Coalescent variant (1675–1780). By the last decades of the eighteenth century, the Plains village pattern had climaxed, and later villages have been assigned to the Disorganized Coalescent (1780–1860). Seven Coalescent tradition sites are included in this survey: Cheyenne

River (39ST1, 1740–1795), Four Bear (39DW2, 1758–1774), Larson (39WW2, 1679–1733), Leavitt (39ST215, 1784–1792), Leavenworth (39CO9, 1802–1832), Mobridge (39WW1, 1600–1700), and Sully (39SL4, 1650–1733). Arikara subsistence was based on horticulture, hunting, and trade (Hurt 1969; Ramenofsky 1987).

Multicomponent sites are particularly informative when examining dynamic change in patterns of morbidity and mortality through time. Sully, a multicomponent site located on the left bank of the Missouri River approximately 21 miles northwest of Pierre, is a good example. This large unfortified village is assigned to the early Postcontact Coalescent variant. There are several discrete burial areas, three (D, A, and E) of which have large samples representing different occupation periods (Owsley and Jantz 1978). Sully spans the time interval when European artifacts were first reaching the Arikara through indirect contact. The percentages of burials with trade beads in these cemeteries are 1.7 (D), 2.6 (A), and 5.1 (E), indicating that trade goods were a relatively new introduction (Jantz and Owsley 1984). These three cemeteries date approximately 1650 to 1700. At Larson, which is slightly later, the percentage of trade beads is 7.3. Given the evidence of abandonment and resettlement indicating several occupations, or at least temporal sequencing of cemeteries, it is pertinent to determine whether the Sully cemetery areas yield significantly different mortality data.

At the Mobridge site, cemeteries 1 and 3 represent late prehistoric (1600–1650), Extended Coalescent populations, and number 2 is an early protohistoric (1650–1700), Postcontact Coalescent site. None of the burials in cemeteries 1 and 3 has trade beads. A total of 109 burial pits were excavated in cemeteries 1 and 3; four pits (3.7%) contained grave artifacts made of metal. Of a total of 168 pits at cemetery 2, 17 burials (10.1%) included metal or glass artifacts (Owsley 1981; Owsley, Bennett, and Jantz 1982).

Central and Southern Plains Villages

To evaluate the Northern Plains data, it is helpful to begin to integrate population data for the Central and Southern Plains, a difficult task because population sample sizes are limited and there has been little paleodemographic study of these groups. Data for two Plains village sites were included: Linwood and McLemore. Linwood (25BU1), in Butler County, Nebraska, was a Grand Pawnee village site with two temporal components—1779–1809 and 1851–1857 (Grange 1968). The majority of the burial sample belongs to the earlier component. The McLemore site (34WA5), in western Oklahoma, provides the largest series available (N = 59) for a Southern Plains population (Owsley, Marks, and Manhein 1989) and adds a special dimension to this study as it represents a pre-Columbian Plains village site. It consisted of a prehistoric Washita River phase village dated to 1150–1375 (Bell 1984; Pillaert 1963). Washita River settlements were small in area, with distributions that suggest "a dispersed, almost rural population, living in small-sized villages or hamlets containing from two or three up to a dozen houses and numbering fewer than 100 individuals" (Bell 1984:311). The subsistence strategy was based on hunting, especially of deer and bison, fishing, gathering, and horticulture. According to Bell (1984), the general impression is that of a marginal subsistence economy, such that surplus resources were uncommon and occurred temporarily only after a rich harvest or a successful hunt.

The demographic data used in this analysis are based on work by Bass and Phenice (1975), Palkovich (1978), Williams (1989), and Owsley (1985–1989). For population comparisons, broad age categories were used to minimize possible interobserver differences in age determinations. Several comparisons are based on total numbers of preadult

(less than 15 years) and adult skeletons. More precise age categories are used in analyses based solely on Owsley's data. These analyses involved comparisons of age-specific adult mortality in prehistoric and postcontact period groups.

DIFFERENTIAL MORTALITY

Figure 1 shows percentages of the mortality distributions of preadults in Plains Woodland and Coalescent tradition populations. The differences among these population samples are statistically significant (chi-square = 53.3, degree of freedom = 4, probability = 0.000), reflecting primarily the pronounced difference between Woodland hunter-gatherers (44–46%) and the more sedentary horticulturists (60–66%).

The basic demographic differences reflected here cannot be explained as a temporal pattern influenced solely by the catastrophic effects of Euro-American contact. Although numerically limited, evidence from McLemore suggests the need for an alternative explanation, as it includes a very high percentage of preadults. The age distribution for this pre-Columbian site implies that these mortality distributions also reflect hazards associated with a sedentary village environment, such as increased population density and sanitary conditions conducive to the spread of disease. Settled village life in the Great Plains was accompanied by increased sub-

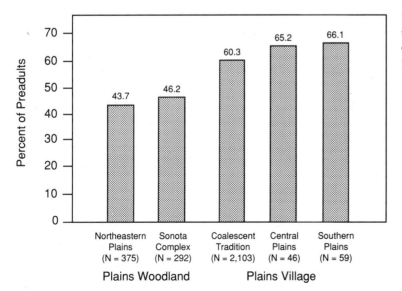

Fig. 1. Percentages of preadults in the mortality distributions of Northern and Northeastern Plains Woodland and Plains Village populations.

adult mortality. However, additional precontact Plains village data are necessary to establish this pattern, as well as to provide better information on variation among precontact populations, as some Woodland groups apparently experienced a high level of preadult mortality, for example, at Jamestown Mounds (Williams 1989) and at the Hanging Valley site (Tiffany et al. 1988).

The percentages of skeletons aged less than 15 years in Northern Plains Coalescent sites varied between 51.2 and 67.9 percent (fig. 2) (chi-square = 29.8, d.f. = 4, p = 0.000). The sites in this illustration are chronologically ordered by date. All are characterized by high rates of infant and childhood mortality, although the Sully site, with archeological components that date primarily to the seventeenth century (cemeteries A, D, and E), has a substantially lower percentage (from about 9 to 17% less than those of the other sites). The highest values occurred during the eighteenth century. As expected, infants constitute much of this childhood mortality. Larson had an especially high mortality rate for perinatal infants, with 40.9 percent of the total sample aged from birth to one year (Owsley and Bass 1979). Preadult mortality accounts for the majority of deaths in Coalescent tradition sites.

There is considerable heterogeneity in the mortality statistics for seventeenth-century sites, as shown in figure 3, which presents data for separate components of the Mobridge and Sully sites. Settle-ments dating from the last half of the century have lower percentages of subadults than those from the first half of the century. The chi-square statistic for the comparison illustrated in figure 3 is 22.0 (d.f. = 5, p = 0.001). Reductions in infant and childhood mortality occur through time at both sites. The difference within Mobridge is statistically significant (chi-square = 12.6, d.f. = 2, p = 0.002), although this is not the case for the Sully cemeteries (chi-square = 1.1, d.f. = 2, p = 0.59).

Adult mortality also changed through time. Figure 4 illustrates age-specific adult mortality in five groups representing Woodland (Boundary Mounds 1, 2, and 3) and Plains Village populations. These sites are displayed in chronological order. The age distribution for the Boundary Mounds shows about the same number of deaths for individuals aged 15–19 years as at prehistoric McLemore but less longevity for older adults. Most adults in the McLemore series were at least 40 years old. This prehistoric Southern Plains adult mortality pattern contrasts markedly with that of the Northern Plains sites. Even Sully, which includes many older individuals (especially in cemetery D) and a lower overall frequency of preadult mortality, aligns with the postcontact period sites. In the following century, the number of deaths of young adults aged 15–19 years increased, while the numbers of older adults declined. After 1740, only 22.1 percent of the population attained the age of 40

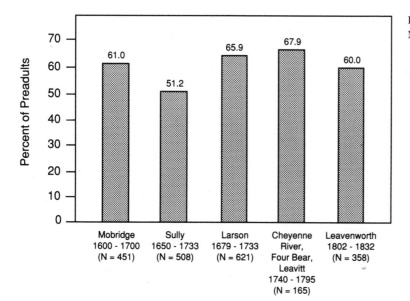

Fig. 2. Percentages of preadult mortality in Northern Plains Coalescent tradition sites.

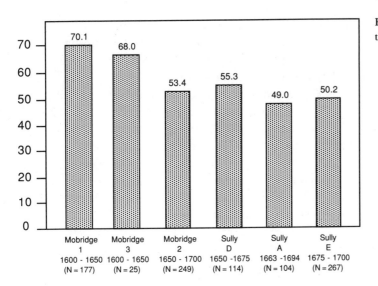

Fig. 3. Percentages of mortality in the cemeteries of Mobridge and Sully.

years. The demography of this time period is characterized by both loss of the older generation and high percentages of preadults.

Selected vital statistics facilitate numerical description of postcontact change in age-specific mortality rates. Table 1 presents three life table values for Sully and a composite late eighteenth to early nineteenth-century series (Four Bear, Leavenworth, and Leavitt) mortality rates. From the age distribution at death (Dx), the life table technique permits calculation of the probability of dying (qx)

between exact age x and exact age x + n; the percentage of deaths (dx); and the percentage of survivors (lx) from one age to the next (Barclay 1958; Acsádi and Nemeskéri 1970). Higher percentages of deaths were found for all ages less than 20 years in the later series. Thus, the portion of the population that survived to age 20 was 43.3 percent at Sully, in contrast to 31.6 percent a century later. Relatively few individuals attained the age of 40 years. The probability of death (qx) is an indicator of age-specific mortality as it expresses the risk of dying in

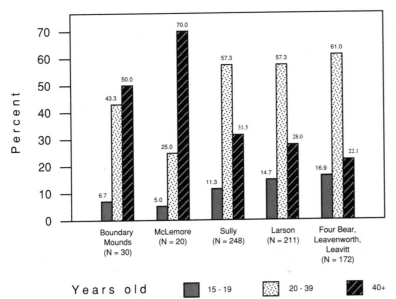

Fig. 4. Age-specific adult mortality for Plains Woodland (Boundary Mounds) and Plains Village populations.

TABLE 1

Abridged Life Table Values for 1650 to 1733 (Sully)
and 1758 to 1832 (Four Bear, Leavenworth, Leavitt)

| | Distribution of Deaths | | | | Survivors | | Probability of Death | |
| | 1650–1733 | | 1758–1832 | | | | | |
Age	N (Dx)	% (dx)	N (Dx)	% (dx)	1650–1733 (lx)	1758–1832 (lx)	1650–1733 (qx)	1758–1832 (qx)
0–4	193	37.99	198	43.81	100.00	100.00	.380	.438
5–9	45	8.86	53	11.73	62.01	56.19	.143	.209
10–14	22	4.33	29	6.42	53.15	44.46	.081	.144
15–19	28	5.51	29	6.42	48.82	38.04	.113	.169
20–29	69	13.58	49	10.84	43.31	31.62	.314	.343
30–39	73	14.37	56	12.39	29.73	20.78	.483	.596
40–49	45	8.86	17	3.76	15.36	8.39	.577	.448
50+	33	6.50	21	4.65	6.50	4.63	1.000	1.000 ·
Total	508		452					

each age interval. The values for this index were higher in late sites for every category until age 40.

DISEASE AND WARFARE

Disease experience varied in different regions of the Americas, depending on the time and nature of Euro-American contact. In the Northern Plains, Indians were geographically isolated from direct contact until early in the eighteenth century. However, trade materials arrived through aboriginal contacts decades in advance of the first Europeans, and historians and archeologists have debated whether the transmission of introduced diseases occurred concomitantly or at an earlier date.

Because adequate mortality data for pre-Columbian village sites in the Northern Plains are not available, late prehistoric sites such as Mobridge, about 1600–1700, seemed to provide a baseline for the evaluation of contact-period demographic change. However, the discussion here has reinforced doubts about the validity of using seventeenth-century data to develop an accurate precontact demographic profile. The limited data available for a Southern Plains prehistoric village—McLemore—indicate a distinctly different demographic profile from that found in the Northern Plains. This difference is not reflected in the numbers of infants represented, because the McLemore

sample includes many newborns; rather, it is apparent in the presence of fewer older children and adolescents, and of more adults of advanced age (Owsley and Jantz 1989).

Composite data based on a number of Northern Plains Woodland sites reveal another pattern for hunter-gatherers, one that is distinguishable from that suggested for later sedentary village populations. Unless markedly biased by burial practices, during the Woodland period infant and childhood mortality as lower and more adults lived past 40 years of age.

The limited demographic data available for the Plains Archaic generally resemble the Woodland pattern. Finnegan (1981), summarizing pooled data for a number of Archaic sites (N = 104 individuals), reported that only 26 percent of the sample was less than 15 years of age. However, this mortality distribution is noticeably deficient in the number of infants, which suggests differential preservation and biases in recovery.

Understanding demographic change during the postcontact period is a complex problem. The available historical information is limited and extends with depth only into the nineteenth century. Yet, paleodemographic analysis can begin to unravel some of the biological issues that archeologists and historians questioned, even without incorporating biological data into their research design.

Temporal variability in mortality profiles is

strongly indicated by statistical analysis of existing collections. Some sites are characterized by tremendous numbers of infants and young adults (Larson); others give the impression of an older population (Sully). Four Bear can be described as a series composed of infants, children, and young adults (Owsley and Jantz 1989). McLemore, although including a large number of infants and small children, has a greater representation of older adults. "This greater longevity and the lack of appreciable numbers of deaths during the ages of 5 to 29 years signifies a different mortality pattern" (Owsley and Jantz 1989:140).

Cemetery samples representing Coalescent tradition Northern Plains villages are heterogeneous in their demographic profiles, and some of this variation is temporally patterned. Historic Leavenworth, representing the fragmented remainder of the Arikara nation, was declining in population, with losses attributable to disease, malnutrition, and warfare. Given the tremendous turmoil experienced by these people during the historic period, it is surprising that the percentage of infants and children was as high two centuries earlier at Mobridge. In a general sense, many of the causes were probably the same. High mortality rates can be related to somewhat marginal climatic and environmental conditions reflected in the archeological record for the Extended Coalescent period (cf. Lehmer 1971, 1977b), to stress imposed by intertribal conflict (Owsley 1989), and, perhaps, also to the introduction of disease.

Early Mobridge was essentially a border outpost, the northern extension of the Arikara during their ascent of the Missouri River. There is considerable archeological and osteological evidence for warfare in these northern villages (Owsley 1989; Owsley, Berryman, and Bass 1977). As the Arikara gained control of new territory, some stability followed, which might partially explain reductions in mortality rates of multicomponent sites through time. However, the occasional transmission of new infectious diseases to the villagers could have caused the high mortality of infants and children.

Without an accurate set of baseline data with which to assess demographic change during the postcontact period in the Northern Plains, the possibility that the earliest components of Mobridge (1 and 3) experienced the effects of introduced infectious disease must be considered. If present these initial disturbances were temporary, for the mortality profiles for later components at this site (Mobridge 2) and at Sully, which was roughly contemporaneous, were less extreme, at least with regard to the representation of preadults. There seems to have been a period of amelioration at these sites, where, following the earliest settlement, later occupations experienced less preadult mortality. Based on demographic and other osteological data and the archeological record, these populations were stable, nutritionally well-off, and perhaps even increasing. This period was a cultural florescence, and the same was true from a nutritional and demographic perspective.

Differences in the demographic profiles of Mobridge 1 and 2 were first reported by Palkovich (1978, 1981), who attributed this disparity to a treponemal infection, tuberculosis, and a malnutrition-anemia condition. The osteological evidence for malnutrition is relatively rare in these populations until after 1800, as indicated by measurements of tubular bone cortical thickness and studies of long-bone growth (Jantz and Owsley 1984; Owsley 1985, 1991). Kelley, Lebesque, and Murphy's (1989) study of tuberculosis in the Arikara presents paleopathologic evidence for its presence in the Mobridge 1 and 2 cemeteries; therefore, communicable diseases, such as measles and smallpox, probably account for the disparity in the mortality distributions. Those who survived the high mortality experienced by the first generation exposed to the disease were immune to subsequent outbreaks, leaving a smaller pool of susceptible hosts, and, in essence, less mortality, at least with regard to that disease. The internal differences noted at both Sully and Mobridge can be explained in this way.

Soon after 1700, the Arikara entered a turbulent era characterized by instability, population mobility, increased morbidity, decline in population, decreasing military strength, and sociocultural deterioration. The temporal pattern evident for later sites such as Larson, Four Bear, and Leavenworth suggests increasing childhood, adolescent, and young adult mortality rates, with fewer adults reaching old age. The increased stress of this disruptive period is evident in various osteological indicators, including fetal and childhood growth rates and femoral cortical thickness (Jantz and Owsley 1984; Owsley 1985, 1991). Early eighteenth-century sites such as Larson were in decline, as both the demographic data and the settlement record show. Successive rebuilding of the earth lodges at Larson reduced the perimeters and sizes of the structures (Bowers 1963). Hoffman (1966) reported two fortification ditches, the inner being stratigraphically more recent and suggesting "a marked contraction in living area (and population?) through time, as well as some strong stimulus that forced the later peoples to rebuild within a prescribed area."

The settlement history for Sully, which dates slightly earlier than Larson, is different. Village growth and an associated increase in population at Sully are indicated by an expansion of the village area through time. This site contains the depressions of nearly 400 earth lodges, more than at any other site in the Northern Plains. Cemetery Area D was dated to relatively early in the history of the site because village debris, such as storage pits, intruded into this area after the burials were made (Bass 1965).

The beginning of the eighteenth century was a turning point in population size for the Arikara, following which there was no recovery until the twentieth century. Although disease was a major factor, social disruption and intertribal warfare played significant roles. Bioarcheological data have shown that the Larson site was abandoned because of warfare; the lodges were burned, and many villagers were massacred (Owsley, Berryman, and Bass 1977). Ethnohistorical accounts frequently mention intertribal conflict, and osteological evidence has demonstrated a large number of traumatic deaths in postcontact populations (Owsley 1989).

SUMMARY

The earliest census counts in the Northern Plains postdated direct contact by more than a half-century. For this reason, the archeological record and skeletal collections are the primary sources of information about the early postcontact experience of the Middle Missouri villagers. Only through paleodemographic research is it possible to document fully the devastating impact of Old World infectious diseases on these people. Using archeologically derived settlement records and epidemic histories for regions adjacent to the Plains to study likely patterns in the transmission of disease, Ramenofsky (1987) concluded that new infectious diseases reached the Middle Missouri by the seventeenth century. The osteological data indicate high mor-

tality rates beginning early in the century, suggesting the early impact of epidemics at Mobridge 1 and 3 (1600–1650). Cemeteries (Mobridge 2, Sully) dating to the late seventeenth century show a reduced effect with lower overall mortality rates for infants and children. The total population was probably increasing until late in the seventeenth century when disease pressure intensified again. Irreversible population decline began with Larson and continued through the eighteenth century as illustrated by changes in age-specific mortality rates.

Many questions remain; a basic one is the extent to which the observed differences in demographic data over time were driven by changes in fertility rates. For example, mortality distributions for the later sites in this series, such as Linwood and Leavenworth, show lower percentages of newborn infants. Although perhaps a sampling effect, such observations suggest a depression in fertility rates during the early nineteenth century. Growth data for perinatal infants born after 1750 also provide evidence of decreased birth size, suggesting increased complications with pregnancy (Owsley and Jantz 1985). Future demographic research should focus on infant and childhood mortality (e.g., Jantz and Owsley 1985; Owsley and Jantz 1985), sex-related mortality (e.g., Owsley and Bradtmiller 1983), and ways of integrating the demographic and skeletal pathology data (e.g., Kelley, Lebesque, and Murphy 1989; Owsley 1989; Palkovich 1981).

REFERENCES

Acsádi, Gy, and T. Nemeskéri
    1970   History of Human Life Span and Mortality. Budapest: Akademiai Kiado.

Barclay, George W.
    1958   Techniques of Population Analysis. New York: John Wiley.

Bass, William M.
    1965   The Physical Anthropology of the Sully Site, 39SL4. (Manuscript submitted to the National Park Service, Omaha, Neb.)

Bass, William M., and Terrell W. Phenice
    1975   Prehistoric Human Skeletal Material from Three Sites in North and South Dakota. Pp. 106–140 in The Sonota Complex and Associated Sites on the Northern Great Plains. *Nebraska State Historical Society, Publications in Anthropology* 6. Lincoln.

Beauregard, Mrs. H. T., ed. and trans.
    1912   Journal of Jean Baptiste Trudeau Among the

Arikara Indians in 1795. *Missouri Historical Society Collections* 4(1):9–48.

Bell, Robert E.
1984   The Plains Villagers: The Washita River. Pp. 307–324 in Prehistory of Oklahoma. Robert E. Bell, ed. Orlando, Fla.: Academic Press.

Bowers, A. W.
1963   Missouri Basin Project Weekly Progress Reports 9 (Summer).

Bradbury, John
1904   Travels in the Interior of America in the Years 1809–1811. In Vol. 5 of Early Western Travels. R. G. Thwaites, ed. Cleveland, Ohio: A. H. Clark.

Campbell, Gregory R.
1989   Plains Indian Historical Demography and Health: An Introductory Overview. *Plains Anthropologist. Memoir* 23:v–xiii.

Dobyns, Henry F.
1983   Their Number Become Thinned: Native American Population Dynamics in Eastern North America. Knoxville: University of Tennessee Press.

Ewers, John C.
1955   The Horse in Blackfoot Indian Culture, with Comparative Material from Other Western Tribes. *Bureau of American Ethnology Bulletin* 159. Washington.

Finnegan, Michael
1981   Archaic Skeletal Remains from the Central Plains: Demography and Burial Practices. *Plains Anthropologist. Memoir* 17:85–92.

Fletcher, Alice C.
1907   Arikara. Pp., 83–86 in Vol. 1 of Handbook of American Indians North of Mexico. Frederick W. Hodge, ed. 2 vols. *Bureau of American Ethnology Bulletin* 30. Washington.

Grange, Roger T., Jr.
1968   Pawnee and Lower Loup Pottery. *Nebraska State Historical Society, Publications in Anthropology,* 3. Lincoln.

Hoffman, J. J.
1966   Larson Site. *River Basin Surveys Weekly Reports* 10:(Summer).

Holder, Preston
[1970]   The Hoe and the Horse on the Plains: A Study of Cultural Development Among North American Indians. Lincoln: University of Nebraska Press.

Hurt, Wesley R.
1969   Seasonal Economic and Settlement Patterns of the Arikara. *Plains Anthropologist* 14(43):32–37.

Jantz, Richard L.
1989   White Traders in the Upper Missouri: Osteological Evidence from the Swan Creek Site. In the Symposium Skeletal Biology in the Great Plains: A Multidisciplinary View. Washington: Smithsonian Institution.

Jantz, Richard L., and Douglas W. Owsley
1984   Long Bone Growth Variation Among Arikara Skeletal Populations. *American Journal of Physical Anthropology* 63(1):13–20.

1985   Patterns of Infant and Early Childhood Mortality in Arikara Skeletal Populations. Pp. 209–213 in Status, Structure and Stratification: Current Archaeological Reconstructions; Proceedings of the Sixteenth Annual Conference of the Archaeological Association of the University of Calgary, Calgary, Alberta.

Kelley, Marc A., Dianne Lebesque, and Sean Murphy
1989   Tuberculosis in the Upper Missouri in Postcontact Native Americans. In the Symposium Skeletal Biology in the Great Plains: A Multidisciplinary View. Washington: Smithsonian Institution.

Lehmer, Donald J.
1971   Introduction to Middle Missouri Archeology. Washington: National Park Service.

1977a   Epidemics Among the Indians of the Upper Missouri. *Reprints in Anthropology* 8:105–111.

1977b   Climate and Culture History in the Middle Missouri Valley. *Reprints in Anthropology* 8:59–71.

Lehmer, Donald J., and David T. Jones
1968   Arikara Archeology: The Bad River Phase. *Smithsonian Institution. River Basin Surveys. Publications in Salvage Archeology* 7. Lincoln.

Nasatir, Abraham P., ed.
1952   Before Lewis and Clark: Documents Illustrating the History of the Missouri, 1785–1804. 2 vols. St. Louis: St. Louis Historical Documents Foundation.

Neuman, Robert W.
1975   The Sonota Complex and Associated Sites on the Northern Great Plains. *Nebraska State Historical Society Publications in Anthropology* 6. Lincoln.

Owsley, Douglas W.
1981   Mobridge Site Cemeteries: Controversy Concerning the Location of the Over and Stirling Burials. *Plains Anthropologist. Memoir* 17:43–48.

1985   Postcontact Period Nutritional Status and Cortical Bone Thickness of South Dakota Indians. Pp. 199–207 in Status, Structure and Stratification: Current Archaeological Reconstructions; Proceedings of the Sixteenth Annual Conference of the Archaeological Association of the University of Calgary, Calgary, Alberta.

1985–   Skeletal Inventories and Demographic Data. (In
1989   author's possession.)

1989 Osteological Evidence for Scalping in Coalescent Tradition Populations of the Northern Plains. In the Symposium Skeletal Biology in the Great Plains: A Multidisciplinary View. Washington: Smithsonian Institution.

1991 Temporal Variation in Femoral Cortical Thickness of North American Plains Indians. In Human Paleopathology: Current Syntheses and Future Options. Donald J. Ortner and Arthur C. Aufderheide, eds. Washington: Smithsonian Institution Press.

Owsley, Douglas W., and William M. Bass
1979 A Demographic Analysis of Skeletons from the Larson Site (39WW2) Walworth County, South Dakota: Vital Statistics. *American Journal of Physical Anthropology* 51(2):145–154.

Owsley, Douglas W., Suzanne M. Bennett, and Richard L. Jantz
1982 Intercemetery Morphological Variation in Arikara Crania from the Mobridge Site (39WW1). *American Journal of Physical Anthropology* 58(2):179–185.

Owsley, Douglas W., Hugh E. Berryman, and William M. Bass
1977 Demographic and Osteological Evidence for Warfare at the Larson Site, South Dakota. *Plains Anthropologist. Memoir* 13:119–131.

Owsley, Douglas W., and Bruce Bradtmiller
1983 Mortality of Pregnant Females in Arikara Villages: Osteological Evidence. *American Journal of Physical Anthropology* 61(3):331–336.

Owsley, Douglas W., and Richard L. Jantz
1978 Intracemetery Morphological Variation in Arikara Crania from the Sully Site (39SL4), Sully County, South Dakota. *Plains Anthropologist* 23(80):139–147.

1985 Long Bone Lengths and Gestational Age Distributions of Postcontact Period Arikara Indian Perinatal Infant Skeletons. *American Journal of Physical Anthropology* 68(3):321–328.

1989 A Systematic Approach to the Skeletal Biology of the Southern Plains. Pp. 137–156 in From Clovis to Comanchero: Archeological Overview of the Southern Great Plains. Jack L. Hofman et al., eds. *Arkansas Archeological Survey Research Series* 35. Fayetteville.

Owsley, Douglas W., Murray K. Marks, and Mary H. Manhein
1989 Human Skeletal Samples in the Southern Great Plains. Pp. 111–122 in From Clovis to Comanchero: Archeological Overview of the Southern Great Plains. Jack L. Hofman et al., eds. *Arkansas Archeological Survey Research Series* 35. Fayetteville.

Palkovich, Ann M.
1978 A Model of the Dimensions of Mortality and Its Application to Paleodemography. (Unpublished Ph.D. Dissertation in Anthropology, Northwestern University, Evanston, Illinois.)

1981 Demography and Disease Patterns in a protohistoric Plains Group: A Study of the Mobridge Site (39WW1). *Plains Anthropologist. Memoir* 17:71–84.

Pillaert, E. Elizabeth
1963 The McLemore Site of the Washita River Focus. *Bulletin of the Oklahoma Anthropological Society* 11:1–114.

Ramenofsky, Ann F.
1982 The Archaeology of Population Collapse: Native American Response to the Introduction of Infectious Disease. (Unpublished Ph.D. Dissertation. Anthropology, University of Washington. Seattle.)

1987 Vectors of Death: The Archaeology of European Contact. Albuquerque: University of New Mexico Press.

Stearn, Esther W., and Allen E. Stearn
1945 The Effect of Smallpox on the Destiny of the Amerindian. Boston: B. Humphries.

Taylor, John F.
1989 Counting: The Utility of Historic Population Estimates in the Northwestern Plains, 1800–1880. *Plains Anthropologist. Memoir* 23:17–30.

Tiffany, J. A., S. J. Schermer, J. L. Theler, D. W. Owsley, D. C. Anderson, E. A. Bettis, III, and D. M. Thompson
1988 The Hanging Valley Site (13HR28): A Stratified Woodland Burial Locale in Western Iowa. *Plains Anthropologist* 33(120):219–259.

Trimble, Michael K.
1979 An Ethnohistorical Interpretation of the Spread of Smallpox in the Northern Plains Utilizing Concepts of Disease Ecology. Lincoln: National Park Service, Midwest Archeological Center.

1989 Infectious Disease and the Northern Plains horticulturalists: A Human Behavioral Model. *Plains Anthropologist Memoir* 23:41–59.

Vehik, Susan C.
1989 Problems and Potential in Plains Indian Demography. *Plains Anthropologist Memoir* 23:115–125.

Will, George F., and George E. Hyde
1917 Corn Among the Indians of the Upper Missouri. St. Louis, Mo.: William Harvey Miner.

Williams, John A.
1989 Health Profiles of Archaic and Woodland Populations from the Northern Plains. In the Symposium Skeletal Biology in the Great Plains: A Multidisciplinary View. Washington: Smithsonian Institution.

Wood, W. Raymond
    1980   Plains Trade in Prehistoric and Protohistoric In-
            tertribal Relations. Pp. 98–109 in Anthropology of
            the Great Plains. W. R. Wood and M. P. Liberty,
            eds. Lincoln: University of Nebraska Press.

Wood, W. R., and T. D. Thiessen, eds.
    1985   Early Fur Trade on the Northern Plains: Canadian
            Traders Among the Mandan and Hidatsa Indians,
            1738–1818. Norman: University of Oklahoma
            Press.

8

Diet and Disease in Late Prehistory

JANE E. BUIKSTRA

The third moon is that of the Small Corn. This moon is often impatiently looked for, their crop of large corn never sufficing to nourish them from harvest to another. (Du Pratz 1972:320)

At the time of contact, maize undoubtedly represented *the* cultivated indigenous plant of the Americas. Variant in size and color, maize was a storable resource that could be prepared in numerous ways—eaten green, parched, popped, ground, boiled, roasted, or even brewed to make beer. Important to daily cuisine, maize also assumed prominence in the ritual life of many Indian peoples. Throughout the Americas, reports of travelers and explorers provide ample evidence for the centrality of this valuable plant.

Unquestionably maize was of central dietary importance throughout the Americas; however, the variability of dependence upon maize through time and region represents an important factor in interpreting variability in nutrition and morbidity. A new, precise technique for estimating the centrality of maize in ancient diets (van der Merwe 1978; van der Merwe and Vogel 1978; Vogel and van der Merwe 1977) is able to determine differences in locality with greater accuracy. Certain tropical grasses, including maize, fix carbon through the C_4 photosynthetic pathway, known as Hatch-Slack, which contrasts with the C_3 or Calvin pathway common to most temperate climate plants. As a result, maize presents $^{13}C/^{12}C$ ratios that are somewhat higher or "heavier" than its less xeric counterparts. This distinction is passed along to consumers and thus leaves a diagnostic $^{13}C/^{12}C$ signature in their tissues. Conventionally expressed as parts per mil (‰) in relationship to the Pee Dee Belemnite standard, $\delta^{13}C$ values derived through the analysis of ancient remains document the amount of carbon derived ultimately from C_4 plants. $\delta^{13}C$ values for the collagen extracted from human bone, for example, are expected to range from -21.5 to -7.5 parts per mil (Chisolm 1989:34). Individuals who have consumed no C_4 plants should present $\delta^{13}C$ values that cluster around -21.5 parts per mil. The influence of C_4-derived carbon will lead to more positive (less negative) values.

Given the fundamental significance of maize throughout the Americas at the time of contact, it is important to determine the degree to which maize intensification may have influenced conditions conducive to depopulation in the face of new, imported pathogens. However attractive maize may have been in terms of storability and yield, early ethnohistoric sources suggest that in some regions maize stores may not have been adequate for supporting populations throughout the annual cycle. Discussions of seasonal inadequacies, frequently associated with disease, are deeply embedded within the calendrics of the ancient Andean region (Poma de Ayala 1944), and they are cited in a 1774 North American account (Du Pratz 1972:320). Although such observations necessarily come from historic sources, the nature of this documentation suggests that similar patterns may be sought in earlier times.

Extreme dependence upon maize can lead to nutritional deficiencies. A sixteenth-century Peruvian writer said that "maize sickness" was among the diseases against which the Inca ordered a ritual attack each spring (Poma de Ayala 1944:253). Though the other conditions cited in the same passage appear metaphorical or at least ambiguous in identity, it is tempting to link the maize sickness or "sara oncuy" to a nutritional disease such as pellagra. Certainly, the poor quality of maize protein, deficient in lysine and tryptophan, has been implicated in health problems wherever maize-dependence is intense (Food and Agriculture Organization 1953).

Within recent history, extremes of maize dependence have been reached in Guatemala, where corn has been reported to furnish 80 percent of the calories and 70 percent of the protein (Flores and García 1960; Bressani, Elías, and Brenes 1972). Health is fragile in these situations; among the most severely compromised are the very young, the elderly, and the pregnant (Scrimshaw and Suskind 1959; Scrimshaw 1964).

After corn was introduced to Europe from the Americas via the Iberian peninsula, maize-induced pellagra proved such a scourge that during the eighteenth century laws were enacted in France to limit the use of this "poor man's cereal" and to encourage instead the consumption of "wheaten bread" (Food and Agriculture Organization 1953). Both historic documents and contemporary surveys illustrate the potential for human groups to suffer poor nutrition and disease as a result of imperfect adaptation to this remarkably versatile and productive resource.

METHOD OF RESEARCH

Relative dependence upon plant and animal resources can be determined by examining $\delta^{13}C$ values for collagen and hydroxyapatite separately (Krueger 1985; Krueger and Sullivan 1984). This argument rests upon the notion that under the influence of lipid-rich proteins, the apatite of carnivores will be isotopically closer to the $\delta^{13}C$ signal of collagen than is the case in herbivores. In herbivores, apatite is fractionated by approximately 12 parts per mil, rather than the $5\%_{00}$ that is characteristic of collagen. Expected C_{13} values for herbivore gelatin, therefore, range between $-14.5\%_{00}$ and $-0.5\%_{00}$. In carnivores, the additional fractionation is only about $3\%_{00}$, with apatite end points thus becoming $-18.5\%_{00}$ and $-4.5\%_{00}$. Thus, the degree of protein enrichment in the diet of omnivores may be estimated by a comparison of the apatite and collagen (gelatin) signals. This strategy has been used by Ericson et al. (1989), Conard (1988), and Krueger (1985).

A factor that complicates interpretation of $\delta^{13}C$ values is the fact that marine resources are 13C enriched, thus paralleling the effect of terrestrial Hatch-Slack pathway plants. Under certain conditions, the effect of terrestrial C_4 plants and marine resources can be decoupled through the investigation of nitrogen isotope ratios ($^{15}N/^{14}N$). Bivariate plots of the $\delta^{13}C$ and $\delta^{15}N$ are widely used as a means of investigating maize contributions to diets that may also include a marine component (Chisolm, Nelson, and Schwarcz 1982, 1983; Ericson et al. 1989; Hayden, Chisolm, and Schwarcz 1987; Schoeninger and DeNiro 1984; Schoeninger, DeNiro, and Tauber 1983; Sealy and van der Merwe 1985; Tauber 1979, 1981; White and Schwarcz 1989). Unfortunately, nitrogen fractionation patterns are less completely understood than those for carbon, and they appear unpredictable in arid environments (Schoeninger 1989; Sillen, Sealy, and van der Merwe 1989; Aufderheide et al. 1988). Given the interior location of the study region, the impact of marine resources can be assumed to be negligible.

A complication of potential importance is the fact that some of the carbon in prehistoric human bones may reflect the consumption of flesh derived from maize-eating herbivores or omnivores such as bison, dog, deer, turkey, bear, beaver, raccoon, woodchuck, and goose (Bumsted 1983; Burleigh and Brothwell 1978; Bender, Baerreis, and Steventon 1981; Conard 1988, Katzenberg 1988a, 1988b; Schoeninger 1989). Of these, the dog consistently shows evidence of C_4 enrichment, whether remains are derived from millennia-old sites in Peru and Ecuador (Burleigh and Brothwell 1978), a fourteenth to fifteenth-century site from South Dakota (Bumsted 1984), or an early historic period site in midcontinental North America (Katzenberg 1988a, 1988b). For example, five domestic dog samples from the historic period Kelley Cambell site, located in southern Ontario, are as C_{13} enriched as human remains from the contemporary Ossossané ossuary in western Ontario (Katzenberg 1988b). Samples from the Crow Creek site, South Dakota, also bracket human values, with a range between -10.5 ‰ and -13.3‰ (Bumsted 1983).

Several other potential animal resources ranging from bears and raccoons to geese and turkeys show little evidence of maize consumption. Conard (1988), basing his interpretations upon $\delta^{13}C$ values from bone apatite as well as collagen derived from materials recovered from the prehistoric Fort Ancient Incinerator site, reports a moderate level of maize consumption for 6 of 10 turkeys sampled in his study. Two of four raccoons and the only squirrel sampled also present slight C_{13} enrichment, with the raccoon $\delta^{13}C$ values for gelatin averaging -17.6‰ and that for the squirrel being a -19.3‰. Similarly, Bumsted (1983:98) reports $\delta^{13}C$ values from -18.1 to 19.7‰ for deer and antelope samples from Middle Missouri river sites. Only a single turkey bone (-19.4‰), among a larger Mississippian sample that included one duck and four deer samples, provides any indication of enrichment in Bender, Baerreis, and Steventon's (1981) analysis.

Schoeninger (1989) estimates that the appropriate $\delta^{13}C$ value for bison meat from the Pecos Pueblo site would have been -13.2‰, based upon a bone value of -17.2‰. This indirect source of C_{13} enrichment figures significantly in the reconstructed diet for the Pecos people, whose $\delta^{13}C$ values average -7.9‰. Such indirect enrichment due to reliance upon bison is also suggested in Lovell, Nelson, and Schwarcz's (1986) study of "bison hunters" from the Gray site in southwestern Saskatchewan, whose dates range from about 3550 to 1500 B.C. The average $\delta^{13}C$ value for 50 remains from the Gray site, which clearly predates the development of local maize agriculture, is -17.5 +/-0.3‰. Significant enrichment of hu-

man tissues, on the order of 4‰, due to the consumption of enriched bison meat has apparently occurred in this skeletal series. Bumsted's $\delta^{13}C$ value for bison is -15.7‰, which would suggest considerable enrichment potential for humans, if Schoeninger's model is followed.

For the purposes of this investigation, given evidence from the studies of Conard (1988) and Katzenberg (1988a, 1988b), negligible C13 enrichment through consumption of animal tissues will be assumed.

MIDCONTINENTAL $\delta^{13}C$ VALUES

As can be seen from the distribution in figure 1, Archaic period skeletal series present averages that cluster around -21.0‰, which is the anticipated value for gelatin containing carbon ultimately derived from C_3 plants. Even though the late portion of this period saw the initial stages of food production based upon indigenous flora, there is no indication that C_4 species were consumed in any quantity. Among the plants subject to early efforts in cultivation are two forms of gourd (*Cucurbita pepo, Lagenaria siceraria*), sumpweed (*Iva annua*), sunflower (*Helianthus annuus*), and chenopods (*Chenopodium berlandieri*) (Asch and Asch 1985; Fritz 1988a; King 1985; Smith and Cowan 1987; Smith 1987; Yarnell 1978).

As indicated in figure 2, similar $\delta^{13}C$ values characterize most of the sites dating to the next millennium, a period that witnessed the cultivation of additional indigenous seed-bearing plants, including maygrass (*Phalaris caroliniana*), knotweed (*Polygonum erectum*), and a little barley (*Hordeum pusillum*). Amaranth species also assumed economic importance during this period. Of the indigenous species common to the prehistoric midcontinent, only amaranths are thought to be C_4 and thus likely to mimic the effects of maize consumption (Buikstra et al. 1988; Schwarcz et al. 1985). In general, the remains of amaranths are less conspicuous in midwestern archeological sites than other weedy grains (Asch and Asch 1985; Cowan 1985; Fritz 1988a; Smith 1987; Watson 1985). However, the consumption of amaranths may be responsible for minor shifts in $\delta^{13}C$ values, such as the -19.4 δ ‰ average for three specimens from the Vine Valley site from central New York state. Although, based upon end-

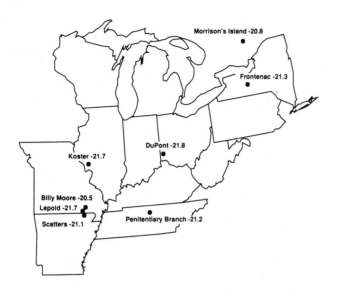

Fig. 1. δ^{13}C values for sites with dates prior to 1000 B.C.

Fig. 2. δ^{13}C values for sites with dates from 1000 B.C. to A.D. 1.

points of −20 and −7, Vogel and van der Merwe (1977:241) argue that there was no C_4 contribution to the diet of Vine Valley site inhabitants, it is now reasonable to infer slight C_4 enrichment. The use of marine resources could, of course, also be reflected in this value, although the site's midstate location and cultural affinities with Ohio Adena (Ritchie 1952:201, 204) would argue against this explanation.

Figure 3 illustrates δ^{13}C values for sites dating

A.D. 1–400. Minor C_4 contributions to the diet of Middle Woodland peoples is indicated for the Donaldson Cemetery 1 and 2 remains from Ontario, which average −19.1‰ (n = 6), and those for the Outlet site in Wisconsin, which average −19.2 (n = 3). In the first case, Schwarcz et al. (1985) suggest that their results are due to the consumption of C_4 plants other than maize, such as amaranth. Baerries and Bender (1984), however, attribute the enrichment evident at the Outlet site to maize consump-

Fig. 3. δ¹³C values for sites A.D. 1–400.

Fig. 3. $\delta^{13}C$ values for sites A.D. 1–400.

Fig. 4. $\delta^{13}C$ values for sites A.D. 400–800.

tion. Given that a few maize kernels dating to the second century A.D. have been recovered from the Edwin Harness (Ford 1987) and Icehouse Bottom (Chapman and Crites 1987) sites, it clearly *is* possible that enrichment due to maize consumption could account for the relatively minor positive shifts in $\delta^{13}C$ values noted here. Even so, it is unlikely that maize was a conspicuous part of the diet for Hopewell peoples from the midcontinent.

Among sites dating between A.D. 400 and 800

(fig. 4) only one presents a $\delta^{13}C$ more positive than those for Middle Woodland series. The value of $-17.2‰$ for the Missionary Island No. 4 site suggests maize dependence beyond that for earlier groups.

A shift in maize consumption patterns is clear in the few documented sites for the period A.D. 800–1000, as illustrated in figure 5. Ohio sites appear more enriched than those to the south and west. Although the estimation of dietary percent-

Fig. 5. $\delta^{13}C$ values for sites A.D. 800–1000.

Fig. 6. $\delta^{13}C$ values for sites A.D. 1000–1150.

ages involves a number of assumptions, the most positive $\delta^{13}C$ value here, $-12.4\%_{00}$, suggests that approximately 50 percent of the dietary carbon originated in C_4 plants. (The technique is that of Schwarcz et al. 1985.)

Sites dating to the period A.D. 1000–1150 (fig. 6) present a range of $\delta^{13}C$ values. Enrichment patterns clearly vary by region, with the Mound Bottom Early Mississippian site from Tennessee presenting the most enriched figure of $-9.3\%_{00}$. In

general, it appears that within a given area, Late Woodland sites present less enriched values than their Mississippian counterparts. Cahokia appears somewhat anomalous in this regard, suggesting that more maize was being consumed in the local Mississippian farmstead communities of production than at the regional center. It should also be noted that the values for Cahokia are derived from remains recovered from Mound 72, in which there is good evidence for status-based dietary distinctions.

Fig. 7. $\delta^{13}C$ values for sites A.D. 1150–1250.

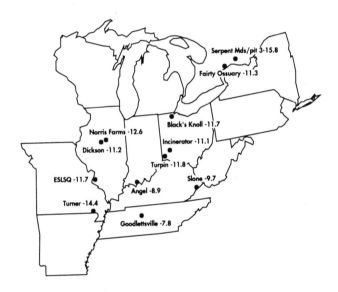

Fig. 8. $\delta^{13}C$ values for sites A.D. 1250–1350.

Individuals who apparently controlled significant resources at the time of death, such as the individual buried on a beaded cape in association with retainers and caches of artifacts, present $\delta^{13}C$ values of $-17.2\%_{00}$ while the remains of females who are thought to represent sacrificial victims show values of $-14.1\%_{00}$, suggesting that the economic and ritual importance of maize did not extend to daily cuisine for persons of high rank (Buikstra, Milner, and Rose 1989).

Evidence of increased maize dependence is obvious in figure 7, which provides $\delta^{13}C$ values for sites dating to the period A.D. 1150–1250. Mississippian, Monongahela, and early Iroquois sites from Ontario are represented here. Figures vary within and between regions, with the $\delta^{13}C$ values for the Mississippian Arnold site being the most enriched at $-7.8\%_{00}$. Mississippian sites from Missouri and Wisconsin present less evidence of maize dependence than those from Illinois.

Fig. 9. δ¹³C values for sites A.D. 1350–1500.

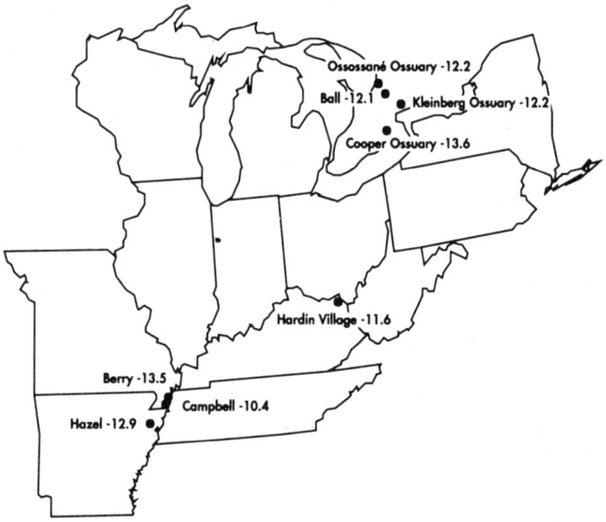

Fig. 10. δ¹³C values for sites with dates A.D. 1500–1650.

More uniform dependence upon maize is indicated for the period A.D. 1250–1350 (fig. 8), although the Missouri and Serpent Mounds values are less positive outlyers. δ¹³C values for this series comprise the most positive cluster for any of the sequences considered thus far, with an average δ¹³C value of −11.5, approximately 1 ppm more positive than the average for the previous century.

The few values for the A.D. 1350–1500 period (fig. 9) indicate a continued high level of maize dependence, with a δ¹³C average of −11.6, which appears to decrease slightly during early historic times (fig. 10). Data points are relatively few for this period. The combined δ¹³C averages for these sites is −12.3‰, more nearly comparable to Middle Mississippian values than those for protohistoric Fort Ancient and Monongahela sites.

Unfortunately, δ¹³C values are available only for two more recent historic period series, including samples from a late eighteenth-century historic

Indian—possibly Ottawa—cemetery where figures of -19.4 and $-19.9\%_{00}$ suggest rather minor dependence upon maize (Bender, Baerreis, and Steventon 1981). By contrast, a late nineteenth century Euro-American Missouri cemetery (Lynott et al. 1986) presents a value of $-13.3\%_{00}$, suggesting a pattern more comparable to pre-Columbian Native Americans.

Among contemporary North Americans, $\delta^{13}C$ values of $-16.5\%_{00}$ are more positive than a European average of $-19.6\%_{00}$ (Bumsted 1983). It is likely that indirect enrichment due to corn-fed beef, along with the use of corn oils and related products, explains the contrastive patterns presented by contemporary Europeans and Americans.

REGIONAL SEQUENCES

A further perspective can be gained by examining local sequences for of $\delta^{13}C$ values, for example, the central Mississippi Valley (Lynott et al. 1986; Rose, Marks, and Tieszen 1990), west-central Illinois (Buikstra et al. 1988; Buikstra, Milner, and Rose 1989), western Ontario (Schwarcz et al. 1985), and the Nashville basin of Tennessee (Buikstra et al. 1988). These present the best combination of regional and temporal coverage for series that also have data available concerning health status. It

should be noted that temporal sequences reported for the western Lake Erie region (Stothers and Bechtel 1987) present values so close to those for western Ontario that only the Ontario has been figured here (fig. 11). The values have been averaged within temporal units in order to simplify the graphs.

This comparison suggests that maize intensification was more rapid and extreme in the Nashville basin than in the other study areas. In other areas the shift in subsistence is relatively gradual and peaks somewhat later, during the very late prehistoric period. In these examples $\delta^{13}C$ values indicate that perhaps as much as 50 percent of the carbon was ultimately derived from C_4 plants (Schwarcz et al. 1985). This clearly contrasts with the Nashville basin example, where the Mississippian tradition and maize agriculture appear together, with $\delta^{13}C$ values in excess of $-8\%_{00}$, which suggests that perhaps as much as 75 percent of the carbon recovered from bone collagen originated in C_4 plants (Decker and Tieszen 1989).

In this context it is of interest to compare these diachronic patterns with those for the Southwest, where maize appears substantially earlier and became a dominant resource during the first millennium A.D. (Berry 1985; Decker and Tieszen 1989). The $\delta^{13}C$ values for the Nashville basin approach those reported for the Southwest, primarily the

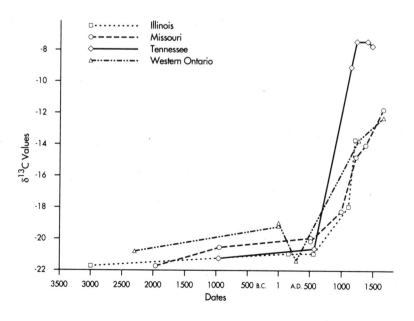

Fig. 11. $\delta^{13}C$ values for selected series from Illinois, Missouri, Tennessee, and Western Ontario.

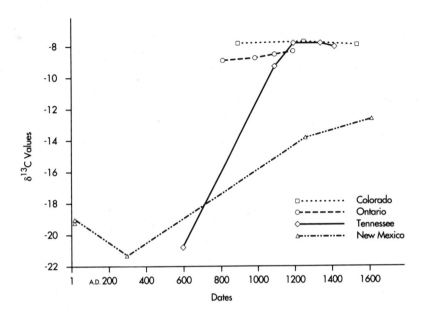

Fig. 12. $\delta^{13}C$ values for selected series from Colorado, New Mexico, Tennessee, and western Ontario.

Four Corners area (Decker and Tieszen 1989; Katzenberg and Kelley 1988; Schoeninger 1989). The figures for Tennessee are approximately 0.5 to 1.0‰ less positive than those for their western contemporaries (fig. 12). According to the dietary translation developed by Decker and Tieszen, this would indicate approximately 5 to 10 percent less dietary dependence upon C_4 sources. In both cases, maize doubtless assumed a dominant dietary role.

Such estimates of dietary dependence are potentially affected by variation in $\delta^{13}C$ signals from C_4 plants. It is possible that the Northern Flint corn of Fort Ancient and perhaps the Late Mississippian peoples of the Nashville basin, apparently a relatively local phenomenon (Fritz 1988b), was a resource that systematically presented enriched $\delta^{13}C$ values (Buikstra et al. 1988; Schwarcz et al. 1985; Wagner 1988), although systematic tests of intraspecies variability in maize are incomplete. Enrichment at the base of the food web would, of course, affect bone collagen values of consumers.

The rapid and relatively extreme intensification of maize agriculture suggested here for the Nashville basin would be compatible with a model proposed by Wagner (1988) for Fort Ancient peoples of Ohio. Basing her interpretation upon paleobotanical evidence, she argues for a "single general introduction of seed" for 8–10 row Northern Flint corn into the Ohio Valley region.

DIET AND HEALTH

What then of long-term trends in health for these regions? In general, the changes noted for the Central Mississippi drainage, west-central Illinois, and western Ontario appear to occur early in the sequence of agricultural intensification when maize dependence is not so extreme.

For west-central Illinois, Cook (1984) has investigated a variety of indicators of health status, including juvenile stature attainment per dental age, porotic hyperostosis, adult stature, cortical bone maintenance, Harris Line frequencies, and age-specific mortality patterns. Increased numbers of deaths during the weaning period, lower rates of stature attainment per dental age, decreased adult stature, and relatively thin long bone cortices all paint a relatively somber picture of juvenile health status during the terminal Late Woodland period when maize agriculture began. During Mississippian times, when maize consumption was at its highest regional levels, there are fewer indications of compromised health, with the exception of a tuberculosis-like pathology. Effective population density is more likely a primary causal factor than diet in explaining the presence of this disease, although its frequency and severity may certainly be affected by nutritional status. Increased prevalence of linear enamel hypoplasias and elevated rates of cribra orbitalia among young infants during Mississippian times is argued to result from the presence of this new infectious disease rather than being attributed to nutritional causes (Cook 1984; Knick 1981).

Farther north along the Illinois river valley, the poor health of Mississippian agriculturalists is compared to the Late Woodland peoples who buried at Dickson Mounds, Illinois (Goodman et al. 1984; Goodman and Armelagos 1985; Lallo 1973; Lallo, Armelagos, and Rose 1978; Lallo, Rose, and Armelagos 1980; Rose, Armelagos, and Lallo 1978). It appears that the severe ill health of the agriculturalists, including elevated rates of porotic hyperostosis, osteoarthritis, infectious lesions, bone fractures, and developmental dental defects, postdates maize intensification and is most likely associated with social and political factors that influence both nutritional adequacy and disease load (Buikstra, Milner, and Rose 1989; Goodman and Armelagos 1985).

Katzenberg's (1988b) investigation of temporally sequential skeletal series from western Ontario provides results that parallel Cook's (1984) inference that health was most severely compromised during the time of transition to maize rather than during the period of highest maize dependence. Based upon specific and nonspecific infection, as well as mortality patterns, Katzenberg infers that individuals buried at the fourteenth-century Fairty Ossuary, Ontario, lived less well and long than early historic period individuals from the same region. Katzenberg's inferences concerning demographic patterning parallel those of Jackes (1986).

Studies of adult remains from diachronic sequences of sites distributed along the lower and central Mississippi valleys implicate population density rather than maize dependence as the key variable associated with the development of infectious pathology (Rose, Marks, and Tieszen 1990). During Late Mississippian times frequencies (66%) for the Central Valley approach those of the most severely affected Fort Ancient populations to the east. Low levels of porotic hyperostosis are reported for populations after maize is introduced; however, the absence of juvenile remains in this sample precludes meaningful analysis. The seeming low frequency of porotic hyperostosis in adults could result from either a true overall low age-specific frequency or high mortality among anemic juveniles.

Unfortunately, the region presenting the contrastive sequence of $\delta^{13}C$ values, the Nashville basin, has the least information available concerning health status. Of the middle Tennessee skeletal series references here, the most intensively studied is that from the Averbuch sites, where analysis has focused upon the rather spectacular evidence for ill health (Buikstra et al. 1988; Eisenberg 1986; Kelley and Eisenberg 1987). High infant mortality and low adult survivorship coupled with striking evidence for infectious pathology and anemia are characteristic of the Averbuch population. Healed and active periostitis and osteomyelitis of the long bones, tuberculosis-like pathology, and cribra orbitalia among juveniles and young adults are conspicuous in the sample (Eisenberg 1986).

It is difficult to fill out the chronological sequence of health-related changes predating the obvious pathology at Averbuch. Although adequate for isotopic work, the other series reported here are, in general, relatively small or poorly preserved. Periosteal remodeling has been observed among the adults at the Early Mississippian Mound Bottom site, while both cribra orbitalia and significant amounts of periostitis have been observed in adults from the Woodland Mansker Creek site in central Tennessee (Buikstra et al. 1988).

The demographic profile for Averbuch requires special comment. The probability of dying pattern is similar to that for the Crow Creek massacre site (Buikstra and Konigsberg 1985), suggesting that it, too, may reflect one or more catastrophic events. While palisades and evidence of burning provide compelling evidence of warfare among Late Mississippian peoples of the Nashville basin (Autry 1983; Klippel and Bass 1984), it is also possible that the Averbuch community may have suffered the impact of epidemics. Such late pre-Columbian events would have, of course, rendered these populations particularly vulnerable to stresses after the time of contact.

In sum, there are two contrasting patterns of maize intensification for the midcontinent, as viewed from the perspective of bone chemistry. In regions such as the Central Mississippi valley and western Ontario, subsistence strategies changed gradually, ultimately reaching a moderate level of maize dependence. Evidence for nutritional stress is noted relatively early, during the time of experimentation with the new crop, rather than in later phases of adaptation. A more subtle and indirect, yet significant impact of maize intensification noted in these areas is the encouragement of increased population densities that, in turn, provide a suitable environment for the development and maintenance of new diseases such as the tuberculosis-like pathology widespread through eastern North America during late prehistory.

Within the Ohio valley and Nashville basin, maize intensification appears to have taken a different course, proceeding rapidly to marked dependency within a few generations. Here there is evidence for severe ill health, perhaps approaching epidemic proportions. While such inferences are speculative, it is clear that compromised health status among late prehistoric peoples is a significant factor in understanding post-Columbian depopulation.

REFERENCES

Asch, D. L., and N. B. Asch
  1985   Prehistoric Plant Cultivation in West-Central Illinois. Pp. 149–203 in Prehistoric Food Production in North America. R. I. Ford, ed. *University of Michigan, Museum of Anthropology, Anthropological Papers* 75. Ann Arbor.

Aufderheide, A. C., L. L. Tieszen, M. J. Allison, J. Wallgren, and G. Rapp, Jr.
  1988   Chemical Reconstruction of Components in Complex Diets: A Pilot Study. Pp. 301–306 in Diet and Subsistence: Current Archaeological Perspectives. B. V. Kennedy and G. M. LeMoine, eds. (Proceedings of the Nineteenth Annual Conference of the Archaeological Association of the University of Calgary, Alberta.)

Autry, W. O.
  1983   Sociopolitical Dimensions of the Mississippian System in the Cumberland River Valley of Middle Tennessee and Western Kentucky: An Analysis of Mortuary Patterns and Skeletal Remains from Mound Bottom, Tennessee. (Report on file, F. H. McClung Museum, University of Tennessee, Knoxville.)

Baerreis, D. A., and M. M. Bender
  1984   The Outlet Site (47 DA 3): Some Dating Problems and a Reevaluation of the Presence of Corn in the Diet of Middle and Late Woodland Peoples in Wisconsin. *Midcontinental Journal of Archaeology* 9(2):143–154.

Bender, M. M., D. A. Baerreis, and R. L. Steventon
  1981   Further Light on Carbon Isotopes and Hopewell Agriculture. *American Antiquity* 46:346–353.

Berry, M. S.
  1985   The Age of Maize in the Greater Southwest: A Critical Review. Pp. 279–307 in Prehistoric Food Production in North America. R. I. Ford, ed. *University of Michigan, Museum of Anthropology, Anthropological Papers* 75. Ann Arbor.

Bressani, R., L. G. Elías, and R. A. Gómez Brenes
  1972   Improvement of Protein Quality by Amino Acid and Protein Supplementation. Pp. 465–540 in Protein and Amino Acid Functions. E. J. Bigwood, ed. New York: Pergamon Press.

Broida, M. O.
  1983   Maize in Kentucky Fort Ancient Diets: And Analysis of Carbon Isotope Ratios in Human Bone. (Unpublished M.A. Thesis in Anthropology, University of Kentucky, Lexington.)

Buikstra, J. E., W. Autry, E. Breitburg, L. Eisenberg, and N. van der Merwe
  1988   Diet and Health in the Nashville Basin: Human Adaptation and Maize Agriculture in Middle Tennessee. Pp. 243–259 in Diet and Subsistence: Current Archaeological Perspectives. B. V. Kennedy and G. M. LeMoine, eds. Calgary, Canada: Proceedings of the Chacmool Conference.

Buikstra, J. E., J. Bullington, D. K. Charles, S. Frankenberg, L. Konigsberg, J. B. Lambert, and L. Xue
  1987   Diet, Demography, and the Development of Horticulture. In Emergent Horticultural Economies of the Eastern Woodlands. W. Keegan, ed. Carbondale: Southern Illinois University, *Occasional Paper of the Center for Archaeological Investigations.*

Buikstra, J. E., and D. C. Cook
  1981   Pre-Columbian Tuberculosis in West-Central Illinois: Prehistoric Disease in Biocultural Perspective. Pp. 115–139 in Prehistoric Tuberculosis in the Americas. J. E. Buikstra, ed. *Northwestern University Archeological Program, Scientific Papers* 5.

Buikstra, J. E., and L. Konigsberg
  1985   Paleodemography: Critiques and Controversies. *American Anthropologist* 87:316–333.

Buikstra, J. E., G. R. Milner, and J. C. Rose
  1989   Archaeological and Isotopic Interpretations of the Central Mississippi Valley. (Paper presented at the Annual Meeting of the Society for American Archaeology, Atlanta.)

Bumsted, M. P.
  1983   Human Variation: $\delta^{13}C$ in Adult Bone Collagen and the Relation to Diet in an Isochronous C_4 (maize) Archaeological Population. Los Alamos, N. Mex.: Publication LA 10259T, Los Alamos National Laboratory.

Burleigh, R., and D. Brothwell
  1978   Studies on Amerindian Dogs. I: Carbon Isotopes in Relation to Maize in the Diet of Domestic Dogs from Early Peru and Ecuador. *Journal of Archaeological Science* 5:355–362.

Chapman, J., and G. D. Crites

1987   Evidence for Early Maize (*Zea mays*) from the Ice-house Bottom Site, Tennessee. *American Antiquity* 52:352–354.

Chisolm, B.

1989   Variation in Diet Reconstruction Based on Stable Carbon Isotopic Evidence. Pp. 10–37 in The Chemistry of Prehistoric Human Bone, T. D. Price, ed. Cambridge: Cambridge University Press.

Chisolm, B. S., D. E. Nelson, and H. P. Schwarcz

1982   Stable Isotope Ratios as a Measure of Marine Versus Terrestrial Protein in Ancient Diets. *Science* 216:1131–1132.

1983   Marine and Terrestrial Protein in Prehistoric Diets on the British Columbia Coast. *Current Anthropology* 24(3):396–398.

Conard, A. R.

1988   Analysis in Dietary Reconstruction. Pp. 112–156 in A History of 17 Years of Excavation and Reconstruction: A Chronicle of 12th Century Human Values. J. M. Heilman, M. C. Lileas, and C. Turnbow, eds. Dayton, Ohio: Museum of Natural History.

Cook, D. C.

1984   Subsistence and Health in the Lower Illinois Valley: Osteological Evidence. Pp. 235–269 in Paleopathology at the Origins of Agriculture. M. N. Cohen and G. J. Armelagos, eds. New York: Academic Press.

Cowan, C. W.

1985   Understanding the Evolution of Plant Husbandry in Eastern North America: Lessons from Botany, Ethnography, and Archaeology. Pp. 205–243 in Prehistoric Food Production in North America, R. I. Ford, ed. *University of Michigan, Museum of Anthropology, Anthropological Papers* 75. Ann Arbor.

Decker, K. W., and L. L. Tieszen

1989   Isotopic Reconstruction of Mesa Verde Diet from Basketmaker III to Pueblo III. (Paper presented at the Plains Conference, Oklahoma City.)

DuPratz, M. LePage

1972   The History of Louisiana. Baton Rouge: Claitor's Publishing Division.

Eisenberg, L. E.

1986   Adaptation in a "Marginal" Mississippian Population from Middle Tennessee: Biocultural Insights from Paleopathology. (Unpublished Ph.D. Dissertation, New York University, New York City.)

Ericson, J. E., M. West, C. H. Sullivan, and H. W. Krueger

1989   The Development of Maize Agriculture in the Viru Valley, Peru. Pp. 68–104 in The Chemistry of Prehistoric Human Bone. T. D. Price, ed. Cambridge: Cambridge University Press.

Farrow, D. C.

1986   A Study of Monongahela Subsistence Patterns Based on Mass Spectrometric Analysis. *Midcontinental Journal of Archaeology* 11:153–179.

Flores, M., and B. García

1960   The Nutritional Status of Children of Pre-School Age in the Guatemalan Community of Amatitlán: 1. Comparison of Family and Child Diets. *British Journal of Nutrition* 14:207–215.

Food and Agriculture Organization

1953   Maize and Maize Diets: A Nutritional Survey. *The Food and Agriculture Organization of the United Nations, FAO Nutritional Studies* 9, Rome.

Ford, R. I.

1987   Dating Early Maize in the Eastern United States. (Paper presented at the Annual Meeting of the American Association for the Advancement of Science, Chicago, 14–18 February.)

Fritz, G. J.

1988a   Early and Middle Woodland Period Paleoethnobotany. (Paper presented at the Annual Meeting of the Southeastern Archaeological Conference.)

1988b   "Newer," "Better" Maize and the Mississippian Emergence: A Critique of Prime Mover Explanations. (Paper presented at the 46th International Congress of Americanists, Amsterdam.)

Goodman, A. H., and G. J. Armelagos

1985   Disease and Death at Dr. Dickson's Mounds. *Natural History* 94:12–18.

Goodman, A. H., J. Lallo, G. J. Armelagos, and J. C. Rose

1984   Health Changes at Dickson Mounds, Illinois (A.D. 950–1300). Pp. 271–305 in Paleopathology at the Origins of Agriculture. M. N. Cohen and G. J. Armelagos, eds. New York: Academic Press.

Hayden, B., B. S. Chisolm, and H. P. Schwarcz

1987   Fishing and Foraging: Marine Resources in the Upper Paleolithic of France. In Regional Perspectives on the Pleistocene Prehistory of the Old World. O. Soffer, ed. [New York: Plenum.]

Jackes, M.

1986   The Mortality of Ontario Archaeological Populations. *Canadian Journal of Anthropology* 5:33–48.

Katzenberg, M. A.

1988a   Stable Isotope Analysis of Animal Bone and the Reconstruction of Human Paleodiet. Pp. 307–314 in Diet and Subsistence: Current Archaeological Perspective. B. V. Kennedy and G. M. LeMoine, eds. (Proceedings of the Nineteenth Annual Conference of the Archaeological Association of the University of Calgary, Calgary, Alberta.)

1988b   Changing Diet and Health in Pre- and Proto-historic Ontario. (Paper presented at the Annual

Meeting of the American Anthropological Association, Phoenix.)

Katzenberg, M. A., and J. H. Kelley
1988   Stable Isotope Analysis of Prehistoric Bone from the Sierra Blanca Region of New Mexico. (Paper presented at the Mogollon Conference, Las Cruces, New Mexico.)

Kelley, M. A., and L. E. Eisenberg
1987   Blastomycosis and Tuberculosis in Early American Indians: A Biocultural View. *Midcontinental Journal of Archaeology* 12:89–116.

King, F. B.
1985   Early Cultivated Cucurbits in Eastern North America. Pp. 73–97 in Prehistoric Food Production in North America. R. I. Ford, ed. *University of Michigan, Museum of Anthropology, Anthropological Papers 75*. Ann Arbor.

Klippel, W. E., and W. M. Bass, eds.
1984   Averbuch: A Late Mississippian Manifestation in the Nashville Basin, 2 vols. (Report submitted to the National Park Service. Department of Anthropology, University of Tennessee, Nashville.)

Knick, S. G.
1981   Linear Enamel Hypoplasia and Tuberculosis in Pre-Columbian North America. *Ossa* 8:131–138.

Krueger, H. W.
1985   Models for Carbon and Nitrogen Isotopes in Bone. (Poster Paper presented at Biomineralization Conference, Airlie House, Warrenton, Va.)

Krueger, H. W., and C. H. Sullivan
1984   Models for Carbon Isotope Fractionation Between Diet and Bone. Pp. 205–220 in Stable Isotopes in Nutrition. J. R. Turnland and P. E. Johnson, eds. *American Chemical Society Symposium Series*, Vol. 258.

Lallo, J.
1973   The Skeletal Biology of Three Prehistoric American Indian Societies from Dickson Mounds. (Unpublished Ph.D. Dissertation, University of Massachusetts, Boston.)

Lallo, J., G. J. Armelagos, and J. C. Rose
1978   Paleoepidemiology of Infectious Disease in the Dickson Mounds Population. *Medical College of Virginia Quarterly* 14:17–23.

Lallo, John W., Jerome C. Rose, and George J. Armelagos
1980   An Ecological Interpretation of Variation in Mortality within Three Prehistoric American Indian Populations from Dickson Mounds. Pp. 203–238 in Early Native Americans: Prehistoric Demography, Economy, and Technology. D. Browman, ed. (*World Anthropology Series*.) The Hague: Mouton Press.

Lovell, N. C., D. E. Nelson, and H. P. Schwarcz
1986   Carbon Isotope Ratios in Paleodiet: Lack of Age or Sex Effects. *Archaeometry* 28:51–55.

Lynott, M. J., T. W. Boutton, J. E. Price, and D. E. Nelson
1986   Stable Carbon Isotopic Evidence for Maize Agriculture in Southeast Missouri and Northeast Arkansas. *American Antiquity* 51:51–65.

Penman, J. T.
1985   Late Woodland Sites in Southwestern Grant County, Wisconsin. *Journal of the Iowa Archeological Society* 32:1–36.

Poma de Ayala, Guaman
1944   Primer nueva coronica y buen Gobierno. La Paz: Instituto "Tihuanacu" de Antropología, Etnografía y Prehistoria.

Reed, D. M., and J. G. Brashler
1988   Health and Status in the Late Prehistoric—the Eastern Fort Ancient Periphery. (Paper presented at the Annual Meeting of the Society for American Archaeology, Phoenix.)

Ritchie, W. A.
1952   The Archaeology of New York State. Rev. ed. Garden City, NY: Published for the American Museum of Natural History by the Natural History Press.

Rose, J. C., G. J. Armelagos, and J. W. Lallo
1978   Histological Enamel Indicators of Childhood Stress in Prehistoric Skeletal Samples. *American Journal of Physical Anthropology* 49:511–516.

Rose, J. C., M. K. Marks, and L. L. Tieszen
1990   Bioarcheology and Subsistence in the Central and Lower Portions of the Mississippi Valley. In What Mean These Bones? The Dynamic Integration of Physical Anthropology and Archaeology in the Southwest. M. L. Powell, A. M. Mires, and P. Bridges, eds. Athens: University of Georgia Press.

Schoeninger, M. J.
1989   Reconstructing Prehistoric Human Diet. Pp. 38–67 in The Chemistry of Prehistoric Human Bone. T. D. Price, ed. Cambridge: Cambridge University Press.

Schoeninger, M. J., and M. J. DeNiro
1984   Nitrogen and Carbon Isotopic Composition of Bone Collagen in Terrestrial and Marine Vertebrates. *Geochimica et Cosmochimica Acta* 48:625–639.

Schoeninger, M. J., M. J. DeNiro, and H. Tauber
1983 $^{15}N/^{14}N$ Ratios of Bone Collagen Reflect Marine and Terrestrial Components of Prehistoric Human Diet. *Science* 220:1381–1383.

Schurr, M. R.
1989   The Relationship Between Mortuary Treatment and Diet at the Angel Site. (Unpublished Ph.D. Dissertation in Anthropology, Indiana University, Bloomington.)

Schwarcz, H. P., J. Melbye, M. A. Katzenberg, and M. Knyf
1985   Stable Isotopes in Human Skeletons of Southern

Ontario: Reconstructing Paleodiet. *Journal of Archaeological Science* 12:187–206.

Scrimshaw, N. S.
1964   Ecological Factors in Nutritional Disease. *American Journal of Clinical Nutrition* 14:112–122.

Scrimshaw, N. S., and R. M. Suskind
1959   Interactions of Nutrition and Infection. *American Journal of Medical Science* 237:367–403.

Sealy, J. C., and N. J. van der Merwe
1985   Isotope Assessment of Holocene Human Diets in the Southwestern Cape, South Africa. *Nature* 315:138–140.

Sillen, A., J. C. Sealy, and N. J. van der Merwe
1989   Chemistry and Paleodietary Research: No More Easy Answers. *American Antiquity* 54(3):504–512.

Smith, B. D.
1987   The Independent Domestication of Indigenous Seed-bearing Plants in Eastern North America. Pp. 3–47 in Emergent Horticultural Economies of the Eastern Woodlands. W. F. Keegan, ed. *Southern Illinois University. Center for Archaeological Investigations, Occasional Paper 7*. Carbondale.

Smith, B. D., and C. W. Cowan
1987   Domesticated *Chinopodium* in Prehistoric Eastern North America: New Accelerator Dates from Eastern Kentucky. *American Antiquity* 355–357.

Stothers, D. M., and S. K. Bechtel
1987   Stable Carbon Isotope Analysis: An Interregional Perspective. *Archaeology of Eastern North America* 15:137–154.

Tauber, H.
1979   C-14 Activity of Arctic Marine Mammals. In Radiocarbon Dating. R. Berger and H. E. Suess, eds. Berkeley: University of California Press.

1981   δ¹³C Evidence for Dietary Habits of Prehistoric Man in Denmark. *Nature* 292:332–333.

Van der Merwe, N. J.
1978   Carbon 12 vs. Carbon 13. *Early Man* 2:11–13.

1982   Carbon Isotopes, Photosynthesis, and Archaeology. *American Scientist* 70:596–606.

Van der Merwe, N. J., and J. C. Vogel
1978   13C Content of Human Collagen as a Measure of Prehistoric Diet in Woodland North America. *Nature* 276:815–816.

Vogel, J. C., and N. J. Van der Merwe
1977   Isotopic Evidence for Early Maize Cultivation in New York State. *American Antiquity* 42:238–242.

Wagner, G. E.
1988   Agricultural Adaptations to Marginal Areas of the Upper Midwest. (Paper presented at the Annual Meeting of the Society for American Archaeology, Phoenix.)

Watson, P. J.
1985   The Impact of Early Horticulture in the Upland Drainages of the Midwest and Midsouth. Pp. 99–147 in Prehistoric Food Production in North America. R. I. Ford, ed. *University of Michigan, Museum of Anthropology, Anthropological Papers 75*. Ann Arbor.

White, C. D., and H. P. Schwarcz
1989   Ancient Maya Diet: As Inferred from Isotopic and Elemental Analysis of Human Bone. *Journal of Archaeological Science* 16:451–474.

Yarnell, R. A.
1978   Domestication of Sunflower and Sumpweed in Eastern North America. Pp. 289–299 in The Nature and Status of Ethnobotany. R. I. Ford, ed. *Anthropological Papers, Museum of Anthropology, University of Michigan 67*. Ann Arbor.

9

Disease and Sociopolitical Systems in Late Prehistoric Illinois

GEORGE R. MILNER

The cultural and demographic transformations set in motion by the collision between Old and New World peoples were played out upon a complex mosaic of Native American cultures known principally through archeological studies. Ongoing research in two parts of Illinois highlights several issues pertinent to studies of postcontact eastern North America: the scale of sociopolitical systems, population density and distribution, the nature of intergroup interactions, and differential disease experience.

Riverine settings in late prehistoric Illinois encompassed many societies that varied greatly in size and organizational complexity. One of the most complex of the pre-Columbian societies north of Mexico was located in the part of the Mississippi River valley near present-day East Saint Louis, Illinois, that is known as the American Bottom. Mississippian period (A.D. 1000–1400) American Bottom society was hierarchically organized, and cemeteries for the elite social stratum were differentiated by burial location, form, and content from those associated with the subordinate stratum (Milner 1984). Skeletons from two nonelite cemeteries have been examined: the Moorehead phase (A.D. 1150–1250) Kane Mounds and the Sand Prairie phase (A.D. 1250–1400) East Saint Louis Stone Quarry sites (Milner 1982, 1983). Both burial areas postdate the Stirling phase (A.D. 1050–1150) peak of Mississippian development in this region.

The central Illinois River valley was a much different social setting. Two skeletal series have been studied: the Dickson Mounds (Goodman et al. 1984) and the Norris Farms #36 (Milner and Smith 1990) collections. The Norris Farms cemetery, an Oneota site dating to about A.D. 1300, is emphasized here because the people who used this burial area belonged to a much smaller scale society than their American Bottom Mississippian counterparts. The better-known Dickson Mounds remains, which span the tenth to fourteenth centuries, are from a series of superimposed mounds having Late Woodland or Mississippian affiliations. The Dickson Mounds results serve as a baseline guide against which other eastern North American skeletal series are evaluated, and they are a critical part of the commonly cited conclusion that prehistoric agriculturalists were generally not so healthy as their hunting and gathering predecessors (Cohen 1989; Goodman et al. 1984). All the late prehistoric Illinois societies discussed here practiced horticulture coupled with gathering, hunting, and fishing (Johannessen 1984; Kelly and Cross 1984; Styles and King 1990).

THE SOCIETIES

American Bottom

Relatively complex forms of sociopolitical organization, typically called chiefdoms and identified archeologically as Mississippian cultures, were present in the Southeast for several hundred years prior to European contact (Smith 1986; Steponaitis 1986). Many of these cultures extended into the protohistoric period and were described in Spanish and French chronicles.

The American Bottom Mississippian society is frequently portrayed as populous, highly organized, and tightly controlled. This interpretation is based largely on Fowler's (1974, 1978) influential separation of settlements into four distinct levels of functionally differentiated and often strategically placed settlements, as well as the supposedly huge population at the paramount site (Gregg 1975). Cahokia, with over 100 mounds and other examples of monumental architecture accompanied by extensive habitation areas, was clearly the premier mound center. The second and third tiers of sites consisted of habitation areas with either multiple or single mounds. Sites conforming to the bottommost level in the settlement hierarchy lacked mounds. Population estimates for Cahokia vary widely but are typically in the low tens of thousands, ranging up to 43,000 for the Stirling phase peak in occupation (Gregg 1975). When the occupants of affiliated sites, including other mound centers, are added to this figure, the society-wide population total reaches unknown, but enormous, proportions.

Although the Cahokia-area cultural system was arguably the most organizationally complex and populous of the Mississippian societies, it is unlikely to have been as highly elaborated, tightly integrated, or as heavily populated as commonly thought. Among the several problems with the existing model is the troublesome fact that the American Bottom mound centers had different occupational histories. Quite simply, the duration and timing of significant periods of occupation varied from one site to another (Milner 1990). Furthermore, the significance of the number of mounds at the second and third tier sites is not understood.

Multimound sites were not necessarily ranked above single-mound centers, except for Cahokia, which greatly exceeded any other site in terms of its size, the amount and dimensions of monumental architecture, and the complexity of its internal structure. Archeological investigations at the second and third tier mound centers have yet to yield evidence indicating that these sites conformed to two discrete nodes in a settlement hierarchy. It is likely that the size and number of mounds, which were often associated with elite-related activities, are better indicators of phenomena such as a center's longevity in a dynamic social landscape than they are reflections of a site's position in a static, longlasting hierarchy of functionally differentiated settlements.

An alternative, comparatively decentralized sociopolitical model was proposed for Cahokia that is more consistent with available archeological data and the organizational characteristics of middle-range societies (Milner 1990). The Cahokia cultural system was probably formed of allied but structurally similar, politically quasiautonomous, and economically self-sufficient territories featuring their own locally important mound centers. For a number of generations, Cahokia dominated the other mound-center-based territories of the region, which for the most part were distributed linearly along the river valley. Throughout this period the regional system remained highly segmented, both spatially and socially. Ties forged among members of leading lineages at the various mound centers presumably formed the basis of regional integration, but most daily interactions were undoubtedly locally oriented, especially for the vast majority of the population at the base of the social hierarchy.

Key members of the elite social stratum at each mound center exercised some degree of control over people who lived in the principal sites as well as in outlying settlements, which consisted of widely separated single-family residences occupied by members of the subordinate social stratum (Milner et al. 1984). Interspersed among these farmsteads were a few feature complexes with distinctive buildings, such as sweatlodges, associated with community-integrating activities. These arrays of features collectively comprised a series of low-density occupation communities.

Population figures in the tens of thousands for Cahokia are also exaggerated. Populations of this magnitude in a settlement measuring about 13 square kilometers imply a high degree of food production capability and bulk commodity transportation efficiency. Assuming that the habitation features in large-scale excavations at outlying sites are representative of floodplain occupation (Milner 1986), then there were simply not enough people around Cahokia to support an enormous population at the paramount site. For example, many excavations in a 15-kilometer-long segment of floodplain south of Cahokia indicate that the population in this part of the valley probably numbered in the low thousands (Milner 1986). Furthermore, a rather generalized, hoe-based horticultural technology, widely dispersed outlying farmsteads, and diverse plant and animal assemblages from both large and small sites do not indicate a marked intensification of food production strategies oriented toward the generation of enormous surpluses.

While commonly cited population estimates for the Cahokia site are too high, the sheer number of habitation sites indicates that the region as a whole was heavily occupied when compared to other parts of the midcontinent. People focused on the river bottoms, but floodplain population density varied over time, reaching its peak in the Stirling phase at Cahokia (Gregg 1975) and outlying communities (Milner 1986). A redistribution of people within the main valley and nearby drainages appears to have contributed to the initial increase in American Bottom population size, and it is probably responsible for the late Mississippian reduction in the occupation of the river bottoms (Milner 1986, 1990; Woods 1986:72; Woods and Holley 1990).

Illinois River Valley

Available information on the distribution of distinctive pottery assemblages and major sites indicates that resource-rich river valleys in Illinois were not occupied to the same extent, and gaps existed between population concentrations. For example, multiple town-and-mound centers are found near Cahokia and in the central Illinois River valley, but not in between (Fowler 1974, 1978; Harn 1978).

In the central Illinois River valley, two cultural traditions, Mississippian and Oneota, were contemporaneous with the American Bottom Mississippian culture. The Dickson Mounds Mississippian society, while hierarchically structured, was much smaller, more areally restricted, and less organizationally complex than its American Bottom counterpart (Harn 1975, 1978, 1980). Norris Farms is one of several sites representing an expansion into the river valley of a distinctive variant of the upper midwestern Oneota cultural tradition (Esarey 1986; Esarey and Santure 1990; Harn 1980:82–83; Smith 1951). The people buried in this cemetery were members of a smaller scale society than that of their Dickson Mounds Mississippian predecessors. The Oneota and Mississippian contrast is especially marked when the Norris Farms group is compared with the American Bottom populations, even those drawn from Cahokia's passage to obscurity.

The Oneota community was part of a social landscape that differed considerably from that of the American Bottom. The cemetery and nearby habitation features represent one of the few Oneota sites in the central Illinois River valley. Regional population estimates are not available, although archeological work since the 1930s indicates that this part of the valley was sparsely occupied when the cemetery was in use, at least in comparison to the American Bottom (Cole and Deuel 1937; Harn 1980). Nevertheless, occupation of this region was risky because of warfare.

The Norris Farms skeletal remains provide the first clear view of the nature and intensity of prehistoric warfare in Illinois. Forty-three (16%) of 264 skeletons from widely distributed graves display damage from trauma, mutilation, and scavengers that, taken together, indicate violent death. Injuries included unhealed fractures resulting in splintered bone and projectile points embedded in various skeletal elements (N = 21). Individuals were scalped (N = 14), crania were removed (N = 11), and postcranial elements were deeply cut (N = 8). Tooth impressions from scavenging carnivores occur on many skeletons in patterns consistent with modern forensic cases (N = 30) (Haglund, Reay, and Swindler 1988; Milner and Smith 1989). Conflict-related mortality, although high, is to some extent underestimated because all such deaths presumably did not result in distinctive bone damage.

The extent of skeletal disarticulation and carnivore damage indicate that some bodies were found soon after death, whereas others were exposed for long periods of time. Marked differences in the condition of skeletons most likely reflect the victims' positions relative to their settlement and, hence, the chances of prompt discovery.

Mostly adults (>15 years) were killed (N = 41). The violent deaths represent 35 percent and 29 percent of all the adult males (N = 52) and females

(N = 62), respectively, for whom a sex could be determined from cranial or pelvic morphology. About half the adult victims (42%) were afflicted by debilitating conditions at time of death, including active infections of bone, rib fractures with new callus formation, markedly deformed femoral heads, or dislocated joints.

The combined osteological and archeological evidence points to chronic intergroup conflict in which vulnerable individuals or small groups of people were killed, often when they were some distance from the protection afforded by their village. This pattern of warfare commonly occurs in ethnographically known tribal-scale societies, although its intensity varies greatly over time and space (Chagnon 1983, 1988; Divale and Harris 1976; Heider 1970; Service 1971:104). It is also consistent with ethnohistorical accounts for eastern North America (Anderson 1987; Hickerson 1970; Sagard 1939:152; Swanton 1946:686–701; Thwaites 1896–1901, 4:199, 10:95, 13:37). Intergroup antagonisms can escalate into chronic hostilities featuring indiscriminate, opportunistic, and retaliatory violence resulting in many deaths. The Norris Farms mortality figures are remarkable because the proportions of males and females who died violently are approximately equal, instead of being heavily weighted toward males (Divale and Harris 1976; Chagnon 1983:79, 1988; Heider 1970:128).

Warfare involving the Norris Farms community was part of a broader regional phenomenon of unknown temporal duration, as indicated by skeletons from nearby sites (Morse 1978: pls. 5, 6; Neumann 1940). Evidence for violent death is spotty throughout the midcontinent, as expected from ethnographically known societies. For example, conflict-related deaths in the American Bottom appear to have been unusual during the Mississippian period, particularly when compared with the central Illinois River valley evidence for warfare.

EVIDENCE OF DISEASE

The disease experience of late prehistoric populations varied throughout eastern North America, but broad patterns are difficult to identify, let alone explain (Buikstra et al. 1987, 1988; Milner 1982; Powell 1988; Rose et al. 1984). In the best of circumstances, comparisons of skeletal collections indicate where a particular prehistoric sample falls along a low to high lesion-frequency continuum.

Many of the Norris Farms skeletons display lesions of the orbits and cranial vault known as cribra orbitalia and porotic hyperostosis, respectively. The lesions have a similar gross appearance, and they occur in the same parts of the skull. These particular skeletal conditions are typically attributed to anemia, usually iron-deficiency anemia in pre-Columbian skeletons from the Americas (El-Najjar et al. 1976; Mensforth et al. 1978; Ortner and Putschar 1985:251–263; Palkovich 1987; Steinbock 1976:213–252; Stuart-Macadam 1985, 1987). However, the identification of the principal determinants of stress is problematic in prehistoric settings because specific deficiencies are frequently only part of a broader pattern of nutritional inadequacy often compounded or precipitated by infection or the presence of intestinal parasites.

The Norris Farm cribra orbitalia and porotic hyperostosis lesion frequencies are high in comparison with other sizable skeletal series. For example, the lesions in an active or, more typically, remodeled state appear on 45 percent (N = 170) of the Norris Farms sample, exceeding figures for the American Bottom Kane Mounds (7%, N = 68) and East Saint Louis Stone Quarry (25%, N = 24) samples. (These specimens include at least one orbit and much of the cranial vault; sample sizes here and below indicate all observable specimens.)

Lesion patterning across age groups is more informative than summary figures. However, rigorous comparisons of the Norris Farms and American Bottom collections are prohibited by the small sizes of the latter and the different age compositions of the samples. Lesion frequency figures are available for juveniles from Dickson Mounds. The percentage of affected juveniles (<15 years) from three sequential Dickson Mounds samples increases from the earliest "Late Woodland" group (14%, N = 44) to the later "Mississippian Acculturated Late Woodland" (31%, N = 93) and "Middle Mississippian" (52%, N = 101) groups (Goodman et al. 1984:289–290). Many more Norris Farms juvenile skeletons (81%, N = 75) have the lesions than their Dickson Mounds counterparts. The proportion of affected adults in the Norris Farms collection (16%, N = 95) is the same as it is in the East Saint Louis Stone Quarry sample (16%, N = 19), although it is larger than the figure for the other American Bottom site (Kane Mounds, 4%, N = 55).

Bone proliferation is the most common form of skeletal response attributable to infectious disease in the Illinois collections. This manifestation of presumably diverse pathological conditions is identified as periostitis or osteomyelitis, depending on lesion severity and the parts of the bone affected. The irregular apposition of reactive bone resulted in the elevation of bone surfaces and, in extreme cases, a distortion of the normal shapes of skeletal elements. The exterior surfaces of affected elements range from the coarse, woven bone characteristic of an active lesion to the smooth, irregularly undulating appearance of well-remodeled pathological bone. Broken bones occasionally reveal thickened, visibly porous cortices along with coarse, disorganized trabeculae filling much or all of the medullary cavity. Small resorptive foci occur occasionally in bones featuring a predominately proliferative pathological bony involvement.

Identifying the etiological bases of pathological bony involvement in prehistoric skeletons is, at best, difficult. Consequently, pathological responses of bone are often grouped together for comparative purposes as a broad category of lesions that have similar gross characteristics but undoubtedly dissimilar causes. In the Illinois samples, most of the proliferative forms of pathological bony involvement presumably resulted from infections, some of which were restricted to single elements whereas others were widely disseminated throughout the body. Some localized pathological foci might have been sequelae to trauma.

Over half (61%, N = 184) the Norris Farms skeletons had predominately proliferative forms of pathological skeletal involvement in either an active or remodeled state. Somewhat fewer of the juveniles (0.5–15 years) were affected than the adults (51%, N = 78 and 68%, N = 106, respectively) (these figures exclude the rib periostitis discussed below). The proportion of affected Norris Farms adults is over two times the corresponding American Bottom figures. Unfortunately, these figures are not directly comparable because the Norris Farms skeletons are better preserved than their American Bottom counterparts. Yet the frequency figure discrepancy remains when only tibiae, the most commonly and severely affected bones, are compared, although this does not completely eliminate difficulties with differential preservation. Of the adult tibiae, 45 percent (N = 220) of the Norris Farms specimens were affected, whereas corre-

sponding figures for the American Bottom samples are 26 percent (Kane Mounds, N = 145) and 29 percent (East St. Louis Stone Quarry, N = 63).

The Norris Farms results are similar to the periostitis and osteomyelitis figures Goodman et al. (1984:291–292) provide for the "Middle Mississippian" Dickson Mounds sample for juveniles (67%, N = 110), adults (68%, N = 111) and all skeletons (67%, N = 221). These figures are over twice as high as those reported for the combined "Late Woodland" and "Mississippian Acculturated Late Woodland" sample (juveniles, 27%, N = 125; adults, 33%, N = 226; all skeletons, 31%, N = 351).

At least some of the proliferative responses to infection in the postcranial skeleton must have been caused by a treponemal disease. The skeletal evidence for such a disease has been debated (Jones 1876), and osteologists are seeking to document the nature of the disease process and its spatial and temporal distribution (El-Najjar 1979; Hackett 1976; Ortner and Putschar 1985:180–218; Powell 1988; Steinbock 1976:86–169).

Lesions in 10 Norris Farms crania approximate patterns of pathological skeletal involvement characteristic of the treponematoses (Hackett 1976; Jaffe 1972:924–951; Ortner and Putschar 1985:180–218; Steinbock 1976:86–169). Six crania have one or more of the following alterations of the normal bony architecture of the nasal-palatal region that are consistent with treponemal gangosa: nasal regions are altered through bone destruction or abnormal remodeling at the piriform aperture; the small bones within the nasal cavity are partially or completely destroyed; and the frontal sinuses and hard palate are penetrated (fig. 1). Furthermore, seven Norris Farms crania, including three with the nasal-palatal involvement, have cranial vault lesions consistent with treponemal infections, but less severe than classic caries sicca. Variations in cranial vault lesion morphology reflects different phases of a bone necrosis and remodeling continuum. A similarly affected adult cranial vault fragment is present in the East Saint Louis Stone Quarry collection.

The existence of tuberculosis in the pre-Columbian Americas has been debated for many years (Buikstra 1981a). This possibility is supported by prehistoric South American mummified remains with characteristic soft tissue lesions (Allison, Mendoza, and Pezzia 1973; Allison et al. 1981) and North American skeletons with lesions resembling those of tuberculosis (Buikstra 1981b).

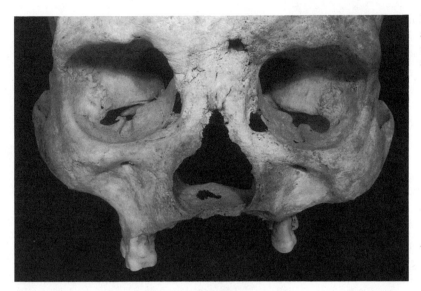

Fig. 1. Nasal-palatal lesion resembling those associated with the treponematoses. From Norris Farms #36 site, Ill. (Ill. State Museum, Springfield, catalog 821230).

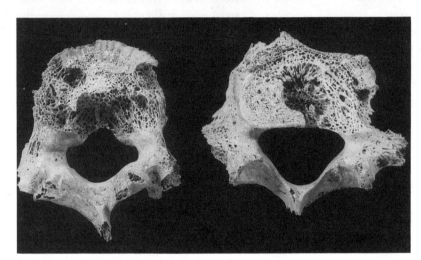

Fig. 2. Vertebral lesions resembling those associated with tuberculosis. From Norris Farms #36 site, Ill. (Ill. State Museum, Springfield, catalog 821246).

Lesions similar to those of skeletal tuberculosis occur in the Illinois samples. Because of superior bone preservation and a high disease load, the lesions are better represented in the Norris Farms than in the American Bottom collections. Osteolytic lesions resulting in the cavitation of presacral vertebral bodies, typically sparing arches, occur in four Norris Farms skeletons (fig. 2). In the most severely affected individual, the destruction of vertebral bodies led to the collapse and bony ankylosis of three lower thoracic vertebrae. Some of the osteolytic lesions with little or no perifocal reactive bone proliferation that occur in sacroiliac joints or the principal limb joints of several juvenile and adult skeletons might have had a similar origin. Le-

sions of the tubular bones of the hands and one foot of six children might represent the early onset of tuberculosis. Periostitis and, occasionally, small osteolytic foci on the internal surfaces of the ribs of 19 skeletons, mostly adults, resemble lesions associated with pulmonary tuberculosis in an autopsy sample (Kelley and Micozzi 1984). Only one skeleton with these forms of rib involvement had osteolytic lesions possibly attributable to tuberculosis elsewhere in the body. The two American Bottom collections include a few specimens with similar vertebral and sacroiliac lesions.

Secure diagnoses for individual specimens remain problematic (Buikstra 1976: Kelley and Eisenberg 1987; Ortner and Putschar 1985), but the late prehistoric people of Illinois were clearly affected by at least two chronic conditions that produced distinctive suites of bone lesions. The Norris Farms population, in particular, must have been characterized by poor health, and much of the population experienced some level of intermittent dysfunction. Debilitating conditions that interfered with strenuous labor associated with group maintenance activities would have reduced further this population's ability to cope with a stressful environment.

IMPLICATIONS FOR POPULATION
AND DISEASE ISSUES

Research in Illinois and elsewhere has identified hitherto undocumented, and often unsuspected, variations in late prehistoric social and demographic landscapes that complicate interpretations of the consequences of Native American contacts with Old World peoples. This work pertains to four aspects of debates about postcontact-era transformations in indigenous societies: estimates of the number of people, the likelihood of pathogen transmission among virgin-soil populations, the advisability of applying recorded mortality rates to different social settings, and community responses to the challenge of new infectious diseases.

Precontact Population

Authoritative estimates of the size of the precontact North American population, excluding much or all of Mexico, range from one million (Kroeber 1939:134) to 18 million (Dobyns 1983:42). These estimates reflect divergent interpretations of sketchy census material and the adjustments needed to project this information back into the precontact era.

The estimate of one million is undoubtedly too small, given evaluations of Mooney's (1928) use of ethnohistorical accounts that served as Kroeber's basic data (Thornton 1987:15–41; Ubelaker 1976a, 1976b, 1988) and revised interpretations of the timing and effects of introduced infectious diseases (Crosby 1972; Dobyns 1966, 1983; Milner 1980; Ramenofsky 1987; Smith 1987; Thornton 1987). Nevertheless, the second estimate is simply implausible. Questions have been raised about Dobyns's interpretation of equivocal ethnohistorical data (Henige 1986), and the high population estimate is predicated upon the frequent and uniform

spread of multiple epidemics throughout North America.

A narrowing of the unacceptably large discrepancy in population estimates will only be accomplished through archeological studies. The associated problems of sample availability and representativeness, chronological precision, and differential efficacy of various estimating methods mean that the derivation of estimates of absolute population size are highly susceptible to error. Nevertheless, these figures serve as a rough yardstick to ascertain whether population estimating procedures provide totals that fall within the realm of likelihood.

For example, in Dobyns's (1983:141, 199–200, 205) influential but controversial assessment of precontact population size, the sixteenth-century Timucua town of Ocali in Florida is said to have been occupied by 60,000 people. However, this town was certainly much smaller and less impressive than Cahokia, for which the maximum—highly unlikely—population estimate is 43,000.

Pandemics

Dobyns's (1983) North American population estimate rests largely on the assumption that newly introduced, high-mortality infectious diseases resulted in regularly occurring pandemics that affected people distributed widely throughout the Americas (cf. Snow and Lanphear 1988). In his reconstruction of the disease experience of the sixteenth and early seventeenth-century Timucuan Indians of Florida, Dobyns (1983:291) identifies no fewer than nine "decisive demographic events" that originated in the distant parts of the Americas that were then colonized and collectively resulted in the Florida population's reduction in little over 100 years to 5 percent of its precontact size.

The critical issue is not whether the Indians of eastern North America and elsewhere experienced devastating, culturally disruptive, disease-induced mortality. This certainly occurred, and newly introduced diseases often had pronounced cultural and demographic consequences before first direct European contact (Crosby 1972; Dobyns 1983; Milner 1980; Ramenofsky 1987; Thornton 1987; Smith 1987). The interpretations differ over the degree to which novel pathogens were regularly transmitted among populations distributed across large portions of the Americas. Quite simply, was the typical pattern one of a series of pandemics sweeping their way both frequently and uniformly through the vastness of North America largely unimpeded by discontinuities in demographic, social, biotic, and physical landscapes? Alternatively, did high-mortality diseases in North America, and in particular the Northeast and Southeast, typically spread irregularly beyond the initial point of introduction, resulting in a spatially erratic distribution of directly affected populations?

The archeological record for the late prehistoric period provides a basis for evaluating the pandemic issue. For example, it has long been recognized that Mississippian populations in the Southeast were not uniformly distributed, and interior populations were oriented toward highly productive riverine environments (Smith 1978). Settlement-oriented research using increasingly fine-grained temporal controls shows that there was considerable heterogeneity over time and space in social and demographic landscapes (Anderson 1987; Anderson, Hally, and Rudolph 1986; Milner 1990; Peebles 1986, 1987; Smith 1978, 1986; Smith 1987; Steponaitis 1986). Extensive, sparsely populated areas existed between often antagonistic Mississippian polities, and all similarly productive environments were not occupied to the same extent. The sixteenth-century Spaniards, for example, noted significant gaps in population distribution that frequently corresponded to disputed territories separating hostile polities with correspondingly limited opportunities for intergroup contact (Hudson, Smith, and DePratter 1984; Hudson et al. 1985; Smith 1987).

Heterogeneous social landscapes, especially discontinuities in the distribution of people as well as social and physical barriers to frequent interaction, would have influenced the magnitude, duration, and timing of postcontact depopulation, much of which occurred in the poorly understood protohistoric period. This is particularly true for the acute herd infections, including smallpox and measles, that are directly transmitted between human hosts. Differential disease experience among separate groups is expected of the opportunistic spread of communicable diseases among people who live in highly segmented social and geographical settings (Black 1966, 1975, 1980; Black et al. 1971). Furthermore, physiographic diversity in a region such as North America would have ensured the irregular distribution of animal reservoirs or vectors neces-

sary for introduced zoonoses. This would have limited the spread of new diseases that are indirectly transmitted to humans or where people serve as opportunistic hosts. Diverse and discontinuous social, demographic, biotic, and physical landscapes make it unlikely that infectious diseases, once introduced, resulted in pandemics that swept both frequently and uniformly throughout vast regions.

Societies and Diseases

Dobyns's (1983:248–295) extrapolation backward through time to reach an enormous Florida precontact population figure is predicated upon a series of sixteenth and early seventeenth-century reductions in Indian numbers, the magnitudes of which are based largely on ethnohistorical accounts of disease-induced mortality elsewhere in the then-colonized Americas. Although this is the only information available, the application of mortality figures to radically different social settings is problematic. Mortality estimates from one context are unlikely to be broadly applicable to other situations where the likelihood of pathogen transmission among susceptibles is quite different. Certainly population density and cultural complexity, which influence the nature and intensity of interindividual contacts, as well as environmental settings, including potential animal reservoirs and vectors, varied greatly across North America.

It is likely that introduced diseases in the Northeast and Southeast did not have the same effect on societies that differed in terms of social organization, population distribution, and density (Dobyns 1983:306–310; Ramenofsky 1987:175). The Southeast chiefdoms would have been highly susceptible to disintegration in the wake of high-mortality diseases (Smith 1987). Newly introduced, widely disseminated, and severe illnesses in virgin-soil populations tend to be associated with inadequate or inappropriate care of the sick, secondary infections, population demoralization, a breakdown in normal social relations, and, consequently, higher than usual mortality (Black et al. 1971; Neel 1970, 1979; Neel et al. 1970). Sudden, unprecedented, unexplained, uncontrollable, and devastating disease episodes would have undermined the hierarchical authority structures and intergroup relationships upon which chiefly polities are built. Furthermore, the nature of interindividual contact affects pathogen transmission among susceptible members of host populations. All other things being equal, the inhabitants of closely affiliated nucleated settlements, such as the often formally linked principal towns of Mississippian polities, would have been at higher risk than the members of less complex cultural systems consisting of small, widely dispersed, and less frequently interacting settlements. Even within Mississippian societies, the socially segmented and geographically localized nature of their populations would have impeded the uniform spread of pathogens that are transmitted directly from person to person.

The movement of diseases into the continental interior, assuming an erratic distribution, would have devastated some groups while leaving others, for a time, unaffected. Differential morbidity and mortality affecting group size, strength, and overall confidence must have been a significant factor contributing to new social relationships and population distributions among the volatile tribal to chiefdom-scale societies of eastern North America. The postcontact era was certainly a time of poorly known population movements coupled with the establishment of alliances and the coalescence of numerically diminished groups in order to remain as viable social entities and to bolster their strength in an increasingly threatening social arena (Brain 1988; Smith 1989).

Norris Farms is an especially clear example of how precontact intergroup antagonisms increased the risks affecting group survival. Conflict increased the likelihood of sudden, premature death for adults who were involved in a wide range of group maintenance activities. The threat of ambushes and raids appears to have played a part in producing hardship in this community, presumably by interfering with food acquisition practices. It is likely that intense intergroup conflict reduced the size of the area available for the procurement of edible resources, thereby diminishing the quantity and diversity of food that could be produced or collected and curtailing the acquisition of alternative but widely scattered resources in times of need. Intergroup hostilities also increase the risks associated with relying on stored foods that are susceptible to destruction by enemies. Finally, the synergism between nutritional inadequacy and infection affects host resistance to pathogens and the subsequent course of infectious diseases. High disease loads reduce further a population's ability to pursue strenuous subsistence-related tasks.

Disruptions in subsistence practices are certainly part of warfare in ethnographically known small-scale societies (Brookfield and Brown 1963: 79, 144; Heider 1970:106, 118–122, 311; Meggitt 1977:36, 94; Netting 1973, 1974). Interference with the consistently effective pursuit of subsistence activities and the need for sentinels, resulting in a diversion of people from direct participation in resource acquisition, also occurred during the historic period in the East (Hickerson 1970; Sagard 1939:155, 164; Swanton 1946:693; Thwaites 1896–1901, 5:93, 10:49–51, 25:107, 31:85, 33:81, 34: 197, 52:175). The disruptive potential of historic warfare in eastern North America that is recorded so vividly in early accounts was certainly aggravated by direct European influence. The precontact archeological record demonstrates that conflict resulting in significant mortality and hardship was not solely a function of competing Old World political and economic agendas.

Differential Response to Disease

Interpopulation differences in hard-tissue lesion frequencies, although quite apparent in the paleopathological literature, are difficult to interpret. Osteological collections tend to be small, sample sizes are typically reduced further by partitioning the skeletal series into biologically meaningful categories, and archeological remains are highly susceptible to sample composition biases. The transformation from lesion frequencies in a skeletal sample to the prevalence of a particular condition in a past population is by no means a straightforward process if the disease indicated by the lesions is associated with an increased risk of death (Wood et al. 1989).

Nevertheless, barring major unrecognized problems stemming from cultural, biological, or archeological biases, it can be stated that experience with disease varied to some extent among the late prehistoric peoples of Illinois. The determination of just how unhealthy some populations were relative to others is a much more problematic proposition. Taken as a whole, however, the available evidence indicates that the Norris Farms population suffered greatly from several diseases. Furthermore, the Illinois results, when coupled with other paleopathological research, have several important implications for studies of postcontact depopulation.

Contrary to romantic portrayals of North America as a disease-free paradise, at least some prehistoric populations experienced a considerable debilitating disease load. The frequently drawn contrast between the health of colonial period Europeans and Native Americans is useful and in many ways accurate, especially given the European cities with which early writers were familiar. Nevertheless, characterizations of the precontact Americas as "relatively disease-free" (Dobyns 1983:34) or "remarkably free of serious diseases" (Thornton 1987:39) should not be taken to mean that all such populations were rather healthy. Certainly some populations were more severely affected by infectious diseases and nutritional inadequacy than were others.

Existing levels of health would have affected host responses to life-threatening challenges posed by novel pathogens. In general, individuals who were already severely stressed by infections or poor nutrition might be expected to display lowered resistance to a new disease, have more complications, and be less likely to survive than more healthy members of the same age and sex cohort. Newly introduced pathogens must have posed the greatest risk to populations with an existing heavy disease load. Excessive mortality and morbidity would have further detrimental effects to the extent that necessary group-sustaining activities were disrupted. In sum, the prevalence of nutritional deficiencies and indigenous infections in populations facing more stressful conditions ultimately traceable to contact with Old World peoples and their novel pathogens must have contributed to differential group survival.

CONCLUSION

Protohistoric demographic collapse and cultural change must have been a complex process (Dobyns 1983; Milner 1980; Ramenofsky 1983; Smith 1987), although the nature and timing of Native American depopulation, cultural disintegration, displacement, and, finally, survival in altogether unprecedented settings is poorly understood. Nevertheless, it is likely that introduced diseases had a differential impact on the peoples of eastern North America. Key factors that undoubtedly affected this process include the frequency of direct contact with Europeans as well as the nature of existing social systems, population density and distribution, intergroup relations, cultural boundaries, and community health. These aspects of the protohistoric and early historic periods are potentially measurable, at least to some degree, in the archeological record.

REFERENCES

Allison, Marvin J., D. Mendoza, and A. Pezzia
  1973   Documentation of a Case of Tuberculosis in Pre-Columbian America. *American Review of Respiratory Diseases* 107:985–991.

Allison, Marvin J., Enrique Gerszten, Juan Munizaga, Calogero Santoro, and Daniel Mendoza
  1981   Tuberculosis in Pre-Columbian Andean Populations. Pp. 49–61 in Prehistoric Tuberculosis in the Americas. J. E. Buikstra, ed. *Northwestern University Archeological Program, Scientific Papers* 5. Evanston, Ill.

Anderson, David G.
  1987   Warfare and Mississippian Political Evolution in the Southeastern United States. (Paper presented at the 20th Annual Chacmool Conference, Calgary, Alberta.)

Anderson, David G., David J. Hally, and James L. Rudolph
  1986   The Mississippian Occupation of the Savannah River Valley. *Southeastern Archaeology* 5:32–51.

Black, Francis L.
  1966   Measles Endemicity in Insular Populations: Critical Community Size and Its Evolutionary Implication. *Journal of Theoretical Biology* 11:207–211.

  1975   Infectious Diseases in Primitive Societies. *Science* 187:515–518.

  1980   Modern Isolated Pre-Agricultural Populations as a Source of Information of Prehistoric Epidemic Patterns. Pp. 37–54 in Changing Disease Patterns and Human Behavior, N. F. Stanley and R. A. Joske, eds. New York: Academic Press.

Black, Francis L., W. Hierholzer, J. P. Woodall, and F. Pinhiero
  1971   Intensified Reactions to Measles Vaccine in Unexposed Populations of American Indians. *Journal of Infectious Diseases* 124:306–317.

Brain, Jeffrey P.
  1988   Tunica Archaeology. Papers of the Peabody Museum of Archaeology and Ethnology, Harvard University 78. Cambridge, Mass.

Brookfield, H. C., and Paula Brown
  1963   Struggle for Land. London: Oxford University Press.

Buikstra, Jane E.
  1976   The Caribou Eskimo: General and Specific Disease. *American Journal of Physical Anthropology* 45:351–368.

1981a   Introduction. Pp. 1–23 in Prehistoric Tuberculosis in the Americas. Jane E. Buikstra, ed. *Northwestern University Archeological Program, Scientific Papers* 5. Evanston, Ill.

———, ed.
1981b   Prehistoric Tuberculosis in the Americas. *Northwestern University Archaeological Program, Scientific Papers* 5. Evanston, Ill.

Buikstra, Jane E., William Autry, Emanuel Breitburg, Leslie Eisenberg, and Nikolaas van der Merwe
1988   Diet and Health in the Nashville Basin: Human Adaptation and Maize Agriculture in Middle Tennessee. Pp. 243–259 in Diet and Subsistence: Current Archaeological Perspectives. Brenda V. Kennedy and Genevieve M. LeMoine, eds. Proceedings of the 19th Annual Conference. University of Calgary Archaeological Association, Calgary, Alberta.

Buikstra, Jane E., Jill Bullington, Douglas K. Charles, Della C. Cook, Susan R. Frankenberg, Lyle W. Konigsberg, Joseph B. Lambert, and Liang Xue
1987   Diet, Demography, and the Development of Horticulture. Pp. 67–85 in Emergent Horticultural Economies of the Eastern Woodlands. William F. Keegan, ed. *Southern Illinois University Center for Archaeological Investigations, Occasional Paper* 7. Carbondale.

Chagnon, Napoleon A.
1983   Yanomamo: The Fierce People. 3d ed. New York: Holt, Rinehart and Winston.

1988   Life Histories, Blood Revenge, and Warfare in a Tribal Population. *Science* 239:985–992.

Cohen, Mark N.
1989   Health and the Rise of Civilization. New Haven, Conn.: Yale University Press.

Cole, Fay-Cooper, and Thorne Deuel
1937   Rediscovering Illinois. Chicago: University of Chicago Press.

Crosby, Alfred W.
1972   The Columbian Exchange: Biological and Cultural Consequences of 1492. Westport, Conn.: Greenwood Press.

Divale, William T. and Marvin Harris
1976   Population, Warfare, and the Male Supremacist Complex. *American Anthropologist* 78:521–538.

Dobyns, Henry F.
1966   Estimating Aboriginal American Population: An Appraisal of Techniques with a New Hemispheric Estimate. *Current Anthropology* 7:395–416.

1983   Their Number Become Thinned: Native American Population Dynamics in Eastern North America. Knoxville: University of Tennessee Press.

El-Najjar, Mahmoud Y.
1979   Human Treponematosis and Tuberculosis: Evidence from the New World. *American Journal of Physical Anthropology* 51:599–618.

El-Najjar, Mahmoud Y., Dennis J. Ryan, Christy G. Turner, and Betsy Lozoff
1976   The Etiology of Porotic Hyperostosis Among the Prehistoric and Historic Anasazi Indians of the Southwestern United States. *American Journal of Physical Anthropology* 44:477–488.

Esarey, Duane
1986   Protohistoric Oneota Material from the Clear Lake Site, Illinois. *Journal of the Iowa Archaeological Society* 33:75–82.

Esarey, Duane, and Sharron K. Santure
1990   The Morton Site Oneota Component and the Bold Counselor Phase. Pp. 162–166 in Archeological Investigations of the Morton Village and Norris Farms 36 Cemetery. *Illinois State Museum, Reports of Investigations* 45. Springfield.

Fowler, Melvin L.
1974   Cahokia: Ancient Capital of the Midwest. An Addison-Wesley Module in Anthropology 48:3–38.

1978   Cahokia and the American Bottom: Settlement Archeology. In Mississippian Settlement Patterns. Bruce D. Smith, ed. New York: Academic Press.

Goodman, Alan H., John Lallo, George J. Armelagos, and Jerome C. Rose
1984   Health Changes at Dickson Mounds, Illinois (A.D. 950–1300). Pp. 271–305 in Paleopathology at the Origins of Agriculture. Mark N. Cohen and George J. Armelagos, eds. Orlando, Fla.: Academic Press.

Gregg, Michael L.
1975   A Population Estimate for Cahokia. Pp. 126–136 in Perspectives in Cahokia Archaeology. *Illinois Archaeological Survey Bulletin* 10. Urbana.

Hackett, C. J.
1976   Diagnostic Criteria of Syphilis, Yaws, and Treponarid (Treponematoses) and of Some Other Diseases in Dry Bones. Berlin: Springer-Verlag.

Haglund, William D., Donald T. Reay, and Daris R. Swindler
1988   Tooth Mark Artifacts and Survival of Bones in Animal Scavenged Human Skeletons. *Journal of Forensic Sciences* 33:985–997.

Harn, Alan D.
1975   Cahokia and the Mississippian Emergence in the Spoon River Area of Illinois. *Transactions of the Illinois State Academy of Science* 68:414–434.

1978   Mississippian Settlement Patterns in the Central Illinois River Valley. Pp. 233–268 in Mississippian Settlement Papers. Bruce D. Smith, ed. New York: Academic Press.

1980   The Prehistory of Dickson Mounds: The Dickson Excavation. 2d ed. *Illinois State Museum, Reports of Investigations* 35. Springfield.

Heider, Karl G.
1970   The Dugum Dani: A Papuan Culture in the Highlands of West New Guinea. *Viking Fund Publications in Anthropology* 49. Chicago.

Henige, David
1986   Primary Source by Primary Source? On the Role of Epidemics in New World Depopulation. *Ethnohistory* 33:293–312.

Hickerson, Harold
1970   The Chippewa and Their Neighbors: A Study in Ethnohistory. New York: Holt, Rinehart and Winston.

Hudson, Charles, Marvin T. Smith, and Chester B. DePratter
1984   The Hernando de Soto Expedition: From Apalachee to Chiaha. *Southeastern Archaeology* 3:65–77.

Hudson, Charles, Marvin T. Smith, David Hally, Richard Polhemus, and Chester B. DePratter
1985   Coosa: A Chiefdom in the Sixteenth-century Southeastern United States. *American Antiquity* 50:723–737.

Jaffe, Henry L.
1972   Metabolic, Degenerative, and Inflammatory Diseases of Bones and Joints. Philadelphia: Lea and Febiger.

Johannessen, Sissel
1984   Paleoethnobotany. Pp. 197–214 in American Bottom Archaeology. Charles J. Bareis and James W. Porter, eds. Urbana: University of Illinois Press.

Jones, Joseph
1876   Explorations of the Aboriginal Remains of Tennessee. *Smithsonian Institution Contributions to Knowledge* 22. Washington.

Kelley, Marc A., and Leslie E. Eisenberg
1987   Blastomycosis and Tuberculosis in Early American Indians: A Biocultural View. *Midcontinental Journal of Archaeology* 12:89–116.

Kelley, Marc A., and Marc S. Micozzi
1984   Rib Lesions in Chronic Pulmonary Tuberculosis. *American Journal of Physical Anthropology* 65:381–386.

Kelly, Lucretia S., and Paula G. Cross
1984   Zooarchaeology. Pp. 215–232 in American Bottom Archaeology. Charles J. Bareis and James W. Porter, eds. Urbana: University of Illinois Press.

Kroeber, Alfred L.
1939   Cultural and Natural Areas of Native North America. *University of California Publications in American Archaeology and Ethnology* 38. Berkeley.

Meggitt, Mervyn
1977   Blood is Their Argument. Palo Alto, Calif.: Mayfield Publishing.

Mensforth, Robert P., C. Owen Lovejoy, John W. Lallo, and George J. Armelagos
1975   The Role of Constitutional Factors, Diet, and Infectious Disease in the Etiology of Porotic Hyperostosis and Periosteal Reaction in Prehistoric Infants and Children. *Medical Anthropology* 2:1–59.

Milner, George R.
1980   Epidemic Disease in the Postcontact Southeast: A Reappraisal. *Midcontinental Journal of Archaeology* 5:39–56.

1982   Measuring Prehistoric Levels of Health: A Study of Mississippian Period Skeletal Remains from the American Bottom, Illinois. (Unpublished Ph.D. Dissertation in Anthropology, Northwestern University, Evanston, Ill.)

1983   The East St. Louis Stone Quarry Site Cemetery. Urbana: University of Illinois Press.

1984   Social and Temporal Implications of Variation among American Bottom Mississippian Cemeteries. *American Antiquity* 49:468–488.

1986   Mississippian Period Population Density in a Segment of the Central Mississippi River Valley. *American Antiquity* 51:468–488.

1990   The Late Prehistoric Cahokia Cultural System of the Mississippi River Valley: Foundations, Florescence, and Fragmentation. *Journal of World Prehistory* 4:1–43.

Milner, George R., and Virginia G. Smith
1989   Carnivore Alteration of Human Bone from a Late Prehistoric Site in Illinois. *American Journal of Physical Anthropology* 79:43–49.

1990   Oneota Human Skeletal Remains. In Archeological Investigations at the Morton Village and Norris Farms 36 Cemetery. *Illinois State Museum, Reports of Investigations* 45:111–153. Springfield.

Milner, George R., Thomas E. Emerson, Mark W. Mehrer, Joyce A. Williams, and Duane Esarey
1984   Mississippian and Oneota Period. Pp. 158–186 in American Bottom Archaeology. Charles J. Bareis and James W. Porter, eds. Urbana: University of Illinois Press.

Mooney, James
1928   The Aboriginal Population of America North of Mexico. *Smithsonian Miscellaneous Collections* 80(7):1–40. Washington.

Morse, Dan
1978   Ancient Disease in the Midwest. 2d ed. *Illinois State Museum, Reports of Investigations* 15. Springfield.

Neel, James V.

1970 Lessons from a "Primitive" People. *Science* 170:815–822.

1979 Health and Disease in Unacculturated Amerindian Populations. Pp. 155–168 in *Health and Disease in Tribal Societies. (Ciba Foundation Symposium 49.)* Amsterdam: Excerpta Medica.

Neel, James V., Willard R. Centerwall, Napoleon A. Chagnon, and Helen L. Casey

1970 Notes on the Effect of Measles and Measles Vaccine in a Virgin-soil Population of South American Indians. *American Journal of Epidemiology* 91:418–429.

Netting, Robert McC.

1973 Fighting, Forest, and the Fly: Some Demographic Regulators Among the Kofyar. *Journal of Anthropological Research* 29:164–179.

1974 Kofyar Armed Conflict: Social Causes and Consequences. *Journal of Anthropological Research* 30:139–163.

Neumann, Georg K.

1940 Evidence for the Antiquity of Scalping from Central Illinois. *American Antiquity* 5:287–289.

Ortner, Donald J. and Walter G. J. Putschar

1985 Identification of Pathological Conditions in Human Skeletal Remains. Revised edition. *Smithsonian Institution Contributions to Anthropology* 28. Washington.

Palkovich, Ann M.

1987 Endemic Disease Patterns in Paleopathology: Porotic Hyperostosis. *American Journal of Physical Anthropology* 74:527–537.

Peebles, Christopher S.

1986 Paradise Lost, Strayed, and Stolen: Prehistoric Social Devolution in the Southeast. Pp. 24–40 in The Burden of Being Civilized. Miles Richardson and Malcolm C. Webb, eds. *Southern Anthropological Society Proceedings* 18. Athens: University of Georgia Press.

1987 The Rise and Fall of the Mississippian in Western Alabama: The Moundville and Summerville Phases, A.D. 1000 to 1600. *Mississippi Archaeology* 22:1–31.

Powell, Mary L.

1988 Status and Health in Prehistory: A Case Study of the Moundville Chiefdom. Washington: Smithsonian Institution Press.

Ramenofsky, Ann. F.

1987 Vectors of Death: The Archaeology of European Contact. Albuquerque: University of New Mexico Press.

Rose, Jerome C., Barbara A. Burnett, Mark W. Blaeuer, and Michael S. Nassaney

1984 Paleopathology and the Origins of Maize Agriculture in the Lower Mississippi Valley and Caddoan Culture Areas. Pp. 383–424 in Paleopathology at the Origins of Agriculture. Mark N. Cohen and George J. Armelagos, eds. New York: Academic Press.

Sagard, Gabriel

1939 The Long Journey to the Country of the Hurons [1632]. Reprinted. H. H. Langton, trans. George M. Wrong, ed. Toronto: The Champlain Society.

Service, Elman R.

1971 Primitive Social Organization. 2d ed. New York: Random House.

Smith, Bruce D.

1978 Variation in Mississippian Settlement Patterns. Pp. 479–503 in Mississippian Settlement Patterns. Bruce D. Smith, ed. New York: Academic Press.

1986 The Archaeology of the Southeastern United States: From Dalton to De Soto, 10,500–500 B.P. Pp. 1–92 in Advances in World Archaeology. Vol. 5. Fred Wendorf and Angela E. Close, eds. Academic Press, Orlando.

Smith, Hale G.

1951 The Crable Site, Fulton County, Illinois. *University of Michigan, Museum of Anthropology, Anthropology Papers* 7. Ann Arbor.

Smith, Marvin T.

1987 Archaeology of Aboriginal Culture Change in the Interior Southeast. *University of Florida, Ripley P. Bullen Monographs in Anthropology and History* 6. Gainesville.

1989 Aboriginal Population Movements in the Early Historic Period Interior Southeast. Pp. 21–34 in Powhatan's Mantle: Indians in the Colonial Southeast. Peter H. Wood, Gregory A. Waselkov, and M. Thomas Hatley, eds. Lincoln: University of Nebraska Press.

Snow, Dean R., and Kim M. Lanphear

1988 European Contact and Indian Depopulation in the Northeast: The Timing of the First Epidemics. *Ethnohistory* 35:15–33.

Steinbock, R. Ted

1976 Paleopathological Diagnosis and Interpretation: Bone Diseases in Ancient Human Populations. Springfield, Ill.: Charles C. Thomas.

Steponaitis, Vincas P.

1986 Prehistoric Archaeology in the Southeastern United States, 1970–1985. *Annual Review of Anthropology* 15:363–404.

Stuart-Macadam, Patty

1985 Porotic Hyperostosis: Representative of a Childhood Condition. *American Journal of Physical Anthropology* 66:391–398.

1987   Porotic Hyperostosis: New Evidence to Support the Anemia Theory. *American Journal of Physical Anthropology* 74:521–526.

Styles, Bonnie W., and Frances B. King
1990   Faunal and Floral Remains from the Bold Counselor Phase Village. Pp. 57–75 in Archaeological Investigations at the Morton Village and Norris Farms 36 Cemetery. *Illinois State Museum, Reports of Investigations* 45. Springfield.

Swanton, John R.
1946   The Indians of the Southeastern United States. *Bureau of American Ethnology Bulletin* 137. Washington.

Thornton, Russell
1987   American Indian Holocaust and Survival: A Population History Since 1492. Norman: University of Oklahoma Press.

Thwaites, Reuben G.
1896–   The Jesuit Relations and Allied Documents, 73
1901   vols. Cleveland: Burrows Brothers.

Ubelaker, Douglas H.
1976a   Prehistoric New World Population Size: Historical Review and Current Appraisal of North American

Estimates. *American Journal of Physical Anthropology* 45:661–665.

1976b   The Sources and Methodology for Mooney's Estimates of North American Indian Populations. Pp. 243–288 in The Native Population of the Americas in 1492. William M. Denevan, ed. Madison: University of Wisconsin Press.

1988   North American Indian Population Size, A.D. 1500 to 1985. *American Journal of Physical Anthropology* 77:289–294.

Wood, James, Henry C. Harpending, George R. Milner, and Kenneth M. Weiss
1989   The Osteological Paradox: Linking Mortality and Morbidity in Skeletal Populations. (Paper presented at the 54th Annual Meeting of the Society for American Archaeology, Atlanta, Ga.)

Woods, William I.
1986   Prehistoric Settlement and Subsistence in the Upland Cahokia Creek Drainage. (Unpublished Ph.D. Dissertation in Geography, University of Wisconsin, Milwaukee.)

Woods, William I., and George R. Holley
1990   Upland Mississippian Settlement in the American Bottom Region. In Cahokia and the Hinterlands: Middle Mississippian Cultures of the Midwest. Thomas E. Emerson and R. Barry Lewis, eds. Urbana: University of Illinois Press.

10

Transformation and Disease

Precontact Ontario Iroquoians

SHELLEY R. SAUNDERS
PETER G. RAMSDEN
D. ANN HERRING

It has sometimes been assumed that American Indian populations experienced calamitous decline after contact as a result of the introduction of Old World pathogens. This supposition has been questioned (Meister 1976; Helm 1980), but few have considered the possibility that substantial social and population changes predating European contact may have already produced infectious disease epidemics.

In effect, the traditional model assumes a culturally and demographically static native population, stabilized in a pure, disease-free natural environment. Consequently, European contact is viewed as the destabilizing, destructive, and "unnatural" source of change in an unchanging world. As expressed by one authority, "Aboriginal times ended in North America in 1520–1524, and Native American behavior was thereafter never again totally as it had been prior to the first great smallpox epidemic" (Dobyns 1983:25). The idea of the Americas and its inhabitants as pristine prior to contact has deep roots in the western European mentality and over the centuries has earned its keep by serving a number of political as well as psychosocial purposes. Most simply, it serves to rationalize the course of White-Indian relations in the centuries following the European invasions of the Americas, and it continues to validate the paternal, dominating role of governments over surviving native populations (Trigger 1985).

This may explain to some extent the distorted use of the epidemiological concept of "virgin soil epidemic" by anthropologists and historians alike. They often describe virgin soil populations as lacking previous exposure to a particular pathogen, such as variola major (smallpox); however, among epidemiologists, the term refers to populations "in which an organism has not been present for many years, if ever" (Mausner and Bahn 1974:27). It is important to recognize that the epidemiological concept includes situations where previous experience of a pathogen has occurred but herd immunity has been lost over time. This explains, for instance, why successive epidemics of tuberculosis wax, wane, and wax again as populations gradually proceed through the various phases of susceptibility and herd immunity, only to revert to susceptibility as the immune portions of the population die (Grigg 1958; Bates 1982). By focusing on the novel, rather than the recurrent dimension of virgin soil epidemics, anthropologists and historians have subtly and unconsciously reinforced the disease-free vision of precontact America (Stewart 1973).

The clear evidence of a radical transformation of host-pathogen relationships in some New World societies following direct or indirect contact with Europeans is not at issue. Rather, the emphasis is on the concept that Native American populations were dynamic and progressive before, during, and after the arrival of Europeans, and, just like populations everywhere in the world, were continually experiencing biological and sociopolitical changes. It would be surprising indeed if such changes did not have implications for human disease ecology, and equally surprising if American Indians were not as capable as people everywhere else of meeting and surviving periodic episodes of epidemic disease. The position taken here is that pathogens were present in the precontact Americas, that social conditions conducive to significant endemic and epidemic diseases were present, and that European contact added new pathogens to the established infection load made possible by precontact patterns of social organization.

Ontario Iroquoia is an appropriate testing ground for this view of the precontact New World because it has a unique combination of evidence that bears on the problem. This includes ethnohistoric records approaching the time of earliest contact, as well as an intensively investigated archaeological record with detailed regional sequences and whole village plans, reasonably good control of dating based on radiocarbon dates, artifact seriation, and early European trade goods (Biggar 1929; Finlayson 1985; Fitzgerald 1982a, 1982b, 1983; Kenyon 1968; Kenyon and Kenyon 1983; Knight 1978; Lennox 1981; Ramsden 1989; Ramsden 1977, 1988; Thwaites 1896–1901; Timmins 1985; Wright 1981, 1986; Wrong 1939). The osteological record is also considered solid, containing as it does a number of large, internally homogeneous ossuary samples (Anderson 1969; Jerkic 1975; Pfeiffer 1986). Careful examination of this evidence supports the contention that epidemiological patterns in southern Ontario were far from static before Europeans arrived in the area.

PRECONTACT PATHOGENS IN THE AMERICAS

The idea that precontact Americans coexisted with a variety of infectious agents is not new. Mycobac-terium tuberculosis was clearly present (Allison, Mendoza, and Pezzia 1973) as were, in all probability, various other atypical mycobacteria in the form of animal pathogens or environmental saprophytes (Clark et al. 1987). Newman (1976:669) further suggests that bacillary and amoebic dysentery, airborne infections like influenza and pneumonia, arthritides, rickettsial and viral fevers, various protozoan diseases like American leishmaniasis and trypanosomiasis, ascarids and endoparasites, bacterial pathogens such as streptococcus and staphyloccus, and salmonella and other foodborne and waterborne pathogens were also constituents of the precontact American microbiological environment.

In this regard, it is important to bear in mind that one class of microorganisms, the K-strategists, were probably producing periodic epidemics among small groups of New World hunter-gatherers and horticulturalists long before the European invasion. K-strategists such as tuberculosis and the treponematoses do not require a large pool of susceptibles to be maintained in endemic form in a population (Fenner 1980). They evade the host's immune response by multiplying slowly and persisting within cells or walled-off lesions. Because they are not eliminated, K-strategists retain the potential to provoke recurrent bouts of disease; indeed, infected individuals can transmit microorganisms to other hosts indefinitely. Clearly, the introduction of European acute community infections like measles, smallpox, and whooping cough (r-strategists) was unlikely to have constituted the first experience of infectious disease among New World peoples.

It is not enough, however, simply to demonstrate the presence of infectious agents or population sizes adequate for their survival and propagation. Pathogens are necessary, but not sufficient, causes of disease (Dubos 1965). Epidemiological theory stresses that

> social arrangements peculiar to specific places are major determinants of the biologic, chemical and physical environments to which the inhabitants are exposed. These arrangements appear to be the main forces in control of the nature and quantity of animal and vegetable species sharing the environment, the frequency and diversity of interpersonal contact, the presence of reservoirs and vectors for the spread of infection, and the degree and kind of physical and chemical addi-

tions to the air and water (MacMahon and Pugh 1970:156).

It therefore must be demonstrated that non-biological, cultural factors enabled microorganisms to flourish in the precontact New World, specifically in Iroquoian Ontario.

THE STUDY REGION: ONTARIO IROQUOIA

The area under investigation encompasses approximately 40,000 square miles between Lakes Huron, Erie, and Ontario (fig. 1). The first European visitors to the area in the early 1600s recognized several major tribal groups: the Huron (between Lake Simcoe and Georgian Bay), the Petun (on the south shore of Georgian Bay), and the Neutral (concentrated around the western shores of Lake Ontario). The Saint Lawrence Iroquoians had apparently disappeared from the shores of the Saint Lawrence River and eastern Lake Ontario prior to the seventeenth century.

The panorama of Ontario Iroquois culture history from the eighth to the seventeenth centuries clearly demonstrates a trend to increasing population size, larger and more numerous villages, and increasing population density within those villages (Warrick 1984). The internal structural elements of Huron villages nevertheless remained relatively stable over time.

The "typical" precontact Ontario·Iroquoian village, exemplified by the earliest stage of the Draper site, which is dated to about 1450 (fig. 2), was occupied year-round, but it was relocated every few decades, owing to resource depletion. Village inhabitants resided in longhouses that were consistently about seven meters wide and ranging in length from about 9 to 90 meters. Conservative calculations of the area of living space available to a family of five individuals average three square meters. The early Draper village contained 11 longhouses, housing some 200–400 people (Finlayson 1985).

Not only was population density high in precontact villages like Draper, but also the longhouses themselves were tightly packed; in fact, spacing between longhouses rarely exceeded three meters. In addition to the crowded living quarters, sanitary conditions would have been less than ideal. Refuse dumps, consisting primarily of organic waste, were distributed throughout the village, along perimeters, and between the houses. Warrick (1984) estimates that an inhabitant never had to walk more than eight meters from his or her house to discard refuse.

Population movements and continued coalescence in the fifteenth and sixteenth centuries are well illustrated by events in the region of Balsam Lake (Ramsden 1988). From the late fifteenth to the early sixteenth century, Hurons in the Balsam Lake area lived in small, widely scattered villages about

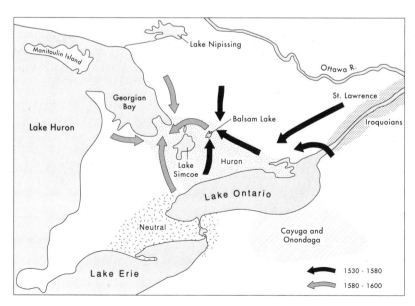

Fig. 1. Late precontact and contact period tribal groups in southern Ontario, with 16th-century population movements into the Balsam Lake area.

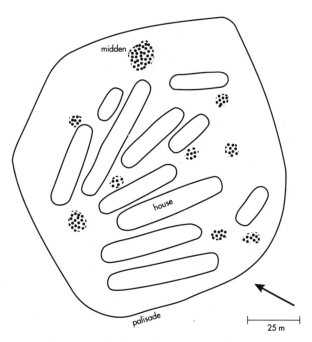

Fig. 2. The Draper site, Phase A, a precontact Ontario Iroquoian village.

creased from approximately 500 to 2,500 people. As a result population density within villages soared from approximately 35 per hectare to an extraordinary 86 per hectare. This trend at Balsam Lake was not unique; rather, it represents a phenomenon common in southern Ontario by the early 1500s, independently reconstructed by a number of archeological surveys. The extent of crowding in Ontario Iroquoia at this time can be better appreciated if one considers that the most generous estimate of population at the Mississippian town of Cahokia is a mere six people per hectare and may be substantially less (Milner 1986).

These population estimates represent more than simple growth. Southern Ontario was not completely covered with villages by the 1600s; rather, the paramount change was in population aggregation. The culmination of the trend includes the well-documented historic concentration of Huron populations in the Simcoe County area, where by 1615 there were 18–25 villages housing 20,000 to 35,000 people (Heidenreich 1971).

IMPLICATIONS FOR DISEASE ECOLOGY

The social and population transformations in precontact southern Ontario undoubtedly affected the disease ecology of the people in a variety of ways. Not only would Ontario Iroquoians have been exposed to indigenous K-strategists, but also the nature of village life at the time would have created conditions conducive to other infectious disease epidemics.

Microorganisms endemic to a population can shift into an epidemic phase under conditions that inhibit the host's ability to mount an effective immune response or that facilitate transmission from

one-half hectare in size, each with an estimated 200–300 people. The villages were not palisaded at this time, nor were they situated in defensible locations. The sites probably represent the remains of two communities that continued to exploit the area over a century or so. The estimated population is 400–600 people.

By the mid-sixteenth century, the area saw the immigration of large numbers of Iroquoians from the south and southeast including the lower and middle Trent River valley, the north shore of Lake Ontario, and the Saint Lawrence valley (fig. 1). As a result, the population size of the Balsam Lake region underwent a five-fold increase. By the late sixteenth century the population, estimated at 2,500, occupied three much larger communities (table 1).

One of these villages, the Coulter site (fig. 3), illustrates several sequences of expansion over a period of five to eight decades (Damkjar 1990). Multiple village palisades suggest that intergroup conflict increased concomitantly with population coalescence.

In sum, there is strong evidence for an increase in population size, density, and crowding in the Balsam Lake region between 1450 and 1580. Over the course of this 130-year period, the population in-

TABLE 1.

Balsam Lake Area Population Estimates

Site	Date	Acres	Houses	Population
Hardrock	1450	2.0	6	180
Jamieson	1500	2.5	10	300
Kirche	1530	4.0	22	660
Coulter, phase 3	1550	3.0	21	630
Benson	1580	3.8	27	810

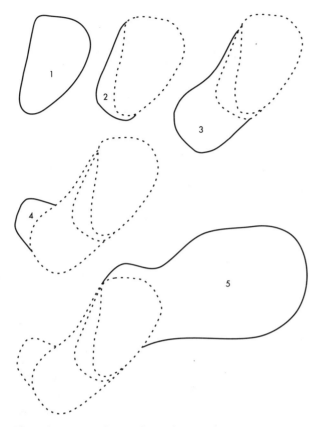

Fig. 3. Sequences of expansion at the 16th-century Coulter site.

person to person or via animal vectors. These are precisely the conditions that existed prior to contact in southern Ontario based on reconstructions of longhouse living. The ubiquitous refuse dumps would have attracted blood-feeding insects such as mosquitoes, ticks, and midges, all of which are known vectors of arbovirus infections (systemic febrile diseases, hemorrhagic fevers, and encephalitides). Scavenging dogs and rodents would have increased the chances of infection with zoonoses like rabies and rickettsial diseases such as typhus. Close and frequent contact among relatively large numbers of people, coupled with poor sanitation, would have created conditions conducive to endemic enteric bacterial infections like dysentery and the transmission of airborne diseases such as pneumonia and tuberculosis. Longhouse living in and of itself can increase the risks of infectious disease as illustrated by a study in Sarawak where a higher prevalence of leprosy and tuberculosis was found among longhouse dwellers compared to single house dwellers (Chen 1988).

The increasing presence of migrants in precontact Iroquoian villages may have heightened the opportunity for infectious diseases to flourish. Studies of morbidity and mortality in living populations have shown that migration tends to put the migrants themselves at higher risk, raising the overall rates of disease and death in the community to which they move (Wessen 1971; Little and Baker 1988). Migrants can further modify disease rates in their new location by disseminating infectious agents from their place of origin (Kaplan 1988). Archeological evidence indicates that Ontario Iroquoia was part of a wide socioeconomic network from the beginning of the Christian era (Spence, Finlayson, and Pihl 1979; Wright 1972). Thus, the region would have been vulnerable to the influx of indigenous pathogens from allies and trading partners from all directions.

In sum, the archeological evidence suggests that the nature and quantity of animal species sharing the environment, the frequency and diversity of interpersonal contact, and the presence of reservoirs and vectors for the spread of infection all would have created conditions favorable for the outbreak of epidemic disease in precontact Ontario Iroquoia. These factors would have enhanced the effects of introduced pathogens (either directly after contact or indirectly through intermediate hosts), leading to the series of epidemics that decimated Huronia in the seventeenth century (Trigger 1976). Examination of the osteological data lends further support to this position.

OSTEOLOGICAL DATA

Skeletal research in southern Ontario has focused on detecting temporal trends in health status and, in particular, the shift from a diffuse to a focal maize-based horticultural economy. This is a consequence of the large body of research that has suggested that subsistence patterns affect population densities and structures, which, in turn, affect the population's susceptibility to disease (Cohen and Armelagos 1984). Nevertheless, the evidence for this shift in southern Ontario is equivocal. The increasing effects of high carbohydrate diets on dental health are apparent from Early through Late Woodland times (500 b.c.–a.d. 1400), but bone isotopic and archeological data argue that the intake of animal protein remained fairly constant over time and that subsistence remained somewhat diverse (Katzenberg and Schwarcz 1986).

This relationship between health and diet is difficult to untangle because the point at which maize became widely cultivated and consumed in southern Ontario is disputed. The isotopic and archeological data confirm that maize entered the diet sometime between A.D. 400 and 1100. Results of carbon isotope studies show a significant increase in $\delta^{13}C$ values from A.D. 500 to 1200. The implication is that maize became a significant component of the diet in the Early Ontario Iroquois period (A.D. 900–1300) and that this change was either stimulated by or contributed to population changes. Maize consumption, based on $\delta^{13}C$ values, appears then to have risen to no more than 50 percent of the diet by 1600 (Schwarcz et al. 1985).

Important though corn may have been to the diet, other food sources may have been providing a nutritionally diverse diet. Published nitrogen isotopic values show no significant change through time, suggesting that beans were not an important protein source (Schwarcz et al. 1985). Beans and squash do not appear in the archeological record in southern Ontario until after A.D. 1400, and seventeenth-century ethnohistoric records do not clearly report their cultivation. On the other hand, dog and deer bones are prevalent in pre- and postcontact faunal samples, and human consumption of corn-eating dogs and certain species of freshwater fish could have biased observed carbon and nitrogen isotope values in Ontario Iroquois bone samples and contributed to nutritionally adequate diets (Katzenberg 1989).

Independent of the nutritional evidence, there are clear indications of compromised health prior to contact. Patterson (1984) examined dental health in three samples dating from the third to the seventeenth century. High rates of tooth trauma were detected in the prehorticultural group. The two horticultural groups showed decreased tooth wear but increased rates of tooth loss as well as rampant caries by 1600. Multiple diachronic skeletal samples confirm a substantial increase in caries incidence over time. High caries rates are seen in the deciduous dentitions of late precontact and historic period samples (Patterson 1984; Hartney 1978). Circular caries of deciduous teeth, associated with growth stress and high carbohydrate diets, were found in this region at a site dated just prior to the fur trade (Saunders and Fitzgerald 1987). The sub-

stantial increase in tooth loss among horticultural groups serves to underline a substantial rise in caries rates just prior to fourteenth-century population movements.

Evidence for disease stress is not limited to the teeth. Samples from two precontact ossuaries (dated 1490 and 1580–1600) have revealed thin subadult and adult cortical bone (Pfeiffer and King 1983; Pfeiffer 1986; Saunders and Melbye 1990). While one study of cortical bone volume (Esler 1989) found no apparent temporal changes in the percent of cortical area in several southern Ontario samples, a carefully controlled densitometric study (Southern 1990) has detected an apparent decrease in Iroquoian adult bone density over time, with below-normal values appearing by the end of the fifteenth century. Nevertheless, Ontario Iroquois precontact and contact skeletal samples also show lower overall bone volumes when compared to twentieth-century North American White samples.

Although dental diseases and bone quality are indirect indicators of health stress and mortality rates, it is difficult to diagnose the magnitude of infectious disease loads in skeletal samples because they are rarely manifested in bone. However, resorptive lesions resembling tuberculosis are detectable on Early Ontario Iroquois sites about the time longhouse villages began to appear (Wright and Anderson 1969). Two studies of the later samples have provided thorough discussions of differential diagnosis—that of Hartney (1981) for the Glen Williams ossuary (approximately 1500) and Pfeiffer (1984) on the Uxbridge ossuary (1490 ± 80, I9865.) Pfeiffer's diagnosis of precontact tuberculosis is particularly persuasive, based as it is on a population approach that identifies the prevalence of tuberculosis in the ossuary sample rather than on the more usual single case description.

Other examples of specific infection include several cases of treponemal disease dated to the late precontact and early historic period (Molto and Melbye 1984; Saunders 1988). The recognition of infectious diseases on the skeleton at this time most probably reflects increases in population growth and aggregation as well as the disproportionate availability of skeletal samples from this time period. An increasingly larger population is able to sustain bouts of acute and chronic infection that then become detectable in the larger skeletal samples.

These difficulties of analysis are not limited to the precontact period. Jackes (1986) has attempted to detect the effects of documented historic-period epidemics on Ontario Iroquoian mortality rates by comparing pre- and postcontact skeletal samples. Standardized life tables were prepared for eight ossuaries, four precontact and four around the time of or after contact. The results are equivocal since some of both earlier and historic sites show low infant and early childhood mortality while other pre- and postcontact sites show a high adolescent mortality pattern. While Jackes argues that the aberrant sites are biased samples, she concludes that Ontario ossuaries generally provide disappointing material for demographic reconstruction. On the other hand, she suggests the possibility of a doubling of childhood mortality between 1600 and 1650, reflecting epidemics from European introduced diseases. Yet a consistent theme running throughout Ontario Iroquois osteological studies is that demographic indicators appear not to be sensitive enough to differentiate samples. A most telling illustration is that there is no instance of the complete excavation of an Iroquoian village along with its associated ossuary to answer questions about sample quality and completeness.

CONCLUSIONS

It is entirely in keeping with the archeological and osteological record to suggest that southern Ontario Iroquoians developed densely populated communities and complex social structures independently of Europeans. It is equally consistent to suggest that these populations experienced both endemic and epidemic episodes of numerous diseases prior to the introduction of whatever new pathogens Europeans may have brought. Clearly, by the second half of the fifteenth century and certainly before the appearance of European trade goods on Ontario Iroquois sites, sociodemographic factors had increased the opportunities for infectious disease in precontact southern Ontario. These factors include the crowded, insalubrious conditions of longhouse-based village structure, the increasing presence of migrants and their possibly distinctive microflora in villages, as well as novel, indigenous pathogens acquired through trading encounters and by virtue of the position of southern Ontario as a nucleus of Iroquoian organization.

The evidence is not consistent with the romantic notion of the New World, mythologized as an unspoiled Eden. The continued assertion of this view of precontact America in the face of the expanding archeological and epidemiological knowledge is scholastically unsound. Ontario Iroquoia provides a good illustration of a society that was both demographically and epidemiologically dynamic prior to European contact.

REFERENCES

Allison, Marvin, D. Mendoza, and A. Pezzia
  1973   Documentation of a Case of Tuberculosis in Pre-Columbian America. *American Review of Respiratory Disease* 107:985–991.

Anderson, J. E.
  1969   The People of Fairty: An Osteological Analysis of an Iroquoian Ossuary. *National Museum of Canada Bulletin* 193. *Contributions to Anthropology* 1961–1962 (Pt. 1). Ottawa.

Bates, J. H.
  1982   Tuberculosis: Susceptibility and Resistance. *American Review of Respiratory Disease* 125(3):20–24.

Biggar, H. P.
  1929   The Works of Samuel de Champlain. Toronto: The Champlain Society.

Chen, P. C. Y.
  1988   Longhouse Dwelling, Social Contact and the Prevalence of Leprosy and Tuberculosis Among Native Tribes of Sarawak. *Social Science and Medicine* 26(1):1073–1077.

Clark, G. A., M. A. Kelley, J. M. Grange, and M. C. Hill
  1987   The Evolution of Mycobacterial Disease in Human Populations: A Reevaluation. *Current Anthropology* 28(1):45–62.

Cohen, Mark N. and George J. Armelagos
  1984   Paleopathology at the Origins of Agriculture. Orlando, Fla.: Academic Press.

Damkjar, E.
  1990   The Coulter Site and Late Iroquoian Coalescence in the Upper Trent Valley. *Occasional Papers in Northeastern Archaeology* No 2. Dundas, Ont.: Capetown Press.

Dubos, R.
  1965   Man Adapting. New Haven, Conn.: Yale University Press.

Esler, J. G.
  1989   An Assessment of Nutritional Health Status of Prehistoric Aboriginal Populations from Southern Ontario. (Unpublished M.A. Thesis, McMaster University, Hamilton, Ontario.)

Fenner, F.
  1980   Sociocultural Change and Environmental Diseases. Pp. 8–26 in Changing Disease Patterns and

Human Behavior, N. F. Stanley and R. A. Joske, eds. Toronto: Academic Press.

Finlayson W. D.
1985   The 1975 and 1978 Rescue Excavations at the Draper Site: Introduction and Settlement Patterns. *National Museum of Man, Ottawa. Mercury Series, Archaeological Survey of Canada Paper* 130.

Fitzgerald, W. R.
1982a   A Refinement of Historic Neutral Chronologies: Evidence from Shaver Hill, Christianson and Dwyer. *Ontario Archaeology* 38:31–46.

1982b   Lest the Beaver Run Loose: The Early 17th Century Christianson Site and Trends in Historic Neutral Archaeology. *National Museum of Man, Ottawa. Mercury Series, Archaeological Survey of Canada Paper* 111.

1983   Further Comments on the Neutral Glass Bead Sequence. *Arch Notes* 83(1):17–25.

Grigg, E. R. N.
1958   The Arcana of Tuberculosis. *American Review of Respiratory Disease* 78(2):151–172, (4):583–603.

Hartney, P. C.
1978   Palaeopathology of Archaeological Aboriginal Populations from Southern Ontario and Adjacent Region. (Unpublished Ph.D. Dissertation, University of Toronto, Toronto, Ontario).

1981   Tuberculous Lesions in a Prehistoric Population Sample from Southern Ontario. Pp. 140–160 in Prehistoric Tuberculosis in the Americas, J. Buikstra, ed. *Northeastern University Archeological Program, Scientific Papers* 5. Evanston, Illinois.

Heidenreich, C.
1971   Huronia: A History and Geography of the Huron Indians, 1600–1650. Toronto: McClelland and Stewart.

Helm, J.
1980   Female Infanticide, European Diseases, and Population Levels Among the Mackenzie Dene. *American Ethnologist* 7:259–285.

Jackes, M.
1986   The Mortality of Ontario Archaeological Populations. *Canadian Journal of Anthropology* 5(2):33–47.

Jerkic, S.
1975   An Analysis of Huron Skeletal Biology and Mortuary Practices: The Maurice Ossuary. (Unpublished Ph.D. Dissertation, University of Toronto, Toronto, Ontario.)

Kaplan, B.
1988   Migration and Disease. Pp. 216–245 in Biological Aspects of Human Migration, C.G.N. Mascie-Taylor and G. W. Lasker, eds. Cambridge: Cambridge University Press.

Katzenberg, M. A.
1989   Stable Isotope Analysis of Archaeological Faunal Remains from Southern Ontario, *Journal of Archaeological Science* 16(3):319–330.

Katzenberg, M. A. and H. P. Schwarcz
1986   Paleonutrition in Southern Ontario: Evidence from Strontium and Stable Isotopes. *Canadian Journal of Anthropology* 5(2):15–21.

Kenyon, W. A.
1968   The Miller Site. *Royal Ontario Museum, Art and Archaeology Division, Occasional Paper* 14.

Kenyon, I. T. and I. Kenyon
1983   Comments on Seventeenth Century Glass Trade Beads from Ontario. Proceedings of the 1982 Glass Trade Bead Conference. *Rochester Museum and Science Center Research Records* 16:59–74.

Knight, D.
1978   The Ball Site: A Preliminary Statement. *Ontario Archaeology* 29:53–63.

Lennox, P. A.
1981   The Hamilton Site: A Late Historic Neutral Town. *National Museum of Man, Ottawa. Mercury Series, Archaeological Survey of Canada Paper* 103.

Little, M. A. and P. T. Baker
1988   Migration and Adaptation. Pp. 167–215 in Biological Aspects of Human Migration, C.G.N. Mascie-Taylor and G. W. Lasker, eds. Cambridge: Cambridge University Press.

MacMahon, B. and T. H. Pugh
1970   Epidemiology. Boston: Little, Brown.

Mausner, J. and A. K. Bahn
1974   Epidemiology. Philadelphia: W. B. Saunders.

Meister, C.
1976   Demographic Consequences of Euro-American Contact on Selected American Indian Populations and Their Relationship to the Demographic Transition. *Ethnohistory* 23(2):161–172.

Milner, George R.
1986   Mississippian Period Population Density in a Segment of the Central Mississippi River Valley. *American Antiquity* 51:468–488.

Molto, J. E. and F. J. Melbye
1984   Treponemal Disease from Two Seventeenth Century Iroquois Sites in Southern Ontario. (Paper presented at the 1984 Paleopathology Association Meeting, Philadelphia, Pennsylvania.)

Newman, M. T.
1976   Aboriginal New World Epidemiology and Medical Care, and the Impact of Old World Disease Imports. *American Journal of Physical Anthropology* 45:667–672.

Patterson, D. K.
1984   A Diachronic Study of Dental Palaeopathology and Attritional Status of Prehistoric Ontario Pre-Iroquois and Iroquois Populations. *National Museum of Man, Ottawa. Mercury Series, Archaeological Survey of Canada Paper* 122.

Pfeiffer, S.
1984   Paleopathology in an Iroquoian Ossuary, With Special Reference to Tuberculosis. *American Journal of Physical Anthropology* 65:181–189.

1986   Morbidity and Mortality in the Uxbridge Ossuary. *Canadian Journal of Anthropology* 5(2):23–31.

Pfeiffer, S., and P. King
1983   Cortical Bone Formation and Diet Among Protohistoric Iroquoians. *American Journal of Physical Anthropology* 60:23–28.

Ramsdcn, C. N.
1989   The Kirche Site: A 16th Century Huron Village in the Upper Trent Valley. *Occasional Papers in Northeastern Archaeology* 1. Dundas, Ont.: Capetown Press.

Ramsden, P. G.
1977   A Refinement of Some Aspects of Huron Ceramic Analysis. *National Museum of Man, Ottawa. Mercury Series, Archaeological Survey of Canada Paper* 63.

1988   A Society Transformed. *Rotunda* 21(4):45–48.

Saunders, S. R.
1988   The MacPherson Site: Human Burials, a Preliminary Descriptive Report. Hamilton, Ontario: McMaster University.

Saunders, S. R. and W. R. Fitzgerald
1987   Life and Death in Sixteenth Century Ontario. (Paper presented at the 1987 McMaster University Symposium, Hamilton, Ontario.)

Saunders, S. R. and F. J. Melbye
1990   Subadult Mortality and Skeletal Indicators of Health in Late Woodland Ontario Iroquois. *Canadian Journal of Archaeology* 14:1–14.

Schwarcz, H. P., F. J. Melbye, M. A. Katzenberg, and M. Knyf
1985   Stable Isotopes in Human Skeletons of Southern Ontario: Reconstructing Paleodiet. *Journal of Archaeological Sciences* 12:187–206.

Southern, B.
1990   An Assessment of Bone Quality and Age-related Patterns of Bone Loss Among Iroquoian Populations. (Paper presented at the Canadian Archaeological Association Meetings, Whitehorse, Yukon.)

Spence, M. W., W. D. Finlayson, and R. H. Pihl
1979   Hopewellian Influences on Middle Woodland Cultures in Southern Ontario. Pp. 115–121 in Hopewell Archaeology: the Chilicothe Conference, D. S. Brose and N. Greber, eds. Kent, Ohio: Kent State University Press.

Stewart, T. D.
1973   The People of America. New York: Charles Scribner's Sons.

Thwaites, R. G., ed.
1896–   The Jesuit Relations and Allied Documents. 73
1901   volumes. Cleveland: Burrows Bros.

Timmins, P.
1985   The Analysis and Interpretation of Radiocarbon Dates in Iroquoian Archaeology. *University of Western Ontario, Museum of Indian Archaeology, Research Report* 19.

Trigger, B. G.
1976   The Children of Aataentsic: A History of the Huron People to 1660. Montreal: McGill-Queen's University Press.

1985   Natives and Newcomers: Canada's "Heroic Age" Reconsidered. Montreal: McGill-Queen's University Press.

Warrick, G.
1984   Reconstructing Ontario Iroquoian Village Organization. *National Museum of Man. Mercury Series, Archaeological Survey of Canada Paper* 124:vi–180. Ottawa.

Wessen, A. F.
1971   The Role of Migrant Studies in Epidemiological Research. *Israel Journal of Medical Science* 7:1578–1583.

Wright, J. V.
1972   Ontario Prehistory, an Eleven Thousand Year Archaeological Outline. Ottawa: National Museums of Canada.

Wright, M. J.
1981   The Walker Site. *National Museum of Man, Ottawa. Mercury Series, Archaeological Survey of Canada Paper* 103.

1986   The Uren Site AfHd-3: An Analysis and Reappraisal of the Uren Substage Type Site. *Monographs in Ontario Archaeology* 3.

Wrong, G. M., ed.
1939   Sagard: The Long Journey to the Country of the Hurons [1632]. Toronto: The Champlain Society.

11

Effects of Contact on the Chumash Indians

PHILLIP L. WALKER

JOHN R. JOHNSON

California Indians experienced a catastrophic population decline following European contact. An estimated precontact population of about 310,000 was reduced to fewer than 25,000 people by 1900 (Cook 1978:91). Historic documentation is particularly good for tribes, such as the Chumash, who converted to Roman Catholicism and entered the California mission system. The Franciscan priests who worked among the Chumash kept careful records of the Indians under their control. These documents allow the social and demographic results of European contact to be reconstructed in considerable detail.

The Chumash economy was based on the intensive exploitation of fish, sea mammals, and other marine resources. Acorns, grass seeds, and root crops were also eaten. These resources were distributed through an exchange system that linked villages on the Channel Islands, mainland coast, and mainland interior. Some island villages specialized in production of shell beads, stone tools, and other manufactured goods. These items were traded to people on the mainland for seeds and other terrestrial resources (King 1976).

This economic system supported an exceptionally dense population. Most Chumash lived along the mainland coast and on the Northern Channel Islands (fig. 1). Much of the inland area, in contrast, was sparsely populated. About 3,200 Chumash lived on the Northern Channel Islands and an additional 12,000 or more on the mainland (Brown 1967:79; Johnson 1982).

The Chumash had a chiefdom level of social organization with an elite group of hereditary leaders. Chumash villages were linked into loosely organized federations that were maintained through the exchange of natural resources, manufactured goods, and marriage partners (Blackburn 1975:12–13; Johnson 1988; Walker and Hudson 1992).

Skeletal studies suggest that the health of the mainlanders was better than that of the islanders. There is evidence that anemia was more common on the islands than on the mainland and that the islanders also more frequently suffered from club wounds (Walker 1986, 1989).

Health conditions and levels of violence also varied through time. Nutritional stress, infectious disease, and traumatic injuries appear to have increased between the early and late prehistoric periods (Walker 1989, 1992; Lambert 1990). Short-term variations in local health conditions also occurred.

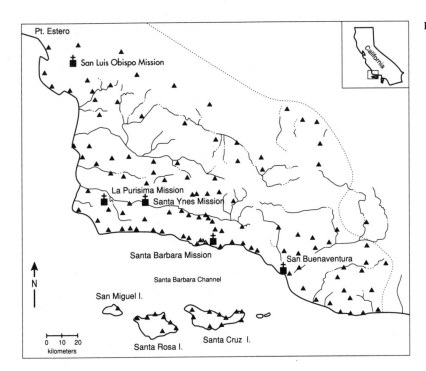

Fig. 1. Chumash territory at Spanish contact.

There is evidence that infectious disease and levels of violence increased significantly during periods of drought and environmental instability (Walker and Lambert 1989).

Certain aspects of Chumash demography and social organization no doubt influenced the effects that European contact had upon them. Their exchange system would rapidly transmit infectious pathogens from village to village. Their high population density and the concentration of people in large villages also would have hastened the spread of disease.

EARLY CONTACTS

The first recorded contact between the Chumash and Europeans occurred in 1542 when the Spanish explorer, Juan Rodríguez Cabrillo, sailed into the Santa Barbara Channel. Others who encountered Chumash Indians were Pedro de Unamuno in 1587, Sebastián Cermeño in 1595, and Sebastián Vizcaíno in 1602. After these early visits, there are no records of the Chumash interacting with Europeans for more than 150 years.

Some undocumented contacts undoubtedly did occur during this period, but their extent and consequences are unclear (Johnson 1982:49; Walker and Hudson 1992). The California coast was followed by ships carrying goods from the Philippine Islands to Mexico during the 1600s (Schurz 1939). It is reasonable to assume that the crews of these ships occasionally interacted with the Chumash when provisioning themselves. European diseases could have been introduced to the Chumash through their contacts with these early explorers. Besides contracting infections directly from Spanish sailors, diseases also may have transmitted to the Chumash along trade routes that tied them to Indians in Mexico (Walker and Hudson 1992). Dobyns (1981:49–50) believes that during the early 1500s smallpox rapidly spread north from central Mexico following Aztec trade routes into northern Mexico and the American Southwest. Diseases spread in this way could have reached the Chumash several decades before the arrival of the first Spanish explorers.

Prolonged contacts between the Chumash and Europeans did not occur until the late 1700s when the Spanish colonization of California began in earnest. This expansion into Alta California was motivated by the Spanish government's desire to prevent Russians from colonizing California (Farris 1989:493). In 1769 a land expedition headed by

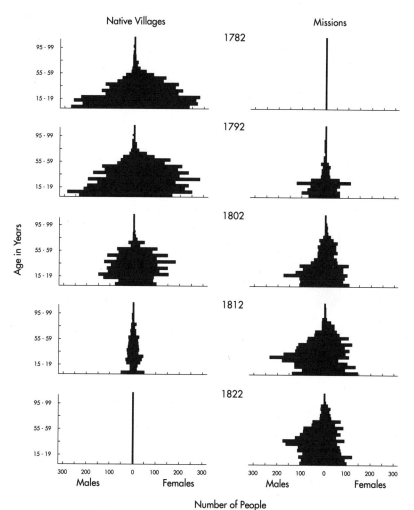

Fig. 2. Population pyramids of baptized Chumash. These population pyramids are based on data from baptismal registers of Santa Barbara, La Purísima Concepción, and Santa Ynes. Records of a person's age at baptism were used to reconstruct the age structure of Chumash who were living at the missions as well as those who were still living in their native villages.

Gaspar de Portolá passed through the Chumash territory. In 1772 the first Chumash mission was built at San Luis Obispo. By 1804 five missions and a fort had been established among the Chumash (fig. 1).

There is evidence that many Chumash died of introduced diseases at the beginning of the mission period. The number of coastal Chumash baptized by the missionaries is about half the number Portolá saw in 1769 (Brown 1967:76; Johnson 1988:84, 113). Nearly all the surviving Chumash were baptized at the missions. If Portolá's figures are accurate, then this discrepancy suggests very high Chumash mortality during the early stages of Spanish colonization.

Mission records provide evidence of the effects these early contacts had on the Chumash. Registers of Indian baptisms, births, marriages, and deaths were kept by the priests at each mission. Using these

registers, population pyramids have been reconstructed for the Chumash who were at the missions as well as those who were still living in their villages but who later were baptized (fig. 2). These demographic reconstructions are based on the ages recorded for Indian converts in the mission baptismal registers.

The year 1782 marks the beginning of intensive Spaniard-Chumash interaction. In this year the Santa Barbara Presidio and Mission San Buenaventura were both founded in the most densely populated portion of Chumash territory. At this time, nearly all Chumash were still living in their villages. The reconstructed 1782 Chumash population pyramid shows some aberrant features that appear to reflect mortality from early epidemics. In a stable population, deaths result in a gradual reduction in the size of successively older cohorts. This produces a population pyramid with a wide base that gradually narrows toward the top. Instead, the 1782 Chumash population pyramid is narrow at its base (fig. 2). There is a significant underrepresentation of children born during the previous 10 years in the 1782 Chumash village population (table 1).

Deaths from diseases introduced by the Spaniards provide the most likely explanation for the small number of surviving children born between 1772 and 1788. Although the explorers did not report epidemics among the Chumash during this period, epidemics were affecting Indians in other parts of California. In 1777, at the San Carlos Borromeo and Santa Clara missions, Costanoan children were dying from influenza (Bolton 1926:4, 161; Milliken 1987:26). At Santa Clara, priests were able to perform many baptisms by simply walking through the villages. The priests "succeeded in sending a great many children (which died almost as soon they were baptized) to heaven" (Palóu 1913:213; see also Cook 1976:18).

A small ratio of adult males to adult females is

another aberrant feature of the reconstructed 1782 Chumash population. Males and females are equally represented in the younger than 15-year-old cohort. This ratio of children contrasts markedly with the nearly two-to-one ratio of women-to-men among adults. Men who would have been between 20 and 30 years old at the time of the Portolá expedition are especially underrepresented in the 1782 population (table 1).

High male mortality in epidemics provides a plausible explanation for the biased sex ratio. Chumash men may have suffered disproportionately in the epidemics because of their role as traders in the intervillage exchange system (Hudson, Timbrook, and Rempe 1978). Through travel to foreign villages on trading missions they would greatly increase their chance of contracting a contagious disease. Modern ethnographic data on isolated populations support this interpretation. The Hagahai, an isolated Papua New Guinea tribe that suffered a series of epidemics, have a sex bias in age structure very similar to that of the 1782 Chumash population (Jenkins 1988:1003). Among the Yanomamo Indians of Venezuela and Brazil, men frequently take long trips to visit or trade with distant groups and are exposed to new diseases long before the people who remain at home. Such groups of men sometimes become seriously ill and die in large numbers before returning to their villages (Chagnon et al. 1970:344).

A disproportionate number of male deaths in warfare also may have contributed to the unusual 1782 Chumash sex ratio. Historic reports document large-scale intervillage warfare in the Santa Barbara Channel area during the early contact period. Between 1769 and 1775 five large coastal villages were either abandoned or newly occupied, or abandoned and reoccupied. Warfare is specifically given as the cause of four of these relocations. When they asked about the burned villages they saw, the Spaniards were told that Indians from the mountains had attacked seven coastal villages and killed many people (Brown 1967:75).

Although the reasons for this warfare were not stated, social disruption caused by epidemics may have been a contributing factor. For example, in April 1801 a war party headed by an Indian named Lihuiasu attacked an enemy village and killed five people. The priest who recorded this incident noted that these Indians were attacked solely because they were relatives or friends of Temiacucat,

TABLE 1

Chumash Population, 1782

Age Group	Males	Females	Total	Sex Ratio	x^2
0–4	256	234	490	1.09	0.99
5–9	218	274	492	0.80	6.37
10–14	247	269	516	0.92	0.94
15–19	222	285	507	0.78	7.83
20–24	122	188	310	0.65	14.05*
25–29	153	209	362	0.73	8.66*
30–34	98	174	272	0.56	21.24*
35–39	111	189	300	0.59	20.28*
40–44	67	123	190	0.54	16.51*
45–49	45	136	181	0.33	45.75*
50–54	37	80	117	0.46	15.80*
55–59	14	51	65	0.27	21.06*
60–64	11	24	35	0.46	4.83
65–69	4	11	15	0.36	3.27
70–74	5	13	18	0.38	3.56
75–79	4	6	10	0.67	0.40
80–84	2	2	4	1	0.00
85–89	0	2	2	0	0.00
90–94	0	1	1	0	0.00
95–99	0	0	0	0	0.00
100+	0	1	1	0	0.00
Total	1,616	2,272	3,888	0.71	110.68

Source: Mission registers.

x^2 = chi-squared value for hypothesis that the number of males and females is equal

* = probability of < .01

an Indian that Lihuiasu held responsible for an epidemic that was killing many at the time (Engelhardt 1932a:7).

THE MISSION PERIOD

The Spanish priests who worked among the Chumash followed a policy of *reducción,* the goal of which was to remove the Chumash from their villages and concentrate them at missions (Hornbeck 1983:46; Hoover 1989:398). At the missions, the Chumash received religious indoctrination and were trained in farming as well as in the other skills necessary to support themselves at the missions. They also had to adopt many new customs that differed radically from those of Chumash culture. This required considerable psychological as well as physical adjustment on their part. The priests insisted that neophytes live together in a common set of buildings. Unmarried women were made to sleep in dormitories. This was done to protect their chastity. As agricultural laborers, the Chumash were required to adopt a work schedule that was more regimented and probably also more time consuming than the one they followed as hunter-gatherers (Hoover 1989:401).

In parts of California, Indians were occasionally removed to missions by force (Cook and Marino 1988:474), even though such activities were explicitly prohibited by Spanish laws, as well as church doctrine. As far as is known, forced conversions did not occur in the Chumash area; however, after Indians moved to the missions they were no longer free to return to their former lives. If Indian converts became dissatisfied with conditions at the mission and fled, soldiers were sent to capture them and make them return (Cook 1976:57–64; Engelhardt 1963:60–61).

The role that physical coercion and forced labor played in maintaining the mission system is a controversial subject. Many Native Americans believe that these were dominant themes in mission life (Costo and Costo 1987; Castillo 1989). There is no doubt that fleeing the mission system was considered a serious offense and punished harshly. In one case, 10 runaways from San Buenaventura Mission who had stolen stock were sentenced to whippings (25 lashes a day for 9 days). In addition they were deprived of meat, imprisoned, and given hard labor (Engelhardt 1930: 29–30; Cook 1976:118).

Physical punishment was not confined to Indians who converted to Christianity. In 1810, 12 unconverted Chumash were sentenced to imprisonment, hard labor, and whippings (Cook 1976:118). Other offenses such as stealing, fighting, drunkenness, and "concubinage" were punished according to the severity of the crime. For such offenses the punishment might be a lashing, a sentence of several days in the stocks, or a few days of imprisonment (Cook 1976:126; Hudson 1979:17).

In cases involving murder, conspiracy, or armed rebellion, Indians were executed (Cook 1976:116–121). Seven Indians were executed for their role in the 1824 Chumash rebellion and 11 others were sentenced to between 8 and 10 years of imprisonment and hard labor (Cook 1976:121; Sandos 1985; Castillo 1989:390). In this insurrection, neophytes from La Purísima Concepción, Santa Ynes, and Santa Barbara Missions took over La Purísima Mission. The revolt apparently was precipitated by the unpaid work the Indians were forced to perform for soldiers (Engelhardt 1932a: 30–33). During the rebellion, 453 Indian neophytes from Santa Barbara fled the mission, but most returned after an absence of several months (Cook 1976:60).

Nearly all Chumash who survived the early epidemics eventually entered the missions. Considering the social disruption, physical punishment, and loss of freedom they faced, why were the priests so successful? Some Indians were undoubtedly attracted by the metal tools, glass beads, and other items of European manufacture that could be obtained at the missions. The social stratification of Chumash society also may explain why some Indians initially entered the missions. The rapidly evolving mission Chumash society would have offered opportunities for the acquisition of social status and material goods that were unavailable to Chumash commoners in their villages (Johnson 1989:366–368; Hoover 1989:397).

It seems likely that, for many Chumash, entering a mission was the lesser of two evils. After the arrival of Europeans, life in Indian villages rapidly deteriorated owing to the effects of epidemics and the disintegration of the Chumash economic system (Johnson 1988; Walker and Hudson 1992). Under these conditions of socioeconomic collapse, the missions would, by comparison, appear to be attractive places to live. Father José Señán, for example, reported that Indians on Santa Rosa Island were eager to go to the missions because they were starving and had heard that meat was plentiful at San Buenaventura (Simpson 1962:86). The failure of Chumash religious leaders to control the epidemics also would have abetted the priests in their conversion efforts. Abandoning the traditional belief system in favor of Christianity would be less difficult because of this disillusionment with Chumash religion (Walker and Hudson 1992).

Diet

At the mission, the diverse native diet was gradually replaced by one composed mainly of corn, wheat, barley, beans, and beef. Typically, a corn gruel was served for breakfast and dinner. A soup made from meat, vegetables, and meal was served for lunch. According to one account, adults were given about eight pounds of food each day (Engelhardt 1923: 75–76).

The transition to a diet of agricultural produce was a gradual one. As late as 1813, native foods were still making important contributions to the Chumash neophyte's diet. The priest at Santa Barbara Mission described their diet as follows:

> The number of meals these Indians eat is beyond count for it can be said that the entire day is one continuous meal. Even at night when they awaken they are wont to reach out for the first thing at hand and eat. The food given them consists of meat, corn, wheat, beans, peas, etc. The missionary fathers give them the eatables in generous amount and the Indians prepare them in the manner that best suits them. Besides the mission food the Indians are also very fond of the food they enjoyed in their pagan state: those from the mountains, venison, rabbits, rats, squirrels or any small animals they can catch; those from the seashore enjoy every species of sea food (Geiger and Meighan 1976:86).

The possibility of supplementing the diet with native foods diminished with the expansion of stock-raising activities. As the mission herds grew, they encroached upon and disrupted the grasslands that were an important source of many Chumash plant foods. The Spanish government also directly interfered with traditional food gathering by banning the Chumash practice of burning grasslands. The Chumash did this to encourage growth of wild seeds and root crops. The Spaniards viewed this practice as destructive because it threatened their settlements and destroyed the pastures their livestock grazed upon (Timbrook, Johnson, and Earle 1982).

For the most part, the missions appear to have produced enough food to feed their neophytes. Beef, in particular, was at times abundant, so much so that cattle were killed only for their tallow and the meat hauled to fields and burned (Geiger and Meighan 1976:86). Some missions were much more productive than others. The annual per capita agricultural production of Mission San Buenaventura, for example, was nearly twice that of Santa Barbara (Costello 1989:445; Cook 1976:37). Food production also varied from year to year. In 1819, for example, the crops failed at Santa Ynes and there was fear of famine (Cook 1976:53).

Physical anthropological studies provide evidence that the mission diet may not have been adequate for the maintenance of optimal growth. The skeletal dimensions of some Chumash neophytes were significantly smaller than those of their prehistoric and protohistoric predecessors (Walker, Lambert, and DeNiro 1989). Although this difference in body size may in part be a result of nutritional deficiencies of the mission diet, infectious diseases and psychological stress (Gardner 1972) undoubtedly also were important.

Disease

The policy of moving the Chumash out of their villages and concentrating them in small areas at the missions created an ideal situation for infections to spread. Respiratory infections spread rapidly in the crowded dormitories where unmarried Indians slept. These same conditions created problems of sanitation and waste disposal that resulted in the contamination of food and water (Cook 1976:30–32).

Venereal disease, tuberculosis, and dysentery were chronic problems that the priests frequently mention in their reports. Of these chronic diseases, syphilis is probably the one that had the most debilitating effects. Instead of killing people outright, venereal disease destroyed the mission Indian population indirectly by causing sterility, miscarriages, and decreasing resistance to acute infections.

The Spaniards who arrived in California were infected with syphilis and quickly spread it to the Indians (Cook 1976:24). As early as 1792, syphilis had made rapid headway among the Indians of

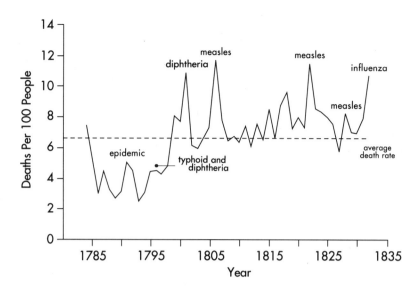

Fig. 3. Death rates for the Mission Chumash population. Data on some Indians from other tribes who entered missions in Chumash territory after 1810 are included.

Alta California (Simpson 1939:32). Reports made between 1813 and 1815 by the priests at the Chumash missions indicate that many of their neophytes were afflicted with venereal disease. The priests at San Luis Obispo Mission wrote in 1814 that venereal disease was "an infirmity with which generally all the Indians are infected to such an extent that any other illness during the various stages of the year kills them. Hence it is to my grief and to all who behold their unhappy fate that there are more deaths than births" (Geiger and Meighan 1976:75).

Similarly, a priest of Santa Barbara Mission wrote that "the sicknesses found among these Indians are those common to all mankind but the most pernicious and the one that has afflicted them most here for some years is syphilis. All are infected with it for they see no objection to marrying another infected with it. As a result births are few and deaths many so that their number of deaths exceed births by three to one" (Geiger and Meighan 1976:74).

Deaths in Epidemics

The death rate of the Indians who lived at the missions can be measured with considerable precision using data from the mission death registers and censuses. The average Mission Chumash mortality rate was 66.5 deaths per 1,000 people. This is an extremely high mortality rate even by eighteenth-century standards. For instance, the average death rate in Sweden for the period 1751–1800 was 27.4

per 1,000 (McKeown 1988:67). In the United States, the age-adjusted mortality rate is now 5.4 per 1000 (Indian Health Service 1989:38).

Mission death records clearly document the terrible effects of the epidemics that swept through the mission population. Six or seven times during the 49 years covered by the mission records, death rates rose precipitously for one or two years and then declined with equal rapidity (fig. 3, table 2). For five of these periods of high mortality, historical accounts provide descriptions of the disease responsible for the epidemic.

The first period of high mortality, between 1790 and 1792, affected Indians at Santa Barbara and San Luis Obispo. At Santa Barbara the death rate peaked at 135 per 1,000 during 1792 (table 2). There is no historical information on the disease responsible for these high death rates. Epidemics were occurring elsewhere in California at this time; in 1792, 40 Costanoan Indian children died in an epidemic at the ranchería associated with Mission San Carlos (Culleton 1950:136).

The next epidemic, in 1796, appears to have affected only the Indians at Mission Santa Barbara, where the death rate nearly doubled from that of the previous year. A 1797 report suggests that several diseases may have been involved: "many cases of typhoid and pneumonia . . . many have died of consumption, which misfortune is very common and principally among the Indians" (Cook 1976:21).

Between 1800 and 1802 there was another epi-

TABLE 2

Deaths per 100 People at the Chumash Missions

Year	San Luis Obispo	La Purísima	Santa Ynes	Santa Barbara	San Buenaventura	All Missions
1784	7.44	—	—	—	—	7.44
1785	5.49	—	—	—	—	5.49
1786	3.05	—	—	—	—	3.05
1787	4.52	—	—	—	—	4.52
1788	3.26	—	—	—	—	3.26
1789	4.15	4.64	—	4.94	—	2.69
1790	3.67	6.47	—	12.78	—	3.12
1791	8.21	5.99	—	7.82	—	5.08
1792	5.98	6.86	—	13.49	—	4.51
1793	2.66	4.76	—	4.81	—	2.50
1794	4.36	3.96	—	5.10	—	3.04
1795	6.42	5.79	—	6.15	—	4.48
1796	6.76	5.95	—	11.46	—	4.51
1797	6.01	4.75	—	6.78	3.13	4.24
1798	7.07	4.46	—	8.54	3.92	4.80
1799	10.18	6.08	—	11.99	8.43	8.06
1800	10.64	5.83	—	8.56	8.17	7.67
1801	11.33	9.95	—	14.68	12.97	10.85
1802	9.73	3.99	—	7.50	6.29	6.04
1803	8.62	3.69	—	7.37	8.16	5.85
1804	6.50	6.38	—	8.97	8.85	6.62
1805	3.85	6.92	—	7.30	—	7.26
1806	10.60	18.87	—	13.35	10.66	11.69
1807	8.05	7.83	6.13	7.28	9.05	7.73
1808	5.77	5.72	5.45	7.24	7.52	6.38
1809	7.31	7.08	3.98	6.94	7.30	6.68
1810	5.91	6.76	5.57	6.64	6.56	6.31
1811	8.02	8.90	10.64	5.89	5.95	7.35
1812	6.50	4.40	4.58	6.60	7.18	6.04
1813	9.48	7.43	6.59	7.01	7.53	7.49
1814	8.15	6.92	5.78	6.31	6.21	6.45
1815	8.36	8.83	9.59	5.61	8.09	8.42
1816	6.42	7.66	6.64	7.70	6.10	6.63
1817	6.49	9.60	11.81	6.53	7.67	8.63
1818	9.51	7.36	10.43	7.76	10.09	9.53
1819	7.16	7.43	9.74	8.46	6.31	7.16
1820	8.93	8.81	7.24	6.36	7.45	7.86
1821	6.02	7.30	10.10	12.80	6.50	7.23
1822	7.71	7.72	7.73	8.32	15.01	11.38
1823	6.28	9.83	8.69	8.73	8.45	8.42
1824	9.03	12.84	10.27	8.02	5.84	8.22
1825	10.89	11.65	5.80	7.34	6.82	7.93
1826	10.25	10.75	7.19	5.42	5.87	7.38
1827	7.56	8.49	5.03	5.79	4.08	5.65
1828	6.10	9.21	7.25	13.52	8.37	8.13
1829	8.39	8.37	5.14	7.60	6.67	6.95
1830	9.89	5.33	4.55	6.61	7.30	6.86
1831	10.19	9.90	7.99	8.84	6.40	7.71
1832	16.45	16.13	10.28	8.76	7.78	10.58

Source: Mission registers; Engelhardt 1923, 1930, 1932a, 1932b, 1963.

demic in California. The infectious disease was probably diphtheria (Cook 1976:19). The epidemic appears to have begun in 1800 at Mission San Gabriel (Kenneally 1965, 2:176, 178, 264). From there it spread north to the Chumash missions. Mortality was especially high at Santa Barbara in 1801, where nearly 15 percent of the Indians died.

At many of the missions the epidemic affected children almost to the exclusion of adults (Cook 1976:18). The low adult mortality is a sign that the neophyte population had been exposed to the disease before. Adults become ill along with children when a population is first exposed to diphtheria. Those that survive gain an immunity to the disease (Weinstein 1970). If another epidemic occurs the only people affected will be children born since the earlier epidemic. Lack of previous exposure may explain differences among the California missions in the effects of the 1800–1802 epidemic. At San Carlos, for example, the mortality rate was much higher than at the Chumash missions; 20 percent of the population died, and adults were the hardest hit (Culleton 1950:164–165).

The first measles epidemic occurred in 1806 (fig. 3). All Chumash missions were affected, and the death rate rose to 117 per 1,000. During a 15-day period, 44 neophytes died at Mission Santa Barbara alone (Cook 1976:19). At Mission La Purísma Concepción 88 people died between February 28 and March 19 (King 1984). This epidemic affected both children and adults. Since exposure to measles confers a long-lasting immunity, this mortality pattern suggests that the mission population had not been exposed to the virus.

The next two major epidemics also were of measles. The first of these, in 1821–1822 (Engelhardt 1930:60; fig. 3), was especially severe at San Buenaventura where the death rate rose to 150 per 1,000. This epidemic does not appear to have been serious at La Purísima and Santa Ynes (table 2). Another measles epidemic occurred in 1827–1828. Its effects were greatest at Mission Santa Barbara where the death rate rose to 135 per 1,000. At Mission San Buenaventura "many died, adults as well as children" (Engelhardt 1930:66).

In 1832 an epidemic of what was probably influenza struck the northern Chumash missions. Santa Barbara and San Buenaventura do not seem to have been affected. In the last three days of the year 15 adults were buried at Mission San Luis Obis-

po, and at Mission La Purísima Concepción the death rate rose to 161 per 1,000 (King 1984) (table 2).

In 1844, the surviving Chumash were devastated by smallpox. By this time, control of the missions had been turned over to secular administrators and the quality of the recordkeeping had deteriorated. At La Purísima Concepción, between July and November 1844, perhaps 150 of the 200 residents died of smallpox (James 1905:206; Storke 1891:23; Engelhardt 1932b:87). A Chumash woman interviewed in the early twentieth century stated that nearly all the Indians at San Luis Obispo and La Purísima Concepción died. Only a few cases appeared at Santa Ynez (Walker and Hudson 1992). This epidemic killed people throughout California (Cook 1939).

Population Pyramids

The effects of European contact can clearly be seen in the changing population pyramids of the mission period Chumash (fig. 2). In 1792, two decades after the first Spanish mission was founded in their territory, most Chumash still lived in their villages. Differences between 1792 native village and mission population pyramids suggest that the earliest Indian converts were predominantly young adults, especially young adult men. By 1792 over half the men and women between the ages of 20 and 25 had entered the mission system. Very few people over 30 converted to Roman Catholicism during this period.

The 1802 population pyramids show the condition of the Chumash one year after the diphtheria epidemic of 1801. By this time there is less of a discrepancy in the ages of the village and mission Chumash. During the previous 10 years many older people, particularly older women, abandoned their villages and moved to missions.

By 1812 nearly all the mainland Indians had been baptized, and the Island Chumash were the only large Chumash enclave living outside the missions. Less than 800 Chumash remained to be converted. The 1812 native village population pyramid provides evidence for the effect of the 1806 measles epidemic on the Island population. Children who would have been less than five years old at the time of the epidemic are especially underrepresented in this population.

By 1822 all surviving Chumash had moved to

the missions. At this time, their population was composed largely of men 30 years of age and older. This predominance of men is a complete reversal of the situation in 1782 (fig. 2, table 1). The sex ratio of the Chumash began to shift in favor of men as soon as most of them had entered the missions. Cook (1976:432), who found this trend toward an increase in the ratio of men to women at all the missions, concluded that high adult female death rates at the missions best explained the change in sex ratios.

In addition to a high female death rate, the fertility of the women that did survive was low. For most of the mission period, the ratio of births to women of reproductive age decreased (Johnson 1989:372). This low fertility may be the result of the prevalence of venereal disease. This low fertility in combination with the high female death rate significantly impaired the reproductive capacity of the mission Chumash population.

THE POST-MISSION PERIOD

In 1834 the missions were secularized by the Mexican government. The Roman Catholic Church was stripped of its holdings, and control of the missions was turned over to hired administrators. The Indians were made free citizens by the Mexican government. Although the Indian neophytes were supposed to get a share of the mission property, this rarely happened (Hudson 1979:32). Those that did sometimes traded the small parcels of land they received for blankets and whiskey (Engelhardt 1963:147).

After secularization, the condition of the Chumash rapidly deteriorated. Many drifted away from the missions and became ranch hands or servants in Santa Barbara and Ventura. For the first time, whiskey became readily available and alcohol-related deaths became common (Hudson 1979:115–120).

Little reliable demographic data is available for the post-mission period. Most of the priests who remained at the missions were elderly or infirm. Many births and deaths went unrecorded, and the census records were no longer kept. Determining the size of the post-mission Chumash population is further complicated by an increase in marriages between Chumash and people outside their tribe. By 1880, at least on paper, the Chumash had been reduced to no more than 200 people (Cook 1976:351).

Some of the surviving Chumash gathered about Indian alcaldes in small settlements where they continued ranching or farming. Beginning about 1840, Chumash enclaves of this sort were established near Saticoy, Ventura, Santa Barbara, and Santa Ynez (Walker and Hudson 1992; Johnson 1992). A few Chumash moved to the Tejón region in the southern San Joaquin Valley were they formed a community with Indians from other southern California tribes.

Living conditions in these settlements were not good. Here is an 1884 description of the community that become the Santa Ynez Indian Reservation:

> The Santa Ynez Indians, some 20 in number, live upon a small stream. . . . The land they occupy belongs to the Church being part of a grant. They have no title whatever to the ground but it is understood they will be allowed to remain here till their final extinction which judging from the report of the death rate will not be a long time. Little . . . is known about them by their white neighbors, who utilize their services so far as convenient and for the rest part let them alone. Judging from appearances they eke out but a scanty livelihood. They live in wretched huts and their household furniture is of the scantiest and poorest kind. They own no stock as a rule. During the week the men are employed about the neighboring ranches and return home on Sunday when they usually have a general drunken spree. For they are all, with the exception of Raphael [the alcalde] greatly addicted to the use of liquor. Every family has its little garden where is raised a little corn, watermelons, garden stuff and fruit. Children appear to be common among them and, so far as appearances go, are healthy. I am told that the mortality among them is, however, very considerable (Heizer 1955:88).

CONCLUSIONS

The introduction of European diseases obviously took a terrible toll on the Chumash. Demographic data show that only about 50 percent of the 1769 population converted to Roman Catholicism and moved to the mission. Most people who did not enter the mission system appear to have died in their native villages during epidemics. These epidemics killed many people directly, and the social disruption they caused resulted in additional fatalities from intervillage warfare.

Epidemics continued to devastate the Chumash who survived long enough to enter the missions. The crowded living conditions at the missions created an ideal environment for the spread of disease. In addition to epidemics of diphtheria, measles, influenza, and smallpox, Chumash also were afflicted by syphilis and tuberculosis. These chronic diseases reduced their resistance to acute viral and bacterial infections, increased mortality during the epidemics, and lowered their reproductive rate. By the end of the mission period only a few thousand Chumash survived from a precontact population of perhaps 15,000 people or more.

REFERENCES

Blackburn, Thomas
    1975   December's Child: A Book of Chumash Oral Narratives. Berkeley: University of California Press.

Bolton, H. E., ed.
    1926   Historical Memoirs of New California, by Fray Francisco Palou, O.F.M. Vol. 2. Berkeley: University of California Press.

Brown, Alan K.
    1967   The Aboriginal Population of the Santa Barbara Channel. Berkeley: University of California Press.

Castillo, Edward
    1989   Native Response to the Colonization of Alta California. Pp. 377–394 in Columbian Consequences, Vol. 1: Archaeological and Historical Perspective on the Spanish Borderlands West. David H. Thomas, ed. Washington: Smithsonian Institution Press.

Chagnon, Napoleon A., James V. Neel, Lowell Weitkamp, Henry Gershowitz, and Manuel Ayres
    1970   The Influence of Cultural Factors on the Demography and Pattern of Gene Flow from the Makiritare to the Yanomano Indians. *American Journal of Physical Anthropology* 32(3):339–349.

Cook, Sherburne F.
    1939   Smallpox in Spanish Mexican California 1770–1845. *Bulletin of the History of Medicine* 8(2):151–191.

    1962   Expeditions to the Interior Valley of California: Central Valley, 1820–1840. *University of California Anthropological Records* 20:151–214. Berkeley.

    1976   The Conflict Between the California Indian and White Civilization. Berkeley: University of California Press.

    1978   Historical Demography. Pp. 91–98 in Handbook of North American Indians. Vol. 8, California. Washington: Smithsonian Institution.

Cook, Sherburne F., and Cesare Marino
    1988   Roman Catholic Missions in California and the Southwest. Pp. 472–480 in Handbook of North American Indians. Vol. 4, History of Indian-White Relations. Washington: Smithsonian Institution.

Costello, Julia
    1989   Variability Among the Alta California Missions: Economics of Agricultural Production. Pp. 435–449 in Columbian Consequences, Vol. 1: Archaeological and Historical Perspective on the Spanish Borderlands West. David H. Thomas, ed. Washington: Smithsonian Institution Press.

Costo, Rupert, and Jeannette Henry Costo
    1987   The Missions of California: A Legacy of Genocide. San Francisco: Indian Historian Press.

Culleton, James
    1950   Indians and Pioneers of Old Monterey. Fresno, Calif.: Academy of California Church History.

Dobyns, Henry F.
    1981   From Fire to Flood: Historic Human Destruction of Sonoran Desert Riverine Oases. *Ballena Press Anthropological Papers* 20. Menlo Park, Calif.

Engelhardt, Zephyrin
    1923   Santa Barbara Mission. San Francisco: James H. Barry.

    1930   San Buenaventura: The Mission by the Sea. Santa Barbara, Calif.: Mission Santa Bárbara.

    1932a   Mission Santa Inés: Virgin y Martir and Its Ecclesiastical Seminary. Santa Barbara, Calif.: Mission Santa Bárbara.

    1932b   Mission La Purísima Concepción de Maria Santísima. Santa Barbara, Calif.: Mission Santa Bárbara.

    1963   Mission San Luis Obispo: In the Valley of the Bears. Santa Barbara, Calif.: W. T. Genns.

Farris, Glenn J.
    1989   The Russian Imprint on the Colonization of California. Pp. 481–491 in Columbian Consequences, Vol. 1: Archaeological and Historical Perspective on the Spanish Borderlands West. David H. Thomas, ed. Washington: Smithsonian Institution Press.

Gardner, Lytt I.
    1972   Deprivation Dwarfism. *Scientific American* 227(1):76–82.

Geiger, Maynard, and Clement Meighan
    1976   As the Padres Saw Them. Santa Barbara, Calif.: Santa Barbara Mission Archive Library.

Heizer, Robert F.
1955   California Indian Linguistic Records: The Mission Indian Vocabularies of H. W. Henshaw. *University of California Anthropological Records* 15(2):85–202. Berkeley.

Hoover, Robert L.
1989   Spanish-Native Interaction and Acculturation in Alta California Missions. Pp. 395–406 in Columbian Consequences, Vol. 1: Archaeological and Historical Perspective on the Spanish Borderlands West. David H. Thomas, ed. Washington: Smithsonian Institution Press.

Hornbeck, David
1983   California Patterns: A Geographical and Historical Atlas. Palo Alto, Calif.: Mayfield Publishing.

Hudson, Travis D.
1979   Breath of the Sun: Life in Early California as Told by Chumash Indian Fernando Librado to John P. Harrington. Banning, Calif.: Malki Museum Press.

Hudson, Travis, Jan Timbrook, and Melissa Rempe
1978   Tomol: Chumash Watercraft as Described in the Ethnographic Notes of John P. Harrington. *Ballena Press Anthropological Paper* 9. Menlo Park, Calif.

Indian Health Service
1989   Trends in Indian Health. Washington: Indian Health Service, Department of Health and Human Services.

James, George W.
1905   In and Out of the Old Missions of California. Boston: Little Brown.

Jenkins, Carol L.
1988   Health in the Early Contact Period: A Contemporary Example from Papua New Guinea. *Social Science Medicine* 26(10):997–1006.

Johnson, John R.
1982   An Ethnohistoric Study of the Island Chumash. (Unpublished M.A. Thesis in Anthropology, University of California, Santa Barbara.)

1988   Chumash Social Organization: An Ethnohistoric Perspective. (Unpublished Ph.D. Dissertation in Anthropology, University of California, Santa Barbara.)

1989   The Chumash and the Missions. Pp. 365–376 in Columbian Consequences, Vol. 1: Archaeological and Historical Perspective on the Spanish Borderlands West. David H. Thomas, ed. Washington: Smithsonian Institution Press.

1992   The Chumash Indians After Secularization. In *The Spanish Missionary Heritage of the United States.* San Antonio, Tex.: National Park Service.

Kenneally, Finbar
1965   Writings of Fermín Francisco de Lasuéun. Washington: Academy of American Franciscan History.

King, Chester
1976   Chumash Intervillage Economic Exchange. Pp. 288–318 in Native Californians: A Theoretical Retrospective. L. J. Bean and T. C. Blackburn, eds. Socorro, N.M.: Ballena Press.

1984   Ethnohistoric Background. Appendix 1: Archaeological Investigation of the San Antonio Terrace, Vandenberg Air Force Base, California. Vol. 4, Report Prepared for the Department of Army, Corps of Engineers, Los Angeles District.

Lambert, Patricia
1990   Changing Health Conditions on Santa Cruz Island. (Unpublished manuscript in author's possession.)

McKeown, Thomas
1988   The Origins of Human Disease. New York: Basil Blackwell.

Milliken, Randy
1987   Ethnohistory of the Rumsen. *Papers in Northern California Anthropology 2, Northern California Anthropology Group.* Berkeley.

Palóu, Francisco
1913   Life of Junipero Serra Mexico, 1787. C. S. Williams, trans. Pasadena, Calif.: G. W. James.

Sandos, James A.
1985   Levantamiento! The 1824 Chumash Uprising Reconsidered. *Southern California Quarterly* 57(2):109–133.

Schurz, William L.
1939   The Manila Galleon. New York: E. P. Dutton

Simpson, Lesley B.
1939   California in 1792: The Expedition of Jose Longinos Martinez. San Marino, Calif.: The Huntington Library.

1962   The Letters of José Señán, O.F.M. Mission San Buenaventura 1769–1823. P. D. Nathan, trans., Ventura, Calif.: Ventura County Historical Society and John Howell Books.

Storke, Yda
1891   A Memorial and Biographical History of Santa Barbara. Chicago: Lewis Butler.

Teggart, Frederick J.
1911   The Portolá Expedition of 1769–1770: Diary of Miguel Costansó. *Publications of the Academy of Pacific Coast History* 2(4).

Timbrook, Jan, John R. Johnson, and David D. Earle
1982   Vegetation Burning by the Chumash. *Journal of California and Great Basin Anthropology* 4(2):163–186.

Walker, Phillip L.

1986   Porotic Hyperostosis in a Marine Dependent California Indian Population. *American Journal of Physical Anthropology* 69:345–354.

1989   Cranial Injuries as Evidence of Violence in Prehistoric Southern California. *American Journal of Physical Anthropology* 80(3):313–323.

1992   Enamel Hypoplasia During 5000 Years of Southern California Prehistory. Health and Disease in the Prehistoric Southwest, II. *Maxwell Museum of Anthropology Papers.*

Walker, Philip L., and Travis D. Hudson

1992   Chumash Healing: Changing Health and Medical Practices in an American Indian Society. Banning, Calif.: Malki Museum Press.

Walker, Phillip L., and Patricia Lambert

1989   Skeletal Evidence for Stress During a Period of Cultural Change in Prehistoric California. Pp. 207–212 in Advances in Paleopathology. Luigi Capasso, ed. *Journal of Paleopathology: Monographic Publication* 1, Chieti, Italy: Marino Solfanelli.

Walker, Phillip L., P. Lambert, and M. DeNiro

1989   The Effects of European Contact on the Health of California Indians. Pp. 349–364 in Columbian Consequences, Vol. 1: Archaeological and Historical Perspective on the Spanish Borderlands West. David H. Thomas, ed. Washington: Smithsonian Institution Press.

Weinstein, Louis

1970   Diphtheria. Pp. 848–854 in Harrison's Principles of Internal Medicine, 6th ed. New York: McGraw-Hill.

12

Impact of Disease on the Precontact and Early Historic Populations of New England and the Maritimes

CATHERINE C. CARLSON

GEORGE J. ARMELAGOS

ANN L. MAGENNIS

Morbidity and mortality among North American aboriginal peoples increased dramatically as a consequence of contact with Old World populations. The way in which this occurred differed regionally in the New World depending upon the nature of contact as well as variation in population settlement and subsistence patterns. In New England and the Maritimes the contact pattern is unique because it is unusually long and sporadic. It lasted for nearly 700 years and consisted of spatially and temporally scattered encounters with the Norse and other European traders, trappers, and fishermen. Only late in the contact period when European settlers colonized the region and began written documentation of their interaction with Native peoples did the deleterious consequences of contact become most evident.

SETTLEMENT, SUBSISTENCE, AND DISEASE

The quality of diet, degree of sedentism and mobility, and population density are all factors that pertain to susceptibility, rate, and intensity of transmission of infections and endemic disease, and to general patterns of health. Ethnohistoric literature from the seventeenth century, along with a variety of archeological studies such as faunal and floral and settlement pattern analyses, have shown that aboriginal settlement and subsistence patterns, both prehistorically and at contact, were based on a generalized, broad-spectrum hunting, fishing, and gathering economy. This included both coastal and terrestrial resources, associated with a seasonally mobile settlement pattern (Carlson 1982, 1988; Kerber 1984–1985; Little 1985; Powell 1981; Ritchie 1969; Spiess, Curran, and Grimes 1984–1985; Waters 1965). In fact, the range of food afforded by this subsistence regime would have provided a varied diet that met or exceeded minimum adequate nutritional needs in terms of proteins, carbohydrates, vitamins, and fats.

The nature and extent to which horticulture played a role in diet and village sedentism in southern New England is poorly understood but clearly requires more research because of its health implications (Bumsted 1980). In general, the prehistoric archeological record of maize (*Zea mays*) kernels and cobs, storage facilities, and agricultural tools is minimal. Fewer than 20 archeological sites in southern New England have shown evidence of maize horticulture, and radiocarbon dates suggest that cultivation began very late in prehistory, about A.D. 1100. Most archeologists adhere to the notion of a generalist subsistence pattern, with horticulture contributing to subsistence only as an additional resource (Bumsted 1980; Ceci 1979–1980; Lavin 1988a, 1988b; McBride and Dewar 1987; Mulholland 1988). The implication for this in terms of diet and health is that the prehistoric Indians of southern New England should not have been suffering the type or degree of nutritional deficiencies and infectious disease seen in maize horticultural communities elsewhere in precontact North America (see Cohen and Armelagos 1984). In northern New England and the Maritimes, aboriginal cultivation was not possible due to climatic constraints.

The practice of maize horticulture and its implied association with sedentism is also unresolved in southern New England but has potential health implications in terms of the spread of crowd infections, sanitation, increased parasite loads, and resource depletion. European accounts do not describe permanent settlements or large sedentary villages. The earliest description of transhumant settlement patterns and horticulture is that of Giovanni da Verrazano, who, in 1524, wrote that Indians on Narragansett Bay "move these houses from one place to another according to the richness of the site and the season" (Wroth 1970:139). Other seventeenth-century writers (Morton 1838:138; Josselyn 1988:91) also mention seasonal mobility in southern New England.

In summary, prehistoric archeological settlement patterns and associated faunal and floral data suggest a mobile hunting, fishing, and gathering lifeway throughout the New England and Maritimes region, with supplementary horticulture of maize and other crops in parts of southern New England. In general, the precontact settlement pattern probably included small bands that made migrations between the coast and inlands to exploit seasonally abundant resources, and, in southern New England, to raise some maize. Populations were generally dispersed, rather than nucleated, and there is little evidence to suggest that large, settled villages occurred in the region until the contact period.

Given this sort of subsistence and settlement system, which generally characterized the entire region even until the colonial period, there are a number of implications that can be derived concerning the health status of these populations. While the nature of maize horticulture in southern New England is poorly documented, its very late arrival in southern New England allowed relatively little time for it to become established and extensively utilized as a subsistence item. Thus, the types of nutritional deficiencies associated with maize as a staple would not have been a health problem for this region prior to European contact. Further, lack of significant proportions of cultigens in the diet, at least up through the precontact period, would suggest good oral health. There is the expectation of a low incidence of infectious disease associated with crowding since there did not appear to be large permanent villages. Finally, nutritional stress episodes would be acute and seasonal, rather than chronic.

After contact, changes in subsistence, settlement, and dietary practices are known to have occurred. In the Micmac region of Nova Scotia and New Brunswick, for example, a heavy dependence upon European trade food (dried peas, beans, and biscuits) developed, and settlements became more sedentary. Miller (1976) has argued that significant mortality among the Micmac populations could have occurred during the sixteenth century even without epidemics of European diseases. She has suggested that the fur trade in the 1500s led to an abrupt shift in the seasonal round, and to a heavy dependence on European foodstuffs, particularly dried food such as peas, beans, corn, prunes, wheat flour, "sea-biscuit" or hardtack, and brandy. Prior to the fur trade, the Micmac spent their summer gathering and preserving meat and plant foods for the winter. Once they began to participate in the fur trade, they no longer could provide adequate stores for the winter and had to rely on traded European foodstuffs (Burley 1981:204; Conkling 1974). Miller (1976:12) cites evidence that the Indians died fairly often from the effects of inferior trade foods and states that "the Indians themselves, as well as European observers, noted the effects of dietary change on health and the fact that lung, chest, and intestinal disorders were increasingly common" (1976:122). Father Pierre Biard wrote in 1611 that, "since the French have begun to frequent their country . . .they do nothing all summer but eat; and the result is that, adopting an entirely different custom and thus breeding new diseases, they pay for their indulgence during the autumn and winter by pleurisy, quincy, and dysentery, which kill them off" (JR 1:177).

In addition to famine in the 1600s due to inadequate stored foodstuffs Micmac participation in the fur trade exposed them to alcohol. Under its influence there was violence, sometimes leading to murder (Conkling 1974:9). The physical effects of alcohol alone may also have had significant impact on reducing family size. Dobyns (1976a:3) advanced the hypothesis that alcohol contributed to impotence, thus reducing population size, and Miller (1976:122) agrees. Along with epidemic infectious disease, nutritional disease, malnutrition, and alcoholism were also contributing to the high mortality rates of Indians following contact.

In New England, there is no documentary evidence to support intensive use of European trade foods during the contact period, but that does not mean that it did not occur. Martin Pring visited Cape Cod in 1603 and noted of the Indians who ate some of his foodstuffs that, "they did eat Pease and Beanes with our men. Their owne victuals were most of fish" (Quinn and Quinn 1983:220). Traditional subsistence practices appear to have persisted into the seventeenth century in the southern New England region as shown by studies of mission documents from the period 1650–1675. Research suggests that while Puritan missionaries were attempting to settle the postsmallpox population of Indians into permanent settlements utilizing European-style farming methods, they had little success because most were still engaged in traditional hunting, fishing, and gathering pursuits (Brenner 1980; Carlson 1986; Salisbury 1974). Corroborating evidence from faunal analysis of an eighteenth century site on Cape Cod has shown the utilization of a mixture of domesticates (cattle, pig, sheep or goat) with wild animals (deer, fish, small mammals, and birds), which may indicate a continued seasonal mobility (Carlson 1989).

SKELETAL EVIDENCE OF DISEASE

Human skeletons have the potential to reveal information about past health, disease, and dietary patterns of individuals and their societies. Many diseases leave their mark on bone, which can then be used to diagnose their occurrence. Certain diseases such as tuberculosis, syphilis, and leprosy have skeletal "signatures" that aid in their diagnosis (Steinbock 1976). However, many pathogens leave only generalized changes in the skeleton, such as periosteal reactions or osteomyelitis. Microorganisms such as staphylococcus and streptococcus can cause skeletal response, but there are many pathogens that leave no evidence on bone. General patterns of nutritional deficiencies can also be diagnosed from bone. For example, there are a number of lesions such as porotic hyperostosis, defects in enamel development, and premature bone loss that, when coupled with evidence of growth retardation, can provide clues to a pattern of nutritional deficiency (Huss-Ashmore, Goodman, and Armelagos 1982; Goodman et al. 1984; Larsen 1988). Interpreting the underlying causes of the observed patterns of nutritional and disease insults must also proceed with complimentary data and analysis from the archeological record.

While skeletal remains can reveal a great deal about the disease history of a population, the skeletal series from the New England and Maritimes region are limited. There is a significant lack of sufficiently large skeletal samples that have been recovered, analyzed, and reported that provide any detailed information concerning the health status and mortality patterns of Indian populations. By far, most of the skeletal samples are comprised of only a few individuals, and many were excavated before the time of controlled archeological investigations. In many instances, only well-preserved bones (primarily crania) were saved for analysis. Given the spotty archeological record for skeletal remains, the picture of morbidity and mortality patterns of native inhabitants before and after contact is very incomplete.

THE PORT AU CHOIX SERIES Anderson (1976) studied this skeletal population of 101 individuals dating to 2340–1280 B.C. of the Maritime Archaic (uncalibrated conversion of radiocarbon assay). Although Anderson's main interest is in the reporting of metric and nonmetric skeletal variation, some data applicable to this study are reported. His examination of porotic hyperostosis was restricted to its occurrence in the orbit; of 30 skulls with orbits, only one individual exhibited a lesion, which would indicate that anemia was not a prevalent stress. In keeping with expectations of a broad spectrum diet low in carbohydrates, dental caries were observed at a very low rate; only four of 863 teeth exhibited carious lesions. Anderson does not report prevalence of lesions indicative of infectious disease, so it is not possible to draw conclusions about disease loads in this population.

THE NEVIN SERIES   Shaw (1988) examined a small sample of skeletons consisting primarily of crania that included nine subadults and nine adults from the Nevin site, dating to 2295–710 B.C. (uncalibrated conversion of radiocarbon assay). Her examination of pathologies indicative of nutritional and disease stress showed that porotic hyperostosis was common. In vault and orbits five of 18 individuals exhibited mild and completely remodeled lesions. Maxillary central incisors and maxillary or mandibular canines from 11 individuals were used to study the prevalence and age-related occurrence of hypoplasias. All 11 individuals exhibited at least one hypoplasia. Although peak age-specific occurrence of hypoplasias for both the canine and incisor occurred between three and four years of age, seven of the 11 individuals exhibited wide continuous bands indicative of chronic, rather than episodic disease or nutritional stress. Not unexpectedly, dental caries were incipient, and only 1 percent of 171 teeth of the 18 individuals showed carious lesions.

THE INDIAN NECK OSSUARY SERIES   Magennis (1986) reported on dental and skeletal pathology from a precontact Late Woodland ossuary (A.D. 1100), with a sample of at least 54 individuals. Both sexes and the entire age range, except those less than 6 months of age, were represented. Cranial and orbital incidences of porotic hyperostosis were recorded. Among the adults, 33 percent demonstrated remodeled lesions, although the expression of the condition is generally mild. Among subadults, lesions were recorded only in the orbits due to the commingled and fragmented remains. Of the subadults aged 0.5–10 years, 11 of 13 individuals exhibited orbital lesions. Of those, only three were unremodeled and occurred in individuals between one and two years of age. The two individuals without lesions were six months to one year of age. Porotic hyperostosis was prevalent but mild, suggesting chronic low level stress associated with anemia.

Postcranial periostitis, indicative of nonspecific infections, was reported for the femora and tibiae. Of the 15 subadult tibiae, six exhibited mild periostitis. Five of 20 subadult femora showed periosteal lesions. The majority of cases were mild. Only one individual exhibited a case that was considered to be a moderate involvement. Among the

14 adult tibiae, two exhibited periosteal reactions. Only one was severe, and it was extensively remodeled. Of the 23 adult femora, only three exhibited mild lesions. Magennis (1986) notes that while the prevalence of infectious lesions is higher than that reported for many hunter-gatherer groups, it is not so high as that reported for populations living in large nucleated settlements.

Like that shown in the Late Archaic samples reported here, the Indian Neck series exhibits a very low caries frequency. Only 18 of 378 teeth showed incipient caries. These incipient caries are slightly more common in the mandibular teeth. Three of 190 maxillary teeth and 15 of 188 mandibular teeth exhibited small caries.

The maxillary central incisor and maxillary canine were used for the analysis of enamel hypoplasia since they were the most frequently occurring teeth. All the incisors exhibited at least one enamel defect, while only one of 26 of the maxillary canines did not exhibit hypoplasia. Peak age of occurrence of hypoplasias on the incisor is 2.5–4.0 years, and for the canine, 3.5–5.0 years of age.

THE RI-1000 SERIES   Kelley, Barrett, and Saunders (1987) and Kelley, Sledzik, and Murphy (1987) examined a seventeenth-century (A.D. 1630–1640) postcontact site from Rhode Island with a sample size of 56 individuals. The entire age range was represented with the exception of children under the age of three years.

Caries are extremely prevalent and severe in this sample. Half of the subadults, 100 percent of the adult males, and 92 percent of the adult females exhibited carious lesions. On a tooth-by-tooth basis, 23.4 percent of all male teeth, and 40.1 percent of all female teeth were carious. These caries frequencies are much higher than those reported for other pre-industrial groups and clearly exceed that reported for the precontact samples. Kelley, Barrett, and Saunders (1987) suggest that the incorporation of sugar and milled flour into the diet is largely responsible for the prevalence and severity of caries in this population.

Hypoplasias in the deciduous dentition are very uncommon; however, in the permanent dentition males exhibited an average of 3.92 defects while females exhibited an average of 3.70 enamel defects (Kelley, Sledzik, and Murphy 1987). Peak age of occurrence of hypoplasias is between the ages of three and four years. Only three cases of mild orbital pitting (porotic hyperostosis caused by iron deficiency anemia) are noted.

Three types of infectious disease-producing skeletal lesions—nonspecific osteomyelitis and periostitis, tuberculosis, and a probable treponemal infection—were observed. Two males and two females (12.5‰ of the adults) exhibited osteomyelitis and/or periostitis lesions in the ulna, tibia, or femur. No nonspecific inflammations were observed in the subadults. A 17–18-year-old female that exhibited an inflammatory lesion of the vomer, inferior concha, superior concha, nasal bones, and internal frontal table is thought to represent venereal syphilis. Spine, rib, or hip lesions exhibited in 17 of 56 individuals are indicative of skeletal tuberculosis (Kelley, Sledzik, and Murphy 1987:14). The researchers concluded that tuberculosis had a major impact on mortality of this population, with a low prevalence of porotic hyperostosis, infectious lesions, and trauma.

HISTORICAL DOCUMENTATION OF DISEASE

The historical documentary record spanning initial European contact through the colonial period provides some understanding of the known and hypothetical prevalence of disease among the northeastern Algonquian-speaking groups following European contact. Technically this would span the Norse period of colonization beginning in A.D. 985, to the French and English colonization of the 1600s. It is only during the colonial period (post-1620) that any substantial historical documentation of diseases affecting the native populations exists, but descriptions are generally vague and often ambiguous concerning the extent of the diseases and their symptoms.

The historic accounts largely pertain to seventeenth-century descriptions of introduced Old World epidemic diseases. One may only speculate on the possibilities for the introduction of disease during the Norse period through the sixteenth century when the area was visited by explorers and countless fishermen, trappers, and traders who left no written records. "Viruses and germs could and did move from tribe to tribe even prior to European contact with a given group" (Dobyns 1976b:98). Furthermore, "permanent colonies are not a prerequisite for disease transmission; mere transient contact will do, and large numbers of contacts have

been recorded for the sixteenth century" (Jennings 1975:23). The possible ways in which disease may have been transmitted from European sailors, fishermen, traders, and explorers to individual Native groups include: the sharing of food or drink; sexual encounters; the trading of European textiles harboring infectious bacteria or viruses; and kidnappings of Native people to Europe and their return, possibly having contracted disease while abroad.

At least one documented precolonial epidemic, 1616–1619, caused a 90 percent mortality in southern New England (Spiess and Spiess 1987). This epidemic substantiates the idea that disease played a significant role in increasing mortality prior to the arrival of European colonists. It is more probable that small localized disease outbreaks, rather than massive catastrophic epidemics, were the norm during the precolonial period.

Norse-Indian Contact

McGhee (1984, 1988) has provided summary reviews of the evidence for the Norse presence in the New World (see also Fitzhugh 1985 and Kaplan 1985). The center of Norse settlement was the southwest coast of Greenland where, by the end of the eleventh century, an estimated 3,000 Norse people had settled in three major colonies carrying on trade in ivory and furs to Europe (McGhee 1988:15).

It appears that Norse contact with native populations was largely with Paleo-Eskimo and Thule groups in Labrador and Greenland, and not with Indians. Along the southern coasts of Labrador and on Newfoundland, however, Indian cultures ancestral to the Montagnais-Naskapi and Beothuk Indians were probably encountered by the Norse (Fitzhugh 1985:25).

The Norse were relatively isolated, and regular trading relationships between them and Native Americans were probably never established (McGhee 1984:21). Therefore, contacts would have been rare, and there are no archeological indicators that European diseases caused depopulation of native groups during this time period.

Fifteenth and Sixteenth Century

The late fifteenth and sixteenth centuries in the far Northeast were critical for the introduction of Old World disease, but is a time period for which there is almost no historical documentation on Native Americans. During this time, numerous expeditions from various parts of western Europe sailed to the area to explore and chart its coastline and evaluate its land, fishing, timber, and fur resources; beginning in 1536, Basque whalers were bringing 2,000 men to the Strait of Belle Isle (between Labrador and Newfoundland); untold numbers of fishing vessels exploited the cod banks off Newfoundland, Nova Scotia, and the Gulf of Maine; and traders and trappers bartering for furs arrived and set up small outposts. Called the protohistoric period because European influences were reaching Native Americans through unrecorded European incursions, or through contact with other Native groups in contact with Europeans, this period is without doubt a "dark century" (Day 1962).

The first fishermen to discover the rich cod fisheries off Newfoundland may have sailed from Bristol, England, in the 1480s (Quinn 1974), but it was not until 1497 that John Cabot wrote the first document that mentioned native peoples on the coast of Newfoundland. In 1501, Gaspar de Côrte-Real captured 51 Indians from Newfoundland or Nova Scotia and took them as slaves to Portugal (Axtell 1988:149). In all probability, European commercial fishing was in progress off the coasts of Newfoundland and Nova Scotia by as early as 1502 (Hoffman 1961). In 1517 "an hundred sail" (Quinn 1979:171) could be seen in Newfoundland harbors; by 1520 fishermen were sailing annually to the Newfoundland banks (Quinn 1974:46). Pierre Biard noted in 1616 that the land of New France (Canadian Maritimes) was first discovered by Bretons in 1504, "and since then they have not ceased to visit" (JR 3: 39).

The voyages of Giovanni da Verrazano in 1524 from France provide the initial firsthand description and maps of the New England region (Morison 1971:303–308). Verrazano described the Indians in Rhode Island as being in good health: "This is the goodliest people, and of the fairest conditions, that we have found in this our voyage . . . they exceed us in bigness" (Morison 1971:305). The next explorer to travel along the Maine coast and provide written documentation was the Spaniard Estévan Gomes. In 1525, he sailed along the coast and captured "a load of Indians" for slaves (probably at Newport, Rhode Island), taking them back to Spain, where the "government forced him to liberate such wretched Indians as had survived the Atlantic

crossing" (Morison 1971:331). Were they returned to New England, perhaps by then as carriers of Old World disease? Jacques Cartier conducted the other major documented voyages of the sixteenth century. During Cartier's second voyage in 1535, he noted scurvy among the Huron (where 50 Indians died), syphilis among the sailors, and sexual intercourse with Indian women (Morison 1971:418).

The earliest explorers—Cabot, Côrte-Real, Verrazano, Gomes, and Cartier—were mostly interested in charting the new waters and coastlines, and recording fauna, flora, and mineral resources. However, they must have made landings for fresh water and firewood or to trade with the natives for foodstuffs such as meat and maize. They often captured Indians during these landings for interpreters and guides, slaves, or "walking souvenirs" (Axtell 1988:148), some of whom were returned, possibly carrying Old World diseases.

The presence of an extensive fur trade, hand in hand with the fishing industry, argues for frequent interpersonal contacts between Indians and Europeans. European fishermen and fur traders did not make records of aboriginal culture or incidents of disease or health, or at least none that has survived (Quinn 1981:3). As early as 1501, when Côrte-Real sailed to Portugal with natives from the Maritimes region, at least one of the Indians was recorded to have been wearing a pair of Venetian silver earrings, and another had a piece of Italian gilt sword (Axtell 1988:154). There are also records that even in the early 1500s, elaborate trade protocols were already established (Axtell 1988), again suggesting that the fur trade predates all records of it.

It is important to recognize the possible effects of untold numbers of anonymous European fishermen in these waters, and trappers and traders on land, upon the nature of Indian contact with Old World diseases. In their zeal to obtain European trade goods, Native Americans undoubtedly

volunteered to work for the landed immigrants, flensing whales, hunting or growing food, and diving for sassafrass. They imitated European words, phrases, and even tunes. . . And as might be predicted of men who had just come off a long, cold voyage, homesick mariners made love with native women. . . European crewmen quickly acquired enough fluency to whisper "Kiss me" or "Let us go to bed," as well as words for phallus, testicles, vagina, and pubic hair (Axtell 1988:178–179).

At what date European commercial fisherman or trappers ventured into the Gulf of Maine waters and the coast of New England is unknown, but it is generally agreed to be earlier than the first records of such activity. For example, when Verrazano landed on the coast of Maine in 1524 he experienced a relatively unfriendly encounter with Indians who exhibited "all signs of discourtesy and disdain, as was possible for any brute creature to invent, such as exhibiting their bare behinds and laughing immoderately" (cited in Morison 1971:309). This suggests that previous negative experiences with earlier European visitors may have instigated such a response, implying that Verrazano, as early as 1524, was not the first European to visit this part of the New England coast.

By the 1570s, colonization of New England was being promoted by Richard Hakluyt to the English Crown (Morison 1971:55). Bourque and White-head (1985) have argued that Europeans in quest of cod and furs did not cruise into the Gulf of Maine until the seventeenth century. They argue that Micmac middlemen controlled the trade between New England and the Maritimes so that interpersonal contact between Europeans and other Indians was virtually nonexistent until the 1600s. Infectious disease may as easily be transmitted through Micmac middlemen as trade goods; therefore, its spread into the New England region very early in the sixteenth century is not improbable.

Roger Williams, in a 1638 letter to John Winthrop, reported on four epidemics that occurred in the sixteenth century among the Narragansetts. His report is based on information from Narragansett elders who associated past epidemics with earthquakes (Spiess and Spiess 1987:77). Some scholars discredit Roger Williams's letter, arguing that the earthquake epidemic "accurately reflects a European notion of disease causation in the seventeenth century" (Snow and Lanphear 1988:20). However, complete dismissal of this account of sixteenth-century epidemics appears unwarranted. The association with earthquakes as disease causation may be questionable, but not the epidemics themselves. It seems reasonable that numerous localized epidemics probably occurred during this century due to contact with traders and fishermen.

Another clue to the prevalence of disease in the sixteenth century is found in a 1611 letter of Pierre Biard, which states that "the people of these countries [Micmac] . . . are very sparsely populated, . . . although Membertou [sagamore] assures us that in his youth he has seen Savages, as quickly planted there as the hairs upon his head. It is maintained that they have thus diminished since the French have been to frequent their country (JR 1:177).

Seventeenth Century

The only actual accounts of diseases affecting the Beothuk in Newfoundland are those of tuberculosis deaths in 1790 and of a smallpox epidemic in 1828 (Marshall 1977:236). Upton (1977 cited in Marshall 1977:235) estimates a precontact Beothuk population of 2,000 and suggests that diseases transmitted by early European fishing crews and traders resulted in a very rapid population decrease by the early seventeenth century.

Samuel de Champlain first traveled to Newfoundland and the Saint Lawrence in 1603 (Champlain 1922:93). From near the mouth of the Saguenay River he wrote that "All these people are well proportioned in body, without any deformity. . ." (1922:118). In accounts of his 1608 return to the Saint Lawrence region (Champlain 1925), he describes the many Indians engaged in the fur trade, and how the Spaniards and Basques were numerous in the region (1925:34). At their settlement at Quebec in November 1608, he stated that "there died of dysentary a sailor and our locksmith, as well as several natives. . ." (1925:52–53) and also that some of his men and the Indians staying at the camp died of scurvy that winter (1925:62–63). During his third voyage to the Saint Lawrence in 1611, he wrote that while waiting for a tribe of Algonquin Indians near Montreal, they were informed that "there would only be twenty-four canoes, inasmuch as one of their chiefs and many of their tribe had died of a fever which had broken out amongst them" (1925:207).

Marc Lescarbot, writing in 1609, describes longevity and the use of sweatbaths to ward off sickness among the Indians of the Bay of Fundy, but that "the ordinary sicknesses are so rare in those parts" (Lescarbot 1907, 3:185, 188–199). Health, he says, is due to their diet, sobriety, and exercise (1907, 3:190), but "since the French bring them kettles, beans, peas, biscuit, and other food, they are become slothful" (1907, 3:195).

The first account of Indian disease is from the Micmac area of Nova Scotia between 1611 and 1613. The Jesuits reported in 1616 that the Indians "are astonished and often complain that since the French mingle and carry on trade with them they are dying fast, and the population is thinning out. For they assert that before this association and intercourse, all their countries were very populous and they tell how one by one the different coasts, according as they have begun to traffic with us, have been more reduced by disease" (JR 3:110). Other diseases, "pleurisy, quincy and dysentery," affecting the Micmac in Nova Scotia and New Brunswick are mentioned (JR 1:177).

A 1672 account of the Micmac mentions the long lives of the Indians (Denys 1908, 2:399) and that "they were not subject to diseases, and knew nothing of fevers. . . They had knowledge of herbs, of which they made use and straightway grew well. They were not subject to the gout, gravel, fevers, or rheumatism. Their general remedy was to make themselves sweat" (Denys 1908, 2:415–416). It claims that "there was formerly a much larger number of Indians than at present" (Denys 1908, 2:403) and that the consumption of alcohol and European foodstuffs has been harmful (Denys 1908, 2:444–450).

Chrétien LeClercq, a Recollect priest who worked among the Micmac settlements of New Brunswick from approximately 1675 to 1687, described the use of herbs and sweatbaths. He said that the Indians "enjoy perfect health right up to a fine old age, for they are not subject to several of the maladies which afflict us in France, such as gout, gravel, scrofula, itch, etc. (1910:296). A French surgeon who lived among the Micmac in 1699 agreed that "they attain to a great age" and that "they cure themselves by profuse sweating" (Dièreville 1933:175–176).

Champlain did not mention disease or health conditions of the people he encountered in New England from 1604 to 1607. His journal is useful principally for the hints it gives of the nature of considerable European contact before him (Champlain 1922:455). He also notes the occurrence of Basque vessels that were trading furs against "his majesty's injunction" (1922:239), a practice that had undoubtedly been going on for quite some time.

The first major known epidemic to occur in the region spread from southern Massachusetts to at least as far as the central Maine coast to Casco or possibly Penobscot Bay (Hoornbeck 1976–1977:42; Spiess and Spiess 1987). Its occurrence from 1616 to 1619 immediately predates the first colonies of Plymouth in 1620 and Massachusetts Bay in 1621. It has been estimated that it did not travel far inland, 20–30 miles (Cook 1973) or 50–60 miles (Bennett 1955). Bradford (1952:87) and Winslow (1830) recorded that the Narragansett, in what is now Rhode Island, were not affected by this epidemic.

There are two firsthand accounts by Europeans of this epidemic. Richard Vines, a physician on Ferdinando Gorges's voyage of 1616–1617, stated that the aboriginal residents of the mouth of the Saco River, Maine, "were sore afflicted with the plague." Although Vines and other Europeans lay in the cabins of those people that died, they were not afflicted (Gorges 1890:24). The other eyewitness, Capt. Thomas Dermer, wrote on May 19, 1619, that he "passed along the Coast where I found some antient plantations, not long since populous now utterly void; in other places a remnant remains, but not free to sickness. Their disease the plague, for wee might perceive the sores of some that had escaped, who described the spots of such as usually die" (Dermer 1906, 19:129).

Squanto, a Pawtuxet, died in 1621 of "an Indian fever, bleeding much at the nose" (Bradford 1952:114). An "infectious fever" that appeared in the Connecticut Valley at the Windsor trading post in 1633 took the lives of 20 colonists, including their physician, and "many of the Indians from all the places near adjoining" (Bradford 1952:260). If this fever was the same as the 1616 epidemic, this would imply that the disease persisted over a period of 17 years, and that both Europeans and Indians were susceptible (Spiess and Spiess 1987:75). In the late 1600s, elderly eastern Massachusetts Indians, who were youths at the time of the epidemic, said that "the bodies all over were exceedingly yellow both before they died and afterward" (Gookin 1972:149).

Other postepidemic accounts describe unburied human skeletons on the ground at abandoned village locations (Bradford 1952:87; Morton 1838; Williams 1973:243). These accounts probably explain the lack of known burials from this time period, as Josselyn (1988:95) wrote in 1673 that "in times of general mortality they omit the Ceremonies of burying, exposing their dead Carkases to the Beasts of prey."

This epidemic, which had an estimated 90 percent mortality (Cook 1973:31), is of an unknown cause. Williams (1909) ruled out smallpox, suggesting that it was bubonic plague. Cook (1973) discredited smallpox and yellow fever because of their vectors. Hoornbeck (1976–1977) discredited smallpox, bubonic plague, yellow fever, and measles and suggested that chicken pox is the only European contagious disease that cannot be ruled out. Spiess and Spiess (1987) argued that the signs of jaundice implicate either yellow fever, which they discount, or hepatic failure, which they strongly suggest.

Smallpox had a wider affect than the 1616 epidemic in that it was not restricted to the New England region or coastal areas. It was first reported from around Boston in 1633 and is described in detail by John Winthrop (1853:137–143). By 1634 it had spread into western Connecticut and Massachusetts (Bradford 1952; Winthrop 1853). It continued to flare up as small epidemics even after the decade 1630–1640; in New England it became almost endemic (Cook 1973:493).

Numerous infections of types other than epidemics of smallpox and "plagues" were common in the Northeast (Cook 1973). These include tuberculosis, respiratory complaints such as pneumonia and influenza, fevers, measles, dysenteries, and syphilis (R. Williams 1973). The last was confirmed by Josselyn (1988:94), who wrote in 1673 that "there are not so many diseases raigning amongst them as our Europeans. The great pox [syphilis] is proper to them. . . ."

As late as 1763, epidemics undiagnosed by local physicians were having a widespread effect on Indian populations. An epidemic of eight-month duration and of unknown cause in the years 1763–1764 on Nantucket Island eliminated 62 percent of the Indian population (Little 1988; Macy 1810; Stackpole 1975). These later epidemics give insight into the patterns of disease transmission and impact during earlier centuries.

SUMMARY

Based on what is known from archeological settlement and subsistence data and from a few skeletal series, the precontact populations in the New England and Maritimes region were largely hunter-fisher-gatherers that were generally healthy. The available prehistoric skeletal series span a 3,000-year period from the Late Archaic (about 2250 B.C.) into the Late Woodland (A.D. 1100). In general, these data suggest that throughout precontact time, populations suffered from mild but probably chronic iron deficiency anemia, at least among coastal groups. Dental enamel hypoplasias are fairly common and indicate a peak in growth disruption due to generalized nutritional and disease stress among 2.5–4-year-old children. Dental caries rates are very low, as are lesions indicative of chronic infectious disease. However, acute disease episodes often leave no evidence on bone.

The critical periods for understanding the impact of European diseases in this region are the protohistoric periods of the Norse, A.D. 985–1450, and the Western European exploration in the sixteenth century. There are no written records of Native Americans from this period. Early explorers and fishermen were largely illiterate and unlikely to have recorded any of this information. In addition, there are no skeletal collections that date to this time period. Theoretically, it is possible that as early as A.D. 985 there was contact with Europeans that could have resulted in some infectious disease transmission. Fishing voyages to the Grand Banks of Newfoundland possibly as early as the 1480s, as well as Basque whaling activities, fur trading, and exploration by John Cabot in 1497, the Côrte-Real in 1501, Verrazano in 1524, and Cartier in 1535 had a direct impact. The historic records of the seventeenth century provide only clues as to the nature and extent of protohistoric contact.

Since the protohistoric period has no documents pertaining specifically to Indian diseases, a protohistoric introduction and spread of infectious diseases can only be inferred from those accounts that intimate what the nature of European contact was prior to colonization. It is uncertain whether this contact was of sufficient degree or intensity to affect the spread of infectious disease. The difficulties lie in predicting what types of diseases may have been introduced and what their effects may have been on immunologically naive populations.

The first epidemic reported by Europeans in New England occurred in 1616–1619, with possible earlier epidemics reported only through oral tradition. While there is no clear evidence of epidemics prior to 1616, there could have been a great deal of impact from diseases as well as significant mortality before this time. The well-recorded epidemics of smallpox beginning in southern New England in 1633 significantly reduced the remaining population of Indians.

The single reported historic skeletal series from the region, from the RI-1000 site, dating 1630–1640, shows evidence of disease that differs from the prehistoric skeletal remains. In particular, the dental caries rate is quite high, indicating a dramatic change in diet. There is also evidence for the occurrence of venereal syphilis. Most striking is the evidence for skeletal tuberculosis. The patterning of skeletal lesions suggests that this highly prevalent disease was a significant underlying cause of mortality, at least among the Narragansett.

REFERENCES

Anderson, James E.
1976   The Human Skeletons. Pp. 124–131 in Ancient People of Port au Choix, by J. A. Tuck. *Newfoundland Social and Economic Studies* 17. University of Toronto Press.

Axtell, James
1988   After Columbus. Essays in the Ethnohistory of Colonial New England. New York: Oxford University Press.

Bennett, M. K.
1955   The Food Economy of the New England Indians, 1605–1675. *Journal of Political Economy* 63:369–397.

Bourque, Bruce J., and Ruth Holmes Whitehead
1985   Tarrentines and the Introduction of European Trade Goods in the Gulf of Maine. *Ethnohistory* 32:327–341.

Bradford, William
1952   Of Plymouth Plantation, 1620–1647. Samuel Eliot Morison, ed. New York: Alfred A. Knopf.

Brenner, Elise
1980   To Prey or To Be Prey: That is the Question. Strategies for Cultural Autonomy of Massachusetts Praying Indians. *Ethnohistory* 27(2):135–152.

Bumstead, M. Pamela
1980   VT-CH-94: Vermont's Earliest Known Agricultural Experiment Station. *Man in the Northeast* 19:73–82.

Burley, David V.
1981   Proto-Historic Ecological Effects of the Fur Trade on Micmac Culture in Northeastern New Brunswick. *Ethnohistory* 28(3):203–216.

Carlson, Catherine C.
1982   Report of the Faunal Analysis of the 1967 Excavations at the Smyth Site, New Hampshire. *New Hampshire Archaeologist* 23:91–102.

1986   Archival and Archaeological Research Report on the Configuration of the Seven Original Seventeenth Century Praying Indian Towns of the Massachusetts Bay Colony. *University of Massachusetts Archaeological Services Report* 22. Amherst.

1988   Where's the Salmon?: A Reevaluation of the Role of Anadromous Fisheries to Aboriginal New England. Pp. 47–80 in Holocene Human Ecology in Northeastern North America. George P. Nicholas, ed. New York: Plenum Press.

1989   Report on the Faunal Analysis of the Historic Simons House Site, Mashpee, Massachusetts. In Archaeological Excavations at the Simons House Site, by Ellen-Rose Savulis and Catherine Carlson. *University of Massachusetts Archaeological Services Report* 99. Amherst.

Ceci, Lynn
1979–   Maize Cultivation in Coastal New York: The Ar-
1980   chaeological, Agronomical, and Documentary Evidence. *North American Archaeologist* 1(1):45–74.

Champlain, Samuel de
1922   The Works of Samuel de Champlain [1604–1607]. Vol. 1. H. P. Biggar, ed. Toronto: The Champlain Society.

1925   The Works of Samuel de Champlain [1608–1613]. Vol. 2. H. P. Biggar, ed. Toronto: The Champlain Society.

Cohen, Mark, N., and George J. Armelagos, eds.
1984   Paleopathology at the Origins of Agriculture. New York: Academic Press.

Conkling, Robert
1974   Legitimacy and Conversion in Social Change: The Case of French Missionaries and the Northeastern Algonkian. *Ethnohistory* 21(1):1–24.

Cook, Sherburne F.
1973   The Significance of Disease in the Extinction of the New England Indians. *Human Biology* 45:485–508.

Day, Gordon M.
1962   English-Indian Contact in New England. *Ethnohistory* 9(1):24–40.

Denys, Nicholas
1908   The Description and Natural History of the Coasts of North America (Acadia) [1672]. William F. Ganong, ed. and trans. Toronto: The Champlain Society.

Dermer, Thomas
1906   To His Worshipfull Friend M. Samuel Purchas, Preacher of the Word, at the Church a Little With-

in Ludgate, London. Pp. 129–134 in Hakluytus Posthumus or Purchas His Pilgrimes, by S. Purchas, 20 vols. Glasgow: James MacLehose and Sons.

Dièreville, Sieur De
1933   Relation of the Voyage to Port Royal in Acadia or New France [1708]. John C. Webster, ed. Toronto: The Champlain Society.

Dobyns, Henry F.
1976a   Native American Historical Demography: A Critical Bibliography. Center for the History of the American Indian Bibliography Series. Chicago: Newberry Library.

1976b   Brief Perspective on a Scholarly Transformation: Widowing the "Virgin" Land. *Ethnohistory* 23(2): 95–104.

Fitzhugh, William W.
1985   Early Contacts North of Newfoundland Before A.D. 1600: A Review. Pp. 23–44 in Cultures in Contact. W. W. Fitzhugh, ed. Washington: Smithsonian Institution.

Goodman, Alan H., Debra L. Martin, George J. Armelagos, and George Clark
1984   Indications of Stress from Bones and Teeth. Pp. 13–49 in Paleopathology at the Origins of Agriculture. M. N. Cohen and G. J. Armelagos, eds. New York: Academic Press.

Gookin, Daniel
1972   Historical Collections of New England [1693]. *Collections of the Massachusetts Historical Society,* 1st series, Vol. 1. Boston.

Gorges, Ferdinando
1890   Sir Ferdinando Gorges and his Province of Maine. James P. Baxter, ed. *Publications of the Prince Society* 2(19). New York: Burt Franklin.

Hoffman, Bernard, G.
1961   Cabot to Cartier: Sources for a Historical Ethnography of Northeastern North America, 1497–1500. Toronto: University of Toronto Press.

Hoornbeck, Billie
1976–   An Investigation Into the Cause or Causes of the
1977   Epidemic Which Decimated the Indian Population of New England 1616–1619. *New Hampshire Archeologist* 19:35–46.

Huss-Ashmore, Rebecca, Alan H. Goodman, and George J. Armelagos
1982   Nutritional Inference from Paleopathology. *Advances in Archaeological Method and Theory* 5:395–474.

JR = Thwaites, Reuben G., ed.
1896–   The Jesuit Relations and Allied Documents: Trav-
1901   el and Explorations of the Jesuit Missionaries in New France, 1610–1791. 73 vols. Cleveland: Burrows Brothers.

Jennings, Francis
1975   The Invasion of America: Indians, Colonialism, and the Cant of Conquest. Chapel Hill: University of North Carolina Press, for the Institute of Early American History and Culture.

Josselyn, John
1988   John Josselyn, Colonial Traveler, A Critical Edition of Two Voyages to New England. Paul J. Lindholt, ed. (Reprint of Account of Two Voyages to New England, published in 1674). Hanover: University Press of New England.

Kaplan, Susan A.
1985   European Goods and Socio-economic Change in Early Labrador Inuit Society. Pp. 45–70 in Cultures in Contact. W. W. Fitzhugh, ed. Washington: Smithsonian Institution.

Kelley, Marc A., T. Gail Barrett, and Sandra D. Saunders
1987   Diet, Dental Disease, and Transition in Northeastern Native Americans. *Man in the Northeast* 33:113–125.

Kelley, Marc A., Paul S. Sledzik, and Sean P. Murphy
1987   Health, Demographics, and Physical Constitution in Seventeenth-century Rhode Island Indians. *Man in the Northeast* 34:1–25.

Kerber, Jordan E.
1984–   Digging for Clams: Shell Midden Analysis in New
1985   England. *North American Archaeologist* 6(2):97–113.

Larsen, Clark S.
1988   Bioarchaeological Interpretations of Subsistence Economy and Behavior from Human Skeletal Remains. *Advances in Archaeological Method and Theory* 10:339–445.

Lavin, Lucianne
1988a   The Morgan Site: Rocky Hill, Connecticut: A Late Woodland Farming Community in the Connecticut River Valley. *Archaeological Society of Connecticut Bulletin* 51:7–22.

1988b   Coastal Adaptations in Southern New England and Southern New York. *Archaeology of Eastern North America* 16:101–120.

LeClerq, Chrestien
1910   New Relations of Gaspesia, with the Customs and Religion of the Gaspesian Indians [1691]. William F. Ganong, ed. and trans. Toronto: The Champlain Society.

Lescarbot, Marc
1907   The History of New France [1609]. 3 vols. W. L. Grant, ed. and trans. Toronto: The Champlain Society.

Little, Elizabeth A.
1985   Prehistoric Diet at Nantucket Island, Massachusetts. *Nantucket Historical Association, Archaeological Studies* 6, Nantucket.

1988   The Indian Sickness at Nantucket. *Nantucket Algonkian Studies* 11. Nantucket Historical Association. Nantucket.

McBride, Kevin, and Robert Dewar
1987   Agricultural Evolution: Causes and Effects in the Lower Connecticut River Valley. Pp. 305–327 in Emergent Horticultural Economies of the Eastern Woodlands. William Keegan, ed. *Center for Archaeological Investigations, Southern Illinois University, Occasional Paper 7.*

McGhee, Robert
1984   Contact Between Native North Americans and the Medieval Norse: A Review of the Evidence. *American Antiquity* 49(1):4–26.

1988   They Got Here First, But Why Didn't They Stay? *Canadian Geographic* 108:13–21.

Macy, Zaccheus
1810   A Short Journal of the First Settlement of the Island of Nantucket (1792). *Massachusetts Historical Society Collections,* series 1, Vol. 3:155–160.

Magennis, Ann L.
1986   The Physical Anthropology of the Indian Neck Ossuary. Part II. Pp. 49–183 in The Indian Neck Ossuary. Chapters in the Archaeology of Cape Cod, V, by F. P. McManamon, J. W. Bradley, and A. L. Magennis. *Cultural Resources Management Study 17, Division of Cultural Resources, North Atlantic Regional Office.* National Park Service, U.S. Department of the Interior. Boston, Mass.

Marshall, Ingeborg
1977   An Unpublished Map Made by John Cartwright Between 1768 and 1773 Showing Beotuck Indian Settlements and Artifacts and Allowing a New Population Estimate. *Ethnohistory* 24(3):223–249.

Miller, Virginia P.
1976   Aboriginal Micmac Population: A Review of the Evidence. *Ethnohistory* 23:177–128.

Morison, Samuel E.
1971   The European Discovery of America. The Northern Voyages A.D. 500–1600. New York: Oxford University Press.

Morton, Thomas
1838   The New English Canaan, or New Canaan: Containing an Abstract of New England Composed in Three Books [1637]. Amsterdam: J. F. Stam.

Mulholland, Mitchell T.
1988   Territoriality and Horticulture, a Perspective for Prehistoric Southern New England. Pp. 137–166 in Holocene Human Ecology in Northeastern North America. George P. Nicholas, ed. New York: Academic Press.

Powell, Bernard W.
1981   Carbonized Seed Remains from Prehistoric Sties in Connecticut. *Man in the Northeast* 12:75–86.

Quinn, David B.
1974   England and the Discovery of America, 1481–1620. New York: Alfred A. Knopf.

1979   New American World: A Documentary History of North America to 1612, Vol. 1. New York.

1981   Sources for the Ethnography of Northeastern North America to 1611. *Canadian Ethnology Service Paper 76. National Museum of Man, Mercury Series,* Ottawa.

Quinn, David B., and Alison M. Quinn
1983   The English New England Voyages 1602–1608. London: Hakluyt Society.

Ritchie, William A.
1969   The Archaeology of Martha's Vineyard. Garden City, N.J.: Natural History Press.

Salisbury, Neal E.
1974   Red Puritans: The 'Praying Indians' of Massachusetts Bay and John Eliot. *William and Mary Quarterly,* 31(1):27–54.

Shaw, Leslie C.
1988   A Biocultural Evaluation of the Skeletal Population from the Nevin Site, Blue Hill, Maine. *Archaeology of Eastern North America* 16:55–77.

Snow, Dean R., and Kim M. Lanphear
1988   European Contact and Indian Depopulation in the Northeast: The Timing of the First Epidemics. *Ethnohistory* 35:15–33.

Spiess, Arthur E., and Bruce D. Spiess
1987   New England Pandemic of 1616–1622: Cause and Archaeological Implication. *Man in the Northeast* 34:71–83.

Spiess, Arthur E., Mary Lou Curran, and John R. Grimes
1984–   Caribou (*Rangifer tarandus L.*) Bones from New
1985   England PaleoIndian Sites. *North American Archaeologist* 6(2):145–159.

Stackpole, Edouard A.
1975   The Fatal Indian Sickness of Nantucket that Decimated the Island Aborigines. *Historic Nantucket* 23(4):8–13.

Steinbock, R. Ted
1976   Paleopathological Diagnosis and Interpretation. Springfield, Ill.: Charles C. Thomas.

Waters, Joseph H.
1965   Animal Remains from Some New England Sites. *Bulletin of the Archaeological Society of Connecticut* 33:5–11.

Williams, Herbert U.
1909   The Epidemic of the Indians of New England, 1616–1620, with Remarks on Native American Infections. *Johns Hopkins University Bulletin* 20:340–349.

Williams, Roger
1973   *Key into the Language of America* [1643]. Edited with a critical Introduction, Notes, and Commentary by John J. Teunissen and Evelyn J. Hinz. Detroit, Mich.: Wayne State University Press.

Winslow, Edward
1830   Good News from New England [1622]. *Collections of the Massachusetts Historical Society,* first series, Vol. 8:239. Boston.

Winthrop, John
1853   The History of New England from 1630 to 1649. From His Original Manuscripts. With Notes by James Savage. 2 vols. Boston: Little, Brown and Company.

Wroth, Lawrence C., ed.
1970   The Voyages of Giovanni de Verazzano, 1524–1528. New Haven, Conn.: Yale University Press.

13

Pre-Columbian Treponematosis in Coastal North Carolina

GEORGIEANN BOGDAN

DAVID S. WEAVER

The human skeletal material from seven pre-Columbian Middle to Late Woodland period (A.D. 350–European contact) coastal North Carolina ossuaries has been analyzed (fig. 1, table 1). Ossuary burial is a collective secondary deposit of human skeletal material representing individuals often initially stored elsewhere. Ossuaries are typical of Late Woodland period sites in the Northeast culture area. The ossuary reburial ceremonies, which probably took place every 8 to 12 years, contained an almost complete representation of all individuals who had died in the contributing population during the culturally prescribed period (Trigger 1969; Ubelaker 1974). Analysis of the ossuary skeletal material focused on findings of patterned skeletal lesions suggesting a probable treponemal infection. The differential diagnosis considered treponematosis, trauma, osteomyelitis, mycotic infection, tuberculosis, leprosy, myeloma, carcinoma, and osteosarcoma as possible conditions causing the skeletal lesions. Treponematosis seems the most likely cause. If the pathological skeletal characteristics are indicative of a treponemal infection, then these data can be added to other evidence of probable endemic treponematosis in pre-Columbian North America (Cook 1976; Powell 1988; Reichs 1989), and the hypothesis that fifteenth-century Europeans brought treponemes to immunologically naive New World people is invalidated.

THE EVOLUTION OF TREPONEMATOSIS: THREE THEORIES

Three theories have been proposed to explain the origin and spread of treponematoses throughout the world (Baker and Armelagos 1988). The Columbian hypothesis states that syphilis was carried to Europe from the New World by Christopher Columbus and his crew in 1493 (Dennie 1962; Crosby 1969; Goff 1967; Harrison 1959). The introduction of this new disease contributed to the epidemics that occurred in Europe during the 1500s. Dennie (1962) proposes that syphilis was virulent after its initial introduction from the New World into a population (Europeans) that had no immunity to it because of no previous exposure to the disease or strain.

In contrast, the pre-Columbian theory states that venereal syphilis was present in Europe prior to Columbus's voyages and was brought to the New

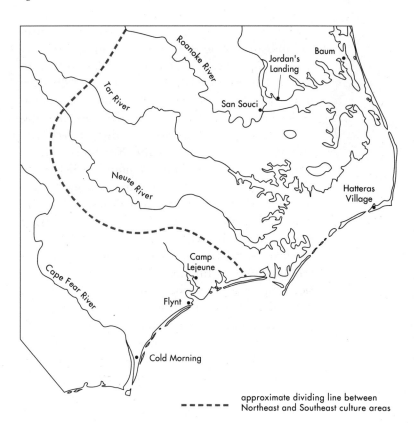

Fig. 1. Locations of the study sites.

- - - - - approximate dividing line between
Northeast and Southeast culture areas

World by Europeans (Hackett 1963, 1967; Holcomb 1934, 1935; Cockburn 1961, 1963). Advocates of this view maintain that venereal syphilis was not distinguished from a number of other diseases grouped under the term "leprosy." They cite descriptions of diseases resembling syphilis in the literature prior to Columbus, including ancient Roman and Greek references and references to "venereal leprosy" in the thirteenth and fourteenth centuries. Modern leprosy never is spread sexually or transmitted congenitally, but these are common features of modern syphilis (Steinbock 1976). Also, the "leprosy" asylums in Europe were established to isolate the "lepers" and prevent the spread of this contagious disease. According to Steinbock (1976) leprosy is not highly contagious and requires an in-

TABLE 1

Ossuary Sites

Site	Dates	Minimum Number of Individuals
Baum site, burial #1 (31Ck9)	Colington phase A.D. 800–1500	58
Hatteras Village (31Dr38)	Colington phase	38
Flynt (31On305)	Late Woodland period, A.D. 800–1650	158
Camp Lejeune (31On309)	Late Woodland	50
Jordan's Landing (31Br7)	Cashie phase, A.D. 800–1715	21
San Souci (31Br5)	Cashie phase	21
Cold Morning (31Nh28)	Oak Island phase, A.D. 800–1715	16
Total		362

cubation period of 3 to 10 years. According to Arnold (1966) leprosy is highly contagious but clinical consequences occur in only a few susceptible individuals. In either scenario, awareness of contagion for leprosy seems unlikely. On the other hand, syphilis is quite contagious and the incubation period is only a few days (Steinbock 1976). Holcomb (1934, 1935) also believes many of the purported cases of leprosy clearly were descriptions of syphilis. Both the appearance and venereal mode of transmission of the historical condition point to syphilis or some similar condition.

The third theory, the unitarian theory, says that syphilis evolved with various human populations and was present in both the Old and New Worlds at the time of Columbus (Hudson 1965; Baker and Armelagos 1988). According to Hudson (1965) pinta, yaws, endemic syphilis, and venereal syphilis are four syndromes in a biological gradient caused by *Treponema pallidum.* "Treponematosis is a single and extremely flexible disease whose permutations are directly related to man's physical and cultural states" (Hudson 1965:890). There have been gradual conversions of one syndrome into another under the influence of environmental change. Hudson maintains that treponemal infection originated in equatorial Africa as yaws, a childhood disease transmitted by skin-to-skin contact. Hunters and gatherers spread yaws throughout the world during their migrations. In the drier zones bordering the tropics the treponemal lesions retreated to the moist areas of the body (mouth, armpits, and crotch), as in endemic syphilis. Yaws probably was regarded as an inevitable and hardly serious childhood event. Endemic syphilis was carried to the New World by the earliest migrants from Asia. When humans reached the heat and humidity of Central and South America endemic syphilis converted back to yaws. The propagation of treponematosis later was enhanced in village settings because of the increase of the number of children, increased frequency and intimacy of childhood contacts, and the overcrowding and unhygienic conditions of village life.

THE RANGE OF DISEASE CONDITIONS

There are four common modern pathological conditions that are caused by the organism *Treponema pallidum.* They are: yaws, pinta, venereal syphilis, and endemic syphilis.

Yaws occurs in the humid tropics usually among rural populations. Yaws usually is acquired in childhood with the lesions affecting both skin and bones.

Pinta occurs in tropical America. Pinta causes skin lesions but usually spares internal organs and bone.

Venereal syphilis has no climatic restrictions and is acquired by adults through sexual intercourse or contact and may be transmitted congenitally. The lesions initially occur on the skin or mucous tissue and may involve internal organs including bone, liver, heart, and brain. The areas of skeletal involvement that are greatly predilected are the tibia, cranial vault, and the bones surrounding the nasal cavity.

Endemic or nonvenereal syphilis usually is found in warm, arid climates. The infecting organism enters the body through abraded areas of skin and sometimes through mucous membranes. The organism replicates and escapes from the local infection site through the lymph system and may be spread hematogenously throughout the body. Modern syphilis may go through three stages. In the primary stage chancres appear; this stage ends with involvement of regional lymph nodes. The secondary stage involves the bloodstream as the organism disseminates through the circulatory system. Bones commonly are involved, and periosteal inflammation was apparent clinically in one-quarter of the cases in the pretreatment era (Musher and Knox 1983). When tertiary syphilis occurs it is characterized by the involvement of the skeleton, skin, soft tissues, cartilage, and certain organs such as the liver and testes. Granulomas and giant cells are present, and central necrosis is seen; these lesions are called gummas (Ortner and Putschar 1985; Musher and Knox 1983). Tertiary syphilitic bone lesions usually develop between 2 and 10 years after the initial infection, but this period can vary. Late stage syphilis of bone frequently affects the tibia and fibula. The tibia is about 10 times more often the site of syphilitic lesions than any other individual bone. When the tibia is involved the result is the typical "saber shin." The tibia is followed by the ulna and radius, clavicle, phalanges, and calcaneus in rapidly decreasing frequency order. The cranial vault, when involved, shows a localized osteitis without extensive destruction. The spine rarely is affected (Steinbock 1976; Ortner and Putschar 1985; Musher and Knox 1983). Pain and swelling are almost always present in the long bones and are consistent with the periosteal location of the granulomatous reaction. The favored sites of long bone lesions are the diaphyses and metaphyses with bone changes rarely affecting the epiphyses. Tertiary skin involvement tends to occur in areas that frequently are subject to trauma or irritation such as the elbows, but the process by which trauma contributes to the development of the lesions is obscure (Musher and Knox 1983; Steinbock 1976). The bone changes that occur can be proliferative or resorptive, and in many cases a combination of the two occurs. Very few infections provoke as much formation of excess bone along with bone destruction as in the bone regeneration reaction of syphilis (Steinbock 1976). The changes may affect only a localized area of bone or an entire bone (Ortner and Putschar 1985). If late syphilis affects the nervous system or neurosyphilis occurs one of a number of syndromes may occur including tabes dorsalis (nerve degeneration associated with syphilis), paresis, dementia, meningitis, or a mixture of these syndromes, depending on which part of the nervous system is involved (Musher and Knox 1983).

Cranial bone changes diagnostic of syphilis range from ectocranial clustered pits to caries sicca (Hackett 1983). The descriptions of long bone lesions in nonvenereal syphilis are identical to those of venereal syphilis and are based on cases of venereal syphilis (Ortner and Putschar 1985; Steinbock 1976). The earliest manifestation of endemic syphilis usually is a localized subperiosteal apposition of bone (periostitis) as a reaction to the periosteal inflammation. The bone reaction occurs mostly on the diaphyses. The localized form of nongummatous periostitis may leave plaquelike exostoses on the bone cortex or circumscribed areas of surface lamellar bone of varying thickness and density. The layers of new bone usually are parallel to the shaft, but in some cases they may project at right angles from the shaft, forming radial subperiosteal spiculation. The entire bone surface, except the cartilage-covered articular facets, may be involved. This diffuse nongummatous osteoperiostitis leaves the bone thick and heavy as if swelling had occurred. If the early lesions progress the medullary cavity may become narrowed or even obstructed by new endosteal bone, particularly in the tibia and the femur. Destruction, in the form of pitting on the surface of long bones, may occur as a result of localized inhibition of the blood supply with necrosis

and not necessarily due to direct destruction from gumma (Steinbock 1976; Ortner and Putschar 1985).

Gummatous osteoperiostitis is a characteristic bone lesion of syphilis. The formation of gumma is the result of the restriction of blood supply to the bone by thrombosed blood vessels with degeneration caused by the products of the treponeme (Steinbock 1976). If the gumma is localized it appears as a tumorlike enlargement of the affected bone area. The hypervascular periosteal bony buildup surrounds a scooped-out defect, extending into the cortex. The margins of the defect are rough and thin, and major sequestra are missing. Gummata of the medullary cavity are large lytic lesions surrounded by perifocal reactive sclerosis (Ortner and Putschar 1985).

Distinctive cranial bone changes do not appear in the 17 crania recovered at the Flynt site, but several stages of Hackett's (1983) diagnostic criteria have been identified in the cranial material from the six other ossuary skeletal samples (Bogdan and Weaver 1989). Unfortunately many crania from the ossuary populations are unavailable for observation; more may have exhibited these bone changes.

Many of the long bones from the ossuary sites are affected with an array of skeletal characteristics that include cavitation, cortical destruction, cortical thickening, swelling, gumma, periosteal plaque, periostitis, radial subperiosteal spiculation, and obstruction of the medullary cavity. These characteristics are multiple in each bone, bilateral, and affect mostly the diaphyses of the long bones. On a few occasions the metaphyses are affected, but the epiphyses almost never are the site of these lesions.

Table 2 shows the total numbers of specific bones at all seven ossuary sites, the number of bones affected with some or all of the pathological characteristics, and the percent frequencies of affected bones.

Eighty-four percent of the offspring of syphilitic mothers are infected congenitally (Steinbock 1976). The newborn may show a variety of signs of the disseminated disease or stillbirth may occur. Radiologic and histologic observations show nearly all infected infants have periostitis and osteochondritis. The disease usually surfaces in the second to sixth week of neonatal life with the initial symptom being the sniffles resulting from involvement of the mucous membranes. Skin and mucous tissue lesions appear, and the patient may be febrile.

TABLE 2

"Treponemal" Lesion Frequency for the Ossuary Sites

Bone	Number of Bones in 7 Sites	Number Affected	Percent Affected
cranium	137	28	20
tibia	297	79	26
fibula	169	63	37
clavicle	194	33	17
ulna	286	30	10
radius	229	22	10
femur	402	76	19
humerus	331	32	10

Source: Bogdan 1989.

Wasting, marasmus, and eventually death will occur. After two years of age late manifestations may develop, including stigmata, apparent in the development of long bones and teeth resulting from earlier damage to these tissues. Other late manifestations are eye and skin lesions, gummas of the nasal and facial bones, periostitis, and central nervous system disease (Musher and Knox 1983). The dental changes are not necessarily pathognomonic signs of the disease unless associated with characteristic bone lesions. The maxillary incisors and first molars often are involved. Hutchinson's incisors are narrowed and variably notched, especially the permanent maxillary central incisors. Mulberry molars—small, rough first molars—occur in cases of congenital syphilis (Steinbock 1976).

Osseous lesions of early congenital syphilis include osteochondritis, periosteal fibrous bone on the diaphyses, foci of osteomyelitis on the medial aspects of both proximal tibiae (Wimberger's sign), and skull lesions with multiple, rounded, destructive foci.

According to Steinbock (1976), although syphilitic females may have several miscarriages due to acquired venereal syphilis, a large proportion of the infants will develop the osseous lesions of congenital syphilis. "A representative skeletal series should present evidence of such lesions" (Steinbock 1976:110). Characteristic congenital and neonatal skeletal lesions do not occur in any of the ossuary skeletal samples in this study.

A differential diagnosis to determine which of several diseases or disorders probably caused the patterned skeletal lesions observed in the material from the ossuaries should compare the known signs of treponematosis, trauma, hematogenous osteomyelitis, mycotic infection, tuberculosis, leprosy, myeloma, carcinoma, and osteosarcoma with the skeletal conditions observed in the ossuary samples. Table 3 illustrates particular characteristics of the nine competing disease models. The bone conditions in the ossuary samples are most similar to the pattern of lesions characterizing the treponematosis model. Figure 2 shows the skeletal distribution of lesions found in the material from the ossuary samples, from Powell's (1988) work at Moundville and Steinbock's (1976) figures of endemic syphilis, yaws, and venereal syphilis. The skeletal distribution of the lesions in the material from the ossuaries is very similar to the distribution in the other four figures, especially to the distribution of the lesions at Moundville.

The probable treponematosis found in the North Carolina ossuaries most likely was an endemic treponemal infection and not a venereal treponemal infection. In more than 360 individuals analyzed from the seven ossuaries, there are no cases of osteochondritis, periosteal cloaking, Wimberger's sign, infant skull lesions, Hutchinson's incisors, or mulberry molars. Of the 245 known subadult long bones, 29 are affected with diaphyseal osteomyelitis and 24 with mild periostitis. Cook (1976) has argued that a high prevalence and specific anatomical distribution of proliferative lesions in subadults and the absence of skeletal and dental lesions pathognomonic of congenital syphilis suggests an endemic nonvenereal syndrome rather than a venereal condition. The bone condition in the ossuary samples was chronic in all age groups, and there is little evidence of the neurologic defects that usually accompany late-stage venereal syphilis in adults.

CONCLUSIONS

The treponemal condition affecting the North Carolina coastal Indians as evidenced in the ossuary skeletal material is similar to modern treponematosis. The host response and coadaptation of the disease and host probably would have been different several hundred years ago for the North Carolina coastal Indians than they would be for a modern population.

TABLE 3

Differential Diagnosis of Skeletal Lesions

	Conditions									
	Ossuary Samples	Treponematosis	Trauma	Osteomyelitis	Mycotic Infection	Tuberculosis	Leprosy	Myeloma	Carcinoma	Osteosarcoma
Location of Lesions										
Cranial	X	X	X				X	X	X	
facial	X	X					X	X		
base								X		
parietal	X	X						X		
occipital	X							X		
frontal	X	X						X		
temporal								X		
endocranial								X		
ectocranial	X	X						X		
Postcranial	X	X	X	X	X	X	X	X	X	X
vertebral			X		X	X		X	X	
flat bone			X	X	X	X		X	X	
long bone	X	X	X	X	X	X	X	X	X	X
diaphyseal	X	X	X							X
metaphyseal	X	X	X	X	X	X		X	X	X
epiphyseal			X		X	X	X		X	X
Occurrence of Lesions										
Bilateral	X	X								
Multiple	X	X		X	X	X	X	X		
Type of Lesion										
Cranial										
punched-out lesions								X	X	
clustered pits	X	X								
confluent clustered pits	X	X								
focal superficial cavitation	X	X								
circumvallate cavitation		X								
radial scar	X	X								
serpiginous cavitation	X	X								
nodular cavitation		X								
caries sicca		X								
Postcranial										
cavitation	X	X				X	X			X
cortical destruction	X	X			X	X	X	X		X
sequestra				X		X				
punched-out lesions								X	X	
cloaca				X						
involucrum				X						
periostitis	X	X		X	X		X			
cortical thickening	X	X	X							X
periosteal plaque	X	X					X			
radial subperiosteal spiculation	X	X		X						
medullary cavity obstructed	X	X								
callus			X							
sclerosis	X	X		X						X
swelling	X	X								
gumma	X	X								

Source: Bogdan 1989: table xv.

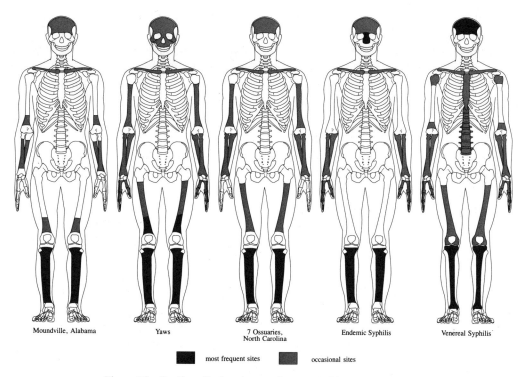

Moundville, Alabama   Yaws   7 Ossuaries,   Endemic Syphilis   Venereal Syphilis
                                                          North Carolina

■ most frequent sites   ■ occasional sites

Fig. 2. Distribution of lesions in 2 study areas and in treponematos

The probable treponemal infection affecting the ossuary populations does not seem to have been transmitted primarily through sexual activity and would have been regarded as part of the normal endemic disease load, an annoyance but not "mortal" or "immoral" (Powell 1988). In most cases this particular disease probably did not contribute directly to the deaths of the people in the ossuary sample (Powell 1988). This is corroborated by modern studies. For example, in Uganda patients with bone lesions from yaws were not severely ill but suffered considerable discomfort (Hackett 1951). In rural Iraqi populations, nonvenereal syphilis did not depress fertility or elevate mortality. The disease manifestations were considered chronic nuisances, not life-threatening afflictions (Hudson 1958). On the biological costs of prehistoric treponematosis in Illinois, Cook (1976) said that mortality probably was not elevated but the level of human misery probably was. An illness described as a "country distemper" or "yaws" among the Carolina Indians in the early eighteenth century (Lawson 1937) seems very similar to modern syphilis. The manifestations of modern venereal syphilis such as visceral, cardiovascular, and central nervous system effects, crippling, blindness, insanity (paresis), and aortic

insufficiency (Brown et al. 1976) probably were not part of the disease symptom load of these coastal ossuary populations.

The proposed diagnosis of endemic treponematosis in these Indians helps inform on the culture of the people. A nonfatal chronic infection such as endemic treponematosis usually will occur in relatively small, rather isolated populations (Cockburn 1963). Affected populations typically are rural with low standards of sanitation and overcrowding. Wearing little clothing, at least seasonally, in this relatively warmer climate would promote skin abrasions and contact with infective lesions, especially among unclothed children. The nature of the villages associated with the ossuaries is confirmed by the archeological data (Phelps 1983), by the ethnohistory (Lawson 1937), and by John White's watercolors of the town of Secotan (Hulton 1984). Lawson (1937) found low standards of sanitation in the villages. White illustrated adults and children wearing little clothing.

A suite of skeletal characteristics in the seven ossuary samples is most consistent with a chronic, endemic treponemal infection. The ossuary material almost certainly dates prior to known European contact. Therefore, the ossuary samples support either the Columbian or unitarian views of treponematosis in North America and argue against the pre-Columbian proposal (Baker and Armelagos 1988).

If the Columbian hypothesis is correct, then Columbus and his crew carried endemic treponematosis back to Europe from their Indian contacts. The Europeans' susceptibility to the disease could have been very high because they previously had not been exposed to it. In Europe the differences in the quality and style of life would have changed the mode of transmission of *Treponema pallidum*. The wearing of clothing would have put the treponeme responsible for endemic treponematosis, transmitted by skin contact, at a disadvantage and a sexually transmitted strain soon would have replaced the endemic strain. This could account for the apparent epidemic of syphilis around 1500 in Europe (Dennie 1962; Crosby 1969; Goff 1967; Harrison 1959). If the unitarian hypothesis is correct, then treponematosis existed in both the Old and New Worlds in different forms, as venereal syphilis in the Old World and endemic syphilis in the New World, and any introduction of New World endemic syphilis probably would not have had a notable effect due to established cross-immunity, although it could have added to the substantial existing disease load in Europe.

What might have been the fate of the New World treponematosis? During the 1700s the North Carolina coastal Indians were removed from their small relatively isolated villages and forced to live on reservations or incorporated into European settlements (Lawson 1937). The change in the Indians' living conditions and the breakdown of their social systems probably affected the transmission of the treponeme. There may have been a change of the endemic syndrome of treponematosis to the venereal syndrome, perhaps accompanied by a transient increase in mortality. With changed living conditions the cycle of childhood infection by endemic syphilis would have been broken, leaving sexual intercourse as the typical means of transmission in adults (Steinbock 1976). If syphilis existed in the New World prior to European contact, in the form of endemic syphilis (Bogdan and Weaver 1988; Bogdan 1989; Hudson 1965; Baker and Armelagos 1988), then the introduction of venereal syphilis by the Europeans to the inhabitants of the New World or the conversion of the existing endemic strains probably would not have had an immediate notable

effect on the Indians. Their susceptibility would have been relatively low because of their previous exposure to *Treponema pallidum*. Therefore, there may not have been an epidemic of venereal syphilis in the New World affecting the Indians.

If the above scenario is correct then the human skeletal material of postcontact coastal Native Americans should exhibit some differences when compared to the skeletal material from the Late Woodland period of the North Carolina coast. Skeletal lesions characteristic of venereal syphilis should begin to appear in the postcontact archeological record of the coastal Indians. Skeletal lesions in adults with acquired venereal syphilis most often would affect the tibia frontal and parietal bones of the cranium, the nasal and palatal regions, sternum, clavicle, vertebrae, femur, fibula, humerus, ulna and radius in that approximate frequency order. Periostitis, osteitis, and gummatous osteomyelitis also would affect the adult skeleton. Although syphilitic females may have had several miscarriages due to acquired venereal syphilis, a large proportion of the infants would have developed the osseous lesions of early and late congenital syphilis including osteochondritis, periosteal cloaking, Wimberger's sign, infant skull lesions, Hutchinson's incisors or mulberry molars (Steinbock 1976; Ortner and Putschar 1985). The archeology and paleodemography also should reveal an increase in fetal and neonatal mortality due to acquired venereal syphilis in females (Steinbock 1976).

REFERENCES

Arnold H. L.
1966   Paradoxes and Misconceptions in Leprosy. *Journal of the American Medical Association* 196:139–142.

Baker, B. J. and G. J. Armelagos
1988   The Origin and Antiquity of Syphilis. *Current Anthropology* 29:703–737.

Bogdan, Georgieann
1989   Probable Treponemal Skeletal Signs in Seven Pre-Columbian Coastal North Carolina Ossuary Samples. (M.A. Thesis in Anthropology, Wake Forest University, Winston-Salem, N.C.).

Bodgan, G. and D. S. Weaver
1988   Possible Treponematosis in Human Skeletons from a Pre-Columbian Ossuary of Coastal North Carolina. *American Journal of Physical Anthropology* 75:187.

Brown, W. J., J. F. Donhue, N. W. Axnick, J. H. Blount, O. G. Jones, and N. H. Ewen
1976   Syphilis and Other Venereal Diseases. London: Harvard University Press.

Cockburn, T. A.
1961   The Origin of the Treponematoses. *Bulletin of the World Health Organization.* 24:221–228.

1963   The Evolution and Eradication of Infectious Disease. Baltimore, Md.: The Johns Hopkins Press.

Cook, D. C.
1976   Pathologic States and Disease Processes in Illinois Woodland Populations: An Epidemiologic Approach. (Unpublished Ph.D. Dissertation in Anthropology, University of Chicago, Chicago).

Crosby, A. W., Jr.
1969   The Early History of Syphilis: A Reappraisal. *American Anthropologist* 71:218–227.

Dennie, C. D.
1962   A History of Syphilis. Springfield, Ill.: Charles C. Thomas.

Goff, C. W.
1967   Syphilis. Pp. 279–293 in Diseases in Antiquity, D. Brothwell and A. T. Sandison, eds. Springfield, Ill.: Charles C. Thomas.

Hackett, C. J.
1951   Bone Lesions of Yaws in Uganda. Oxford, England: Blackwell Scientific Publications.

1963   On the Origin of the Human Treponematosis. *Bulletin of the World Health Organization* 29:7–41.

1967   The Human Treponematoses. Pp. 152–169 in Diseases in Antiquity, D. Brothwell and A. T. Sandison, eds. Springfield, Ill.: Charles C. Thomas.

1983   Problems in Paleopathology of the Human Treponematoses. Pp. 106–129 in Disease in Ancient Man, G. D. Hart, ed. Toronto: Clarke Irwin.

Harrison, L. W.
1959   The Origin of Syphilis. *British Journal of Venereal Diseases* 35:1–7.

Holcomb, R. C.
1934   Christopher Columbus and the American Origin of Syphilis. *United States Naval Medical Bulletin* 32:401–430.

1935   The Antiquity of Syphilis. *Medical Life* 42:275–325.

Hudson, E. H.
1958   Non-veneral Syphilis, a Sociological and Medical Study of Bejel. Edinburgh: E. and S. Livingston.

1965   Treponematosis in Perspective. *Bulletin of the World Health Organization* 32:735–748.

Hulton, P.
1984   America 1585, The Complete Drawings of John White. London: University of North Carolina Press and British Museum Publications.

Lawson, J.
1937   Lawson's History of North Carolina. Richmond, Va.: Garrett and Massie Publishers.

Musher, D. M. and J. M. Knox
1983   Syphilis and Yaws. Pp. 101–120 in Pathogenesis and Immunology of Treponemal Infection, R. F. Schell and D. M. Musher, eds. Boston: Little, Brown and Company.

Ortner, D. J. and W. G. J. Putschar
1985   Identification of Pathological Conditions in Human Skeletal Remains. Washington: Smithsonian Institution Press.

Phelps, D. S.
1983   Archaeology of the North Carolina Coast and Coastal Plain: Problems and Hypothesis. Pp. 1–49 in The Prehistory of North Carolina, M. A. Mathis and J. J. Crow, eds. Raleigh: North Carolina Division of Archives and History, Department of Cultural Resources.

Powell, M. L.
1988   Status and Health in Prehistory: A Case Study of the Moundville Chiefdom. Washington: Smithsonian Institution Press.

Reichs, K. J.
1989   Treponematosis: A Possible Case from the Late Woodland of North Carolina. *American Journal of Physical Anthropology* 79:289–303.

Steinbock, R. T.
1976   Paleopathological Diagnosis and Interpretation. Springfield, Ill.: Charles C. Thomas.

Trigger, B. G.
1969   The Huron Farmers of the North. New York: Holt, Reinhart and Winston.

Ubelaker, D. H.
1974   Reconstruction of Demographic Profiles from Ossuary Skeletal Samples. *Smithsonian Contributions to Anthropology* 18. Washington.

14

Summary on Disease before and after Contact

ARTHUR C. AUFDERHEIDE

This review of the paleopathology evidence of the pre- and post-Columbian eras sheds light on the existence and extent of disease during these periods, its severity, and the response of the Indian populations to new diseases. The paleopathology chapters here, together with many others in the anthropological literature, clearly document the presence of malnutrition, anemia, and a variety of tuberculoid, trepanematoid, and other infections as well as trauma and degenerative conditions. This body of data is now so well established that the concept of a pristine, disease-free, pre-Columbian New World environment is no longer credible.

As is true with most human endeavors, closer examination reveals the need to accommodate a greater degree of complexity than had been conceived when less information was available. The populations studied by Walker and Johnson and by Milner, for example, are reminders that a population's health status does not respond to independent imperatives but instead is commonly linked to sociocultural behavior. The case of the Chumash demonstrates that, in the decades preceding contact, the southern California population was in a state of social and health flux due to agricultural intensification and associated sedentism, with its commonly accompanying negative health effects. The postcontact deterioration in health is augmented by new, contact-related influences. Stodder and Martin show that some isolated populations escaped, or at least postponed, the epidemic infectious consequences of contact suffered by neighboring groups. Milner's study of several contemporary populations also reveals that substantial differences in health status may enable certain groups to cope with an infectious threat better than others.

It is not surprising, then, that the response to contact influences was not uniform. The toll of violence, infection, and social disruption accompanying the campaign of Hernando de Soto and possibly other Spanish explorers was more than the La Florida people could overcome, and Larsen documents their relatively rapid extinction. On the other hand, changes in cortical thickness indicate that the Arikara Indians reported by Owsley thrived during their initial, postcontact interval, probably due to their role as middlemen traders, suffering catastrophic effects only later when the turbulence of social disruption engulfed them.

These, and other studies reported here, clearly

demonstrate the peril of extrapolating isolated observations of disease-related demographic changes to the population of an entire region or even a continent.

These same studies also reveal that paleopathology methods are burdened with some very real constraints. Ortner explains that the acute viral infections of smallpox and measles produce no diagnostic morphologic skeletal changes, yet it is precisely these viral infections that are perceived as the principal agents of the known and postulated postcontact epidemics. Until immunology, molecular biology, or other disciplines create means permitting viral identification in archeological bone, viruses will continue to escape detection, except indirectly through distinctive mortality profiles.

Before contact, Native Americans had developed an immunity to certain infections such as tuberculoid and trepanematoid conditions, which was sufficient to convert them to chronic illnesses resulting in characteristic, and sometimes diagnostic, skeletal alterations. These must have contributed a significant burden to the affected populations, but their demographic effects would have been expressed primarily through decreased fertility, detectable only over a period of many generations. Further, if a disease such as tuberculosis existed in a given population during precontact years and flourished following contact, present methodology cannot identify whether the increase was on an immunological basis or due to dramatically altered social conditions. Finally, few skeletal collections can be dated reliably to the special period of interest—just before or just after contact.

In summary, then, the bioanthropologic studies reported here provide unmistakable evidence of a substantial disease burden suffered by Native Americans prior to 1492. Much of this is due to chronic bacterial infections, while the remainder includes the effects of traumatic, degenerative, and congenital conditions. Their prevalence, severity, and chronology fluctuated enormously, were probably static in any one community only transiently, and responded to both biological and environmental conditions. Present paleopathologic methodological limitations include the absence of reliable markers for epidemic viral infections and the paucity of skeletal collections reliably dated to specific periods of special interest relating to contact time.

II

Population Size before and after Contact

15

North American Indian Population Size

Changing Perspectives

DOUGLAS H. UBELAKER

Why is it important to study population size in the New World in the fifteenth century? An accurate evaluation of population size contributes to an understanding of adaptation and history of the Americas. In one sense, population size and rate of change in population size offer a direct measure of some aspects of adaptational success. Growth in numbers may represent the demographic product of increased fertility, life expectancy, fecundity, survivorship, immigration, and decreased disease exposure or susceptibility. The relationship of population size to available resources can help explain change in technological migration patterns and social systems.

In long-term historical perspective, population size figures offer an opportunity to evaluate the impact of culture contact and arguments for relationships among peoples separated in time. In this sense, assessment of American Indian population numbers is of paramount interest (Johansson 1982). Minimal estimates of pre-European American population size suggest less mortality impact of European contact, while very large estimates imply demographic catastrophe (Ramenofsky 1987). On the other hand, large estimates of aboriginal population weaken the ability of some contemporary American Indians to trace their ancestry back to the tribes identified at contact or to what has been called the ethnographic present. Thus, assessments of American Indian population numbers and other demographic profiles not only serve academic interest but also contribute to broad interpretations of population history and the historical identity of contemporary American Indian groups.

METHODOLOGICAL APPROACHES

Unfortunately, demographic data on American Indian population size from pre-European times to the present are incomplete and subject to interpretation. There is no perfect approach to estimating population size; all available data bases are flawed to some extent and require assumptions and interpretations to generate estimates (Ubelaker 1981). Archeological approaches look at site surface areas, house and mound frequency, quantity of refuse, settlement patterns, and poorly defined concepts such as ecological resource potential. Population estimates generated from such sources must guess how long houses were occupied, how many persons lived in a house, just how many oysters make a meal or to what extent populations exploited their environment. In some regions, data are available to support such interpretations (Asch 1976); in others assumptions must be made.

Ethnohistorical approaches largely rely upon estimates made by early Europeans in contact with American Indian populations. Even if such data were accurate, they may underestimate the pre-European population size since some major epidemics may have preceded actual European contact or at least contact by the particular European making the estimates. On the other hand, memories of those epidemics would have been fresh and perhaps were communicated to the European who enjoyed sufficient rapport. Needless to say, all estimates by early European travelers must be evaluated by scholars familiar with that person's reputation for accuracy, his exposure to the groups being evaluated, and the political context of his estimates.

Given the inadequacy and variable quality of census data during the period of initial historic contact, it is not surprising that scholars have turned to a variety of methods of estimating population size. Some have relied on estimates of death rates utilizing early historic sources or epidemiological analogy, for example, assuming a particular disease impact and working back from a fixed historic estimate. This approach overcomes some problems of spotty census data during the early periods of contact, but it unjustifiably assumes uniformity in population decline and susceptibility to disease. This approach takes the form of computer modeling, which allows more sensitive manipulation of variables and their impact on estimates but does not dispense with and in some cases masks the original underlying assumptions.

Contributions from physical anthropology involve demographic reconstruction from skeletal samples and delineation of disease profiles that augment ethnohistorical and archeological evidence (Buikstra 1976; Ubelaker 1974). Such studies are limited primarily by sampling problems and the frustrations of obtaining accurate estimates of age at death and differential diagnosis of disease.

VARIATION IN ESTIMATES

As a consequence of the weak primary data and multitude of methodological approaches, estimates of New World population size have varied greatly. In 1541, Bartholomé de Las Casas argued that 15 million Indians died in the West Indies between 1500 and 1540 (MacNutt 1909); Kroeber (1939) estimated that just over 8 million Indians occupied the entire Western hemisphere in 1492.

Table 1 documents how estimates of early population size of the United States, North America, and the entire Western hemisphere have varied. Remember that these estimates reflect not only contrasting methodology and assumptions but also different definitions of the geographic areas involved. For example, most scholars define North America as north of Mexico or north of the Rio Grande; however, for Dobyns (1983), the area is "north of Civilized MesoAmerica." I have followed the usage of the *Handbook of North American Indians* in defining it as "north of the urban civilizations of central Mexico" (vol. 7:xiii).

The dates offered for population size show similar variation, further complicating direct comparison. Spinden's (1928, 1930) estimates are offered for the date A.D. 1200. Willcox (1931) focused on the middle of the seventeenth century, and Dobyns (1983) on the "early years of the sixteenth century." Rivet's (1924) estimate refers to the "moment of discovery," which presumably is 1492. In reality, there were many individual "moments of discovery" as European contact with American Indian groups gradually moved from east to west. This temporal variation in early contact was identified in the Mooney-Kroeber estimates since their "early figures" varied from 1600 in New England, the coastal Southeast, and eastern Canada to as late as 1845 for the Central Mountain area (Ubelaker 1976b).

The first and some would argue the most thorough attempt to estimate early American Indian population size was by Smithsonian ethnologist James Mooney (1910, 1928). In contributing to the Smithsonian's *Handbook of American Indians North of Mexico* and in preparation for a monograph to be published in the Bureau of American Ethnology series, Mooney attempted a tribe-by-tribe estimate of American Indian population size. He supplied a minimal estimate for the data described largely based on ethnohistorical sources (Ubelaker 1976b). For many tribes he utilized original census data and primary ethnohistorical sources. For tribes of other areas, he relied upon secondary sources and compilations of statistical data that he considered trust-

TABLE 1

Estimates of Early New World Population Size

	United States	North America	Western Hemisphere
Mooney 1910	846,000	1,148,000	—
Sapper 1924	2,000,000–3,000,000	2,500,000–3,500,000	40,000,000–50,000,000
Rivet 1924	—	1,148,000	40,000,000–45,000,000
Spinden 1928	—	—	50,000,000–75,000,000
Mooney 1928	849,000	1,153,000	—
Willcox 1931	294,000	1,002,000	13,101,000
Kroeber 1939	—	900,000	8,400,000
Rosenblat 1945	—	1,000,000	13,385,999
Steward 1945	770,000	1,000,000	13,170,000
Ashburn 1947	—	2,000,000–2,500,000	—
Steward 1949	—	1,000,880	15,590,880
Rivet, Stresser, and Loukotka 1952	—	1,000,000	15,500,000
Driver 1961	—	1,000,000–2,000,000	—
Borah 1964	—	—	100,000,000
Dobyns 1966	—	9,800,000	90,043,000
Mörner 1967	—	—	33,300,000
Ubelaker 1976a	—	2,171,125	—
Denevan 1976	—	4,400,000	43,000,000–72,000,000
Thornton and Marsh-Thornton 1981	1,845,183	—	—
Dobyns 1983	—	18,000,000	—
Thornton 1987	5,000,000	7,000,000	72,000,000
Ubelaker 1988	—	1,894,350	—

worthy or at least amenable to interpretation. For tribes in the southern Plains and California, he utilized estimates made by colleagues Herbert E. Bolton and C. Hart Merriam, whose knowledge of those areas he respected. By 1913, he had assembled most of the information, completed estimates for most tribes, and even drafted text for some areas. At that point, his research on the problem was interrupted and never completed. Following Mooney's death in 1921, Smithsonian colleague John R. Swanton discovered and published Mooney's tribal tabulations (Mooney 1928). Kroeber (1939) used the Swanton-published Mooney estimates as the basis for his well-known monograph on culture areas of North America. In computing density statistics for different areas of North America, Kroeber utilized all Mooney's figures except those for California, where he substituted his own data. Through these publications, the Mooney estimates influenced thinking on population numbers for decades.

Spinden (1928, 1930) offered a contrasting early approach utilizing ecological and archeological evidence. Mound frequency in North America and other evidence suggested to him that as many as 50 to 75 million Indians occupied the Western hemisphere at about 1200. Spinden did not suggest a specific population size but claimed that Mooney's figures were much too conservative. His estimates also communicate his apparent belief that American Indian population size had declined between 1200 and the time of European contact, a point of view relevant to issues being discussed today.

Borah (1964) and Dobyns (1966) introduced an influential new perspective on the population issue. Emphasizing the catastrophic effect of disease on a resistence-free New World population, they utilized projection techniques to increase hemispheric estimates to the 90 million to 100 million range. Much of their projection procedure involved working backward in time from a fixed point of nadir and assuming a generalized rate of population decline. They also assumed that the mortality impact of epidemics long preceded actual contact or at least historic documentation and thus American Indian populations had dramatically reduced in size prior to the first accounts recorded by Europeans. Dobyns's (1966) population estimate of just under 10 million for North America was increased by him to 18 million in 1983.

As table 1 shows, later estimates of population size are substantially higher than generally acknowledged in Mooney and Kroeber's time, reflecting an increased appreciation for the devastating impact of disease and the relatively late date of Mooney's estimates. However, there is little agreement on the magnitude of the early population decrease.

SMITHSONIAN ESTIMATES

Analysis of essays in the Smithsonian's *Handbook of North American Indians* (Sturtevant 1978–) offers an opportunity to measure scholarly sentiment on this issue. For each of the tribal chapters, specialists were invited to consider temporal change in population numbers. Logically, this effort makes available fresh estimates for each tribe offered by specialists who best know the primary sources. In 1976, I evaluated articles submitted for publication at that time, utilizing only those that could be directly compared with Mooney's estimates and those that presented evidence of a fresh evaluation, not just a direct utilization of the Mooney estimates (Ubelaker 1976a). Estimates that merely cited Mooney or Kroeber were not considered unless they critically evaluated the evidence and agreed with Mooney's figures. The 45 articles that at that time met the above criteria showed an average increase of 98 per-

cent over the original Mooney estimates. If projected to all of North America, Mooney's estimate of 1,152,950 would be raised to 2,171,125, a dramatic increase but still far short of that suggested by Dobyns.

In 1985, I returned to the *Handbook* tribal chapters to utilize the individual tribal population estimates as a data base along with information assembled from other sources. This effort culminated in new estimates (table 2) of North American population size at the time of initial European contact for all tribes in each of the 10 culture areas covered by the *Handbook* (Ubelaker 1988). These new estimates reflect early ethnohistorical data, archeological evidence, assessment of the likely impact of early epidemics, and ecological factors. All estimates for each tribe were made independently and later summed to obtain regional totals. Areas occupied by tribes were measured using the tribal maps available in the *Handbook* files. Densities were then calculated for each tribe and culture area (table 2).

The relative density calculations compare favorably with those offered by Kroeber (1939). California clearly shows the greatest density, followed closely by the Northwest Coast. Predictably, the Subarctic, Arctic, Great Basin, and Plains show the sparsest population. A minimum and maximum population size is given for each culture area at the time of initial European contact, reflecting the range in interpretation of data available for that

TABLE 2

Estimates of North American Population Size at Initial European Contact

Region	Area/ 100 km²	Minimum		Ubelaker Estimate		Maximum	
		Number	Density/ 100 km²	Number	Density/ 100 km²	Number	Density/ 100 km²
Arctic	23,779	56,575	2	73,770	3	94,350	4
Subarctic	56,261	69,400	1	103,400	2	151,850	3
Northwest Coast	3,260	102,100	31	175,330	54	210,100	64
California	2,963	128,400	43	221,000	75	287,300	97
Southwest	16,116	287,300	18	454,200	28	679,000	42
Great Basin	9,002	25,700	3	37,500	4	45,500	5
Plateau	5,093	42,500	8	77,950	15	96,700	19
Plains	30,056	140,700	5	189,100	6	284,900	10
Northeast	18,937	205,000	11	357,700	19	503,200	26
Southeast	9,095	155,800	7	204,400	22	286,000	31
Total	174,562	1,213,475	7	1,894,350	11	2,638,900	15

Source: Ubelaker 1988:291.

TABLE 3

Estimates of North American Indian Population Size, 1500 to 1970

Area	1500	1600	1700	1800	1850	1900	1925	1950	1960	1970
Arctic	73,700	73,700	73,700	59,190	49,905	34,994	35,928	51,928	61,186	73,304
Subarctic	103,400	103,400	99,750	76,350	55,960	45,535	46,145	57,286	76,115	98,892
Northwest Coast	175,330	175,330	175,000	98,333	50,338	29,785	25,906	33,311	40,337	47,798
California	221,000	221,000	221,000	200,000	82,980	14,825	11,005	10,542	13,341	16,140
Southwest	454,200	420,000	276,260	215,950	176,740	158,283	180,010	214,845	263,400	312,129
Great Basin	37,500	37,500	37,500	33,905	26,097	14,606	11,874	14,406	16,964	19,562
Plateau	77,950	77,950	77,950	70,000	46,300	18,720	18,649	25,045	60,245	35,682
Plains	189,100	189,100	189,100	120,330	103,136	62,656	76,591	123,513	169,613	211,701
Northeast	357,700	345,700	149,360	117,260	106,110	95,457	120,346	159,257	200,803	244,327
Southeast	204,400	157,400	105,125	60,370	73,415	61,701	79,578	109,826	122,263	137,932
Total	1,894,280	1,801,080	1,404,745	1,051,688	770,981	546,562	606,032	799,959	994,267	1,197,467

Source: Ubelaker 1988:292.

group. Totals of these figures suggest a minimum population size for North America between 1,213,475 and 2,638,900. My own estimate of 1,894,350 more than doubles Kroeber's (1939) figure of 900,000, is about 65 percent greater than Mooney's (1910) estimate of 1,148,000, is slightly lower than my 1976 projection of the then-available *Handbook* data, and is far short of the Borah (1964) and Dobyns (1983) projections.

As part of the *Handbook* project, I also traced the population history of each culture area through time (table 3). Of course, in the nineteenth century, these data become complicated by the mass movement of Indian people, intermarriage among tribes, intermarriage between Indians and non-Indians, as well as the shifting definitions of tribes. With time, census procedures improved, but the definitions of Indian and tribe changed, sometimes dramatically. Following population reduction and relocation, new tribal definitions and reservations evolved that incorporated remnants of pre-existing tribes.

To assess the size of the contemporary Indian population, I turned to four data bases: the 1980 United States census based upon projections from a sampling of self-declared Indian citizens, 1980 Department of Commerce statistics on Indian residents on or near reservations, 1981 tribal enrollment numbers provided by the Bureau of Indian Affairs, and 1985 tribal enrollment provided directly by the tribes (table 4). Note that the reservation figures included all American Indians,

Eskimos, and Aleuts residing on each reservation, including those who may be enrolled elsewhere.

The 1985 enrollment figures result from a questionnaire and subsequent telephone inquiries directed to the elected officials of all federally recognized United States tribes and their enrollment offices. For the few tribes who did not respond, numbers were projected from the 1981 figures provided by the Bureau of Indian Affairs, in consideration of the rate of change documented for neighboring groups. American Indian communities and organizations that were not recognized by the United States were not included.

Tribal requirements for membership in the United States today vary widely. These requirements specify from one-sixteenth to five-eighths "blood quantum" traceable to known members of the tribe, or to members on tribal rolls at a particular date, certificates issued by the Bureau of Indian Affairs, individual judgment by the tribal council, and matrilineal or patrilineal descent from a known member.

Data on Canadian bands were provided by the Canadian federal government (Canada, Department of Indian Affairs and Northern Development 1980, 1982, 1985). Data on 1985 population size of Mexican Indian groups living in that portion of northern Mexico included within the Southwest were provided by the Instituto Nacional Indigenista of Mexico City.

These data plotted through time show that population reduction in North America was quite

TABLE 4

Estimate of United States Indian and Eskimo Populations in the 1980s

Area	1980 Census	1980 Reservation	1981 Enrollment	1985 Enrollment
Arctic and Sub-arctic	64,103[a]	—[b]	81,366[a]	—[b]
Northwest Coast	31,848	7,815	18,222	22,202
California	30,682	6,758	22,302	28,323
Southwest	270,071	180,922	262,869	282,203
Great Basin	26,384	15,293	22,962	28,432
Plateau	27,499	18,383	26,774	30,968
Plains	172,087	69,132	179,021	204,306
Northeast	179,118	30,962	152,592	179,573
Southeast	371,714	10,210	126,179	174,048
Total	1,173,506	339,475	892,287	950,055

Source: Modified from Ubelaker 1988:293.

[a]All Alaska Natives—Indians, Eskimos, and Aleuts.

[b]Data not available for Alaska.

variable (tables 3 and 5). California populations suffered the greatest reductions (95 percent) even though they were among the last populations to sustain major disease impact. Reductions at nadir were least among Arctic and Subarctic populations. The numbers at nadir for all areas total 515,757, indicating an overall reduction of 73 percent. However, because the average dates of nadir range from 1800 to 1940, the actual nadir from North America probably was about 530,000 around 1900, a 72 percent reduction.

The modern data document the remarkable population recovery among American Indians as well as the difficulty of defining "Indian" in contemporary society (table 4). The 1980 United States census estimated American Indian population size at nearly 1.5 million. Passel and Berman (1985, 1986) suggest that this large figure is affected by the incorporation of former non-Indians into the Indian sample as well as shifts of census procedures.

In contrast, only 339,475 Native Americans were living on United States reservations in 1980 (excluding Alaska), and in 1981, 892,287 were enrolled in United States federally recognized tribes.

TABLE 5

Variability in Population Reduction among North American Culture Areas

Area	Number at Contact	Number at Nadir	Approximate Date of Nadir	Reduction	Percentage Reduction
Arctic	73,770	35,000	1900	38,770	53%
Subarctic	103,400	45,500	1900	57,900	56
Northwest Coast	175,330	20,000	1910	155,330	89
California	221,000	10,000	1940	211,000	95
Southwest	454,200	158,000	1900	296,200	65
Great Basin	37,500	11,800	1920	25,700	69
Plateau	77,950	18,000	1910	59,950	77
Plains	189,100	62,000	1900	127,100	67
Northeast	357,700	95,457	1900	262,243	73
Southeast	204,400	60,000	1800	144,400	71

Source: Ubelaker 1988:293.

The following are examples of how these figures are reflected at the individual tribal level. The Cherokee of the Southeast numbered between 22,000 and 40,000 at the time of initial contact, implying a density between 21 and 39 persons per 100 square kilometers. They reached their nadir in about 1839 with a population of about 18,000, a reduction of 7,000 or 28 percent. In 1980, the census indicated a Cherokee population of 232,002. In contrast, only 4,844 were living on reservations, while enrollment for the North Carolina Cherokee, Shawnee Cherokee, and Tahlequah Cherokee totaled 55,368. In 1985, the enrollment increased to about 77,977. Put another way, of the 232,002 Americans who declared themselves to be Cherokee during the 1980 census, only 24 percent were actually enrolled and only two percent were living on a reservation.

In the Southwest, enrollment of the Quechan in 1981 was 1,875 with 1,099 living on the reservation in 1980; yet only 1,237 appeared on the 1980 census projections. Elsewhere in the Southwest, 35,715 Americans considered themselves Apache in the 1980 census, while only 22,257 were enrolled, and 16,396 were living on reservations.

Enrollment in 1985 increased over the 1981 figures by approximately 17 percent in the United States and 8 percent in Canada, documenting the continuing rapid growth of North American Indian populations. The combined United States, Mexican, and Canadian data would suggest a total 1985 population of 1,354,868 using the U.S. reservation figures, 1,612,966 using the United States enrollment data, and over 2.5 million using the United States census self-declaration figure. Whatever figures one uses, the conclusion is the same. The American Indian population suffered a devastating reduction during the nineteenth century; nevertheless, in spite of cultural disruption and continued health and economic problems, Indians are in the midst of a remarkable population recovery. This recovery is so extensive that by some counts they may have surpassed their original numbers in 1492. All demographic indicators suggest this growth will continue into the foreseeable future.

REFERENCES

Asch, D.
1976   The Middle Woodland Population of the Lower Illinois Valley: A Study in Paleodemographic Methods. *Northwestern University Archeological Program, Scientific Papers* 1. Evanston.

Ashburn, P. M.
[1947]   The Ranks of Death, a Medical History of the Conquest of America. New York: Coward-McCann.

Borah, W.
1964   America as Model: The Demographic Impact of European Expansion upon the Non-European World. *35th Congreso Internacional de Americanistas Acts y Memorias.* Vol. 3: 379–387. Mexico, D.F.

Buikstra, J.
1976   Hopewell in the Lower Illinois Valley: A Regional Approach to the Study of Human Biological Variability and Prehistoric Mortuary Behavior. *Northwestern University Archeological Program, Scientific Papers* 1. Evanston.

Canada. Department of Indian Affairs and Northern Development
1980   Linguistic and Cultural Affiliations of Canadian Indian Bands. Ottawa.

1982   Registered Indian Population by Sex and Residence for Bands, Districts, Regions, and Canada. December 31, 1981. Ottawa.

1985   Registered Indian Population by Sex and Residence, for Bands, District, Regions, and Canada. December 31, 1983. Ottawa.

Denevan, W. M.
1976   Epilogue. Pp. 289–292. In The Native Population of the Americas in 1492. W. M. Denevan, ed. Madison: University of Wisconsin Press.

Dobyns, H. F.
1966   Estimating Aboriginal American Population: An Appraisal of Techniques with a New Hemispheric Estimate. *Current Anthropology,* 7(4):395–416.

1983   Their Number Became Thinned: Native American Population Dynamics in Eastern North America. Knoxville: University of Tennessee Press.

Driver, H. E.
1961   Indians of North America. Chicago: University of Chicago Press.

1968   On the Population Nadir of Indians in the United States. *Current Anthropology* 9(4):330.

Johansson, S. R.
1982   The Demographic History of the Native Peoples of North America: A Selective Bibliography. *Yearbook of Physical Anthropology* 25:133–152.

Kroeber, A. L.
1939   Cultural and Natural Areas of Native North America. *University of California Publications in American Archaeology and Ethnology* 38:1–242. Berkeley.

MacNutt, F. A.
1909 Bartholomew de las Casas: His Life, His Apostolate and His Writings. Cleveland, Ohio: A. H. Clake.

Mooney, J.
1910 Population. Pp. 286–287 in Vol. 2 of Handbook of American Indians North of Mexico. F. W. Hodge, ed. *Bureau of American Ethnology Bulletin 30*. Washington.

1928 The Aboriginal Population of America North of Mexico. *Smithsonian Miscellaneous Collections* 80:1–40. Washington.

Mörner, M.
1967 Race Mixture in the History of Latin America. Boston: Little, Brown, and Company.

Passel, J. S., and P. A. Berman
1985 An Assessment of the Quality of the 1980 Census Data for American Indians. Proceedings of the Section on Survey Research Methods. *American Statistical Associate:* 50–59.

1986 Quality of 1980 Census Data for American Indians. *Social Biology* 33(3–4):163–182.

Ramenofsky, Ann F.
1987 Vectors of Death: The Archaeology of European Contact. Albuquerque: University of New Mexico.

Rivet, P. G.
1924 Langues Américaines. Pp. 597–712. in *Les Langues du Monde, Vol. 16*. A. Meillet and M. Cohen, eds. Paris: Société de Linguistique de Paris.

Rivet, P. G., P. Stresser, and C. Loukotka
1952 Les Langues de l'Amérique. Pp. 941–1160. in *Les Langues du monde*. A. Meillet and M. Cohen, eds. Paris: Centre National de la Recherche Scientifique.

Rosenblat, A.
1945 *La Poblacíon indígena de América desde 1492 hasta la actualidad*. Buenos Aires: Institución Cultural Española.

Sapper, K.
1924 Die Zahl und die Volksdichte der indianischen Bevölkerung in Amerika von der Conquista und in der Gegenwart. Pp. 95–104. in *Proceedings of the 21st International Congress of Americanists*, Pt. 1. The Hague, Leiden: E. J. Brill.

1948 Beiträge zur Frage der Volkszahl und Volksdichte der vorkolumbischen Indianerbevölkerung. Pp. 456–478. in Reseña y Trabajos Científicos del XXVI Congreso Internacional de Americanistas. Sevilla, 1935. Madrid: S. Aguirre.

Spinden, H. J.
1928 The Population of Ancient America. *The Geographical Review* 28:641–661.

1930 The Population of Ancient America. Pp. 451–471 in *Annual Report of the Smithsonian for 1929*. Washington.

Steward, J. H.
1945 The Changing American Indian. Pp. 282–305. in The Science of Man in the World Crises. Ralph Linton, ed. New York: Columbia University.

1949 The Native Population of South America. Pp. 655–688. in The Comparative Ethnology of South America Indians. vol. 5 of Handbook of South American Indians. *Bureau of American Ethnology Bulletin 143*. Washington.

Sturtevant, W. C.
1978– *Handbook of North American Indians*. 20 vols. Washington: Smithsonian Institution.

Thornton, R.
1987 American Indian Holocaust and Survival: Population History Since 1492. Norman: University of Oklahoma Press.

Thornton, R., and J. Marsh-Thornton.
1981 Estimating Prehistoric American Indian Population Size for United States Area: Implications of the Nineteenth Century Population Decline and Nadir. *American Journal of Physical Anthropology* 55(1):47–53.

Ubelaker, D. H.
1974 Reconstruction of Demographic Profiles from Ossuary Skeletal Samples: A Case Study from the Tidewater Potomac. *Smithsonian Contributions to Anthropology* 18. Washington.

1976a Prehistoric New World Population Size: Historical Review and Current Appraisal of North American Estimates. *American Journal of Physical Anthropology* 45:661–665.

1976b The Sources and Methodology for Mooney's Estimates of North American Indian Populations. Pp. 243–288 in The Native Population of the Americas in 1492. W. M. Denevan, ed. Madison: University of Wisconsin Press.

1981 Approaches to Demographic Problems in the Northeast. Pp. 175–194 in Foundations of Northeast Archaeology. D. R. Snow, ed. New York: Academic Press.

1988 North American Indian Population Size, A.D. 1500 to 1985. *American Journal of Physical Anthropology* 77(3):289–294.

Willcox, W. F.
1931 Increase in the Population of the Earth and of the Continents Since 1650. Pp. 33–82 in International Migrations. Vol. 2, W. F. Willcox, ed. New York: National Bureau of Economic Research.

16

Disease and Population Decline in the Northeast

DEAN R. SNOW

The Mohawk Valley is a nearly ideal region in which to study paleodemography by archeological and ethnohistorical means. Perhaps the most favorable aspect of the research conditions has to do with the Mohawk settlement pattern. Beginning in the late fifteenth century, small scattered Mohawk villages began to nucleate into a few large and archeologically well-defined communities. The practice was for each community to remain at a particular village location until soil productivity and firewood supplies declined to a point that made trips to active fields too long to be practicable. As villages grew to become towns, and these processes worked more rapidly, this interval shortened to around two decades. Because communities tended to move their villages to new locations on which there were few or no remains from earlier occupations, the practice left a large number of well-defined single component sites of brief duration.

Village population sizes can be derived from measurements of village areas (Snow and Starna 1989), using the ratio of warrior counts to total populations, average nuclear family sizes, and the number of people per unit of longhouse space. Warriors accounted for 25 percent of the total population, there were five people per nuclear family, and there were on average 10 people (2 families) per longhouse compartment. Prior to A.D. 1500 villages tended to allow about 20 square meters per person. From that time to around 1633 the ratio was at a more dense level of about 12 square meters per person. Thereafter it went back to 20 square meters per person. All these ratios have been tested in various ways (Snow 1987) and have been found to be accurate within 10 percent.

The seventeenth-century Mohawks are fairly well understood because there are good documentary sources from around 1625 on. Evidence from these and archeological sources has established that there must have been an aggregate population of no fewer than 8,100 Mohawks in 1633 (Snow and Starna 1989). There were no exogenous epidemics of measurable severity prior to that year (Snow and Lanphear 1988).

Starting with the archeologically known population at around 1550 and assuming a rate of endogenous growth that is consistent with known growth rates for Iroquoian communities, the population could not have reached 8,100 by 1633. This means that the Mohawk population of 1633 must have been augmented to some degree by in-migration.

Mohawk population growth through in-migration is consistent with what is known about regional population shifts from the fifteenth century on. Prior to nucleation, Northern Iroquoians were broadly distributed in small villages in southern Ontario and New York. By the late sixteenth century, the small villages had nucleated into larger ones, and the larger villages had clustered into 13 settlement areas—Huron, Petun, Neutral, Wenro, Erie, Seneca, Cayuga, Onondaga, Oneida, Mohawk, Susquehannock, and two groups of Saint Lawrence Iroquoians (Coe, Snow, and Benson 1986:61). In this process, large areas were abandoned together, but with no apparent overall population decline. For example, the areas just north of Lake Ontario and Jefferson County, New York, just east of Lake Ontario both had sets of large prehistoric villages, but these were abandoned before the first traces of European trade goods began to arrive. Archeological evidence suggests that both these groups joined other Ontario Iroquoians west of Lake Simcoe to become the nation known historically as the Huron.

This process continued through the sixteenth century. Saint Lawrence Iroquoian communities were visited by Jacques Cartier in the 1530s and 1540s, but they had disappeared by the seventeenth century. Similarly, the Susquehannock abandoned their villages on the upper Susquehanna River, some of them dispersing while others reestablished villages in southern Pennsylvania. Trigger (1985: 144–148) and Pendergast (1989) both suggest that the western Saint Lawrence Iroquoians were dispersed and partly absorbed by the Huron, while those from modern Montreal to Quebec were dispersed and partly absorbed by the Mohawk. Some Susquehannocks probably also went to the Mohawk Valley, and these influxes might account for the rapid growth of Mohawk villages prior to 1633.

SEVENTEENTH-CENTURY EPIDEMICS

It is known that epidemics ravaged the Mohawks from 1634 on. The epidemic that nearly wiped out the Indians of southeastern New England between 1616 and 1622 did not reach what is now New York. Its identity has been debated for years, but compelling arguments have used evidence of hepatic failure to focus attention on viral hepatitis (see Spiess and Spiess 1987, with references).

The failure of this epidemic to spread westward beyond the Connecticut River represents the first occurrence in the Northeast of a pattern of severe but localized outbreaks. Later epidemics tended to be similarly severe but localized, sometimes taking years to spread across the entire region. The sporadic pattern of spatially limited outbreaks contradicts the pattern of widespread pandemics proposed by Dobyns (1983).

An unidentified epidemic, perhaps measles, was reported during the summer of 1633 in and around the trading post established by Plymouth on the Connecticut River (Bradford 1908:302–303). Measles later struck various Northern Iroquoian communities during 1634 and 1635 (JR 7:221, 8:43, 87–89, 12:265).

During the winter of 1634–1635, in a fort on the upper Connecticut, over 900 of 1,000 Indians resident there became ill, and half of them died. A contemporary account implies that the disease was smallpox, and the mortality rate is consistent with that identification. In spring 1635, Indians around the Plymouth trading house on the lower Connecticut also became sick, and the disease was explicitly identified as smallpox (Bradford 1908:312–313).

The smallpox epidemic had also reached the Mohawks. The Dutch had been permanently settled at what is now Albany since 1624, having traded sporadically there since 1609. The fur trade suddenly dried up in 1634, prompting the Dutch to send their first small expedition into Mohawk country to find out what was wrong. They suspected that French traders were diverting the furs that would normally pass through Mohawk country to Fort Orange. They were so worried that they sent a small expedition up the Mohawk River to visit Mohawk and Oneida villages. Van den Bogaert's 1634–1635 (1988) journal of this trip provides the first documentary glimpse of the Mohawks. What he found was a population staggered by the effects of its first smallpox epidemic. His description of the villages clearly indicates that an epidemic had only recently ravaged their populations. He was especially struck by the large number of new graves outside the village of Canagere (Van den Bogaert 1988:5).

Smallpox spread to the other Iroquois nations, but it is nearly certain that it did not reach the Huron for six years. Measles, but apparently not smallpox, attacked the Huron in 1635 (JR 8:87–

89). The Jesuits were consistent and accurate in reporting smallpox, but they avoided using that word to describe this epidemic. Nevertheless, the disease was lethal. In 1635 "hardly one of the savages escaped . . . the infection of a certain plague, by which very many were destroyed" (JR 11:9).

In 1636, a new epidemic made its way to the Mohawk, and from there it spread to the Huron. The reports of the Jesuits for 1636 to 1637 are filled with details regarding fatalities among the Indians around their Huron missions. However, those details focus mainly on successes and failures in the constant effort to baptize dying Indians (JR 11:13–17). The Jesuit chroniclers rarely describe the symptoms of the disease, and almost always refer to it vaguely as a contagion or a malady (JR 13:145, 15:13, 23, 43). Whatever the disease was, the Hurons and the Jesuits had definite ideas about its origin. The malady had come from the Mohawks, who had contracted it from the Susquehannock (JR 14:9). What few comments are made about the disease itself indicate that it was characterized by a very high fever and delirium in the terminal stage. Rashes or other external signs of disease are almost never mentioned. With smallpox and other epidemic diseases having visible diagnostic symptoms, the telltale signs are customarily mentioned, and the failure to mention them in this case is evidence that none was manifest. Le Mercier (JR 14:51) seems to misdiagnose this epidemic as malaria (*mauvais air*), but this is just a mistranslation of words meaning "bad air." Malaria is not carried by the mosquitos of northeastern North America. Elsewhere, Le Mercier refers to the epidemic as a "*maladie*" or "*contagion*" "which has spared hardly any one" (JR 14:82–83), suggesting that these are all general terms for a disease he could not identify with certainty.

The Jesuits themselves fell ill during the 1636 epidemic (JR 13:95–101). The Jesuits' own experience with the epidemic indicates that it was characterized by a high fever that came and went episodically over the course of one or two weeks. The patient was apparently flushed during these episodes, and the worst of them were serious enough to cause death. The epidemic worsened in Huron villages during the winter of 1636–1637 (JR 13:145). The intensification of the epidemic during the winter is consistent with the behavior of streptococcal infections, commonly referred to as scarlet fever. The few symptoms described are also consis-

tent with this identification. The tendency for such infections to spread by means of contaminated food is consistent with the communal eating habits of Iroquoians. Families often ate from the same pots, using common utensils. This would also explain why the disease bypassed some families, some longhouses, and some villages, but often infected either everyone or no one within a particular dining unit. The epidemic abated by the summer of 1637.

Smallpox at last came to Quebec in 1639 (JR 18:91) and made its way westward into Huron country during 1640. There was high mortality among children under seven years of age, 360 of which died in one village (JR 19:79, 127). Smallpox was probably not the only disease afflicting the Huron at this time, but it was probably the primary cause of death (JR 20:25).

By 1644 the Jesuits despaired of salvaging anything from their mission (JR 25:105–109). However, by 1648 at least some Jesuits were more optimistic (JR 32:253). At least some of their enthusiasm was zealous hyperbole, but it is interesting to note that a major epidemic had not returned to Huron country in the nine years between 1639 and 1648.

The preepidemic population of the Huron has been variously estimated. Heidenreich (1971:103) concludes that it was about 21,000 but allows the possibility that it was as low as 14,000. Trigger once put the total at 18,000 but has allowed for both higher and lower figures (Trigger 1969:11–13, 1985:234). Whatever the original number, by the 1640s, the Huron had been reduced to 7,000–9,000 (Trigger 1976:589, 1985:234), a loss of 35 to 67 percent depending upon the original figures chosen.

In 1643 there were for the Mohawk "only three villages, comprising about seven or eight hundred men of arms" (JR 24:271). This figure suggests a maximum Mohawk population of 2,800–3,200, a reduction of at least 60 percent over the course of a decade. There were no fewer than 2,000 Mohawks, probably more, in 1644 (JR 26:49).

There was a general epidemic, a "malignant fever" that "took them like a cold" (Winthrop 1908, 2:267, 326) in 1646–1647 in New England. It struck the Europeans as well as the Indians. A relatively mild disease, perhaps the same one, hit the Huron in 1653 (JR 39:125–127). The disease was rapid and affected virtually all the Jesuits and the Hurons. Yet while the Jesuits recovered quickly, it was lethal to many of the Hurons. Winthrop (1908, 2:267) remarks that in the New England epidemic "some died in five or six days, but if they escaped the eighth they recovered." He explains that "such as bled or used cooling drinks died; those who took comfortable things, for most part recovered, and that in a few days" (Winthrop 1908, 2:326). These observations, like those of the French Jesuits, all suggest that variations in treatment led to pronounced variations in severity and mortality.

By 1656, Donck (1968:64), writing of all the Indians of coastal and interior New Netherland, reported that they had experienced a 90 percent population loss overall by this time. By 1660 there were no more than (as opposed to no fewer than) 2,000 Mohawks (JR 45:207), a net loss of 75 percent in 25 years. However, if Donck's overall estimate is anywhere near correct, the Mohawks experienced a net loss that was substantially less than overall losses in New Netherland during the same period.

The Jesuits estimated that there were about 8,800 Iroquois surviving in 1660, 2,000 of which were Mohawks (JR 45:207). These numbers are derived by multiplying their warrior counts by four to obtain overall population sizes. The Jesuits also noticed the changing structures of Iroquois populations. The Iroquois nations had clearly incorporated many people from other nations by 1660, former allies and former enemies alike (JR 45:207).

Smallpox returned and destroyed over half the Montauk of Long Island in 1658 (Ruttenberg 1872). Smallpox spread to the interior and killed 1,000 Iroquois in 1662 (JR 47:193, 50:63). About 23 percent of the Iroquois were Mohawks at this time, and perhaps the same proportion of the deaths, or 230 people, were Mohawks. The mortality rate among the Iroquois was around 12 percent, about what one should expect for a smallpox epidemic returning after an absence of 28 years. There would have been few susceptibles over 28 years of age, and case fatality rates would probably have been below 30 percent for all but infants (Benenson 1984:551). Two years after this, in 1664, a smallpox epidemic killed many Massachusett Indians (Potter 1835).

In 1668, smallpox or measles was again among the Montagnais and Algonquin, but Huron refugee settlements escaped with minor losses (JR 53:123–124). The low mortality suggests that although smallpox may well have attacked some groups, the Huron were afflicted by something milder, perhaps

measles. The same epidemic attacked at least some of the Iroquois, namely the Seneca (JR 54:79–81). There is no mention of smallpox. Furthermore, given that there had been a severe smallpox epidemic among the Iroquois only six years earlier, in 1662, it seems unlikely that enough new susceptibles could have been present among the Senecas to allow it to get a foothold at this time.

Epidemics occurred sporadically elsewhere in New France in 1669–1670 (JR 53:71–81). The disease (if it was only one) is not identified but appears to have led to high fever and dementia in at least some cases. What sounds like the same disease broke out among the Mohawk in 1672 (JR 57: 81–83).

Influenza (rheum) spread to the Huron in 1676 (JR 60:175). An epidemic of smallpox was said to be among the Iroquois in 1678 (JR 63:205). The reported low incidence and mortality again probably had to do with smallpox having broken out there only 16 years earlier, in 1662. There were probably few, if any, susceptibles over the age of 16, and of these the older children would have had a good chance of recovery.

Perhaps the same outbreak of smallpox was noted by Dutch sources. It was said to have caused many deaths among the Iroquois in the winter of 1679–1680 (Dankers and Sluyter 1867:277; cf. Danckaerts 1959:181). The reason for the apparent delay of a year between the Jesuit notice of 1678 and the Dutch one of 1679 might be that the Jesuits were among the Senecas while the Dutch observers dealt mainly with the Mohawks. The lags in disease spread in the Northeast over the previous half century indicate that it could take a year for the epidemic to spread from the westernmost to the easternmost of the Five Nations.

There was measles or smallpox among the Huron in 1682 (JR 62:145) but no more references to epidemics for the remainder of the seventeenth century. Table 1 summarizes documentary evidence of Mohawk population decline through the seventeenth and eighteenth centuries.

COMPUTER SIMULATION OF DISEASE

The archeological evidence for the seventeenth century is consistent with documentary sources. In order to carry the research forward beyond these empirical findings, computer simulations of disease

Population of Mohawk Villages in the Mohawk Valley

Year	Villages	Warriors	Population	Sources
1634	8		8,110	Van den Bogaert 1908
1640–1641	3			JR 21:21
1642–1643	3	700–800	2,800–3,200	JR 24:271
1643–1644			>2,000	JR 26:49
1644	3			Megapolensis 1909
1645–1646	4			JR 29:51
1653	4			Donck 1968:map
1659	3(1 named)			NYCD 13:112
1659–1660	3–4	500	2,000	JR 45:207
1660–1662	3	200	800	JR 47:93
1663–1665	2–3	300–400	1,200–1,600	JR 49:257
1666	4			JR 50:203
1666	5(1 named)			NYCD 3:135
1667–1668	6(3 named)			JR 51:185–203
1669–1670	6(3 named)			JR 53:137–139, 153
1672–1673	3	400 "souls"	?	JR 57:91, 111
1677	5(4 named)	300	1,200	NYCD 3:250
1679		<400	<1,600	Hennepin 1903, 2:511
1685		200	800	NYCD 9:282
1689		270	1,080	NYCD 4:337
1698		>110	>440	NYCD 4:337, 345
1700	4			Romer 1700
1700	2			NYCD 4:654
1701	2			NYCD 4:907
1705	2			Lydekker 1938:19
1709		150–155	600–620	Wraxall 1915:69, 91
1711		150–155	600–620	Wraxall 1915:69, 91
1713	2			Lydekker 1938:37
1713	3[a]		580	Lydekker 1938:40
1736		>80	>320	NYCD 9:1056
1750	2[b]		418	Lydekker 1938:68
1763	3[a]	160	640	DHSNY 1:24
1763	2[b]	160	640	NYCD 7:582
1770	3[a]		420	Johnson 7:877
1773	2[b]		406	NYCD 8:458
1774	3[a]?		406	DHSNY 1:766
1779		100	400	Jefferson 1964

[a]Includes Schoharie.
[b]Excludes Schoharie.

dynamics can provide additional insights. Dynamo, a computer program that allows one to specify initial conditions and rates of change for any number of variables operating over a specific period, simulates complex dynamic systems for the purpose of predicting subsequent trends. Because initial demographic conditions, the processes of epidemics, and the historic outcomes are already known, careful simulations can be used to fill out the details of epidemics.

Figure 1 shows a simple simulation of an influenza epidemic in which everyone is susceptible, everyone gets sick, but no one dies. Such a simulation requires one to specify incubation period, the average length of illness and contagion, cure rate, and infection rate. The last is determined by the frequency of contacts between contagious people and susceptible people multiplied by the frequency with which such contacts lead to infection. The epidemic as shown here plays itself out in under 100 days. The most informative aspect of the simulation is that it demonstrates that variation of the infection rate only hastens or delays the process. One cannot reduce the number of people becoming ill and then

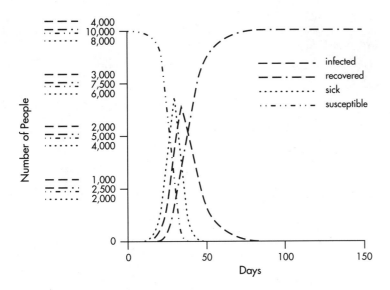

Fig. 1. A sample influenza epidemic simulated by Dynamo, in which there are no deaths.

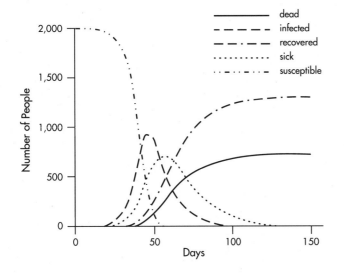

Fig. 2. Simulation of a smallpox epidemic in a village of 2,000. While the lines were produced by computer simulation, all known details of the Mohawk epidemic of 1634 are consistent with this more detailed representation.

recovering by reducing the infection rate. When the infection rate is reduced far enough a threshold is reached below which no one gets sick at all. The message is that if a population is composed entirely of susceptibles, the only way in which a portion of the population can be saved from infection and held in reserve as susceptibles for the next appearance of the same strain of influenza is for them to be out of town for the duration of the epidemic. Even strict quarantine will not stop an influenza epidemic because infected people not showing symptoms are already contagious.

Figure 2 shows a smallpox epidemic and its effects on a Mohawk village population of 2,000. Some new variables are specified in this case. There

is now a death rate, which leads to an accumulation of deceased people and a reduction in the population. Incubation time and the duration of symptoms differ from those of influenza. Once again, however, everyone is initially susceptible and everyone eventually gets sick from this highly contagious disease unless there is an unrealistically effective quarantine or some portion of the population is out of town. In the case of smallpox, people are not contagious until after they show symptoms, but the disease is so contagious and longhouse villages so densely packed that no susceptible Mohawk could have reasonably been expected to escape it.

Figure 3 shows a simulation of the 1633 smallpox epidemic among the 8,100 Mohawks using val-

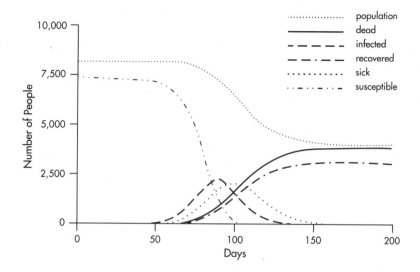

Fig. 3. Simulation of a general smallpox epidemic in a Mohawk population of 8,100. The simulation assumes that 10% of the population was absent.

ues derived from various sources. Standard medical sources indicated that the incubation period of smallpox averages 12 days from the time a person contracts the disease. During this time the person is infected but neither sick nor contagious. The disease is acute and the patient is contagious for 14 days following this. In the worst case epidemic in recent recorded history, 36 percent of those becoming sick died. Benenson (1984:551), following Dixon (1962), allows for the probability that populations having had no previous experience with smallpox would have initially had people present that were genetically very vulnerable. "Vulnerable" here means likely to become infected and likely to die if infected. Although they have not found the rapid natural selection implied by the impressions offered by Dixon and Benenson, Vogel and Chakravartti (1966) have shown that infection rates and mortality vary to some extent by blood groups. They have also documented 50 percent mortality rates in India for the years 1964–1966. These individuals would have been selected out quickly during the first epidemic, leaving few if any descendants having the same high vulnerability. Consequently, Bradford's (1908:312–313) very high death rate of 50 percent has been used in this simulation of the initial Mohawk epidemic. In later smallpox epidemics the death rate among those falling ill might have dropped to 30–40 percent and might have varied by season, but the data from India suggest that this was not necessarily the case.

The 1633 smallpox epidemic simulation explored the range of possible variation in the number of contacts occurring between contagious and susceptible people by varying rates in repeated runs. The possible variation in the fraction of those susceptibles contacted by contagious people that might actually become infected was also explored in repeated runs. These are the two most important variables that one is unable to derive from either medical or historical sources. The outcome changed somewhat when either the number of contacts or the fraction becoming sick was changed. As in the case of influenza, even if the fraction becoming sick was small, the number of contacts between sick and susceptible people ensured that everyone eventually became sick. This could be modified if the fraction becoming sick was made very small, but as soon as it fell below a certain threshold it was too small for anyone to become sick at all. In other words, simulation reveals that if everyone is susceptible but only some fraction of the population actually becomes sick, it is because the people not falling ill have somehow avoided all contact with the sick.

In the simulation in figure 3, Bradford's (1908) observation that 10 percent avoided infection by being away was employed. The equations in the simulation representing the number of contacts and the fraction of contacted susceptibles becoming sick serve to control he length of the epidemic, not the size of the fraction of the total population that eventually become sick. The simulation has shown that 10 percent of the community could have avoided infection only by being away at the time. This initially surprising discovery seemed to fly in the face of the documentary record. Close examination of the documentary record for the seventeenth century reveals that smallpox did not strike everywhere in the same years. The progress of the disease must have been swift and pervasive in any particular community, yet it appears to have had difficulty spreading *between* communities.

Thus smallpox did not spread initially as a regional pandemic. Further, it did not return to any locale until enough new susceptibles were available to allow it to gain a foothold. The Mohawks experienced a smallpox epidemic in 1634. They experienced a second one in 1662 and a third in 1679. This pattern is seen elsewhere in the Northeast, but it occurred in different years for different groups. Smallpox appears to have been unable to cycle more rapidly in any local population because not enough new susceptibles could have been born in that much time to allow the disease to establish itself as an epidemic. Unfortunately, there were other diseases to fill these gaps with their own epidemic cycles.

If migration is added to a larger regional simulation, it explains why some older people remained susceptible and why some nations fared much worse than others through the century. There is plenty of evidence that in this era many Mohawks, especially but not exclusively men, were out of town on almost any particular day. Rare exceptions might have been the days of the Midwinter Festival and other periodic holidays. Second, village fissioning

and the departure of disaffected factions was an established tradition that could have saved uninfected groups even while infected individuals carried the disease to other communities in the region.

There are additional factors at the level of regional simulation. Some out-migrating Mohawks probably did not die for many years, but their departures still contributed to the gross decline of the Mohawk population. Some in-migrating non-Mohawks probably contributed to the pool of susceptibles available in 1637.

Thus at the regional level, there is a relatively simple picture of steady population decline. Even assuming, unrealistically, that in-migration balanced out-migration in every locale, the curve of population decline varied according to the scale of analysis. At the local level, as shown in table 1, decline was prompt and steep. Meanwhile, at the regional level delay in the spread of the disease and the effects of migration cause a more gradual decline. At the continental scale the decline was very close to being linear ("North American Indian Population Size: Changing Perspectives," table 3, this vol.).

Smallpox and other diseases raised the overall mortality rate. Meanwhile, the fertility rate appears not to have changed much if at all (Engelbrecht 1987). The regional population shifted from a mode of modest net growth to dramatic net decline. However, it seems clear that the history of any par-

TABLE 2

Iroquois Population Estimates, 1630–1770

Year	Seneca	Cayuga	Onondaga	Oneida	Mohawk	Canada	Total
1630	4,000	4,000	4,000	2,000	8,000	0	22,000
1640	4,000	2,000	2,000	1,000	3,200	0	12,200
1650	4,000	1,200	1,200	600	2,000	0	9,000
1660	4,000	1,200	1,200	400	2,000	0	8,800
1670	4,000	1,200	1,300	600	1,200	400	8,700
1680	4,000	1,200	1,400	800	800	800	9,000
1690	4,000	1,280	2,000	720	520	400	8,920
1700	2,400	800	1,000	280	400	1,400	6,280
1710	4,000	600	1,400	480	600	800	7,880
1720	2,800	520	1,000	800	640	800	6,560
1730	1,400	480	800	400	320	1,200	4,600
1740	2,000	500	800	400	320	1,200	5,220
1750	2,000	500	800	800	320	1,200	5,620
1760	4,200	504	544	1,000	456	1,200	7,904
1770	4,000	1,040	800	800	420	1,200	8,260

Source: Tooker 1978:421 and table 1 sources.

ticular local population is not simply some fraction of this larger picture. Some populations were more successful than others at taking in migrants. These remained stable or even grew slightly as others declined quickly and disappeared. Furthermore, some local populations were lucky, receiving migrants who were not incubating smallpox or some other disease. Other communities were unlucky hosts to people who fell ill soon after their arrival.

In a simulation of several epidemics at a regional scale, chance variations in local histories would smooth out in the overall picture. People who survived smallpox would still be susceptible to influenza, measles, or whatever, and the net regional decline would quickly approach the 90 percent level described by Donck (1968). However, as terrible as the diseases were, individually and collectively, a perhaps unexpectedly large fraction of the population survived. By itself, the smallpox epidemic of 1634 probably would not have killed more than 50 percent of the population. Yet it is known from the documents that some nations disappeared completely while others seemed to suffer relatively modest losses. The discrepancy appears to be best explained by migration, and a pattern of migration already well established in Iroquoia. Nucleation and homeland abandonment were processes that began before 1500. In the later epidemics surviving nations were by definition net migration gainers while those that did not survive were net migration losers. If a model were controlled adequately for migration, there would almost certainly be little variation in the overall effects of the epidemics.

Of the Northern Iroquoian nations known to exist in 1633, most of those that survived the century were members of the Five Nations Iroquois political confederacy—Mohawk, Oneida, Onondaga, Cayuga, and Seneca. The Saint Lawrence Iroquoians were already gone, their remnants absorbed by the Hurons and others.

The Eries and Wenros disappeared completely, probably absorbed by the Neutrals and Senecas. The Petuns gradually moved into the sphere of the Huron confederacy, while the Neutral confederacy held out nearer the Niagara frontier. All of them were losers in their wars with the stronger Iroquois confederacy. By the middle of the century all these people were either dispersed westward or absorbed by one or another of the five Iroquois nations.

The Susquehannocks shrank to a very small number. They dwindled and disappeared by the middle of the eighteenth century. Meanwhile the Senecas maintained their population level at around 4,000 for most of the century, even while suffering the same epidemics as those experienced by other nations. The Mohawks, who had been net gainers from the migration of the sixteenth century, continued to take in migrants, but not enough to offset losses from epidemics. Table 2, which summarizes data from many sources, shows these differing effects within the Iroquois confederacy over time. However, it is significant that the nations of the Iroquois confederacy all survived the century, while most of those outside it did not.

REFERENCES

Benenson, A. S.
1984 Smallpox. Pp. 541–568 in Viral Infections of Humans: Epidemiology and Control. A. S. Evans, ed. New York: Plenum Medical Book Company.

Bradford, W.
1908 Bradford's History of Plymouth Plantation. W. T. Davis, ed. New York: Barnes and Noble.

Coe, Michael, Dean Snow, and Elizabeth Benson
1986 Atlas of Ancient America. New York: Facts on File.

DHSNY = O'Callaghan, E. B., ed.
1849– Documentary History of the State of New York. 4
1851 vols. New York: Parsons.

Danckaerts, J.
1959 Journal of Jasper Danckaerts [1679–1680]. B. B. James and J. F. Jameson, eds. New York: Barnes and Noble.

Dankers, J., and P. Sluyter
1867 Journal of a Voyage to New York and a Tour in Several of the American Colonies in 1679–80. Henry C. Murphy, trans. and ed. Brooklyn: Long Island Historical Society.

Dixon, C. W.
1962 Smallpox. London: J. & A. Churchill.

Dobyns, H. F.
1983 Their Number Become Thinned: Native American Population Dynamics in Eastern North America. Knoxville: University of Tennessee Press.

Donck, A. van der
1968 A Description of the New Netherlands. T. F. O'Donnell, ed. Syracuse: Syracuse University Press.

Engelbrecht, W. E.
1987 Factors Maintaining Low Population Density Among the Prehistoric New York Iroquois. *American Antiquity* 52:13–27.

Heidenreich, C.
1971   Huronia: A History and Geography of the Huron Indians 1600–1650. Ottawa: Ontario Ministry of Natural Resources.

Hennepin, Louis
1903   A New Discovery of a Vast Country in America [1698]. R. G. Thwaites, ed. 2 vols. Chicago: A. C. McClurg.

JR=Thwaites, R. G., ed.
1959   The Jesuit Relations and Allied Documents 1610–1791. 73 vols. New York: Pageant.

Jefferson, Thomas
1964   Notes on the State of Virginia [1787]. T. P. Abernethy, ed. New York: Harper and Row.

Johnson, William
1921–   Papers of Sir William Johnson. J. Sullivan et al.,
1965   eds. 15 vols. Albany: University of the State of New York.

Megapolensis, Johannes
1909   A Short Account of the Mohawk . . . . 1644. Pp. 163–180 in Narratives of New Netherland, 1609–1664. J. Franklin Jameson, ed. New York: Charles Scribner's Sons.

NYCD = O'Callaghan, E. B., ed.
1853–   Documents Relative to the Colonial History of the
1887   State of New York; Procured in Holland, England and France, by John R. Brodhead. 15 vols. Albany: Weed and Parsons.

Pendergast, J.
1989   Emerging St. Lawrence Iroquoian Settlement Patterns. Symposium on Saint Lawrence Iroquoian Archaeology, Northeast Anthropological Association Meetings, Montreal, March 1989.

Potter, E. R., Jr.
1835   The Early History of the Narragansett Country. Rhode Island Historical Society Collections 3:1–315.

Romer, C.
1700   A Mappe of Colonel Romer's Voyage to ye 5 Indian Nations. New York State Archives Collection, Ser. 1, vol. 3: map 15.

Ruttenberg, E. M.
1872   History of the Indian Tribes of Hudson's River. Albany: J. Munsell.

Snow, D. R.
1987   Variables and Constants in Iroquoian Settlement

Patterns. Toronto: Society for American Archaeology.

Snow, D. R., and K. M. Lanphear
1987   European Contact and Indian Depopulation in the Northeast: The Timing of the First Epidemics. Ethnohistory 35:15–33.

Snow, D. R., and W. A. Starna
1989   Sixteenth Century Depopulation: A View from the Mohawk Valley. American Anthropologist 91:142–149.

Spiess, A. E., and B. D. Spiess
1987   New England Pandemic of 1616–1622: Cause and Archaeological Implication. Man in the Northeast 34:71–83.

Tooker, Elizabeth
1978   The League of the Iroquois: Its History, Politics, and Ritual. Pp. 418–441 in Handbook of North American Indians. vol. 15: Northeast. B. G. Trigger, ed., W. C. Sturtevant, gen. ed. Washington: Smithsonian Institution.

Trigger, B. G.
1969   The Huron: Farmers of the North. New York: Holt, Rinehart and Winston.

1976   The Children of Aataentsic: A History of the Huron People to 1660. 2 vols. Montreal: McGill-Queen's University Press.

1985   Natives and Newcomers: Canada's Heroic Age Reconsidered. Montreal: McGill University Press.

Van den Bogaert, Harmen M.
1988   A Journey into Mohawk and Oneida County, 1634–1635. Charles T. Gehring and William A. Starna, trans. and eds. Syracuse: Syracuse University Press.

Vogel, F., and M. R. Chakravartti
1966   ABO Blood Groups and Smallpox in a Rural Population of West Bengal and Bihar (India). Humangenetik 3:166–180.

Winthrop, J.
1908   Winthrop's Journal "History of New England." 2 vols. J. K. Hosmer, ed. New York: Barnes and Noble.

Wraxall, P.
1915   An Abridgement of the Indian Affairs Contained in Four-Folio Volumes, Transacted in the Colony of New York, for the Year 1678 to the Year 1751. C. H. McIlwain, ed. (Harvard Historical Studies 21) Cambridge, Mass.: Harvard University Press.

17

Depopulation in the Southeast after 1492

RUSSELL THORNTON

JONATHAN WARREN

TIM MILLER

What was the size and density of Indian population in the Southeast in 1492? Scholars have used knowledge of depopulation from early diseases to estimate exceedingly large and dense Indian populations (Dobyns 1983). It is probably generally agreed that Old World diseases were the primary cause of the initial depopulation of the Southeast. Beyond that, there may be little consensus. There are arguments that smallpox was the first, deadly killer of Indians in the Southeast (Dobyns 1983:11–16; Thornton 1987:63–65), though subsequent diseases were important in the depopulation (Dobyns 1983:16–24, 254–271; Thornton 1987:44–47). Did an immense smallpox epidemic sweep the Southeast and elsewhere in 1520 or even earlier (Dobyns 1983:11–16), causing massive and widespread population reduction? Or were the initial impacts of smallpox more local and less severe "episodes," whenever they may have occurred?

ABORIGINAL CHIEFDOMS

Accounts of the expeditions of Hernando de Soto and other early European explorers in the Southeast (Bourne 1922; Swanton 1985, 1979:33–59; Garcilaso de la Vega 1951) as well as archeological evidence (Thomas 1985; Muller 1978; Smith 1978, 1986; Steponaitis 1986) indicate that Indian populations in the Southeast in the sixteenth, seventeenth, and early eighteenth centuries were typically organized as "chiefdoms," though considerable diversity among chiefdoms existed (DePratter 1983:2).

Chiefdoms represented, more or less, the territorial province controlled by a chief; lesser chiefs controlled smaller areas within the chiefdoms (DePratter 1983:20). It has been suggested that Southeast chiefdoms had been rising and declining since about A.D. 900 (DePratter 1983:210). Among the more well known of the chiefdoms were the Natchez, the Coosa (Hudson et al. 1985), the Calusa, the Apalachee, and the Cofitachiqui.

A chiefdom may be generally defined "as a centralized polity that organizes a regional population in the thousands" (Earle 1989: 84; see also Service 1962; Fried 1967; Earle 1987). The characteristic contrasting them from less "developed" types of societies is that they have permanent, institutionalized leadership positions. The distinction may be made between "simple" chiefdoms and "complex" chiefdoms: the former have only one subordinate political level; the latter have two or more subordinate political levels. Moreover, the various political levels are generally associated with geographically discrete central settlements (Steponaitis 1978:419–421).

Population increases in areas of land scarcity have been suggested as the primary cause for the development of highly centralized chiefdoms (Carneiro 1970; Harner 1975; cf. Earle 1989: 84). Population density is probably important in the development of chiefdoms but does not seem to be determinant. For example, it has been argued that low population density was characteristic of the Black Warrior Valley, Alabama (Earle 1989:84). However, a shift to large-scale maize agriculture by Southeast Indians between A.D. 800 and 1200 was probably an important foundation for the development of the chiefdoms; and maize agriculture itself was possibly a response to population pressures (Steponaitis 1986:388–389).

The chronicles of the Hernando de Soto expedition of 1539–1543 (Bourne 1922; Garcilaso de la Vega 1951; also Swanton 1985) indicate that the expedition often encountered large, dense Indian populations organized in complex societies. The settlement pattern described in the chroniclers' writings "was one of discrete territorial units comprised of towns and villages varying in size, and arranged in a hierarchical order of political and presumably economic significance" (Milner 1980:41). The archeological record also indicates "core" settlement patterns within provinces along portions of river drainage systems and scattered villages, towns, and farmsteads throughout the remainder of the province. The geographically small province of Calusa reportedly contained between 40 and 70 towns, and the highly developed Natchez chiefdom may have contained 60 towns (DePratter 1983:22, 24).

The Southeast was not homogenous. The societies and cultures of the interior Southeast seem to have been quite different from those of the coastal areas and the south Florida area, at least in part because of different environments and adaptations to them (Larson 1980:229). Settlement patterns varied: "some groups preferred aggregated settlements, others remained predominantly dispersed, and yet others adopted a flexible strategy that combined both options" (Steponaitis 1986:390).

The geographic areas of the chiefdoms were typically surrounded by unoccupied or sparsely oc-

cupied lands or "deserts" (DePratter 1983:34–36, table 1). These consisted of natural barriers and sociocultural "buffer zones," which frequently corresponded to linguistic differences between the Indian peoples. One such natural area was described on the De Soto expedition. After leaving Apalachee the expedition marched for a week or so through what was described as "desert country" or "wilderness" before reaching the province of Cofitachiqui (Bourne 1922, 2:12, 91). This area comprised part of the "pine barrens sector" of the southeastern coastal plain. The sector stretches from central Florida into and along southern Alabama and Georgia and northward along the Atlantic coastal area into North Carolina (Larson 1980: 5, fig. 1). The entire sector may be considered one of the great "deserts" of the aboriginal Southeast: it contained apparently little population as few food resources were available there (Larson 1980: 35–65). While undesirable areas such as the pine barrens constituted some buffer zones, other buffer zones consisted of environmentally desirable areas and arose because of sociocultural differences. In such instances, the lack of population may have created richer natural resources in the buffer zone (and, perhaps, more reason for rival chiefdoms to contest the area).

The "deserts" of the Southeast served to isolate one chiefdom from another, for example, the " 'desert of Ocute' was a large buffer zone between two antagonistic chiefdoms" (Hudson, Smith, and DePratter 1984:72). Contact between various chiefdoms existed, but little is known about the nature and extent of such contact beyond the fact that some of it occurred through warfare and trade (Milner 1980:41). Warfare was apparently frequent, as all four narratives of the De Soto expedition contain many references to it (DePratter 1983:31).

ABORIGINAL POPULATION SIZE AND DECLINE

Swanton's Estimate

Swanton (1979:11), summarizing Mooney (1910, 1928) and Kroeber (1939), arrived at a population "from the Chesapeake to Texas, including the Caddo and Shawnee and excluding the Atakapa, of 171,900" for the approximate period 1600–1650. Using his own, independent estimates, Swanton arrived at essentially the same figure, though he was inclined to reduce figures somewhat for some specific tribes (Swanton 1979:11). He did not conclude that there was much depopulation prior to 1600–1650, though he did note a depopulation in certain areas (Swanton 1979:12–14).

Ubelaker's Estimate

Ubelaker (1988:292) established a figure for the Southeast of 204,400 for the year 1500. His figure was derived by summarizing population sizes from tribal chapters of the Smithsonian Institution's *Handbook of North American Indians* (Sturtevant 1978–). Ubelaker established a Southeast population of 157,400 for the year 1600, a decline of slightly less than 25 percent during the previous century. He also estimated the Indian population of the Southeast at 105,125 for 1700 and at 60,370 for 1800.

Dobyns's Estimate for Florida

Standing in contradiction to Swanton's and Ubelaker's figures is Dobyns's (1983:291–295) estimate based on depopulations from disease for only the Timucuan-speaking populations of Florida, which total 722,000 for the year 1517 or 807,500 before contact (Dobyns 1983:205, table 22). Added to this, according to Dobyns (1983:294), *could* be a Calusa population of 100,000 and an Apalachee population of 100,000 for an aboriginal population of 922,000 for the state of Florida alone! This is in marked contrast to other estimates of the Timucuan-speaking population: Mooney (1928:8) estimated 13,000 for circa 1650; Kroeber (1939:139, table 7) estimated only 8,000 at the aboriginal period; other estimates range from less than 10,000 to as many as 20,000 for about the mid-1500s (see Dobyns 1983:149, table 20). Mooney (1928:8) estimated 3,000 Calusa and 7,000 Apalachee and related groups; Kroeber (1939:138–139, table 7) estimated 3,000 Calusa and 12,000 Apalachee and related groups. Dobyns (1983:293, table 28) additionally argued that the Timucuan-speaking populations had declined to 361,000 by 1519–1524, to 180,500 by 1528–1533, to 158,000 by 1545–1548, to 150,000 by 1559, to 135,000 by 1564–1570, to 121,500 by 1585, to 97,200 by 1586, to 72,900 by 1596, and to 36,450 by 1613–1617. This represents

a 95 percent decline by 1617. No figures were given for subsequent depopulation, but the Timucan speakers declined to virtual extinction by 1763, according to Dobyns (1983:284).

Rates of Decline

The depopulation rates for the estimates of Swanton, Ubelaker, and Dobyns present very different pictures of Indian depopulation (in part, of course, because they are for somewhat different time periods and areas). Swanton's rates show more or less population stability up to 1600–1650, and then an asserted, though unmentioned population decline. Ubelaker's depopulation rates show a gradually increasing rate of population decline from 1500 to 1800. Dobyns's depopulation rates show a generally decreasing rate of population decline from 1517 to the mid-1500s and then a gradually increasing rate of population decline into the 1600s.

Using exact figures, Ubelaker's data show a decline of 23.0 percent from 1500 to 1600, of 33.2 percent from 1600 to 1700, and of 42.6 percent from 1700 to 1800. Hence, according to Ubelaker, the greatest population decrease in the Southeast occurred during the eighteenth century, followed by the decrease during the seventeenth century, with the initial depopulation during the sixteenth century being the smallest decrease of the 300-year period. In contrast, Dobyns's data show large decreases during the early 1500s, the late 1500s and early 1600s, and around the mid-1700s, but particularly low decreases during the approximate mid-1500s. Timucuan-speaking populations declined, according to Dobyns, by 78.1 percent from 1517 to 1545–1548, by 23.1 percent from 1545–1548 to 1585, by 70.0 percent from 1585 to 1613–1617, and by virtually 100 percent from 1613–1617 to 1763. The lowest mortality, it should be noted, is for the period between the De Soto expedition of 1539–1543 and the arrival of Tristan de Luna in 1559–1560. According to Dobyns (1983:293, table 28), the Timucuan-speaking population declined by only 5 percent between 1545–1548 and 1559! Yet, as Dobyns (1983:291–293) discusses, this was a period of some population collapse, as documented by comparing the observations of the De Luna expedition with those of the De Soto expedition. (In fact, this mere 5 percent mortality was "introduced" by Dobyns precisely to account for the collapse—Dobyns 1983:291.)

INITIAL DEPOPULATION

Ethnohistorical and archeological evidence indicates depopulation of the aboriginal southeastern chiefdoms during the 1500s and 1600s as well as migrations and settlement shifts (Brain 1978; Peebles 1978). Some depopulation may have occurred during the early 1500s, prior to Hernando de Soto's arrival in Florida in 1539 (Wright 1981:44). Certainly, considerable depopulation had occurred between the expeditions of Alvar Nuñez Cabeza de Vaca in 1527–1536 and Juan Pardo in 1566–1568 (DePratter, Hudson, and Smith 1983; Hudson 1987). Up until about 1670 there was little further penetration by Europeans into the interior of the Southeast, but reports after that date indicate that considerable demographic and sociocultural change had occurred. Still, "adequate recording of epidemic disease and its impact on the Indian population of the Southeast does not occur until the eighteenth century" (Milner 1980:40). At issue is the early, initial depopulation of the region, and consequently the shape of the depopulation curve.

Ethnohistorical Evidence

Accounts of European contact with the Southeast and what is now Texas indicate possible depopulation due to disease in the early 1500s. Cabeza de Vaca (1961:60, 103; see also Snow and Lanphear 1988:17–18; Henige 1986:296) reported a possible typhoid epidemic on the coast of Texas in 1528 and in 1535 noted the effects of a possible smallpox epidemic in the interior of Texas. Some writings of the De Soto expedition contain a piece of information that possibly indicates depopulation due to epidemic disease. The Gentleman of Elvas wrote with regard to De Soto's arrival in 1540 at the chiefdom of Cofitachiqui (in present-day South Carolina): "About the place, from half a league to a league off, were large vacant towns, grown up in grass, that appeared as if no people lived in them for a long time. The Indians said that, two years before, there had been a pest in the land, and the inhabitants had moved away to other towns" (Bourne 1922, 2:66). Garcilaso de la Vega (1951:298) wrote from "eyewitness accounts" in his book, completed in 1599, that "a great pestilence with many consequent deaths had ravaged their province during the past year, a pestilence from which their town [Cofitachiqui] alone had been free."

He also wrote that in the nearby abandoned town of Talomeco, there were "four large houses" in the town "filled with the bodies of people who had died of the pestilence" (Garcilaso de la Vega 1951:325). This disease episode of 1538, if it occurred, seems to be the first documented one in the Southeast. Its nature and origin are unknown, and its existence could certainly be disputed (see Henige 1986:301). If it actually happened, possibly the disease came from members of the Lucas Vazquez de Ayllon colony on the coast of South Carolina in 1526. If so, it took the disease a dozen years to arrive from less than 200 miles away.

Dobyns (1983:254–62, 270, table 25) has suggested the possibility of an epidemic of an unknown disease (possibly malaria) in Florida in 1513–1514 and argued for epidemics there of smallpox in 1519–1524, of measles or typhoid fever in 1528, and of an unknown disease in 1535–1538 (Dobyns 1983:259–264, 270, table 25). However, none of these was demonstrated to have definitely occurred, and the chroniclers of the early expeditions to the north do not document any effects of the diseases (except the possible disease episode around Cofitachiqui). The same could be said for Dobyns's epidemics of bubonic plague in 1545–1548, of typhus in 1549, of mumps in 1550, and of influenza in 1559 (Dobyns 1983:264–270, table 25; cf. Henige 1986). Subsequent ethnohistorical accounts indicate some depopulation in Florida and elsewhere due to disease during the late 1500s (see Milner 1980:44; Dobyns 1983:275–290, table 27; Snow and Lanphear 1988:18–20). From then on, many Southeastern Indian populations were depleted for various reasons, including disease (see Milner 1980:44–46; Thornton 1987:65–70, 76, 79, 86, 91–92, 104–105, 113–118).

Archeological Evidence

In the chiefdoms of the "interior" Southeast, "both population and political collapse" occurred "by no later than the first third of the seventeenth century" according to Smith (1984:xiv), who describes population collapse as leading to political collapse. He also argued that depopulation and cultural change resulted from epidemic disease (Smith 1984:1). Smith examined both mass and multiple burials, population curves, site size, and population movements but found little archeological evidence to support this thesis of population collapse as a result of European disease (see Smith 1984:75–121). He did find considerable evidence for the disintegration of the chiefdoms by the early seventeenth century (see Smith 1984:122–155).

Ramenofsky (1987) found archeological evidence of population collapse during the late sixteenth century in the lower Mississippi valley. She argued for its being a result of introduced European diseases, given the ethnohistorical record (Ramenofsky 1987:42–71).

DISEASE DIFFUSION: THE PATTERN OF SMALLPOX

The pattern of initial disease diffusion is important in the debate regarding aboriginal Southeast population size and subsequent depopulation. Particularly important in this regard is whether the introduction of European disease into the Southeast resulted initially in widespread epidemics in the region or only isolated disease episodes. Arguments for the pandemics include the "virgin soil" nature of Southeast populations whereby almost everyone is infected by a new disease; dense populations that were able to sustain disease and facilitate their diffusion throughout a wide area; European expeditions and explorations in the Southeast, which may have spread diseases to wide areas; the migrations of Indian peoples after exposure to diseases, which resulted in other American Indian peoples being exposed; and, of course existing, pre-European patterns of contact between Indian peoples such as warfare and trade, which may have spread diseases without European intervention. In contrast, arguments for localized disease episodes include the possible isolation of the Southeast chiefdoms because of existing hostilities and large "buffer zones," both of which acted to contain diseases; relatively low population densities in many areas, which hindered the spread of diseases as well as their continuation because of small pools of susceptibles; and the relatively short infection periods of many diseases (Joralemon 1982; Dobyns 1983; Thornton 1987; Snow and Lanphear 1988).

Smallpox may have been the first disease introduced into the Southeast, perhaps initially causing a large-scale epidemic. However, the first serious disease in the New World may have been swine influenza (Guerra 1988). It is certain that smallpox was introduced in 1518 and shortly thereafter caused huge population losses in the Caribbean, present-day Mexico, and Central and South America (Joralemon 1982; Gibson 1964). It has not been demonstrated that smallpox arrived in the Southeast at about this time, though it could have. It has also not been demonstrated that smallpox initially was epidemic over a wide area of the United States, though this too has been argued (Dobyns 1983; Upham 1986).

Smallpox was officially eradicated in the world as of December 9, 1979, after a global history of perhaps over 3,000 years. The World Health Organization recognizes two forms of smallpox: variola major, the classic form, which contains various types, and, since the late 1800s, variola minor. Distinctions between the two forms are based on fatality rates; distinctions among the types of variola major are based on the density of the rash (Fenner et al. 1988:4–5; see also Dixon 1962:5–66).

The incubation period of smallpox is usually less than two weeks, followed by fever, the onset of rash, and either death or recovery after another two weeks or more. Smallpox is typically transmitted via the respiratory tract, through either the nose or mouth (or through inoculation) and is usually spread by the shedding of virus from an erupted pox (Fenner et al. 1988:191). Generally, it is spread through coughing or sneezing; sometimes it can be spread from erupted pox on the surface of the skin. Infectivity is during the initial week of the rash, or from about two to three weeks after the infected person was exposed. Typically, infection occurs by direct contact through the inhalation of the virus or by the transfer of the virus via the fingers or objects.

The possibility of infection from smallpox virus on objects in the environment and how long smallpox virus may exist in the environment are important topics, as much of the focus upon smallpox among Indians, especially during the first century or two after European contact, argues that transfer from the environment was an important way Indian populations first contacted the disease. According to the World Health Organization, "even under favorable conditions of low temperature and humidity, the virus did not survive for more than a few days or weeks in a form which could induce infection, unless inoculated, as in variolation" (Fenner et al. 1988:480). If this is actually the case, and it may not be as other studies indicate a much longer survival time (Dixon 1962:296–318), then smallpox diffusion throughout the Southeast—an area of relatively high temperatures and humidity—was probably far more dependent upon direct human transmission than upon transmission via objects in the environment.

In unvaccinated populations, outbreaks of variola major have typically had a fatality rate of 5 to 25 percent; variola minor had a fatality rate of 1 percent or less (Fenner et al. 1988:5). In so-called virgin-soil populations, episodes of smallpox had an incidence rate approaching 100 percent for all age groups, and there are reported fatality rates of 30 to 50 percent and higher (Fenner et al. 1988:229, 237). Under such conditions, smallpox eventually died out in a population because of a lack of susceptible individuals.

Recovery from smallpox typically results in lifetime immunity; however, smallpox reoccurred in a population that acquired a large enough pool of new susceptibles, through birth and immigrations. Smallpox may also become endemic as a disease of children (Fenner et al. 1988:178–179, 215, 224).

Smallpox introduced into the "virgin soil" aboriginal Southeast undoubtedly resulted in incidence rates approaching 100 percent and fatality rates of perhaps 50 percent. At issue is whether smallpox initially became widespread throughout the Southeast, or whether its impacts were localized. It has been argued (Snow and Lanphear 1988) that the "buffer zones" around Southeast chiefdoms hindered, if not actually prevented, the diffusion of smallpox throughout the Southeast. It has also been argued (Snow and Lanphear 1988; Ramenofsky 1988) that smallpox may have "burned itself out" in large, dense Indian populations before it had the opportunity to diffuse from one population to another.

It may be concluded that the more dense the population, the more rapid the spread of smallpox within that community and the sooner smallpox outbreaks terminated (Fenner et al. 1988:196).

Some calculations may demonstrate this. They are based generally on population size, the number of possible close contacts per week per person (a measure of density), the period of infectivity of individuals with smallpox, the removal rate of susceptible individuals from the population due to infection, and the removal rates of infected individuals from the population due to death or recovery (immunity) from smallpox infection. Specifically, calculations are based on the Hamer-Soper model (Bailey 1975). This is a deterministic model of epidemics for a closed community assumed to be comprised of three classes of individuals: those susceptible to infection, those currently infected, and those who have recovered or died from infection. Simple transition rates are used to determine the flow of susceptibles to infected, and of infected to recovered or dead. The model assumes homogeneous mixing of the population; that is, any individual is as likely to meet any other individual. This assumption certainly fails as the population size increases: For example, in a village of 100, a person is just as likely to meet one villager as another, but in a city of 100,000 there are some whom an individual may never meet. This means that for large populations epidemics probably affect fewer people and occur more rapidly than the model would indicate.

Simulations of smallpox epidemics that vary the size of the local population and number of close contacts per individual show different results in terms of numbers infected, sick, recovered, and dead ("Disease and Population Decline in the Northeast," figs. 1–3, this vol.). A close contact is a contact that is close enough and long enough to result in infection if one of the individuals was infected. The number of close contacts per week varies with density: the more dense a community, the more close contacts per week. The other parameters of the simulation are fixed for all simulation runs: an average infectious period of 10 days and a simulation interval length of one week.

Table 1 calculates the time it takes smallpox outbreaks to terminate in different-size populations assuming different numbers of contacts per week. The table clearly indicates the importance of population density in determining the length of an epi-

TABLE 1

*Variance of Length of Smallpox Epidemics
in Different Populations*

Close Contacts per Week	Length of Epidemic in Weeks Population Size		
	30,000	10,000	3,000
9	12	11	10
7	13	11	10
5	13	13	10
3	15	15	12
1	53	49	36

Note: Length of the epidemic is measured until only 0.1% of the population remains infected.

demic. Thus, nine close contacts per week produces an epidemic of 12 weeks duration in a population of 30,000, while only one close contact per week produces an epidemic lasting 53 weeks in the population.

As these calculations indicate, smallpox will "burn itself out" fairly quickly in dense populations, particularly under "virgin soil" conditions of virtually 100 percent infection rates. This, of course, supports arguments that smallpox outbreaks among the Southeast chiefdoms may have terminated before diffusion to other chiefdoms. On the other hand, smallpox outbreaks in populations with low density may have been longlasting and spread very slowly. In fact, this has been observed in rural and nomadic populations (Fenner et al. 1988:200–201, 205). Thus, "buffer zones" between the chiefdoms of the Southeast may have acted as reservoirs of smallpox, slowing, but not necessarily eliminating the spread of the disease from one chiefdom to another. Under such conditions, the pattern of initial smallpox diffusion in the Southeast may have been one of spurts and busts as the disease infected a chiefdom, spreading rapidly throughout the population until "buffer zones" were encountered. If it entered such zones, the outbreak may have then progressed slowly, eventually either terminating or spreading to another chiefdom, where it would have spread rapidly once again.

CONCLUSIONS

Very little is known about the initial depopulation of the Southeast. It is clear that by the beginning of the eighteenth century a depopulation of Southeast Indians had occurred, probably mainly because of disease (see Milner 1980:40; DePratter 1983). It also seems clear that by the beginning of the seventeenth century a depopulation of areas within the Southeast had occurred, probably, here again, because of disease. And it is also possibly true that some tribes had experienced disease episodes by the time De Soto arrived in 1540. This, however, is a long way from documenting a massive depopulation of Indians in the Southeast or parts of it during the first half or even during the last half of the sixteenth century.

Analysis of smallpox indicates support for either isolated episodes or a slowly developing epidemic of smallpox throughout the region or parts of it. Little support is obtained for a sudden pandemic throughout the Southeast. Smallpox may have diffused throughout the region, but it probably did not do so in a short span of time. Actually, the "model" of smallpox diffusion developed here fits very well with the ethnohistorical record. Certainly, a pandemic of smallpox could have occurred if these buffer zones did not exist or if they were effectively neutralized via, for example, Indian trade routes or traveling European explorers spreading smallpox virus in a condition that could infect susceptible Indians. If such conditions existed, then a pandemic was possible; if they did not, then the model indicates that a pandemic was unlikely.

Ubelaker's (1988) pattern of increasing rates of population decline from about 1500 to 1800 is supported here or at least is consistent with it. The notion of greater population decline from 1700 to 1800 than from 1600 to 1700 and from 1600 to 1700 than from 1500 to 1600 would seemingly indicate a pattern of increasing exposure of Indian populations to disease from about 1500 through the 1700s. Thus, early disease in the Southeast would be characterized by either isolated disease episodes or slowly developing epidemics than by sudden pandemics.

REFERENCES

Bailey, Norman T.
  1975   The Mathematical Theory of Infectious Diseases and Its Application. 2d ed. London: Griffin.

Bourne, Edward G., ed.
  1922   Narratives of the Career of Hernando de Soto. 2 vols. New York: Allerton Book Company.

Brain, Jeffrey P.
  1978   Late Prehistoric Settlement Patterning in the Yazoo Basin and Natchez Bluffs Regions of the Lower Mississippi Valley. Pp. 331–368 in Mississippian Settlement Patterns. Bruce D. Smith, ed. New York: Academic Press.

Cabeza de Vaca, Alvar Nuñez
  1961   Adventures in the Unknown Interior of America. Cyclone Covey, trans. and ed. New York: Collier Books.

Carneiro, Robert
  1970   A Theory of the Origin of the State. *Science* 169:733–738.

Crosby, Alfred W., Jr.
  1976   Virgin Soil Epidemics as a Factor in the Aboriginal

Depopulation in America. *William and Mary Quarterly* 33:289–299.

DePratter, Chester B.
1983   Late Prehistoric and Early Historic Chiefdoms in the Southeastern United States. (Unpublished Ph.D. dissertation in Anthropology, University of Georgia, Athens.)

DePratter, Chester B., Charles M. Hudson, and Marvin T. Smith
1983   The Route of Juan Pardo's Explorations in the Interior Southeast, 1566–1568. *The Florida Historical Quarterly* 62(2):125–158.

Dixon, C. W.
1962   *Smallpox.* London: J. & A. Churchill.

Dobyns, Henry F.
1983   Their Number Become Thinned: Native American Population Dynamics in Eastern North America. Knoxville, Tenn.: The University of Tennessee Press.

1989   More Methodological Perspectives on Historical Demography. *Ethnohistory* 36(3):285–299.

Earle, Timothy
1987   Chiefdoms in Archaeological and Ethnohistorical Perspective. *Annual Reviews in Anthropology* 16:279–308.

1989   The Evolution of Chiefdoms. *Current Anthropology* 30(1):84–88.

Fenner, F., D. A. Henderson, I. Arita, Z. Jezek, and I. D. Ladnyi
1988   Smallpox and its Eradication. Geneva: World Health Organization.

Fried, Morton
1967   The Evolution of Political Society. New York: Random House.

Garcilaso de la Vega, the Inca
1951   The Florida of the Inca. John G. Varner and Jeannette J. Varner, trans. and eds. Austin: University of Texas Press.

Gibson, Charles
1964   The Aztecs under Spanish Rule. Stanford, Calif.: Stanford University Press.

Guerra, Francisco
1988   The Earliest American Epidemic: The Influenza of 1493. *Social Science History* 12:305–25.

Harner, Michael
1975   Scarcity, the Factors of Production, and Social Evolution. Pp. 123–38 in Population, Ecology, and Social Evolution. Steven Polgar, ed. The Hague: Mouton.

Henige, David
1986   Primary Source by Primary Source? On the Role of Epidemics in New World Depopulation. *Ethnohistory* 33(3):293–312.

1989   On the Current Devaluation of the Notion of Evidence: A Rejoinder to Dobyns. *Ethnohistory* 36(3):304–7.

Hudson, Charles
1987   Juan Pardo's Excursion Beyond Chiaha. *Tennessee Anthropologist* 12(1):74–87.

Hudson, Charles, Marvin T. Smith, and Chester B. DePratter
1984   The Hernando De Soto Expedition: From Apalachee to Chiaha. *Southeastern Archaeology* 3:65–77.

Hudson, Charles, Marvin T. Smith, David Hally, Richard Polhemus, and Chester B. DePratter
1985   Coosa: A Chiefdom in the Sixteenth-Century Southeastern United States. *American Antiquity* 50(4):723–737.

Joralemon, Donald
1982   New World Depopulation and the Case of Disease. *Journal of Anthropological Research* 38(1):108–27.

Kroeber, Alfred L.
1939   Cultural and Natural Areas of Native North America. *University of California Publications in American Archaeology and Ethnology* 38(1):1–142. Berkeley.

Larson, Lewis H.
1980   Aboriginal Subsistence Technology on the Southeastern Coastal Plain During the Late Prehistoric Period. Gainesville: University Presses of Florida.

Milner, George R.
1980   Epidemic Disease in the Postcontact Southeast: A Reappraisal. *Mid-Continental Journal of Archaeology* 5:39–56.

Mooney, James
1910   Population. Pp. 286–287 in Handbook of American Indians North of Mexico, F. W. Hodge, ed. *Bureau of American Ethnology Bulletin* 30, pt. 2. Washington.

1928   The Aboriginal Population of America North of Mexico. *Smithsonian Miscellaneous Collections* 80:1–40. Washington.

Muller, Jon D.
1978   The Southeast. Pp. 281–325 in Ancient Native Americans. Jesse D. Jennings, ed. San Francisco: W. H. Freeman.

Peebles, Christopher S.
1978   Determinants of Settlement Size and Location in the Moundville Phase. Pp. 369–416 in Mississippian Settlement Patterns. Bruce D. Smith, ed. New York: Academic Press.

Ramenofsky, Ann F.
1987   Vectors of Death: The Archaeology of European Contact. Albuquerque: University of New Mexico Press.

Service, Elman
1962   Primitive Social Organization. New York: Random House.

Smith, Bruce D., ed.
1978   Mississippian Settlement Patterns. New York: Academic Press.

1986   The Archaeology of the Southeastern United States: From Dalton to de Soto, 10,500–500 B.P. Pp. 1–92 in Advances in World Archaeology. Fred Wendorf and Angela E. Close, eds. Orlando, Fla.: Academic Press.

Smith, Marvin T.
1984   Depopulation and Culture Change in the Early Historic Period Interior Southeast. Unpublished Ph.D. Dissertation, University of Florida, Gainesville.

Snow, Dean R., and Kim M. Lanphear
1988   European Contact and Indian Depopulation in the Northeast: The Timing of the First Epidemics. *Ethnohistory* 35:15–33.

1989   More Methodological Perspectives: A Rejoinder to Dobyns. *Ethnohistory* 36:299–304.

Steponaitis, Vincas P.
1978   Location Theory and Complex Chiefdoms: A Mississippian Example. Pp. 417–53 in Mississippian Settlement Patterns. Bruce D. Smith, ed. New York: Academic Press.

Sturtevant, William C., gen. ed.
1978–   Handbook of North American Indians. 20 vols. Washington: Smithsonian Institution Press.

Swanton, John R.
1979   The Indians of the Southeastern United States [1946]. Washington: Smithsonian Institution Press.

1985   Final Report of the United States De Soto Expedition Commission [1939]. Washington: Smithsonian Institution Press.

Thomas, Cyrus
1985   Report on the Mound Explorations of the Bureau of Ethnology [1894]. Washington: Smithsonian Institution Press.

Thornton, Russell
1987   American Indian Holocaust and Survival: A Population History Since 1492. Norman: University of Oklahoma Press.

Ubelaker, Douglas H.
1988   North American Indian Population Size, A.D. 1500 to 1985. *American Journal of Physical Anthropology* 77(3):289–94.

Upham, Steadman
1986   Smallpox and Climate in the American Southwest. *American Anthropologist* 88(1):115–28.

Wright, J. Leitch, Jr.
1981   The Only Land They Knew: The Tragic Story of the American Indians in the Old South. New York: The Free Press.

18

Prehistoric Population Density in the Amazon Basin

BETTY J. MEGGERS

Before the end of the seventeenth century, the combined impacts of slave raids and smallpox epidemics had exterminated most of the indigenous inhabitants along the Amazon, and those surviving on the terra firme (land not subject to renewal by annual inundation) are generally considered to be depleted relicts and thus unrepresentative of the pre-Columbian situation. The potentially high productivity of manioc, the apparent surfeit of land suitable for cultivation, and the lack of protein shortage among such populations have been cited as evidence of underexploitation of resources, implying higher potential carrying capacity. Pre-Columbian population density has consequently been inferred using early ethnohistoric accounts and calculating rates of attrition, duration of attrition, and rates of recovery. Different sources and methods of evaluation have produced estimates for the population of Amazonia at the time of European contact ranging from 500,000 (Moran 1974: 137) to 10,000,000 (Comas 1951:256), representing densities from 0.12–0.75 (Steward 1949: 659) to 29.00 per square kilometer (Denevan 1976:218).

The intensification of national and international efforts to "develop" the neotropical lowlands makes the potential carrying capacity of the region for humans a matter of more than academic interest. If 10 million inhabitants could be sustained using local resources prior to European contact, this density might be matched or exceeded using modern technology. However, if the surviving indigenous groups represent sustainable exploitation, the prognosis is very different.

The obvious source of evidence for reconstructing prehistoric demography is the archeological record. The existence of extensive accumulations of black soil (terra preta) containing fragments of pottery, especially along the Amazon floodplain, has been noted by both archeologists (Myers 1973; Roosevelt 1989) and ecologists (Smith 1980). On the assumption that their dimensions equate with the areas of prehistoric villages, it has been asserted that "there have been relatively dense settlements along the Ucayali and other rivers of Amazonia for at least 4,000 years" (Smith 1980:564). It has also been estimated that the pre-Columbian population of Manacapuru, west of Manaus, was 18,000 and that "the overall population of the Marajoara society [on eastern Marajó] would have been at least 100,000 and probably more," with "many mounds . . . occupied more or less continuously for hundreds of years" (Smith 1980; Roosevelt 1989:78).

Until the 1970s archeological investigations were insufficient to evaluate these interpretations. Even along the relatively accessible lower Amazon, few sites had received more than casual examination. The major tributaries were unknown and carbon-14 dates were few and scattered. In 1976 a systematic plan was adopted for exploring sectors of the principal tributaries within Brazil by the Programa Nacional de Pesquisas Arqueológicas na Bacia Amazônica, cosponsored by the National Research Council of Brazil and the Smithsonian Institution. Uniform procedures were established for collecting and analyzing ceramics. Concurrent investigations were undertaken in northeastern Bolivia.

Sufficient spatial and temporal information has been accumulated to permit preliminary assessment of pre-Columbian settlement behavior and population dynamics. Three topics will be considered: whether the way of life characterizing surviving unacculturated indigenous groups is pre-Columbian, whether population pressure on the varzea (flood plain of a whitewater river) was relieved by migration up the tributaries to the terra firme, and whether potential carrying capacity was realized.

METHODOLOGY

Survey has been restricted to the present channels of rivers, except where roads facilitated access inland. Most sites are shallow, and cultural remains are usually limited to fragments of pottery. Surface dimensions were recorded and surface collections made at all sites; where depth of refuse exceeded 10 centimeters, one or more small test pits were excavated in 10 or 20-centimeter levels. The pottery, principally undecorated, was classified by temper and decorative techniques. Quantitative differences in the undecorated types were used to construct seriated sequences. Samples compatible with interdigitation into a single sequence define a phase; phases sharing a set of diagnostic decorated techniques comprise a tradition. Ethnographic and theoretical considerations indicate that phases are the prehistoric counterparts of communities among contemporary indigenous groups (for detailed discussion, see Meggers et al. 1988).

THE ANTIQUITY OF THE SHIFTING SETTLEMENT PATTERN

About 100 phases have been recognized, representing numerous ceramic traditions. Contemporary phases have contiguous spatial distributions that resemble the territories of surviving terra firme groups (figs. 1–2). Differences in pottery-type frequencies among successive levels of stratigraphic excavations are usually sufficiently great to require their separation in the seriation, implying discontinuous occupation. This interpretation is compatible with the settlement histories of contemporary communities, which are characterized by frequently moved villages and reoccupation of former sites (Gross 1983:439; Vickers 1983:471). Chronological and spatial correlations among sites of the same phase usually produce a pattern of centripetal movement within a territory resembling that documented among surviving terra firme groups (figs. 3–4; cf. Meggers and Evans 1979).

The maximum area potentially assignable to each episode of occupation can be estimated by correlating contemporary levels of multiple stratigraphic excavations in the same site. For example, three stratigraphic excavations in AM-MA-9 on the lower Negro reveal the presence of two successive phases of the Polychrome tradition, the Pajurá phase with at least four occupations and the Apuau phase with two. The phases are distinguished by different trends and relative frequencies of the undecorated types. The presence of decoration by painting, double-line incising, and excising affiliates them with the Polychrome tradition.

The lower levels of AM-MA-9, Cut 3, seriate into the Pajurá phase and the upper levels into the Apuau phase, indicating the Pajurá phase to be the earlier. This assessment is supported by a carbon-14 date of A.D. 825 (SI-2751) for the Pajurá phase and dates of A.D. 1545 (SI-2752) and 1560 (SI-4052) for the Apuau phase. The maximum area of the earliest occupation by the Pajurá phase is established by its restriction to Cut 2, providing a standard for estimating the areas of subsequent occupations (fig. 5). The probability that more episodes would be detectable from additional excavations is suggested by the settlement history of AC-CS-5 in western Acre, reconstructed from 10 stratigraphic excavations. These reveal successive occupation by five phases of the same tradition, with two to eight episodes during each phase. Nine stratigraphic excavations in

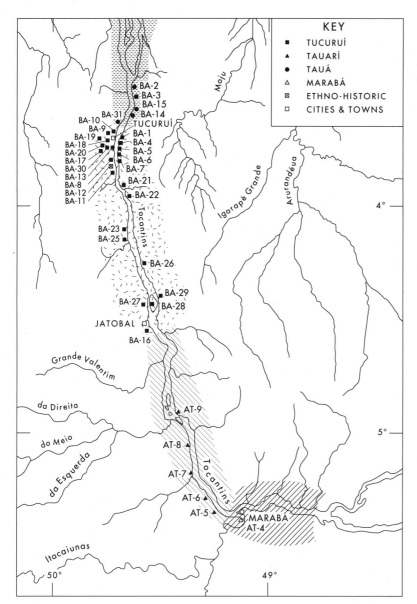

Fig. 1. Habitation sites recorded on the lower Rio Tocantins, the easternmost tributary of the right bank of the Amazon. The first rapid marks the boundary between the Tauá phase of the Polychrome tradition and the Tucuruí phase (unaffiliated). The Tauarí and Marabá phases belong to the Itacaiunas tradition. The absence of overlap in the distribution of the sites suggests that the phases occupy contiguous territories.

AM-CA-7 on the middle Juruá produced a similar history. In this case, six successive phases of a regional subtradition of the Polychrome tradition could be distinguished, each with multiple reoccupations. Ten carbon-14 dates indicate a time span of some 1,700 years.

In summary, the similarities of the settlement behavior reconstructed from pre-Columbian habitation sites to that among surviving indigenous groups of the terra firme indicate this way of life has existed for at least two millennia without significant alteration in village size and permanence.

EVIDENCE OF EXPANSION FROM THE VARZEA

The central Amazon has been envisaged as a region of continuous population increase, creating pressure that was relieved by migration up the various tributaries (Lathrap 1970:94–98). Survey data from the Tocantins, Xingu, and Madeira reveal sites of the Polychrome tradition to be confined below the first rapid, which marks the northern limit of the Brazilian Shield (fig. 1). Sites above the first rapid represent phases of other traditions, and their contemporaneity with those downriver is es-

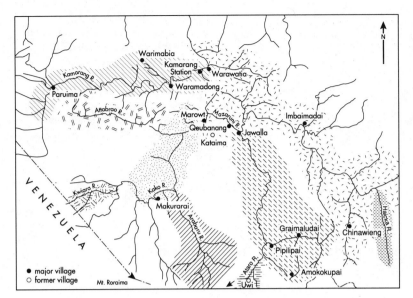

Fig. 2. Territorial differentiation among Akawaio communities along the headwaters of the Mazaruni River in west-central Guyana. Their general configurations resemble the territories reconstructed for the archeological phases on the Rio Tocantins (after Colson 1983–1984:108).

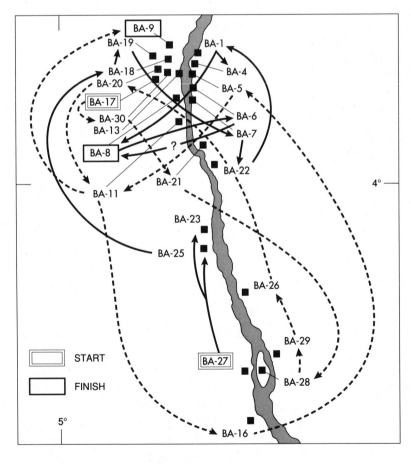

Fig. 3. Village movement during the Tucuruí phase, Rio Tocantins, reconstructed from the seriated sequence. The similarity in the relative frequencies of samples from the two initial sites suggested two villages, one at PA-BA-27 and the other at PA-BA-17. Since many sites are represented only by surface collections, the actual situation is more complex, but restriction of movement within the boundaries of the territory indicates that additional stratigraphic information would not alter the centripetal pattern.

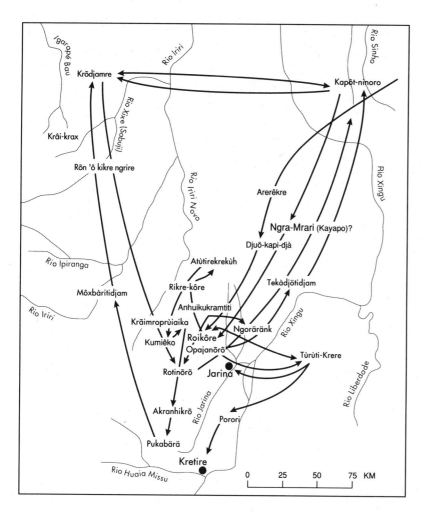

Fig. 4. Settlement history of the Mekragnoti, a Kayapó-speaking group on the upper Rio Xingu, during a 77-year period beginning in 1900, based on information from informants. The centripetal pattern, the combination of long and short moves, the fissioning and fusing, and the reoccupation of several locations are characteristics inferred from the seriated sequence of the Tucuruí phase (after Verswijver 1978).

tablished by numerous carbon-14 dates. This situation is particularly clear on the lower Xingu, where it is documented by sequences of phases both above and below the first rapid. Occasional sherds with decoration diagnostic of one region in the other may reflect trade, but there is no example of site intrusion from either side of this ecological barrier. The failure of either tradition to expand into the territory of the other implies adaptation to different resources.

In general, the settlement behavior inferred from the seriated sequences for phases of the Polychrome tradition is not significantly different from that reconstructed along clear and black-water tributaries of the terra firme. Settlements may have been somewhat larger, more permanent, and more numerous along the Amazon and Solimões, but if population expansion occurred it was confined within the region dominated by sediment-rich white-water rivers.

REALIZATION OF CARRYING CAPACITY

Carrying capacity can be evaluated independently of the archeological record by assessing the productivity of subsistence resources. This is governed by topographic, edaphic, and climatic conditions. The high plateaus of the Guyana Shield and the annually inundated flood plains constitute large areas unsuitable for human settlement. Another 12 percent within Brazil is unproductive savanna (Soares 1953:78). Only 7 percent of the basin is considered free from major edaphic constraints (Nicholaides et al. 1984:10). Furthermore, the fertility of the best soils is low compared to other tropical regions (Moran 1981:39; Fearnside 1986).

Numerous investigations are revealing significant annual and short-term variations in the timing, duration, and intensity of the rainy season. These inhibit the flowering or fruiting of many plants, reducing the food supply for various kinds of ani-

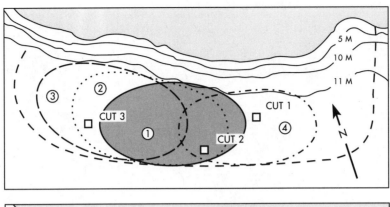

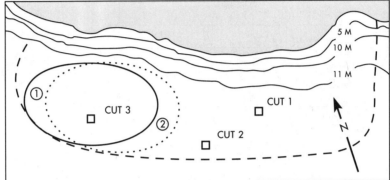

Fig. 5. Estimated areas of successive occupations at AM-MA-9 by the Pajurá and Apuau phases of the Polychrome tradition on the lower Rio Negro. Correlating contemporary levels of three stratigraphic excavations implies four occupations by the Pajurá phase (top). Since the first episode is represented only in Cut 2, its limits are defined by the locations of Cuts 1 and 3. The second episode is represented in Cuts 2 and 3, the third only in Cut 3, and the fourth in Cuts 1 and 2. The maximum extent of the initial occupation has been used as a standard for the areas allocated to later episodes. Two episodes by the Apuau phase are represented only in Cut 3 (bottom). Although each occupation may have covered a larger area than shown, neither could have exceeded more than about half the site, which extends 500 m along the riverbank.

mals, which respond by failing to reproduce, by low survival of offspring or by starvation of adults (Foster 1982; Mori and Prance 1987:74–75). Animal populations tend to stabilize at densities sustainable during lean years, and humans dependent on both plants and animals for subsistence must accommodate to these realities (Rindos 1984:277; Wilson 1981). Plant domestication permits larger and more sedentary communities but increases their vulnerability to environmental perturbations (Flowers 1983:358).

In addition to annual fluctuations, Amazonia has experienced several episodes of climatic change sufficiently intense to alter the vegetation significantly. Pollen profiles indicate that forest was replaced by savanna in several parts of the lowlands

during much of the first millennium B.C. (Bigarella and Andrade-Lima 1982:35; Absy 1985:fig. 4.9). In most of the region, the earliest existing dates for pottery follow this long episode. On Marajó, where it was adopted prior to the first millennium B.C. there is a hiatus of some 700 years between the end of the Mangueiras phase and the inception of the Formiga phase about the beginning of the Christian era (Meggers and Danon 1988:fig. 2). Briefer episodes about A.D. 500, 700, and 1200, detected in pollen records, correlate with cultural discontinuities throughout the lowlands (Meggers 1987). These turnovers imply population displacements, presumably provoked by subsistence stress. Repeated displacements are also reflected in the disjunct distributions of the principal lowland languages:

Arawakan, Cariban, and Tupian (Migliazza 1982). Drastic reduction in the productivity of primary foods would have made it necessary to exploit secondary resources more intensively, and the remarkable detailed knowledge of the vegetation characteristic of surviving Amazon groups becomes intelligible in this context. Several investigators have suggested that domestication of bitter manioc may have been a by-product of increased dependence on what was originally a minor food (Williams 1988; Sanoja 1989).

In short, Amazonia is a counterfeit paradise with severe limitations for human exploitation under conditions prevailing in the late twentieth century. Pre-Columbian populations appear to have achieved a stable and sustainable accommodation to these conditions but were subjected to severe subsistence stress during at least four episodes of climatic fluctuation during the past four millennia that caused temporary abandonment of the affected regions or significant reduction in population size, concentration, and mobility.

CONCLUSION

The ecological, ethnographic, and archeological data conflict with the ethnohistorical accounts that have been primary sources for estimating pre-Columbian population size. These describe settlements extending for leagues along the banks of the Amazon, organized into provinces ruled by powerful chiefs. Such descriptions are also difficult to reconcile with the topography. With a few notable exceptions, the river channel passes through floodplain, out of sight of the high banks occupied today and in the past. The varzea narrows west of Manaus, but the favored location for settlement remains along the unflooded margins of lakes invisible from the channel. Although large parts of the lowlands are unknown archeologically, there is little reason to expect that future work will alter the existing picture significantly. The conclusion that early eyewitness accounts exaggerate the indigenous population density seems inescapable.

The similarity in settlement behavior between pre-Columbian and surviving indigenous groups suggests population sizes and concentrations were also similar. The present densities on the terra firme, which comprises 98 percent of the lowlands, range from 0.04 to 1.0 per square kilometer with a mean of about 0.3 per square kilometer. Sustainable densities calculated using protein resources fall into the same range. Although higher concentrations could have existed on the varzea, these are offset by large uninhabitable regions. Depending on the boundaries employed, an average density of 0.3 per square kilometer gives a pre-Columbian population between 1,500,000 and 2,000,000 for Amazonia as a whole.

It is instructive to compare these estimates with those provided for North America by Ubelaker (1988 and this volume). He suggests a range of 0.17 to 0.31 per square kilometer for the southeastern United States, the region most comparable environmentally to the Amazonian terra firme. The density estimated for the American Southwest, which was characterized by numerous relatively large and permanent settlements, is similar. His total of 1,894,350 for North America is within the range that I suggest for Amazonia.

Ecological evidence for low sustainable productivity of critical resources, archeological evidence for relatively small settlements and discontinuous occupation, and ethnographic evidence for fine-tuned integration with the ecosystem favor the conclusion that the population of Amazonia had stabilized before European contact. The impression that carrying capacity had not been reached appears to reflect misunderstanding of the complex interactions between the soil, climate, and biota that characterize this unique and remarkable region.

REFERENCES

Absy, Maria Lucia
　1985　Palynology of Amazonia: The History of the Forests as Revealed by the Palynological Record. Pp. 72–82 in Amazonia. G. T. Prance and Thomas E. Lovejoy, eds. Oxford: Pergamon Press.

Bigarella, João José, and Dárdano de Andrade-Lima
　1982　Paleoenvironmental Changes in Brazil. Pp. 27–40 in Biological Diversification in the Tropics. G. T. Prance, ed. New York: Columbia University Press.

Colson, Audrey Butt
　1983–　The Spatial Component in the Political Structure
　1984　of the Carib Speakers of the Guiana Highlands: Kapon and Pemon. *Antropológica* 59–62:73–124.

Comas, Juan
　1951　La Realidad del trato dado a los indígenas de América entre los siglos XV y XX. *América Indígena* 11(4):323–370.

Denevan, W. M.

1976   The Aboriginal Population of Amazonia. Pp. 205–234 in The Native Population of the Americas in 1492. W. M. Denevan, ed. Madison: University of Wisconsin Press.

Fearnside, Philip M.

1986   Human Carrying Capacity of the Brazilian Rainforest. New York: Columbia University Press.

Flowers, Nancy M.

1983   Seasonal Factors in Subsistence, Nutrition, and Child Growth in a Central Brazilian Indian Community. Pp. 357–390 in Adaptive Responses of Native Amazonians. Raymond B. Hames and William T. Vickers, eds. New York: Academic Press.

Foster, Robin B.

1982   Famine on Barro Colorado Island. Pp. 201–212 in The Ecology of a Tropical Forest. E. G. Leigh Jr., A. S. Rand, and D. M. Windsor, eds. Washington: Smithsonian Institution Press.

Gross, Daniel R.

1983   Village Movement in Relation to Resources in Amazonia. Pp. 429–449 in Adaptive Responses of Native Amazonians. Raymond B. Hames and William T. Vickers, eds. New York: Academic Press.

Lathrap, Donald W.

1970   The Upper Amazon. New York: Praeger.

Meggers, Betty J.

1987   Oscilación climática y cronología cultural en el Caribe. Pp. 23–54 in Actas del Tercer Simpósio de la Fundación de Arqueología del Caribe. Washington.

Meggers, Betty J., and Jacques Danon

1988   Identification and Implications of a Hiatus in the Archeological Sequence on Marajó Island, Brazil. *Journal of the Washington Academy of Sciences* 78:245–253.

Meggers, Betty J., and Clifford Evans

1979   An Experimental Reconstruction of Taruma Village Succession and Some Implications. Pp. 39–60 in Brazil: Anthropological Perspectives. Maxime L. Margolis, ed. New York: Columbian University Press.

Meggers, Betty J., Ondemar F. Dias, Eurico Th. Miller, and Celso Perota

1988   Implications of Archeological Distributions in Amazonia. Pp. 275–294 in Proceedings of a Workshop on Neotropical Distribution Patterns. P. E. Vancolini and W. R. Heyer, eds. Rio de Janeiro: Academia Brasileira de Ciências.

Migliazza, Ernest C.

1982   Linguistic Prehistory and the Refuge Model in Amazonia. Pp. 497–519 in Biological Diversification in the Tropics. G. T. Prance, ed. New York: Columbia University Press.

Moran, Emilio

1974   The Adaptive System of the Amazonian Caboclo. Pp. 136–159 in Man in the Amazon. Charles Wagley, ed. Gainesville: University Presses of Florida.

1981   Developing the Amazon. Bloomington: Indiana University Press.

Mori, Scott A., and G. T. Prance

1987   Species Diversity, Phenology, Plant-animal Interactions, and Their Correlation with Climate, as Illustrated by the Brazil Nut Family (Lecythidaceae). Pp. 69–89 in the Geophysiology of Amazonia. R. E. Dickinson, ed. New York: Wiley Interscience.

Myers, Thomas P.

1973   Toward the Reconstruction of Prehistoric Community Patterns in the Amazon Basin. Pp. 233–252 in Variation in Anthropology. D. W. Lathrap and Jody Douglas, eds. Urbana: Illinois Archaeological Survey.

Nicholaides, J. J., III, D. E. Gandy, P. A. Sánchez, J. H. Villachica, A. J. Coutu, and C. S. Valverde

1984   Continuous Cropping Potential in the Upper Amazon Basin. Pp. 337–365 in Frontier Expansion in Amazonia. Marianne Schmink and Charles C. Wood, eds. Gainesville: University of Florida Press.

Rindos, David

1984   The Origins of Agriculture: An Evolutionary Perspective. Orlando, Florida: Academic Press.

Roosevelt, Anna C.

1989   Lost Civilizations of the Lower Amazon. *Natural History* 98:74–83.

Sanoja, Mario

1989   Origins of Cultivation Around the Gulf of Paria, Northeastern Venezuela. *National Geographic Research* 5:446–458.

Smith, Nigel J.

1980   Anthrosols and Human Carrying Capacity in Amazonia. *Annals of the Association of American Geographers* 70(4):533–566.

Soares, Lúcio de Castro

1953   Limites meridionais e orientais da área de ocorrência de floresta amazônica em território brasileiro. *Revista Brasileira de Geografia* 15:3–122.

Steward, Julian H.

1949   The Native Population of South America. Pp. 655–688 in Vol. 5 of Handbook of South American Indians. *Bureau of American Ethnology Bulletin* 143. Washington.

Ubelaker, Douglas H.
    1988   North American Population Size, A.D. 1500 to 1985. *American Journal of Physical Anthropology* 77 (3):289–294.

Verswijver, Gustaf
    1978   Separations et migrations des Mekrognoti: Groups Kayapó du Brésil Central. *Société Suisse des Américanistes Boletin* 42:47–59.

Vickers, William T.
    1983   The Territorial Dimensions of Siona-Secoya and Encabello Adaptation. Pp. 451–478 in Adaptive Responses of Native Amazonians. Raymond B. Hames and William T. Vickers, eds. New York: Academic Press.

Williams, Denis
    1988   The Archaic of Northwestern Guyana and the Beginnings of Agriculture. (Paper delivered at the Quincentennary Symposium "Prehistoric South Americans," Smithsonian Institution, October 1988.)

Wilson, David J.
    1981   Of Maize and Man: A Critique of the Maritime Hypothesis of State Origins on the Coast of Peru. *American Anthropologist* 83(1):93–120.

19

Impact of Disease in the Sixteenth-Century Andean World

NOBLE DAVID COOK

The Andean reeled, as other native peoples of the western hemisphere, from the disastrous impact of Old World disease. Knowledge of the epidemic history of Andean South America is neither so detailed nor so accurate as for some regions farther north, particularly Mesoamerica, where the native written tradition was strong and can be tapped to correlate with later European reports. Although Andean *quipocamayos* (keepers of the quipu) recorded on the knotted-string quipu important statistical and historical information, by the time it was written in ink much meaning had been lost. Information about the earliest epidemics followed the actual disease occurrences by a number of years.

The Inca ruler Huayna Capac succumbed to European infection in the 1520s, before direct contact with the outsiders. Given the clear-cut nature of the spread of disease, other preceding germ contact might have taken place in the Andean world. The appearance of Christopher Columbus in the Caribbean in October 1492 led to the rapid introduction of epidemic disease into the Americas. The Native American possessed virtually no natural immunity to several important disease strains. For 25 years following the establishment of the Antilles base, Spaniards managed to explore and settle the islands, to set up some small posts on the coast from Venezuela to almost the Yucatan, as well as to reconnoiter a modest section of the Florida peninsula under Ponce de Léon. The initial quarter century brought with it the virtual extinction of the native population of the islands. Whichever estimate is chosen, the unrealistically high eight million (Borah and Cook 1971–1979) for the island of Hispaniola or the unrealistically low figure of 60,000 (Rosenblat 1967), the consequence is the same—the disappearance of the island Taino.

MEANS OF DISEASE TRANSMISSION

This chapter attempts to establish an accurate chronology of disease in the sixteenth-century Andean world. Several spearheads of European exploration took place there. The most important was the northern approach, beginning as early as 1509, when Alonso de Ojeda embarked on exploration of the coast of Veragua. Francisco Pizarro, who went to the Indies with Gov. Nicolás de Ovando in 1502, was with Ojeda. Blasco Nuñez de Balboa's discovery of the "Southern Sea" in 1513, with Pizarro again present, was followed quickly by settlement of the isthmus of Panama in 1514. In 1522 the southward reconnaissance was led by Pascual de Andagoya. What was the impact of this almost continuous European presence on the Panamanian isthmus? The thrust was northward toward Nicaragua, but all the activity there must have provided a disease focus that could act as a springboard. In 1514 some 700 New Darién settlers on the Gulf coast of Panama died in a single month, of hunger and an "unidentified disease" (Crosby 1967:330). Furthermore, two million Indians died in Panama between 1514 and 1530. Antonio de Herrera reported more than 40,000 Indians died from disease in Panama City and Nombre de Dios in a 28-year period during the sixteenth century (Crosby 1967:330).

The southern approach also came early, with the voyage of Ferdinand Magellan who sailed clear of the straits that took his name toward the end of 1520. Woodrow Borah (personal communication 1988) has posited that the epidemic that raged in Cuzco, taking the lives of so many of the Inca elite, may have resulted from infection from the stop of Magellan at the Rio de la Plata, rather than from introduction via the isthmus of Panama. The southern approach was not pursued. The coasting piratical expedition of Francis Drake that began in 1577 was one of a mere few penetrations that the Spanish so feared but rarely had to face directly during the sixteenth century. Drake returned to the Indies in 1585, heading a fleet that has been linked by some researchers to the passage of one of the most formidable pandemics of the sixteenth-century Andean world. Portuguese involvement on the Brazilian coast to the east came early, in 1500. But 3,000 miles of difficult tropical rain forest terrain separated the Portuguese world from the Spanish.

Could epidemic disease have been introduced into the Andean region early? Might the 1493 epidemic that seems to have afflicted the Caribbean island population so catastrophically (Guerra 1985, 1988) have flowed to the north shore of South America, then followed native trade routes into the interior, there to ravage an unprotected population? On the western coast of South America, the ocean, when the technological level of Native Americans allowed evolution of a sea-faring capability, did act as a relatively free avenue for the transfer of cultural artifacts. That technological level was reached in pre-Columbian times (Rostworoski de Diez Canseco 1981). The coastal *caballitos*, small

reed boats similar to the larger versions still plying the waters of Lake Titicaca, allowed short-distance exchange of fish and other products. But the larger, more seaworthy balsa rafts, encountered by the Pizarro reconnaissance, could carry 20 or more people, as well as trade goods, over longer distances, perhaps from coastal Ecuador to Nicaragua. Although movement in the interior along the Andean chain was difficult, travel along the western edge was relatively easy and must have contributed to exchange of both wanted and unwanted items in the years immediately preceding the physical arrival of Francisco Pizarro.

Archeology cannot pinpoint what took place in the Andes from 1492 to 1530 with enough accuracy to allow reliable conclusions. Did the region suffer no disease, or was there disease that simply went unrecorded? In both the rural Andean parish of Yanque from the late seventeenth century, and in the urban parish of Yanahuara next to Arequipa in the mid-eighteenth, there were a number of small, localized epidemic outbreaks that were not reported by secular or religious authorities. Only the most devastating of infections caused enough mortality for notice to be given.

THE FIRST ANDEAN EPIDEMIC AND THE DEATH OF HUAYNA CAPAC

In a sense the demise of the Inca leader Huayna Capac is the first confirmable death from European disease in the Andean region. Information on this occurrence comes from the knotted-string quipu, then the oral tradition that quickly evolved around the event and became part of the common knowledge of the Andean past. In the early 1540s, a group of *quipocamayos* was questioned by Gov. Cristobal Vaca de Castro about the origin and history of the Inca rulers. Their account is unequivocal: the Inca ruler died "of the pestilencia of smallpox" (Urteaga 1920:22–23). Early in the next decade, two Spanish soldier-scholars, Juan de Betanzos and Pedro de Cieza de Léon, prepared careful histories of the Incas and the European conquest. Betanzos described the fatal sickness of Huayna Capac as "such that it removed his judgment and understanding, and it gave him a *sarna* [cutaneous disease] and *lepra* [leprosy] that made him very debilitated" (Betanzos 1987:200–201). He died within four days, and his infant son "died of the same illness of lepra as his father." Betanzos did not use the word smallpox to identify the disease. He probably was translating from the Quechua two known diseases whose symptoms parallel those of smallpox, by the time they become fatal. The transfer of the corpse of Huayna Capac to the imperial city of Cuzco must have further spread infection. In Pedro de Cieza de Léon's account (1984, 1:219–220), the smallpox was "so contagious that more than two hundred thousand souls passed away in all the surrounding districts."

Pedro Pizarro's history, completed about 1571, is the account of a soldier-settler, who served in the first ranks of the conquest. In his version the Incas were visited with "a sickness of smallpox, never seen among them before, which killed many Indians" (Pizarro 1978:48–49).

Two principal accounts from the early 1570s and 1580s, those of Miguel Cabello Balboa and Pedro Sarmiento de Gamboa, introduce the origin of the epidemic. Sarmiento de Gamboa (1988:148–149) was in charge of the collection of the "official" history of the Incas for the colonial version of the story and in Cuzco had the opportunity to interview a series of *quipocamayos*, on which to base his version. Several points of the version of Sarmiento are worthy of note. First, he dates the death of Huayna Capac at the end of 1524. While in the north, at the time of the conquest of the Huancavilcas, he learned that there was in Cuzco "a great pestilencia, from which his governors Apu Hilaquita, his uncle, and Auqui Tupac Inca, his brother, and his sister Mama Cuca, with many other of his relatives," had died. Sarmiento called Huayna Capac's disease "an illness of fevers, although others say that it was of smallpox and measles."

Cabello Balboa's account is particularly interesting, for he knew the north coastal sector of Peru, where the events took place, better than some other chroniclers. He had come to America about 1566, took holy orders in 1571, residing in various spots from New Granada and Quito. He participated in several of the late entradas into the interior, serving often as chaplain. He began collecting the material for his history in 1576, and finished the manuscript about 1586. Cabello Balboa (1951:393) relates that Huayna Capac "received news of great sadness from Cuzco, from where they advised him that there was an incurable and general illness" that had taken his brother and uncle, whom he had left as governors, his sister, and other principal lords of his

lineage. Huayna Capac died from "deadly fevers . . . in the year 1525" (Cabello Balboa 1951:394). The close parallels between the accounts of these two historians indicate intensive borrowing, if not plagiarism. Why do earlier accounts not document the prior passage of the epidemic in Cuzco?

The later accounts of native historians Poma de Ayala (1980, 1:93), and Santa Cruz Pachacuti Yamqui do not shed new light on the answer. Poma de Ayala does not mention a Cuzco origin, and he identifies the illness as measles, not smallpox. Santa Cruz Pachacuti fails to mention Cuzco, and states the disease was measles, although his description of symptoms indicates smallpox. The famous mestizo chronicler, Garcilaso de la Vega (1966:576) modified the account to attribute Huayna Capac's death to a chill, followed by a fever.

The illness that took Huayna Capac and so disrupted the Inca empire was probably smallpox. The toll it extracted allowed Francisco Pizarro's subsequent conquest relatively easy victory. One other serious epidemic may have reached southward into the interior highlands prior to the direct march on Cajamarca, and that took place in 1531. The epidemic was concentrated on the isthmus of Panama.

> From a ship that has arrived from Nicaragua the *pestilencia* has struck this land, and it has been so great that although it has not yet ended, two parts of all the people that there are in this land have died, native Indians as well as slaves, and among them some Christians. I attest to Your Majesty that it is the most frightening thing that I have ever seen, because even the strongest does not last more than a day and a half, and some two or three hours, and now it reigns as at the beginning, and has become concentrated in Panama. The clerics are organizing processions, and praying, but not even these pleas to Our Lord have lifted his ire, to the point that I don't think there will remain alive a single person in all the land (Porras Barrenecha 1959:22).

In early September, the town council of the city of Panama notified the ruler that few Indians remained after the passage of the *pestilencia* and requested permission to use Indians from Nicaragua, Tumbez, and Peru, who had been condemned to death, as slaves (Porras Barrenecha 1959:24). In September 1532 measles was noted as having arrived in Santiago de Guatemala, from New Spain, but there is no indication that this was the outbreak experienced in Panama in 1531. Indeed, the speed of death and the fact that all segments of the population were liable to become infected in the Panamanian isthmus epidemic of 1531 indicates it was not measles (Porras Barrenecha 1959:33).

FROM PANDEMIC TO ENDEMIC DISEASE

The disease chronology for Colombia fits generally with what is known to have happened in Peru. Villamarin and Villamarin (1988:1) report "Epidemic disease was an important factor in the almost continuous decline in the native population throughout the colonial period, in the Sabana de Bogota and in Colombia generally." The earliest epidemic indeed may have occurred prior to 1537, when the first face-to-face contact took place in the Chibcha homeland. The Chibcha exchanged goods with peoples down the Magdalena River and had indirect contact with coastal groups in years immediately preceding the conquest. Although disease could have been introduced, no archival evidence exists to prove such was the case.

Perhaps the first historical record of epidemic disease for Colombia is given by Cieza de Léon (1984:127), who reported a "pestilencia en las casas" in Popayan in 1539, which coincided with famine, caused the death of 100,000, and led to an increase in cannibalism. Herrera reported it was "peste" and caused sudden death of those who contracted it. Northward, in the province of Cartagena, Friede (1955–1960, 5:148) claimed measles and smallpox struck there. There is no reason to assume the epidemic might not have spread southward toward Quito, for the district between Popayan and Quito was coming under control of Europeans in the period from 1536 to 1540. In 1546, Cieza de Léon (1984:26) reported for the Quimbaya province of Colombia, a "pestilencia" that caused high fever and headache, with pain concentrating in the left ear, and frequently death at the second or third day. The 1546 epidemic was rampant throughout the northern Andes, if not beyond. Much dispute exists over its identification. The two most likely candidates are typhus and plague, probably pneumonic. The fact that llamas and sheep were infected at the same time shifts the balance in favor of pneumonic plague. Friede (1967:339) was cautious in his assessment of the extent of the 1546 epidemic, stating that the usually reliable Cieza de Léon erred when

he indicated this illness reached the province of Cartago in New Granada.

Villamarin and Villamarin (1988) document the first major outbreak of Old World disease in Colombia with a smallpox epidemic of 1558. This was introduced by slaves purchased on the island of Hispaniola by the bishop of Sante Fe, Juan de los Barrios. Mortality was low for Europeans, but high for the Native Americans, with over 400,000 Indian deaths. The epidemic that entered Ecuador in 1557 was accompanied by catarrh, afflicted both Europeans and Native Americans, and may have been associated with the 1558 Colombia epidemic. The cough was probably a secondary infection coming on the heels of the weakened victims of measles and smallpox (Alchon 1984:54). An Old World source seems clear, as influenza buffeted Spain in 1557. The combination was both lethal and lingering. In Cuenca, in 1562 nearly all Indians were ill with smallpox (Newson 1988).

The next two decades saw less in the way of major epidemics at the regional level in Ecuador (Newson 1988). A localized outbreak of smallpox may have occurred in Almaguer in south highland Colombia in 1566, perhaps touching eastern sectors of Colombia in 1568 and 1569. But substantiation of this epidemic is needed. Smallpox and measles appear to have settled down to an endemic form. In 1582, for example, in the *relaciones geográficas* report for the province of Cuenca, Hernando Pablos reported that they were appearing "por sus temporadas" (Jiménez de la Espada, 1965, 2:266). A localized smallpox outbreak coincided with the Cuenca investigation.

THE CRISIS OF 1585–1591

One of the most devastating epidemic series of the entire sixteenth century occurred in the period from about 1585 to 1591. If a relatively disease-free era existed for some two decades, it was broken at this juncture. The duration and the impact of the 1585–1591 series clearly reflect not one, but two or more disease components. Dobyns (1963) pointed out that one epidemic moved from Lima and Cuzco to Quito, whereas another spread south from Ecuador (?). Part of the problem of identification is the accurate dating of the series. Dobyns (1963:501–502) reports smallpox, measles, and perhaps mumps striking Lima and Cuzco 1585–1586. An epidemic, variously dated for Quito as 1586–1589, hit the city with a vengeance, killing 4,000, especially children, within about three months. It is described as "high fevers, smallpox and measles." No agreement exists on the passage to America, but two routes seem most likely. One possibility is introduction by Black slaves in the Cartagena market, spreading into the interior, to Mariquita, and the entire Andes. If so, it arrived in Quito in 1587, then spread to the south, Cuenca, Loja, and into Peru, at Paita, and finally Trujillo. The other theory as to source is that it came via Francis Drake's infected crew. After touching in the Canaries, several hundred of Drake's men became ill and died. He managed to enter the Caribbean, attack, and take Cartagena. There he stayed for some six weeks into early 1586. By then the expeditionary force was so weakened by disease that it was deemed best to return to the homeland (Newson 1988). In Quito, 30,000 of 80,000 people died. Various of the *relaciones geográficas* report high mortality in Ecuador during this period. "In the early 1590s, Indians around Cuenca and Loja were said to have 'consumido y acabado' as a result of smallpox, measles and dysentery" (Newson 1988). Similar depopulation took place in nearby provinces. The *relaciones geográficas* illuminate the process in the southern Ecuadorian sector. Some 20,000 Indians had worked the mines in Zaruma, but after the epidemics only 500 remained. Across the frontier in Peru, in the province of Jaén, smallpox (*mal de viruelas*) stripped Indian numbers from 30,000 to 1,000. Devastating epidemics in Yaguarsongo and Pacamoros spread eastward into the lowlands of Loyola and Santiago de las Montanas. Mortality may have reached one-third. Along the Ecuadorian coast the 1589 epidemic resulted in the virtual extinction of the Huancavilca (Jiménez de la Espada 1965, 2:208–309).

The 1585 series of diseases was devastating in the area of Quito. The second of the waves is documented in Quito in July 1587. For the next nine months the number of deaths was elevated (Alchon 1984:55). The epidemic lingered in the highlands of Ecuador, well into 1590. By 1591, when the epidemics subsided, "they left behind a trail of death and destruction unsurpassed by even the 1558 outbreak. In fact, the sharpest drop in Quito's native population during the sixteenth century occurred between 1560 and 1590; the epidemics of 1585–91 were primarily responsible" (Alchon 1984:56).

Perhaps better known is the nature of the course of part of the series, which afflicted Colombia in 1588. Smallpox lasted six months, afflicting Indian and European. It came from the coast by way of Mariquita, and it was carried by a female Black slave. From central Colombia it spread into Popayan, then southward into Peru, and even reached Chile. Mortality was particularly high for "boys, girls, the youth" (Villamarin and Villamarin 1988:28). In 1626 Simon (1882–1892, 3:271–272) said the 1588 bout was "one of the most unfortunate that the natives have experienced." It took more than one-third, hitting Spaniards as well as Indians, to the point it was necessary to inter 100–200 corpses at a time in common graves. In a series of regional reports prepared in 1594, several caciques recall the impact of the smallpox epidemic that had passed through in 1588. A number stressed the difficulty of the reduced number of living to pay the tribute assessment of the earlier, larger population (Villamarin and Villamarin 1988:29).

Lastres (1951, 2:77) reports the appearance in Lima of smallpox, which particularly attacked young people. During this epidemic the hospitals of Lima were filled with the ill and convalescing.

In the central Peruvian sector, Dobyns (1963) has provided a full account of the 1588 epidemics. When the epidemic reached Trujillo, in March 1589, the viceroy established a commission to combat continued spread southward. Two physicians advised the viceroy to recommend the use of sugar, oil, honey, raisins, and meat, in order to help block infection. Bleeding was also recommended as a useful prophylactic. More important, the viceroy suggested that the clothing of the victims who died should be burned. Nevertheless, by June 1589 the epidemic afflicted Lima. By the end of the year, the contagion reached Cuzco (Alchon 1984:55–56), and a "peste de tumores o bubas" decimated the city's population (Porras Barrenechea 1986:630). The cadavers would not fit into the churches or cemeteries, and the sick overflowed the rooms of the hospitals. Montesinos (Lastres 1951, 2:76–77) refers to the arrival of smallpox and measles in Cuzco, in the form of a "peste universal" in 1585. The vaguely described "dolor de costado" was present at the same time, and the illness came with such a malignancy that those who came down with it suffered intensely. The epidemic recurred in Cuzco in 1590, with many Indian and Creole victims.

A study of the community of Aymaya, in Upper Peru, examines the effects of the 1580s series by using copies of parish registers, which are rare to find for years prior to the 1640s in the Andean world. The average annual number of community burials in the 1580s was in the 20s. Then, in 1590, the number exploded, with 194 deaths, slightly more than 20–25 percent of the community's total population (Evans 1988). Some 147 of the deaths that year were specifically ascribed to smallpox.

Also available is a detailed account of the late 1580s series as it hit the city of Arequipa in the south Peruvian Andes.

> The onset of the disease brought severe headaches and kidney pains. A few days later, patients became stupefied, then delirious, and ran naked through the streets shouting. Patients who broke out in a rash had a good chance to recover, reportedly, while those who did not break out seemed to have little chance. Ulcerated throat killed many patients. Fetuses died in the uterus. Even patients who broke out in a rash might lose chunks of flesh by too sudden movement. . . No count of victims was possible in Arequipa, where they had to be interred in open ditches in the public squares during the three month long episode (Joralemon 1982:114).

The outbreak is identified almost certainly as smallpox, "a combination of fulminating and malignant confluent (variola major) smallpox" (Joralemon 1982:121). Mortality was up to 30 percent for cases of variola major. Also important is the age-specific mortality, which has been reported "as recently as 1885" "for ages 0–4 . . . 60 percent, and for ages over 40 the rate exceeded 40 percent" (Dixon 1962:326).

CONCLUSION

Crosby (1967) identified the 1518–1521 pandemic as a major factor in the conquest of the Aztec and Inca empires, noting that domination of the American Indian would have been much more difficult had not alien disease coincided with the sword of the outsiders. On the other hand, Friede (1967:341), in his own study of the mining community of Muzo in Colombia, concluded that "when there were epidemics in Spanish America, these were neither general nor of identical consequences throughout the regions affected, contrary to what might be gathered from reading the various reports and chronicles of the colonial era." To what then does Friede ascribe severe depopulation? "There are numberless documents which definitely attribute the decrease of the Indian population to excessive work, malnutrition, flight, segregation of the sexes, ill-treatment, cruelty, conscription for expeditions, enslavement, the mita, etc." (Friede 1967:339).

Friede, as many other scholars, did not accept the significance of the disease factor, primarily because it had not been documented well enough. Further, many epidemics that occurred in the sixteenth century simply were not recorded in the official documents, the ones most widely used by historians. The lesser epidemic went unrecorded, except in the parish registers. Even Alfred Crosby and Henry F. Dobyns, who have done so much work in the field of epidemic history, may have missed the first major epidemic to strike the New World. When attempting to explain initial depopulation of the island of Hispaniola prior to the first smallpox epidemic, Crosby (1967:326) stated "Indians apparently suffered a steady decline in numbers, which was probably due to extreme overwork, other diseases, and a general lack of will to live after their whole culture had been shattered by alien invasion." As Guerra (1988) suggests, a major epidemic may have struck the island's people shortly after the second Colombus expedition returned in late 1493 and early 1494. The Black Legend, which stresses exploitative overwork and genocide, cannot explain all that historians see in the documentary record. It is clear that epidemics played a major role in the demographic collapse of native America.

REFERENCES

Alchon, Suzanne Austin
  1984   The Effects of Epidemic Disease in Colonial Ecuador. (Unpublished Ph.D. Dissertation in History, Duke University, Durham, N.C.

Betanzos, Juan de
  1987   Suma y narración de los Incas. Madrid: Atlas.

Borah, Woodrow, and Sherburne F. Cook
  1971–   Essays in Population History. 3 vols. Berkeley:
  1979   University of California Press.

Cabello Balboa, M.
  1951   Miscelánea antártica. Lima: Universidad de San Marcos.

Cieza de Leon, Pedro de
1984– Obras completas. 2 vols. Madrid: Consejo Superi-
1985 or de Investigaciones Científicas.

Cook, Noble David
1981 Demographic Collapse: Indian Peru, 1520–1620.
New York: Cambridge University Press.

1982 People of the Colca Valley: A Population Study.
Boulder, Colo. Westview Press.

Cook, Noble David, Jose Hernandez Palomo, Maria Luz Pena
Fernandez, and Alexandra Parma Cook
1988 Epidemics in the Parish of Santa Ana de Triana:
1665–1850. (Paper presented at the 46th International Congress of Americanists. Amsterdam, 4–8
July.)

Crosby, Alfred W.
1967 Conquistador y Pestilencia: The First New World
Pandemic and the Fall of the Great Indian Empires. *Hispanic American Historical Review* 47:321–
337.

1972 The Columbian Exchange: Biological and Cultural Consequences of 1492. Westport, Conn.: Greenwood Press.

Dixon, C. W.
1962 Smallpox. London: J. and A. Churchill.

Dobyns, Henry F.
1963 An Outline of Andean Epidemic History to 1720.
Bulletin of the History of Medicine 37:493–515.

Evans, Brian
1988 Death in Aymaya of Upper Peru, 1580–1623. (Paper presented at the 46th International Congress
of Americanists, Amsterdam, 4–8 July.)

Friede, Juan
1955– Documentos inéditos para la historia de Colombia.
1960 10 vols. Bogotá: Academia Colombiana de Historia.

1967 Demographic Changes in the Mining Community
of Muzo after the Plague of 1629. *Hispanic American Historical Review* 47:338–359.

Garcilaso de la Vega, the Inca
1966 Royal Commentaries of the Incas and General
History of Peru. Austin: University of Texas Press.

Guerra, Francisco
1985 La Epidemia americana de influenza en 1493. *Revista de Indias* 46:41–58.

1988 The Earliest American Epidemic: The Influenza
of 1493. *Social Science History* 12(3):305–325.

Jiménez de la Espada, Marcos, ed.
1965 Relaciones geográficas de Indias, Peru. 3 vols.
Madrid: Atlas.

ɔralemon, Donald
1982 New World Depopulation and the Case of Disease.
Journal of Anthropological Research 38(1):108–127.

Lastres, Juan B.
1951 Historia de la medicina peruana. 3 vols. Lima: San
Marcos.

Newson, Linda
1988 Old World Epidemics in Early Colonial Ecuador.
(Paper presented at the 46th International Congress of Americanists, Amsterdam, 4–8 July.)

Pizarro, Pedro
1978 Relación del descubrimiento y conquista del Peru.
Lima: Universidad Católica.

Poma de Ayala, Felipe Guaman
1980 El primer nueva corónica y buen gobierno. J. V.
Murra and R. Adorno, eds. 3 vols. Mexico: Siglo
Veintiuno.

Porras Barrenechea, Raul
1959 Cartas del Peru. Lima: Edición de la Sociedad de
Bibliofilos Peruanos.

1986 Los cronistas del Peru (1528–1650) y Otros En-
sayos. Franklin Pease G. Y., ed. Lima: Banco de
Crédito del Peru.

Rosenblat, Angel
1955 La Población indígena y el mestizaje en America. 2
vols. Buenos Aires: Editorial Nova.

1967 La Población de America en 1492. Mexico.

Rostworoski de Diez Canseco, Maria
1981 Recursos naturales renovables y pesca. Siglos XVI
y XVII. Lima: Instituto de Estudios Peruanos.

Santa Cruz Pachacuti Yamqui, Juan de
1968 Relación de antiguedades deste reyno del Piru.
Madrid: Ediciones Atlas.

Sarmiento de Gamboa, Pedro
1988 Historia de los Incas. Madrid: Ediciones Polifemo.

Simon, Pedro
1882– Noticias historiales de las conquistas de tierra
1892 firme en las Indias Occidentales. 5 vols. Bogotá:
Imprenta de Medardo Rivas.

Urteaga, Horacio H., ed.
1920 Informaciones sobre el antiguo Peru. Lima: San-
marti.

Villamarin, Juan, and Judith Villamarin
1988 Epidemic Disease in the Sabana de Bogotá, 1536–
1810. (Paper presented at the 46th International
Congress of Americanists. Amsterdam, 4–8 July.)

——— 20 ———

Native American Trade Centers as Contagious Disease Foci

HENRY F. DOBYNS

Native American trading centers have been defined very much in terms of culturally patterned behaviors. For example, on the Plains, "barter between hunting and gardening peoples enabled each group to supplement its economy with the products of the other's labor" (Ewers 1954:433). Native American commerce at trading centers had epidemiological consequences of fundamental demographic importance, especially during post-Columbian times. Trading center merchants conducted fairs attracting trading partners from many societies. Mandans, for example, attracted Assiniboine, Plains Cree, Crow, Cheyenne, Arapaho, Kiowa, Kiowa-Apache, and Comanche customers. Those traders engaged in a very important disease-transmission activity. Foreign merchants increased trading center population, in itself a demographic shift conducive to contagion.

Intimate interpersonal interaction during trading-center fairs favored direct aerosol transmission of viruses. By feeding a multitude of traders, merchants' wives and female relatives risked giving them dysentery transmitted by human or insect vectors. United States treaty negotiating sessions are a historic analog for trading fairs. In 1825, for example, natives "flocked to the treaty ground from all quarters," even the Dakotas. "Dysentery supervened . . . some died on the ground, and a great many perished on the way from Prairie du Chien" (Snelling 1868:124). Members of female work groups hosting foreign traders were themselves at increased risk from pathogens the traders carried (Trimble 1989:57).

ACCELERATED NINETEENTH-CENTURY DISEASE TRANSMISSION

Native trading centers inevitably became foci of communicable diseases. Like magnets, trading centers attracted infectious merchants or transportation workers who placed trading-center residents at risk. The reality of that risk is well illustrated by 1837 Mandan, Hidatsa, and Arikara losses to smallpox. Both crew members (Schoolcraft 1851, 1:257) and passengers (Coues 1898, 1:132) aboard the river steamboat *St. Peters* have been identified as transmitting smallpox rapidly up the Missouri River from Fort Leavenworth. Mandan population reportedly plummeted from about 1,600 to 125 or else 75 percent mortality (Howard 1960:30). Both

Hidatsa and Arikara suffered 50 percent mortality, declining from 1,000 to 500 and from 3,000 to 1,500 respectively. After 1837, remnant Mandans amalgamated with remnant Arikaras and Hidatsas to form the Three Affiliated Tribes.

The biological impact of variola major on Mandans in 1837 appears particularly horrible because such high mortality was preventable. In fact, contract physicians hired by the United States Indian Service had effectively vaccinated several thousand Dakota speakers during the half-decade immediately preceding the 1837 epidemic. The Mandan tragedy lay in the failure of any contract physician to travel up the Missouri River far enough to vaccinate them (Trimble 1983). Vaccination had become available when Edward Jenner published in 1798 the results of his clinical investigation revealing that cowpox, a mild ailment, conferred immunity to smallpox, a deadly one (Saunders 1982). Mandan mortality in 1837 occurred, therefore, under biological conditions representative of those all over the world prior to 1798.

There is a second demographic dimension of native trading centers as historic foci of contagious disease transmission. Foreign merchants visiting a sedentary trading center during an epidemic were, as part of the crowd at a populous fair, at risk along with their local trading partners. Those who were attacked by a pathogen ravaging the trading center's populace frequently carried the virus or germ back to their homes and relatives. Again, the 1837 northern Plains smallpox epidemic illustrates epidemiological consequences.

The riverine Mandan, Hidatsa, and Arikara transmitted variola major to their Assiniboine trading partners, who carried it home. Consequently, whole Assiniboine villages were "nearly annihilated." Absaroka traders contracted smallpox in riverine trading centers and carried it home; they lost about one-third of their population. The disease spread to the Blackfeet, thought by newcomers to have lost 6,000–8,000 persons (Schoolcraft 1851, 1:257).

The demise of the ethnic Mandan trading center occurred in the aftermath of one of the most studied and best-recorded smallpox epidemic episodes in North American history (Crosby 1976; Quaife 1930). From ancient times until 1837, Mandans operated their own trading centers, although newcomer traders invaded Mandan territory and usurped much native commerce during the final few years.

Steamboat travel was in 1837 a new condition greatly accelerating the rate of travel on streams crossing the Great Plains. Such rapid movement of infectious individuals had not existed during earlier decades. Rather than imply too much from the Mandan-Hidatsa-Arikara cases, therefore, this chapter analyzes other Indian trading centers.

NINETEENTH-CENTURY OVERLAND DISEASE TRANSMISSION

The Pecos River is not conducive to steamboat navigation. Native and newcomer merchants visiting Pecos Pueblo traveled on foot, horse or muleback, or on wagons. Like the Mandan, Hidatsa, and Arikara, the Pecos Indians had in 1837 operated a trading center through recorded historic times. Like the Missouri Trench natives, the Pecos felt impelled in the wake of their 1837 epidemic mortality to amalgamate with members of another ethnic group. In 1838, the remnant Pecos traders migrated halfway across New Mexico to reside with fellow Towa speakers in Jemez Pueblo.

The first Europeans who entered Pueblos described Pecos merchants engaging in "farther-ranging contact," as Trimble (1989:56) labels such behavior. After Francisco Vázquez de Coronado occupied Hawikkuh Pueblo, "some Indians came to Cibola [Zuñi] from a village which was 70 leagues east of this province, called Cicuye [Pecos]." The leader offered friendship and "a present of tanned hides and shields and head-pieces" (Castañeda 1896:430, 490). Later the Spaniards learned that Cicuye Pueblo conducted trans-Plains commerce with Wichita in the Mississippi River basin.

Missionaries who resided at Pecos Pueblo while trying to convert its natives to Roman Catholicism recorded a long series of disease epidemics that depopulated it. Mission records identify smallpox at Pecos Pueblo in 1640, 1696, 1738, 1780–1781, 1800, 1816, and 1831–1832. Measles struck in 1728–1729, and other lethal ailments in 1669, 1704, 1748, 1759, and 1826 (Kessell 1979:163, 225, 378, 457). General Pueblo susceptibility to contagious diseases emphasizes that mortality had been higher in the Pecos trading center than in other pueblos in order to force its 1838 abandonment.

The Northern Panya trading center (Dobyns 1984) seems to have flourished on the lower Colorado River from the sixteenth century until 1827

(Dobyns, Ezell, and Ezell 1963). In 1821–1827, Northern Panya entrepreneurs added a disease transmission "farther-reaching contact" by serving as couriers between Sonora and California (Ezell 1968). Panya couriers exposed themselves to measles, which was epidemic in Sonoran villages* (Escalante 1826) and New Mexico Pueblos (Aberle, Watkins, and Pitney 1940:170; Kessell 1979:378) in 1826. Breaking out in central Mexico in 1825 (Brading and Wu 1973:14, 29), measles spread to California (Cook 1943:20) in 1827. Indeed, Panya couriers may have transmitted the virus from Sonora to California, as well as to their own relatives. Disproportionately high disease mortality in their trading center led to the 1827 Northern Panya exodus from the Colorado River.

The numerical attrition of the people around this trading center from 1775 to 1850 reportedly was from 10 to one. In 1775, the intrepid Franciscan explorer Francisco Garcés (1965:89) estimated Halyikwamai at 2,000, Kahwan at 3,000, Northern Panya at 2,500, and Southern Panya at 2,500, a total of 10,000 persons. By 1840, these peoples had amalgamated into the "Maricopa" (Spier 1933:18), numbering a reported 1,000 individuals in 1850 (Hayes 1929:45).

EIGHTEENTH-CENTURY OVERLAND DISEASE TRANSMISSION

In the Southeast, the historic demise of the Eno trading center becomes intelligible in "farther-reaching contact" terms. The Eno "hired out to their neighbours, who employ them as carryers or porters." Gardening industriously, the Eno raised three maize crops each summer "and out of their granary supply all the adjacent parts." Eno storage capacity is one criterion of a trading center: "to each house belongs a little hovel made like an oven, where they lay up their corn and mast, and keep it dry" (Alvord and Bidgood 1912:156–157). Evidently the Eno trading center suffered such disease mortality that only a few score Eno survived into the

eighteenth century. By 1743, the remnant amalgamated into the Catawba, and the Eno language was but one of twenty dialects spoken by shattered ethnic groups amalgamated under the "Catawba" rubric (Swanton 1946:131; Hudson 1970:47–48; Adair 1930:236).

When European colonists first learned in mid-seventeenth century about the Ocaneechi, they "devoted themselves largely to trade, as is testified by the fact that their language had become the trade jargon over a considerable extent of territory" (Swanton 1946:739). Their trading center was militarily secure on an island in the Roanoke River. Across the stream "upon the north-shore they yearly reap great crops of corn, of which they always have a twelve-months supply aforehand" (Alvord and Bidgood 1912:154). Ocaneechi merchants resorted to violence to block European traders' access to natives south of their trading center. They "owed their existence to trade" (Hudson 1970:36–37).

Ocaneechi suffered the same fate as the Eno. In 1676, Saponi, Tutelo, and Conestoga migrated to Ocaneechi territory. Nathaniel Bacon attacked that year, and the natives fled south to Eno River, North Carolina, by 1701. Around 1714 they were at Fort Christianna with the Manahoac, possibly motivated to amalgamate by scarlet fever epidemic mortality in 1708–1710 (Dobyns 1983:22). Epidemic measles in 1717–1728 perhaps reduced the Ocaneechi. A smallpox epidemic among Southeast natives during 1738–1739 surely did (Dobyns 1983:15, 17). By 1740, the amalgam group was called "Saponi" (Swanton 1946:164).

LATE SEVENTEENTH-CENTURY TRADING CENTER ABANDONMENT

The differentially high mortality rate characteristic of trading centers appears to have motivated about 1672 the abandonment (Hayes 1981:8) of Pueblo de los Jumanos. The Spanish name indicated that this pueblo was a trading center. "[I]t is called Xumanas, because this nation often comes there to trade and barter" (Benavides 1945:66). Until 1671, it was the southeastern gateway to the Pueblo market. In 1666–1669, a severe drought in colonial New Mexico caused famine conditions, which continued in 1670. Malnutrition exacerbated the impact of "a great pestilence, which . . . carried off many people and cattle" in 1671 (Hackett 1937,

---

*At Cocóspera Mission on the Panya trail to Arispe, 10 of the year's 15 deaths occurred during April, indicating that was when the virus invaded (Anonymous 1822–1836). Measles raged through Papagos at Caborca and Pitiquito in northwestern Sonora in late June (Anonymous 1826).

3:188). Livestock scarcity stimulated raiding by Apaches (DiPeso 1974, 3:864). The disease may have been smallpox, which was epidemic in 1669–1671 among Ontario Algonquians, Montagnais, Mohawks (Hurlich 1983:156; Kellogg 1968:162; Stearn and Stearn 1945:29, 31), and Susquehannocks (Hanna 1911, 1:35) and caused an archeologically identifiable phase shift about 1675 in southern Appalachia (Smith 1987:80) as well as the 1676 Saponi, Tutelo, and Conestoga migrations.

New Mexico's severe domestic livestock epizootic killed large numbers of horses, including those of Apacheans who had been trading peacefully with Pueblo merchants. Earlier trades turned into 1672 raids. So Pueblo de los Jumanos merchants abandoned their homes and migrated to Piro-speaking pueblos on the Rio Grande.

Colonial New Mexico's seventeenth-century epidemiology may be traced in missionary reports concerning diseases that decimated Pueblo peoples prior to their 1680 militant nativistic movement. Bubonic plague struck, apparently about 1617–1619 (Dobyns 1989a:173; Hackett 1937, 3:108), followed by scarlet fever in 1637 and smallpox in 1640 (Reff 1987:705; Upham 1987:709).

Mortality during these epidemics was so high that it caused a number of pueblos to amalgamate in a sharply reduced number of settlements. In 1582, Antonio de Espejo (1966:223) described Old Zia Pueblo as "a very large pueblo" with eight plazas. In 1598, Juan de Oñate (1953, 1:346) referred to four Zian pueblos on Jemez River besides Santa Ana de Tamaya. Rio Grande Paint Glaze E ceramic vessels recovered from the ruins of LA 28 (the ruin under modern Zia Pueblo), La Rinconada (LA 241), Old Sia (LA 384), and LA 374 (Mera 1940:4, 25) indicate that they were occupied until after 1620. La Rinconada yielded Glaze F sherds, indicating that it was, like Pueblo de los Jumanos, abandoned around 1672, following the 1669–1671 biological crisis. The Glaze E sherds indicate that Old Sia, LA 374, and LA 28 were abandoned after 1620 and before 1669 as a result of 1633–1640 epidemic disease mortality. On the eve of the 1680 Pueblo Revolt, only Santa Ana and Zia were still inhabited. Indeed, the "1613–40 period constituted a major demographic watershed in Greater Southwestern history" (Dobyns 1989a:173). Its rapid demographic decline caused the abandonment of several trading centers.

EARLY SEVENTEENTH-CENTURY ABANDONMENTS

Changes in native trading occurred not only in Pueblo and Piman markets, but also in the Great Lakes area. European observers there left written records dating a 1638 disruption of ancient trading relationships across the isthmus separating Lakes Ontario and Erie. That year, surviving members of the Wenro tribe, which had occupied the key territory between the Neutrals and Senecas, migrated to Huronia. "An epidemic was also causing depletion of their numbers. Some died along the way and others continued to die for two moths after their arrival in Huronia" (White 1978:407, 409).

Weakened by disease mortality, the more populous Neutrals, famed for their trading operations, proved unable to defend their Grand Island and isthmian territory. Initial Neutral response to drastic depopulation appears to have been three military campaigns between 1640 and 1643, during which they captured and took home over 1,000 Huron Confederacy prisoners (Trigger 1985:260). Schlesier (1976:129–145) suggested that replacing deceased relatives motivated Iroquoian warfare. Certainly Iroquois armies attacked key villages in 1650 and 1651 and destroyed Neutral will to resist. These preeminent traders fled westward along the south shore of Lake Erie and to Michigan during the 1650s (White 1978:410).

Some Huron Confederacy remnants fled along parallel routes. The very Five Nations that militarily destroyed Huron trading centers absorbed other remnants. Like the Wenro, Neutral, and other Great Lakes peoples, the Hurons suffered drastic depopulation during the "killing years" 1634, 1636, 1637, and 1639 (Trigger 1985:229–231).† The year smallpox broke out, 1639, Mohawks began buying guns from English traders in the Connecticut River valley, motivating Dutch officials along the Hudson River valley to relax their prohibition on selling firearms to natives. While French colonists responded by trading muskets to natives, they sold them only to Christian Huron converts. By 1648, Iroquois enjoyed a 500+ to <120 gun advantage over Hurons. "Throughout the 1640s the Hurons

---

†Trigger (1985:230 following Thwaites 1896–1901, 13:131–133, 165) identifies from Jesuit descriptions a 1636 influenza outbreak that began in August in the St. Lawrence Valley and persisted for about 6 weeks in each community.

suffered escalating losses as a result of Iroquois at-tacks," beginning in 1642 with the destruction of an Arendahronon village (Trigger 1985:262–263). After the 1647 harvest, the Arendaronons near Lake Simcoe migrated west to other confederacy villages (Trigger 1985:164–165). In July 1648 an Iroquois army destroyed two Attigneenongnahac settlements, taking hundreds of prisoners to re-plenish their own numbers. On 16 March 1649, a large Iroquois army seized Taenhatentaron Town, turning it into a base for operations against hamlets in Sturgeon Valley (Trigger 1985:266–267). Within two weeks after the Iroquois retreated, Hurons "de-serted all of their remaining settlements, which they burned to prevent them from being used by Iro-quois raiders." Refugees scattered to seek refuge with Algonquin, Petun, or Neutral trading part-ners. The Tahontaenrats moved as a group to Neu-tral country. For several years, large numbers of ref-ugee Hurons voluntarily joined the Iroquois (Trigger 1985:268–269).

Military defeat by numerically superior and better-armed Iroquois was the immediate cause for the demise of the Great Lakes region's premier traders. Without detracting from the strategic sig-nificance of Iroquois superiority in muskets, one can perceive that the "killing years" created the de-mographic conditions leading to Iroquois military superiority. The Five Nations appear to have been at least as populous as the Hurons before 1634–1639. "Even after the epidemics, they may have had several thousand more people, which would have given them an advantage in warfare that has not hitherto been adequately considered" (Trigger 1985:236). This analysis suggests that, during the "killing years," professional Huron traders suffered disproportionately higher mortality than the less commercialized Iroquois.

SIXTEENTH-CENTURY PUEBLO AND PIMA TRADING CENTER ABANDONMENTS

Ceramic evidence indicates that the Northern Pan-ya merchants once maintained a resident enclave at the Salt River valley settlement known to archeolo-gists as Las Colinas. The residence of known traders and the relative abundance of marine shell identify Las Colinas as a Piman-speaking trading center (Ur-ban 1981). Other ceramic evidence—Black Mesa

Hopi trade wares—dates final habitation of Las Colinas around 1650 (Crown 1981:143–147).

Up the Verde River tributary of Salt River, a hilltop stronghold known to archeologists as Tuzigoot formerly housed merchants importing from Salt River valley trading partners worked ma-rine shell originating on the Gulf of California coast (Caywood and Spicer 1935:87–89, pl. XVII). Tuzigoot's traders also imported abalone shell and marine mammal peltries from Northern Panya partners over an almost due east-west trail between the lower Colorado and middle Verde rivers (Fore-man 1941:190–225). The same types of Black Mesa Hopi trade ceramics that help to date final occupa-tion at Las Colinas date the demise of Tuzigoot to the same seventeenth-century period (Caywood and Spicer 1935:48–49, 56–57, 61, pls. XII, XIV).

Black Mesa Hopis in the early twentieth cen-tury could precisely describe the ancient foot trail between Tuzigoot and the ruined pueblo trading center in Chavez Pass south of the middle Little Col-orado River (Colton 1964:91–94). That pass pueblo functioned as the western gateway to the Pueblo market for Pacific coast commodities traded east-ward on the Rio Grande–Pacific Trail. The "gateway" label emphasizes the concept that all pueblos constituted a culturally and economically distinctive market, as Upham's (1982:181–183) "port of trade" label does not. The quantity of im-ported marine shell at Nuvaqueotaka is greater than that found in the ruins of other pueblos (Fewkes 1904, 1896) except Pueblo frontier trading centers such as Pecos (Kidder 1932:183–194). This differential distribution of highly valued marine shell helps to identify the Chavez Pass Pueblo as having functioned as a gateway pueblo like Taos, Pecos, and Pueblo de los Jumanos (McKusick 1981:40–42). The same Black Mesa Hopi trade ce-ramics that date the final days of Las Colinas and Tuzigoot date them at Chavez Pass (Upham 1982:169).

After 1650, the Northern Panya necessarily ad-justed to profoundly altered demographic condi-tions. Instead of dealing in a Salt River valley port-of-trade, merchants traveled episodically to ethnic Kohatk Shodak shon on the middle Gila River (Bur-rus 1971:344). Instead of visiting Tuzigoot, North-ern Panya traders exchanged precious commodities with Northeastern Pai relatives who carried them over circuitous trails to Oraibi Pueblo (Dobyns and

Euler 1976:22–26). Oraibi traders trod those round-about routes to acquire raw cotton and coastal commodities from the Northern Panya. Despite Oraibi's limited food production, its traders prospered by charging their Pueblo customers far more for east-bound commodities than they paid their Pai and Panya trading partners for them. (For example, Hopis purchased red hematite from Havasupais for $5 per pound but resold it to other Pueblos at 25 cents per teaspoonful—Colton 1941:309.) Oraibi replaced Chavez Pass as the western gateway to the Pueblo market. The 1613–1640 demographic decline caused attrition among native trading centers, and traders shifted to longer major trading paths. It did not disrupt trade "beyond repair" (Riley 1976:44).

CONCLUSION

The dates when Indians abandoned trading centers—1838, 1827, 1675–1672, 1650, 1649, 1638—show that merchants abandoned hitherto prosperous trading centers a year or so after a final demoralizing epidemic disease episode, and imply that trading-center populations differed in their exposures to Old World diseases. Some scholars perceive the demographic impact of the "killing years" alone as sufficient to cause such changes (Snow and Lanphear 1988). The paucity of written records for earlier decades encourages this view. One may infer that greater demographic decline than occurred during the "killing years" was required to bring down an established native trading center (Dobyns 1983:313–327, 1989b:293–296).

REFERENCES

Aberle, Sophie B. D., J. H. Watkins, and E. H. Pitney
    1940   The Vital History of San Juan Pueblo. *Human Biology* 12(May):2.

Adair, James
    1930   History of the American Indians. Samuel C. Williams, ed. Johnson City, Tenn.: Watauga Press.

Alvord, Clarence W., and Lee Bidgood, eds.
    1912   *The First Explorations of the Trans-Allegheny Region by the Virginians 1650–1674.* Cleveland: Arthur H. Clark.

Anonymous
    1822–   Libro de Entierros de Santiago de Cocospera,

    1836   1822–1836. (In Bancroft Library, University of California, Berkeley.)

    1826   Libro de Bautismos de San Diego del Pitiqui, No. 3. (In Bancroft Library, University of California, Berkeley.)

Benavides, Alonso de
    1945   Fray Alonso de Benavides' Revised Memorial of 1634. Frederick W. Hodge, George P. Hammond and Agapito Rey, eds. Albuquerque: University of New Mexico Press.

Brading, D. A., and Celia Wu
    1973   Population Growth and Crisis: Leon, 1720–1860. *Journal of Latin American Studies* 5(1):1–36.

Burrus, Ernest J., ed.
    1971   Kino and Manje, Explorers of Sonora and Arizona: Their Vision of the Future, a Study of Their Expeditions and Plans. Rome: Jesuit Historical Institute.

Castañeda de Nacera, Pedro de
    1896   Relación de la Jornada de Cibola. Pp. 413–546. George P. Winship, trans. in *14th Annual Report of the Bureau of Ethnology for the Years 1892–93, Pt. 1.* Washington: U.S. Government Printing Office.

Caywood, Louis R., and Edward H. Spicer
    1935   Tuzigoot: The Excavation and Repair of a Ruin on the Verde River Near Clarkdale, Arizona. Berkeley, Calif.: National Park Service.

Colton, Harold S.
    1941   Prehistoric Trade in the Southwest. *Scientific Monthly* 52(4):308–319.

    1964   Principal Hopi Trails. *Plateau* 36(3):91–94.

Cook, Sherburne F.
    1943   The Conflict Between the California Indians and White Civilization. Pt. 1: The Indian versus the Spanish Mission. *Ibero-Americana* 21. Berkeley, Calif.

Coues, Elliott, ed.
    1898   Forty Years a Fur Trader on the Upper Missouri: The Personal Narrative of Charles Larpenteur, 1833–1872. New York: Francis P. Harper.

Crosby, Alfred W., Jr.
    1976   Virgin Soil Epidemics as a Factor in the Aboriginal Depopulation in America. *William and Mary Quarterly,* 3d ser., Vol. 33(2):289–299.

Crown, Patricia L.
    1981   Analysis of the Las Colinas Ceramics. Pp. 87–170 in The 1968 Excavations at Mound 8, Las Colinas Ruins Group Phoenix, Arizona. Laurens C. Hammack and Alan P. Sullivan, eds. *University of Arizona, Arizona State Museum, Cultural Resource Management Section, Archaeological Series,* 154. Tucson.

DiPeso, Charles C.
    1974   Casas Grandes, A Fallen Trading Center of the

Gran Chichimeca. Gloria J. Fenner, ed. *Amerind Foundation* 9. Dragoon.

Dobyns, Henry F.

1983   Their Number Become Thinned: Native American Population Dynamics in Eastern North America. Knoxville: University of Tennessee Press.

1984   Trade Centers: The Concept and a Rancherian Culture Area Example. *American Indian Culture and Research Journal* 8(1):23–35.

1989a   Native Historic Epidemiology in the Greater Southwest. *American Anthropologist* 91(1):171–174.

1989b   More Methodological Perspectives on Historical Demography, *Ethnohistory* 36(3):285–299.

Dobyns, Henry F., and Robert C. Euler

1976   The Walapai People. Phoenix: Indian Tribal Series.

Dobyns, Henry F., Paul H. Ezell, and Greta S. Ezell

1963   Death of a Society, *Ethnohistory* 10(2):105–161.

Escalante, Manuel

1826   23 de Agosto de 1826. Arispe. Archivo del Gobierno de la Mitra de Sonora, Hermosillo, Mexico, Legajo de los Años 1825 a 1831.

Espejo, Antonio de

1966   Report. Pp. 213–231 in The Rediscovery of New Mexico 1580–1594. George P. Hammond and Agapito Rey, trans. Albuquerque: University of New Mexico Press.

Ewers, John C.

1954   The Indian Trade of the Upper Missouri Before Lewis and Clarke: An Interpretation. *Missouri Historical Society Bulletin* 10(4):429–446.

Ezell, Paul H.

1968   The Cocomaricopa Mail. Pp. 28–34 in *Brand Book Number One*. Ray Brandes, ed. San Diego: San Diego Corral of the Westerners.

Fewkes, Jesse W.

1896   Pacific Coast Shells from Prehistoric Tusayan Pueblos, *American Anthropologist* 9(11):359–367

1904   Two Summers' Work in Pueblo Ruins. Pp. 3–195 in *22d Annual Report of the Bureau of American Ethnology for the Years 1900–1901*. Washington: U.S. Government Printing Office.

Foreman, Grant, ed.

1941   A Pathfinder in the Southwest: The Itinerary of Lieutenant A. W. Whipple During His Explorations for a Railway Route from Fort Smith to Los Angeles in the Years 1853 & 1854. Norman: University of Oklahoma Press.

Garcés, Francisco

1965   A Record of Travels in Arizona and California 1775–1776. John Galvin, trans. Berkeley, Calif.: John Howell-Books.

Hackett, Charles W., ed.

1937   Historical Documents Relating to New Mexico, Nueva Vizcaya, and Approaches Thereto, to 1773, Collected by Adolph F. A. Bandelier and Fanny R. Bandelier. Washington: Carnegie Institution of Washington.

Hanna, Charles A.

1911   The Wilderness Trail. New York: G. P. Putnam's Sons.

Hayes, Alden C.

1981   Excavation of Mound 7, Gran Quivira National Monument, New Mexico. *National Park Service, Publications in Archaeology* 16. Washington.

Hayes, Benjamin

1929   Pioneer Notes from the Diaries of Judge Benjamin Hayes. Marjorie T. Wolcott, ed. Los Angeles: Privately printed.

Howard, James H.

1960   Butterfly's Mandan Winter Count: 1833–1876. *Ethnohistory* 7(1):28–43.

Hudson, Charles M.

1970   The Catawba Nation. *University of Georgia Press Monograph* 18. Athens.

Hurlich, Marshall G.

1983   Historical and Recent Demography of the Algonkians of Northern Ontario. Pp. 143–199 in Boreal Forest Adaptations: The Northern Algonkians. A. T. Steegmann, Jr., ed. New York: Plenum Press.

Kellogg, Louise Phelps

1968   The French Regime in Wisconsin and the Northwest. New York: Cooper Square Publishers.

Kessell, John L.

1979   Kiva, Cross, and Crown: The Pecos Indians and New Mexico 1540–1840. Washington: National Park Service.

Kidder, Alfred V.

1932   Artifacts of Pecos. *Yale University Press, Papers of the Southwestern Expedition* 6. New Haven, Conn.

McKusick, Charmion R.

1981   The Faunal Remains of Las Humanas. Pp. 39–66 in Contributions to Gran Quivira Archeology. Alden C. Hayes, ed. *National Park Service Publications in Archeology* 17. Washington.

Mera, H. P.

1940   Population Changes in the Rio Grande Glaze-Paint Area. *Laboratory of Anthropology Archaeological Survey Technical Series, Bulletin* 9. Sante Fe.

Oñate, Juan de

1953   Don Juan de Oñate, Colonizer of New Mexico, 1595–1628. George P. Hammond and Agapito Rey, eds. Albuquerque: University of New Mexico Press.

Quaife, M. M.
    1930   The Smallpox Epidemic on the Upper Missouri. *Mississippi Valley Historical Review* 17(2):278–299.

Reff, Daniel T.
    1987   The Introduction of Smallpox in the Greater Southwest. *American Anthropologist* 89(3):704–708.

Riley, Carroll L.
    1976   Sixteenth Century Trade in the Greater Southwest. *Southern Illinois University, Museum, Research Records* 10. Carbondale.

Saunders, Paul
    1982   Edward Jenner, The Cheltenham Years 1795–1823, Being a Chronicle of the Vaccination Campaign. Hanover, N.H.: University Press of New England.

Schlesier, Karl
    1976   Epidemics and Indian Middlemen: Rethinking the Wars of the Iroquois, 1609–1653, *Ethnohistory* 23(2):129–145.

Schoolcraft, Henry R.
    1851   Historical and Statistical Information Respecting the History, Condition and Prospects of the Indian Tribes of the United States. 6 vols. Philadelphia: Lippincott, Grambo.

Smith, Marvin T.
    1987   Archaeology of Aboriginal Culture Change in the Interior Southeast: Depopulation During the Early Historic Period. *University of Florida Press, Florida State Museum Bullen Monograph* 6. Gainesville.

Snelling, William J.
    1868   Early Days at Prairie de Chien and Winnebago Outbreak of 1827. *Wisconsin Historical Collections* 5. Madison.

Snow, Dean R., and Kim M. Lanphear
    1988   European Contact and Indian Depopulation in the Northeast: The Timing of the First Epidemics, *Ethnohistory* 35(1):15–33.

Spier, Leslie
    1933   Yuman Tribes of the Gila River. Chicago: University of Chicago Press.

Stearn, E. Wagner, and Allen E. Stearn
    1945   The Effect of Smallpox on the Destiny of the Amerind. Boston: Bruce Humphries.

Swanton, John R.
    1946   The Indians of the Southeastern United States. *Bureau of American Ethnology Bulletin* 137. Washington.

Thwaites, Reuben G., ed.
    1896–   The Jesuit Relations. Cleveland: Burrows Bros.
    1901

Trigger, Bruce G.
    1985   Natives and Newcomers: Canada's "Heroic Age" Reconsidered. Montreal: McGill-Queen's University Press.

Trimble, Michael K.
    1983   Cycles of Infectious Disease on the Upper Missouri: A Preliminary Chronology and Case Study. (Paper presented at Conference on Native American Historic Demography, The Newberry Library, Chicago, December.)

    1989   Infectious Disease and the Northern Plains Horticulturists: A Human Behavior Model. Pp. 41–59 in Demography and Health: Perspectives, Interpretations, and Critiques. Plains Indian Historical Gregory R. Campbell, ed. *Plains Anthropologist* 23:34–124.

Upham, Steadman
    1982   Politics and Power: An Economic and Political History of the Western Pueblos. New York: Academic Press.

    1987   Understanding the Disease History of the Southwest. *American Anthropologist* 89(3):708–710.

Urban, Sharon F.
    1981   The Las Colinas Shell Assemblage. Pp. 308–336 in The 1968 Excavations at Mound 8 Las Colinas Ruins Group Phoenix, Arizona. Laurens C. Hammack and Alan P. Sullivan, eds. *University of Arizona, Arizona State Museum, Cultural Resource Management Section, Archaeological Series* 154. Tucson.

White, Marian E.
    1978   Neutral and Wenro. Pp. 407–411 in Volume 15 of Handbook of North American Indians. Bruce G. Trigger, ed. William C. Sturtevant, gen. ed. Washington: Smithsonian Institution.

— 21 —

Population and Spanish Contact in the Southwest

STEADMAN UPHAM

The size and structure of native populations in the Americas is a topic of interest to scholars of the contact period because of the possibility that catastrophic population decline occurred as a result of diseases introduced by Spaniards. This chapter describes the demographic history of one region, the American Southwest, at the time of the Spanish entradas and during the immediately preceding prehistoric period, approximately A.D. 1450 to 1600. Because the course of Spanish exploration prior to 1600 was limited to specific areas of New Mexico and central and northern Arizona, the contact history of only these areas is examined.

THE SPANISH NARRATIVES OF CONTACT

The narratives written prior to 1600 contain important information related to Indian populations and are especially valuable for illustrating the difficulties that are encountered in reconciling Southwestern population estimates (Bolton 1916; Winship 1896; Hodge 1907; Hackett 1923–1927, 1942; Hammond and Rey 1928, 1929, 1940, 1953, 1966). These narratives include the correspondence of Francisco Vásquez de Coronado written in 1540, the accounts of the 1540 Coronado expedition written by Pedro de Castañeda in 1565; the Gallegos Lamero relation of the 1581 Agustín Rodriguez–Francisco Sanchez Chumascado expedition written in 1582; two different narratives of the 1582 Antonio Espejo expedition, one written by Diego Perez de Luxan sometime before 1602 and another written by Espejo in 1583; and the *memoria* of Gaspar Castaño de Sosa written in 1592. Other important information about population size and structure can also be gleaned from the letters, narratives, and accounts of Marcos de Niza in 1539, Hernando de Alarcon (1540), Juan de Oñate in 1598–1599, and the secondary account of various Spanish expeditions to the Southwest written by Baltasar de Obregon in 1584.

Data presented in table 1 summarize population estimates from these Spanish narratives for different Pueblo groups. The estimates vary widely because the Spaniards used three different means to estimate population in the Southwest: they counted men or warriors, they counted houses and pueblos, and, more rarely, they estimated the total population of a pueblo, province, or entire region.

TABLE 1

Pueblo Population Estimates from Sixteenth-Century Spanish Narratives

Narrative	Date	Group or Region	Population Estimate
Coronado	1540	Zuni	740 houses
Francisco López de Gomara	1550	Zuni	4,000 men
Castañeda	1565	Rio Grande region	20,000 men 66? (71) pueblos
		Hopi and Zuni	3,000 to 4,000 men 14 pueblos
		Pecos	500 warriors
Martín de Pedrosa	1581	Rio Grande region	6,861 multistoried houses; 61 pueblos
Gallegos Lamero	1581	Piro territory	more than 12,000 people
		Rio Gande region and Zuni	6,301 multistoried houses; 58 pueblos
Perez de Luxan	1582	6 Piro Pueblos	350 houses 2,800 inhabitants
		Zia Pueblo	1,000 houses; more than 4,000 men over 15 years of age
		Hopi	12,000 inhabitants plus Querechos
		San Cristobal Pueblo	over 1,500 warriors
		Pecos Pueblo	about 2,000 armed men
Espejo	1582	Zuni	20,000 inhabitants
		Hopi	50,000 inhabitants
		Tompiros	40,000 inhabitants
		Keresan Pueblos	15,000 inhabitants
		Tiwa Pueblos	no estimate
		Zia	20,000 inhabitants
		Jemez	30,000 inhabitants
		Acoma	6,000 inhabitants
		Province of Ubates	20,000 inhabitants
		Tanoan Pueblos	40,000 inhabitants
Obregon	1584	Pueblo region	117,300 Indians 78? (64) pueblos 22,400? (7,467) houses
		Zuni region	in two hours 30,000 men could be assembled
Oñate	1598	Rio Grande region	70,000 Indians
		Acoma	3,000 Indians

Men or Warriors

Given the perceived threat to the safety of the Spaniards during the first expeditions to the Southwest, and the often hostile intentions of the Indian inhabitants, it is natural that Spanish explorers counted the number of fighting men or warriors in a given pueblo or province. These estimates are perplexing because to estimate total population from them one must make certain assumptions about the age-sex structure, fertility, and mortality of a given population, using life tables developed from anthropological data (Weiss 1973) and data from the analysis of large burial populations, like those from the late prehistoric occupations of Pecos (Hooton 1930), Arroyo Hondo (Palkovitch 1980), and Grasshopper (Hinkes 1983; Cordell, Upham, and Brock 1987; Brock 1988).

Data from Weiss's (1973:134) life table MT:22.5–35, for example, approximate what is known about mortality and survivorship at the three sites mentioned above.* As determined from the Pecos burial population, life expectancy at age 15 was 21.5 more years, that is, someone living at Pecos in 1500 who had reached the age of 15 could expect to survive to age 36 or 37. Weiss's table provides a demographic profile of a population whose life expectancy at 15 was 22.5 more years, a close approximation to that of Pecos. Juvenile survivorship at age 15 equaled 35 out of 100 births, meaning that 65 in a cohort of 100 did not survive to age 15. At Grasshopper juvenile survivorship at age 15 equaled 45 of 100 births, and at Arroyo Hondo, 41, meaning that slightly lower mortality before age 15 is indicated at these sites. The table provides additional corroborating evidence in the form of data on life expectancy at birth. For example, life expectancy at birth is shown to be 14.8 years, suggesting relatively high infant mortality rates. This figure is remarkably close to that reported for the large skeletal series recovered from the fourteenth and fifteenth-century sites of Grasshopper Pueblo, where life expectancy at birth equals 14.1 (Brock 1988), and Arroyo Hondo, where it equals 16.23 (Palkovitch 1980:33). Consequently, Weiss's (1973:134) life table appears to provide a reasonable approximation of the profile of known prehistoric Southwestern populations, although Palkovitch (1980:36) notes important divergences from the model data that can result from population growth or decline and migration. Important details from Weiss's (1973) life table are presented in table 2.

Data from the table can be used to estimate the size of a few contact period populations that the Spaniards described. The terms "men" and "warriors" are assumed to identify individuals of fighting age, all males between the ages of 15 and 40, a proportion determined from the life table to constitute 21.2 percent of the total population given a sex ratio of 0.50.

Population estimates vary widely for the same site. Pecos Pueblo, for example, said to contain 500 warriors in 1540 (Castaneda writing in 1565), would have an estimated 2,359 inhabitants by this formula

---

TABLE 2

Demographic Data Extrapolated from the Sites of Pecos, Arroyo Hondo, and Grasshopper

Crude birth rate	0.0677
Index of growth regulation	0.3636
Completed family size (gross reproductive rate)	4.66
Mean family size	5.71
Generation length	26.98
Adult survivorship	24.30
Proportion of population under age 15	46.8%
Proportion of population 15 to 50	45.6%
Proportion of population over 50	7.7%
Dependency ratio	1.2
Average age of the population	20.7
Average age of adults	33.1

Source: Weiss 1973:134.

---

or 9,434 inhabitants using Perez de Luxan's 1582 figure of 2,000 "armed men" (table 1). Similarly, the Hopi and Zuni Pueblo population would be between 14,000 and 19,000 inhabitants using Castaneda's numbers. Yet Francisco López de Gomara's figures for 1550 would yield an estimate that the six Zuni pueblos alone contained nearly 19,000 inhabitants; and some 30 years after that, Obregon's "30,000 men" would mean the entire Zuni region was estimated to contain more than 141,000 people, a wholly unrealistic count.

These inconsistencies would appear to suggest that the Spanish population estimates based on counting "men" or "warriors" are unreliable. In many cases, however, the number of "men" or "warriors" represent aggregate population estimates that may combine segments of several different local populations. The conflation of different local populations by the Spaniards tends to indicate that demographic instability and population movements occurred frequently during this phase of exploration (Palkovitch 1985:417).

It is clear, for example, that one reaction of the Pueblos to visitation by the Spaniards was to band together to present a unified front and superior numbers. This process of temporary population aggregation is obvious during the visits of Coronado and subsequent explorers to Zuni, Hopi, and to several Rio Grande Pueblos (Hodge 1907:308, 321–322; Bolton 1916:185–186; Hammond and Rey 1966:281).

---

*According to Ann L. W. Stodder (personal communication, 1989), based on data from the site of San Cristobal, all the population estimates here need to be increased by 1.5% to conform to Weiss's (1973) life table MT:20–65 as a better approximation of late prehistoric Pueblo populations.

Houses and Pueblos

Counting houses or pueblos was often the best method of population estimation because in some regions a few or all of the inhabitants of particular villages had fled in anticipation of the Spaniards' arrival. Consequently, the architectural details of villages often provided the only means of assessing the likely size of particular populations.

Most frequently, the Spanish counted the number of pueblos in different provinces and then sought to estimate the number of house (or households) in each pueblo. Such counts have resulted in four different lists of Rio Grande pueblos prepared prior to 1596, and a few other estimates for individual villages or provinces (table 1). Based on descriptions of house size by Gallegos Lamero, who describes Rio Grande pueblo houses as "two, three, or four stories high, with eight or ten rooms" (Hammond and Rey 1966:101), population can be projected. Using Martín de Pedrosa's 1581 figures of 61 Pueblos and 6,861 houses, 54,888 rooms can be estimated for the Rio Grande region. Using Gallegos Lamero's 58 Pueblos and 6,301 houses leads to an estimated 50,408 rooms. Coronado's 1540 count of 740 houses in 6 Zuni Pueblos amounts to 5,920 rooms, and Perez de Luxan's 1582 count of 1,000 houses yields 8,000 rooms. However, it is important to point out that what the Spaniards called "houses" may not be direct analogs to the Western concept of "house." Rather, the houses described by the Spaniards may be "households" or may be constellations of rooms used for different purposes by different groups of people at different times (Adams 1983:48–55). Moreover, certain categories of rooms probably were communal and, therefore, "houses" composed of such rooms cannot be related directly to occupancy by a nuclear or extended family. Finally, Wilk and Netting (1984) have demonstrated that houses and "households" bear no necessary correspondence to one another and that houses, numbers of occupants, and the social and biological relationships of such occupants must be determined independently of each other.

Thus, there is no facile conversion from the number of "houses" estimated by the Spaniards to the number of people in a particular pueblo. The unique style of pueblo architecture coupled with the fact that interconnections between rooms in pueblo houses are veiled from public view created confusion among the explorers who sought to describe these structures. Obregon, who wrote that more than 22,000 houses existed in the 64 pueblos he described, appears to have been confused by the multistory character of pueblo architecture. Obregon's *historia* of Spanish explorations of the Southwest is a secondary account compiled from notes, documents, and other narratives. It appears he believed that each separate tier of rooms in a pueblo represented a separate story of distinct houses. It also appears that he presumed that an average of three stories was the norm for most Rio Grande pueblos. This postulated compounding error (by a factor of three) becomes more plausible in light of Obregon's statement that the majority of pueblos were "three stories high" with each house "containing three inhabitants" (in Hammond and Rey 1928:340). To account for this possible error, Obregon's estimate of houses is here reduced by two-thirds, from 22,400 to 7,467, a figure that is in closer agreement with those of Pedrosa and Gallegos Lamero (table 1).

Total Inhabitants

Among the various estimates made by the Spaniards are those that relate directly to the total population of a pueblo, or province. Two population estimates exist for the entire Pueblo region (that is, the Rio Grande pueblos as well as the Keresan and Western Pueblos), one made in 1582 by Antonio de Espejo and another made in 1584 by Baltasar de Obregon. Oñate's 1598 population estimate pertains strictly to the Rio Grande region and omits some of the Keresan and Western Pueblo groups.

These estimates vary widely and present major interpretative problems for those interested in reconstructing the demographic characteristics of contact period Puebloan populations.

Evaluation of the Estimates

Spanish population estimates have been the subject of controversy for decades, with many anthropologists believing that such figures are inflated and represent substantial exaggerations (e.g., Hodge 1907–1910, 1:561). One of the principal reasons for this view is that the Spaniards described populations in some regions of the Southwest that appear unrealistically large in the face of what is known about population size during later historic periods (table 3). The estimates indicate that the

TABLE 3

Pueblo Population, 1793–1821

Pueblos	1793	1797–1798	1805	1810	1821
Acoma	820	757	731	818	477
Cochiti	720	505	656	701	339
Galisteo	152	—	—	—	—
Isleta	410	479	419	498	511
Jemez	485	272	264	299	330
Laguna	668	802	940	1,016	779
Nambe	155	178	143	196	231
Pecos	152	189	104	135	54
Picuris	254	251	250	226	320
Pojoaque	53	79	100	48	93
Sandia	304	236	314	372	405
San Felipe	532	282	289	331	310
San Ildefonso	240	251	175	283	525
San Juan	260	202	194	199	232
Santa Ana	356	634	450	511	471
Santa Clara	139	193	186	216	180
Santo Domingo	650	1,483	333	726	726
Taos	518	531	508	537	753
Tesuque	138	155	131	162	187
Zia	275	262	254	290	196
Zuni	1,935	2,716	1,470	1,602	1,597
Total	9,216	10,457	7,911	9,166	8,716

Sources: Dozier 1970a:122; Simmons 1979:185.

total Pueblo population, without Hopi, varied between 8,000 and 11,000 from 1793 to 1821, figures that contrast dramatically with the estimates of Espejo, Obregon, and Oñate made some 200 years earlier. Moreover, total Pueblo population around 1915–1932 was only 15,327 (Parsons 1939).

Much of the existing ethnographic work on Pueblo groups was conducted in the first half of the twentieth century. Consequently these lower population figures have served as a kind of demographic baseline for descriptions of the Puebloan peoples, who are typically depicted as small-scale societies (Benedict 1930, 1934; Dozier 1954, 1970a; Eggan 1950; White 1932a, 1932b, 1935, 1942, 1960; Titiev 1944). Such descriptions no doubt prompted historians like Bolton (1930:216) to claim that Oñate's count of 70,000 Indians in the Rio Grande region in 1598 was "an exaggerated estimate." It is also the case that many ethnographers of this period believed that the Pueblo were relatively unchanged by the contact experience, that nearly 500 years of colonial domination had little effect on the demographic size and structure of Pueblo groups (e.g., Dozier 1970b). As a result, many anthropologists and historians viewed the eighteenth through twen-

tieth century population estimates as accurate reflections of population size during the preceding several centuries. For example, Hodge (1907:359) believed that Castaneda's estimate of "20,000 men" in the Rio Grande region should have been 20,000 total inhabitants.

Owing largely to the pathbreaking work of Henry Dobyns, Alfred Crosby, and a handful of other anthropologists and historical demographers, scholars have begun the task of examining the biological consequences of European contact in the Americas. This work indicates the biological consequences of contact were often catastrophic for the native peoples. The spread of European-introduced acute crowd infection, such as smallpox, measles, and influenza, to completely susceptible Indian populations often resulted in extremely high levels of mortality in very short periods of time.

In the Southwest, there are lacuna in the contact history of the sixteenth century. No historical records exist for the years following initial European contact in central Mexico (1519 to 1539), or for the years between 1540 and 1580, 1582 and 1591, and 1591 to the establishment of the Spanish garrison at the junction of the Rio Chama and Rio Grande in 1598. In other words, historical records are based on a total of less than four years of sporadic contact and observation during an 80-year period. As a result, it has been suggested that epidemics could have ravaged Puebloan populations a number of times in the sixteenth century, and historical documentation would not exist to record the introduction and spread of disease (Upham 1980, 1982, 1986).

In the Southwest, support for unrecorded epidemics comes primarily from the fields of archeology and quantitative epidemiology (Upham 1980, 1982, 1986; Lycett 1984; Rushforth and Upham 1989). On the basis of such information, some anthropologists have argued that mortality following epidemics in the sixteenth-century Pueblo Southwest may have been as high as 80 percent of the total population following the first 50 years of contact. Other anthropologists have used sixteenth-century Spanish records from other areas, especially those from the Jesuit-controlled areas of West Mexico, to identify diseases, to infer the occurrence of epidemics, and to estimate likely mortality rates in the Southwest (Dobyns 1983; Reff 1986, 1987). Both approaches indicate that epidemic diseases spread within Indian interaction networks and had catastrophic consequences on Southwestern populations.

If such epidemics did occur, then the magnitude of depopulation can be determined by comparing Spanish population estimates with those from later historic periods. Using an average total Pueblo population of 12,500 during the years 1775–1850, the approximate period of population nadir, a depopulation rate of between 95 percent (Espejo) and 90 percent (Obregon) is indicated for the entire Pueblo region, and a depopulation rate of 87 percent (Oñate) for the Rio Grande pueblos alone. These figures are remarkably close to Dobyns's (1966) generalized hemispheric depopulation ratio of 20:1, or 95 percent, and Ubelaker's estimate of a 91 percent population reduction among the Pueblos (Ubelaker 1986).

PUEBLOAN POPULATIONS AT 1500

The fourteenth and fifteenth centuries in the central and northern Southwest witnessed profound change in the structure of Puebloan settlement and the distribution of Puebloan populations. At the beginning of this period, large, nucleated pueblos were constructed in the Rio Grande Valley and the Western Pueblo zone of occupation. By the end of the period, settlement in much of the Western Pueblo region had contracted to a few areas around the Hopi mesas, along the Zuni River, and at the rock of Acoma. In contrast, by 1500 in the valleys of the Rio Grande, Chama, and Pecos rivers, across the Jemez region, and in the Galisteo Basin and Salinas areas, Puebloan populations had expanded greatly. These populations built very large pueblos; sites dating to this period are among the largest found anywhere in the Southwest. All these settlements were built in the characteristic pueblo style; all were sustained by relatively intensive agricultural systems, including the use of elaborate irrigation networks; all were linked in varying degrees to formal and informal interaction networks that archeologists have termed "alliances" (Plog 1984; Upham 1982; Upham and Reed 1989).

The Rio Grande Pueblos

Mera (1940) described the demographic structure of the late prehistoric and early contact period in the Southwest by focusing on changes in Glaze-paint ceramic styles in the central and northern Rio Grande region to develop a chronological scheme for dating site occupations. Based on this scheme, Mera dated more than 200 large pueblos to five different periods. These pueblos were built, occupied, and in some cases abandoned between 1350 and 1700. During the period 1350 to 1450, many medium (250 to 500 rooms) and large pueblos (500 to 2,000 rooms) were built, occupied, and abandoned. At the close of this period, "seventy-four sites were deserted leaving only seventy inhabited villages" (Mera 1940:39). From 1450 to 1490, population aggregation resulted in the formation of very large sites (as large as 3,000 rooms). Mera (1940:39) states that "no villages were abandoned and no new ones founded," during these years. This is in approximate agreement with the total number of pueblos (in both Eastern and Western Pueblo areas) reported by Castañeda following the 1540 Coronado expedition, the earliest firsthand count of occupied pueblos. By the end of the period 1490–1515, population movement and the founding of new communities is evident in the archeological record, but the total number of settlements remained the same. From 1515 to 1650, population dispersal into smaller communities and population loss; the founding of new settlements in concealed, well-protected locations; and a change in the total number of sites is indicated. The change from approximately 70 pueblos in 1540 to more than 130 at 1600 (Schroeder 1979:254) tends to corroborate Mera's assertion regarding the dispersal of population and the founding of new but smaller communities during this period. That population estimates following 1600 reflect a precipitous decline in the size of Pueblo groups also lends support to the notion that disease and disruptions to native social and economic systems were responsible for this demographic collapse.

Reed (1988) has undertaken an analysis of site occupations in the Rio Grande region, focusing specifically on Pueblo settlement in six major areas: Albuquerque, Galisteo Basin, Jemez, Sante Fe, Pajarito Plateau–Tewa, and Abiquiu-Chama. Reed (1988:118–119) identifies 72 pueblos that were occupied during the fifteenth and sixteenth centuries and estimates the number of rooms in each (excluding the Piro and Tompiro Pueblos). Because some of these sites were occupied for as long as three centuries, one cannot assume that each room in the pueblo was occupied during the entire occupation. Rather, the architecture of a pueblo evolves as the population grows and as activities dictate changes in room function (Adams 1983). Archeologists have argued that the number of rooms in use in different pueblos at any one time varied between 50 and 90 percent of the total (Hill 1970; Plog 1974; Watson, LeBlanc, and Redman 1980; Smith, Woodbury, and Woodbury 1966; Upham 1982; Kintigh 1985).

At the living pueblo of Zuni, Kroeber (1917:110–116) found an occupancy rate of 81 percent. Occupancy rates at two living Hopi pueblos, Walpi and Shongopavi, have been recorded as being 75 percent and 90 percent, respectively (Stubbs 1950:91–119). Kintigh (1985) adopted the figure of 65 percent of the total number of rooms as a generalized and conservative estimator of site occupancy at Zuni. This conservative figure is adopted here in recognition that all the pueblos described by Reed may not have been occupied or may not have had a peak occupation at 1500. Consequently, the figure of 65 percent accounts for pueblos not yet built or abandoned, as well as portions of a pueblo that were built early in the site occupation that fell into disuse as new portions of the pueblo were built and occupied. It also accounts for later episodes of remodeling and addition to a site following peak occupation. The use of a 65 percent occupancy figure probably has a tendency to underestimate the proportion of a site that was occupied in cases where sites were built very rapidly. Rapid construction of many pueblos is indicated in some areas of the Rio Grande valley during the fourteenth, fifteenth, and sixteenth centuries (Cordell 1984).

Based on this assumption, one could estimate that a total of 39,423 rooms were occupied at 1500. This figure represents 65 percent of the 60,650 total rooms in Reed's (1988:118–119) list of pueblos. Using a random sampling strategy to correct for different sizes of sites, a simulation yielded the suggestion that nearly 39,747 of the 60,650 total rooms in the central and northern Rio Grande might have been in use. The Piro and Tompiro regions must be added to this hypothesized figure. Based on the ceramic data from Marshall and Wait's (1984) study, an estimated 22 sites were occupied about 1500. These sites range in size from 8 to 750 ground-floor rooms, containing a total of 2,788 ground-floor rooms. Because virtually all the sites were multistory structures built in the traditional

pueblo architectural style, the total number of rooms is larger than this figure, but by how much is unknown. Comparable data do not exist for the Tompiro region and a similar comparison is not possible.

On the basis of the above data, it appears that a minimum of approximately 42,500 rooms were occupied in 1500 in the Rio Grande pueblos. This figure is conservative because the Tompiro region has been omitted from consideration and room counts for the Piro region only take into account the number of ground-floor rooms.

What remains, then, is to convert the number of rooms occupied in the Rio Grande pueblos at 1500 into an estimate of total inhabitants. Various estimators have been suggested to calculate total population from the number of rooms at sites. Hill (1970) has summarized much of the information on the number of people per occupied room for Pueblo groups. He documents a high of 4.6 people per room, a low of 2.0 people per room, and a mean of 3.1. In a study based on an analysis of domestic ceramic containers, Turner and Lofgren (1966) derived a figure of 5.2 people per room for the Pueblo IV period on the Colorado Plateau, 1300 to 1450. This figure represents a high and has been criticized as unrealistic by Nelson (1981).

Given the range of estimates, Hill's mean of 3.1 people per room is adopted here, with the acknowledgment that this number is probably conservative. Using this figure, it is estimated that a minimum of 131,750 people occupied the Rio Grande pueblos, excluding the Tompiro region, at 1500.

The Western Pueblos

Upham (1982, 1986, 1987) has described the demographic characteristics of Western Pueblo populations at contact and provided estimates of immediately precontact population size. The primary purpose of this work was to assess the demographic consequences of epidemic disease on the populations of Hopi, Zuni, and Acoma. As a result, population reconstructions for these groups were based on a variety of methods, including quantitative epidemiological measures, Dobyns's (1966) depopulation ratio, and comparative data from other New World groups.

Upham (1982, 1986, 1987) has provided population estimates for Hopi, Zuni, and Acoma that are tied to a baseline data of 1520. The population for these three groups of pueblos totals 66,967 on the eve of Spanish contact. This figure includes a population of 29,305 for the eight Hopi villages, 24,662 for the six Zuni villages, and 13,000 for the large village of Acoma and its satellite farming villages.

Evaluation of the Estimates

The different methods of estimating used above leave much to be desired in terms of data comparability. This problem is exacerbated by the lack of comparability between the archeological measures of population and those estimates provided by the Spaniards. Nevertheless, the calculations allow for a tentative conclusion regarding the size of Rio Grande and Western Pueblo population about 1500. Approximately 200,000 (actual calculation 198,717) people occupied the more than 90 pueblos in the Rio Grande valley and at Hopi, Zuni, and Acoma.

This figure for the entire Pueblo region is less than Espejo's 1581 estimate of 241,000 people and greater than Obregon's 1584 estimate of 117,300. The estimate of 131,750 people for the Rio Grande pueblos is also greater than Oñate's 1598 estimate of 70,000 and the estimate of 94,340 obtained by calculation from Weiss's (1973:134) table using Castañeda's estimate of "20,000 men." One way to account for such discrepancies is to attribute them to depopulation following Spanish contact due to the introduction of acute European crowd infections. If this assumption is correct, total population was reduced approximately 50 percent in the first 100 years of contact. Compared to other New World groups contacted by the Spaniards, a 50 percent population reduction following the first 100 years of contact would be considered relatively low (Dobyns 1966; Cook 1943; Cook and Borah 1968; Upham 1982). Reductions of approximately 80 percent during the first 50 years of contact were more common among groups for which better historical documentation exists.

The estimate here of the number of occupied rooms (42,500) in the Rio Grande pueblos is much lower than any estimates derived from the Spanish narratives. This discrepancy is due to the method of estimating rooms from data in the narratives (using a constant of eight rooms per "house") and to the fact that the several large Tompiro and Humanas pueblos of the Salinas region are omitted from the analysis. Despite these inconsistencies, the above population estimates represent realistic approximations of the total population residing in pueblo-style sites at 1500.

NON-PUEBLOAN POPULATIONS— A TRIAL FORMULATION

Using archeological data to estimate the size and density of hunter-gatherer populations is difficult. The reason for this, of course, is that hunter-gatherers do not leave obtrusive archeological remains on the landscape. Instead, they produce unobtrusive, nonarchitectural sites and low visibility remains—the kind of sites referred to by archeologists as "artifact scatters" or "limited activity sites."

The large, multistoried pueblos are the most conspicuous reminder on the landscape of the Southwest that the Pueblo were once much more numerous and widely distributed than during the later historic period. Other data also suggest that populations residing in the large pueblos were but one component of a far more complex demographic structure in the Southwest. Perhaps the most striking aspect of the earliest descriptions of the Pueblo region is the numerous references to populations that *did not* live in pueblos, but were mobile; who were not heavily committed to maize agriculture, but who hunted and gathered. These groups occupied both the peripheries and interstices of the Puebloan region and engaged in well-structured exchange relationships with different Pueblo groups (Bolton 1916:183). Groups occupying the interstices of the Eastern and Western Pueblo regions were identified prior to 1598 generically as Querechos, Jumanos, *indios rayados,* or *chichimecos,* terms that apparently referred to the character of their adaptation rather than to their specific ethnic or cultural identity (Amsden 1932:194; Schroeder 1952:140). Many different groups also occupied the peripheries of the Pueblo core area, including the Julimes (Passaguates or Cabris), Conchos, Cholomes, Sumas, Teyas, and Manso. These groups could not have been Athapaskans but were instead indigenous Southwestern populations (Upham 1982, 1984).

The regions inhabited by non-pueblo-dwelling populations, as reported by the Spaniards between 1540 and 1600, were on the peripheries of the Puebloan zone of occupation in the Rio Grande valley, south of the modern town of Socorro, New

Mexico and east of the southern Rocky Mountains, and in the interstitial regions of the Western Pueblo area, the little Colorado and Verde valleys and Mogollon Rim country. The numerous references to these groups suggest that they occupied fairly widespread territories, lived in relatively large groups whose camps or villages consisted of "rancherias and straw houses" (Hammond and Rey 1966:218), subsisted by hunting, gathering, and fishing, and obtained trade goods, including maize and buffalo hides, from neighboring Pueblo groups. By comparing the different narratives, it is also clear that these groups moved their camps, perhaps seasonally. Groups living south of the Piro region who were reported by members of the Rodríguez-Chumascado expedition in August 1581, for example, were in different locations in December and in January 1582, when they were described by members of the Espejo expedition.

Worldwide, the population density for hunter-gatherers rarely exceeds one person per square mile; between .01 and .25 per square mile is most common (Lee and DeVore 1968:11). Population density near the middle range would be roughly .10 per square mile or 0.04 persons per square kilometer (Wrigley 1969:44–45).

The region where members of the Rodríguez-Chumascado and Espejo expeditions identified the first hunting and gathering populations in the American Southwest today encompasses nearly all of Dona Ana County, New Mexico, a region occupied by the Manso during historic times and by groups known as the Jornada Mogollon during the late prehistoric period. Dona Ana County contains approximately 9,857 square kilometers. Based on the above figures, one might estimate that between 400 and 3,800 hunter-gatherers occupied the region in the 1500s.

The computerized Archaeological Records Management site file at the Laboratory of Anthropology, Museum of New Mexico, contains information on more than 60,000 archeological sites in the state of New Mexico. The information is coded using a variety of different variables, including site location, site type, site size, period of occupation, and cultural affiliation. In Dona Ana County, 1,605 prehistoric archeological sites are recorded in the data base.

In order to partition the data from Dona Ana County to evaluate the above population estimate, sites had to be ordered by time period. Because of the way that sites are recorded in the data base, it is not possible to identify a target date of 1500. In fact, the latest target date one can reasonably obtain from the coded data is about 1300, and this "date" has a standard deviation of some 200 years. Thus, the actual target date is 1300 ± 200 years. This problem is lessened somewhat by two conditions. First, artifact scatters as a class of sites are usually dated to very broad temporal periods. In Dona Ana County, 704 of the 1,605 sites are classified as artifact scatters, and 35 percent of these artifact scatters measure more than 10 square meters. Such sites, common in southern New Mexico, are believed to represent the locations of repeated visitation over long periods of time by groups of hunter-gatherers.

Second, by 1300 in Dona Ana County, as well as in the remainder of the Jornada Mogollon region, more sedentary occupation in adobe pueblos was rare (Carmichael 1984). In fact, sedentary occupation throughout the Jornada sequence (about 600 to 1400) is uncommon; that is, permanent habitation sites are rare in the archeological record of the area (Upham 1984). Consequently, the adaptive pattern of past populations who occupied Dona Ana County at 1300 was probably quite similar to that seen by the Spaniards some 200 years later. In Dona Ana County, 199 artifact scatters comprising a total site area of 1,293 square kilometers can be associated with the target date of 1300. An additional 178 such scatters are listed in the site file as "unknown temporal affiliation." Apportioning these undatable artifact scatters based on a pro rata basis adds another 22 sites and 121 square kilometers of site area to the total. At a 65 percent rate of occupancy, 144 sites and 919 square kilometers of site area are presumed to have been occupied on the target date.

Between 10 and 15 square meters of living space is cleared and used by each member of a hunter-gatherer group at a camp during a single visit (Binford 1968:247; Isaac 1968:258). It is in this space that cultural debris accumulates. Given these data and assumptions, it is possible to figure an approximate population for the site data in Dona Ana County. Presuming an annual round with return trips to the same location on a yearly basis, the maximum amount of cleared space in which debris accumulates during an individual's lifetime at any one location is approximately 300 square meters (10 square meters of debris times 30 visits). Therefore, over the duration of the 400-year period of the tar-

TABLE 4

*Population Estimates for Southern
and Eastern N. Mex.*

County	Number of Artifact Scatters	Area in km²	Estimated Population	Density per km²
Dona Ana	1,440	9,194	2,298	0.233
Sierra	813	4,787	1,196	0.109
Luna	995	5,486	1,372	0.179
Grant	689	2,591	648	0.063
Otero	2,113	10,018	2,505	0.146
Eddy	1,853	12,006	3,002	0.277
Lea	982	6,314	1,579	0.139
Chaves	1,860	7,107	1,777	0.113
San Miguel	1,620	1,317	329	0.027
Colfax	1,800	1,852	462	0.047
Total			15,168	0.131

Note: Insufficient data exist to generate comparable population estimates for Hidalgo, De Baca, Roosevelt, Guadalupe, Curry, Quay, Mora, Harding, and Union counties.

get date (approximately 13 generations), the total area of debris that might exist if sites were used repeatedly would be approximately 4,000 square meters. This figure would represent the area of debris for one individual standardized over the entire 400-year period.

The sites recorded in Dona Ana County represent survey coverage of roughly 1 percent of the total county area; however, large areas of the county are characterized by extremely steep and rugged terrain that would not prove suitable for even temporary habitation. Consequently, it is estimated that the 144 target date sites represent approximately 10 percent of the total artifact scatters in Dona Ana County that fall within the range of the target date. Therefore approximately 1,440 artifact scatters and 9,194 square kilometers of site area were in use at 1300 ± 200. Using the above assumptions, an estimated population of 2,298 is obtained for an overall population density of 0.233 persons per square kilometer (0.604 persons per square mile), a figure in the upper-middle of the expected range.

Using these same assumptions and calculations, one can obtain similar population estimates for the remaining portion of southern and eastern New Mexico, areas on the periphery of Puebloan occupation that were inhabited by mobile, non-pueblo-dwelling populations. These calculations

suggest that approximately 15,168 people might have inhabited the 11-county area listed in table 4, for an overall population density of 0.131 persons per square kilometer (0.339 persons per square mile). At this same population density, 7,962 additional people are projected for the nine counties for which insufficient sample data existed. In other words, more than 23,000 hunter-gatherers are estimated to have occupied regions adjacent to the Rio Grande Pueblos. Comparable data do not exist for the Western Pueblo region, but it is presumed that a few thousand non-pueblo dwellers were present in areas above the Mogollon Rim and between the Verde Valley and Acoma.

CONCLUSIONS

The total population of the Pueblo Southwest at 1500 is estimated to have been approximately 220,000 people. This estimate includes 131,750 people living in the Rio Grande pueblos (excluding the Tompiro region), 66,967 people living in the Western Pueblo area, and approximately 23,000 hunter-gatherers occupying territories to the east and south of the Rio Grande pueblos. These estimates contrast with those made by anthropologists who presumed demographic continuity in the Pueblo region from past to present. It is now clear that disease and other colonial disruptions severely impacted the demographic structure of Southwestern groups.

The estimates made here are comparable to other reconstructions of aboriginal population. Ubelaker (1988), for example, has offered a population estimate for the Greater Southwest (including north and west Mexico) of 454,200 people at 1500. In another paper (Ubelaker 1986), he concludes on the basis of textual information that the Pueblo region contained approximately 150,000 people at the time of initial Spanish contact. However, this figure does not include the mobile, hunting and gathering component of the population in the Pueblo region. The estimates made here for the pueblo-dwelling portion of the population are larger than Ubelaker's by approximately 40,000 people, based on archeological data that suggest a larger sedentary population at 1500 than heretofore recognized. Based on archeological and epidemiological data, I also believe that a larger population occupied the Western Pueblo region. The slightly higher estimates for these two regions along with the addition of some 23,000 non-pueblo-dwelling people account for the differences between Ubelaker's and my estimates.

The Spanish estimates of total population, including those of Espejo, Obregon, and Oñate, appear to reflect enumeration inconsistencies and the frequent movement of population between pueblos. This kind of population flux is described in the Spanish narratives and led the Spaniards to adopt imprecise techniques of estimating population, such as counting "houses," and estimating the number of men or warriors. The frequent movement of population between regions no doubt accounts for some of the enumeration inconsistencies made for the same locations at different points in time. More importantly, the frequent movement of people between pueblos was probably a powerful mechanism for spreading newly introduced diseases among these virgin-soil groups and may have resulted in more rapid population loss than would have occurred under demographically stable conditions.

Based on estimates of total population generated from archeological data, it appears that depopulation of the Pueblo Southwest is tied to the arrival of the Spaniards. In 1500 an estimated 131,750 people occupied the Rio Grande region (not counting Tompiros). In 1540 approximately 95,000 people occupied the same region. By 1598, Oñate estimated that only 70,000 people remained in the Rio Grande pueblos. If these figures are correct than roughly half the original precontact Pueblo population succumbed during this period. Comparative data from other New World regions suggest that a 50 percent reduction following contact is low; more extreme rates of decline are likely. Although textual data providing references to epidemic disease among the Pueblos are lacking during the 1540–1598 interval, it appears that only the acute crowd infections brought by the Spaniards could effect this magnitude of population loss.

The number of occupied pueblos in the Rio Grande region noted in the sixteenth century accords well with archeological data. The number of occupied pueblos appears to be between 72 and 79 (an additional 15 were occupied in the Western Pueblo region at 1540). Unfortunately, only limited success has been achieved in linking the Spanish names for the different pueblos with the actual sites recorded by archeologists.

Although the Spaniards overestimated the number of "houses" in pueblos, for the reasons discussed here they often underestimated total population because of their methods of estimation. This fact, along with enumeration inconsistencies, obfuscates any attempt to use the data from the narratives in an uncritical manner.

REFERENCES

Adams, E. Charles
  1983   The Architectural Analogue to Hopi Social Organization and Room Use, and Implications for Prehistoric Northern Southwestern Culture. *American Antiquity* 48(1):44–61.

Amsden, C. A.
  1932   Navajo Origins. *New Mexico Historical Review* 7(3):193–209.

Benedict, Ruth
  1930   Psychological Types in the Cultures of the Southwest. Pp. 572–581 in Proceedings of the 23d International Congress of Americanists, New York.

  1934   Patterns of Culture. Boston and New York: Houghton Mifflin.

Bolton, Herbert E.
  1916   Spanish Explorations in the Southwest 1542–1706: Original Narratives of Early American History. New York: Charles Scribner's and Sons. (Reprinted 1930 and 1952.)

Brock, Sharon L.
  1988   Addendum. *American Antiquity*. 53(2):385.

Carmichael, David
  1984   Possible Evidence for Nonlinear Culture Change in the Southern Tularosa Basin, New Mexico. Pp. 13–27 in Recent Research in Mogollon Archaeology. Steadman Upham et al., eds. *New Mexico State University Occasional Papers of the University Museum* 10. Las Crucas.

Cook, Sherburne F.
  1943   The Conflict Between the California Indian and White Civilization. *Ibero-Americana* 21. Berkeley.

Cook, Sherburne F., and W. Borah
  1968   The Population of Mixteca Alta 1520–1960. *Ibero-Americana* 50. Berkeley.

Cordell, Linda S.
  1984   Prehistory of the Southwest. Orlando, Fla. Academic Press.

Cordell, Linda S., Steadman Upham, and Sharon L. Brock
  1987   Obscuring Cultural Patterns in the Archaeological Record: A Discussion from Southwestern Archaeology. *American Antiquity*. 52(3):565–577.

Dobyns, Henry F.
1966   Estimating Aboriginal American Population: An Appraisal of Techniques with a New Hemispheric Estimate. *Current Anthropology* 7(4):395–416; "Reply," 440–444.

1983   Their Number Become Thinned. Knoxville: University of Tennessee Press.

Dozier, Edward P.
1954   The Hopi-Tewa of Arizona. *University of California Publications in American Archaeology and Ethnology* 44(3):259–376. Berkeley.

1970a   The Pueblo Indians of North America. New York: Holt, Rinehart, and Winston.

1970b   Making Inferences from the Present to the Past. Pp. 202–213 in Reconstructing Prehistoric Pueblo Societies. William A. Longacre, ed. Albuquerque: University of New Mexico Press.

Eggan, Fred R.
1950   Social Organization of the Western Pueblos. Chicago: University of Chicago Press.

Hackett, Charles W., ed.
1923–   Historical Documents Relating to New Mexico,
1927   Nueva Vizcaya, and Approaches Thereto, to 1773. Adolf F. A. Bandelier and Fanny R. Bandelier, colls. 3 vols. *Carnegie Institution of Washington Publication* 330. Washington.

1942   Revolt of the Pueblo Indians of New Mexico and Otermin's Attempted Reconquest, 1680–1682. Charrnion C. Shelby, trans. 2 vols. Albuquerque: University of New Mexico Press.

Hammond, George P., and Agapito Rey, eds. and trans.
1928   Obregon's History of Sixteenth Century Explorations in Western America. Los Angeles: Wetzell.

1929   Expedition into New Mexico Made by Antonio de Espejo, 1582–1583 as Revealed by the Journal of Diego Perez de Luxan. *Quivira Society Publication* 1. Los Angeles.

1940   Narratives of the Coronado Expedition, 1540–1542. Albuquerque: University of New Mexico Press.

1953   Don Juan de Onate, Colonizer of New Mexico, 1598–1628. Albuquerque: University of New Mexico Press.

1966   The Rediscovery of New Mexico, 1580–1594: The Explorations of Chumascado, Espejo, Castano de Sosa, Morlete, and Leyva de Bonilla and Humana. Albuquerque: University of New Mexico Press.

Hill, James, N.
1970   Broken K Pueblo: Prehistoric Social Organization in the American Southwest. *Anthropological Papers of the University of Arizona* 18. Tucson.

Hinkes, M. J.
1983   Skeletal Evidence of Stress in Subadults: Trying to Come of Age at Grasshopper Pueblo. (Unpublished Ph.D. Dissertation in Anthropology, University of Arizona, Tucson.

Hodge, Frederick W.
1907   The Narrative of the Expedition of Coronado, by Pedro de Castaneda. Pp. 273–387 in Spanish Explorers in the Southern United States. F. W. Hodge and T. H. Lewis, eds. New York: Charles Scribner's Sons. (Reprinted: State Historical Association, Austin, 1984.)

———, ed.
1907–   Handbook of American Indians North of Mexico.
1910   2 vols. *Bureau of American Ethnology Bulletin* 30. Washington. (Reprinted: Rowman and Littlefield, New York, 1979.)

Hooton, Earnest A.
1930   The Indians of Pecos Pueblo: A Study of Their Skeletal Remains. New Haven, Conn.: Yale University Press.

Kintigh, Keith W.
1985   Settlement, Subsistence, and Society in Late Zuni Prehistory. *Anthropological Papers of the University of Arizona* 14. Tucson.

Kroeber, Alfred L.
1917   Zuni Kin and Clan *Anthropological Papers of the American Museum of Natural History* 18:39–205. New York.

Lee, Richard B., and Irven DeVore, eds.
1968   Man the Hunter. Chicago: Aldine Publishing Company.

Lycett, Mark
1984   Social and Economic Consequences of Aboriginal Population Decline from Introduced Disease. (Paper presented at the 49th Annual Meetings of the Society for American Archaeology, Portland, Ore.)

Marshall, M. P., and H. J. Wait
1984   Rio Abajo: Prehistory and History of a Rio Grande Province. Sante Fe: New Mexico Historical Preservation Program.

Mera, H. P.
1940   Population Changes in the Rio Grande Glazepaint Area. *New Mexico Archaeological Survey, Laboratory of Anthropology, Technical Services Bulletin* 11. Sante Fe.

Nelson, Ben A.
1981   Ethnoarchaeology and Paleodemography: A Test of Turner and Lofgren's Hypothesis. *Journal of Anthropological Research* 37(2):107–129.

Palkovitch, Ann M.
1980   Pueblo Population and Society: The Arroyo Hon-

do Skeletal and Mortuary Remains. Sante Fe: School of American Research Press.

1985   Historic Populations of the Eastern Pueblos: 1540–1910. *Journal of Anthropological Research* 41(4):401–426.

Parsons, Elsie Clews
1939   Pueblo Indian Religion. 2 vols. Chicago: University of Chicago Press.

Plog, Fred
1974   The Study of Prehistoric Change. New York: Academic Press.

1984   Exchange, Tribes, and Alliances: The Northern Southwest. *American Archaeology* 4(3):217–233.

Petersen, William
1961   Population. New York: Macmillan.

Reed, Paul F.
1988   A Spatial Analysis of the Northern Rio Grande Region, New Mexico: Implications for Sociopolitical and Economic Development from A.D. 1325–1540. (Unpublished Master's Thesis in Anthropology, New Mexico State University, Las Cruces.)

Reff, Daniel T.
1986   The Demographic and Cultural Consequences of Old World Disease in the Greater Southwest, 1520–1660. (Unpublished Ph.D. Dissertation in Anthropology, University of Oklahoma, Norman.)

1987   The Introduction of Smallpox in the Greater Southwest. *American Anthropologist* 89(3):704–708.

Rushforth, Scott, and Steadman Upham
[1989]   A Social History of the Hopi: Anthropological Perspectives on Sociocultural Persistence and · Change. (Manuscript in preparation.)

Schroeder, Albert H.
1952   Documentary Evidence Pertaining to the Early Historic Period of Southern Arizona. *New Mexico Historical Review* 27(2):137–167.

1979   Pueblos Abandoned in Historic Times. Pp. 236–254 in Handbook of North American Indians. Vol. 9: Southwest. Alfonso Ortiz, vol. ed. William C. Sturtevant, gen. ed. Washington: Smithsonian Institution.

Simmons, Marc
1979   History of the Pueblos Since 1821. Pp. 206–223 in Handbook of North American Indians. Vol. 9: Southwest. Alfonso Ortiz, vol. ed. William C. Sturtevant, gen. ed. Washington: Smithsonian Institution.

Smith, Watson, Richard B. Woodbury, and Nathalie F. S. Woodbury
1966   The Excavation of Hawikuh by Frederick Webb Hodge: Report of the Hendricks-Hodge Expedi-

tion. *Museum of the American Indian, Heye Foundation Contributions* 20. New York.

Stubbs, Stanley A.
1950   Bird's Eye View of the Pueblos. Norman: University of Oklahoma Press.

Titiev, Mischa
1944   Old Oraibi: A Study of the Hopi Indians of Third Mesa. *Papers of the Peabody Museum of American Archaeology and Ethnology.* Harvard University 22(1) Cambridge, Mass.

Turner, Christy G., and L. Lofgren
1966   Household Size of Prehistoric Western Pueblo Indians. *Southwestern Journal of Anthropology* 22(2):117–132.

Ubelaker, Douglas
1986   North American Indian Population Size. (Manuscript in author's possession.)

1988   North American Indian Population Size, A.D. 1500 to 1985. *American Journal of Physical Anthropology* 77(3):289–294.

Upham, Steadman
1980   Political Continuity and Change in the Plateau Southwest. Ann Arbor, Mich.: University Microfilms.

1982   Polities and Power: A Political and Economic History of the Western Pueblo. New York: Academic Press.

1984   Adaptive Diversity and Southwestern Abandonment. *Journal of Anthropological Research* 40(2): 235–256.

1986   Smallpox and Climate in the American Southwest. *American Anthropologist* 88(1):115–127.

1987   The Tyranny of Ethnographic Analogy in Southwestern Archaeology. Pp. 265–280 in Coasts, Plains and Deserts: Essays in Honor of Reynold J. Ruppé. Sylvia Gaines, ed. *Arizona State University, Anthropological Research Papers* 38. Tempe.

1989   Regional Systems in the Central and Northern Southwest: Demography, Economy, and Sociopolitics Preceding Contact. Pp. 57–76 in Columbian Consequences: Archaeological and Historical Perspectives on the Spanish Borderlands West. David Hurst Thomas, ed. Washington: Smithsonian Institution.

Watson, Patty Jo, Steven A. LeBlanc, and Charles L. Redman
1980   Aspects of Zuni Prehistory: Preliminary Report on Excavations and Survey in the El Morro Valley of New Mexico. *Journal of Field Archaeology* 7(2):201–218.

Weiss, Kenneth M.
1973   Demographic Models for Anthropology. *Memoirs of the Society for American Archaeology* 38(2). Salt Lake City, Utah.

Wendorf, Fred, and Eric K. Reed
 1955   An Alternative Reconstruction of Northern Rio
         Grande Prehistory. *El Palacio* 62(5–6):131–173.

White, Leslie A.
 1932a   The Pueblo of San Felipe. *Memoirs of the American
         Anthropological Association* 38. Menasha, Wis.

 1932b   The Acoma Indians. Pp. 17–192. *47th Annual Re-
         port of the Bureau of American Ethnology for the Years
         1929–1930*. Washington.

 1935   The Pueblo of Santo Domingo, New Mexico.
         Memoirs of the American Anthropological Association
         43. Menasha, Wis.

 1942   The Pueblo of Santa Ana, New Mexico. *Memoirs of
         the American Anthropological Association* 60. Men-
         asha, Wis.

 1960   The World of the Keresan Pueblo Indians. Pp. 53–
         64 in Culture in History: Essays in Honor of Paul
         Radin. Stanley Diamond, ed. New York: Columbia
         University Press.

Wilk, Richard R., and Robert McC. Netting
 1984   Households: Changing Forms and Functions. Pp.
         1–28 in Households Comparative and Historical
         Studies of the Domestic Group. Robert McC Net-
         ting, Richard R. Wilk, and E. J. Arnould, eds.
         Berkeley: University of California Press.

Winship, George P.
 1896   The Coronado Expedition, 1540–1542. Pp. 329–
         613 in *14th Annual Report of the Bureau of American
         Ethnology for the Years 1892–1893*, Pt 1. Wash-
         ington.

Wrigley, E. A.
 1969   Population and History. New York: McGraw-Hill.

22

Yellow Fever and the Africanization of the Caribbean

KENNETH F. KIPLE

BRIAN T. HIGGINS

Few today would dispute that the single most important reason for the extinction of the Indians in the Caribbean islands was the sudden and relentless assault of pathogens that accompanied the Spaniards and their animals. Only the details of the assault are blurred. A major question has to do with the magnitude of the demographic disaster. Other questions have to do with the disease that precipitated it. Perhaps swine flu was the first epidemic to take a heavy toll. Typhus and measles were doubtless present very early on. Smallpox arrived at least by 1518. Yet even by this early date the indigenous peoples were already in rapid decline and it was in that year that King Charles I of Spain yielded to the pleas of the colonists for substitute laborers by authorizing the importation of Black slaves directly from Africa (Cook and Borah 1971; Rosenblat 1967; Guerra 1988:305–325; Crosby 1972; Kiple 1984).

Yet, despite the fact that the Spanish islands were the original terminus of the transatlantic slave trade, that trade did not lead to the islands' "Africanization" (defined as a population in which the African phenotype predominates). Curtin (1969: 25) has estimated that during the first 120 years of the traffic, when Spaniards imported about 185,000 slaves to the Americas, the overwhelming majority was sent to the mainland. Early attempts by the Spaniards to develop a sugar industry on Hispaniola based on slave labor came to little, and after this there was not much demand for slaves in the Spanish Caribbean. Thus counts in the last half of the seventeenth century indicate about 3,835 Blacks in Santo Domingo (1681), 1,000 slaves and free *pardos* in Puerto Rico (1673), and some 5,000 slaves in Cuba out of an estimated total of 50,000 inhabitants. In fact, as late as 1774 Cuba had a population of only 44,000 slaves and another 31,000 individuals classified as free colored as against almost 10,000 classified as white. In Puerto Rico in 1765 there were only 5,000 slaves out of a population of 45,000 individuals mostly of mixed blood, whereas in Santo Domingo in 1783 there were only 14,000 slaves out of a population of 117,000 persons, again mostly of mixed blood although one-third of the population was classified as white (Mintz 1986:34–35; Larrazabel Blanco 1975:97; Lopez Cantos 1975:22–23; Perez 1988:46; Marrero y Artiles 1971, 3:49; Kiple 1976:4; Diaz Soler 1952:194–195).

Similarly, despite the tremendous volume of Africans brought to Cuba during the first six decades of the nineteenth century only 26 percent of the population at mid-twentieth century was classified as mixed or African in origin. Puerto Rico, which was also the focus of a lively late eighteenth and early nineteenth century slave trade, nonetheless classified only 20 percent of its population as mixed or African in origin. In fact, of the former Spanish islands, only the Dominican Republic had a population that was classified as predominantly Black, and this was due more to the Africanizing influence of nineteenth-century invaders from Haiti than it was to slave importations (Kiple 1984:184–185, table 8; Logan 1968:12–13).

THE NON-SPANISH ISLANDS

Thus, to speak of an extensive Africanization of the Caribbean is to speak of the non-Spanish Caribbean islands such as Jamaica or Barbados where, in 1990, 5 percent or less of the population was White. The Africanization of these islands did not begin until a century and a half after the first Africans were delivered to Hispaniola, and it is solidly embedded in the literature that the process was the result of what has been termed the "sugar revolution." This revolution began about the middle of the seventeenth century as the Dutch, who learned the secrets of sugar cultivation and manufacture in Brazil, brought those secrets to a relative handful of English and French interlopers who had settled on a few islands of the eastern Caribbean that the Spaniards had largely ignored. In the most important of these islands, Barbados, the settlers had become small tobacco planters raising their crop with the help of a few White indentured servants who hoped to survive their period of indenture, acquire land, and become planters themselves (Parry and Sherlock 1971:63–80).

Yet the tobacco of Barbados could not compete well in either quantity or quality with that of Virginia. Thus, after the introduction of sugar to the island in 1637, it was soon apparent that sugar was by far the more profitable crop. But unlike tobacco, which could be grown in small plots, sugar (because the cane needs to be processed quickly after cutting and thus demands an investment in a mill) lends itself to large-scale cultivation. As a consequence individuals who were able to secure the financing

(often from the Dutch) began buying up the lands of those who could not. The result was consolidation of land and a concomitant increased demand for labor (Parry and Sherlock 1971:63–80).

But White labor, so the argument goes, was not in adequate supply, its cost of transportation from England was expensive, and, perhaps more importantly, land consolidation destroyed the hope of indentured servants ever acquiring their own land. Thus planters turned increasingly to Black labor, and "the economic triumph of sugar meant the demographic domination of the Negro" (Williams 1970:110). However, this is not strictly true. Sugar was of enormous importance later on in Cuba and Puerto Rico, yet these islands did not experience Black "demographic domination," suggesting that something may be missing from the traditional view of the sugar revolution and the switch to Black labor.

Just as imported disease played a substantial role in rearranging Caribbean demography by ushering the Indians out, it also played a substantial role in ushering Blacks into the region. Malaria has been discussed in this connection, both in the Caribbean and in the United States, and West Africans did and do possess genetic defenses against falciparum and vivax malaria. Yet malaria was never a problem on some of the islands that became Africanized, such as Barbados. Yellow fever was; it is on this disease, the timing of its arrival, and the timing of the decline of the White and the growth of the Black populations in the sugar islands that this chapter will focus (Sheridan 1985:9–10; Kiple 1984;15–16; Kiple and King 1981:51–57; Wood 1974; Rutman and Rutman 1976:31–60; Savitt 1978:17–34).

YELLOW FEVER REACHES THE WEST INDIES

In 1643, shortly after the adoption of sugar cultivation in Barbados, there were perhaps as many as 37,000 Whites on the island and about 6,000 Black slaves (Anonymous 1925:338–339). By 1655 the White population had decreased to an estimated 23,000 while the slaves had increased to 20,000. In the traditional view, this dramatic demographic turnabout, which by 1668 had reduced the Whites to 20,000 and increased the slaves to 40,000, has been credited exclusively to demographic changes wrought by the sugar revolution. But entirely overlooked in this view is that in 1647 yellow fever slammed into Barbados for the first time, and this disease alone was reported to have reduced the 1643 White population by 6,000 or 16 percent in just the mortality it inflicted. In addition it doubtless reduced that population considerably more by driving many others away and discouraging still others from coming to the island. On the other hand yellow fever did not drive away slaves who had no means of fleeing. But then, the disease did not kill them either. Those of West African origin or ancestry proved remarkably refractory to yellow fever throughout its career in the Americas (Dunn 1972:312, table 26; Findlay 1941:145–146; Ligon 1657:21; Hunter, Frye, and Swartzwelder 1966:31; Sawyer 1949, 5:738).

It is now generally accepted that the cradle of yellow fever was West Africa. Arguments for its pre-Columbian presence in the Americas have faltered in the face of both immunological and entomological evidence. Immunologically, both humans and nonhuman primates in West Africa have historically demonstrated steadfast resistance to the disease, indicating a long and intimate relationship. In the New World, by contrast, the disease killed Indians just as quickly as it did Whites (in Brazil, reportedly even more quickly) and monkeys, too, were susceptible. Moreover, entomological evidence strongly suggests that the most efficient vector of yellow fever, *Aedes aegypti*, was also not present in the New World prior to Columbus. Today, in Africa, there are many species of mosquitos that are more or less closely allied to *Aedes aegypti;* however, no other member of the subgenus Stegomyia is native to the Americas, suggesting, of course, that *Aedes aegypti* is not either (Carter 1931; Strode 1951; Downs, Shope, and Kerr 1981:1–27; Kiple and Cooper 1991).

Thus the strong probability is that both virus and vector had to be imported, and the many challenges facing the pair in making a transatlantic voyage and taking root in the Americas probably account for the relatively late debut of yellow fever in the Caribbean. Yellow fever is normally a disease of nonhuman primates. In this enzootic form, called jungle or sylvan yellow fever, the disease is spread from monkey to monkey in the treetops by mosquitos that do not generally look to humans for blood meals. But when the virus does get down to ground level it changes mosquitos, entering the female *Aedes aegypti*, which depends almost entirely on humans for those meals (Downs, Shope, and Kerr 1981:1–27).

Because yellow fever is a disease that confers immunity against future attacks on those who survive it, the young in areas where the virus frequently descends from the treetops normally constitute the only important pool of nonimmunes, and yellow fever treats the young considerably more kindly than it does adults—meaning that they generally survive their attack and by doing so gain immunity against another one. In such areas, where a considerable portion of the population has acquired yellow fever immunity, the disease is said to be endemic (Kerr 1957:391–399; MacArthur 1957:146–149).

The epidemic form of the disease occurs when the virus is brought to a sizable population of nonimmunes, providing a number of mosquito or vector-related requirements are met. *Aedes aegypti* likes hot weather, will refuse to bite when the thermometer falls below 62°F, and will be driven into hibernation by extended low temperatures. The human population must also be closely packed, for the range of the female *Aedes* is short, seldom exceeding more than a few hundred yards in her lifetime. Finally, there has to be plenty of standing water about, for the mosquito cannot survive long without water and breeds best in water-filled artificial containers such as barrels and discarded pots (Kiple 1984:17–20; Downs, Shope, and Kerr 1981:8).

Doubtless huge numbers of *Aedes aegypti* arrived in the West Indies with early slaving voyages. A slave ship in tropical waters with many individuals in a confined space, and water casks close at hand provided the migrating insects with a nearly ideal habitat. But after winging their way ashore the mosquitos would have frequently found hardship because of a lack of densely packed humans available for blood meals and the absence of discarded human junk to provide good breeding places. In fact, the growth of the *Aedes* population must have been a direct function of the growth of the human populations of the islands (Goodyear 1978:5–21; Uttley 1960:187–188).

Doubtless too, the virus made many early voyages, although not so easily as its mosquito vector. Presumably the virus would have boarded a ship in the bodies of nonimmune sailors or slaves (most likely the very young) during the first three to five days of illness when that virus is still in the blood and yellow fever is virtually symptomless. It is also during this early period of viremia that one or more of the female *Aedes* aboard would have had to have bitten the victim, for after the virus leaves the blood and yellow fever's distinctive features of hemorrhage, high fever, jaundice, and black vomit appear, the patient is no longer infective (Rhodes and Van Rooyen 1968:703–704).

Next, the infected mosquitos would have had to survive for the generally requisite 9 to 12 days necessary to incubate the virus (although the period can be as long as 30 days depending on the temperature) before they could pass it along to another human aboard ship. After the incubation period, the mosquito remains infectious for whatever remains of a lifetime that generally lasts a month, although life spans of three and four months have been recorded. Many, of course, would have been blown away by the wind, and others would have perished for a wide variety of reasons. In addition to these obstacles to virus transmission there was another very large one: many of the slaves would have originated from areas of endemic yellow fever and consequently, because of an acquired immunity, could not host it (Downs, Shope, and Kerr 1981:8).

Added to these difficulties for the virus was the problem of time. In the late eighteenth century, the sailing time to, say, Jamaica from the yellow fever areas of West Africa varied from 52 days from Sierra Leone to 68 days from the Bight of Biafra; and these ships were faster and more specialized than the cumbersome vessels of a century and a half earlier. Still, Barbados is much closer to Africa than is Jamaica and what sailing times are known for the seventeenth century suggest an average elapsed time from various points on the African coast of about 50 days, although mention was made of passage from the Gambia River to Barbados in just three weeks. Obviously lightning-like crossings of this nature were those most likely to deliver the virus to the Americas. On slower ships at least two or three generations of mosquitos would have been required during the voyage to keep the virus moving through human bodies in serial fashion. Indeed, it would have to have moved in such a fashion because an epidemic would have defeated the virus by quickly converting nonimmunes into either immunes or corpses (Klein 1978:157, table; Donnan 1930–1935, 1:141–145; Phillips 1732, 6:97; McKay 1967:25; Mannix 1962:112). Finally, even when the complicated symbiotic relationship among vector,

virus, and human host was maintained throughout the voyage, ashore the virus (like the vector) would have been frequently thwarted by the absence of a densely packed population, perhaps reaching a victim or two and then dying out.

Thus a critical mass of both humans and mosquitos on an island was required before yellow fever could burst forth in urban form, which means that one may be justifiably skeptical of assertions of early epidemics in the Caribbean such as the one alleged to have driven the British out of sparsely populated San Juan in 1598. Similarly, it is highly unlikely that whatever attacked the original 550 French settlers of Guadeloupe in 1635 (the same year that they arrived) was yellow fever, nor would yellow fever have been the disease that struck the same island five years later (Burns 1954:171; Johnson 1910:211–212; Guerra 1966:31; Hirsch 1883–1886, 2:318; Kiple 1984:164; Carter 1931:182–186).

CARIBBEAN EPIDEMICS

The critical mass of humans and mosquitos was reached in 1647 when the still mostly White (and consequently nonimmune) population of Barbados had attained a density of 200 people per square mile, and it was in that year that yellow fever made its first successful documented transatlantic crossing via the slave trade. Then, having established a New World beachhead on Barbados (where it appears to have lingered until 1655), the yellow fever virus was within easy sailing distance of other Caribbean populations and in 1648 began a northerly march with the invasion of Guadeloupe where it reportedly killed almost 6,000 Whites or about one-third of the population. From there it journeyed to St. Kitts where it allegedly killed "most" of the Whites (Ligon 1657:21; Burns 1954:32; Scott 1939:287; Findlay 1941:145–166; Lloyd and Coulter 1957–1963, 2:66; Lopéz Cantos 1975:21–22).

Then, still in 1648, the disease jumped from San Juan to the Yucatan Peninsula before backtracking to Cuba to prune the civilian and garrison populations there by at least one-third. Yellow fever returned to St. Kitts for another assault in 1652 and then left Barbados to mount an attack on the English invaders of Jamaica in 1655. Following this date the disease became a regular visitor to the slave-importing islands of the Caribbean (Lopéz de Cogolludo 1867, 2:561–562; Leroy y Cassa 1930;

Pezuela y Lobo 1868, 2:106–109; Hirsch 1883–1886, 1:338–340).

It is doubtful that yellow fever became endemic to the region. Very few of the islands had monkey populations large enough to sustain the virus, especially after they were cleared of their forests to make way for sugar cultivation and fuel the boilers of the sugar mills. It did at some time or another become endemic in the jungles of Central and South America, where it reached out occasionally to the Caribbean. But for the slave-importing islands, the major source of yellow fever continued to be West Africa.

Goodyear (1978) argued that yellow fever plagued the sugar islands in particular for still another reason—that of the presence of sugar itself and its synergistic relationship with *Aedes aegypti*. In addition to blood meals, the mosquito is attracted to and nourished by sweet fluids; and thus it is conceivable that the growth of the sugar industry in the West Indies assisted the *Aedes* in becoming acclimated to its new surroundings. Certainly the boiling of cane juices, the reboiling of molasses, and the piling of waste stalks (bagasse) around a plantation would have made much sucrose available to mosquitos on a more or less year-round basis. In addition, other features of sugar production would have assisted in mosquito proliferation, especially the use of artificial containers such as clay pots, which when discarded or simply left outdoors to be filled with rain water became ideal breeding vessels.

Perhaps for this reason, as well as the slave trade conduit that linked the sugar islands with the home of the disease, yellow fever provided those islands with much unwanted attention. However, after its initial assaults of the 1640s and 1650s, it seems to have subsided for about 30 years, with epidemics recorded only for Jamaica in 1671; San Juan, Puerto Rico, in 1673; and Martinique in 1688. Doubtless the lull was due in no small part to a lack of nonimmune individuals. But such were present again in the 1690s as yellow fever erupted once more in Martinique and Barbados and then swept the entire West Indies. This widespread epidemic occurred at precisely the same time that, at least for the British sugar islands, a considerable percentage of their White residents vanished. Barbados, for example, lost some 25 percent of its White population, the British Leewards 36 percent, and even Jamaica, which was experiencing a huge influx of slaves and had become a center of great potential wealth, saw

its White population decline slightly (Hirsch 1883–1886, 1:318–338). Interestingly, by contrast, Antigua, whose first recorded yellow fever epidemic did not occur until 1729, had its White population increase by 26 percent (table 1).

Also by contrast, save for a reported outbreak in Santiago de Cuba in 1695, Cuba suffered no recorded yellow fever outbreaks from that of 1649 until 1761 when it was apparently imported from Vera Cruz. San Juan was invaded twice, once in 1689 and again in 1698, and Santo Domingo in 1690 and 1696. Yet as table 2 indicates, the Spanish islands were very lightly punished when compared with British or French counterparts. One reason for this has to do with the size of the islands in question. On tiny Barbados, for example, the population was dense and the disease could and did sweep the entire island. But in the larger Spanish islands, the disease was generally confined to port cities. The other reason, of course, has to do with the slave trade that linked the sugar islands directly with the African reservoir of yellow fever. When the disease broke out in the Spanish islands, it generally arrived in secondhand form, not from Africa, but from the slave-importing islands (Anonymous 1842:30; Ashburn 1947:135; Hirsch 1883–1886, 1:338–340).

Thus it would seem that perhaps yellow fever

TABLE 1

Changes in the Population of British West Indian Colonies, 1670s–1700s

Colony	White Population		
	1670s	1700s	Percentage
Antigua	2,308	2,898	+26%
Barbados	20,500	15,400	−25%
Jamaica	8,000	7,300	−6%
Montserrat	2,682	1,544	−42%
Nevis	3,521	1,104	−68%
St. Christopher	1,897	1,670	−12%
	Black Population		
Antigua	2,172	12,937	+495%
Barbados	44,900	50,100	+11%
Jamaica	7,300	42,000	+475%
Montserrat	992	3,571	+278%
Nevis	3,860	3,676	−5%
St. Christopher	1,436	3,258	+126%

Sources: Abenon 1987; Bridenbaugh and Bridenbaugh 1972; Carter 1931; Chauleau 1966; Dunn 1972; Galenson 1986; Higham 1921; Roberts 1957; Wells 1975.

TABLE 2

*Yellow Fever Outbreaks in the Caribbean
in the 17th Century
(Spanish possessions in italics)*

Year	Location
1647	Barbados
1648	Guadeloupe
1649	*Cuba*
1652	St. Kitts
1655	Jamaica
1656	*Santo Domingo*
1665	St. Lucia
1671	Jamaica
1673	*San Juan*
1688	Martinique
1689	*San Juan*
1690	Barbados
	Santo Domingo
	Santa Cruz
1692	Barbados
1693	Martinique
1694	Barbados
1695	St. Domingue
	Santiago de Cuba
1696	*Santo Domingo*
	Martinique
	Other islands
1698	*San Juan*
1699	West Indies generally

Sources: Burns 1954; Carter 1931; Chauleau 1966; DuTetre 1667–1671; Hirsch 1883–1886; Hughes 1750; Humboldt 1856; Lloyd and Coulter 1957–1963; Labat 1742; Ligon 1657; Lopez Cantos 1975; St. Michael 1657; Moreau de St. Mary 1784–1790; Moseley 1789; Scott 1939; Trapham 1679.

deserves some overdue credit for the Africanization of the non-Spanish Caribbean if for no other reason than that, on the one hand, it held down the number of Whites in the sugar islands by killing them, and on the other, it quickly garnered for those islands such a reputation for deadliness that it forestalled European immigration. But there is still another reason for the credit, and this is that yellow fever spared Blacks (Beckles 1969:238).

YELLOW FEVER RESISTANCE AMONG BLACKS

The question of Black resistance to yellow fever is a complicated one that has yet to be satisfactorily resolved. In Brazil, and in the United States as well as in the West Indies, Africans, whether newly imported or Creole-born were regarded by observers to be incredibly resistant to its ravages. Some claimed that they "were not at all subject to it" and called them "perfect nonconductors" of the disease. During the last half of the eighteenth century, a physician in Jamaica stated that "it has never been observed that a negroe immediately from the Coast of Africa, has been attacked with the disease" (Jackson 1791:249–250). Others noticed that Blacks did become ill during epidemics, but unlike Whites they suffered only mildly and seldom died of yellow fever (Teixeira 1895:12–13; Pereira Rego 1873:39; Couto and Rezende 1912:28; Ferreira 1892; Kiple and King 1981:29–49; Stewart 1808:26; Pincknard 1816, 2:475; Chisolm 1799:19; Pouchet 1864:59; Belot 1879:39).

Physicians of the time explained the phenomenon as a "natural immunity," whereas many of their modern counterparts speak of an "innate resistance." At least one modern doctor feels that the important factor in resistance to yellow fever has had to do with virus-protecting antibodies acquired by infection by other flaviviruses such as the dengue virus. Others have speculated that for some reason *Aedes aegypti* prefer Whites to Blacks for blood meals. The blood of Blacks a century earlier was thought to contain some sort of yellow fever protection; one physician, writing in the Brazilian medical journal *O Progresso Medico* in 1878, wondered if transfusions of this blood to Whites would transfer the protection as well (Moscoso Puello 1977:48; Burnet and White 1972:245; Taylor 1951; Hunter, Frye, and Swartzwelder 1966:31; Uttley 1960:187; Ashburn 1947:136–137; Carter 1931:270).

Certainly nineteenth-century data on yellow fever cases and mortality seem to point to some kind of genetic protection, as the following few examples should make clear. In the Rio de Janeiro hospital of São Sebastião, of 14,545 cases of yellow fever admitted during the years 1892 to 1899, only 126 of the patients were Black (Seidl 1900:181–183). In Puerto Rico an average mortality rate of 12 percent of the Whites in all epidemics has been calculated, but the number of blacks lost to yellow fever was "insignificant" (Quevado y Baez 1946–1949, 1:156–157). During the New Orleans yellow fever epidemic of 1853 Whites died at a rate of 75 per thousand, Blacks at a rate of 3 per thousand. During an epidemic in Savannah the following year Whites died at a rate of 72 per thousand, Blacks at a rate of 2 per thousand (Kiple and King 1981:42).

The usual argument against the involvement

of some protective genetic factor is centered on immunity, which both Blacks and Whites could have acquired by long residence in areas frequently visited by yellow fever. It is true that most of the Whites who were doing the dying from the disease throughout the hemisphere were not born and raised in these areas. Rather, they were adult outsiders. Of the 14,545 yellow fever cases admitted to the hospital of São Sebastião in Rio de Janeiro, for example, fully 95 percent were listed as foreigners (Seidl 1900:181–183). Similarly, of the 3,414 cases treated by the Howard Association during the New Orleans epidemic of 1858, only 11 percent were listed as "citizens of the United States," with a great many Germans and Irish among the victims (Kiple and King 1981:41). In the Caribbean of the eighteenth century it was the European armies, which crossed and crisscrossed the region, that provided most of the fodder for yellow fever. Moreover, it is true that Whites who had been born and raised in these areas justifiably felt themselves sufficiently safe that they called the disease "strangers' fever." But what is missed in this argument is the notice on the part of physicians and laymen alike that Blacks did contract the disease as adults. Obviously, then, they had not acquired immunity to the disease. But they did have an ability to escape its deadliness, which White counterparts did not (Guerra 1966:23–35).

It was only in the beginning of the twentieth century that the conventional wisdom regarding Black yellow fever resistance was called into question. Investigating a small outbreak of yellow fever in Barbados during 1908 and 1909, Boyce (1911) discovered that of the 86 cases suffered on the island (other reports put the number of cases at about 100), 54 of these occurred in Black individuals. From this he leaped to two conclusions. One was that Blacks had suffered more severely than Whites during the epidemic, while the other was that Blacks had no special ability to resist the disease after all (Boyce 1911:106–107). Unfortunately, Boyce's argument was abstracted by the *Yellow Fever Bulletin* without the case numbers Boyce had used, and it was reported only that "in Barbados, the negroes in 1909 suffered more severely from yellow fever than the white population." Actually, of course, those numbers made a very convincing case for inherited Black yellow fever resistance. As Boyce pointed out, yellow fever had been absent from the island since 1881 (27 years), and thus all of

those born since that epidemic could not have acquired yellow fever immunity. Nonetheless, the 32 cases that occurred among 12,000 Whites provide a case ratio of roughly 3 per thousand, while the 54 cases that occurred among 118,000 blacks and 41,000 individuals classified as "mixed" yield a case ratio of (again, roughly) about 3 per 10,000. In other words, Whites were some 10 times more likely than blacks to develop recognizable symptoms of the illness (Yellow Fever Commission [West Africa] 1913:83–84; Boyce 1910:83–121, 1911:106–107; Siler 1915:49).

Another argument that Blacks are not resistant to yellow fever has been put forth on the basis of heavy mortality generated among them in yellow fever epidemics in the Nuba Mountains of Sudan in 1940 and again in 1959, in Ethiopia in 1960, and Senegal in 1965. Yet these areas are outside the region of yellow fever endemicity in Africa. Their inhabitants would have had no selective encouragement to develop resistance to the disease over the centuries, as would West Africans who mostly resided well inside that region. Certainly in Africa, as in the Americas, that resistance consisted of something more than acquired immunity. A Rockefeller Foundation yellow fever worker in Africa during the 1930s reported that a great number of specimens taken from the inhabitants of Nigerian towns within the endemic yellow fever zone had revealed that only about 50 percent of those aged 30 or more years had suffered from the disease at one time or another. Despite the fact that only one-half the population enjoyed acquired immunity, "we have not . . . been able to recognize clinically a single case of yellow fever in the West African Native" (Beeuwkes 1933). In the words of one of yellow fever's conquerors, Henry Rose Carter (1931:270), the West Africans' "reaction to yellow fever is just what one would expect to have been evolved in a race for many generations in Africa subject to that infection" (Downs, Shope, and Kerr 1981; Downs 1982a:179–185; Burnet and White 1972:245).

Thus, the fact that many thousands of mostly Black cases developed in the Trinidad epidemic of 1954 should not be taken as evidence that those of West African descent are not "immune" to the disease. Rather, the phenomenon provides still more evidence of a special ability on the part of those of West African ancestry to entertain the disease and survive it today as they did yesterday because most of these cases were "subclinical or mild" (Downs

1982b:16). Similarly, it is true that a 1969 outbreak of yellow fever on the Jos plateau in Nigeria killed 40 percent of an estimated 252 patients hospitalized by the disease. On one hand this kind of case-fatality ratio is certainly not suggestive of any special ability to host yellow fever and survive it. On the other hand, those who investigated the outbreak estimated that up to 100,000 cases of the disease had occurred during the epidemic, which certainly is suggestive (Carey et al. 1972:645–651).

In 1987 there was another yellow fever epidemic in Nigeria, this in the states of Benue and Cross River, which it was estimated had killed 11,000 individuals and where it was apparently, as of January 1991, still smoldering (Cleveland *Plain Dealer*, May 28, 1987). However, a health official in the region pointed out that the term "yellow fever" in these areas is used by the inhabitants to denote any febrile illness accompanied by jaundice, such as malaria, hepatitis, or pneumonia. In fact, investigators from the United States Centers for Disease Control could not isolate yellow fever virus during the epidemic. They did identify 126 cases of "probable yellow fever" and were convinced by epidemiological and immunological evidence that these represented the tip of an iceberg, which in the Oju region of Benue state was composed of an estimated 9,800 cases with jaundice, and thus severe cases, and 5,600 deaths. How many mild cases may have occurred was not estimated, but obviously, if the estimates of severe cases and yellow fever mortality represent anything more than a wild guess, then for the first time Blacks within the endemic yellow fever zone are suffering severe cases of the illness in large numbers (Einterz 1988:39–40; De-Cock et al. 1988:630–632).

If true, some may see this as proof that West Africans were not innately resistant to yellow fever after all. Yet there are other explanations. The most likely one is that, since the end of the civil war in Nigeria, many victorious peoples from the north on the edge of the yellow fever zone have moved south directly into it, and presumably they, like the Senegalese or Ethiopians, would have had little evolutionary encouragement for developing resistance to the illness. Another explanation is that the yellow fever virus may have changed in such a way as to surmount innate defenses. Significant in this regard may be the fact that *Aedes aegypti* has not been the major vector in any of the recent epidemics, meaning that the virus is incubating in any number

of African mosquito species. The dynamics and implications of this phenomenon are simply not understood at present (World Health Organization Expert Committee on Yellow Fever 1971:14–15; DeCock et al. 1988:631–632).

Unless or until some genetic mechanism is discovered there will probably always be lingering doubts about innate Black yellow fever resistance. However, history makes a very compelling case for it. As table 3 shows, in Cuba in August 1649, at the start of yellow fever's career in the Americas, only the White death rates rose precipitously during the yellow fever assault on Havana. Yet at this time Cuba had become a backwater and was not importing any slaves to speak of. Thus Whites and Blacks were both presumably equally "virginal" in the face of the disease, if acquired immunity were the only protective factor.

Again in 1878, toward the end of yellow fever's career, the disease ascended the Mississippi River to fall upon Blacks and Whites in Memphis who were previously safe from the disease that had mostly confined its attention to coastal areas. As in Cuba, both Blacks and Whites were "virginal" in confronting the disease, which Blacks quickly proved as fully 78 percent of them became infected. But only 9 percent died. In contrast, of the 6,000 Whites who had the disease, 70 percent perished from it (Kiple and King 1981:45–46). Moreover, whenever Blacks died during epidemics it was generally claimed that they were in fact mulattoes and that "intermixture with even a small amount of white blood makes the

TABLE 3

Deaths in Havana by Race, 1649

Month	Whites	Blacks
January	7	1
February	10	—
March	3	—
April	3	—
May	4	—
June	2	2
July	7	5
August	208	4
September	235	8
October	24	3
November	20	—
December	13	3
Total	536	26

Source: Leroy y Cassa 1930.

Negro just as susceptible as whites to yellow fever" (Lewis 1942:211).

Thus the following pattern emerges: Blacks in the Caribbean (as elsewhere) were resistant to yellow fever in a way that Whites were very definitely not. The disease struck the British and French islands just as the sugar revolution was getting underway, and the waves of disease that followed throughout the last half of the seventeenth century coincided with rapidly shrinking White populations and swelling Black populations. Yellow fever, then, would appear to have played a role in creating a demographic profile for the non-Spanish Caribbean in which Blacks quickly came to be overwhelmingly dominant in numerical terms.

This contrasts substantially with the experience of the Spanish islands, which, because they had little to do with sugar until much later on, were not linked via a slave trade with the African source of yellow fever. Thus, on the one hand they were not inundated with unwilling immigrants from Africa and on the other hand, not inundated with a disease that vigorously killed Whites. The result in the case of Cuba was that the island continued to receive immigrants from Europe as well as from elsewhere in Spanish America, and by the time its sugar revolution began the White population base was sufficiently large that despite the return of yellow fever and despite a thriving nineteenth-century slave trade, the island was never Africanized to the extent that the earlier sugar islands had been and have continued to be.

REFERENCES

Abenon, Lucien R.
1987   La Guadeloupe de 1671 a 1759: Etude politique, économique et sociale. Paris: Editions L'Harmattan.

Anonymous
1842   Antigüedad del vómito negro en la isla de Cuba. *Repertorio Medico-Habanero* (August).

1925   A Briefe Discription of the Ilande of Barbados [1647]. Pp. 338–339 in Colonizing Expeditions to the West Indies and Guiana, 1623–1667. Vincent T. Harlow, ed. London: Haklyut Society.

Ashburn, P. M.
1947   The Ranks of Death: A Medical History of the Conquest of America. New York: Coward McCann.

Beckles, Hilary M.
1969   Sugar and White Servitude: An Analysis of Indentured Labour During the Sugar Revolution of Barbados 1643–1655. *Journal of the Barbados Museum and Historical Society* 36:238–247.

Beeuwkes, Henry
1933   [Letter to F. F. Russel Dated July 20, 1933] (In Rockefeller Archive Center, International Health Division 1:1, series 495, box 2, folder 12.)

Belot, Charles
1879   The Yellow Fever at Havana; Its Nature and its Treatment. Savannah, Ga.: Morning News Steam Printing House.

Boyce, Rubert
1910   Health Progress and Administration in the West Indies. London: John Murray.

1911   Note Upon Yellow Fever in the Black Race and its Bearing Upon the Question of the Endemicity of Yellow Fever in West Africa. *Annals of Tropical Medicine and Parasitology* 5:106–107.

Bridenbaugh, Carl, and Robert Bridenbaugh
1972   No Peace Beyond the Line. New York: Oxford University Press.

Burnet, Macfarlane, and David O. White
1972   Natural History of Infectious Disease. Cambridge: Cambridge University Press.

Burns, Alan
1954   History of the British West Indies. London: George Allen and Unwin.

Carey, D. E. et al.
1972   Epidemiological Aspects of the 1969 Yellow Fever Epidemic in Nigeria. *Bulletin of the World Health Organization* 46:645–651.

Carter, Henry R.
1931   Yellow Fever: An Epidemiological and Historical Study of its Place of Origin. Laura Armistead Carter and Wade Hampton Frost, eds. Baltimore, Md.: Williams and Wilkins.

Chauleau, Liliane
1966   La Société à la Martinique au XVIIe siècle (1635–1713). Caen.

Chisolm, Colin
1799   An Essay on the Malignant Pestilential Fever. Philadelphia: Thomas Dobson.

Cook, Sherburne, and Woodrow Borah
1971   Essays in Population History: Mexico and the Caribbean. Berkeley: University of California Press.

Couto, G., and C. de Rezende
1912   Control of Infectious Diseases in Brazil and Especially in Rio de Janeiro. Rio de Janeiro: Pimenta de Mello.

Crosby, Alfred W.
  1972   The Columbian Exchange: Biological and Cultural Consequences of 1492. Westport, Conn.: Greenwood Publishing Company.

Curtin, Philip D.
  1969   The Atlantic Slave Trade: A Census. Madison: University of Wisconsin Press.

DeCock, K. M. et al.
  1988   Epidemic Yellow Fever in Eastern Nigeria. Lancet (March 19): 630–632.

Diaz Soler, Luis
  1952   La Historia de la esclavitud negra en Puerto Rico. San Juan: Editorial Universitaria.

Donnan, Elizabeth, ed.
  1930–   Documents Illustrative of the History of the Slave
  1935   Trade to America. 4 vols. Washington: Carnegie Institution of Washington.

Downs, Wilbur G.
  1982a   History of Epidemiological Aspects of Yellow Fever. The Yale Journal of Biology and Medicine 55:179–185.

  1982b   The Rockefeller Foundation Virus Program: 1951–1971 with Update to 1981. Annual Review of Medicine 3:16.

Downs, Wilber G., Robert E. Shope, and J. Austin Kerr
  1981   Yellow Fever. In Clinical Medicine. John A. Spittell, Jr., ed. Philadelphia: Harper and Row.

Dunn, Richard
  1972   Sugar and Slaves: The Rise of the Planter Class in the English West Indies, 1624–1713. Chapel Hill: University of North Carolina Press.

DuTetre, Jean-Baptiste
  1667–   Histoire générale des Antilles habitées par les
  1671   François. Paris.

Einterz, Ellen M.
  1988   'Yellow Fever' in Eastern Nigeria. Lancet (July 2):39–40.

Ferreira, Luiz Augusto
  1892   Acclimaçño nos paizes quentes, especialmente no Brasil. (Unpublished Ph.D. Dissertation in Medicine, University of Rio de Janeiro, Brazil.)

Findlay, G. M.
  1941   The First Recognized Epidemic of Yellow Fever. Transactions of the Royal Society of Tropical Medicine and Hygiene 35:145–146.

Galenson, David W.
  1986   Planters, Traders and Slaves: Market Behavior in Early English America. Cambridge: Cambridge University Press.

Goodyear, James
  1978   The Sugar Connection: A New Perspective on the History of Yellow Fever. Bulletin of the History of Medicine 52:5–21.

Guerra, Francisco
  1966   The Influence of Disease on Race, Logistics and Colonization in the Antilles. Journal of Tropical Medicine and Hygiene 69:31.

  1988   The Earliest American Epidemic: The Influenza of 1494. Social Science History 12:305–325.

Higham, C. S. S.
  1921   The Development of the Leeward Islands Under the Restoration, 1660–1688: A Study of the Foundations of the Old Colonial System. Cambridge: Cambridge University Press.

Hirsch, August
  1883–   Handbook of Geographical and Historical
  1886   Pathology. 3 vols. Charles Creighton, trans. London: New Sydenham Society. (Original: Handbuch der Historischen Geographischen Pathologie, Erlangen, Germany, 1860–1864).

Hughes, Griffith
  1750   A Natural History of Barbados. London: Printed for the author.

Humboldt, Alexander von
  1856   The Island of Cuba. New York: Derby and Jackson.

Hunter, George W., William W. Frye, and J. Clyde Swartzwelder
  1966   A Manual of Tropical Medicine. 4th ed. Philadelphia: Saunders.

Jackson, Robert
  1791   A Sketch of the History and Cure of Febrile Diseases. London: Baldwin, Craddock and Joy.

Johnson, Harry
  1910   The Negro in the New World. New York: Macmillan.

Kerr, J. Austin
  1957   The Clinical Aspects and Diagnosis of Yellow Fever. Pp. 391–399 in Yellow Fever. G. K. Strode, ed. New York: McGraw-Hill.

Kiple, Kenneth F.
  1976   Blacks in Colonial Cuba, 1774–1899. Gainesville: University Presses of Florida.

  1984   The Caribbean Slave: A Biological History. Cambridge: Cambridge University Press.

Kiple, Kenneth F., and Donald B. Cooper
  1991   Yellow Fever. In The Cambridge History and Geography of Human Disease. Kenneth F. Kiple, ed. Cambridge: Cambridge University Press. In press.

Kiple, Kenneth F., and Virginia H. King
  1981   Another Dimension to the Black Diaspora: Diet, Disease and Racism. Cambridge: Cambridge University Press.

Klein, Herbert S.
  1978   The Middle Passage: Comparative Studies in the
          Atlantic Slave Trade. Princeton, N.J.: Princeton
          University Press.

Labat, Jean-Baptiste
  1724   Nouveau voyage aux îsles de l'Amérique. 2 vols. La
          Haye.

Larrazabel Blanco, Carlos
  1975   Los Negros y la esclavitud en Santo Domingo. San-
          to Domingo: J. D. Postigo.

Leroy y Cassa, Jorge
  1930   La Primera epidemia de fiebre amarilla en la
          Habana en 1649. Havana: La Propagandista.

Lewis, Julian H.
  1942   The Biology of the Negro. Chicago: University of
          Chicago Press.

Ligon, Richard
  1657   A True and Exact History of the Island of Bar-
          bados. London: P. Parker and T. Guy.

Lloyd, Christopher, and J. L. S. Coulter
  1957–   Medicine and the Navy, 1200–1900. 4 vols. Edin-
  1963   burgh: E&S Livingstone.

Logan, Rayford W.
  1968   Haiti and the Dominican Republic. New York: Ox-
          ford University Press.

López Cantos, Angél
  1975   Historia de Puerto Rico (1650–1700). Sevilla: Es-
          cuela de Estudios Hispano-Americanos.

López de Cogolludo, Diego
  1867   Historia de Yucatan. 2 vols. Mexico: Manuel Al-
          dana Rivas.

MacArthur, William P.
  1957   Historical Notes on Some Epidemic Diseases Asso-
          ciated with Jaundice. *British Medical Bulletin*
          13:146–149.

McKay, F. G.
  1967   The Shameful Trade. London: Longmans.

Mannix, Daniel P.
  1962   Black Cargoes: A History of the Atlantic Slave
          Trade. New York: Doubleday.

Marrero y Artiles, Levi
  1971   Cuba: Economía y sociedad. 13 vols. Madrid: Edi-
          torial Playor.

Mintz, Sidney W.
  1986   Sweetness and Power: The Place of Sugar in Mod-
          ern History. New York: Viking Press.

Moreau de St. Mary, Meredic Louis E.
  1784–   Lois et constitutions des colonies françoises de
  1790   l'Amérique sous le vent. 6 vols. Paris.

Moscoso Puello, Francisco Eujenio
  1977   Apuntes para la historia de la medicine de la isla de
          Santo Domingo. Santo Domingo: Libreria Domin-
          icana.

Moseley, Benjamin
  1789   A Treatise on Tropical Diseases: Or Military Oper-
          ations and the Climate of the West Indies. London:
          Printed for T. Cadell, in the Strand.

Parry, J. H., and Philip Sherlock
  1971   A Short History of the West Indies. 3d ed. Lon-
          don: Macmillan.

Pereira Rego, Jose
  1873   Memória histórica das epedemias da febre
          amarella e cholera morbo que tem reinado no
          Brasil. Rio de Janeiro: Typ. Nacional.

Pérez, Louis A., Jr.
  1988   Cuba Between Reform and Revolution. New York:
          Oxford University Press.

Pezuela y Lobo, Jacobo de la
  1868   Historia de la Isla de Cuba. 4 vols. Madrid: C.
          Bailly-Balliere Hermanos.

Phillips, Thomas
  1732   A Journal of a Voyage Made in the Hannibal of
          London, 1693–94 [1695]. Pp. 97–100 in A Collec-
          tion of Voyages and Travels. John Churchill, ed. 6
          vols. London: J. Walthoe.

Pincknard, George
  1816   Notes on the West Indies, Including Observations
          Relative to the Creoles and Slaves. 2d ed. 2 vols.
          London: Baldwin, Craddock and Joy.

Pouchet, G.
  1864   The Plurality of the Human Race. H. J. Beauvau,
          trans. London: Longmans Green. [Original
          French title unknown].

Quevado y Baez, Manuel
  1946–   Historia de la medicina y cirugía de Puerto Rico. 2
  1949   vols. Santurce.

Rhodes, A. J., and C. E. Van Rooyen
  1968   Textbook of Virology. 5th ed. Baltimore: Williams
          and Wilkins.

Roberts, George W.
  1957   The Population of Jamaica. Cambridge: Cam-
          bridge University Press.

Rosenblat, Angél
  1967   La Población de America en 1492. Mexico: Colegia
          de Mexico.

Rutman Darret B., and Anita H. Rutman
  1976   Of Agues and Fevers: Malaria in the Early
          Chesapeake. *William and Mary Quarterly* 36:31–60.

Savitt, Todd L.
  1978   Medicine and Slavery: The Diseases and Health

Care of Blacks in Antebellum Virginia. Urbana: University of Illinois Press.

Sawyer, Wilbur A.
1949   Yellow Fever. Pp. 738 in vol. 8 of The Oxford Medicine. Henry A. Christian, ed. New York: Oxford University Press.

Scott, H. Harold
1939   A History of Tropical Medicine. 2 vols. London: Edward Arnold.

Seidl, Carlos
1900   Dados estatisticos ao estudo etiologico da febre amarella. O Brazil-Medico 181–183.

Sheridan, Richard B.
1985   Doctors and Slaves: A Medical and Demographic History of Slavery in the British West Indies, 1680–1834. Cambridge: Cambridge University Press.

Siler, J. F.
1915   Medical Notes on Barbados, British West Indies. American Journal of Tropical Diseases 3:49.

Stewart, John
1808   An Account of Jamaica. London: John Churchill.

Strode, G. K., ed.
1951   Yellow Fever. New York: McGraw-Hill.

Taylor, Richard M.
1951   Epidemiology. In Yellow Fever. G. K. Strode, ed. New York: McGraw-Hill.

Teixeira, Jose Maria
1895   Febre amarella nas crianças. Rio de Janeiro: Typ. Nacional.

Trapham, Thomas
1679   A Discourse on the State of Health in the Island of Jamaica. London: Printed for R. Boulter.

Uttley, K. H.
1960   The Mortality of Yellow Fever in Antigua, West Indies, Since 1857. West Indian Medical Journal 9:187–188.

Wells, Robert V.
1975   The Population of the British Colonies in America Before 1776. Princeton: Princeton University Press.

Williams, Eric
1970   From Columbus to Castro: The History of the Caribbean 1492–1969. New York: Andre Deutsch.

Wood, Peter H.
1974   Black Majority: Negroes in Colonial South Carolina from 1670 Through the Stono Rebellion. New York: Knopf.

World Health Organization. Expert Committee on Yellow Fever.
1971   Third Report of the World Health Organization Expert Committee on Yellow Fever. WHO Technical Reports Series. Geneva.

Yellow Fever Commission (West Africa)
1913   Yellow Fever Bulletin 1:83–84.

23

Population Decline from Two Epidemics on the Northwest Coast

ROBERT BOYD

Direct contact by Indians of the Northwest Coast culture area with Euro-Americans began very late, in 1774. Therefore, documentation of the contact process is relatively good. It appears that the introduction of Old World diseases was similarly late and coincided with contact. Although Campbell (1989), using archeological data, has made a case for penetration of the Northwest Coast by the hemispheric smallpox epidemic of the 1520s, all other evidence (archeological, historical, Indian oral tradition) for Northwest disease introduction postdates 1774. That evidence is considerable, with nearly the full list of high mortality infectious diseases introduced in rapid fire sequence, with accompanying heavy mortalities strongly suggesting that these diseases were new to the area, or at least present again after a very long absence.

Smallpox epidemics appeared roughly every generation—the first, in the late 1770s following direct contact, over the entire coast, and others in 1801, 1836–1838, 1853, and 1862–1863 in more limited regions (Boyd 1990:137–143). This interesting sequence appears to have been created by the dual factors of introduction from an outside source plus presence of a large enough pool of non-immune susceptibles in the Northwest born since the last epidemic. Evidence for depopulation from the initial outbreaks is limited to descriptions of abandoned villages and native recollections, but high mortalities from the later epidemics are well documented in the Indian censuses and estimates compiled by the Hudson's Bay Company and by early government officials. Besides smallpox, malaria was introduced to and became endemic in a sizable portion of the southern coast, and records indicate considerable population decline concurrent with its introduction. Other "new" diseases that contributed to Northwest Coast Native American population decline included measles, influenza, dysentery, whooping cough, and (in a different way) tuberculosis and venereal diseases (Boyd 1985, 1990).

This is the situation for the region as a whole. This chapter will discuss the records on population decline associated with two localized outbreaks—on the lower Columbia in the decade following the introduction of malaria in 1830, and in the Queen Charlotte Islands during the years of the last great smallpox epidemic, 1862–1863. The two epidemics appear to qualify as virgin soil or near virgin soil; malaria had not been known in the Northwest prior to 1830, and smallpox had been absent from the Charlottes since the late 1770s. The data on depopulation in these two instances are remarkably good and may provide clues to patterns of depopulation in similar virgin soil situations in other places and at earlier dates in the Americas.

MALARIA ON THE LOWER COLUMBIA, AFTER 1830

The Lower Columbia drainage, here defined as the area from the river mouth to near The Dalles and including the basins of large tributaries such as the Willamette and Cowlitz, was home to several Indian groups. The two largest, Chinookans on the banks of the Columbia and Kalapuyans in the Willamette Valley, are also the most completely documented as far as population decline is concerned; and they are used as the base of discussion here.

In the late 1820s the population of these two peoples approximated 18,580; within a decade it had dropped to 2,433, or 13 percent of the initial number. Detailed discussions of the sources for these numbers have been given elsewhere (Boyd 1985, 1990, 1991a; Boyd and Hajda 1987); suffice it to say that the preepidemic estimates are from Meriweather Lewis and William Clark and the Hudson's Bay Company, and the postepidemic numbers are from the 1841 U.S. Exploring Expedition.

What caused this monumental decline in Lower Columbia populations? The contemporary sources (a large body of data) uniformly ascribe it to the disease called "fever and ague" by Americans and "intermittent fever" by the British. Despite some controversy over the identity of this disease (e.g., Cook 1955; Taylor and Hoaglin 1962), epidemiological evidence strongly suggests that it was malaria (Boyd 1975), described most often in later accounts (e.g., Townsend 1839:197; Brackenridge 1931:141, 221; J. R. Dunn 1846) as the tertian form (*Plasmodium vivax* and *P. falciparum*). The sources are unanimous in stating that this disease was new to the area, and unknown before 1830 (e.g., McLoughlin 1941:88). This points to a virgin soil situation. Malaria, as has been fully established by research (F. Dunn 1965; Wood 1975), is an Old World disease, which was introduced in sequence to different regions of the Americas, where suitable vectors, mosquitoes of the genus *Anopheles,* were native (Harrison 1978). Once introduced, it became endemic. In the unbroken tropical and subtropical regions of the Amazon, circum-Caribbean, and Southeast United States this introduction was early and apparently has gone unrecorded (Ashburn 1947:112–123; Friedlander 1969). In the Lower Columbia and adjacent California central valley (Cook 1955) malaria arrived late and was both observed and recorded.

The statistics from the area are unambiguous in documenting a dramatic population decline following the introduction of "fever and ague." What remains unclear are the dynamics of this decline. Such high mortalities are not characteristic of endemic malarial regions today, nor of those occasional instances where a combination of factors inflate mortality rates in endemic areas to numbers that merit the term "epidemic" (Wood 1979:260). It is essential to remember that on the Lower Columbia the outbreak was a virgin soil epidemic, and virgin soil outbreaks of whatever disease are almost by definition unusually virulent (Crosby 1976). This may be part of the answer to the large decline. Three other contributing factors are: the Indian means of dealing with the alternating spells of chills and fever characteristic of the disease, secondary diseases that precipitated mortality, and fertility decline directly or indirectly associated with malaria.

A small, consistent, yet independently written body of sources from the earliest years of the epidemic ascribe the high mortality to inadequate treatment of the disease. During the fever spells, Indians would plunge into cold water; when chills came they retreated to sweat lodges. Sudden death followed. The phenomenon is securely documented; the actual dynamics of death are not (Boyd 1979). Quinine sulfate, the medicine used by Whites, was in short supply in the early 1830s (Allan 1882:79; McLoughlin 1941). Factor two: Modern malaria is a disease of complications; death, when it comes, is usually from a secondary illness superimposed on a weakened malarial constitution (Brown 1983:65). Children, in endemic regions, form the bulk of casualties (Wood 1979:258–259). Though evidence is sparse, deaths listed in the record book of an 1830s Willamette Valley mission school, for instance are ascribed to such secondary diseases (including influenza and tuberculosis) introduced to Indian children chronically ill from malaria (Shepard 1922). It seems likely that much of the mortality in later years may have been due to secondary illnesses.

These two factors, in combination, appear to

have contributed to the mortality side of the population equation in the Lower Columbia valley. But it appears that there may have been a decline in fertility as well in this newly malarial population. Post-malaria Chinookan and Kalapuya censuses (Hudson's Bay Company 1838; Spalding 1851; Boyd 1985: chart 26) incorporate information on population structure, specifically age and sex. Censuses of groups within the epidemic focal area show low—below 30—percentages of children. Elsewhere in the Northwest, among Indian populations counted by the Hudson's Bay Company but not subjected to disease, the percentages are much higher, generally in the 30–40 percent range. In the case of the 1851 counts, mortality from the 1848 measles epidemic (Boyd 1991b) decreased the percentage of children even more. But in 1838 and 1851, two underlying explanations for fertility decline also seem likely. First, in immediate postepidemic years (MacArthur 1961:8), there was a sudden drop in fertility due to disrupted marital units. Second, there was considerable malaria-caused anemia, which, among women of child-bearing age, led to spontaneous abortions and stillbirths (Wood 1979:258).

The approximate 87 percent decline in Lower Columbia Indian populations in the decade following the introduction of malaria therefore appears not to have been a simple process. Inappropriate Indian treatments precipitated deaths in cases where proper treatment would have resulted only in temporary debilitation; secondary ailments moved in and pushed weakened malarial cases on to death, particularly among the very young; and maternal anemia is likely to have caused spontaneous abortions and miscarriages, resulting in a drop in fertility. The decline was regular and cumulatively dramatic: in 1841 an American physician, resident since 1835, estimated that the population of the Willamette Valley Indians diminished by one-quarter annually (Bailey in Wilkes 1926:57), a proportion fully in keeping with before (late 1820s) and after (1841) Kalapuyan population figures.

Socially, after 1841, most Chinookan and Kalapuyan populations were approaching extinction as viable and ethnically distinct entities. Inhabitants of Chinookan winter villages, tied to their local land base, remained in place with minimal regrouping (Dart 1851) until they were reduced to a few survivors or overwhelmed by migrants from more robust populations (Sahaptin or Salishan) from the peripheries of the endemic malaria zone (Tappan

1854). The 1851 Kalapuya census showed that these people likewise remained in their local band territories, with negligible regrouping. The average band size in 1851 was a mere 53 people, and the bands were evenly spread over the entire valley. As on the Columbia, more robust outsiders (Sahaptin Klikitat) had begun to move in, and by 1851 they were equivalent in numbers to the sum total of the Willamette Valley indigenes. The Kalapuyan population nadir was reached in the 1850s, and numbers (in what was a highly mixed population) began to increase again only after enforced concentration on the Grand Ronde Reservation and regular access to Western medicines.

SMALLPOX IN THE QUEEN CHARLOTTE ISLANDS, 1862–1863

The steady population decline of the Lower Columbia Indians following the introduction of malaria was very different in nature from the sudden catastrophic drop of the Haida population of the Queen Charlottes caused by the 1860s smallpox epidemic, even though the percentage losses were comparable.

The 1862–1863 British Columbia smallpox epidemic has been documented (Yarmie 1968; Pethick 1978). Over 20,000 Indians, nearly 60 percent of the pre-epidemic total, died in British Columbia and the Alaska Panhandle (Duff 1964; Boyd 1985, 1990:142–144). In classic fashion, the disease arrived with an infected individual on a ship from San Francisco. The ship docked at Victoria, and the disease spread rapidly to the crowded Indian encampment on the city's outskirts. Instead of quarantining the Indians, the authorities evicted them, and fleets of Haida, Tlingit, Tsimshian, and Kwakiutl traders sailed back to their homelands, taking the epidemic with them.

On the densely populated (relatively speaking) and isolated Queen Charlotte Islands, the effect was rapid and devastating. A Hudson's Bay census dating from 1839–1842 showed a total of 8,428 Haidas (table 1); there is no evidence that this number changed significantly in the next 20 years. The people were concentrated in several winter villages spread along the coastline in areas of heavy resource concentration (especially halibut, the local staple). Each village was associated with a particular matriclan.

TABLE 1

Haida Village Populations

Village	1839–1842[a]	1882–1884[b]	1915–1920[c]
Ninstints	308	30	
Tanu	545	150	
Skedans	439	12	
Cumshewa	286	60	
Kaisun	329		
Chaatl	561	108	
Skidegate	738	100	238
Aseguang	120		
Hiellan	280		
Tian	196		
Kung	122		
Kiusta	296		
Masset	2,473	350	350
Kaigani	234		
Koianglas	148	62	
Howkan	458	287	
Klinkwan	417	125	
Sukkwan	229	141	
Hydaburg			335
Kasaan	249	173	126
Total	8,428	1,598	1,049

[a]Douglas (1878).

[b]Chittenden (1884) for the Queen Charlotte villages; Petroff (1882) for the Kaigani villages.

[c]Skidegate and Masset (1915) from VandenBrink (1974:109); Hydaburg (1916–1917) from Vaughan (1985:186); New Kasaan from U.S. Bureau of the Census (1921:681).

Censuses of the Haida taken 1882–1884 (Chittenden 1884; Petroff 1882) show 1,598 survivors, or a population drop of over 80 percent, nearly all of which must on present evidence be assigned to the smallpox epidemic. This exceedingly large loss was due to several factors. First, the strain of smallpox virus in the 1860s epidemic was particularly virulent; second, Haida settlement was (relatively) dense and continuous, facilitating transmission; third, the Queen Charlotte population was particularly vulnerable, as there was no segment with acquired immunity, as was the case with most other British Columbia Indian populations. Whereas Tsimshian, Tlingit, and others had experienced an outbreak 24 years prior, the Haida had not known the disease for more than 90 years (Boyd 1985; Blackman 1981:23; cf. MacDonald 1983:17). It was, in essence, a virgin soil experience for them. A fourth factor was vaccine. While sizable numbers of Tlingit and some Kwakiutl had been vaccinated in the 1830s, and the Metlakatla Tsimshian in 1862,

none of the Haida had been vaccinated (Boyd 1985, chapter 4 and appendix).

The Queen Charlotte Islands population figures are the obverse of those from the Lower Columbia: the "before" numbers preserve important information on population structure; the "after" numbers are less specific. For instance, the pre-smallpox percentage of children was a high 48 percent, certainly associated with the reliable resource base (Frisch 1982) and the fecundity of Haida women (Fleurieu 1801:454), but equivalent figures for the remnant population are not known (despite anecdotal statements indicating a paucity of both children and marriageable women) (O'Reilly 1882; Crosby in VandenBrink 1974:66).

What is most interesting for the Haida are statistics on average village size in pre- and post-epidemic years. Haida people, for whatever reason, appear not to have been so closely tied to their land base as were the Chinookans and Kalapuyans. When village numbers dropped below a certain threshhold, the survivors moved and consolidated into multilineage villages. In pre-epidemic times Haida villages ranged in size from 120 to 738 people (excluding Masset) (table 1). In the 1880s many villages were already abandoned; other formerly populous settlements had dropped to dangerously low numbers. By the second decade of the twentieth century only four towns (Skidegate, Masset, Kasaan, and the newly established Hydaburg) remained, all with populations at or above the pre-contact minimum. Although movement to these centers was certainly prompted by White-introduced attractions (trading posts, missions, schools, and canneries), the failure of villages below the pre-contact minimum of 120 to survive is notable and may relate to continuing culturally determined limits on numerical size. Some of these possibilities are minimal sizes of subsistence-related task groups (Smith 1981), traditional rules of exogamy and available mates (Yengoyan 1972), and minimal sizes of ceremonial groups (Wagley 1951).

The Haida nadir population of 1,049 was reached in the 1910s (VandenBrink 1974:109; Vaughan 1985:186) and has recovered slowly since then. Unlike the Lower Columbia peoples, who remained scattered in small population units among larger and more robust populations, the Haida regrouped and persisted in a few, fair-sized settlements, relatively isolated from contact with outsiders. Disease history, environment, sociocultural characteristics, and contact history, which militated against the continued survival of the Lower Columbia peoples, were more favorable for the viability of the Haida, despite the fact that both had experienced population drops of similar magnitude after their most important virgin soil experience.

CONCLUSIONS

What do these two epidemics show? They indicate that, in certain cases, the hypothesis of catastrophic population decline with virgin soil epidemics holds. They also indicate that the type of disease introduced is in many ways as important as the virgin soil experience itself. The decline associated with a particular instance of malaria introduction was deliberate and cumulative, with continuing effects on mortality and fertility, while that associated with the smallpox case was sudden and discrete, without longlasting fertility and mortality effects. It is also clear that disease-related mortality, fertility, and population survival are strongly related to cultural practices such as the adequacy of indigenous health care systems (for example, the cold plunge and febrile diseases), and the ability of social systems to readjust after important perturbations (such as the village consolidation model).

REFERENCES

Allan, George
  1882   Reminiscences of Fort Vancouver, Extracts from a Letter of 1832. Pp. 75–80 in Transactions of the Oregon Pioneer Association, 1881.

Ashburn, Percy
  1947   The Ranks of Death: A Medical History of the Conquest of America. New York: Coward-McCann.

Blackman, Margaret
  1981   Window on the Past: The Photographic Ethnohistory of the Northern and Kaigani Haida. *Canada National Museum of Man, Mercury Series, Ethnology Service Paper* 74. Ottawa.

Boyd, Robert
  1975   Another Look at the "Fever and Ague" of Western Oregon. *Ethnohistory* 22(2):135–154.

  1979   Old Cures and New Diseases: The Indian Sweat Bath and Febrile Diseases in the Pacific Northwest During the First Century of Contact. (Manuscript in possession of the author.)

  1985   The Introduction of Infectious Diseases Among the Indians of the Pacific Northwest, 1774–1874. (Unpublished Ph.D. Dissertation in Anthropology, University of Washington, Seattle.)

  1990   Demographic History, 1774–1874. Pp. 135–148 in Handbook of North American Indians, Vol. 7: Northwest Coast, Wayne Suttles, vol. ed. William C. Sturtevant, gen. ed. Washington: Smithsonian Institution.

  1991   Kalapuya Disease and Depopulation. In What Price Eden? The Willamette Valley in Transition, 1812–1855. *Northwest Anthropology* (In preparation.)

Boyd, Robert and Yvonne Hajda
  1987   Seasonal Population Movement Along the Lower Columbia River: The Social and Ecological Context. *American Ethnologist* 14(2):309–326.

Brackenridge, Charles
  1931   The Brackenridge Journal of the Oregon Country. O. B. Sperlin, ed. Seattle, University of Washington.

Brown, Peter
  1983   Demographic and Socioeconomic Effects of Disease Control: The Case of Malaria Eradication in Sardinia. *Medical Anthropology* 7(2):63–87.

Campbell, Sarah
  1989   [Abstract of] Post-Columbian Culture History in the Northern Columbia Plateau: A.D. 1500–1900. *The Thunderbird: Archaeological News of the Northwest* 9(1):6.

Chittenden, Newton
  1884   Hyda Land and People: Official Report of the Exploration of the Queen Charlotte Islands for the Government of British Columbia. Victoria.

Cook, Sherburne
  1955   The Epidemic of 1830–33 in California and Oregon. *University of California Publications in Archaeology and Ethnology* 43(3):303–326.

Crosby, Alfred
  1976   Virgin Soil Epidemics as a Factor in the Aboriginal Depopulation in America. *William and Mary Quarterly* 33(2):289–299.

Dart, Anson
  1851   [Letter of May 14.] (In Oregon Superintendency of Indian Affairs, National Archives, Washington, microfilm copy at Oregon Historical Society Library, Portland.)

Douglas, James
  1878   Census of the Indian Population on the N.W. Coast . . . transcription by Ivan Petrov. (In Private Papers, Second Series. Microfilm A92, Suzzallo Library, University of Washington, Seattle, original in Bancroft Library, University of California, Berkeley.)

Duff, Wilson
1964   The Indian History of British Columbia, Vol. 1:
        The Impact of the White Man. *Anthropology in Brit-
        ish Columbia Memoir* 5. Victoria.

Dunn, Frederick
1965   On the Antiquity of Malaria in the Western Hemi-
        sphere. *Human Biology* 38:385–393.

Dunn, J. R.
1846   Journal on H. M. S. Fisgard: Admiralty 101/100.4
        XC A/3930. Kew, Surrey: Public Record Office.

Fleurieu, Claret
1801   Voyage Round the World Performed During the
        Years 1790, 1791 and 1792 by Etienne Marchand.
        London: T. N. Longmans and O. Rees.

Frisch, Rose
1982   Demographic Implications of the Biological De-
        terminants of Female Fecundity. *Social Biology*
        29:187–192.

Harrison, Gordon
1978   Mosquitoes, Malaria and Man. New York: E. P.
        Dutton.

Hudson's Bay Company
1838   Census of Indian Population at Fort Vancouver:
        Klickitat Tribe, Cathlacanasese Tribe, Cath-lal-
        thlalah Tribe. Hudson's Bay Company Archives B.
        223/z/1, folios 26–28. Winnipeg, Manitoba.

MacArthur, Norma
1961   Introducing Population Statistics. Melbourne: Ox-
        ford University Press.

MacDonald, George
1983   Haida Monumental Art: Villages of the Queen
        Charlotte Islands. Vancouver: University of Brit-
        ish Columbia Press.

McLoughlin, John
1941   McLoughlin's Fort Vancouver Letters: First Series,
        1825–38. E. E. Rich, ed. *Publications of the Hudson's
        Bay Record Society*, Vol. 4. London.

O'Reilly, P.
1883   [Letter of 10/27/1882 to the Indian Reserve Com-
        mission, Victoria.] Pp. 106–109 in *Canada Sessional
        Paper* 5. Ottawa.

Pethick, Derek
1978   1862: The Smallpox Epidemic. Pp. 11–23 in Brit-
        ish Columbia Disasters. Langley, Wash.: Stage-
        coach Publishing.

Petroff, Ivan
1882   Report on the Population, Industries, and Re-
        sources of Alaska. 10th Census: 1880. Wash-
        ington: U.S. Government Printing Office.

[Shepard, Cyrus]
1922   The Mission Record Book of the Methodist Epis-
        copal Church, Willamette Station, Oregon Ter-
        ritory. Charles Carey, ed. *Oregon Historical Quar-
        terly* 23(3):230–266.

Smith, Eric
1981   The Application of Optimal Foraging Theory to
        the Analysis of Hunter/Gatherer Group Size. Pp.
        36–65 in Hunter/Gatherer Foraging Strategies:
        Ethnographic and Archaeological Analyses. Eric
        Smith and Bruce Winterhalder, eds. Chicago:
        University of Chicago.

Spalding, Josiah
1851   Letters of March 22 and August 27 to Anson Dart.
        (In Oregon Superintendency of Indian Affairs.
        National Archives, Washington.)

Tappan, William
1854   Annual Report, Southern Indian District, Wash-
        ington Territory. (In Washington Superintenden-
        cy of Indian Affairs, National Archives, Wash-
        ington; microfilm copy at Oregon Historical
        Society Library, Portland.)

Taylor, Herbert and Lester Hoaglin
1962   The Intermittent Fever Epidemic of the 1830's on
        the Lower Columbia River. *Ethnohistory* 9:160–
        178.

Townsend, John
1839   Narrative of a Journey Across the Rocky Moun-
        tains to the Columbia River. Philadelphia. (Re-
        printed: University of Nebraska Press, Lincoln,
        1978).

U.S. Bureau of the Census
1921   14th Census of the United States. Vol. 1: Popula-
        tion 1920, Number and Distribution of Inhabi-
        tants. Department of Commerce. Washington:
        U.S. Government Printing Office.

VandenBrink, J. H.
1974   The Haida Indians: Cultural Change Mainly Be-
        tween 1876–1970. Leiden: E. J. Brill.

Vaughan, James
1985   Towards a New and Better Life: Two Hundred
        Years of Alaskan Haida Culture Change. (Un-
        published Ph.D. Dissertation in Anthropology,
        University of Washington, Seattle.)

Wagley, Charles
1951   Cultural Influences on Population: A Comparison
        of Two Tupi Tribes. *Revista do Museu Paulista* 5:95–
        104.

Wilkes, Charles
1926   Diary of Wilkes in the Northwest. Edmund Meany,
        ed. *Washington Historical Quarterly* 17(1):43–65.

Wood, Corinne
1975   New Evidence for a Late Introduction of Malaria

into the New World. *Current Anthropology* 16(1):93–104.

1979   Human Sickness and Health: A Biocultural View. Palo Alto, Calif.: Mayfield Publishing Company.

Yarmie, Andrew
1968   Smallpox and the British Columbia Indians: Epi-demic of 1862. *British Columbia Library Quarterly* 31(3):13–21.

Yengoyan, Aram
1972   Biological and Demographic Components in Ab-original Socio-Economic Organization. *Oceania* 63(2):85–95.

24

The 1832 Inoculation Program on the Missouri River

MICHAEL K. TRIMBLE

Several key historically documented episodes directly affected the demographic transition associated with the smallpox epidemic of 1837–1838—an epidemic that decisively altered the demographic profile of the Great Plains. The smallpox epidemic of 1831, the Vaccination Act of 1832, and the 1832 Great Plains vaccination campaign all directly affected the morbidity and mortality rates associated with the Great Plains smallpox epidemic of 1837–1838.

Epidemiology and ethnohistory can be used as complimentary research orientations. An epidemiological paradigm provides a body of theory centering around a number of variables that influence disease process. Ethnohistory provides the diachronic and synchronic data that are examined within the framework of a disease model. Although these orientations can generate generalizations that summarize a volume of disease episodes, a fine-grained regional analysis, as espoused here, may ultimately be of more utility for a comprehensive understanding of the dynamic nature of epidemic episodes in the Americas.

THE 1837 SMALLPOX EPIDEMIC ON THE NORTHERN PLAINS

In 1837, a smallpox epidemic swept through the northern Plains. Its results were catastrophic to the Indian tribes. It turned the entire Missouri River Valley into "one great grave yard" (Trimble 1979:79–83).

The epidemic in the upper Missouri region of the northern Plains began almost simultaneously at three widely separated places. By the first of July 1837 the disease had already broken out and was rapidly spreading among the Yankton and Santee Sioux Indians at Sioux Subagency, in central South Dakota (Trimble 1979:73). A few days later, cases of the disease were reported at the American Fur Company trading post, Fort Union, at the mouth of the Yellowstone River, almost 1,000 miles upstream (Abel 1932:294; Lapenteur 1933:132). On July 14, the first recorded death from the disease occurred in the Indian village at Fort Clark, a fur trading post on the Missouri River, between the other two places (fig. 1) (Abel 1932:121). Within a few more weeks, the pestilence spread to the Assiniboine and Blackfeet Indians around Fort Union, and to the Man-

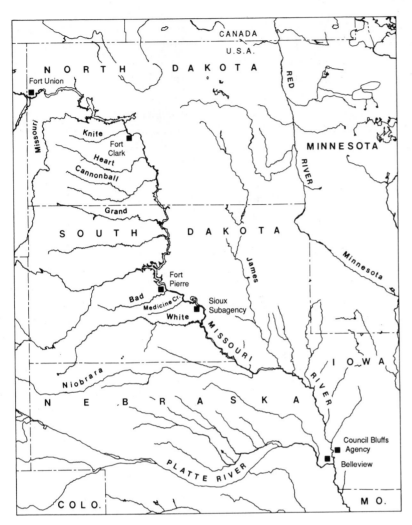

Fig. 1. Parts of the northern and central Plains where smallpox was epidemic in 1831 and 1837 and where the federal War Department conducted an inoculation program in 1832.

dan, Arikara, and Hidatsa living near Fort Clark (Meyer 1977).

The accounts of the terror, suffering, and death caused by this disease are ghastly, and there is little reason to suspect exaggeration. Within the short period of three months, it was raging "with the greatest destruction possible," in the words of Jacob Halsey, an eyewitness at Fort Union (Abel 1932:394). He reported that 10 out of every 12 Indians in his area were dead and that even though he had been unable to keep pace with the number of victims, he presumed at least 700 Blackfeet and perhaps 800 Assiniboine were dead (Abel 1932:394–395). Alexander Culbertson, another eyewitness, estimated that more than half the Assiniboine tribe fell victim to the disease and about two-thirds of the Blackfeet tribe (DeVoto 1947:289–291). Before the snows fell in the high country that winter, these two large and powerful Indian tribes along the head-

waters of the upper Missouri were shattered into tiny, starving remnants (Ewers 1961:72).

Downstream at Fort Clark, the toll from the disease was even more dreadful. By August 11, François Chardon, the clerk at the fort, had recorded in his daily journal that the Mandans were dying so fast that it was impossible for him to keep a record (Abel 1932:126). The disease spread to the Arikara and Hidatsa, and they died as rapidly as the Mandan. On September 19, Chardon recorded that as many as 800 Mandans were dead from the small-pox (Abel 1932:132), and in one of the Mandan villages located near the fort, only 14 people were left alive from a former population of more than 600. By the end of that month, he speculated that the disease had destroyed as much as seven-eighths of the Mandan tribe, and one-half of the Arikara and Hidatsa (Abel 1932:137–138).

By early spring of 1838, the smallpox epidemic

had died out almost as rapidly as it had started. In its aftermath, perhaps as many as 17,000 people were dead (DeVoto 1947:294–295).

The data just presented permit the following generalizations to be made. A smallpox epidemic broke out over a three- to seven-month period along the Missouri River from Fort Leavenworth in present-day Kansas, to Fort Union on the head-waters of the Missouri. There appears to be a rough patterning associated with the direction of the out-breaks—south to north—and in the severity of the epidemic among various tribal groups. Severe mor-tality was associated with this epidemic, which left several cultural groups as fractions of their former sizes.

Mode of Introduction

A critical evaluation of archival data (Trimble 1979:35–44), combined with an epidemiological analysis of smallpox transmission among "virgin soil" populations leads to the conclusion that the in-troduction and rapid dissemination of this particu-lar epidemic can be traced to, and was a function of, the fur trade.

Documentary sources reveal that the crew of the steamboat *St. Peters* experienced an outbreak of smallpox while on a provisioning tour up the Mis-souri River to certain fur trading posts and federal government agencies. The virus was subsequently passed on to the passengers aboard the vessel (Na-tional Archives and Records Service 1838). An epi-demic of this type would usually not spread so rapidly as this one did over a wide geographic area. The virus's spread was facilitated by the steamboat captain's refusal to quarantine the crew and pas-sengers, because he feared that his schedule would be unnecessarily delayed (Meyer 1977:92–99). The result was that the localized smallpox outbreak on board the *St. Peters* was rapidly transported upriver.

Many Plains tribes became infected, and an epidemic occurred when passengers who were still capable of transmitting the disease disembarked and came into contact with Indians at the docking points (Trimble 1979:32–39). At Council Bluffs Agency elements of the Otoe, Omaha, and Pawnee are reported to have been exposed. The next stop, Sioux Subagency, directly exposed the Yankton and Santee Sioux (National Archives and Records Ser-vice 1838). There was a stop at Fort Pierre, but there is no mention of which groups were exposed. At

Fort Clark, smallpox apparently was introduced to the Mandan, Hidatsa, and Arikara by two Arikara women who disembarked to visit relatives and were still in an infectious state (Meyer 1977; Trimble 1979:38).

The final groups directly infected with small-pox from the *St. Peters* passengers were the Black-feet and Assiniboine who were awaiting trading goods and government annuities at Fort Union (De-Voto 1947).

In the remarkably brief time span of seven weeks (first week of May to third week of June), the smallpox epidemic of 1837–1838 was introduced into almost every major tribe living on or near the Missouri Valley. Through continued intertribal contact, the introduction developed into a pan-demic on the Plains.

Morbidity and Mortality

What factors appear to be the key elements in deter-mining why this disease became epidemic? What ac-counts for the varying morbidity and mortality estimates among and between tribes? A number of reasonably accurate explanations can be offered to suggest reasons why this disease became such a vir-ulent epidemic while exhibiting such variable mor-bidity and mortality rates among tribes.

First, it is clear from a wealth of published liter-ature (Burnet and White 1972; Dixon 1962) that smallpox is highly contagious. Unless the initial host is isolated from others, or the general population has an acquired immunity either through past con-tact or inoculation, a single case can rapidly develop into an epidemic. Not only were the initial victims unquarantined, but also there were many Native Americans living on the upper Missouri River who had no immunity, acquired or conferred, to the dis-ease (National Archives and Records Service 1838a). It is also clear that the long period of com-municability of smallpox provided the potential (which was realized) for the prolonged transmission of the disease. All the aforementioned factors con-tributed to the small outbreak's becoming an areal epidemic.

Second, living in large, nucleated communities as opposed to small, fragmented, hunting and gathering groups imposed a distinct disadvantage on the sedentary populations. These densely popu-lated communities not only increased the chances of an epidemic occurring but also facilitated this one. In such an environment, a virus could easily be transmitted through an entire village in a number of days. Once an epidemic began in this type of community, the entire group suffered. Planting and harvesting schedules requiring close cooperation between a number of family groups were disrupted, guaranteeing nutritional stress and increased mortality.

Conversely, the nomadic populations of the Plains were built on a foundation of self-sufficiency achieved through the cooperation of significantly fewer family groups. These bands only united to become tribes—and hence large population groups—during corporate endeavors such as the summer bison hunt. When an epidemic struck a tribe or even a band, the group dissolved into small family units to escape the disease. This strategy could not prevent an epidemic, but it often diminished its impact. Dispersing behavior among nomadic tribes many times had the effect of a general quarantine. Morbidity and mortality were often confined to small bands, reducing the chances of transmission to other nomadic groups. The community disruption suffered by the sedentary populations because of the loss of specialists was virtually unknown among the nomads.

Third, contrasting living practices of the nomads and the sedentary populations also provides data that help to explain the differential morbidity and mortality that occurred among these cultural groups. The sedentary villagers were more likely to experience a crowd-disease epidemic simply by virtue of the fact that many more individuals lived and slept in an earthlodge than in the smaller tepees of the nomads. Transmission rates are greatly enhanced when a large number of people interact within a small area. The permanence of the villages additionally increased the chances of an epidemic's being introduced. Most of the sedentary village populations were visited on a regular basis by Whites and Indians for trading purposes. As permanent entities, these villages and their inhabitants were continuously exposed to microbes carried by visiting traders. The same cannot be said for the nomadic groups, which visited trading posts but did not live in them. The fact that they led a nomadic life insured far fewer contacts with potential infecting agents. The smaller number of inhabitants housed in their portable living quarters, as well as their ability to disperse easily, provided

fewer chances for an acute crowd infection to establish itself among nomads.

The aforementioned variables are all certainly crucial to any discussion of the morbidity and mortality suffered by the Indian tribes of the Plains in 1837–1838; however, questions remain as to why there was such a disproportionate case fatality rate among the sedentary villagers and nomads of the upper Missouri (above present-day Ft. Pierre, South Dakota), as opposed to Indians of the lower Missouri.

Two events clearly account for the disproportionate morbidity and mortality rates experienced by aboriginal populations in the Plains during the 1837–1838 smallpox epidemic. These events are: the 1831 smallpox epidemic; and the federal government's response to this epidemic, the Vaccination Act of 1832 and the resulting 1832 Plains vaccination program.

THE 1831 SMALLPOX EPIDEMIC ON THE CENTRAL PLAINS

In 1831 a smallpox epidemic swept through the central Plains. Although not widely reported, the epidemic was particularly devastating for the Pawnee Indians living in present-day south-central Nebraska.

The first major report on the virulence of the epidemic was delivered by John Dougherty, the Indian agent for the region, to Superintendent William Clark (U.S. Congress. Senate 1831). Dougherty estimated that 50 percent of the Pawnee were dead: "They told me that not one under thirty-three years of age escaped the monstrous disease, it having been that length of time since it visited them before."

On October 31 Dougherty wrote Clark describing the plight of the Omaha (U.S. Congress. Senate 1831a) who had also suffered a number of smallpox deaths.

Further evidence of the range of this epidemic in the central Plains is revealed in a letter received by Secretary of War Lewis Cass from Rev. Isaac Mc-Coy in March 1832 (U.S. Congress. Senate 1832). McCoy reported that while surveying Kansas and portions of southern Nebraska in the summer and fall of 1831 he observed widespread smallpox outbreaks among the Shawnee, Delaware, Osage, and

Pawnee. McCoy reported that all tribes save the Pawnee were vaccinated in great numbers by the fur trading companies. It was his observation that perhaps as many as 3,000 Pawnees perished, a figure that he stated represented approximately one-half of their population.

McCoy (U.S. Congress. House of Representatives 1832a) further detailed the events of the smallpox epidemic of 1831–1832 as it affected the Pawnee, Otoe, Omaha, and Ponca. This time he estimated that 4,000 deaths occurred and that all save 160 can be attributed to the Pawnee. This letter is significant in that for the first time McCoy proposed a federally funded vaccination program to save these populations.

McCoy was persistent in his reporting to Cass on the smallpox epidemic (U.S. Congress. House of Representatives 1832b). He continued to argue for federally funded vaccination campaigns and to outline its organization (U.S. Congress. House of Representatives 1832c). On May 5, 1832, the Vaccination Act of 1832 became law (U.S. Congress. House of Representatives 1832; U.S. Congress. Senate 1832b).

THE VACCINATION ACT OF 1832

The Vaccination Act of 1832 was a significant piece of legislation for its time. It not only set a precedent for the federal government in assuming responsibility for the vaccination of Indians but also by its very nature assured that future smallpox epidemics would be influenced by the government's effectiveness in carrying out the mandate. The law was the product of intensive lobbying by the religious community and no doubt from fur trading concerns (U.S. Congress. Senate 1832).

The official title of the act was: An Act to Provide the Means of Extending the Benefits of Vaccination, as a Preventative of the Smallpox, to the Indian Tribes, and Thereby as far as Possible, to Save Them from the Destructive Ravages of that Disease. Its charge to the superintendencies that were responsible for Indian relations was brief but all encompassing. The agents and subagents were to convene all Indian tribes at appropriate "places" so that they could be vaccinated for smallpox. The secretary of war was empowered to employ as many physicians as were needed to accomplish the task and was directed to offer compensation of $6.00 a day to the physicians. The secretary of war was responsible for supplying all agents and physicians with "genuine vaccine matter," and all agents were required to make monthly returns to the secretary of war listing the names of those vaccinated, their tribal affiliation, and an estimate of age. Twelve thousand dollars was appropriated by Congress to carry out this national campaign in 1832 (U.S. Congress. Senate 1832a).

THE 1832 PLAINS VACCINATION PROGRAM

The field implementation of the Vaccination Act of 1832 was initiated in August 1832. John Dougherty, the senior Indian agent at the Council Bluffs Agency, was responsible for administering the program (National Archives and Records Service 1832). The two physicians he hired, Dr. M. Martin, and Dr. D. H. Davis, were dedicated men who relentlessly pursued their charge—to vaccinate as many Indians as they could along the Missouri River.

The diaries these men produced and the rosters of tribes vaccinated from August until October 1832 are exhaustive and contain several key units of data. First, the doctors report on their activities: where they went, who they saw, and difficulties they encountered. Second, the most useful component of their reports is the exhaustive rosters of the tribes they vaccinated (tables 1–2). These rosters are organized by tribes, and within this unit individual names are phonetically recorded along with the estimated age of the individual vaccinated. Gender is not recorded.

Dr. Martin vaccinated elements of the Iowa, Otoe, Yankton, Yanktonai, Omaha, and Teton (National Archives and Records Service 1832a).

Although Martin and Davis arrived at Fort Leavenworth in mid-July ready to begin work, Dougherty did not arrive until August 2, 1832. On August 3 all three departed for Bellevue, arriving August 10. There were no Indians. Martin and Dougherty then left for the Otoe trading post at Council Bluffs, arriving on August 14. Government vaccine "crusts" were used to vaccinate 28 individuals among the Iowa, Omaha, and Otoe.

They returned to Bellevue on August 18 and proceeded up the Missouri to the Sioux Subagency where they arrived on September 5. They began vaccinating the Yankton and Teton Sioux, but the vaccination did not "take." There was something

TABLE 1

Vaccinations Recorded by Age and Tribe

| | Age Group | | | | | | | | | | | | |
	0–1	2–4	5–7	8–10	11–15	16–20	21–25	26–30	31–40	41–50	51–60	60+	Total
Omaha band[a]		2		2	3		3	2					12
Omaha band[a]	41	39	27	7	4	11	4						133
Otoe band[a]		1		2	3		3	2					11
Otoe band[a]	39	11	4	10	4	14	16	4					102
Iowa		4	1		1								6
Sioux bands	21	37	26	17	35	29	23	27	44	14	8	13	294
Yanktonai band[a]	11	25	21	24	18	10	13	7	17	12	4	10	172
Yanktonai band[a]	5	8	5	3	14	11	12	13	12	1			84
Yankton Sioux	135	97	69	108	153	108	71	155	101	30	17	19	1,063
Grand Pawnee	52	1		1	2	1							57
Republican Pawnee	66				1	2							69
Loup Pawnee	63			6	4	5							78
													2,081

Source: National Archives and Records Service 1832a.
[a]When two lines are given for one tribe, this indicates that the doctors administered the vaccine to a different group of the tribe.

TABLE 2

Age Distribution of Recorded Vaccinations in 1832 by Percentage

	0–1	2–4	5–7	8–10	11–15	16–20	21–25	26–30	31–40	41–50	51–60	60+
Omaha band[a]		17%		17%	25%		25%	16%				
Omaha band[a]	31%	29	20%	6	3	8%	3					
Otoe band[a]		10		18	27		27	18				
Otoe band[a]	38	11	4	10	4	14	15	4				
Iowa		66	17		17							
Sioux bands	7	12	9	6	12	10	8	9	15%	5%	3%	4%
Yanktonai Sioux band[a]	6	15	12	14	10	6	8	4	10	7	2	6
Yanktonai Sioux band[a]	6	10	6	4	17	13	14	15	14	1		
Yankton Sioux	13	9	6	10	14	10	7	15	9	3	2	2
Grand Pawnee	90	2		2	4	2						
Republican Pawnee	96				1	3						
Loup Pawnee	81			8	5	6						

Source: National Archives and Records Service 1832b.
[a]When two lines are given for one tribe, this indicates that the doctors administered the vaccine to a different group of the tribe.

defective with the vaccine material, and Martin ceased using the vaccine. Though he is unclear as to where he procured viable vaccine material (no doubt from the fur trade concerns) he did "procure more virus" and re-vaccinated all 294 individuals. On September 21 he visited the Santee Sioux, who refused to be vaccinated. Predictably, the Santee were devastated during the 1837–1838 epidemic.

To obtain vaccine to continue his work, Dr.

Martin returned to the Sioux Subagency to harvest the attenuated scabs from those he had previously vaccinated.

On September 29, Dr. Martin departed for Fort Pierre on the Bad River, where he vaccinated 172 Yanktonai by October 2. At Fort Tecumseh (several hundred meters from Ft. Pierre) on October 3 he vaccinated an additional 84 Yanktonai.

Having completed his work among the

Yanktonai Dr. Martin returned to the Sioux Sub-agency on October 5. He then left immediately to vaccinate the Teton who were assembled at the head of Medicine Creek. At this rendezvous he estimated that he vaccinated approximately 900 Tetons. However, their names do not appear in the journal as there was no time to record them. They were anxious, Martin records, to return to the Plains to hunt bison; many individuals were not vaccinated owing to lack of time.

Dr. Martin then returned to the Sioux Sub-agency, arriving on October 12. From October 13 to 16 he vaccinated 1,063 Yanktons. Martin estimated that at this vaccination session he vaccinated only one-half of the assembled Indians, the other half refusing because they were fearful of its consequences.

Martin concluded his report by asking to return the following year to complete his work, but he was not sent back. He declared that a great number of Indians remained to be vaccinated, specifically those residing north of Fort Pierre. The populations most affected by the 1837–1838 epidemic resided above that point.

Dr. D. H. Davis's efforts included the vaccination of the Otoe, Omaha, Grand Pawnee, Republican Pawnee, and Loup Pawnee (National Archives and Records Service 1832b).

Dougherty and Davis encountered a large Otoe encampment (location not described) and vaccinated 102 individuals on September 25. Davis then proceeded to the Pawnee villages located on the Loup River. On October 1 he vaccinated 57 individuals at the Grand Pawnee village. On October 3–4 he visited the Republican Pawnee, vaccinating 69 individuals. And on October 6 he entered the Loup Pawnee village, vaccinating 78 individuals.

From the Pawnee he proceeded to the Omaha encampment (location not described) and on October 10 vaccinated 133 individuals. He then returned to Bellevue.

SUMMARY AND CONCLUSIONS

In 1831 a massive smallpox epidemic occurred on the central Plains. It does not appear to have spread into the northern Plains. The response to this epidemic was the passage of a vaccination act in 1832 and its implementation as best as could be achieved in the summer and fall of 1832. Tribes were vacci-

nated in the Missouri River valley, but no groups above Fort Pierre were vaccinated.

Specifically, elements of the Iowa, Otoe, Yankton, Omaha, Teton, Yanktonai, Grand Pawnee, Republican Pawnee, and Loup Pawnee were vaccinated. In all approximately 3,000 individuals were vaccinated (National Archives and Records Service 1832a), although only 2,081 were recorded (table 1). At that time of the year, these Indians were living on the Missouri River below Fort Pierre. Because of the delays, tribes living on the upper Missouri—notably the Mandan, Hidatsa, Arikara, Assiniboine, Cree, and Blackfeet—were not vaccinated. Epidemiological theory would suggest that the selective vaccinations served to insure that the lower Missouri River groups had a reduced probability of experiencing an epidemic should they have been exposed to the smallpox virus. Conversely, those groups that had not acquired immunity through vaccination or recent epidemic episodes could expect to experience higher morbidity and mortality rates should they come into contact with smallpox. This is in fact what occurred during the 1837–1838 smallpox epidemic. The vaccination programs of the early 1830s best served the nomadic and sedentary tribes of the lower Missouri River, while the unvaccinated horticulturists and nomads of the upper Missouri river were at far greater risk.

The nomadic groups of the lower Missouri River, especially bands of the Sioux, were the main beneficiaries of the vaccination program and as such suffered the lowest mortality of the major Plains tribes. The Yankton, Yanktonai, and Teton were the most heavily vaccinated, and in terms of conferred immunity among the Plains tribes they clearly were at an advantage during the 1837–1838 epidemic. The upper Missouri River horticulturists and nomads lacked this immunity. The result was tremendous morbidity and mortality among upper Missouri River tribes during the 1837–1838 epidemic. The vaccination campaign of 1832 thus more clearly defines regional and tribal reactions to the 1837–1838 smallpox epidemic.

REFERENCES

Abel, A. H., ed.
  1932   Chardon's Journal at Fort Clark, 1834–1839. Pierre: State of South Dakota, Department of History.

Burnet, M., and D. O. White
1972   Natural History of Infectious Disease. 4th ed. Cambridge: Cambridge University Press.

DeVoto, Bernard
1947   Across the Wide Missouri. Boston: Houghton-Mifflin.

Dixon, C. W.
1962   Smallpox. London: Churchill.

Ewers, J. C., ed.
1961   Five Indian Tribes of the Upper Missouri: Sioux, Arickaras, Assiniboines, Crees, Crows. Norman: University of Oklahoma Press.

Larpenteur, C.
1933   Forty Years a Fur Trader on the Upper Missouri. M. M. Quaife, ed. Chicago: Donnelley and Sons.

Meyer, R. W.
1977   The Village Indians of the Upper Missouri: The Mandans, Hidatsas, and Arikaras. Lincoln: University of Nebraska Press.

National Archives and Records Service
1832   [Letter of December 6, from John Dougherty to Lewis Cass.] (Microcopy No. 234, roll 750. Washington.)

1832a   [Letter of November 28, from M. Martin to Lewis Cass.] (Microcopy No. 234, roll 750. Washington.)

1832b   [Letter of October 21, from M. Davis to Lewis Cass.] (Microcopy No. 234, roll 750. Washington.)

1838   [Letter of February 5, from Joshua Pilcher to William Clark.] (Microcopy No. 234, roll 884, frame 0273–0275. Washington.)

1838a   [Letter of February 27, from Joshua Pilcher to William Clark.] (Microcopy No. 234, roll 884, frame 0293–0295. Washington.)

Trimble, Michael K.
1979   An Ethnohistorical Interpretation of the Spread of Smallpox in the Northern Plains Utilizing Concepts of Disease Ecology. (Unpublished Master's Thesis, in Anthropology, University of Missouri, Columbia.)

U.S. Congress. House of Representatives
1832   [Journal of House Activities, March–May.] Pp. 526–705 in 22d Congress, 1st sess., House Document No. 215. Washington.

1832a   Letter of March 23, from Isaac McCoy to Lewis Cass. P. 3 in 22d Congress, 1st sess., House Executive Document No. 190, Vol. 5. (Serial No. 220) Washington.

1832b   Letter of March 27, from Isaac McCoy to Lewis Cass. P. 3 in 22d Congress, 1st sess., House Executive Document No. 190. Vol. 5. (Serial No. 220) Washington.

1832c   Letter of April 20, from Isaac McCoy to Lewis Cass. Pp. 8–15 in 22d Congress, 1st sess., House Executive Document No. 190. Vol. 5. (Serial No. 220) Washington.

U.S. Congress. Senate
1831   Letter of October 29, from John Dougherty to William Clark. Pp. 718–719 in 23d Congress, 1st sess., Senate Executive Document No. 512. Vol. 2. (Serial No. 245) Washington.

1831a   Letter of October 31, from John Dougherty to William Clark. Pp. 719–721 in 23d Congress, 1st sess., Senate Executive Document No. 512. Vol. 2. (Serial No. 245) Washington.

1832   Letter of March 6, from Isaac McCoy to Lewis Cass. Pp. 230–241 in 23d Congress, 1st sess., Senate Executive Document No. 512. Vol. 3. (Serial No. 246) Washington.

1832a   Journal of Senate Activities, May 18. P. 283 in 22d Congress, 1st sess., Senate Document No. 211. Washington.

1832b   Journal of Senate Activities, April 10–May 3. Pp. 230–269 in 22d Congress, 1st sess., Senate Document No. 211. Washington.

25

Contact Shock in Northwestern New Spain, 1518–1764

DANIEL T. REFF

Controversy persists regarding the impact of Old World diseases on American Indian populations during the sixteenth and seventeenth centuries. The debate has intensified with Dobyns's (1983; cf. Reff 1989) suggestion that many disease episodes that affected central Mexico and Inca Peru reached pandemic proportions, affecting almost the entire Western hemisphere. Native populations from New England to the Amazon are said to have been largely destroyed prior to 1600, often before sustained contact with Europeans.

Dobyns's hypothesis is provocative. If what happened in Meso-America and Peru occurred elsewhere, then many assumptions and inferences about the size as well as the structure and functioning of American Indian populations in 1492 require revision. Moreover, because of archeological reliance on ethnographic analogies, empirical evidence of disease-induced changes in aboriginal culture would cast a shadow on current interpretations of the archeological record. Affirmation of Dobyns's pandemic hypothesis would likewise require reexamination of processes of enclavement and acculturation, which also have been analyzed largely without regard for Old World diseases and their consequences during the early historic period (Jennings 1976; Reff 1987).

This chapter summarizes the results of research that has documented the demographic and cultural consequences of Spanish-introduced disease in northwestern Mexico and, to a lesser extent, the American Southwest (Reff 1986, 1987, 1991). The evidence from the Greater Southwest is significant for several reasons. First, the region's proximity to central Mexico makes it a logical area to look for evidence to evaluate Dobyns's hypothesis that early epidemics in central Mexico spread northward, reaching pandemic proportions. Second, because the aboriginal population of the Greater Southwest was representative of Indian populations as a whole, with respect to population densities and economic and sociopolitical systems, the consequences of disease might be illustrative of changes that affected Indian populations elsewhere in the Americas. In this regard, central Mexico and Inca Peru were not especially representative; both regions had the highest population densities and the most extensive and well traveled trade and transport networks in the Americas. From an epidemiological perspective, the two civilizations were ideal environments for Old World diseases.

Conditions for the spread of disease were far less favorable in the Greater Southwest in 1500. At that time, the aboriginal population was divided among rancherias, villages, and towns, ranging in size from several dozen to several thousand people. Like most areas of the Americas, the Greater Southwest lacked state-level polities with institutionalized craft production, markets, and related infrastructures (Ford 1983; Riley 1982). Trade, although extensive, did not daily link communities separated by great distances, as was the case in Inca Peru and Meso-America.

In addition to its representativeness vis a vis New World populations, the Greater Southwest was a region in which many groups largely escaped exploitation by encomenderos or other Spaniards. Researchers have argued that European exploitation rivaled or surpassed Old World diseases as a cause of Indian population decline (Denevan 1976; Johansson 1982). In 1591, the Jesuits were given a virtual monopoly on the control of the Indian population of a large part of northern Mexico. The Jesuits largely were free of the vices that characterized their countrymen, especially mine operators and encomenderos. Indeed, the Jesuits' greater respect for Indian life contributed to one of the most successful mission enterprises in the Americas (Dunne 1951:123). Between 1591 and 1678 they baptized more than 500,000 people and established missions throughout northwestern Mexico (Alegre 1956–1960; Perez de Ribas 1896, 1944).

The Jesuits generated a wealth of documents that are replete with references to disease and epidemics. The Jesuit materials also include numerous censuses and reports with anecdotes on Indian life, all of which facilitate an assessment of both the demographic and cultural consequences of introduced disease. This is particularly true for the period after 1591, when the Jesuits initiated mission activities along the eastern and Pacific slopes of the Sierra Madre, in Sinaloa and Durango. Although there is a relative paucity of historical documents from the period 1518 to 1590, reflecting the limited Spanish presence in the region, Spanish explorers penetrated many areas of the Greater Southwest between 1530 and 1565. The exploration chronicles, when examined along with the archeological record and the later writings of the Jesuits, are an invaluable source for reconstructing the size and structure of aboriginal populations. A comparison of the explorers' observations and the later writings

of the missionaries also make it possible to determine whether disease episodes that are known to have affected central Mexico spread northward during the decades immediately following Hernando Cortés's conquest.

DISEASE EPISODES, 1518–1630s

Several researchers have suggested that the Greater Southwest was affected by the smallpox pandemic of 1518 to 1525 (Dobyns 1983:12–13; Nixon 1946:53; Upham 1986); however, there is little or no evidence to support this inference (Reff 1987a). Rather, the evidence, particularly the favorable descriptions of Indian life in western Mexico that were supplied by participants in Diego de Guzman's expedition of 1530 to 1531 (Carrera Stampa 1955; Sauer and Brand 1932), suggest that smallpox and other maladies did not spread much beyond the northwestern border of the Tarascan empire.

It was during Guzman's conquest of Nueva Galicia that Old World diseases first were unleashed along the southern margins of the Greater Southwest. In September 1530, while Guzman's army was encamped at Aztatlan, along the Rio Acaponeta, an epidemic of what appears to have been malaria, typhoid, or dysentery, killed 8,000 of Guzman's Indian allies and left the province of Aztatlan largely depopulated (Carrera Stampa 1955:108–109, 138–139, 154, 185; Pacheco and Cardenas 1870, XIV:439). As was the case in other lowland regions of America (Sauer 1948; Thompson 1970), malaria, typhoid, and dysentery subsequently became endemic or semi-endemic along the west coast of Mexico. Occasionally, one or more of these chronic infectious maladies reached epidemic proportions, often in the company of other chronic as well as acute infectious diseases.

In 1534, for instance, measles, which had raged for several years in central Mexico, spread northward to coastal Nayarit and central and southern Sinaloa (Tello 1891:251–255). Over 130,000 Indians were reported to have died from measles and what was termed "bloody stools," presumably dysentery, typhoid, or a combination, which were introduced several years earlier. Again, in 1545 to 1548, Nueva Galicia, which included Nayarit and southern and central Sinaloa, suffered from one or more maladies, including what appears to have been typhus (Bancroft 1886:529–530; Beaumont

1932, 2:141; Grijalva 1924:213–215; Tello 1891:509–510, 524–527). Largely as a result of disease, the aboriginal population of northern Nayarit and southern and central Sinaloa was reduced by over 90 percent by about 1600, from a population of at least several hundred thousand to perhaps 40,000 (see Arregui 1946:29; Bancroft 1886:552–553; Sauer and Brand 1932).

The mountains and central plateau regions of Zacatecas, Durango, and southern Chihuahua were next affected by disease, after coastal Nayarit and Sinaloa. The region's fate was sealed in 1546 when vast mineral deposits were discovered in and around Zacatecas. During the following years, thousands of Spaniards and free Indians from the south flocked to the burgeoning mining frontier. Almost immediately, an extensive Spanish transport network developed (Bakewell 1971; Moor-

head 1958; Powell 1952; West 1949; West and Parsons 1941), which facilitated the northward movement of disease agents that had become endemic or semi-endemic in Meso-America (Cook 1939).

At the heart of the network was the Camino Real, the major highway of the interior, which by 1607 stretched some 1,500 miles from Mexico City to Sante Fe, New Mexico (fig. 1). People, goods, and disease agents also traveled to the northern frontier from Meso-America via Guadalajara and the Pacific coast road. The coastal and interior roads were connected by several mule trails that spanned the Sierras, the most important of which was the Topia Road. Major arteries and lesser trails all were frequented primarily during the winter or dry season (Mota y Escobar 1940:99–100; Paso y Troncoso 1939, 4:183). This is precisely when acute infectious

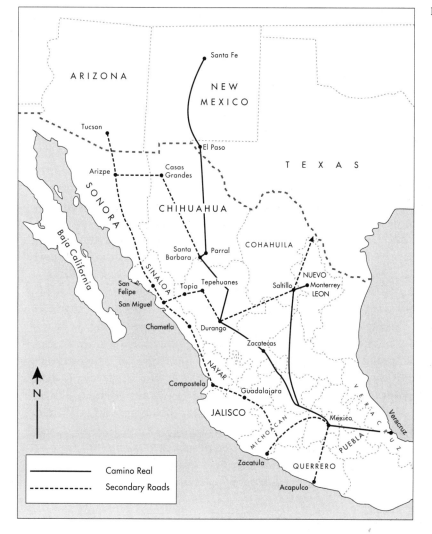

Fig. 1. Spanish colonial transport networks.

diseases, such as smallpox and influenza, have their highest incidence (Busvine 1976; Dixon 1962) and when many epidemics began in central Mexico during the early historic period (Cooper 1965; Gibson 1964:137).

During the third quarter of the sixteenth century, when the mining frontier and Spanish transport networks expanded dramatically, central Mexico experienced a respite from major epidemics (Cook and Simpson 1948:14; Mendieta 1945:174; Ocaranza 1934:85). There are several lines of evidence, particularly documents relating to Francisco de Ibarra's exploits in the north (Hammond and Rey 1928; Mecham 1927), which make little or no mention of disease, and which suggest that much of northwestern Mexico also was spared the ravages of smallpox and other maladies during the period 1550 to 1575. The situation began to change dramatically in 1576. That year typhus became epidemic in Meso-America and quickly spread northward, apparently along the coastal road in Nayarit and Sinaloa as well as northward along the Camino Real to Zacatecas and other Spanish and Indian settlements in Durango and southern Chihuahua (Bakewell 1971:126–127; Florencia 1955:257; Mota Padilla 1924:311; Powell 1952:168; Tello 1891:623).

It is difficult to determine how far typhus or other diseases spread in 1576 to 1581 without the records of missionaries. In the early 1590s, when the Jesuits began working in the Sierras and along the eastern slopes of the Great Divide, they encountered a variety of behaviors and beliefs, and in one instance a mass burial, that suggests that the Zacatec, Xixime, Irritila, Acaxee, and Tepehuan all were affected by typhus or other introduced diseases prior to 1591 (Alegre 1956–1960, 3:108; DHM 1598:48; Perez de Ribas 1944, 3:263–264). By contrast, the Jesuits who began working on the Pacific slopes of the Sierra in 1591 reported that the Cahita proper and Guasave in northern Sinaloa and southern Sonora largely were unaffected by disease. Indeed, when first affected by smallpox in 1593, the Indians complained that it was only after they accepted baptism that they suffered from disease (AGN 1593; Alegre 1956–1960, 1:393; Dunne 1940:32). It would appear, then, that epidemics such as the measles epidemic of 1530 to 1534 or the typhus epidemic of 1575 to 1581 did not spread much beyond the Tahue of northern Sinaloa.

The vast mission system that was erected by the Jesuits after 1591 became an important link in the chain of disease transmission. Acute and chronic infectious diseases that were carried northward from central Mexico along the coastal and interior roads to Durango and San Felipe, where the Jesuits had their headquarters, quickly spread throughout the mission system. The annual reports of the Jesuits indicate that smallpox, measles, typhus, pneumonia, and other maladies returned as epidemics at regular intervals, in 1593–1594, 1601–1602, 1607–1608, 1612–1613, 1617, 1623–1625, and on numerous occasions during the decades that followed (Reff 1986). Not surprisingly, as the mission system grew, incorporating increasing numbers of Indian communities, the epidemics became more destructive and far reaching. The spread of disease was not limited to the mission system; peoples beyond the mission frontier invariably were affected by Old World diseases. For instance, in January 1615, 350 Lower Pimas left their homes along the middle Rio Yaqui and traveled over 100 kilometers to Jesuit headquarters along the Sinaloa River to petition for priests and baptism (Perez de Ribas 1944, 2:34). During the spring of the following year, another large group of Pimas left their village in the sierras, as did a third group late in 1616 (AGN 1615; Alegre 1956–1960, 3:563–569). Although the Jesuits attributed this exodus to impatience for baptism, it is apparent that the Pima had suffered from typhus or another malady that had raged during the previous years among the mission population. Perez de Ribas (1944, 2:255–256), in fact, noted that three adults who came south in January 1615 died en route, and another five died after they reached San Felipe. One man who came south in January arrived at San Felipe in a "death trance . . . so leprous that there was not a part of his body, from his head to his feet, that was free of disease."

The Lower Pima experience is one of many instances where introduced disease spread far in advance of the Jesuits themselves. There were occasions as well when epidemics in northwestern Mexico spread to the American Southwest. During the mid 1630s, for instance, many thousands of Pueblo Indians died from smallpox and other maladies (Hackett 1923–1937, 3:108), which apparently were carried northward along the Camino Real from Zacatecas and Parral (AGN 1638; Bakewell 1971:200; Reff 1987a). There is good reason to believe that the mission caravan, which passed through Zacatecas in 1625, also was responsible for the introduction of one or more maladies that previously had killed many thousands of Indians in northwestern Mexico (AGN 1625:137; Reff 1986). More specifically, it is known that approximately half of the pueblos in the Rio Grande Valley were abandoned between 1600 and 1643 (Schroeder 1972:55), and that communities such as Pecos, which persisted, nevertheless lost 40 percent of its population (Kessell 1979:170). Vetancurt's (1961: 276) observation that the Hopi were greatly reduced by disease prior to 1629 further implicates disease in Pueblo abandonment and the general decline in the Pueblo population during the early seventeenth century.

THE DEMOGRAPHIC CONSEQUENCES OF INTRODUCED DISEASE

During the course of their tenure in northwestern New Spain the Jesuits compiled a number of reports that shed light on the rate and extent of population decline in northwestern Mexico between 1591 and 1764. For instance, in 1638, the Jesuits reported that while they had baptized 300,000 Indians, only one-third survived (AHH 1638; Hackett 1923–1937, 3:100). After about 1638, when a new wave of epidemics began in northern New Spain, many thousands more perished. The continuing population decline is reflected in a detailed report compiled by the Jesuit Visitor, Juan Zapata, in 1678 (AGN 1678). At this time, Jesuit baptisms in the north approached 500,000. Nevertheless, the entire mission population numbered approximately 63,000. Thereafter, the mission population continued to decline. At the time of the Jesuit expulsion from the New World, in 1767, the mission population numbered no more than 30,000 (AHH 1764; Tamaron y Romeral 1937).

Baptismal and census figures for individual groups clarify that many populations largely were destroyed within a decade or two of missionization. This was particularly true of the Zacatec, Tepehuan, Acaxee, and Irritila. The aboriginal homelands of each of these groups were invaded at an early date by Spanish miners and were crisscrossed by the Camino Real and the Topia Road. The Irritila, in the Jesuit missions of Parras, to the north and west of Zacatecas, are thought to have lost one-third of their population prior to missionization, in 1598. At that time, the Irritila numbered between 16,000 and 20,000 (Perez de Ribas 1944, 3:293). Following missionization, and as a consequence of disease, particularly the epidemics of 1607 and 1623 to 1625, the Irritila declined to 1,569 in 1625 (Hackett 1923–1937, 2:152–159).

The rapid diminution of the Irritila was not unusual. Neighboring groups in the Sierras and along the eastern slopes of the Sierra Madre all suffered dramatic population reductions during the opening decades of the seventeenth century. Indeed, by 1678, the Zacatec, Irritila, Tepehuan, Acaxee, and Xixime were too few in number to survive as distinct cultural entities (Reff 1986).

While most Sierran groups largely were destroyed, the Tarahumara survived many of the dislocations of the early historic period, and as late as 1944 numbered approximately 44,000. Although it has been suggested that the Tarahumara population remained relatively stable during the historic period (Pennington 1963:23–24), the Jesuit materials clarify that the Tarahumara repeatedly suffered from disease (AGN 1638, 1647; DHM 1645, 1662). How is it then that the Tarahumara survived when others did not? The answer is that the Tarahumara abandoned much of their aboriginal homeland during the late sixteenth and seventeenth century, withdrawing to the largely inaccessible barranca country of southwestern Chihuahua (Pennington 1963). It was only after this withdrawal and the adoption of distance-maintaining behaviors (Sheridan and Naylor 1979:79) that the Tarahumara population rebounded from earlier losses.

Because of the rather late date (1593) of the first epidemic in northern Sinaloa and Sonora, the rate and extent of population decline among groups such as the Yaqui, Mayo, Guasave, Lower Pima, and Opata were retarded relative to Sierran groups, such as the Acaxee or Irritila. Nevertheless, most populations in northern Sinaloa and Sonora largely were destroyed by 1678 (Reff 1986). One of the few groups to weather the demographic collapse of the seventeenth century was the Yaqui. From a population of around 60,000 in 1565, the Yaqui declined to approximately 30,000 at the time of missionization, in 1617 (Perez de Ribas 1944, 2:64). By 1678 the Yaqui population had dropped to around 8,000 (AGN 1678). After reaching a nadir about 1720, the Yaqui population rebounded sharply, growing to over 22,000 in 1759 (Tamaron y Romeral 1937). These gains were made possible, at least in part, by regular food surpluses and general good health (see Spicer 1980), and more than a century of exposure to disease.

A brief consideration of data for the Pueblos clarifies the extent to which epidemics in northwestern Mexico affected Indian peoples in the American Southwest during the seventeenth century. Though a wide range of figures has been suggested for the aboriginal Pueblo population, a figure of 100,000 for both the Eastern and Western Pueblos would appear reasonable (Simmons 1979; Upham 1982). Between 1608 and 1638 the Franciscans baptized 60,000 Pueblo Indians, one-third of whom reportedly perished from disease (Hackett 1923–1937, 3:108). Between 1638 and 1660, the Pueblo population was reduced by an additional 42 percent to approximately 24,000 (Vetancurt 1961:269). By the time of the Pueblo Revolt of 1680, the population of both the Eastern and Western Pueblos had declined to around 17,000 (Simmons 1979:186). The Pueblo population, in effect, declined by over 80 percent between 1608 and 1680, much as populations did in northwestern Mexico.

DEMOGRAPHIC TRENDS AND PARALLELS

It is apparent that many disease episodes in central Mexico did in fact spread northward during the early historic period, affecting Indian peoples in northwestern Mexico and the American Southwest. At the same time, the evidence does not support the hypothesis that epidemics in central Mexico invariably swept northward, infecting many or most native populations in the Greater Southwest and subsequently spreading throughout North America. Early epidemics in central Mexico, such as the measles epidemic of 1530 to 1535 and the typhus and/or plague epidemic of 1545 to 1548, did not penetrate the Greater Southwest. It was not until after about 1575, when a suitable infrastructure was in place, that Old World diseases spread northward with regularity, reaching epidemic proportions in northwestern Mexico and, after 1600, in the American Southwest. Even then, the spread of disease was uneven and conditioned by a number of factors, in-

cluding a population's history of exposure to disease, uprisings, and other intangibles (Reff 1986, 1991).

Nevertheless, it is true that Old World diseases largely destroyed the Indian population of northwestern New Spain during the early historic period. The earliest and most profound losses occurred along the southern margins of the Greater Southwest, in Nayarit and southern and central Sinaloa. Between 1530 and 1590, Old World diseases, notably malaria and dysentery, reduced the Totorame and Tahue from a population of several hundred thousand to less than 40,000. Comparable losses were sustained by Sierran groups between 1575 and 1625. Populations along the Pacific slopes of the Sierras, in northern Sinaloa and Sonora, as well as the Pueblos of the American Southwest, were exposed to disease at a much later date, after 1593. West-coast populations and the Pueblos nevertheless were reduced by more than 90 percent by 1680. Only a handful of groups rebounded during the second quarter of the eighteenth century.

The precipitous decline in the Indian population of northwestern New Spain parallels demographic trends in Peru and Central Mexico. In all three regions, disease-induced reductions frequently began before sustained contact with Spaniards. The Yaqui experience, characterized by population losses of almost 50 percent prior to missionization in 1617, exemplifies the reductions that many groups sustained prior to regular contact with the Jesuits or other Spaniards. The population nadir for the Yaqui as well as other native groups in Sinaloa and southern Sonora occurred between 1720 and 1750, over a century after the nadir in central Mexico and Inca Peru. Again, this difference in timing reflects the fact that most groups in northern Sinaloa and Sonora were not affected by disease until after 1593.

In northwestern Mexico as in Meso-America, the initial "contact shock" period—when populations declined precipitously—spanned a period of 30–40 years, followed by a brief respite from devastating epidemics. In central Mexico, this respite occurred between 1550 and 1575. In northwestern Mexico, the respite came between 1626 and 1638. After a lull, both regions experienced another round of major epidemics. Predictably, the losses sustained during this second wave of epidemics largely were due to a high infant and child mortality rate. In central Mexico, more than half the children born alive during the colonial period died during their first year of life; close to three-quarters died in infancy (Gibson 1964:141–142).

In northwestern New Spain the infant mortality rate varied from year to year and from one settlement to another, depending on the currency of disease, its virulence, and how often a community had been exposed to different maladies. Initial encounters with smallpox, measles, and typhus often resulted in mortality rates of 50 to 75 percent. During the epidemic of 1593 in Sinaloa, for instance, Father Gonzalo de Tapia commented that two-thirds of the children that he had baptized died during the epidemic (Shiels 1934:142). By the early eighteenth century the infant and child mortality rate had abated for many groups, depending on their history of exposure to disease. For instance, reports from 1720, following an epidemic of smallpox, generally indicate that the older a mission community, and the more it had been exposed to disease, the lower its infant mortality rate (Alegre 1956–1960:491–518). Because the mission frontier generally moved in a northerly direction over time, the mortality rates also exhibit a distinct spatial patterning. The mortality rates range from a low of around 12 percent in the south at Santa Maria Tepuspe (Batuc) to a high of almost 60 percent at the mission of Bavispe, which was founded in 1645.

High infant mortality was coincident with a higher mortality rate for women, particularly married women, relative to aboriginal conditions. The Jesuit reports frequently mention women who suffered during childbirth and were comforted with medals, relics, specialized prayers, and basic care. The report of 1621, for instance, related how a woman who had been in labor for three days finally gave birth to a healthy child after the resident priest placed a medal of San Ignacio around her neck. The report tells of another women near death, who gave birth to a healthy child ("without any lesions") upon receiving the last rites and a medal of San Ignacio (AGN 1621:275–276). Similar "edifying cases" involving pregnant women can be found in many Jesuit reports (AGN 1620:253, 1628:344, 1635:264, 1636:2).

It is not surprising, then, that many male converts objected to Jesuit insistence on monogamy, fearing that they would end up widowers (Perez de Ribas 1944, 2:227). The high mortality rate for married women (relative to aboriginal conditions) apparently resulted in pressure for women to marry at an earlier age. Writing in the mid 1700s, Father Joseph Och noted that girls married much too early and often died with their first birth. Och commented that he often was called upon to marry 13-year-old girls who had a child the following year (Treutlein 1965:135).

The occurrence of major epidemics every five to eight years during the seventeenth century meant that children aged 4 to 12 also were particularly susceptible to disease. This cohort included children born since the last disease episode and infants who were being breast fed at the time of the last epidemic, who benefited from maternal antibodies. The susceptibility of children is reflected in Jesuit reports from 1678 that show that the infant/child mortality rate in five Opata communities ranged from 37 to 59 percent (AGN 1678a, 1678b). In four of the five communities, over half those who were born died before they reached puberty.

The high mortality rates for infants, children, and pregnant women largely were responsible for a decrease in household size during the early historic period. Aboriginally, most peoples in northwestern Mexico and the American Southwest apparently lived in households with a nuclear family of around five or six (Beals 1932; Ortiz 1983; Sauer 1935). Household counts and total population figures (AHH 1638; Hackett 1923–1937, 3:97) indicate that the average household in Sonora and Sinaloa decreased to 4.9 in 1638. As a consequence of repeated exposure to disease, many of these households necessarily included a husband and wife, one or two of their children, and one or more relatives who were left homeless by previous epidemics (Reff 1991).

The size of the average household varied considerably during the remainder of the seventeenth and eighteenth centuries, depending on the recency of disease. The trend was decidedly in a downward direction until the late 1600s or early 1700s, when, depending on a group's particular disease history, household size tended to increase. Data from 1720 (Alegre 1956–1960, 4:491–519) suggest that the average household had 4.2 members. Although the average in 1765 for 111 communities discussed by Tamaron y Romeral (1937) was only 3.2, this figure is misleading because large numbers of adult males were working away from the missions (see also Pennington 1980:73–91). If these males who worked on Spanish farms and ranches were counted, the average household among groups such as the Yaqui probably would have numbered between five and six.

CONCLUDING THOUGHTS

During the eighteenth and nineteenth centuries groups such as the Yaqui, Tarahumara, and Pueblos continued to rebound from the tremendous losses of the early contact period. The resiliency of these groups has been misconstrued by researchers, who have implied or explicitly stated that Old World diseases did not have a profound impact on Indian peoples during the early historic period (Basso 1979:14–15; Hu-DeHart 1981:51; Pennington 1963:24). The failure to acknowledge or explore the evidence of disease is attributable, at least in part, to what Jennings (1976) has called the "civilization-savagery myth"—the belief that native American societies were less populous and advanced than their European counterparts (Reff 1987).

The myth has prompted many researchers to discount the early observations of Spanish explorers, who indicated or suggested that many areas of the Greater Southwest were well populated with sophisticated cultures (DiPeso 1974:IV; Reff 1991; Riley 1982). The explorers' statements often have been rejected or ignored in favor of the observations of missionaries and mission historians who wrote in the eighteenth and nineteenth centuries (Bolton 1948; Nentvig 1980; Treutlein 1949, 1965). Unlike early missionaries such as Perez de Ribas, these later missionaries and historians did not witness the contact-shock losses of the seventeenth century, nor were they disposed intellectually to acknowledge the effects of disease.

Too few researchers have critically examined the Jesuit materials and other primary sources that have a bearing on aboriginal culture; most Southwesternists have relied on secondary sources that pertain to Indian societies that had been profoundly altered by Old World disease. The failure to acknowledge the evidence of disease has had important implications for the understanding of more than demographic trends during the sixteenth and seventeenth centuries. The disease evidence, for example, has never figured in archeological interpretations of the widespread abandonment of sites throughout the Greater Southwest during the protohistoric period. Most archeologists continue to assume that this "collapse" occurred *prior to* European contact and was the result of warfare, deleterious climatic shifts, and other nondisease factors (Cordell 1984; El Zur 1965; Gumerman and Haury 1979; Wilcox and Masse 1981). For their part, ethnologists and ethnohistorians have inferred that Indians' interest in and acceptance of missionization was a logical consequence of their recognition of the inherent benefits that accrued to missionization. Both historians and anthropologists (Bolton 1917, 1932; Spicer 1962, 1980) have cast the Jesuits in a role analogous to modern extension agents. The Jesuits are said to have been the source of "thousands of innovations" that revolutionized aboriginal culture, making possible for the first time in many areas permanent houses, towns, crop surpluses, craft production, trade, and other advances in economic and sociopolitical organization (Spicer 1962:58, 292–297, 1980:32, 86).

The Jesuits' own letters and reports clarify that European innovations such as wheat, chickens, and plows were of little or no consequence during the early historic period (AGN 1657; AHH 1638; Hackett 1923–1937, 3:95–127). Only cattle, which provided a ready source of meat protein during epidemics (Hackett 1923–1937, 3:100), when Indians could not hunt, was truly significant. The Jesuit materials clarify that Indian acceptance of missionization followed and was coincident with epidemics that destroyed or altered the fabric of Indian society. Jesuit success was due largely to the fact that the Jesuits acted in a managerial capacity, supervising productive activities and the redistribution of surpluses and trade goods, much as caciques had done prior to the introduction of smallpox and other maladies that undermined aboriginal adaptive strategies (Reff 1987, 1991). Similarly, through the practice and advocacy of Roman Catholicism, the Jesuits filled a void left by the death or failure of Indian leaders and shamans to chart a course through uncertain and inexplicable times.

In summation, Old World diseases had a profound impact on not only the size but also the structure and functioning of Indian societies, which, in turn, greatly influenced Indian and Jesuit relations. Though there is little or no evidence of pandemics, Old World disease did spread in advance of the mission frontier, destroying or altering the fabric of Indian society prior to sustained contact with Spaniards.

REFERENCES

Documents

AGN (Archivo General de la Nacion, Mexico City)

1593   *Misiones 25. Anua del ano de mil quinientos de noventa y tres.*

1615   *Historia 15. Memoryas Para la Historia de la Provincia de Synaloa. Carta del Padre Diego de Guzman al Padre Provincial de Septiembre de mil seiscientos veinte y neube.* (Note: Although the title for this letter, as it appears in the *Memoryas*, indicates it was written in 1629, internal evidence indicates it was written in 1615).

1620   *Historia 15. Memoryas Para la Historia de la Provincia de Synaloa. Anua del ano de mil seiscientos y veinte.*

1621   *Historia 15. Memoryas Para la Historia de la Provincia de Synaloa. Anua del ano de mil seiscientos y veinte y uno.*

1625   *Misiones 25. Carta Annua de la Provincia de la Compania de Jesus de Neuva Espana, Juan Lorencio.*

1628   *Historia 15. Memoryas Para la Historia de la Provincia de Synaloa. Carta del Padre Juan Varela al Padre Provincial, 16 de Febrero 1628.*

1635   *Misiones 25. Puntos para el Anua del ano de 1635, destas misiones de San Ignacio Nuestro Padre en la Provincia de Cinaloa, Thomas Basilio, 26 de Marzo 1636.*

1636   *Misiones 25. Puntos para el Anua del ano de 1636 destas misiones de San Ignacio Nuestro Padre en la Provincia de Cinaloa, Thomas Basilio, 9 de Abril 1637.*

1638   *Misiones 25. Copia de una carta del Padre Gaspar de Contreras para el Padre Provincial, Santiago Papasquiaro, 5 de Augusto 1638.*

1647   *Missiones 26. Annua del Pueblo de Santa Catalina de Tepeguanes.*

1657   *Historia 316. Apologetico Defensorio y Puntual Manifesto que los Padres de la Compania de Jesus, Missioners de las Provincias de Sinaloa y Sonora, Francisco Xavier de Faria.*

1678   *Misiones 26. Relacion de los Missiones que la Compania tiene en el Reyno y Provincias de la Nueva Viscaya en la Nueva Espana echa el ano de 1678 con ocasion de la Visita General dellas que por orden del Padre Provincial Thomas Altamirano hizo el Padre Visitador Juan Hortiz Zapata de la misma Compania.*

1678a   *Jesuitas (Fichero II-4). Untitled Informe for the Partido of San Miguel de Oposura, Juan Martinez.*

1678b   *Missiones 26. Numero de los Bauptizmos, cassamientos,*

y entierros deste Partido de Guepaca, Banamatzi, y Sinoquipe deste el ano de 1675 hasta el ano de 78, Munoz de Burgos.

AHH (Archivo Historico de Hacienda, Mexico City)

1638   *Temporalidades 2009-1. Memorial al Rey para que no se recenga la limosna de la Misciones y consierva al Senor Palafox en las relaciones a la Compania, Andres Perez de Ribas, 12 de Septiembre 1638.*

1764   *Temporalidades 17–22. Noticias de las Missiones que Administran los Padres de la Compania de Jesus de Nueva Espana, M. Aguirre.*

DHM (Documentos Para la Historia de Mexico, Cuarta Serie, Tomo III, Mexico, 1857)

1598   *Anua del Ano de 1598.*

1645   *Relacion de los sucedido en este reino de la Vizcaya desde el ano de 1644 hasta el de 45 acerca de los alzmientos, danos, robos, hurtos, muertos y lugares despoblados de que se saco un traslado para remitir al padre Francisco Calderon, provincial de la provincia de Mexico de la Compania de Jesus . . . Nicolas de Zepeda, San Miguel de las Bocas, Abril 28 de 1645, mas addendum de 11 de septiembre de 1645.*

1662   *Puntos de Anua de estos diez anos que he asistido en este partido de San Pablo, de la mision de Taramuras y Tepehuanes (de unas y otras hay), desde el ano de 1652 hasta este de 1662 sumariamente lo que ha pasado cuanto a lo espiritual.*

Publications

Alegre, Francisco J.
1956–   Historia de la Provincia de la Compañia de Jesus
1960   de Nueva España [1780]. 4 vols. Ernest J. Burrus and Felix Zubillaga, ann. Rome: Bibliotheca Instituti Historici S.J.

Arregui, Domingo Lazaro de
1946   Descripcion de la Nueva Galicia [1621]. Sevilla: Escuela de Estudios Hispano Americanos de la Universidad de Sevilla.

Bakewell, P. J.
1971   Silver Mining and Society in Colonial Mexico: Zacatecas 1546–1700. Cambridge: Cambridge University Press.

Bancroft, Hubert H.
1886   The Works of Hubert Howe Bancroft. Vol. 10: History of Mexico; Vol. 2: 1521–1600. San Francisco: A. L. Bancroft.

Basso, Keith
1979   History of Ethnological Research. Pp. 14–21 in Handbook of North American Indians. Vol. 9: Southwest. Alfonso Ortiz, vol. ed. William C. Sturtevant, gen. ed. Washington: Smithsonian Institution.

Beals, Ralph L.
1932   The Comparative Ethnology of Northern Mexico Before 1750. *Ibero-Americana* 2. Berkeley, Calif.

Beaumont, Pablo
1932   Crónica de Michoacan [1873–1874]. 3 vols. *Publicaciones del Archivo General de la Nación: 17–19.* Mexico.

Bolton, Herbert E.
1917   The Mission as a Frontier Institution in the Spanish-American Colonies. *American Historical Review* 23:42–61.

1932   The Padre on Horseback. San Francisco: Sonora Press.

————, trans.
1948   Kino's Historical Memoir of Pimeria Alta. Berkeley: University of California Press. (Originally published in 1919 by A. H. Clark).

Busvine, J. R.
1976   Insects, Hygiene and History. London: Athlone Press.

Carrera Stampa, Manuel, ed.
1955   Memoria de los Servicios que Habia Hecho Nuno de Guzman, Desde que fue Nombrado Gobernador de Panuco en 1525. Mexico: Jose Porrua e Hijos.

Cook, Sherburne F.
1939   The Smallpox Epidemic of 1797 in Mexico. *Bulletin of the History of Medicine* 7:937–969.

Cook, Sherburne F., and Lesley B. Simpson
1948   The Population of Central Mexico in the Sixteenth Century. *Ibero-Americana* 31. Berkeley, Calif.

Cooper, Donald B.
1965   Epidemic Disease in Mexico City, 1761–1813. Austin: University of Texas Press.

Cordell, Linda S.
1984   Prehistory of the Southwest. New York: Academic Press.

Denevan, William M.
1976   Estimating the Unknown. Pp. 1–12 in The Native Population of the Americas in 1492. William M. Denevan, ed. Madison: University of Wisconsin Press.

Di Peso, Charles C.
1974   Casas Grandes: A Fallen Trading Center of the Gran Chichimeca. 8 vols. *Amerind Foundation Publication* 9. Dragoon, Ariz.

Dixon, C. W.
1962   Smallpox. London: J. and A. Churchill.

Dobyns, Henry F.
1983   Their Number Become Thinned. Knoxville: University of Tennessee.

Dunne, Peter Masten
1940   Pioneer Black Robes on the West Coast. Berkeley: University of California Press.

1951   Andres Perez de Ribas. New York: The United States Catholic Historical Society.

El Zur, Arieh
1965   Soil, Water and Man in the Desert Habitat of the Hohokam Culture: An Experimental Study in Environmental Archaeology. (Unpublished Ph.D. Dissertation in Anthropology, University of Arizona, Tucson.)

Florencia, Francisco de
1955   Historia de la Provincia de la Compañia de Jesus de Nueva España [1694]. Mexico: Editorial Academia Literaria.

Ford, Richard
1983   Inter-Indian Exchange in the Southwest. Pp. 711–723 in Handbook of North American Indians. Vol. 10: Southwest. Alfonso Ortiz, vol. ed. William C. Sturtevant, gen. ed. Washington: Smithsonian Institution.

Gibson, Charles
1964   The Aztecs Under Spanish Rule. Stanford: Stanford University Press.

Grijalva, Juan de
1924   Cronica de la Orden de N. P. S. Augustin en las Provincias de la Nueva Espana . . . de 1533 hasta el de 1592 [1624]. Mexico: Imprenta Victoria.

Gumerman, George J., and Emil W. Haury
1979   Prehistory: Hohokam. Pp. 75–90 in Handbook of North American Indians. Vol. 9: Southwest. Alphonso Ortiz, vol. ed. William C. Sturtevant, gen. ed. Washington: Smithsonian Institution.

Hackett, Charles Wilson
1923–   Historical Documents Relating to New Mexico,
1937   Nueva Vizcaya and Approaches Thereto, to 1773. Adolph F. Bandelier and Fanny R. Bandelier, colls. 3 vols. Washington: Carnegie Institution of Washington.

Hammond, George P., and Agapito Rey, trans.
1928   Obregon's History of 16th Century Exploration in Western America. Los Angeles: Wetzel Publishing Company.

Hu-DeHart, Evelyn
1981   Missionaries, Miners and Indians. Tucson: University of Arizona Press.

Icazbalceta, Joaquin Garcia
1866   Colección de Documentos para la Historia de Mexico. Vol. 2. Mexico: J. M. Andrade.

Jennings, Francis
1976   The Invasion of America: Indians, Colonialism, and the Cant of Conquest. New York: W. W. Nor-

ton. (Originally published in 1975 by University of North Carolina Press, Chapel Hill.)

Johansson, S. Ryan
1982 The Demographic History of the Native Peoples of North America: A Selective Bibliography. *Yearbook of Physical Anthropology:* 25:133–152.

Kessell, John L.
1979 Kiva, Cross, and Crown, the Pecos Indians and New Mexico. Washington: National Park Service.

Mecham, John L.
1927 Francisco de Ibarra and Nueva Vizcaya. Durham, North Carolina: Duke University Press.

Mendieta, Geronimo de
1945 Historia Eclesiástica Indiana [1596]. Mexico: Editorial Salvador Chavez Hayhoe.

Moorhead, Max
1958 New Mexico's Royal Road. Norman: University of Oklahoma Press.

Mota Padilla, Matias de la
1924 Historia de la Conquista del Reino de la Nueva Galicia [1742]. Guadalajara: Talleres Graficos de Gallardo y Alvares del Castillo.

Mota y Escobar, Alonso de la
1940 Descripcion Geografica de los Reinos de Nueva Galicia, Nueva Vizcaya y Leon [1605]. Mexico: Editorial Pedro Robredo.

Nentvig, Juan
1980 Rudo Ensayo [1764]. Alberto F. Pradeau and Roberto R. Rasmussen, trans. and ann. Tucson: University of Arizona Press.

Nixon, Pat I.
1946 The Medical Story of Early Texas, 1528–1853. Lancaster, Pennsylvania: Lancaster Press.

Ocaranza, Fernando
1934 Historia de la Medicina en México. Mexico.

Ortiz, Alfonso, ed.
1983 Handbook of North American Indians. Vol. 10: Southwest. William C. Sturtevant, gen. ed. Washington: Smithsonian Institution.

Pacheco, Joaquin F., and Francisco de Cardenas, eds.
1864– Coleccion de Documentos Ineditos Relativos al
1884 Descubrimiento, Conquista y Colonización de las Posesiónes Espanoles en America y Oceania. 42 vols. Madrid.

Paso y Troncoso, Francisco del
1939 Epistolario de Nueva España 1505–1818. Vols. 4–6. Mexico: Jose Porrua e Hijos.

Pennington, Campbell W.
1963 The Tarahumar of Mexico: Their Environment and Material Culture. Salt Lake City: University of Utah Press.

1980 The Pima Bajo of Centràl Sonora, Mexico. Vol. 1: Their Material Culture. Salt Lake City: University of Utah Press.

Perez de Ribas, Andres
1896 Coronica y Historia Religiosa de la Provincia de la Compañia de Jesus de Mexico [1655]. 2 vols. Mexico: Sagrado Corazon.

1944 Historia de los Triunfos de Nuestra Santa Fe Entre Gentes las Mas Barbaras y Fieras del Nueve Orbe [1645]. 3 vols. Mexico: Editorial Layac.

Powell, Philip W.
1952 Soldiers, Indians & Silver: The Northward Advance of New Spain, 1550–1600. Berkeley: University of California Press.

Reff, Daniel T.
1986 The Demographic and Cultural Consequences of Old World Diseases in the Greater Southwest, 1519–1660. Ann Arbor, Mich.: University Microfilms.

1987 Old World Disease and the Dynamics of Indian and Jesuit Relations in Northwestern Mexico, 1520–1660. Pp. 85–95 in Ejidos and Regions of Refuges in Northwestern Mexico. N. R. Crumrine and P. C. Weigand, eds. *Anthropological Papers of the University of Arizona* 8. Tucson.

1987a The Introduction of Smallpox in the Greater Southwest. *American Anthropologist* 89:704–708.

1989 Disease Episodes and the Historical Record: A Reply to Dobyns. *American Anthropologist* 91(1):174–175.

1991 Disease, Depopulation and Culture Change in Northwestern New Spain, 1520 to 1764. Salt Lake City: University of Utah Press.

Riley, Carroll L.
1982 The Frontier People. *Southern Illinois University Center for Archaeological Investigations. Occasional Paper* 1. Carbondale.

Sauer, Carl O.
1935 Aboriginal Population of Northwest Mexico. *Ibero-Americana* 10. Berkeley, Calif.

1948 Colima of New Spain in the Sixteenth Century. *Ibero-Americana* 29. Berkeley, Calif.

Sauer, Carl O., and Donald E. Brand
1932 Aztatlan: Prehistoric Mexican Frontier on the Pacific Coast. *Ibero-Americana* 1. Berkeley, Calif.

Schroeder, Albert
1972 Rio Grande Ethnohistory. Pp. 41–70 in New Perspectives on the Pueblos. Alfonso Ortiz, ed. Albuquerque: University of New Mexico Press.

Sheridan, Thomas E., and T. Naylor, eds.
  1979   Raramuri, a Tarahumara Colonial Chronicle 1607–1791. Flagstaff, Ariz.: Northland Press.

Shiels, W. Eugene
  1934   Gonzalo de Tapia (1561–1594), Founder of the First Permanent Jesuit Mission in North America. New York: United States Catholic Historical Society.

Simmons, Marc
  1979   History of Pueblo-Spanish Relations to 1821. Pp. 178–193 in Handbook of North American Indians. Vol. 9: Southwest. Alfonso Ortiz, vol. ed. William C. Sturtevant, gen. ed. Washington: Smithsonian Institution.

Spicer, Edward H.
  1962   Cycles of Conquest, the Impact of Spain, Mexico, and the United States on the Indians of the Southwest, 1533–1960. Tucson: University of Arizona Press.

  1980   The Yaquis: A Cultural History. Tucson: University of Arizona Press.

Tamaron Y. Romeral, Pedro
  1937   Demostración del Vatisimo Obispado de la Nueva Vizcaya—1765. Mexico: Anitgua Librereia Robredo.

Tello, Antonio
  1891   Libro Segundo de la Cronica Miscelanea de la Santa Provincia de Xalisco. Guadalajara: La Republica Literaria.

Thompson, J. Eric
  1970   Maya History and Religion. Norman: University of Oklahoma Press.

Treutlein, Theodore E., trans.
  1949   Sonora, a Description of the Province, by Ignaz Pfefferkorn. Albuquerque: University of New Mexico Press.

————, trans.
  1965   Missionary in Sonora, the Travel Reports of Joseph Och, S. J., 1755–1767. San Francisco: California Historical Society.

Upham, Steadman
  1982   Polities and Power: An Economic and Political History of the Western Pueblo. New York: Academic Press.

  1986   Smallpox and Climate in the American Southwest. American Anthropologist 88(1):115–128.

Vetancurt, Augustin de
  1961   Teatro Mexicano: Descripcion Breve del los Sucessos Exemplares de la Nueva-España en el Mundo Occidental de la Indias. Vol. 3: Chronica de la Provincia del Santo Evangelio [1697]. Madrid: Jose Porrua Turanzas.

West, Robert C.
  1949   The Mining Community in Northwestern New Spain: The Parral Mining District. Ibero-Americana 30. Berkeley, Calif.

West, Robert C., and J. L. Parsons
  1941   The Topia Road: A Trans-Sierran Trail of Colonial Mexico. The Geographical Review 31:406–413.

Wilcox, David R., and W. B. Masse
  1981   A History of Protohistoric Studies in the North American Southwest. Pp. 1–27 in The Protohistoric Period in the North American Southwest, A.D. 1450–1700. David Wilcox and W. Bruce Masse, eds. Arizona State University Anthropological Research Papers 24. Tempe.

26

Summary on Population Size before and after Contact

ALFRED W. CROSBY

Starting in the 1930s, scholars such as Carl O. Sauer, Lesley Byrd Simpson, and the two giants of American Indian demographic history, Sherburne F. Cook and Woodrow Wilson Borah, began to change the way we look at the history of *Homo sapiens* in the Americas. Most particularly, these scholars (often collectively known as the Berkeley School) changed the way we now see the contact between the first great wave of humans to come to the New World, the American Indians, and the second wave, Whites and Blacks, who arrived after 1492. For generations prior to the advent of the Berkeley School, the Euro-Americans, the dominant people of the Americas, had accepted the testimony of their own eyes that there were relatively few American Indians (at least in the temperate zones, where most Euro-Americans lived and published) as evidence that there had never been many of them at any time. The great anthropologist, Alfred L. Kroeber, had offered a meager figure of 8.4 million for their total in 1492. By the 1960s Cook and Borah were estimating that the population of Meso-America alone when Hernando Cortés debarked there was about triple that figure. In 1966 Henry F. Dobyns, after considering masses of material on the subject, original and secondary, put forth the hypothesis that Indian population at the time of contact with the invaders in a given area had been commonly about 20–25 times their lowest number after the ensuing population crash. Dobyns offered an estimate of an Indian total for 1492 of 90–112 million, a number that was compatible with the Cook and Borah estimates but that riled students of the subject who clung to their traditional views of demographic history.

The disparities between the estimates of Indian numbers around 1492 are so enormous that there has obviously not been enough work on the subject. We need meticulous research and rigorous analysis of the demographic histories of specific areas, like those Cook and Borah made of Meso-America and the Caribbean islands, rather than additional blowzy accounts of what happened to Indians as a whole.

The papers presented at the Smithsonian Institution entitled collectively "Population Size Before and After Contact" are a major answer to the demand for precise scholarship. The picture that these papers proffer does not clash with the work of the demographic historians who claim that Indian populations crashed after contact, but it does clearly show that the details differed enormously from place to place and time to time. There is no doubt that the Euro- and Afro-Americans carried diseases deadly to Indians, but said diseases did not rain down uniformly and all at once on all the original peoples of the New World. The differences enabled some peoples to survive and, some, eventually, to return to their pre-Columbian densities. Others disappeared forever with a swiftness that must chill our spines if we are capable of any empathy at all for our fellow creatures.

Dobyns, not content with the admiration and malice he has aroused thus far, has continued his labors and now tells us that trading centers were major foci of new infections, much like the cities of the Old World, and that Indians involved in trade usually suffered imported diseases earlier and probably more severely than their less commercial cousins. Meggers, also loath to rest on her laurels, has applied the most rigorous techniques to the problem of how many lived in Amazonia at first contact; and while she grants an appalling population crash after that contact, finds insufficient evidence to indicate precontact densities as high as earliest eyewitnesses claimed. Several other participants—Cook, Upham, Kiple, Boyd, and Reff—contend that where climate and food supplies allowed, quite large precontact populations existed and that they suffered profound losses following contact. Ubelaker, Snow, Trimble, and Thornton (in the cases of Snow and Thornton with the aid of a sophisticated computer program) examine relatively small-scale and regional histories and discover that these histories did not proceed uniformly, that population crashes did not take place in unison, and, by clear implication, that additional exacting studies like their own are needed. The arrival of invaders from the Old World did, in the long run and on the whole, bring disaster to all incumbent Americans, but such fuzzy concepts of "in the long run and on the whole" serve better as inspirations for questions than as answers per se. If further work ensues in the vein of which these papers are such fine examples, we may, along with Borah (1976:30), look forward to the day when, after generations of scholarship, our hemispheric estimate will be accurate to a tolerance of plus or minus 30–50 percent!

REFERENCE

Borah, Woodrow W.
   1976   The Historical Demography of Aboriginal and Colonial America: An Attempt at Perspective. Pp. 13–34 in The Native Population of the Americas in 1492. William M. Denevan, ed. Madison: University of Wisconsin Press.

27

Conclusion

DOUGLAS H. UBELAKER
JOHN W. VERANO

This volume constitutes a testimonial to the ongoing need for interdisciplinary research in scientific subfields relating to the problem of the biological impact of European contact with the New World. Clearly scholars in physical anthropology, demography, history, epidemiology, medicine, archeology, ecology, paleopathology, and related disciplines have a lot to teach one another. Collectively, and in some cases individually, essays in this volume touch on the diverse scholarship involved and the importance of interpreting individual data sets in wide biocultural, historical perspective. Clearly, an accurate impression of the sweep of demographic history of the Americas must take into account much of the scholarship presented here, although these essays represent only a sampling of the diversity of current research in the field. While these essays may not present "the final word" on what happened in the Americas, they do offer a convincing portrayal of the problems involved in researching the issues. They also indicate that the issues are more complex than has been assumed by many previous workers.

The assumption held by many that prior to 1492 populations of the New World were living in a "disease-free paradise" clearly can be put to rest. Evidence for pre-Columbian disease in the New World indicates that many areas of the New World prior to 1492 experienced significant levels of morbidity and mortality related to problems of population density, diet, and sanitation. Most of this evidence stems from the study of well-dated archeologically recovered samples of human remains, coupled with archeological evidence for diet, social organization, and population size and density.

Identifying and interpreting disease conditions in human remains is not a simple process. As Ortner points out in his essay in this volume, many diseases can leave similar marks on bone, and several diseases may affect the skeleton simultaneously, complicating diagnosis. Interpretation of skeletal lesions requires considerable training and experience and frequently interdisciplinary interpretations. Physical anthropologists usually have the most experience in differentiating disease conditions from "pseudo pathology" or taphonomic (postmortem environmental) factors that mimic disease conditions. Radiologists offer important expertise in the interpretation of radiographic evidence, once taphonomic factors can be controlled. Pathologists, especially orthopedic pathologists, offer unique perspective on the interpretation of bone lesions, but many such specialists are unfamiliar with the appearance of lesions in dry bone.

Efforts in paleopathology have moved forward to enable more sophisticated diagnosis of individual disease in ancient bone or mummified tissue. New techniques in histology and bone chemistry, CAT, and other computer-enhanced imaging techniques all have contributed to this advance. In addition, an increasing number of anthropologists employ paleopathological techniques as part of their routine analysis of ancient bone samples. As a result, there is increasing information on the frequency of specific skeletal pathologies in prehistoric populations and how these frequencies changed through time in relation to cultural factors such as changes in diet, residence patterns, and population density. These data, coupled with sophisticated chemical approaches to the reconstruction of past diet have substantially increased our ability to assess the impact of diet and disease in past populations.

In this volume, several scholars demonstrate what these techniques reveal about geographic and temporal variability of morbidity within the pre-1492 New World. Powell, Bogdan and Weaver, Verano, Milner, Buikstra, and Larsen et al. document that in Andean South America, and Southeast, Northeast, and Plains North America, morbidity was on the increase through time. This temporal trend apparently was related to increases in population size and density, as well as to dietary shifts. Essays by Buikstra, Milner, and Verano also argue for considerable geographic variability in the manifestation of disease. Clearly, patterns of morbidity for the American Southeast do not apply to the Plains or to Andean South America. Even within a general geographic area, considerable variability may have occurred in response to varying cultural factors. The Buikstra essay offers a case in point, demonstrating how differences in the extent to which maize agriculture was adopted by prehistoric societies in North America resulted in distinctive patterns of generalized stress and infectious disease.

In the Andean area, Verano argues from skeletal data that health deteriorated through time prior to 1492 as a result of increased population density as well as dietary problems. In addition, Verano notes that the great geographical diversity of the Andean area produced variability of morbidity.

Samples of human skeletal remains from coastal sites show higher frequencies of some disease conditions than do highland sites, apparently reflecting the fact that the coastal environment is more favorable to certain pathogens, especially intestinal parasites such as hookworm.

As Milner notes from his study of prehistoric Illinois, social structure and population size contributed to dietary factors in influencing the expression of disease in pre-1492 America. Milner found considerable variability in morbidity in skeletal samples from sites with markedly different social systems.

Saunders, Ramsden, and Herring note that in southern Ontario, populations had been transformed by high levels of infectious disease long before European contact and the historically recorded epidemics of the early 1600s.

Essays by Bogdan and Weaver and by Powell present evidence for the role of specific diseases in the patterns of morbidity within the New World. Differential diagnosis clearly indicates that high population density and living conditions in some areas of the New World led to significant morbidity and mortality from tuberculosis and treponemal disease. There seems little doubt that both conditions evolved in the New World and were major health problems prior to 1492 in areas where population density was relatively high.

There is substantial evidence that by 1492, many populations of the New World had already experienced high levels of mortality and morbidity due to disease conditions related to population density, subsistence, and culture. However, the years immediately following 1492 brought diseases and levels of mortality unknown before in the New World. At least in the Caribbean area, the impact of these diseases was swift and harsh with epidemics beginning perhaps as early as 1493. There is general scholarly agreement that mortality from introduced disease proceeded from east to west loosely following the sequence of European contact. However, as is emphasized in Ubelaker's essay on North American Indian population estimates, scholars disagree on the magnitude of the population decline, the existence and impact of pandemics, and the extent of variability in population response. Collectively, the essays in this volume argue for considerable variability in the timing and effect of introduced disease in the New World.

Upham (Southwest), Thornton (Southeast),

Carlson, Armelagos, and Magennis (Northeast) and Cook (Andean area) all point out the difficulty in interpreting the evidence for very early epidemics. All admit the possibility and likelihood that disease spread in advance of European contact in many areas. Such a pattern leaves little opportunity for the historical record to capture the evidence. The very earliest European contacts produce inconsistent accounts of early epidemics and are very difficult to interpret. As Dobyns points out, it is easy to visualize how the excitement of culture contact could have brought Europeans laden with communicable disease in contact at trading centers with representatives of different tribes. In his essay, Dobyns argues that such trading centers served to transmit disease, crosscutting other cultural barriers to the spread of illnesses. In contrast, Milner argues that such factors may have been formidable barriers to the spread of disease during historic times. Milner notes that the frequency of direct contact, the nature of existing social systems, population density, intergroup relations, cultural boundaries, and community health all were influencing factors. Reff, Thornton, and Cook find no evidence for pandemics in the North American Southwest, Southeast, and Andean South America; but they note that sporadic localized epidemics ultimately produced tremendous mortality in those areas.

Clearly an important element in understanding the impact of European disease in the New World is to elucidate the myriad of influencing factors. For example, in the Plains area, Trimble points out how the United States government policy of vaccination influenced the impact of epidemics on Plains Indian populations. Trimble argues that complexities of the policy benefited tribes of the lower Missouri River and left those of the upper Missouri at greater risk.

Kiple argues that the dynamics of economic and immigration history of the Caribbean affected the course of epidemics and population shifts in that area. He notes that yellow fever struck particularly hard in the British and French islands, where the slave trade followed the sugar revolution, bringing in large numbers of Black African immigrants. Kiple argues that the Black populations enjoyed a resistance to the disease not shared by the populations of European origin. The result was great mortality among the White population and a further increase in the percentage of Black residents. Such

was not the case in nearby Cuba, where a different pattern of immigration and involvement in the sugar industry reduced the impact of yellow fever and culminated in a population with proportionally more individuals of European descent.

Essays by Snow and by Thornton illustrate the use of computer modeling as a research tool in demographic reconstructions. Simulation programs offer the opportunity to explore various scenarios in detail before making interpretations. Such an approach suggests to Thornton that in the American Southeast epidemics were localized and gradual. Computer modeling helps Snow document the timing of population decline in the Northeast.

Overall, essays in this volume indicate that while the continent-wide effect of introduced diseases was devastating, populations demonstrated considerable regional variability in their response. Upham notes that in the American Southwest, depopulation was tied to the arrival of the Spaniards. Reff notes that in New Spain, populations demonstrated a remarkable resiliency in the eighteenth and nineteenth centuries but suffered great loss earlier. In New Spain as probably elsewhere, mortality from Old World disease epidemics led not only to population decline but also to major changes in social structure. Cook utilizes the excellent early colonial period documentary sources for epidemics in the Andean area to document the tremendous mortality associated with them. Similarly, Boyd notes great mortality on the Northwest Coast, noting that malaria had a cumulative long-term demographic effect, whereas smallpox mortality was more sudden and discrete. Boyd also notes the important role of cultural practices on the impact of disease. Walker and Johnson draw upon detailed mission records to document the precipitous decline of the Chumash Indians in California in the late eighteenth and early nineteenth centuries. They demonstrate that multiple factors, including cultural disruption, resettlement in missions, epidemics of measles, diphtheria, and smallpox, as well as high frequencies of chronic diseases such as tuberculosis and syphilis led to a major decline of the native population by the end of the mission period.

Analysis of skeletal samples dating from the historic period offers information on the impact of European introduced disease. In the Plains area of the United States, Owsley presents a synthesis of his demographic analysis of historic samples to indicate that high mortality hit the Plains in the early 1600s but lessened in the late 1600s. His data suggest that populations were increasing until the late 1600s and then began a strong decline that continued through the nineteenth century.

Larsen notes that in Southeast samples, bone chemistry indicates that within the historic period diet was becoming more restricted and lower in nutritional quality. During historic times, epidemic disease obviously had a major impact, but other factors such as excessive work load, reduced nutritional quality, warfare, soil depletion, poor sanitation, population nucleation, and social disruption were important as well.

In the American Southwest, Stodder and Martin's analysis of skeletal samples suggests that during the historic period rates of nutritional stress, infectious disease, and trauma all increased. In agreement with Larsen, they feel that many factors in addition to infectious disease are responsible.

Meggers's essay on prehistoric population density in the Amazon Basin addresses the problem of reconciling ethnohistorical information on disease and population size with the archeological record. In her essay, Meggers presents the results of long-term archeological testing of settlement pattern and concludes that the population density of Amazonia was substantially less than previous workers have suggested using ethnohistorical data. She further suggests that the carrying capacity of the area is far less than others have indicated.

In total, the essays in this volume attest to the complexity of the issues involved and the diversity of ongoing research in the field. They provide few answers to the difficult questions of the size of the New World population in 1492 and the timing of the epidemics that followed. However, they do indicate that while many of these problems may never be resolved, much can be learned through interdisciplinary research and careful research design. We hope that this volume will serve to stimulate further dialogue between researchers and to suggest new approaches to these issues.

Contributors

GEORGE J. ARMELAGOS
Department of Anthropology
1350 Turlington Hall
University of Florida
Gainesville, FL 32611

ARTHUR AUFDERHEIDE
Department of Pathology
University of Minnesota at Duluth
10 University Drive
Duluth, MN 55812

GEORGIANN BOGDAN
Department of Anthropology
Wake Forest University
Winston-Salem, NC 27109

ROBERT BOYD
1039 S.E. 25th Street
Portland, OR 97214-2811

JANE E. BUIKSTRA
Department of Anthropology
University of Chicago
1126 E. 59th Street
Chicago, IL 60637

CATHERINE C. CARLSON
Department of Anthropology,
   Sociology, and Geography
Cariboo College
P.O. Box 3010
Kamloops, B.C. V2C 5N3
Canada

NOBLE DAVID COOK
History Department
University of Bridgeport
Bridgeport, CT 06601

ALFRED CROSBY
American Studies and American
   Civilizations Programs
University of Texas
Austin, TX 78712

HENRY F. DOBYNS
Department of Anthropology
University of Oklahoma
Norman, OK 73019

ANN HERRING
Department of Anthropology
McMaster University
1280 Main Street West
Hamilton, ON L8S 4L9
Canada

BRIAN T. HIGGINS
Department of History
Bowling Green State University
Bowling Green, OH 43403

DALE L. HUTCHINSON
Department of Anthropology
University of Illinois
Urbana, IL 61801

JOHN R. JOHNSON
Department of Anthropology
Santa Barbara Museum of Natural History
2559 Puesta del Sol Road
Santa Barbara, CA 93105

KENNETH F. KIPLE
Department of History
Bowling Green State University
Bowling Green, OH 43403

CLARK SPENCER LARSEN
Department of Sociology and Anthropology
Winthrop E. Stone Hall
Purdue University
West Lafayette, IN 47907

ANN L. MAGENNIS
Department of Anthropology
Colorado State University
Fort Collins, CO 80523

DEBORAH MARTIN
School of Natural Sciences
Hampshire College
Amherst, MA 01002

BETTY MEGGERS
Department of Anthropology
MRC NHB-112
Smithsonian Institution
Washington, D.C. 20560

TIM MILLER
Department of Demography
University of California
Berkeley, CA 94720

GEORGE R. MILNER
Department of Anthropology
409 Carpenter Building
Pennsylvania State University
University Park, PA 16802

DONALD J. ORTNER
Department of Anthropology
MRC NHB-112
Smithsonian Institution
Washington, D.C. 20560

DOUGLAS W. OWSLEY
Department of Anthropology
MRC NHB-112
Smithsonian Institution
Washington, D.C. 20560

MARY L. POWELL
Museum of Anthropology
University of Kentucky
Lafferty Hall
Lexington, KY 40506

PETER RAMSDEN
Department of Anthropology
McMaster University
1280 Main Street West
Hamilton, ON L8S 4L9
Canada

DANIEL T. REFF
Department of Anthropology
Ohio State University
Columbus, OH 43210

CHRISTOPHER B. RUFF
Department of Cell Biology and Anatomy
School of Medicine
Johns Hopkins University
725 N. Wolfe Street
Baltimore, MD 21205

SHELLEY R. SAUNDERS
Department of Anthropology
McMaster University
1280 Main Street West
Hamilton, ON L8S 4L9
Canada

MARGARET J. SCHOENINGER
Department of Anthropology
University of Wisconsin
Madison, WI 53706

DEAN R. SNOW
Department of Anthropology
University of Albany, SUNY
1400 Washington Avenue
Albany, NY 12222

ANN L. W. STODDER
Paul H. Rosendahl, Ph.D., Inc.
Hilo, HI 96720

RUSSELL THORNTON
Department of Sociology
410 Barrows Hall
University of California, Berkeley
Berkeley, CA 94720

MICHAEL TRIMBLE
U.S. Army Corps of Engineers
St. Louis District Planning Division
1222 Spruce Street
St. Louis, MO 63103

DOUGLAS H. UBELAKER
Department of Anthropology
MRC NHB-112
Smithsonian Institution
Washington, D.C. 20560

STEADMAN UPHAM
Dean, Graduate School
University of Oregon
Eugene, OR 97403

JOHN W. VERANO
Department of Anthropology
MRC NHB-112
Smithsonian Institution
Washington, D.C. 20560

HERMAN J. VIOLA
Office of Quincentenary Programs
MRC NHB-117
National Museum of Natural History
Smithsonian Institution
Washington, D.C. 20560

PHILLIP L. WALKER
Department of Anthropology
University of California
Santa Barbara, CA 93106

JONATHAN WARREN
Department of Sociology
410 Barrows Hall
University of California
Berkeley, CA 94720

DAVID S. WEAVER
Department of Anthropology
Wake Forest University
Winston-Salem, NC 27109

Index